THE EMPEROR'S OLD CLOTHES

SPEKTRUM: Publications of the German Studies Association
Series editor: David M. Luebke, University of Oregon

Published under the auspices of the German Studies Association, *Spektrum* offers current perspectives on culture, society, and political life in the German-speaking lands of central Europe—Austria, Switzerland, and the Federal Republic—from the late Middle Ages to the present day. Its titles and themes reflect the composition of the GSA and the work of its members within and across the disciplines to which they belong—literary criticism, history, cultural studies, political science, and anthropology.

Volume 1
The Holy Roman Empire, Reconsidered
Edited by Jason Philip Coy, Benjamin Marschke, and David Warren Sabean

Volume 2
Weimar Publics/Weimar Subjects
Rethinking the Political Culture of Germany in the 1920s
Edited by Kathleen Canning, Kerstin Barndt, and Kristin McGuire

Volume 3
Conversion and the Politics of Religion in Early Modern Germany
Edited by David M. Luebke, Jared Poley, Daniel C. Ryan, and David Warren Sabean

Volume 4
Walls, Borders, Boundaries
Spatial and Cultural Practices in Europe
Edited by Marc Silberman, Karen E. Till, and Janet Ward

Volume 5
After The History of Sexuality
German Genealogies with and Beyond Foucault
Edited by Scott Spector, Helmut Puff, and Dagmar Herzog

Volume 6
Becoming East German
Socialist Structures and Sensibilities after Hitler
Edited by Mary Fulbrook and Andrew I. Port

Volume 7
Beyond Alterity
German Encounters with Modern East Asia
Edited by Qinna Shen and Martin Rosenstock

Volume 8
Mixed Matches
Transgressive Unions in Germany from the Reformation to the Enlightenment
Edited by David Luebke and Mary Lindemann

Volume 9
Kinship, Community, and Self
Essays in Honor of David Warren Sabean
Edited by Jason Coy, Benjamin Marschke, Jared Poley, and Claudia Verhoeven

Volume 10
The Emperor's Old Clothes
Constitutional History and the Symbolic Language of the Holy Roman Empire
Barbara Stollberg-Rilinger
Translated by Thomas Dunlap

The Emperor's Old Clothes

Constitutional History and the Symbolic Language of the Holy Roman Empire

BARBARA STOLLBERG-RILINGER

Translated by
THOMAS DUNLAP

Published by
Berghahn Books
www.berghahnbooks.com

English-language edition
© 2015, 2020 Berghahn Books
First paperback edition published in 2020

German-language edition
© 2008 Verlag C.H.Beck oHG, München
Des Kaisers alte Kleider

All rights reserved. Except for the quotation of short passages for the purposes of criticism and review, no part of this book may be reproduced in any form or by any means, electronic or mechanical, including photocopying, recording, or any information storage and retrieval system now known or to be invented, without written permission of the publisher.

The translation of this work was funded by Geisteswissenschaften International – Translation Funding for Humanities and Social Sciences from Germany, a joint initiative of the Fritz Thyssen Foundation, the German Federal Foreign Office, the collecting society VG WORT and the Börsenverein des Deutschen Buchhandels (German Publishers & Booksellers Association).

Library of Congress Cataloging-in-Publication Data

Stollberg-Rilinger, Barbara.
 [Des Kaisers alte Kleider. English]
 The emperor's old clothes : constitutional history and the symbolic language of the Holy Roman Empire / Barbara Stollberg-Rilinger ; translated by Thomas Dunlap.
   pages cm. — (Spektrum: Publications of the German Studies Association)
 Includes bibliographical references and index.
 ISBN 978-1-78238-805-0 (hardback : alk. paper) — ISBN 978-1-78238-806-7 (ebook)
 1. Holy Roman Empire—Civilization. 2. Holy Roman Empire—Kings and rulers. 3. Holy Roman Empire—Symbolic representation. 4. Political customs and rites—Germany. 5. Constitutional history—Holy Roman Empire. I. Dunlap, Thomas, 1959– translator. II. Title. III. Title: Constitutional history and the symbolic language of the Holy Roman Empire.
 DD125.S72513 2015
 943'.02—dc23
                                                                                   2015003129

British Library Cataloguing in Publication Data

A catalogue record for this book is available from the British Library

Printed on acid-free paper

ISBN: 978-1-78238-805-0 (hardback)
ISBN 978-1-78920-798-9 (paperback)
ISBN: 978-1-78238-806-7 (ebook)

CONTENTS

List of Illustrations	vi
Acknowledgments	viii
List of Abbreviations	ix
Introduction	1
Chapter 1. Creation and Presentation of the Empire: Worms, 1495	15
Chapter 2. Cleavage of the Sacral Community: Augsburg, 1530	80
Chapter 3. More Strife than Ever Before: Regensburg, 1653/54	121
Chapter 4. Parallel Worlds: Frankfurt-Regensburg-Vienna, 1764/65	203
Conclusion. The Symbolic Logic of the Empire	269
Bibliography	285
Index	327

ILLUSTRATIONS

Figure 1. Coronation regalia: alb, coronation mantle, and belt for the imperial sword. Johann Adam Delsenbach, colored copper engraving, 1751, © KHM, Vienna. — 2

Figure 2. Coronation regalia: stocking, two pairs of gloves, three pairs of shoes. Johann Adam Delsenbach, colored copper engraving, 1751, © KHM, Vienna. — 3

Figure 3. Hans Burgkmair the Elder, *Quaternionen* eagle, woodcut (detail), 1495, Nuremberg, Staatsarchiv. — 23

Figure 4. Maximilian I in the circle of the electors, woodcut, 1495, Nuremberg, Staatsarchiv. — 40

Figure 5. Nicolaus Hogenberg, *Entry of Charles V with Pope Clemens VII into Bologna in 1530 for the Imperial Coronation* (detail), 1532, © Herzog August Bibliothek Wolfenbüttel. — 88

Figure 6. Jörg Breu the Elder, *Entry of Charles V into Augsburg in 1530*, Brunswick, Anton-Ulrich-Museum, Inv. No. 5350b. — 89

Figure 7. Investiture of Archduke Ferdinand by Charles V in 1530. Title-page woodcut from Kaspar Sturm, *Wahrhafftig anzaygung wie Kayser Carl der fünfte ...*, Augsburg 1530, Vienna, Österreichische Nationalbibliothek. — 109

Figure 8. The emperor in the circle of the electors. Single-page broadsheet entitled *Abbildung Unsers heutigen Deutschlands und der höchstgewünschten Vereinigung*, copper engraving by Abraham Aubry after Johann Toussin, 1653/54. — 127

Figure 9. The entry of Ferdinand III into Regensburg on 12 December 1652. Single-sheet broadsheet by Melchior Küsel, Germanisches Nationalmuseum Nuremberg, Graphische Sammlung. — 137

Figure 10. Solemn session of the imperial diet, 1653. Single-page broadsheet entitled *Eigentlicher Abriss der Reichstags-Solennitet, so den 13.–23. Juny Anno 1653 in Regensburg auf dem gewöhnlichen großen Rathauß-Saal, bey Eröfnung der kaiserlichen Proposition angestellet und gehalten worden*, Germanisches Nationalmuseum Nuremberg, Graphische Sammlung. 167

Figure 11. The entry of Emperor Francis I and Joseph II into Frankfurt am Main, 1764. Workshop of Martin van Meytens the Younger (Johann Dallinger von Dalling, 1741–1806, et alia), Vienna, around 1765, © KHM, Vienna. 205

Figure 12. The coronation meal of Joseph II in the *Römer*, 1764. Workshop of Martin van Meytens the Younger, Vienna, around 1764, © KHM, Vienna. 216

Figure 13. Old and new city halls in Regensburg. Oil on canvas, Historisches Museum der Stadt Regensburg, Inv. No. AB 274. 221

Figure 14. Andreas Geyer, *Re- und Correlationssaal des Regensburger Reichstags*, around 1725. 222

Figure 15. Salomon Kleiner, *Entry of the Envoys into the Hofburg in Vienna, Inner Court*. Vienna, Österreichische Nationalbibliothek, © ÖNB Bildarchiv, Vienna, NB 902.35b-A/B. 252

Figure 16. Diagram of the throne investiture of Liege at the Viennese court, 12 December 1765. Vienna, HHStA OMeA ZA 30, fol. 377v. 253

Figure 17. Title-page copper engraving from Johann Carl König, *Abhandlungen von denen Teutschen Reichs-Tägen*, Nuremberg, 1738. 275

~: ACKNOWLEDGMENTS :~

This book arose out of a long collaboration with my Münster colleagues in the Special Research Center 496, "Symbolic Communication and Social Value Systems from the Middle Ages to the French Revolution." I am indebted to them above all for the perspective of understanding the Old Empire from its medieval past. This is especially true of Gerd Althoff, who constructively accompanied the evolution of this study and read the manuscript with a critical eye. I am grateful to the collaborators at the University of Münster, especially the generation that created the Special Research Center, for countless theoretical discussions and the unerring readiness to contradict: Antje Flüchter, Marian Füssel, Michael Sikora, and Thomas Weller. A special thank you to André Krischer and Johannes Kunisch for their critical reading of parts of the manuscript and their encouragement during times of doubt. Aloys Winterling gave me important and stimulating suggestions from his perspective as a historian of Roman Antiquity. Katrin Keller and Lothar Höbelt were generously willing to provide me with unpublished source transcriptions; Susanne Friedrich allowed me to consult her important book about the Regensburg diet before it was published.

The English translation owes its existence to the foundation Geisteswissenschaften International, which financed it. It would hardly have happened without the very generous reference from Thomas Brady. My longtime friend David M. Luebke and the publisher Marion Berghahn made it possible for the book to be included in the series Spektrum. Adam Capitanio oversaw the project with great professionalism. The translator, Thomas Dunlap, was able to find the right turn of phrase throughout. Hendrik Holzmüller compiled the index with particular care. Nina Hagel was a great help during the final edit with her superb feel for linguistic clarity. To them go all my heartfelt thanks.

I dedicate this book to Georg Rilinger, my constant guide in understanding the foreign academic culture in the United States.

Barbara Stollberg-Rilinger
Münster, August 2014

ABBREVIATIONS

ÄZA	Ältere Zeremonialakten (Older Ceremonial Records)
AVA	Allgemeines Verwaltungsarchiv (General Administrative Archive)
BAV	Biblioteca Apostolica Vaticana
CR	Corpus Reformatorum
fl	Gulden
fol.	folio
GF FT	Gratialia et Feudalia, Fürstliche Thronbelehnungen (Princely Investitures)
GF TZ	Gratialia et Feudalia, Thronbelehnungen und Zeremonialanstände (Investitures and Ceremonial Records)
HHStA	Haus-, Hof- und Staatsarchiv Wien
HJB	*Historisches Jahrbuch*
HRG	*Handwörterbuch zur deutschen Rechtsgeschichte*
HStA	Hauptstaatsarchiv (Central State Archive)
IPO	Instrumentum Pacis Osnabrugense
JRA	Jüngster Reichsabschied (Recent Imperial Recess)
MEA	Mainzer Erzkanzler Archiv (Archive of the Archchancellor of Mainz)
MGH	*Monumenta Germaniae Historica*
MÖStA	*Mitteilungen des Österreichischen Staatsarchivs*
NTSR	*Neues Teutsches Staatsrecht*
OMeA	Oberhofmeisteramt (Office of Lord Chamberlain)

ÖNA	Österreichisches Nationalarchiv (Austrian National Archive)
ÖNB	Österreichische Nationalbibliothek Wien (Austrian National Library, Vienna)
RHR	Reichshofrat (Imperial Court Council)
RK	Reichskanzlei (Imperial Chancery)
RKG	Reichskammergericht (Imperial Chamber Court)
RT	Reichstag (Imperial Diet)
RTA	Reichstagsakten (Imperial Diet Files)
RTA ÄR	Reichstagsakten Ältere Reihe (Imperial Diet Files, Older Series)
RTA JR	Reichstagsakten Jüngere Reihe (Imperial Diet Files, Younger Series)
RTA MR	Reichstagsakten Mittlere Reihe (Imperial Diet Files, Middle Series)
TSR	*Teutsches Staatsrecht*
WA	Weimarer Ausgabe (Weimar Edition)
WK	Wahl- und Krönungsakten (Election and Coronation Records)
ZA	Zeremonialakten (Ceremonial Records)

Introduction

Four years before the Holy Roman Empire of the German Nation ceased to exist, a young Hegel wrote that the Germans had been fastidiously preserving all signs of the German polity for centuries, while the thing itself, the state, had vanished. The Empire was an entity only in form, not in substance. Hegel referred to "[t]his German superstition regarding purely external forms and ceremony, so ridiculous in the eyes of other nations," which passed off" this immutability of form … as immutability of substance." This was expressed in exemplary fashion by the emperor's old clothes: "The constitution in fact seems to have undergone no change at all during the thousand years which have elapsed since the time of Charlemagne, for at his coronation, the newly elected Emperor bears the crown, sceptre and orb of Charlemagne, and even wears his shoes, coat, and jewels. An Emperor of modern times is thus identified with Charlemagne as Emperor to such an extent that he even wears the latter's own clothes." And he went on: "In the preservation of these forms, the German convinces himself that he can discern the preservation of his constitution."[1]

This, precisely, is the subject of the present book: the relationship between the imperial constitution and its external, symbolic-ritual forms. It is indeed true that the Empire was characterized in its late phase by the fact that the actors had an extraordinarily ambiguous relationship to it: on the one hand, they took the symbolic objects and gestures in which the Empire embodied itself so seriously that they were engaged in endless quarrels about them. On the other hand, this did not prevent them, circumstances being favorable, from simply shunting elementary rules of the imperial system aside if it served their interests.

The emperor's old clothes are a metaphor for the entire symbolic system of the Empire. On the one hand, it was known in the eighteenth century—for scholars had demonstrated as much with their critical historical methodology—that the emperor's clothes were by no means as old as they appeared.[2] Many made fun of them and thought the "musty junk" ridiculous.[3] On the other hand, they were not abandoned; on the contrary the right to store them, handle them during the coronation, and dress and undress the emperor with them was jealously guarded. That calls for an explanation.

Figure 1. Coronation regalia: alb, coronation mantle, and belt for the imperial sword. Johann Adam Delsenbach, colored copper engraving, 1751, © KHM, Vienna.

This book is not only about the emperor's clothes, but about the totality of the symbols, gestures, rituals, and procedures in which the system of the Empire concretely embodied itself. The ritual act of dressing, the investiture with the regalia—crown, orb, scepter, and sword (figures 1 and 2)—stands pars pro toto for all actions in which the Empire manifested itself visibly. At the same time, as suggested by the title derived from Andersen's fairy tale,[4] this book is above all concerned with the question of how a society is kept under the spell of a collective fiction—even if many, quietly and in their own minds, might not believe in it at all.

Fictions and Symbols

The premise of the book is drawn from cultural sociology and asserts the following: every institutional order needs symbolic-ritual embodiments and rests on the shared belief in fictions. Here fiction refers to the social construction and collective imputation of meaning on which every social order is based. Unlike the fairy tale about the emperor's *new* clothes, fiction has nothing to do with lies or deception. According to the basic premise, an institutional system consists in the final analysis of nothing else than the permanent, reciprocal ex-

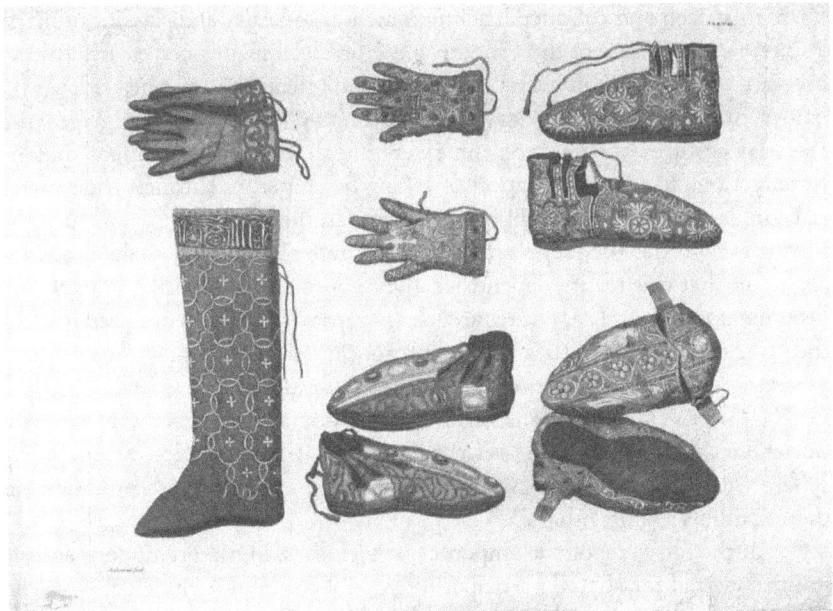

Figure 2. Coronation regalia: stocking, two pairs of gloves, three pairs of shoes. Johann Adam Delsenbach, colored copper engraving, 1751, © KHM, Vienna.

pectations of those who participate in it: each individual believes in the functioning of the system as something completely self-evident, and posits just as self-evidently that everyone else believes in it as well. Social order functions on the basis of "expectations about expectations": each individual is guided in his actions by the expectation that the others will do likewise.[5]

What plays a crucial role is how justified these expectations are in the long run. For example, if rulership is ultimately based on the expectations of those subject to it that physical force will be used should the situation warrant it, the system can be undermined and toppled if that expectation is never met. However, that does not happen very easily. Institutional systems are also characterized by the tendency to become increasingly stable over time. Maintaining them is far easier than changing them. After all, institutions create normative expectations that are maintained even if they are violated in individual cases.[6]

Even though they are made up of reciprocal expectations and collective imputations of meaning, which individuals use to guide their conduct, institutions (i.e., systems that are stable over long periods) usually strike people as something fixed and objective, largely inaccessible and removed from their influence. That is because institutions confront the individual at every turn with symbolic forms. Those forms adhere to a collective code, which the individual learns by growing up in a specific system and which he or she in turn reproduces in speech and conduct. The fundamental concepts and classifications of a system—in the case of the Empire: emperor, electors, princes, estates, and so on—are omnipresent in every manner of symbolization: starting with terms, names, titles, and forms of address, moving on to physical symbols, images, and everyday gestures of deference, and extending all the way to complex, solemn, ritual actions like the coronation of a king or emperor. Through their material concreteness, their perception by the senses, these symbolizations turn the institutional order they represent into a concrete reality. They make individuals forget that this reality depends on their continuously creating it anew and bringing it to life, and they surround the system with an "aura of necessity."[7] At the same time, however, these symbolizations are never unambiguous, and the perceptions and mental pictures in the minds of individuals are never identical. Often, various interpretations compete with one another openly or covertly. Societal struggles are waged over the attempt not only to colonize the public sphere with one's own symbols, but also to assert one's own interpretations of these symbols against others.[8]

As in the fairy tale of the emperor's new clothes, in the premodern empire it was above all the shared participation in public symbolic-ritual acts—*solemnities*—on which institutional fictions were erected: royal and imperial coronations, enfeoffments, ceremonies of homage, the opening of an imperial diet. Everyone's open and visible participation turned those present into reciprocal eyewitnesses of their faith in this order. Anyone who participated in a public symbolic-ritual act affirmed his consent and announced that in the future he would live up to the expectations this entailed.[9] Presence meant acceptance. If one wanted to obviate this effect, one had to either avoid participation or make a demonstrative display of protest. But all those in attendance affirmed by their mere physical presence and witness the effect of the act—and for this the inner attitude did not matter, as long as it was not visible.[10]

Symbolic-ritual acts can generate this kind of effect for an institutional order above all if that order rests on the personal interactions of those involved, if the individuals come face-to-face on specific occasions. In the premodern world this was the case in local societies, for example, a village, a city, or a princely court. But to some extent it was true also of the princely society of the Empire, whose members met in person at least occasionally, and at the end of the Middle Ages and the dawn of the modern era with ever greater frequency and in ever larger numbers. We are dealing with a "culture of presence," which rested first and foremost on the personal presence of the rulers themselves, and only secondarily on written communication and representation by proxy.[11] What characterized this order was the fact that its fundamental structures had to be symbolically and ritually enacted on certain solemn occasions. This changed slowly over the course of the early modern period. Describing the specific logic of this culture of presence and its transformation is the purpose of this book.

The collective belief in the necessity, self-evident nature, and inviolability of an institutional order never holds sway entirely unchallenged. What usually accompanies phases of heightened criticism of an institution is that the symbolic forms in which it embodies itself are unmasked as an "empty semblance," its sacral aura is stripped away, and its rituals enacted—if at all—only with an ironic distance.[12] In the eighteenth century, this attitude indeed grew stronger among the educated vis-à-vis the Old Empire. For many, the dignity of the old order now seemed attached only to the imperial garments, which had long since become ridiculous. If the officeholders were ever stripped of their splendid regalia, as happened during the French Revolution, it was very difficult to forget this disenchanting sight. Already in the late eighteenth century, and even more so after the fall of the Holy Roman Empire, people liked to speak about this complex entity in metaphors of barbarian ruins,[13] of an old house threatened by collapse,[14] a Gothic monstrosity,[15] and a chimera.[16] The questions are these: When and why was the trust in the old forms lost, and why did they nevertheless continue to be enacted for so long, indeed, with even heightened fastidiousness? How did the ambivalent situation diagnosed by Hegel come about, a situation that is reminiscent of Andersen's fairy-tale emperor? Why did nothing change until the Empire was toppled from the outside by Napoleon's troops? To answer these questions, however, one has to ask even more basically: What actually constituted the institutional order of the Empire? To what extent and in what way was it bound together into a whole capable of acting? How were its institutional structures positioned to last? On what expectations of the actors did it rest? Wherein did it embody itself as a political entity? And what role did symbolizations of every kind play in this process—words, images, objects, gestures, ceremonies, and rituals?

The Idea of Constitution and Constitutional History

Hegel's charge was that "[i]n the preservation of these forms, the German convinces himself that he can discern the preservation of his constitution."[17] In Hegel's time, the concept of the constitution had taken on an entirely new meaning;[18] in the American and especially the French Revolutions, *constitution* had turned emphatically into a highly charged political slogan. "Constitution" no longer referred in general terms to the condition of a body (human or political), but to a construct of basic laws and especially individual basic rights that was construed with the criteria of political rationality and invariably took concrete form in a written charter. "A constitution is not a thing in name only, but in fact. It has not an ideal, but a real existence; and wherever it cannot be produced in a visible form, there is none," wrote the revolutionary Thomas Paine.[19] This concept of constitution, which is essentially still ours today, describes a system of abstract, supreme norms, a basic order of the state fixed in writing that regulates the operation of the organs of the state, specifies the rights and duties of citizens, and thus brings the state into existence as a legal system. What characterizes such modern constitutions, above all else, is that they stipulate how new laws are created, indeed, how they themselves can be altered.[20] This, precisely, was not yet the case in the premodern world.

One of the salient features of modern constitutions is that we are dealing with a text, namely, a published, printed text. Even if observers speak of constitutional *reality*, they define it by the way it deviates from the constitutional *text*.[21] Traditional scholarship on constitutional history was long shaped by this concept—even though scholars knew full well that in the Middle Ages and the early modern period there were no constitutional texts of the kind we have today. Still, historians for the most part dealt with premodern constitutions as though they were abstract systems of norms enacted by a legislator and put down in writing. It was implied that their meaning was unambiguous, that they were arranged systematically and free of contradictions, and that they met with consensus.[22] If even modern constitutions hardly fulfill this criterion upon closer inspection, this is all the more true for the constitution of the Empire. Measured against this yardstick, the Empire had to appear as an incomplete, weak, monstrous, and deficient state. The medievalist Peter Moraw, one of the founders of a new constitutional history of the Empire, already noted as much in 1989: "Notwithstanding all the skill of the jurists, [in the late Middle Ages and early modern period] there did not exist a secure 'constitutional' and procedural consensus that would have been based—as in the constitutional state of modernity—on basic norms and procedures that created the state power in the first place, and would have been construed with logical consistency and fully legally actionable. To think of such things for the more distant past ... would be anachronistic." And he continues: "What we call constitution was back then often a relationship among grandees, for whom princely renown matters a good deal more than texts on paper, or better: these were incommensurable factors."[23] But what Peter Moraw does not yet take into consideration are the symbolic-ritual acts in which one can see a premodern equivalent to the written constitution of modernity—an equivalent, however, that followed a logic all its own.

It is extremely difficult, though, to disregard the familiar and seemingly self-evident cosmos of formally established written legal norms through which we continuously move in the modern world. Yet when historians posit categories like constitution, state, sovereignty, state organ, state law, and so on, they are employing concepts that were not yet known in the early modern period, or were accorded an entirely different meaning. If one uses these categories, it is all but unavoidable that one will also project the structures they designate into earlier eras.[24] Between us and the Old Empire stand legal positivism and constitutionalism, which mislead one—looking back in time—into treating the imperial constitution as a closed, autonomous system of legal norms that can be clearly distinguished from actual political praxis. Many of the questions that modern historians pose from this perspective thus lead one astray, because they can have no clear answers. They presuppose precise conceptual distinctions that actors at the time did not themselves make. One such question, for example, is whether or not certain rituals of power—investiture, homage, coronation, and so on—were legally constitutive acts. But what is the general yardstick against which one should measure this? Concrete symbolic acts are *all* that existed; there was no concrete constitutional text that could have endowed these acts with or stripped them of constitutive meaning. Symptomatic of such an anachronistic perspective is the complaint of the older constitutional historiography that the conceptualization of the sources is vague and diffuse, and that the sources deal much more with representative externalities than with constitutional law. This was seen as superficiality, naïveté, and an incapacity for abstraction on the level of state theory. But both of these qualities—carelessness about concepts and careful attention to ceremonies and rituals—are exactly what was characteristic of the premodern world.[25] The precision that mattered to the actors themselves all the way into the seventeenth century was the precision of concrete, symbolic-ritual "externalities," not the precision of abstract concepts. Instead of abstract categories, this book therefore deals first of all with concrete phenomena, with the media in which they were conveyed to the observers, and with the meanings that the participants ascribed to them.

Characteristic of the treatment of the Holy Roman Empire by earlier generations of historians was also that they either ignored a great deal of the symbolic-ritual phenomena that the sources talked about—everything that was colorful, ostentatious, ceremonial, and demonstratively staged—or assigned it to the realm of "culture" instead of politics. This included not only court feasts, tournaments, weddings, and banquets, but also ceremonial enfeoffments, entrances, and acts of homage. Although it was understood, and occasionally mentioned, that all of these phenomena held great importance to the actors themselves, they were not addressed as *political* events. Behind this focus on "real" politics, that is, on everything that did not take place on the public stage, stood the unspoken yardstick of a later political style that was characterized by objectivity, soberness, writing, and professionality. This political style of the "gray suit," to which the bourgeois historians of the nineteenth and twentieth centuries felt committed and which enjoyed their sympathies, was the political style of their own age. It presupposed that the political had established itself as an autonomous social functional system with a behavioral logic all its own. However, that was not yet the case in the early modern period. Political, social, religious, and economic systems were not yet separated one from the other. Relations between the members of the Empire were not anonymous and abstract like those between functionaries in the modern state or other formal organizations: instead, they still rested to a high degree on personal closeness, kinship, and patronage. But as long as the political was not separated from other societal functions, political actions always entailed simultaneously a demonstration of a person's economic wealth, social affiliation, and rank.

To preempt these misunderstandings, one could try, first of all, to look at this past order as something other, something not self-evident—the way in which an ethnologist approaches a distant, foreign culture. Of course, this comparison falls short: after all, the past epochs of their own culture are never completely foreign to historians, who are linked to them through traditions and lines of structural continuity. Instead, the "ethnological view" is a methodological fiction, an artifice, which consists of initially looking at everything one encounters in the sources not as self-evident, but in need of interpretation.[26] One should not overlook that this perspective, too, like any other, highlights certain aspects of the object under examination (exotic, archaic ones), while allowing others (more familiar and modern ones) to recede into the background. Still, this perspective seems fruitful and informative, especially with respect to the Empire.

It is no accident that this kind of new approach to the premodern era is being sought out today. We live in a time when sovereign statehood is waning. The modern nation-state of the nineteenth and twentieth centuries is no longer the primary political point of reference, no longer the only point of convergence of political action. Transnational, global, but also regional references have become more important. The old model of modernization, which proceeded from a progressive rationalization of the world, has become less convincing. The ideal-type model of the bureaucratic, institutionalized state, conceived as a thoroughly rationalized enterprise, has itself been demystified. Sociologists have long since discovered that modern organizations, too, do not function as envisioned by their statutes.[27] All of this has created distance to the modern concepts of state and constitution, and it opens up a perspective on the degree to which modern notions—which have been shaped by several myths of rationality—still obscure a view of premodern politico-social structures.

Constitutional History as Ritual History?

Already in the seventeenth and eighteenth centuries, historians were stumped by the imperial constitution and felt unable to tell a coherent story about it: they found that the Empire was too heterogeneous to be cast into a narrative form. When Johann Gottfried Herder pondered why a national history of the Germans was not as easy to write as one of the French, English, or the ancient Romans and Greeks, his explanation was that "the Holy Roman Empire is still today in its arrangement the most peculiar in Europe: for centuries it went through chaos … ; its history a history of rank, law, and quarrels." Much like Hegel later on, Herder also saw it as characteristic of the Germans "to take an interest in ceremonial rank, in this or that chartered sign of authority, in one law or another, not because it was advantageous, but because it was a legal imperative, to allow themselves to become interested, often to break their necks. The history of Germany, too, will not refute this character."[28] For a long time, constitutional history of the modern era tended to smile condescendingly upon the "fringes of this ceremonial canopy" and hardly took it seriously. By now this has thoroughly changed. Symbolic representations of every kind, images and symbols, ceremonies and rituals, feasts and celebrations, have become a very popular topic of historical scholarship.[29] However, they are still treated separately from "real" political history: the "soft" themes of symbolic communication confront the "hard" themes of political decision making.[30] But the issue is precisely to bring these two areas together.

This does not mean, though, that one should simply turn the tables—as though the constitution of the Empire rested solely on symbols, ceremonies, and rituals. Rather, one can distinguish various ways in which the order of a community is secured over the long run: first, in positive legal ways, that is, through treaties and laws; second, through concrete administrative praxis, that is, through the actual procedures of collectively binding consensus formation and decision making; third, theoretically and discursively, that is, through learned interpretation and systematization; and fourth, symbolically and ritually, that is, through the continuously renewed, solemn, and explicit symbolism of public rituals of power, as well as through the implicit symbolism of everyday behavior.[31] The institutional order of the Empire, its constitution in the broadest sense, was based on all of these forms of consolidation, and all of them will be addressed in this book. The symbolic-ritual form is undoubtedly the oldest, most archaic type of institutionalization. It corresponds to a culture of personal presence, and one can assume that its function waned the more the use of written media became customary and the more efficient formal procedures asserted themselves. And yet, as is expressed by the quotes from Hegel and Herder, these forms did not fade away in the Empire of the early modern period; on the contrary, they grew increasingly complex. The question is therefore how the various forms of institutional consolidation related to one another in the Empire and how those relationships changed over the course of the early modern era.

This book is not intended as an alternative constitutional history. Its goal is merely to open up a new perspective on that history.[32] It does *not* proceed from abstract institutional categories that had seemingly been always and immutably fixed (i.e., emperor, electors, princes, estates), but from events in which these categories became visible and were sometimes also newly negotiated. This book is also not concerned with drawing up an inventory of all key symbols and rituals of the Empire. Such symbols existed at every level of the political system: from church prayers for the emperor in village parishes, to the imperial eagles and coats of arms on the town halls of imperial cities, to images of the emperor and electors on patents of nobility, all the way to the sumptuous imperial halls in the residences of prince-bishops or imperial prelates. These symbols of presence were found throughout the territories and cities of the Empire, by means of which especially less powerful members of the Empire demonstrated their membership in the whole.[33] All of this must be left aside here. Instead, the focus is on the central solemn acts and procedures in which "the Empire" became visibly manifested as a political body.

The structure of the book is neither systematic nor consistently chronological. Instead, it contains four successive individual snapshots. Four times, the microhistorical magnifying glass will be focused on particularly significant symbolic dates: the so-called Reform Diet of Worms in 1495, the Augsburg imperial diet of the *Confessio Augustana* of 1530, the first imperial diet following the Peace of Westphalia in Regensburg in 1653/54, and the years of the royal election, coronation, and succession of Joseph II in 1764/65. The choice of these dates calls for an explanation. Traditionally, the imperial diets of 1495, 1530, and 1653/54 and the years 1764/65 have been seen as the milestones of German constitutional history. The four dates selected here were historical moments in which the situation seemed particularly open to change, something that some of the actors involved were also fully aware of.

The imperial diet of Maximilian I in Worms in 1495 represents a phase of heightened institutionalization, which earlier historians referred to as "reform of the Empire." At this diet, a number of institutional regulations were negotiated and fixed in writing, regulations that would shape the Empire of the early modern period. Charles V's imperial diet in Augsburg in 1530, where the Protestants met the emperor in person for the first time in nearly a decade and handed over the *Confessio Augustana* to him, marks a turning point in the history of the Reformation; here the relationship between estates bent on reform and the emperor was placed on a new foundation. The imperial diet that Ferdinand III summoned to Regensburg in 1653 in the wake of the Peace of Westphalia was in some sense the real end of the Thirty Years' War in the Empire; here the emperor and the estates sought to resolve the questions that had remained open and to balance out the future order of peace. The years 1764/65, finally, stand for several turning points. The Seven Years' War had just come to an end and had redistributed power. Within the Empire, two rival major powers now confronted each other permanently, powers that were able to draw upon large territorial complexes outside of the Empire. Joseph II's election as Roman king in 1764 put onto the throne in 1765 (as his father's successor) a man who had a new understanding of rulership and of emperorship. Henceforth, the most tradition-bound secular office of European Christendom was held by one of the most determined anti-traditionalists and anti-ritualists.

The choice of these symbolic dates in no way means that these were the only or the most important milestones in the history of the Empire. The selection could have been different, and many crucial developments are not adequately encompassed by them. But all of these dates have one thing in common: shortly before, external conflicts had been resolved (at least temporarily), and the order of the whole was being challenged to a greater degree than usual. Thus, the expectations of the actors had to be newly calibrated. What was at stake in these moments in various respects was to define what "the Empire" really was, and to assert, defend, or even alter one's own position within the whole. And it is my thesis that all of this transpired not least through symbolic means.

Until the second half of the seventeenth century, the most important stage on which these symbolic confrontations took place were the *Hoftage* (court days) or imperial diets—assemblies and simultaneously embodiments of the entire Empire at changing locations. Here "the Empire" became temporarily a perceptible, concrete reality. This was not only where deliberations took place on the most important shared concerns; the imperial princes were also invested with their territories, and the Roman king or the emperor was elected and crowned. The ceremonial opening of the imperial diet, the conferment of the princely imperial fiefdoms, and the election and coronation of the king were the central rituals of power of the empire. By taking place in traditional symbolic-ritual forms, they were a reminder of earlier actions and placed those involved into a system that was older than they. Leopold von Ranke already saw it this way: "Solemn acts of this kind have the characteristic that the meaning they possess at the moment connects them directly to the most distant centuries."[34] Paradoxically enough, this was true also—and especially—when the traditions had in fact been interrupted or the stability of the system was under threat: rituals bridged such ruptures and symbolically created a permanence that might not have existed at all without them.

In the course of the early modern period these various symbolic-ritual acts—coronations, imperial diets, enfeoffments—became increasingly separated in space and time. As a result, in the later period one can no longer find a specific event in a specific year at a specific place that could have been considered *the* stage for the empire. Instead, in the eighteenth century the imperial diet took place exclusively in Regensburg, the enfeoffments exclusively at the imperial court in Vienna, and the elections and coronations exclusively in Frankfurt am Main. Chapter 4 will therefore not focus on *one* symbolic event, but will address all of these various locations as venues of the empire.

The primary sources for the present account are official descriptions of the ceremonies by the heralds and masters of ceremonies, illustrated broadsheets, and pamphlets—that is to say, written and pictorial representations of the ritual acts either commissioned by the actors themselves and circulated at the courts, or produced by publishers independently for a broader market. These sources are symbolic duplications of the solemn acts in a different medium, representations of representations, symbolizations of the second order. Other sources are written reflections of the concrete acts: protocols, correspondence, diaries, and so on. The obvious perspective assumed by the various accounts should not be regarded—as it often is—as a methodological problem. After all, the issue here is, precisely, to gain a view of the different interpretations and competing conceptions of what the order of the empire was.

That is also why our gaze will be directed less at the normal case and more at ruptures and conflicts. For it was on these occasions that the participants had reason to address the rules of the game, which they otherwise observed for the most part tacitly in their actions. In this way the flexible character of the symbolic praxis comes into view, and one can see how in any given case the politicosocial boundaries are newly drawn, order categories are newly defined, and claims to validity are newly fine-tuned. Even if the tradition-bound rituals suggested as much, the constitution of the empire was *not* a static, fixed, and objective entity, but something that was calibrated by the players through their actions—though of course not without preconditions. It was a "doing" more than a "being."[35] The manner in which this happened changed considerably over the course of three centuries. The patterns of actions became more rigid, the possibilities of change smaller. Using the individual points in time, this book intends to illustrate what all of this meant to the actors involved, how this Holy Roman Empire of the German Nation appeared to them, and how they brought it forth time and again in their actions.

Notes

1. Hegel, "Die Verfassung Deutschlands," 85–86. English translation: Hegel, *Political Writings*, text available at http://www.marxists.org/reference/archive/hegel/gcindex.htm.
2. Roeder, *De fatis klinodiorum*; see Kirchweger, "Reichskleinodien."
3. Heine, *Deutschland, ein Wintermärchen*, chapter 17.
4. Koschorke, Frank, and Lüdemann, *Des Kaisers neue Kleider*; Berns, "Der nackte Monarch."
5. In this I follow institutional theory, especially that of Rehberg: "Weltrepräsentanz," "Institutionswandel," and "Institutionen als symbolische Ordnungen." In reference to the empire, see Rehberg, "Stabilisierende 'Fiktionalität,'" 406. See the fundamental work of Schütz, *Der sinnhafte Aufbau der sozialen Welt*; Berger and Luckmann, *The Social Construction of Reality*; Giddens, *Constitution of Society*; but also Luhmann, *Funktionen und Folgen formaler Organisation*. On the concept of "fiction," see also Reinhard, *Krumme Touren*. In general on the theoretical approach, see Stollberg-Rilinger, "Symbolische Kommunikation" and "Die zeremonielle Inszenierung des Reiches."
6. Luhmann, *Rechtssoziologie*, 1:40–52.

7. Drawing on a formulation of Karl-Siegbert Rehberg.
8. Pierre Bourdieu calls this "symbolic violence"; see Bourdieu, *Logic of Practice*, 122–35.
9. Althoff, *Macht der Rituale*, 85.
10. Rappaport, "The Obvious Aspects of Ritual."
11. See on this the systems theory concept of "communication among those present" according to Luhmann, in Kieserling, *Kommunikation under Anwesenden*; the concept of "culture of presence" (*Präsenzkultur*) in Rehberg, "Weltrepräsentanz"; Gumbrecht, "Reflections on Institutions and Re/Presentation"; Schlögl, "Vergesellschaftung" and "Politik beobachten"; see also Habermas's concept of the "representative public" in *The Structural Transformation of the Public Sphere*.
12. This critical stance is today widespread toward "media democracy"; see the fundamental work of Edelman, *Symbolic Uses of Politics*; most recently, see Nullmeier, "Nachwort," in Edelman, *Politik als Ritual*, 199–219; Meyer, *Politik als Theater* and *Inszenierung des Scheins*; Dörner, *Politainment*. However, by now we have learned to understand the mandatory nature of such enactments: every order needs visibility, but at different times in different ways. See, for example, Münkler, "Visibilität der Macht"; Soeffner and Tänzler, *Figurative Politik*.
13. See Schmidt, "Die gotische Ruine."
14. Schiller, *Deutsche Größe*.
15. Classic formulation in Pufendorf, *Die Verfassung des deutschen Reiches*, 106–7; thereafter, see Goethe, for example, *Dichtung und Wahrheit*; other examples in Schmidt, "Die gotische Ruine"; testimonies from the perspective of English travelers in Geyken, *Gentlemen auf Reisen*.
16. Wekhrlin, *Anselmus Rabiosus Reise durch Oberdeutschland*.
17. Hegel, "Die Verfassung Deutschlands," 86.
18. Schmale, "Constitution, Constitutionnel"; Mohnhaupt and Grimm, "Verfassung."
19. Paine, "Rights of Man," 309–10.
20. Luhmann, "Verfassung als evolutionäre Errungenschaft."
21. See Koselleck, "Begriffsgeschichtliche Probleme." For criticism from the field of political science, see Vorländer, "Integration durch Verfassung?" and "Verfassung als symbolische Ordnung"; Blänkner, "Integration durch Verfassung?"; Boldt, *Verfassungsgeschichte*. Early criticism of a purely normative-legal understanding of constitution can already be found in Smend, *Verfassung und Verfassungsrecht*; Heller, *Staatslehre*; see Lhotta, *Integration des modernen Staates*.
22. Luhmann, "Funktionen und Folgen formaler Organisation," 54, and "Verfassung als evolutionäre Errungenschaft."
23. Moraw, "Hoftag und Reichstag," 11, 20.
24. See, to begin with, the fundamental critique by Brunner, *Land und Herrschaft*; on the history of constitutional historiography, see Grothe, *Zwischen Geschichte und Recht*; on the controversy about the statehood of the empire, see Schmidt, "Das frühneuzeitliche Reich"; Schilling, "Das Alte Reich"; Stollberg-Rilinger, "Die zeremonielle Inszenierung des Reiches"; most recently see Haug-Moritz, *Verfassungsgeschichte*, 7–37.
25. Moraw, "Hoftag und Reichstag"; fundamental is the critique of the older constitutional history by Moraw, "Versuch" and *Von der offenen Verfassung*; Isenmann, "Kaiser, Reich und deutsche Nation."
26. This is the concern of the more recent "culturalist" political history; on this concept, see Mergel, "Kulturgeschichte"; Frevert, "Neue Politikgeschichte"; Landwehr, "Diskurs—Macht—Wissen"; Reinhard, "Politische Kultur"; Jussen, *Die Macht des Königs*;

Stollberg-Rilinger, *Was heißt Kulturgeschichte des Politischen?*; with reference to the empire, see Stollberg-Rilinger, "Die zeremonielle Inszenierung des Reiches"; for a critical opposing view, see Rödder, "Klios neue Kleider."
27. See above all Luhmann, "Funktionen und Folgen formaler Organisation"; Weick, *Der Prozeß des Organisierens*; Meyer and Rowan, "Institutionalized Organizations"; Brunsson, *Organization of Hypocrisy*.
28. Herder, "Über die Reichsgeschichte"; see Völkel, "The 'Historical Consciousness.'"
29. Fundamental is Daniel, "Clio unter Kulturschock" and *Kompendium Kulturgeschichte*; for a survey of the scholarship, see Stollberg-Rilinger, "Zeremoniell, Ritual, Symbol" and "Symbolische Kommunikation."
30. Symptomatic for this misunderstanding is Kraus and Nicklas, *Geschichte der Politik*.
31. On the distinction between explicit and implicit symbolism, see Krischer, "Inszenierung und Verfahren"; similarly, see Schlögl, "Symbole in der Kommunikation."
32. For the following, see the general introductions: Willoweit, *Deutsche Verfassungsgeschichte*; Duchhardt, *Deutsche Verfassungsgeschichte*; Neuhaus, *Das Reich*; Gotthard, *Das Alte Reich*; Wilson, *The Holy Roman Empire*; Stollberg-Rilinger, *Das Heilige Römische Reich Deutscher Nation*. For a history of the scholarship on the empire, see Schnettger, "Reichsverfassungsgeschichtsschreibung"; Eichhorn, *Deutsche Staats- und Rechtsgeschichte*; Nicklas, "Müssen wir das Alte Reich lieben?" On constitutional history in general, see Grothe, *Zwischen Geschichte und Recht*; Haug-Moritz, *Verfassungsgeschichte*.
33. See, for example, Müller, *Bilder des Reiches*.
34. Ranke, *Reformation*, 534.
35. Drawing on Ernst Cassirer, see Daniel, *Kompendium Kulturgeschichte*, 90ff.; Stollberg-Rilinger, "Die zeremonielle Inszenierung des Reiches," 238–39.

CHAPTER 1

Creation and Presentation of the Empire
Worms, 1495

A Milestone of Constitutional History?

"Item Anno 1495 on Wednesday after *Reminiscere* [18 March], the king of the Romans Maximilian came to Worms and held a great diet with the electors, princes, cities, and all estates, sacred and secular, to make a common peace," the mayor of Worms recorded in his diary.[1] There are various reasons for considering this "day of the king and the Empire," which lasted into August, a very special event. It was the first imperial assembly called by King Maximilian I following the death of his father and his own accession to the throne in 1493, after he had already been elected and crowned Roman king in 1486 and before he intended to journey to Rome and have himself crowned emperor by the pope (a plan that did not come to fruition). The threat to the Empire from external enemies and internal strife was acute, and the new king felt the need to restore the old imperial authority, which was confronting two challenges: first, from the French king, who had invaded Italy, prompting the pope and the Italian princes to call for help; second, from the Turks, against whom the new king was envisaging a new pan-European crusade. For all of this Maximilian required an extraordinary amount of money. This offered the group of princes around the Elector of Mainz, Berthold of Henneberg, imperial arch-chancellor, an opportunity to put forth their own ideas about participation in governance. Their concern was to establish secure and lasting institutions of conflict resolution that would function independently of the king himself: a permanently staffed high court, a universal tax, and a permanent estate-based imperial government. The negotiations were "indeed hard and peculiar, rambling and errant; if action is taken today, changes are made tomorrow," and for a long time it seemed to observers that a "unanimous resolution would not be found."[2] It was only at the end of July that a makeshift compromise was arrived at; the goal of establishing an imperial *Regiment* of estates was thwarted by opposition from the king. But after months of deliberations, the participants were able to accomplish what had not been possible at similar assemblies over the past two decades: to adopt fundamental reform resolutions by fixing them in writing in a joint imperial recess (*Reichsabschied*). The Worms imperial diet of 1495 is thus seen by historians as a milestone of German constitutional history, the turning point from the Middle Ages to the early modern era. Here, scholars have argued, momentous regulations for the internal and external pacification of the Empire were debated and adopted, regulations that significantly advanced the institutional consolidation of the imperial order.[3]

The diet is considered a milestone not only because of the substantive results, but also because of its form, for here the imperial estates and King Maximilian I came together and negotiated in a way that shaped the future procedures. The assembly in 1495 not least made itself into a topic of discussion in that it resolved, among other things, to meet regularly once a year in the future. Former constitutional historians maintained that this concluded the transformation from the emperor's court assembly (*Hoftag*) to the imperial diet (*Reichstag*): the Empire had placed itself vis-à-vis the king as a separate political body capable of acting collectively; the imperial diet had become the "crucial instrument of the will of the Empire."[4]

But what was this "will of the Empire"? In fact, what was "the Empire" to contemporaries: as a concept, an idea, a notion, a fact? When historians say that "the Empire" did this or that, they implicitly take for granted that it was a political whole with a collective "will," capable of collective action. But that is precisely the blind spot the present study addresses. This chapter will ask whether, to what extent, and in what way contemporaries themselves made such attributions. In other words, the Empire is to become discernible as something that was first and foremost created by individual persons, both through their visible reciprocal actions and through the meanings (by no means always unambiguous and consistent) they attributed to these actions. In what way did the actors *create* the Empire as an entity, how did they *imagine* it, and how did they *represent* it? What turned an assembly of individuals into an assembly of "the Empire"? How was the Empire enacted, directly through actions and indirectly through media? How was it demarcated against the outside world, and how were its component parts organized and classified? What divergent situational interpretations collided in the process, and how were conflicts of interpretation resolved? The assembly at Worms in 1495 offers a particularly good example for investigating these questions.

The first diet (*Tag*) of a new ruler was always a special gathering. Maximilian could invoke the old custom "that is due and proper to us and every king of the Romans at the beginning of his governance of the Holy Empire, that we can summon all and every one of our and the Holy Empire's electors, princes, and other estates of the same to a joint assembly and make known to them the affairs of the Holy Empire."[5] For a system still largely based on personal relationships, every change of ruler meant a rupture that had to be ritually bridged. Even though Maximilian had already been elected and crowned king of the Romans seven years earlier, and had attended the imperial assemblies as such, it was only after his father's death that he assumed the role of the overlord of the Empire, the holder of the *imperium*.[6] This meant that the ties between the new sovereign of the Empire and its immediate members had to be publicly re-established as personal ties. That was the purpose of the first ceremonial *Hoftag* (*curia solemnis*) of the new regent.[7]

Maximilian seems to have been fully aware that this meeting with the members of the Empire possessed unusual symbolic character. A whole host of measures reveals his intent to use this assembly to make visible and assert the order of the Empire as he saw it. The other participants, too, were aware that the manner in which they presented themselves publicly not only expressed their place within the whole order, but was critical for determining that place going forward. As a result, they had to be very intent on protecting their own claims to status and aligning them with those of the other participants. The fundamental questions—who was really part of the Empire, how participants dealt with one another, what rank they held vis-à-vis one another, and above all how decisions binding on all could arise out of their joint actions—could not be answered in the abstract. The answers were nowhere put down authoritatively in writing; instead, they emerged out of concrete praxis. And that praxis was still very much in flux. The assembly of 1495 was particularly important in this regard, because more persons came together than ever before, at least more than contemporaries asserted they could remember: "This assembly in Worms was called the great assembly, for it is believed that no king of the Romans in a hundred years had had such an imperial diet."[8] The importance of the matters to be dealt with, and their relevance to a large circle of participants far beyond the Empire, ensured that a great many nobles appeared in person with a large retinue or at least sent delegates. The assembly itself developed a social magnetic force: one wanted and needed to be present to assume one's place. This created conflicts in many respects, bringing into contact persons who might never have met before and whose reciprocal expectations about their place within the whole did not converge. It was one thing to posit in ideal fashion that the Empire constituted a harmonious, hierarchical system, and another to have to create this hierarchical order de facto by sitting, walking, standing, and proceeding. In many cases, therefore, one had to negotiate ahead of time how to behave toward one another in the external forms of outward conduct.

There was another reason why this was of new and extraordinary importance: the ways of presentation and supraregional transmission of what transpired at such a "royal assembly and assembly of the Empire" had changed, and participants were becoming increasingly aware of this. The heralds of the kings and princes,[9] whose primary task traditionally had been to ensure the orderly arrangement of persons according to coats of arms, ranks, and titles at tournaments and other public events, now occasionally began to document this order in writing and publish it in the new medium of printed broadsheet. This gradually transformed the limited public of those personally present in the same location into a border-spanning, vast, and impersonal public of broadsheets.[10] For all these reasons the assembly in 1495 was also a milestone with respect to the visible staging of the Empire. Here "the Empire" was *represented* in the twofold meaning of the word: as an entity it was both symbolically *depicted* ("*dargestellt*")—in public rituals, images, participant lists, and symbols—and *constituted* ("*hergestellt*") in the strict legal sense of the word, namely, through the adoption of resolutions that claimed to be binding on all its members. Both of these aspects related to each other and belonged together.

Place and Time

That a "day" (*Tag*) of the king and the Empire had to have a specific place and a specific time, a beginning and an end, may seem like a trite statement. It is not. Rather, the question is how it was made clear to the participants that such an assembly was one of "the Empire" and not just a random meeting between some princes and lords and the king. An imperial diet was not an institution with a stable location in a concrete building of the same name, but an event in time, a "day." To be identified as a "day of the Empire," it had to be lifted demonstratively out of the flow of daily activity, and the assembly had to be symbolically marked in space and time.

The royal summons extended an invitation for a specific time at a specific place—at "the Purification of Our Dear Lady" (i.e., 2 February 1495) in the free city of Worms. The assembly was "not to exceed 14 days."[11] The location itself was not arbitrary: since the king was the host, the assembly had to take place between the walls of a civic community that had the king as its immediate overlord. However, the status of Worms as an immediate subject of the Empire and its relationship to the bishop as the former overlord was problematic at this time. Already in the previous year Maximilian had received the homage of the citizenry, under protest from the bishop. Now the free imperial status of the city was additionally affirmed symbolically by the summons to the imperial assembly, which the mayor of Worms had urgently requested from Maximilian.[12] The community's festive reception of the king as lord of the city and host of a

Hoftag was a potent manifestation of the city's legal claim; it defined Worms as a free imperial city.[13]

The city, already a separate legal sphere, possessed a special, temporary legal status during the assembly. It was marked out in an elevated sense as a city of the Empire, making it clear to all involved that the king was temporarily exercising his direct sovereignty over the city, and at the same time his sovereignty over the entire Empire. Maximilian had issued regulations intended to guarantee the peace, security, and maintenance of the many outside visitors, numbering in the thousands. Food prices were fixed to prevent profiteering. What was usually forbidden to the citizens was explicitly permitted to the noble lords—for example, to let minstrels perform and put on games of chance. Residents were called upon not to mock foreigners "who are not like us," and all were prohibited from harassing or harming the Jews in Worms.[14] Hereditary Imperial Marshal Pappenheim, not the city council, was in charge of implementing these regulations and punishing violations, and to that end he was authorized to employ city personnel.

How the king's legal sovereignty over the city manifested itself is revealed by the execution of a verdict during the imperial diet. On the public square in front of the New Mint, the council's newly acquired meeting house—a place that served for the staging of judicial sovereignty as the embodiment of all sovereign rights—a Dutchman was placed into an iron collar and branded on his face by the city's executioner. An official of the Hereditary Imperial Marshal "had him burned on his check by a city executioner in the iron collar and he branded him with an iron … and there was an eagle on it." The Dutchman's crime was "having spoken ill of the king."[15] The background to this was presumably opposition to Maximilian's succession in Burgundy. His insulted majesty was restored through an act of symbolic and also very real physical violence: by permanently and visibly branding the vilifier of the king with the symbol of the latter's authority—the imperial eagle, which similarly marked coins, banners, and seals[16]—the executioner inscribed the power of the king irreversibly upon the body of the culprit, and by doing so turned it into its medium. In this way, the king's legitimate sovereignty and penal authority put itself menacingly on display: the wounded violator of the king's dignity became a living symbol of the restored majesty.

This was the most extreme physical form in which the royal claim to authority manifested itself in the city. The eagle in general marked and represented the presence of the royal majesty. Thus, the traditional lodging of kings, the bishop's court, the highest-ranking location in the city, was transformed into the king's court for the duration of his stay by having his crest affixed above the door. In this way the king assumed the place of the city's overlord. The same transformation occurred through the tournament tent he had erected, and through the public royal throne at the Upper Market, on which he performed enfeoffments and knightings *in maiestate*. The eagle was an essential element of what was meant by appearance in maiestate, "in royal adornment and honor." The crest was not only a sign that referred to an object beyond itself; it was also a symbol of presence that itself practically embodied what it represented: where the imperial eagle appeared on a crest or banner, "it was as though we [the king or emperor] were present in our very own body."[17]

The electors and princes also used their coats of arms to mark the lodgings where they and their retinue took quarters, mostly the houses of city councilors in the case of secular princes and those of canons in the case of ecclesiastical princes.[18] This indicated that these houses, together with all the persons therein, temporarily constituted a separate sphere of law and were subject to the authority of those residing in them. It is variously attested that enclosed wooden walkways were erected between neighboring lodgings, allowing their residents to visit each other without appearing in public. This was motivated not only by the wish to visit even after dark, for it was otherwise forbidden to leave one's lodgings at night, but also by the desire to carefully stage any appearance in the public sphere of the city. Kings and princes, after all, were public persons in the sense that they were compelled to demonstrate their status at all times and everywhere through their mere public appearance. This symbolic burden could be lessened only if they appeared in public as rarely as possible.

When did the imperial diet begin? There was still no standardized temporal order of absolute and universally binding validity to which all participants could have been bound. As a result, no one had arrived as of 2 February, the date specified in the summons. The king himself had been delayed by the war in the Netherlands. He did not arrive until 18 March, the first to do so, accompanied by Berthold of Henneberg, the Elector of Mainz and arch-chancellor of the Empire. The king, we read in the mayor's diary, "was properly received by the council and with the baldachin, as was customary."[19] This referred to the king's festive entry as the city's overlord, though in this instance we are not told much about the details. At such a ritual reception, the council usually received the ruler outside the city, handed him the keys as a sign of voluntary submission to his authority, offered him an obligatory series of gifts, and escorted him to his lodgings under a baldachin.[20]

With this, the king took public possession of his city and henceforth resided there as the host himself. Subsequently, it was he who in turn received the high-ranking guests by riding out to meet them as they gradually arrived, in great splendor with his own retinue and accompanied by the princes who were already in residence.[21] These elaborate meetings, which took place in front of a large urban public, followed an intricate grammar of reverence and made it possible, through subtle distinctions and deviations in detail, to specify the mutual relationship with great precision. This was especially significant when dealing with persons whose place within the Empire's system of political-social classification was uncertain or contested. That was the case, for example, with Duke René II of Lorraine, whose circumstances we will examine in detail later.[22] Following such a reception, it was the unspoken (though no less universally recognized) rule that those already present and the newcomer visit one another in their lodgings, whereby the sequence of these visits contained a clear indication about the rank of the visitors.

The envoys at the Worms diet interacted very differently with one another than did the high-ranking lords in person among themselves and with the king. If the status of princely councilors was fundamentally different from that of the princes themselves, that was even more so for city delegates, who represented alien social elements within the courtly environment. While princes performed reciprocal receptions and visits in their lodgings, there was no such ritual of personal notification for the envoys of princes and for city delegates. The counterpart of this ritual was the presentation of their credentials through the letters of accreditation from their masters. In Worms, most of these letters were still addressed to the king, and not—as became customary later—to the archbishop of Mainz as the arch-chancellor of the Empire and organizer of the imperial diet deliberations. The royal chancellery verified the envoys' letters of credentials before the hereditary imperial marshal invited them to the deliberations.[23] While the interactions of princes and other high-ranking lords rested on the fiction of personal proximity and took place in the social forms of friendship and kinship, the fundamentally different status of the civic councilors was marked by the fact that they had to prove their identity in writing and legitimize their participation with a mandate.

There was thus a series of rituals of beginning: the reception of the king, the mutual solemn greeting of the king and arriving princes, and—in a very different way—the notification of the envoys. However, this did not provide an unambiguous beginning to the deliberations in the sense, for example, of modern parliamentary proceedings. New participants continued to arrive after the meetings had long been underway, while others were already departing.

The sources on the Worms diet reveal nothing about the ritual of beginning that was prescribed in the Golden Bull for a new king's first *curia solemnis* (*Hoftag*), a ritual with which most "common days" (*gemeine Tage*) of the fifteenth century had begun and which was also used to open the proceedings of the imperial assemblies in the sixteenth century: a mass of the Holy Spirit. This mass began with a solemn procession in which the participants picked up the king or emperor at his lodgings and proceeded jointly to the city hall, where the proposition with the king's demands was read out. This usually formed the sacred starting point to the deliberative proceedings in the narrower sense. The invocation of the Holy Spirit served as the "blessed opening" of an imperial assembly; it was considered "the necessary foundation of the entire act," anchoring it within the divine order and endowing it with sacral authority.[24] Even if the sources for the Worms diet of 1495 do not explicitly mention such an opening mass, they do report the joint celebration of Palm Sunday and Easter mass.[25] The fact that no formal opening mass *De Sancto Spiritu* seems to have taken place reveals how little the events at this diet were formalized and just how much everything was still focused on the physical presence of the king, who was at the heart of it all. In retrospect we are told that the assembly began "on Wednesday after Sunday *Reminiscere* [18 March] … when His Royal Majesty arrived in Worms."[26] In other words: his festive arrival was considered the real beginning.

The Order of Persons in Text and Space

Who actually belonged directly to "the Empire" in Worms in 1495? What does "belonging" mean in the first place? And how can it be determined beyond a doubt? It is not possible to provide unambiguous answers to these questions. To be sure, there were persons whose membership was utterly beyond question, who were imperial vassals and traditionally appeared at the imperial diets; but there were also those whose relationship to the Empire was disputed. The participants certainly held very divergent ideas about the immediate membership of persons and communities. But that became a growing problem only in the course of the fifteenth century, when the demand was first raised that "all estates of the Empire" be invited to the assemblies.[27] Depending on which criteria one applied, "all" could mean very different things. The attempts in Worms in 1495 to create an orderly scheme in this regard were accordingly diverse: in writing, images, and ceremonies.

Some of the answers that struck contemporaries as meaningful and reasonable seem completely absurd to modern constitutional historians. For example, on the occasion of his elevation to the rank of an imperial prince in 1495, the Count and soon-to-be Duke of Württemberg inquired from his persevant Jorg Rugen who the actual members of the Empire were. (A persevant was a low-ranking herald whose task it was to ensure the proper order of persons at all festive, public occasions.) His written response astounds modern readers. Under the heading "Electors, dukes, princes, counts, barons, knights, and servants [*knecht*] of the Holy Roman Empire of the German Nation," we read the following:[28]

> Item four electors of secular rank.
> Item four princes and supreme magistrates [*öberst amptleut*] of the Empire.
> Item four counts palatine and councilors of the Empire.
> Item four archdukes of the Holy Empire.
> Item eight barons [*Freiherren*] of the Holy Empire.
> Item twelve hereditary dukes of the Empire.

Item four margraves of the Empire.
Item four landgraves of the Empire.
Item four burgraves of the Empire.
Item four *hergravenn* of the Empire.
Item four *flugelgraven* of the Empire.
Item fifty-two princes, hereditary and free counts of the Empire, who according to the order hold offices, names, and titles.

This list, which adheres to a rigid scheme of fours, has nothing to do with the situation that prevailed de facto at the imperial diet. It includes neither those summoned nor those present; it accords with none of the many participant lists or registers that existed at the time. Rather, it is a symmetrical scheme that resembles what we encounter in many pictorial depictions of the Empire, the so-called *Quaternionen* (figure 3).[29]

Evidently contemporaries as knowledgeable as the Württemberg herald held an idea of the Empire that was not derived from firsthand observation, but from a very different way of knowing. The scheme of fours, repeated across every kind of estate, created an image of both diversity and symmetry. Other versions of the *Quaternionen* depicted different groups of fours and sought to integrate also the three ecclesiastical electors. This had nothing to do with

Figure 3. Hans Burgkmair the Elder, *Quaternionen* eagle, woodcut (detail), 1495, Nuremberg, Staatsarchiv.

empirical perception. In fact, such a perception would have been difficult to achieve. To begin with, the Empire had dimensions that far exceeded the possibilities of personal perception. Unlike in premodern rural or urban communities, it was hardly possible for everyone to meet and become cognizant of everyone else. Moreover, empirical clarity was difficult to attain because there was simply no clear and binding criterion of membership of the kind that we are familiar with today from formal organizations.[30] In a written membership list one could have unequivocally looked up who was a member of the Empire and who was not. But empirical accuracy was evidently not at all the concern of the *Quaternionen* model. Rather, the intent was to provide a symbolic visualization that the Empire, for all its extraordinary diversity, was nevertheless a harmonious and hierarchically ordered whole. At any rate, the herald obviously considered the scheme an appropriate and adequate answer to the duke's question. The strangeness of this answer to modern readers reveals that the criteria we consider self-evident have not always been the only criteria for correct knowledge. Contemporaries had a way of envisioning the makeup of "the Empire" that was very different from an inductively arrived at description of systematic completeness: rather, this way was symbolic and pars pro toto.

However, a systematic, complete, and accurate list was increasingly needed when it came to soliciting military aid or, better still, money to resolve the urgent problems of the Empire or the imperial dynasty. The ancient feudal core of this bond was the duty of imperial vassals to provide military support for the king's journey to Rome, and this fiction was formally maintained.[31] (That is why *Römermonat* was still the measure for imperial aids.) All those who stood in a direct relationship to the king—either as imperial vassals or, in the case of the cities,[32] as subjects—were required to help defray the burdens of the Empire. Yet who belonged to this "all" was precisely the question. From the early fifteenth century on, the assembled princes had been drawing up registers (*Matrikularanschläge*) to allocate the military aid demanded by the emperor among themselves, that is, lists of contributors and their shares.[33] As expected, this generated considerable disagreement. Many of those included on the lists rarely if ever appeared at the imperial assemblies and in fact never contributed to the expenses. As a result, at the imperial diet in 1486 a register was created of those at the periphery of the Empire whose membership was uncertain: e.g., it included the Duke of Savoy, the Duke of Burgundy, and the King of Bohemia. Just how unclear the circumstances were is revealed by the fact that one occasionally encountered on these lists estates "that one cannot find," for example, a mysterious Duke of the Maas.[34]

In Worms, the king—at the end of May 1495—submitted a preliminary proposal for the "urgent aid" against the Turks and for his Italy campaign. The electors turned it down and replaced it with a list of their own. In the traditional way, the royal register had been arranged according to estate groups, not contribution levels: first ecclesiastical and secular electors, secular princes, counts, and lords, then archbishops and bishops, abbots, abbesses, and provosts, and finally cities. By and large the sequence of the names corresponded—with deviations—to the seating order that could be observed at public gatherings.[35] The register presented by the electors, by contrast, was new and unusual in that it compiled only three large groups that were roughly graduated according to financial capacity and comprised members of very diverse estate rank—from electors down to cities. Both proposals were originally rejected by the estates. A list that was universally accepted by all participants and would have been incorporated into the concluding recess was not produced.[36] What has come down to us, though, is a comprehensive list of those who had not yet furnished the required aid by October.[37]

In fact, these registers were not member lists that documented an established state of affairs. Rather, they were wish lists that formulated expectations and tried to create in the first place what they were describing, namely, a fixed circle of Empire members in the full sense of the word. In 1521, at another imperial diet at Worms, an Imperial Register (*Reichsmatrikel*) was finally adopted that claimed lasting validity. This list, too, still contained a multitude of controversial entries—not only with respect to the level of the assessments, but also with respect to the persons themselves. That applied especially to the less powerful estates, whose status as direct imperial subjects was challenged by their princely neighbors, or to estates that were located at the periphery of the Empire. But even princes who in fact never contributed anything to aid the Empire, like Lorraine, continued to appear on the register.[38] Nevertheless, these registers created new facts and could be used as arguments, should the need arise. If a bishop, count, or prelate was not on the list, the prince on whose territory his lordship was located had every right to claim him as *landsässig*, that is, he could summon him to his own territorial diet (*Landtag*) and tax him. Conversely, anyone who was listed in the register could invoke this as an argument to escape the tax and sovereignty claims of a neighboring prince.

One significant example is the duchy of Pomerania-Stettin, whose status as a fief of the electors of Brandenburg had long been in dispute. Until 1481 it had appeared on all the imperial registers (*Reichsanschläge*), but in 1486 and 1487 it did not. In 1489 the Elector of Brandenburg was able to use that fact to claim the Duke of Pomerania-Stettin as his vassal, while the king in turn called upon him to contribute aid to the Empire (*Reichshilfe*). The elector resisted that attempt, "lest Duke Buxla [Bogislav of Pomerania] thereby indirectly assert his liberty." But the elector himself also did not pay the *Reichshilfe*. As a result, in 1495 the Duke of Pomerania-Stettin found himself back on the lists as an imperial prince.[39] However, he did not show up at the imperial diet, nor was he enfeoffed by the king.

This exemplary case reveals that the registers were at all times merely one argument alongside others when it came to the question of direct membership in the Empire. Actual participation in the deliberations was another, far more potent argument. Added to this was the criterion of imperial vassalship, which was based on the letter of enfeoffment and above all on the act of public investiture itself. In the process, written documents and ritual acts (which were in turn documented in writing) could be played off one against the other. It was by no means the case, as one might be inclined to assume from a modern perspective, that the written document in principle counted more than the public ritual. We shall see this exemplified further on in the case of Pomerania-Stettin.

We encounter lists of a very different nature in the various registers of participants at the Worms assembly. Just how important such lists were becomes evident if one considers how little the various participants actually knew about one another, and how important it was to them to be appropriately recognized. *Hoftage* were not only *the* relevant forum for being recognized as a member of the Empire; they also offered the most effective arena for demonstrating one's own status through ostentatious pomp: by means of sumptuous banquets and balls, hunts, and tournaments, but especially through the size and outfitting of the retinue at festive enfeoffments.[40] It was this that the registers of participants documented: they were account books of symbolic capital.[41]

Two printed accounts have come down to us from the Worms diet. In essence they consist of such lists, and they report the order of persons, their names and titles, but also their outward appearance in stereotypical manner and—to modern readers—exhausting detail. The brand-new tool of printing had been employed for the first time within the Empire in 1486 at the coronation of Maximilian as king of the Romans. It had imparted an entirely new quality of communications technology to the herald's traditional task of arranging the correct public enactment of the social hierarchy.[42] In the case of Worms it was Ulrich Burkgraf, herald of the Margrave of Brandenburg-Ansbach, who had a detailed description of the solemn events—in essence, the acts of homage (*Thronbelehnungen*)—printed in Nuremberg; a second, even more exhaustive printed version was produced in Speyer.[43] These accounts are visual representations of the ceremonial acts: either they make the procession of participants pass before the reader's eyes in the temporal sequence of their appearance, or they describe the spatial arrangement of the persons such that the reader can let his gaze scan the scene, beginning with the pinnacle of the hierarchy, the king.[44] Not only the electors and princes were painstakingly recorded, but so were their retinues (*Hofgesinde*), by name where possible. Delegates who wrote home from Worms referred to these printed registers or enclosed them with their letters.[45]

The correctness of these descriptions was exceedingly important to the participants. Wherever they appeared together in public, they assumed a linear order—whether in walking, standing, sitting, or speaking, but also in the medium of writing—and invariably gave symbolic expression to their rank on a hierarchical scale. The arrangement in space was always read as a rank order. Once it was determined where the hierarchical center in a space was located, in this case the king, it was impossible to escape the comparatively clear symbolic effect of a spatial sequence. This made conflicts unavoidable.[46] Whenever the imagined social hierarchy was translated into concrete praxis in the form of processions, assemblies, and written lists, it turned out that the ideas of order, and especially the notions of one's own place within that order, were never in agreement in the minds of the actors and first had to be negotiated and worked out in detail. The social logic of space was compelling. The public appearance at the ceremonially elevated royal diet and its representation in the printed text had a performative effect: it was in this way, and only in this way, that the hierarchical order of the Empire became objective.

As a result, the order in the text had to represent the order in space with the greatest possible exactitude. The written—and even more so the printed—lists of participants enhanced the effectiveness of the visible acts and increased the possibility of invoking them as demonstrable precedents in case of conflict. It was no easy task for the heralds to ensure, in haste and under pressure of timely reporting, to completely record all names and titles and accurately reproduce the arrangement in the procession and seating orders. After all, they could not possibly know all the participants and were forced to draw on information furnished by others. Evidently they did not rely only on what they saw, but had the quartermasters of the princely participants provide them with lists of the names of their respective retinues. Still, it was unavoidable that the published lists contained errors, or perhaps depicted a hoped-for procession and not one that actually took place. In any case, the lists created a potent social reality of their own.

In subsequent years, the heralds were increasingly aware of the responsibility that this imposed upon them. On the one hand, they responded by trying to be as diligent as possible. For example, the imperial herald Kaspar Sturm felt compelled to produce a second and third version of his account of the imperial diet of 1530 to correct mistakes in his initial description. The title of the third version states explicitly: "Thus everything is truthfully indicated and described in summary herein, with additional information, especially in the naming of persons gathered in accordance with the dignity of every estate (respecting which there may previously have been a deficiency on account of haste)." He explicitly corrected errors, for example, concerning the order of the electoral delegates when seated and entering on horseback, and he conceded that in the previous reports many participants "had not been arranged and mentioned properly and in correct order according to their rank and character."[47] On the other hand, the authors felt obligated to introduce their reports with escape clauses to relieve themselves of responsibility. For example, in his description of the imperial diet of 1548, the Habsburg court historiographer Nikolaus Mameranus wrote explicitly that one could not use his information as the basis of legal claims.[48] This reveals, conversely, how seriously those involved took the documentary value and the binding effect of the reports.

This was true not only of the order of the processions, but even more so of the seating order (*Session*), especially during deliberations. Ever since the imperial assemblies of the 1470s and 1480s, the session order had slowly begun to solidify. The place that every person assumed in relationship to everyone else was regarded as a legal right; the seating order became an order of possession. This solidification was furthered by the fact that the events were documented in writing with ever greater precision and that the assemblies occurred in ever shorter intervals. Unlike the ceremonial order of the electors, which was regulated in the Golden Bull of 1356, a precise order of the other princes and estates still needed to be determined. In Worms in 1495, a few cases illustrate how this was done.

In addition to the heralds' accounts, what has come down to us is a list of "those who were then at the imperial diet in Worms," which Hereditary Imperial Marshal Pappenheim, as the responsible official, ordered to be reconstructed around 1507/8 based on the seating order in 1495.[49] This list is a graphic representation of the session at public acts and is organized according to estate groups and rank; the courtly retinues are absent. However, the list includes not only those who participated in the deliberations, but also persons who, as explicitly stated in other sources, "were neither summoned to counsel nor went."[50] At the top in the center stand the king and queen; below them in the center are the electors, among them the count palatine "with 6 sons." Next there follow, also in the center, the papal delegation, the *welsch* (that is, Romanic) kings and princes or their delegations (including Maximilian's son Philip as king of Castile; even the king of Denmark is counted among them). On the king's right, the more honorific side (i.e., to the left on the list), are the ecclesiastical princes and the abbots, on the opposite side the secular princes and the counts. In the center at the very bottom are listed the "delegations" of the cities, though not by name and incomplete. If one compares this list with another one drawn up at the Worms diet itself, which was appended to the draft of the imperial recess (*Reichsabschied*) and which records "who appeared in person at this diet ... and those who sent their delegations, and all of their names, those who were in the council and held session," quite a few differences are evident in the number and sequence.[51] Praxis thus seems to have been still relatively fluid, such that even the hereditary imperial marshal was unable to reconstruct it unambiguously.

It was by no means left to the discretion of every person to choose a place; instead, one had to have a seat assigned by the hereditary imperial marshal. For example, after his elevation in rank, the Duke of Württemberg was given a new place among the princes.⁵² If a participant did not agree with his assigned seat, he would usually consult the archives to find out where he had most recently been seated. This was an obvious way to resolve seating disputes: after all, in the traditional society of the premodern era, demonstrable, uncontroverted tradition was the surest and most challenge-resistant foundation for a claim to ownership.⁵³ However, problems could not always be solved in this way, because an unquestioned tradition often did not exist. Either one could not find the answer in the written record,⁵⁴ or there were contradictory testimonies. But one could also challenge the binding nature of the precedents or invoke altered circumstances that called for a change in the seating order. Already at the *Große Christentag* of 1471, the emperor, "on account of the disorderly seating," had a decree affixed to the door of the assembly hall declaring that nobody was to have his traditional rights insulted by the seat assigned to him here. Such escape clauses were soon established to allow persons to communicate at all in the face of irreconcilable claims.⁵⁵ For all that, the criteria according to which such a ranking order should be devised were in reality completely vague and disputed. Anyone could invoke different arguments on his side if he were to insist that he merely wished to assume, in all humility, the place that was his proper due.

We can see how such disputes unfolded in the case of Duke Heinrich of Brunswick-Lüneburg. In Worms in 1495, it was he, above all others, who refused to accept the seat assigned to him. The notes of his councilor Vicentius reveal that the duke, following his reception in the city, initially lingered in his lodgings, waiting for the king and electors to agree on how "all and the estates of the Empire should be properly organized."⁵⁶ When that was some time in coming, he first approached the electors—through his councilor—and the king himself with the request that he be accorded the rank that was his due; under that condition he was willing to agree to all the decisions of the assembly. Various proposals were discussed: Brunswick and Brandenburg should take daily turns in assuming the contested seat; on the other days they should send only their councilors. At his most demanding, the Duke of Brunswick wanted to be seated ahead of Duke Albrecht of Saxony, possibly also on the opposite side of the hall ahead of the archbishops, but at least directly behind them in front of the bishop of Bamberg. However, realistically there was "fearful doubt" that the highly meritorious old Duke Albrecht would put up with this any more than the archbishops of Salzburg and Magdeburg, who for their part were busy fighting over precedence on the ecclesiastical bench.⁵⁷ The Duke of Brunswick's argument was that he was among the "four dukes on which majesty was founded [*darauf die Majestät gewidemet*]." This somewhat opaque formulation appealed to the above-mentioned *Quaternionen* model, the most common version of which listed Brunswick among the "*quatuor duces Imperii*" alongside

Swabia, Bavaria, and Lorraine. The dukes of Saxony, Bavaria, and Brandenburg, on the other hand, invoked a very different criterion, asserting that, as members of electoral dynasties (if in collateral lines), they should be sitting together on the princes' side at the very front. There now began a complicated back and forth (which we can reconstruct only in part) between the king, his chancellor Stürzel, the hereditary imperial marshal, the electors, and the councilor of the Duke of Brunswick, during which the latter kept away from the assemblies. Eventually he succeeded in having a special chair set up for him in the general council assembly across from Duke Otto of Bavaria. But at soon as the princes were among themselves, he was passed over again during the polling of the individual votes. Once more he approached the king, pressuring him with the announcement that he would not permit his public enfeoffment until he had been given his rank.[58] This touched on a sensitive issue: it mattered a great deal to the king that he personally invest all princes in solemn ceremony. As negotiations became further protracted, the duke put pressure on the king and the electors by threatening to depart; the royal councilors submitted proposals that the other princes in turn refused to accept. In the meantime, the assemblies took place mostly "without order" and with the participants standing so as to avoid additional conflicts. In the end the Duke of Brunswick did consent to being invested (though with some delay), but shortly thereafter he prepared to leave. The king offered one more compromise, with the reminder that "the entire nation and all of Christendom" were interested in the success of this assembly. However, the Duke of Brunswick was no longer willing to accede to the proposed compromise, a continual rotation with the Margrave of Brandenburg: he declared that "for all eternity he would not sit among any margrave who was not an elector" and left Worms. As was usually the case, the resolution of the problem was postponed to a later assembly.

That conflicts over rank were by no means limited to the sphere of princes is evident from very similar occurrences among the city delegates. The Aacheners contested the right of their counterparts from Cologne to sit at the very front of the bench of free cities—only one example of many other quarrels that usually involved neighboring cities.[59] While the Cologne delegates pointed to the custom at the imperial assemblies in the 1470s and documented it with the old imperial recesses, the Aacheners invoked their rank as Charlemagne's coronation city, their place at Maximilian's coronation feast in 1486, and an imperial charter (which they did not have with them, though).[60] This was an old quarrel over rank that flared up at every opportunity, impeding the communication at every assembly of the cities and remaining unresolved until the very end of the Empire. In seeking to mediate, the other city envoys produced numerous precedents in favor of Cologne. The delegate from Straßburg asserted that he, too, should sit ahead of the Aacheners, but that in the interest of the important business of the assembly he would give them priority this time. The Aacheners even rejected the offer to sit in the very middle of the council chamber between the other city envoys. Even though there were "intense and friendly talks with them," they left the assembly and departed for home. Evidently, maintaining their collective social status, which was based on the tradition of being a coronation city, mattered more to the Aachen councilors than exerting influence on the deliberations.

It was in fact still a fairly flexible ranking order that was being worked out in Worms. In their disagreements, the participants continued to move their seats back and forth argumentatively, submitted compromise proposals, and offered situational solutions. But the order that actually materialized depended substantially on who was present, in person and in a timely manner, and could therefore assert himself more successfully. We read, for example: "Duke Hans ... was the first prince of Bavaria at the diet, and at that time no duke of Saxony was present, that is why he was seated at the very top."[61]

Conflicts over the seating order generally manifested a characteristic dilemma of the premodern validity of norms. Concrete, visible praxis exerted a potent normative force. Assuming a particular seat was not by accident *the* metaphor for the assertion of legal claims as such. Something that was taken possession of—in the literal meaning of the Latin roots, something that was "sat upon" (German: *besessen*) in the literal sense of the Latin *sedere* ("to sit")—was regarded as a *possessio*, property (*Besitz*). Rank and honor, too, were immaterial goods (*res incorporales*) which could be objects of ownership, of *quasi-possessio*. And *possessio* established a legal claim that could be overturned only on very good grounds. This was reflected also in the procedural praxis of Roman law: in cases of conflict, the *possessor* always had the better chance of prevailing, since the burden of proof rested on the person challenging the *possessio*, the *petitor*.[62] Contemporaries tried to escape this normative force of the factual by officially protesting against a particular public act, and putting it on record that it must not diminish one's own rights; that is to say, it was performed only *salvo jure*, "harmless" to the rights of the person lodging the protest. The upshot of this—particularly with seating arrangements, but not limited to them—was a kind of dual reality: the de facto praxis was always hedged about with a multitude of escape clauses documented in writing, though in the long run these were not able to prevent a new custom from establishing itself.

Why was it so important to occupy a particular seat? More so than anything else, the position in space that a person assumed among others on particularly elevated occasions embodied his status. The issue was one's *standing* (*status*, *Stand*) in the literal sense. In the premodern culture of presence, status was not yet the sort of abstraction it is in sociological theory today. Instead, it consisted first and foremost in the concrete symbolic-ritual acts of standing, sitting, and walking, which manifested social dignity and political participation in equal measure. Status needed to be demonstrated, lest one lose it. Needless to say, a person's status did not simply depend on the seat he took, for he could take a specific seat only because he had lordship, kinship, material resources, and so on. Yet these underlying factors were merely necessary, not sufficient, conditions for a particular status within the overall structure of the Empire. Added to them must be the recognition of others, especially the king and the *pares*, one's peers. This recognition was manifested precisely in the fact that participants at an imperial diet jointly assumed a visible spatial relationship to one another. "Estates of the Empire" (*Reichsstände*)—the term established itself beginning in the 1480s—were not yet legal subjects in an abstract, institutional sense; instead, in a very concrete sense they were the ones who assumed an uncontested place at an imperial diet. While a modern, formal organization with fixed criteria of membership can exist even if its members never meet in person,[63] this was not the case with the Empire. Political participation at imperial diets rested on the status of the person or family as the bearer of authority, which was, in turn, inseparable from the social rank of the person in question. Conversely, rank and status in turn depended on concrete participation in the assemblies. Everything was reciprocally conditioned and visualized. That is why the seating order always had to be taken seriously. Its assertion was a genuine motive of sociopolitical action that was accorded high priority—sometimes even higher priority than all other topics of deliberation.

Constitutional historians usually see the seating order at imperial diets as a disruptive element, an obstacle to the actual adoption of decisions, because it was prone to conflict. This is an anachronistic perspective, one that confuses rule and exception and overlooks the specific efficacy of this symbolic-ceremonial order. Not only did this order ensure a clear definition of the status of participants, it also provided for an orderly casting of votes, namely, during the procedure of the *Umfrage* (polling of the participants). There simply was no other order available that could have assured the uniformity of the process. A technical-instrumental procedural order that abstracted from the differing status of the participants did not—and could not—exist. Under these circumstances, it was the ceremonial order of sitting and speaking according to rank that created a kind of certainty of expectation in the first place and structured the process of the assemblies.

The Order of Deliberation

When constitutional historians speak about an imperial diet, they usually refer only to the deliberations between the king and the estates. However, from the perspective of the participants themselves, this made up only a small part of what happened. In Worms, as at any such gathering of the members of the Empire, a *solemnis curia*, the king did much more: he held court, celebrated masses, sat as a judge, acted as conciliator and mediator, granted privileges and other demonstrations of royal favor, performed enfeoffments and knightings, hosted banquets and tournaments—indeed, in spectacular fashion he even participated in knightly duels himself.[64] It would be a complete misunderstanding of the character of all these acts if one separated aristocratic "entertainment" as mere phenomena of cultural and social history from "serious" political business. Rather, in this way Maximilian carried out and enacted both his role as monarch and his role as the (highest-ranking) member of the high nobility, whose demands of virtuous and knightly conduct he appropriated for himself, ratcheting it up in unprecedented ways.[65] That he took council with "the Holy Roman Empire's electors, princes, and other estates, in order to make known to them … the matters of the Holy Empire, as well as its troubles, and to arrange and forestall these things according to their council" was *one* element of this role alongside others, *one* element of holding court in solemn fashion.[66]

Conceptually, the deliberations in the narrower sense were distinguished from the "diet of the king and the Empire" as a whole, and were usually referred to as an "assembly" (*sambnung*) or as "going to council" (*zu Rat gehen*). Contemporaries thus definitely perceived them as something distinguishable.[67] However, the deliberations did not follow firmly institutionalized procedures; instead, the latter only emerged gradually over time. An important role in this process was played by Berthold of Henneberg, the Elector of Mainz and archchancellor, whose concern was to fuse the imperial estates into a political whole capable of taking action.[68] As a result, the deliberations in Worms still had a dual structure: in part they followed the social logic of a royal diet, and in part they already separated themselves from it and developed their own, independent procedural script. The archchancellor was intent on giving the deliberations a structural autonomy within the meetings between the king and his vassals.[69]

This is evident above all from the changing location of deliberations: the estates usually met in the town hall, but they could also be invited to the royal court. Depending on the location, the situation was defined differently: the town hall was the arena of action for the estates in their totality; here the proceedings were directed by the archchancellor, and the king only joined in on occasion. The king's residence, by contrast, was his own arena of action, where he selectively received individual estates or groups of estates. The difference was significant. Whereas Frederick III had still preferred to consult selected princes individually at his discretion, since the 1480s the policy of Berthold of Henneberg was aimed at having the estates confront the emperor as a collective. The precondition for this was the creation of a separate space for the deliberations of the estates.[70] In Worms, the two methods were still used alternately:

Item, the electors as well as other princes held council at the Burgerhof, which is the city's town hall, and every elector also has his own chamber for his councilors at the hall, and afterward they went as a group into the large chamber; the free and imperial cities were often also present at council with the princes in this town hall; and the king, too, was sometimes at council with the princes in the hall, and the princes were often at council with the king at his court; and the imperial cities were also with the royal majesty at his court.[71]

The outward organization of all meetings—like the arrangements for the entries, investitures, and other solemn acts—was in the hands of the imperial marshal, the hereditary official of the Elector of Saxony as the arch-marshal of the Empire. He rode from house to house and personally invited everyone. There was no formal beginning that was clearly demarcated symbolically. Since there was also no clearly defined circle of participants, one had no criterion for how many participants had to be assembled before one could properly begin. On 26 March, the king for the first time summoned the electors, princes, and other estates who had by then arrived to the town hall, where he had his councilors present to them the topics of the deliberation. After a few days of back-and-forth talks, those present complained that too few princes had arrived as of yet. The participants waited a week, and on 7 April the Elector of Mainz gave a new signal to commence the proceedings. He documented his organizing oversight by requesting that all "delegations and envoys" present their letters of accreditation. On 24 April another general assembly took place, where the royal councilors once again presented Maximilian's agenda.[72]

The negotiations took the form of a dialogue between the king and his councilors on the one hand and the estates on the other. The king spoke to the assembly of the electors, princes, and other estates either in person or through his chancellor; his subjects deliberated together or—as was mostly the case already in Worms—they broke up into estate-based groups, "each in its order: the electors, in particular, with a number of their councilors, and the princes, princely delegations, prelates, counts, and so forth also separate, and the envoys of the cities also separate."[73] The two "upper estates" subsequently exchanged views one or more times and formulated a joint response to the king; the cities were not specifically heard. This deliberative praxis gradually gave rise to three distinct estate groups, "councils" (*Räte*), or curias (*Kurien*) of the Empire. But it could also happen that the king convened only the electors and the princes or singled out individual princes,[74] or that the archchancellor summoned the city envoys before himself separately. For specific, particularly complicated issues of deliberation, committees were set up composed of members of various estates. The joint assembly of estates could be sought out and addressed directly by envoys from foreign potentates, like the kings of Naples.[75] In those instances, the assembly was both conceived as an acting entity and treated as such in practice. In keeping with this praxis, the expression "estates (of the Empire)" was highly ambiguous. It could designate every person who had a seat and voice in the assembly, as well as the group of peers who met and took counsel together. Moreover, in the phrase "electors, princes, and estates," the last word was also a vague collective term for the members of the Empire below the princes, whereby it was not even clear at all times whether that included the cities as well.[76]

Writing was slow to make its way into the deliberations. Initially it was above all the city envoys and some princely delegates who compiled careful and regular records, because they had to report back to their masters at home. In 1486, the Mainz chancellery had begun to produce protocols.[77] However, protocols about the internal deliberations of the various estate groups were not yet kept, and the respective negotiation positions were also rarely put into writing. One way in which the archchancellor of Mainz asserted his control over the deliberations was by monopolizing the use of writing in the deliberative procedures.[78] When the royal councilors asked for a copy of the response of the estates to the king's proposition, the archchancellor turned them down by arguing that "until now such a thing has not been customary."[79] It would appear that in other ways, too, the archchancellor shied away from putting things in writing during the course of the negotiations. For example, we read this in a report by two city envoys about the deliberations regarding the (especially touchy and controversial) plans to establish an estate-based government (*ständisches Regiment*): "They [the assembled estates] requested to be given such in writing, but [the Elector of Mainz] turned it down. But he offered ... that someone be sent to him, and he would relate everything to him."[80]

The deliberations within the various groups usually took place in the form of a poll (*Umfrage*): that is, the highest-ranking member was asked first for his opinion by the moderator of the assembly, after which one proceeded according to the seating order, with the right (ecclesiastical) and left (secular) sides alternating.[81] The importance of the votes corresponded to the dignity and rank of the participants; there was no formal majority rule in which all votes carried equal weight.[82] Politically the most influential role fell to the person who conducted the poll and was the last to speak. This function was contested between the Elector of Mainz as the arch-chancellor and the Elector of Saxony as the arch-marshal of the Empire. At the assembly in Nuremberg in 1487, the two men had agreed that Mainz would conduct the poll among the electors, and Saxony the poll among the princes. This dispute would erupt again repeatedly in later years.[83] The crucial point is that the poll was a ceremonial rank order and an instrumental constitutional procedure in one. The order of the deliberation followed the seating order and thus obeyed the same hierarchical logic as the king's *Hoftag* as a whole.

The circle of persons summoned to the general deliberations in the city hall was quite different from the large circle of all who had journeyed to Worms for the royal diet. That presupposed at least implicit criteria of participation.

As recently as the *Großer Christentag* in 1471, it had not been clear who was allowed to be present at the first general assembly and who was not: "Now, our lord the margrave said and shouted out too loudly that anybody who was not among the electors, princes, envoys of princes, or delegations of cities, should leave. But in the end he announced that the electors, princely councilors, the envoys sent by the princes, as well as all counts, free lords, knights, and servants, and the delegations of the cities should remain inside."[84]

In Worms, too, it was not entirely settled who should and could take part in the deliberations. Above all, it was by no means a given that the delegations from the imperial cities were invited. As the envoys from the Swabian League wrote with an air of satisfaction: "It should be especially noted that the cities were permitted at the proceedings of this diet, they were not excluded, and their concerns were heard."[85] All imperial cities were first invited in 1471 and again in 1489, but it did not become customary until 1495.[86] At some of the previous assemblies, city envoys, though not invited, had appeared on their own initiative and had been included after all. Ambiguous also was the status of the many counts and lords who had come to Worms in the retinue of a prince. Revealing in this respect is the already mentioned draft of the imperial recess (*Reichsabschied*), which recorded only those who had "held session in council": it names two counts "on behalf of all counts and barons,"[87] while the other participant lists always mention a large number of other counts and barons. The draft also records the abbot of Schussenried as "on his own behalf and on behalf of the abbots from the land of Swabia." These formulations suggest that individuals were treated as representatives of their peers. This did not yet reflect any formalized procedures of delegated authority. Rather, it was only the numerous imperial assemblies during this period that prompted the counts and prelates to join together more closely and organize themselves collectively so as to be able to appoint representatives jointly and send them to the imperial diets.[88]

In the late medieval culture of presence, it was the exception that someone did *not* act "on his own behalf." The royal diet demanded in principle the presence of the imperial vassals in person, for the king was, after all, also holding court in person. The city envoys represented a special case, since communes could not act in any other way except through representatives. From all others, however, the king demanded their personal presence in his summons. Absenteeism had to be excused on good grounds.[89] Especially the cases of Dukes Albrecht and Georg of Bavaria, but also those of the Elector of Brandenburg, the Duke of Holstein, and many others, reveal how eager Maximilian, in particular, was to ensure that the princes appeared in person.[90]

There were good reasons for this. Only he who participated in the deliberations in person and by his own right obligated himself fully and could later be held to what had been agreed upon. "Letters of authorization" (*Gewaltbriefe*), even if they contained a *plena potestas*, never granted their holders complete freedom of action. Such delegates were further restricted by instructions, and frequent consultations with those back home were customary.[91] Those who acted only on behalf of someone else could always maintain that their "authority" was not sufficient for unforeseen decisions—an evasion of which both city envoys and princely delegates liked to make tactical use. The lack of unencumbered and free mandates was repeatedly the target of criticism, and not only at the imperial diets, for it impeded the capacity of any assembly to take action. That masters did not wish to entrust an unrestricted mandate to their delegates for fear of losing control of a situation was only one aspect. Another was that the delegates, in turn, were not treated by those they dealt with as full representatives of their lords. The estate-based order did not—or only to a very limited extent—allow a person of lower rank to fully represent someone higher up: that is to say, to assume his place within the visible order of the world and speak publicly with his voice. In other words, functional role and personal status were not completely separated.[92]

That the authorized agents of a prince were not accepted as his representatives in the fullest sense was evident in multifarious ways. In a literal sense, the delegates were not allowed to take their master's place, that is, they could not occupy his place in public processions and meetings. It was "customary that every envoy sit behind the princes, and no one intruded upon his lord's place." This had already been laid down by the Golden Bull.[93] During the deliberations as well, envoys were treated differently than the princes in person. In some cases they were even excluded entirely. For example, the councilors of the electors of Brandenburg complained to their lord in writing that "His Royal Majesty has entered into deliberations with all the electors and princes; we were told to wait outside. We sent word … to His Royal Majesty: because we are separated from other electors and princes outside the door, we did not wish to cause our lord this detriment, but instead wished to go to our lodgings."[94] The elector's envoys were thus not treated according to their lord's high status, but according to their own, lower rank, and they were set back relative to the princes present in person; indeed, they were excluded from the princes' circle—they had to wait outside the door. They in turn interpreted this as an insult—not so much against themselves, but against their lord, the elector. Two competing interpretive patterns collided here. The "great" lords treated each other differently than they did their councilors. It was not compatible with the social grammar of the high nobility, which rested on personal presence, to regard envoys who were commoners or otherwise unequal in rank as in every respect equal to their lords by the fiction of representation and treat them accordingly. The councilors had a different perspective: they considered themselves representatives of their lords in the fullest sense of the word and felt that what was being done to them was being done to their lords—at least as long as they were active as their authorized agents. That presupposed a clear awareness of different social roles, an awareness that the princes themselves did not possess. As long as delegates and princes in person interacted at the imperial diets, such clashing interpretations happened time and again. It was only much later, once the envoys of the princes were among themselves during deliberations, that a uniform situational definition could establish itself. However, a complete separation of roles between the personal and professional status of the envoys never happened in the Empire until the very end.[95]

The treatment of the envoys also reveals that the boundaries between the deliberations and the other solemnities of a court diet were fluid. Both were dominated by the rules of social interaction among persons of noble rank. But that restrained the ability of the assembly to make collective decisions, that is, impeded its procedural autonomy. To push through his far-reaching reform plans, the archchancellor must have been interested in creating a circumscribed sphere of deliberation within which participants could negotiate freely and with no regard for status problems and dependencies. The technical procedural instrument to that end was the implementation of the secrecy of deliberations.

Secrets organize, structure, and, indeed, often make communication possible in the first place by drawing a boundary between those in the know and everyone else.[96] The secrecy of deliberations shields the sphere of those engaged in them against the outside and conceals their internal clashes. This renders individual participants more independent from their environment, and, conversely, it leads to the group being perceived by the outside world as a single entity. And it is only this that makes it possible to ascribe the decisions that are made to the group as a whole, that is, to make it appear as an effective collective with a *single* common will. In other words, the secrecy of deliberations endows the decision-making process with autonomy and transforms a collection of discrete participants into a *single* political body.

That, at any rate, was the goal the arch-chancellor sought to accomplish for the first time at the Nuremberg diet in 1487.[97] After some initial hesitation, the city delegates and princely envoys promised to keep all deliberations secret and—this was unheard of—not to report back to their masters "until an agreement had been reached." The Straßburg delegate captured it in a nutshell: everyone, be they princes, princely envoys, or cities, pledged themselves to secrecy, "because we now belong together in the Holy Empire."[98]

In Worms in 1495 as well, "all in the entire assembly" had to promise secrecy, namely, each person individually, by shaking the arch-chancellor's hand.[99] With the secrecy of deliberations he was seeking to shield the assembly of the estates not so much from the city's public as from the king. Most of all, however, the goal was to undercut the ties that bound delegates to their mandate. Secrecy created a boundary that cut across the structures of the surrounding environment: it was intended to separate the deliberations from the diet as a whole, envoys from their cities, the delegates from their princes, and all participants together from the king. At the same time, it was supposed to bridge the hierarchical boundaries between the highly unequal participants, from electors down to city envoys, and temporarily fuse those engaged in deliberations into a single unit of action. Such a unit of action was one of the preconditions for the assembly to *represent* the Empire as a whole, that is, to make decisions that were attributed not only to those who had been personally involved in them and had explicitly agreed to them in person, but to the totality.

Opposed to this were the loyalties of the individual participants. As a result, the secrecy of deliberations could hardly be implemented in Worms. The archchancellor had to permit the delegates at least to report back to their masters. It was not possible—or only incompletely so—to create an assembly that was set apart from its environment and functioned according to its own rules, an assembly that could have integrated the Empire into an efficient whole capable of taking action. In Worms, "the Empire" continued to make itself manifest in actions differently than through the assembled estates sitting "in council" separated from the surrounding world: namely, through the public sitting of the king and electors *in maiestate*.

Sitting *in Maiestate*

How the Empire presented itself visually in Worms is evident from the title woodcut of one of the contemporary tracts about the imperial diet of 1495. The image is the representation of a representation, a second-order depiction, as it were. What it shows is *the* central act of the embodiment of the Empire at that time: the king sitting *in maiestate*, meaning "in his royal adornments and dignity." The picture provides an idealized notion, abstracted from all accidental circumstances, of what contemporaries understood by *maiestas imperialis*, the majesty of king *and* Empire in a still indistinguishable sense.[100]

What we have become accustomed to regard as an abstraction from a modern perspective—"the majesty of the Empire"—appears here as something very concrete: namely, as a ritual act that could in turn be represented pictorially. Seating *in maiestate*, "in royal adornments and dignity"—this was the fixed formula in the sources—meant that the king appeared in very specific forms, which marked and certified the act as one that was elevated and particularly important: namely, in royal regalia with the imperial treasures of the crown, scepter, orb, and sword (which was sometimes absent, as in this instance), elevated on a throne under a baldachin, seated in the midst of his electors (figure 4). In this case they are—identified by name scrolls—the Elector of Mainz to the king's right, the Elector of Cologne to his left, the Elector of Trier opposite, in addition the Count Palatine on the right and on the left the Electors of

Figure 4. Maximilian I in the circle of the electors, woodcut, 1495, Nuremberg, Staatsarchiv.

Brandenburg and Saxony, which does not accord entirely with the arrangement documented in the written sources.[101]

This seating *in maiestate* was a dominant pictorial motif of the late fifteenth and early sixteenth centuries. The illustration accompanying the account of 1495 is only one example among many. We are dealing with an ideal-typical pictorial scheme, a fixed code that must not be misunderstood as the realistic depiction of a specific act. The pictorial type always shows the Empire or king in his regalia with a crown, seated on an elevated throne, with the electors in their electoral garb on his right and left. The precise arrangement of the electors can vary, as can the more or less detailed elaboration of the scenery. Usually these were woodcuts that, if they were not published as broadsheets, nearly always served as an illustration for printed law codes: for example, the *Sachsenspiegel*, the *Schwabenspiegel*, the *Layenspiegel*, the *Institutes of Justinian*, the *Libri Feudorum*, the Bamberg *Halsgerichtsordnung*, the *Constitutio Criminalis Carolina*, the *Reichspoliceyordnung*, and not least the Golden Bull.[102] This is highly revealing: the pictorial type stages the *maiestas imperialis* as a source of legitimacy, a point of reference, and a sanctioning authority of the law—precisely *not* in the form of the totality of the imperial estates, but solely in the shape of the king or emperor and college of electors, who jointly form *unum corpus*, that is, they can act as *one* body with a single will.[103] Pars pro toto, this constellation depicted the Empire as a whole.

In accord with the pictorial type was a real scene that constituted the solemn heart of every royal diet, a ritual staging that stood before the eyes of the spectators like a living picture. That was the case also in Worms in 1495, where, between 14 and 21 July, the king sat *in maiestate* on several occasions "behind the Swan's at the dance house," on the northeastern side of the Upper Market, elevated on a specially erected platform splendidly decorated with tapestries and a gold canopy: "with all the accouterments that behoove a king of the Romans, in the presence of the most reverend, serene, highborn electors, princes, and so on … with His Royal Majesty's garments, as befit a king of the Romans."[104]

Already the sitting as such was a posture of lordship; it elevated the king and his electors over all the others, who had to stand.[105] Sitting *in maiestate* meant first of all specific garb. Thus, the printed accounts of the heralds state emphatically that the king and the electors initially retired to a chamber set up specifically for this purpose in order to put on their garments, "as was fit and proper for everyone according to his status [*Stand*]."[106] In the case of the electors this was the electoral garb: a scarlet cloak trimmed with ermine and a red, ermine-trimmed beret. The electoral envoys were not allowed to wear this garb.[107] In the case of the king the regalia consisted of quasi-liturgical vestments. Like the episcopal garb, after which it was modeled, the ritual dress imparted to its wearer a transpersonal, quasi-sacral quality. At the coronation itself, the emperor wore the pontifical regalia from the thirteenth century that were considered the robes of Charlemagne and were guarded in Nuremberg as part of the imperial treasure: alb, dalmatic, pallium, cope, shoes, stockings, and gloves.[108] It would appear that it was in fact these clothes that Maximilian wore in Worms, for the sources stated that one still had to wait for the "royal pontificalia."[109] In most instances, however, it was the regalia of his own house that the king put on for solemn occasions in order to sit "in his adornments and dignity [*zier und würde*]." The words *zier und würde* have a characteristic dual meaning; one can understand them simultaneously in concrete and abstract terms: the material signs (the vestments) and the object designated (the office) were inseparably merged here. By putting on the clothing, the king assumed the role and office of the king. The change of clothes before the act was thus by no means a minor matter. Rather, it defined the situation unambiguously, transformed the actors, and marked the beginning of the solemn act, just as the disrobing marked its end.[110] Everyone who described such an act—be it a herald in the official performance of his office or a random witness in his account—thought it important to mention that the king or emperor and the electors assumed their vestments "as was proper."

In Worms for the first time the king also prescribed precisely how the princes should dress for the solemn acts as a way of making the order of the Empire visible. So that "the princes in princely garb look that much more dignified before the foreign delegations and the attending folk, His Royal Grace has drawn up a register what kind of clothing a duke, landgrave, margrave, archbishop, a bishop who has land and people, as well as a regular bishop, should have and use": namely, floor-length red sateen cloaks with lining and a collar of weasel fur and a matching hat for the dukes, brown damask cloaks with gray fur collars and matching hat for the landgraves—and on it went with finely graded distinctions.[111] Maximilian had his hereditary imperial marshal hand every prince a slip of paper depicting the prescribed garb so he could dress himself accordingly.

It was customary for princes to mark their retinue by dressing their men and horses in uniform fabrics and colors and having them bear uniform standards and coats of arms, something that contemporary accounts always describe in elaborate detail. Maximilian himself spent considerable sums on having his court uniformly attired several times a year.[112] On the other hand, the princes and city councils were increasingly concerned that their subjects were outdoing each other in their luxurious dress, and they prescribed which materials, cuts, and adornments a given person could wear and which he could not. At the diet in Worms as well, this was the topic of deliberations; in the end, the imperial estates agreed that with respect to "the excessive dress and other unseemly costliness ... a common order throughout the Empire must be enacted for the honor, benefit, and distinction of all estates."[113] However, that dress codes were issued for the princes themselves was a novelty, and it attests to Maximilian's ambition to direct his first diet and turn it into a high point of the staging of royal power. Such a dress code for the princes remained the exception, even though it would appear that all of them adhered to the king's guidelines.[114]

There was, however, one exception: Margrave Frederick V of Brandenburg-Ansbach did not wish to be classified among the simple margraves, as this was incompatible with the special honor of the margraviate of Brandenburg as an electoral princedom. Although the Frankish and Brandenburg territories of the Hohenzollerns had been divided up among three brothers in 1473, the Frankish margraves also wanted to benefit from the symbolic capital of the status of elector. Their partition of the inheritance upset the system of classification on which Maximilian's dress code was based, just as it had already caused problems during the arrangement of the session and would lead to further problems at the solemn enfeoffment itself. The margrave therefore handed the slip of paper back to the hereditary imperial marshal and had him negotiate with the king about it. Maximilian eventually conceded that "Brandenburg was an electoral house and did not belong among the common margraviates," and he gave the Margrave of Brandenburg permission to dress like a duke.[115]

Like the clothes, the presence of specific objects established the majesty of the Empire. These insignia of power—especially the crown, orb, scepter, and sword—were occasionally referred to simply as "imperium," because that is exactly what they embodied. A Nuremberg chronicle called them "the jewels of Emperor Charlemagne of blessed memory, which belong to the adornment of a king of the Romans when he sits in his majesty."[116] In actuality this was a fiction of continuity: the objects were of varying provenance and age.[117] After 1423, most of the imperial insignia were kept, by virtue of an imperial privilege, in Nuremberg (according to the Golden Bull actually the location of the first royal diet following the coronation), and since then they were defended as the pledge of the city's special status vis-à-vis Aachen and guarded with the utmost care. From then on, they were no longer interchangeable—as they had been in the early Middle Ages—but unique and distinctive objects surrounded by a sacral aura. Although the insignia of crown, scepter, orb, and sword were not salvation-bestowing relics like the Holy Lance and the Holy Cross, which were also part of the imperial treasure, they, too, had a sacral character because they shared in the majesty of Charlemagne, who was venerated as holy. Kings and emperors could by no means dispose freely of these precious objects, but had to borrow them, which they did in the early modern period only on the occasion of the coronation. For other acts of majesty they therefore had a house crown and house insignia fashioned. Still, the imperial insignia were not tokens that were readily interchangeable. Rather, they were symbols of presence in the sense that they established the presence of something that could only be experienced through this symbolic embodiment.[118]

Not least, it was the ceremonially regulated participation of specific persons that constituted the sitting *in maiestate*: specifically, the presence of all or at least a few of the electors. The imperial regalia were simultaneously attributes of the electors and symbols of their participation in lordship. The fact that they had to hold the regalia during the ritual and present them to the king or emperor spoke to their elevated status and endowed them with a share of the imperial majesty: the Count Palatine the orb as the insignia of the world, the Margrave of Brandenburg the scepter, the Duke of Saxony the sword, and the

King of Bohemia the crown. The holders of the imperial hereditary offices, vassals of the respective electors, assisted them or acted in their stead, though they were not permitted to sit in their lord's place, but had to stand behind them. The three ecclesiastical electors, as archchancellors for Germania, Gaul, and Italy, carried the imperial seals, which were both symbols and instruments of their offices.

The sitting *in maiestate* at the imperial diet in Worms followed forms that had been precisely regulated long before, namely, in the Golden Bull of 1356, which had fixed the status of the electors as the elevated circle of the privileged electors of the king. This law code of Charles IV, considered one of the fundamental laws of the Empire throughout the early modern period, prescribed in detail not only the procedure for the election of the king, but also the ceremonial details at all solemn occasions on which the emperor or the king assembled with the electors "for the benefit of the Empire."[119] These regulations concerned, for one, the order of the electors among themselves, namely, when seated, in procession, and at liturgical acts, and, for another, their shared preeminence over all other princes of the Empire and the exercise of their arch offices. The occasions that were ceremonially regulated were not only the election and coronation of the king, but—far beyond that—the jurisdiction (*iudicia*), consultations (*consilia*), enfeoffments (*collaciones feudorum*), meals (*refectiones mensarum*), and all other occasions of solemn meetings, that is, occasions where the majesty of the Empire was manifested.[120]

Beginning in the eighteenth century, jurists dismissed the detailed ceremonial regulations for the most part as a mere sideshow, or even as "contemptible trivialities and trifles."[121] Most constitutional historians followed their lead; at any rate, they hardly asked about the function of these regulations and their systemic connection with the other prescriptions of the Golden Bull. It therefore did not come into focus that the privileged status of the electors as the kingmakers and their role as representatives of the Empire could not be separated from their ceremonial elevation. That the circle of the electors was closed and its procedural forms were regulated in an obligatory manner was the precondition for ensuring that the election of the king produced sure and universally binding decisions—and that, in turn, was the precondition for the body of the electors representing the entire Empire in the fullest sense of the word.[122]

The electors could represent the Empire jointly with the emperor or alone (during the election of the king), namely, in the strict technical-legal sense that whatever they decided together in the prescribed forms was obligatory for the entire Empire. Late medieval jurists referred to this circumstance as *representatio identitatis*. A body at the top of the system, commissioned by no one and singled out, represented this system as a whole.[123] It *was* the Empire, because this was the way the Empire could take collective action. In order to successfully assert representational character, it was necessary that the electors in turn constitute a body capable of acting. This notion had already been clearly formulated in the fourteenth century as part of the legal corporation theory.[124] Such a capacity for corporate action in turn presupposed, first, that a binding process of decision-making existed, second, that membership in the body was exclusive, clearly defined, and not subject to arbitrary changes, and third, that the corporate action by the electoral college as a whole could be distinguished from the action of its individual members. That precisely was the goal of the regulations laid down by the Golden Bull: they were supposed to secure the electors' capacity for political action as a *single* body, thereby empowering them to represent the whole. That end was by no means served only by the elements that appear from our perspective today as the constitutional-legal "core" of the law code—such as the indivisibility of territories, the majority principle in the election process, or safe conduct to the site of the election—but also by the ceremonial regulations that stipulated how the electors should stand, walk, sit, and serve the king symbolically.

These ceremonial regulations also contributed concretely to the capacity for corporate action. For one, they did so by demonstrating that the electors were elevated above the other princes, and that jointly with the king they formed a single body with one (fictive) will created by orderly procedures—in the words of the king, that they "themselves are part of our body [*ipsi partes corporis nostri sunt*]."[125] In addition to the handling of the imperial regalia, it was above all the exercise of the four classic court offices, the arch offices of chamberlain, marshal, steward, and cupbearer, through which the secular electors participated visibly in the *maiestas imperialis*. In the process the Empire appeared symbolically as the expanded household of the king. Even more, it was only these highly ceremonial *officia* that qualified the electors in the eyes of contemporaries as representatives of the Empire in the first place. The only way one could explain the elevated status of the secular electors above all other imperial princes in the thirteenth and fourteenth centuries was by saying that they had held these four classic offices at the king's court since time immemorial.[126] For another, the ceremonial rules served to prevent conflicts among the electors over precedence as a potential disturbance to the process. Finally, and above all, they served to characterize the joint actions by the electors—either alone or together with the king or emperor—as corporate actions *ut universi* on behalf of the Empire, as distinguished from their individual actions *ut singuli*; in other words, to define an act as a representative act in the first place. It is therefore impossible to separate the supposedly "real," "rational" constitutional procedural forms from the "merely" symbolic-ritual forms of the Golden Bull. Rather, the latter were the constitutive conditions for marking an action as an act of the Empire. The Golden Bull thus regulated for the college of the electors everything that was *not* regulated for the assembly of the imperial estates as a whole, as we have seen. That is why the college of the electors was collectively capable of taking action, much more than the imperial estates taken together.[127]

The appearance of the king within the circle of the electors, sitting *in maiestate* in accordance with the rules of the Golden Bull, thus constituted the core of the Worms diet of 1495 as a solemn *Hoftag*, a *curia solemnis*. In the eyes of later historians, this act merited for the most part no more than a passing remark; it appeared alongside courtly "masquerades" and tournaments, beyond the realm of serious politics.[128] We learn from the Basel jurist Peter von Andlau that an imperial assembly was described primarily as such a *curia solemnis* also in the fifteenth century: his *Libellus de Caesarea Monarchia* of 1460 depicted a solemn diet still exclusively after the model of the Golden Bull, without mentioning the deliberations.[129] These forms may have seemed archaic already in the fifteenth century,[130] but precisely that made them valuable, since it suggested that the order symbolized by the rituals was unchangeable and unassailable.

The word *solemnis* did not simply mean that the diet was especially festive and splendid, that is to say, that it set itself apart from the day-to-day court in the display of its splendor. In Roman law, *solemnis* originally meant something that returned annually and adhered to certain prescribed formalities (from *solus annus*).[131] Thus, *curia solemnis* also designated that the king or emperor appeared in specific forms that marked the act as significant and binding. The solemn forms were signs that brought about what they depicted—just like sacraments did in the teachings of the early church: *efficiunt quod figurant*. They manifested the majesty of the emperor and the Empire and simultaneously established it by ensuring that a publicly performed act was considered a sovereign act of the Empire, an *actus maiestatis imperialis*.

Sitting *in maiestate* was public in a twofold sense: First, it took place in a generally visible way—either out in the open in a public place, or at least in an accessible location like city hall, but in any case in the presence of qualified persons, namely, princes, counts, lords and their retinues, envoys from foreign potentates, and, finally, the citizenry of the imperial city. Second, all acts were simultaneously public in the sense that they claimed to be universally binding. The one was the result of the other: what happened demonstratively before qualified eyewitnesses in fixed ritual forms was authenticated by these eyewitnesses; it could not be denied by any of the participants. The crucial point was that by their mere participation in such a demonstrative and formal act, all participants affirmed their consent to what was transpiring and what it meant for the future.[132] Their personal presence, therefore, had consequences. The question was whether and, if so, how one could escape this binding effect. There were two possibilities: First, one could lodge a protest against the proceedings, namely, during the act itself in ritual and public form.[133] Second, one could leave the place of the proceedings or not appear at all, and thus contest the binding nature of the acts performed by others with the argument that one had not agreed to them in person. In other words, the solemn diets still followed entirely a logic of personal presence, which permitted only limited possibilities of surrogacy.

Solemn Enfeoffments

Enfeoffments and elevations in rank were the central solemn acts with which the king all but compelled the electors and princes to attend in person in Worms, and at which he sat *in maiestate*. This was the ritual core of the entire Worms diet; it was this, above all else, that made the diet into an event that allowed the Empire to manifest itself in real presence.

The feudal system constituted one of the oldest strata of the imperial system.[134] The king or emperor as the supreme feudal lord was the head of an association of persons in which the control over land and people, goods and sovereign rights, was linked to a personal relationship of allegiance between the lord and his vassals, and as such was always newly enacted and accepted. The unity of the association as a whole became visible in the relationship between the person of the king or emperor as the highest feudal lord, in whom all these bonds ideally came together, and his immediate princely vassals. Each single ritual of enfeoffment, on whatever level of the association it took place, constituted the same relationship as the one that existed between the top, the king, and his imperial princes, and it thereby endowed the feudal association with a homogenous structure down to the very lowest branches.

Since the thirteenth century, the imperial princes had been symbolically and ritually singled out by the fact that only they were enfeoffed with their regalia and territories by the head of the Empire in person and in front of his throne. All electors and princes were imperial vassals. But the reverse was not the case: by no means were all imperial vassals imperial princes. Conversely, imperial princes could also receive fiefs from others besides the emperor and the Empire. In addition to the imperial princes, all manner of other persons, communities, or ecclesiastical corporations possessed fiefs from the emperor. The objects of imperial fiefs were not only territories and princely and electoral honors, but also every kind of goods, offices, and benefits; even single farms, houses, mills, fields, or pastures could be received from the Empire as fiefs.[135]

In keeping with medieval feudal law, it was imperative at every so-called *Herrn- und Mannfall*, that is, upon the death or change of feudal lord or vassal, for the latter to petition for the renewal of the feudal relationship and receive the enfeoffment anew from his lord. That the claim of princes to their fiefs had become de facto hereditary already since the Middle Ages changed nothing about the necessity of repeating the enfeoffment every time—that is, of reestablishing the relationship as a personal bond of fealty between feudal lord and vassals by means of an oath. The renewal of the fief, the investiture, regularly endowed existing relationships of power and property with a ritual stamp of legitimacy. If that legitimation did not take place, this could potentially have consequences for the vassal's position in his own territory; for example, the territorial estates could take it as an opportunity for their part to refuse the oath of homage to him.

Following Maximilian's ascension to the throne, all imperial vassals were obliged to petition him for a renewal of their fiefs. In Worms a larger number of letters of enfeoffment (*Lehnbriefe*) were issued, which documented such an investiture in writing and contained a list of all enfeoffed objects. The feudal oath (*Lehnseid*) could be performed in a variety of ways, depending on the status of the vassals. The lower-ranking ones, such as counts and knights, were for the most part asked in writing to swear the feudal oath to a neighboring prince, individual citizens swore their oath to the council of their city.[136] But the king could also dispatch commissioners who accepted the feudal oath in his stead. That is what happened in 1495 in the case of the controversial enfeoffment of Ludovico Sforza with the duchy of Milan, which was performed three times in front of different audiences, but which was supposed to be repeated once again by the emperor in person during his trip to Italy—or at least this prospect was held out to the duke.[137] Higher-ranking vassals either sent representatives to the king[138] or appeared in person. Counts, who were located on the feudal hierarchy between the princes, on the one side, and lords and knights, on the other, sometimes appeared in person for the enfeoffment; sometimes (in most cases) they swore the oath to a designated neighboring prince.[139] The investiture in person, in turn, could take place either within the emperor's lodgings[140] or *in maiestate* with great public pomp and circumstance. Although this solemn form was essentially reserved for electors and princes, in Worms in 1495 two counts of Henneberg were also enfeoffed in this way.[141]

Maximilian must have had a profound interest in the personal appearance of the princely vassals before his throne. The exercise of his office as the supreme feudal lord manifested—visible to everyone—the authority of the ruler as the head of the system and—next to God—the highest source of legitimacy.[142] The legitimacy of the entire system depended—pars pro toto—on the legitimacy of its leader. The princes, too, had therefore a fundamental interest in the recognition of royal authority, because on it depended simultaneously the recognition of their own elevated status. Thus, the right to solemn investiture of the imperial vassals with the regalia constituted the inviolable core of royal power within the Empire. How elementary this right was is revealed, not least, by the fact that even in the most radical reform plans of this time, this right remained fundamentally spared from the grasp of the estates. The right of investiture was, alongside the right of promotion to a higher rank, the sole prerogative that would be excluded from the authority of the planned *Reichsregiment* and left to the king or emperor alone.[143]

Added to this was a special reason for Maximilian's insistence on personal enfeoffment: since the Middle Ages, one of the traditional feudal obligations of the imperial vassals was to accompany the new king on his first journey to Rome. And Maximilian's most urgent goal at the diet of Worms was, after all, to set out as quickly as possible on this journey to expel the French king from Italy and acquire the dignity of Roman emperor. The personal investiture of the imperial vassals in Worms was thus to represent the prelude to the *Romzug* and induce the princes to the immediate performance of their feudal oath.

For the vassals, the solemn enfeoffment entailed immense material expenses. It therefore tended to be the rule that princes requested permission to perform the feudal oath in front of a representative or through a delegate.[144] But in Worms most electors and princes appeared personally in spite of—or also because of—the great expenditures. After the king had expressly requested that everyone appear in person for the enfeoffment and not send envoys, the process gradually unfolded a certain self-reinforcing effect: if so many came to be enfeoffed in person, others did not want to remain at home. "Thus we also hear that the electors and princes are willing to receive their fiefs and regalia from His Royal Majesty, and to that end the throne has been made and erected. Since this is also being done by others, we are of the opinion ... that we should also receive our two fiefs and regalia," the Elector Frederick of Saxony wrote to his brother.[145]

In his position as the supreme feudal lord, and with his absolute control over investiture, the king held in his hands an instrument to coerce recalcitrant princes to appear in Worms in person. Another reason this was of fundamental interest to him is because—as we have seen—the personal consent of the princes was essential to the binding nature of the decisions made in Worms, especially the financial commitments. Examples of how Maximilian employed enfeoffment as leverage can be found in the correspondence of the Dukes Georg and Albrecht of Bavaria, the Duke of Cleves-Mark, and the Elector of Brandenburg. For instance, Maximilian sent word to the envoy of the Duke of Cleves that unless his lord appeared in person, he would not enfeoff him at all.[146] The councilors of Lower Bavaria also urged their lords to come "so that Your Honor's regalia will not be missed out on because of this."[147]

Once nearly all princes were assembled, Maximilian stalled the solemn investitures. At the beginning of June, the councilors of electoral Brandenburg wrote to their lords that they, like the other princes, would have to wait to receive their fiefs "until the royal business has been settled," that is, until an agreement had been reached on the king's demands.[148] The great spectacle of the solemn throne investitures did not take place until the second half of July, after a rudimentary compromise had been found in the negotiations and the *Reichshilfe* had been approved in principle, though the most far-reaching reform plans had failed.

Enfeoffments and deliberations must therefore be seen in conjunction. Investiture was a service of the king toward the princes, but also a service of the princes toward the king. It was a ritual that constituted—through its performance—the unity of the Empire and the legitimatory ground of princely rule, thereby allowing the conflict-ridden negotiations to disappear, in the interests of all participants, behind the staging of a consensus. This staging should not be misunderstood as "mere appearance."[149] Instead, it was a representation collectively borne by all, a precondition for the legitimacy of joint action that nobody could do without.

On 14 July, the king began with the solemn enfeoffments *in maiestate* in accordance with the stipulations of the Golden Bull for a *solemnis curia regalis sive imperialis*.[150] The first to be invested were the electors of Mainz, Cologne, the Palatinate, and Saxony. They were followed the next day by the Elector of Trier, Duke Albrecht of Saxony, the Elector of Brandenburg, who was represented by an envoy, and his brother, the Margrave of Brandenburg. Two days after that came the two Landgraves of Hesse, the Prince of Anhalt, and Count Wilhelm of Henneberg. Finally, after two more days, it was the turn of the Duke of Brunswick, Count Otto of Henneberg, and Count Eberhard of Württemberg, who was elevated to the rank of duke by the investiture. All princes and estates stood, with choreographic precision, "in their order" to the right and left of the royal throne, at the very front the envoys of the foreign powers Spain, Naples, Hungary, Milan, and Montferrat. The king had mustered more than one hundred soldiers with halberds who kept the assembled people under control, and "also many other fellows such as heralds, adventurers, and all manner of servants."[151]

The ritual followed the extraordinarily elaborate and ostentatious form that had emerged at the beginning of the fifteenth century.[152] The atmosphere resembled that of a tournament. Every one of the men to be invested appeared with hundreds of retainers, all on horseback and with pennants and clothes in the colors of their lord. It began with the retinue of the lord to be invested galloping around the royal chair three times.[153] Later accounts of the events point out explicitly that the military might of the vassals was being staged here: hundreds of knights, all of them "brave, experienced warriors of nobility," with their banners gathered around the red flag, "as was customary on the battlefield."[154] After the first round, the highest-ranking relatives and friends of the vassals stepped forward as advocates and presented the request for enfeoffment to the king while genuflecting three times.[155] Following a brief ritual dialogue with the king, the Elector of Mainz passed the imperial consent on to the advocates; they expressed their thanks and brought the answer to the lord, who had so far been standing off to the side. Only after this dialogic sequence did the vassal step onto the stage himself, kneel before the throne, and hand his feudal banners to the Empire—the red blood-flag (*Blutfahne*), which symbolized high justice as the core of all regalia, and one banner for each of his territories with the appropriate coat of arms.[156] The territories were embodied in the banners: one knight "carried Thuringia," another "carried the Palatinate," and so on. The ecclesiastical electors also received the imperial seals as the insignia of their arch offices, while the secular electors had bestowed on them a banner with the insignia of their electoral honor.

The special status of a family's jointly held feudal property was also manifested very precisely in the form of the ritual, namely, in the joint enfoeffment (*zur gesamten Hand*). In accordance with their father's succession arrangements, the two heirs of the Hohenzollern house—Elector Johann and Margrave Frederick[157]—held the lordship over the Frankish territories and the Mark Brandenburg jointly, while the electoral honor belonged only to the older brother.[158] These details were very precisely staged. Only the envoys of the elector received the electoral banner, and all other banners were handed to both men jointly, that is, both grasped every banner pole at the same time. Later sources described the *Samtbelehnung* (joint investiture), where all vassals took hold of each other's mantles.[159]

On his knees, the vassal swore the feudal oath, which the archchancellor of Mainz recited for him, and in so doing he entered into an unspecified, unlimited, vague, and all-encompassing fealty toward the emperor and the Empire. After that the banners were handed back to him, one at a time, and then they were thrown from the investiture stage down into the crowd. The surrounding people tried to get control of them in an act of ritualized violence, in the process of which they were usually torn to pieces. It was considered a lucky omen if someone from the vassal's retinue was able to save the banner. This is what happened in the case of the banner of Hesse, which the soldiers of the landgrave subsequently dedicated in the cathedral of Worms to Our Lady.[160] At the conclusion of the ritual, the vassal kissed the pommel of the imperial sword, which the imperial archmarshal presented to him, and, still on this knees, delivered a brief speech of thanks. Then he climbed down from the stage and rode back to his lodgings with his retinue.

The symbolic value of the ritual was reciprocal. Subjecting himself to the king on his knees, the vassal symbolically accepted his status as a member of the Empire and simultaneously affirmed the overall imperial order. Both sides profited from the splendor of the scene, which manifested the centuries-old sacral authority of the Holy Roman Empire. The vassal acknowledged the majesty of the king and the Empire as the source of his own lordship, but in so doing he simultaneously participated in its traditional legitimacy and its supreme rank within Christendom. To the vassals the act offered the opportunity to muster their social capital in the form of their advocates, and to display their military and economic power in the form of their knightly retinue. The banners made visible to all which territories the vassal controlled. That is why the ritual was also the locus where public protests had to be lodged if someone felt aggrieved in his lordship rights by the investiture.

The investitures in Worms, too, did not come off without conflict. It was not only the Duke of Brunswick, notorious for fighting for a better place, who upset the enfeoffment proceedings.[161] Problems also arose from the fact that Elector Johann of Brandenburg had himself represented by an envoy, Herr von Reppin.[162] The latter's lower personal status was already expressed in the fact that he was not allowed to sit next to the king *in maiestate* or participate alongside the margrave in the storming of the royal chair. It was incompatible with the personal honor of the electors and princes who were present to rank behind an envoy, no matter whom he represented. That is why the Elector of Saxony successfully refused to be enfeoffed *after* the Elector of Brandenburg, against which the envoy from Brandenburg in turn lodged a formal protest.

It was the solemn act of investiture by the king that defined the status of the vassal publicly and authoritatively and situated him within the Empire's system of political-social classification. Three cases in Worms illustrate this vividly, because they were borderline cases in different ways: the investiture of Count Eberhard with the territory of Württemberg elevated into a duchy, the investiture of Duke René II of Lorraine, and finally, the investiture of the Elector of Brandenburg with the duchy of Pomerania-Stettin.

Elevation in Rank: Württemberg

The elevation of the Count of Württemberg into the princely rank on 21 July 1495 was an intervention in the status structure of the Empire, one that took place within the forms of an investiture in the true sense of the word, that is, as an act of dressing. Little is known about the preparation for this act.[163] As with other enfeoffments, the king sat *in maiestate* within the circle of the electors. Instead of the king, his councilor, Veit von Wolkenstein, delivered a "long, graceful speech" about the merits of the house of Württemberg to the emperor and the Empire, and about the fact that the princely estate was therein already "brought forth and contained in praiseworthy manner," so that the elevation in rank in a sense merely helped the true order of things to become outwardly valid and visible.[164] After that, the king dressed the count kneeling before him with the ducal frock, mantel, and hat of red satin. By bestowing upon him all ducal and princely honors, we read in a Württemberg source, the king also transformed the "land of Württemberg" into a duchy and principality, whereof the house henceforth bore the title, name, and coat of arms. Finally, the king placed a sword into Count of Württemberg's hand and thereby endowed him with "the right also to protect widows and orphans and punish injustice, and to display and carry the sword as a duke and prince."[165] After the new duke "had done his duty," the Elector of Saxony, in his capacity as the hereditary imperial marshal, took him by the hand and led him to his new place among the princes, "where he should now and henceforth be seated," namely, between the Duke of Jülich and the Landgrave of Hesse, that is, immediately behind all the other dukes and before all margraves and landgraves, "as he had been seated at the above-mentioned diet in front of all [*vor allermenngklich*] and as he and his descendants shall be seated in the future."[166] Subsequently the advocates of the future duke opened the usual ritual of investiture with the threefold "storming," during the course of which he was invested with the banners of Württemberg, Teck, and Mömpelgart, with the blood banner, and with the imperial storm flag. In the evening, the king and the queen together held a banquet for the new duke, in which the electors and the other princes participated. With this, the king was following the usual practice of concluding an act of status change—just like every ritual of transition—with a shared meal with all those on whose consent the success of the status change depended. The shared meal was (and is) probably the most elemental social act of community formation. A person who participated affirmed his agreement with what was happening.[167]

An act of "social magic" transformed the count into a duke.[168] The sequence of the ritual thus effected three transformations simultaneously: First, it changed the appearance and character of the person himself by bestowing on him the insignia of his new dignity, which the duke henceforth wore on his body and carried before him during solemn acts. Second, the ritual, through the bestowal of new crests, altered the territories and combined them into a new entity, the principality, from which the name and title of the person was derived. Third, the ritual altered the overall system of the Empire by assigning the prince a new place within it. That was not possible without the consent of those whose rights were affected by it. With the new duke assuming his place among the assembled princes, the latter simultaneously professed their agreement and accepted the Duke of Württemberg literally within their ranks.[169] The elevation of a prince thus had three dimensions: a personal one, a factual one, and a collective one; the ritual changed the person or the family, the territory, and the entire order of the princes. However, such an alteration fundamentally required legitimation, since changeability was regarded as a mark of worldly imperfection. To be sure, the king arrogated to himself the right to decide on his own about the order of the estates, just as his predecessors had already "arranged and furnished princes and other estates in their nature." However, he did not let this appear as arbitrary change, but as a necessary measure to preserve the "adornment and majesty" of the Empire, as a way of adjusting the worldly conditions to the eternal order. Since "by the exigencies of this temporal, transient world many have been lost and have expired," the king is entitled to replace the extinct families with others and thus restore the order.[170]

Compared with the princely elevations of rank in later centuries, the act was fairly uncontroversial. Evidently the authoritative power of the king in the circle of his electors was sufficient to ensure its efficacy. Even though we have no information about extensive negotiations leading up to the investiture, no formal protest stirred against the placement of the new prince, and he was able to assume his new place also in the deliberations without challenge.[171] However, this change of status, too, was not entirely free of points of conflict. The Elector Frederick of Saxony "did not want to allow" the Württemberger to be invested with the storm banner of the Empire, a stance he justified by invoking an ancient privilege granted by Emperor Ludwig the Bavarian in 1336. An eyewitness account relates that the conflict was resolved by the king and the other electors[172]—but not permanently, for the honorary service of carrying the imperial storm banner in war was later repeatedly a cause of conflict.[173]

Although the ritual did not change anything with respect to the *fundamentum in re* of the lordship, its material resources, it did change everything that concerned social standing, public appearance, and treatment by third parties. The new place in processions and sessions, whether during deliberations, masses, or enfeoffments, with the claim to a different title, a different coat of arms, and different ceremonial treatment from the other princes, also entailed a different mode of political participation—and a higher assessment for imperial contributions. The claim to ducal standing had to be redeemed in public appearance through a luxury appropriate to the estate; economically, the prince had to invest in symbolic capital. There were different opinions about whether or not this investment paid off. Württemberg's councils and *Landstände* (territorial estates), who in the end would have to pay for all of this, complained that they would have to trade in a rich count for a poor duke, and they criticized Eberhard's elevation in status soberly: "Now, however, he would have to contribute like a duke, represent the princely fief, as well as maintain a princely status and court with knights, noblemen, councilors, horses, and court retainers, and for these things bear much greater expenses"—and all of this even though nothing had in fact changed about the material fundament of the lordship: "after all, the princely income, the usufruct and the receipts, have not been increased, neither has anything been added in terms of land or people." The duke, the source goes on to tell us, received these statements with extreme disfavor and great displeasure, "as though they begrudged him this honor he had attained." Another chronicle reports that the critical councilors had to leave the court.[174] The elevation in rank evidently followed a logic different from an economic cost-benefit analysis; for the man who held it, the princely existence was a value in and of itself. Since the historians of the nineteenth and twentieth centuries felt greater affinity with the values of the learned councilors than with those of princely society, this aspect was for a long time not properly appreciated.

Ambiguity: Lorraine

The reception of Duke René II of Lorraine from the house of Anjou with the title of King of Jerusalem and Sicily in Worms on 30 April struck observers with amazement. Maximilian and the duke sought to outdo each other with demonstrations of honor. The king had already sent the Elector of Cologne to meet the duke, and now he and all the other electors, princes, counts, and lords, along with their retinues, rode out to welcome him in front of the city gate. When they met each other, "the King of Sicily leapt off his horse and advanced toward the King of the Romans on foot three or four paces, then the King of the Romans also wanted to be off his horse; the King of Sicily caught him and hoisted him back into the saddle before he came down to the ground."[175] However, this scene, somewhat strange to modern eyes, did not follow a spontaneous impulse, but corresponded to the customary practice between the king and the electors. When the king and the electors met, it was an act of ritual convention that the king, as he was getting ready to dismount, be prevented from doing so by the electors.[176] After this, the Duke of Lorraine rode in the midst of the three archbishops and the king, ahead of the Elector of Saxony. This special distinction did not escape observers, since it violated the rules of the order of procession in the Golden Bull, according to which the electors need not allow anyone to ride between themselves and the king or emperor.[177] The Duke of Lorraine was thus given a treatment in Worms equal to that of an elector. If Duke René proceeded toward the king on foot for a few paces, and even physically prevented him from dismounting, this kind of ceremonial self-diminishment should by no means be confused with a binding subordination. Instead, what characterized especially the rules of politeness among equals was, paradoxically enough, that individuals sought to outdo each other with demonstrative debasement: that is what distinguished voluntary courtesy from coerced submission.[178] With gestures of courtesy one could playfully invert an existing rank order, as happened, for example, when men gave ceremonial precedence to women, which, as everyone knew, in no way abrogated the gender hierarchy. In this instance it was clear to all observers that René of Anjou was being treated, and behaving, in a way that was usually reserved for electors. That Duke René had no intention of actually submitting himself to Maximilian became evident when it came to the ritual of his enfeoffment.

The fact was that René's status between France and the Empire was exceedingly ambiguous.[179] The *welsch* duke from the French royal house of Anjou was a vassal of the French king for one part of his territories, the Duchy of Bar. By contrast, what sort of feudal relationship he had to the Empire and which territories he possessed as fiefs from the emperor, was not a question that could be easily answered. What was true is that René II's grandfather, René I, had been solemnly enfeoffed with the Duchy of Lorraine by Emperor Sigismund *in Caesareo solio sub apparatus Imperialis Maiestatis*, on the imperial throne and in the forms of majesty.[180] As a result, the duke was assessed for imperial aid in all registers of the fifteenth century. In actual fact, though, he never paid his contributions.[181] Such an ambiguous status was characteristic of lordships at the periphery of the Empire, where the sphere of influence of the great dynasties intersected in multifarious ways, and the smaller princes, to the advantage of their own independence, tacked back and forth between the neighboring monarchs. René's treatment at the imperial diet was thus of the utmost significance, for the issue at stake was to reframe his relationship to the Empire and clarify his status as a vassal.

Maximilian was concerned with bringing the duke over to his side in the struggle against the French king, to which end he held out the prospect of the kingdom of Naples and Sicily, as well as the imperial vicariate over Italy.[182] Likewise, the archchancellor of Mainz and the other princes, in the interest of their reform plans, must have been interested in demarcating Lorraine's affiliation with the Empire more clearly than before. As early as 1488, an imperial councilor had been dispatched to the western periphery of the Empire to summon the imperial vassals there to renew their fiefs and accept their feudal oaths in the emperor's stead.[183] René II had asked Maximilian, the successor to the throne, to enfeoff him in the form of a procurator. Maximilian had rejected this on the grounds that this was not his privilege, but the emperor's; the duke should appear in person at the next imperial diet. However, he did not do so, but sent an envoy.[184]

The duke's personal visit to the Worms diet thus carried special significance. A report described from the perspective of Lorraine the form of the investiture.[185] After it had been determined that the charters of enfeoffment would be drawn up in line with the older documents presented by René (that is, not as in 1434, when his grandfather had been invested with the duchy as a whole[186]), the Duke of Lorraine and Bar had two princes escort him before the king. The latter was seated in the circle of the electors of Cologne, Mainz, Trier, and Saxony, the Margrave of Brandenburg, and several other princes, and was holding in his hands the scepter that was regarded as the scepter of Charlemagne. The duke went down on his knees, touched the evangelary, and swore the oath of fealty to the Empire, the king, and his successors—or more precisely, *fidelitatem, subiectionem et obedientiam*, with the addition *secundum tenorem litterarum feodorum meorum*, that is, in accordance with the stipulations of his bills of enfeoffment. This formula had previously been the topic of intensive arguments. The Elector of Mainz had demanded that the Duke of Lorraine allow himself to be enfeoffed like any other imperial prince and swear the same unrestricted oath of fealty. The latter, however, refused to utter the usual general formula, because it expressed too great an obligation (*laquelle estoit trop de plus grande obligation et expression*) and invoked the *liberté* of the Duchy of Lorraine. The duke was granted his wish only after long debates over the precise nature of the fiefs, which could not be precisely documented. The report points out that it had been a special favor of the king to allow the Duke of Lorraine to swear the feudal oath at a place *à part* and *sans solemnité*, and to spare him the elaborate ritual on horseback and involving the banners, as was customary with the other princes.[187] And the bills of enfeoffment that were issued to the duke did not concern the Duchy of Lorraine, but only the Margraviate of Pont-à-Mouson and a few other, small imperial fiefs.[188]

This case illustrates the importance of the outward form of the ritual for the scope of the obligations that were taken on, and the relationship that existed between ritual and writing. The act of investiture was anything but an expendable ceremony; rather, it constituted a special legal relationship, one that did not presuppose the validity of the old bills of enfeoffment, but guaranteed them in the first place. Documents could not replace the ritual, especially since in this case various bills of enfeoffment with contradictory content existed. At the same time, it becomes clear just how seriously the public of such an act was taken: it could be done only *à part*, under the eyes of the electors and imperial princes and the retinue of Lorraine; printed herald reports of it were not disseminated. As a relative of the French king, the duke had also not agreed to the spectacular tournament ritual in front of the throne in the open. But given the way the act was performed, with a kind of semi-public and modified obligation of fealty, he could continue his policy of charting a course between two lords, and continue to benefit from the fact that both the French and the Roman king competed for his support. Any clarity, of the kind the arch-chancellor of Mainz had called for (and modern constitutional historians also desire), was avoided. The Duke of Lorraine continued to be listed in the register, and he continued to be essentially remiss on the imperial aid.[189] Lorraine was also placed within the Imperial Districts (*Reichskreise*) created in 1521, but the duke refused to recognize the jurisdiction of the newly established Imperial Chamber Court (*Reichskammergericht*). His status was and remained ambiguous, very much to his advantage.[190]

Conflict: Pomerania

Another, equally significant special case, this one at the northeastern periphery of the Empire, was the Duchy of Pomerania. For centuries it had been a point of controversy between the electors of Brandenburg and the dukes of Pomerania whether the Pomeranians were vassals of the emperor and the Empire, and thus imperial princes with a seat and vote at the imperial assemblies, or instead *Landsassen* and vassals of Brandenburg. The history of the conflict between the two dynasties, antagonists related by marriage, is long and eventful. The ritual of enfeoffment played a central part in it. In the fourteenth century, the dukes of Pomerania had been solemnly invested by the emperors as direct vassals of the Empire; before 1486 they had always been included in the registers of the Empire.[191] However, already from the beginning of the fifteenth century, the Hohenzollerns tried to restore their feudal overlordship, among other things by arguing that the dukes of Pomerania had failed to receive their fief from the emperor in person and had thereby forfeited their right as imperial vassals. Above all, they were concerned with asserting a hereditary claim to the Duchy of Pomerania-Stettin. The Elector Albrecht of Brandenburg succeeded in 1470 to have himself invested with all of Pomerania by Frederick III. A peculiar treaty came about with the dukes of Pomerania in 1472: it stated that the dukes would retain the greater part of their lands under their lordship but take it from Brandenburg as a fief, though without solemn investiture, only through a handshake and without a feudal oath. The Elector of Brandenburg would also be allowed to carry the title and coat of arms of a Duke of Pomerania, though he should not use them when dealing with the traditional dukes of Pomerania. Should their line die out, the land would fall to the Mark Brandenburg as a discharged fief.

When the new Duke Bogislav X of Pomerania-Stettin assumed the throne in 1474, the conflict flared up again: violent clashes alternated with negotiations. In 1479, the duke once again had to accept Brandenburg feudal suzerainty in a treaty. At the Nuremberg diet of 1487, the three Brandenburg brothers, Elector Johann and Margraves Frederick and Sigmund, appeared in person to have Emperor Frederick III confirm the treaty with the Duke of Pomerania. The staging of their material and social capital left observers dumbstruck: they had with them seven hundred and fifty "enormous horses well equipped," and this was only the noble retinue, not counting "cook and cellarer and useless folk."[192] They conveyed to the emperor the urgent request for a speedy solemn investiture, explicitly promising in return that they would not immediately depart afterward, but would also participate in the deliberations. Already before their arrival they had their delegates negotiate the formalities of the enfeoffment in all their details; the Elector of Mainz had recommended that they receive the territories—with the exception of the electoral honor—together as joint holders, "so as to avoid much future complaint."[193] On 2 May 1487, Frederick III bestowed upon them their lands in the form of ten "coat of arms-banners," which they all grasped together as a sign of their undivided lordship, including also the banners of Pomerania, Stettin, Rügen, Wenden, and Kashubia.[194]

However, they had to assert this title against the Duke of Pomerania by prevailing upon him in turn to receive the duchy from them as a fief. But Bogislav refused to do so. What worked in his favor was Maximilian's need for money. Even during his father's lifetime, the king tried to extract financial benefit from the Pomeranian duke's ambition by calling upon him in 1489 to render direct imperial aid in spite of his feudal dependence on Brandenburg. The Brandenburgers had to try and prevent that with every means possible. As a result, at the imperial diet in Nuremberg in 1491, Elector Johan, after balking for a long time, assumed the Pomeranian share of the imperial aid.[195] The Brandenburgers even contemplated using military force to compel Bogislav to swear the feudal oath to the elector, but in the end they considered it too risky. Eventually, they concluded a treaty with him in 1493, in which they affirmed their hereditary claim (*Erbanwartschaft*) but renounced receiving the personal feudal oath, on the condition that Bogislav not take the Duchy of Pomerania as a fief from anyone else, including the king.[196] They thus exchanged the obligation of the Pomeranian duke through the traditional personal ritual for a mere obligation through a treaty charter—something that would prove a bad trade.

In this situation, the events at the Worms diet took on fundamental importance for the relationship between the king, Brandenburg, and Pomerania. Unlike his brother, Margrave Frederick, Elector Johann of Brandenburg had sent only his councilors to Worms; his intention was not to receive the fief in person, but to ask for a postponement. But after their arrival in Worms, the two councilors reported back that the Elector of Mainz and other well-intentioned individuals were urging that he "not seek to postpone the fief," but receive the investiture in person and publicly like the other princes in order to avoid harm and disadvantage. Word had reached the Brandenburg councilors that the Duke of Pomerania-Stettin, alarmingly enough, had once again been invited to Worms as a prince of the Empire and had been directly assessed for imperial aid.[197] Apparently, however, the letter of summons had been intercepted by two bribed imperial court officials and had been held back. Brandenburg now had to make sure to be invested with the Duchy of Pomerania by the king himself as soon as possible, all the while keeping Duke Bogislav from being able to bring that request to the king in the first place. "It is therefore all the more necessary to receive the fief, so that he [Bogislav] would not achieve anything prejudicial in the meantime," the councilors warned the elector.[198] The interception of the royal summons seems to have been successful; in any case, the Duke of Pomerania did not appear at the diet and was therefore unable, by having a seat and vote in the deliberations, to assert his claim to being a member of the Empire. And even though the Elector of Brandenburg also did not appear in person in Worms, but had himself represented by his brother, Margrave Frederick, he was still able to influence matters in his interest. When the Brandenburgers were publicly and jointly invested with the banners, those of Pomerania and Stettin were once more among them.[199] No wonder that it was the herald of Brandenburg who published a broadsheet with a detailed description of this ritual.

Still, during the period that followed, Bogislav continued to seek personal enfeoffment from Maximilian, and he eventually succeeded with his successor.[200] At his first solemn diet in 1521 in Worms, Charles V bestowed upon the two Brandenburg brothers, Elector Joachim and Margrave Kasimir, their fief in solemn form, including also the banners of Pomerania.[201] But in spite of the urgent pleas of the elector, the Duke of Pomerania also received a letter of enfeoffment from the emperor, was included in the registers, was incorporated into the new district system, and from 1522 on held a seat and vote at the imperial diet in Nuremberg, over the protests from Brandenburg.[202] Charles V pursued a dual strategy, the goal of which was to extract the imperial taxes from both princes.

The dispute subsequently occupied the imperial government, which represented the emperor during his absence from the Empire. Lawyers on both sides exchanged learned briefs, which concerned, among other things, the precise form of the investitures. The government formulated a decision, which Brandenburg rejected. After Bogislav's death in 1523, his sons carried on the quarrel. There were renewed negotiations, the imperial diet in Speyer in 1526 took up the matter, and other princes and the king of the Romans, Ferdinand, Charles V's deputy, became active as intercessors. None of this had any lasting success until the two adversaries met in person in 1529 in Grimnitz, Pomerania, and negotiated a treaty.[203] From a modern perspective, this agreement is quite strange. By the standards of the day, however, it is highly revealing. The agreement envisaged that the Elector of Brandenburg accept Pomerania's immediate subjection to the Empire (*Reichsunmittelbarkeit*), in return for which his expectant hereditary claim to the duchy was guaranteed. However, before every investiture of the Pomeranians, the emperor had to inform the elector in a timely manner so that the latter could appear in person and also take a hold of all the banners. The same would apply to the hereditary homage of the Pomeranian territorial estates (*Landstände*): in every case an envoy from Brandenburg should be present to receive the homage jointly with the dukes of Pomerania. The elector would likewise be allowed to be enfeoffed by the emperor with his claim to Pomerania and also bear the title and coat of arms of a Duke of Pomerania—except for those instances when the Duke of Pomerania himself was present. Finally, the entire treaty would be guaranteed by being renewed in writing at every change of ruler and being mentioned in every letter of enfeoffment.

When Charles V, at the diet of Augsburg in 1530, held court once again in person and in the greatest splendor, this treaty was put into practice. In the presence of the Hohenzollerns, the emperor invested the two dukes of Pomerania publicly and in due form with the banners. How this unfolded is described in great detail by the imperial herald Kaspar Sturm in a printed diary.[204] After the emperor and the electors had taken their seats and had passed the imperial regalia on to the holders of the hereditary offices, Elector Joachim of Brandenburg rose "from his seat, stepped before His Imperial Majesty, and orally delivered in person a very gracious and skilled speech, to the effect that he publicly protested and objected that he would not further consent to the investiture of the dukes of Pomerania that was about to take place. Instead, he offered during the enfeoffment to take hold of every banner and to jointly receive the totality and justice," that is, to be jointly enfeoffed alongside the Duke of Pomerania. The emperor informed him through the arch-chancellor that he would consider his protest. Thereupon Margrave Georg of Brandenburg also stepped forward and likewise wanted to "have a speech delivered in the form of a protest" by his councilor, but he was blocked from doing so with the argument that one could no longer put off the princes who were waiting on the track in their armor.[205] In spite of the protest, the ritual of the storming began. The dukes of Pomerania were able to muster as their advocates the dukes of Brunswick and Mecklenburg, and their retinue carried the banners of Pomerania, Stettin, Kashubia, Wenden, Barth, Rügen, Wolgast, Usedom, and Buckow. When the emperor, following the feudal oath, wanted to hand the banners over to the kneeling dukes, the Elector of Brandenburg rose from his seat once again, "stepped in front of the emperor next to the oft-mentioned princes of Pomerania and with his hands also took hold of every banner," and reiterated his protest. The dissent of the Brandenburgers was thus coenacted, as it were, in the previously agreed-upon form. That is also what happened at later diets.[206]

What strikes modern eyes as an exceedingly strange handling of the conflict was thus that the competing legal claims existed permanently side by side and were symbolically and ritually reaffirmed time and again and kept in memory. Both the electors of Brandenburg *and* the dukes of Pomerania were enfeoffed with *the same* territories; both received the hereditary homage of the Pomeranian *Landstände*, and both bore *the same* title and coat of arms, even though the Brandenburgers at no point exercised actual lordship over the Duchy of Pomerania. The compromise that the two princes had negotiated left the core issue in a sense unresolved and kept the conflict in abeyance in a ritualized form. The ritual of enfeoffment always enacted simultaneously the transfer of lordship and the opposition to it. That was necessary in order to maintain the competing claim of the Brandenburgers for the future in a contrafactual fashion, that is, against actual practice. Over the long term the strategy proved the right one for the Hohenzollerns. The ducal house of Pomerania died out in 1637, and their hereditary claim could be revived even after being dormant for centuries.

These three examples—Württemberg, Lorraine, and Pomerania—are revealing in various ways. They show how flexible the order of the Empire still was. Changes in status were possible and occurred fairly frequently, namely, in the form of performative solemn acts. Stabilizing the order depended on having it symbolically and ritually enacted. It was not sufficient to have it written down somewhere, since contemporaries did not yet place much trust in the written documentation of legal claims. Dealings with the written form were not very professionalized and therefore very uncertain. Archives were disorganized; important documents were often impossible to find. Even great noble dynasties like the Habsburgs, the Hohenzollerns, or the Lorrainers did not yet have proper record offices; documents were mostly scattered in disorganized fashion in many locations and had to be laboriously searched for if one wanted to appeal to them.[207] It therefore seemed safer to uphold claims in a symbolic-ritual way in front of witnesses. This changed only gradually through the increasingly experienced handling of writing, that is, as people began to collect written records more systematically, archive documents more carefully, and develop a historical-critical method in dealing with them. Still, the relationship between the emperor and the imperial estates, the Empire's web of statuses, remained profoundly dependent on ritual enactments. Every significant deviation in ritual action could in turn exert a structure-shaping effect and become a point around which a new claim could crystallize.

On the other hand, it is striking that people clung stubbornly to their claims even if they had little chance of enforcing them de facto. Constitutional historians have referred to this as the "conservative" feature of the imperial constitution. The case of Pomerania reveals that contemporaries dealt with competing claims differently from what seems self-evident to a modern perspective. Conflicts did not necessarily have to be clearly settled, but could remain permanently unresolved. Evidently people at the time were not even counting on unambiguous decisions. After all, which authority could have made and enforced them even against powerful princes? Instead, the parties involved could often get along permanently and perfectly well with ambiguous situations. They were chiefly concerned with preserving their respective claims and waiting for more favorable circumstances. And that, precisely, is what symbolic-ritual means offered. Salvatorius clauses, protestations, the bearing of coats and arms and titles—all of this made it possible to preserve the memory of claims in ritualized form. The result was a largely disconnected existence alongside actual practice on the one hand, and a multitude of competing counterfactual claims on the other. That Lorraine, for example, remained on the imperial register (*Reichsmatrikel*) even though the duke never paid taxes, or that the margraves of Brandenburg bore the coat of arms and title of the dukes of Pomerania even though they never held the lordship there, is highly significant for the structure of the Empire as a whole. We will encounter similar phenomena more often: ambiguity where today one would expect clarity, and a lack of resolution where today one would consider a definitive decision a necessity.

This applies also to the conclusion of the Worms diet. Its results were by no means as clear, and its decisions by no means as binding, as a modern observer might expect from "reform laws."

Departure

"Taking leave" (*Abschied nehmen*) means departing from a meeting place with mutual agreement. "Bidding farewell" is more than a mere separation; the phrase describes a form of parting that implicitly signals the intent—and establishes the reciprocal expectation—of maintaining the respective relationship beyond the separation.[208] That was and is the meaning of ritualized forms of parting, of bidding farewell, from the simple handshake to the solemn audience of leave-taking. Conversely, separating without a word of greeting could and can be intended (and be interpreted) as the abrogation of friendly relations, a hostile signal. In other words, rituals of leave-taking maintain social bonds beyond spatial and temporal separation, or at least create the precondition of meeting again later on the same footing.[209]

For premodern diets it was even more so the case that none of the invited participants could simply depart without taking their leave, that is, without having received from the king permission to leave (*urlaub*). For example, in Worms the Duke of Brunswick asked the king three times for a "gracious leave." After "it had been denied for the third time in humiliating fashion," he departed without it, though he transferred to his brother the "authority" and obliged himself ahead of time to agree to the decisions of the estates. That he did not wish to break all contact with the Margrave of Brandenburg in spite of the above-mentioned seating conflicts was attentively noted by his councilor: "Yet in parting outside of the king's chamber, he [the Duke of Brunswick] and Margrave Frederick shook hands."[210] The formal departure of the duke was a significant act, because the personal presence of the princes was so important to the binding nature of the decisions that were made.

From the ritualized act of taking leave, the term *Abschied* was transferred to the document that recorded the joint decision at the end—that is, everything those assembled had agreed upon and wished to consider binding for the future. *Abschied* meant "the resolution adopted and publicized at the solemn dismissal of an assembly, at the end of a transaction." Its Latin equivalent was the *recessus* (from *recedere*, or "withdraw").[211]

For the capacity of the assembly to make a decision, the formal demarcation of its end was just as important as that of its beginning. One had to ensure that what had been "transacted" had come to an end, namely, in the concrete sense that all participants committed themselves to the outcome and recognized it as valid. That end was served by symbols and rituals of ratification: the public, solemn reading of the joint resolution on the one hand, and the signing and sealing of the document on the other.[212] In accord with the old legal principle *quod omnes tangit ab omnibus approbetur* (whatever touches all must be approved by all), such a recess was binding only on those who had been present. Anyone who had left early and had not participated in the ratification rituals could contest their binding force on him—and that applied even more to those who had not shown up at all and had not even sent delegates to represent them. This stood in conflict with the interest of the assembly to make their joint decision generally binding also on those who had been absent. Beginning in the 1480s and 1490s, this topic was intensively discussed at the imperial diets, and the claim had been put forth that recesses should also apply to those who had been invited but had failed to show up.[213] Already at the imperial diet of 1480, the estates had asserted that they had made their decisions "on behalf of the [entire] nation,"[214] and they called upon the emperor to impose severe sanctions on those who resisted. With that they were seeking to redefine themselves as an assembly of "the Empire" in the strict sense, namely, a body that was able to act and make decisions in the name of the Empire as a whole that would be binding upon all its members, comparable to what the college of the electors was able to do at least in the act of electing the king. One reflection of this development is that one began to speak, beginning in the 1480s, of "the Empire" as a collective actor.[215]

But in Worms in 1495, the archbishop of Mainz was still unable to successfully assert this claim. To be sure, a document was drawn up about what had been "agreed and decreed." What marked it as a joint recess was that the king sealed it and the imperial archchancellor signed it, whereas at the previous "common days" (*gemeine Tage*) there had been at most unilaterally composed recess documents.[216] However, no consensus could be reached about its universally binding nature. The delegates of the princes refused, in particular, to affix their seals to the resolutions about imperial aid; instead, the consent was to be procured by means of a special letter separately for each prince who was not present in person.[217] Notwithstanding, Maximilian had his councilors summon the estates on 1 September, hand them the recess document, and at the same time grant them formal leave. As he had been at the opening, the king was in charge at the closing; he alone could legitimately terminate the deliberations.

When constitutional historians debate whether or not there was an "official imperial recess with the force of law" at Worms,[218] they are applying an anachronistic criterion. After all, a clear and universal obligation was a claim that had to be successfully asserted going forward. However, a category such as "force of law" already presupposes the formal procedures of decision making and sanctioning, which some were trying to establish here in the first place against resistance. In fact, it would turn out that the personal consent of all the princes to the Worms recess was indispensable if its stipulations were to be put into practice.

Those stipulations, in turn, contained provisions aimed at boosting the binding nature of the recesses in the future through greater personal presence. For the purpose of "administering peace and law," it was specified that an imperial assembly was to meet every year, at which all electors and princes should appear in person, or if they did not, excuse themselves and at least send delegates. In addition, it was decreed that participants could depart only with permission, not from the king, but from the assembly itself, or rather, the majority of those assembled—a rule that would have greatly enhanced the autonomy of the assembly vis-à-vis the king. But this was one of the rules that proved impossible to enforce subsequently. The public nature of the Empire was and remained a selective, temporally limited public assembly. Once participants had taken their leave, it dissolved again, and it required considerable exertions to place it on a permanent footing through representation or written transactions. The dilemma was this: on the one hand, the assembly was still following the logic of personal presence; on the other hand, an entity as complex and far-flung as the Empire could not be durably stabilized and integrated into a single whole by way of personal presence alone.

Interim Summary

The fifteenth century has been described as an age of structural consolidation:[219] expanding supraregional communication networks, growing potential for conflict, increasing need for money, greater literacy, an intensification of political power by means of legally trained personnel—these are only the most important indicators. Humans entered into contact with one another that was ever more frequent, intensive, and continuous. That did not happen without conflict, and the result was that reciprocal relationships were newly calibrated and fixed more precisely for the future than before. What people referred to as "the Empire" was being developed into a more stable political-social system of classification. This happened in a variety of ways: first, through large-scale solemn rituals of enfeoffment, which defined the status of individual princes in the society of the high nobility (sometimes in a completely new way), and second, through the growing participation in shared burdens and problem-solving procedures. The imperial diet of 1495 shows this in exemplary fashion.

For a long time, constitutional historians told the story of the Worms diet differently than contemporaries did. Highlighting this difference in perception is not to deny the historical significance of the reforms, but merely to place them into a different perspective. The imperial diet was not a state organ and no "visible representation of the German nation."[220] No collective actor was active here; no "imperial will" was being articulated. Rather, the action was being done by individual persons of varying status and capacity for action, whom the king, their shared overlord, had summoned. The events were by no means unstructured, but they followed the logic of direct personal presence rather than the logic of formal organization.[221] What imparted structure to the assembly and ensured stability of expectations were not formalized procedures that could have produced collective decisions without regard to a person's status, but instead symbolic-ritual rules.

The Worms diet was the object of intense and contentious efforts at enactment, just as it was the object of intense and contentious deliberations. Participants were not only concerned with discussing the questions of how funds could be raised for the fight against the French and the Turks and the how the inner peace could be secured; at the same time, the issue was always—explicitly and implicitly—negotiations over the questions of what "the Empire" was and where each person would find a place within it.

The assembly was simultaneously *Hoftag* and imperial diet; from different perspectives, it was sometimes seen as one, and sometimes as the other. The king was holding a "royal day," that is, he gathered his vassals, relatives, and friends around himself for advice and aid. A group of imperial estates, and especially the elector of Mainz, used the same occasion to take counsel with each other and turn it into an "imperial diet" in the later sense. They practiced forms of deliberation and decision making that bound the king himself institutionally or were even independent of his person, and sought to make them permanent. Through their actions they gradually created and changed—in a conflict-ridden way—the rules of acting together.

Two different modes of representation can be grasped in the ritual of sitting *in maiestate* and in the processes of the estate deliberations. The stable, institutional core of the entire meeting was formed by the solemn acts at which the king appeared publicly in the circle of the electors "in his adornment and dignity." In the ritual of the *repraesentatio identitatis*, in the forms of the fourteenth and fifteenth centuries (public, sacrally superelevated, qualified by the *appropriate* clothing, objects, gestures, and persons), the king, together with the electors, embodied pars pro toto the majesty of the Empire. Sitting *in maiestate* was a ritual that made an existing consensus about the shared order symbolically manifest. But if that consensus was missing, or if the participants had not negotiated an agreement *before* the performance of the ritual, the ritual itself could not bring about a decision that would have also bound the dissenters (as the majority principle was able to do at the election of the king, for example). All the actors could do was to ritually express their dissent in the form of the *protestatio*, the public declaration of disagreement. The spectrum of acts that could be carried out in the ritual of sitting *in maiestate* was limited: enfeoffments and status elevations were acts that, while they changed the status of the individual person within the overall system, simultaneously integrated that person into the overall system, and in the process enacted and affirmed that system as an institutional order that persisted above all changes in persons.

Against this older form of identity representation, a very differently structured procedure of deliberating—secret, open as to the outcome, aimed at producing binding decisions also vis-à-vis dissenters—could prevail only with difficulty. The assembled estates—without the king—formed on their own only the beginnings of an autonomous process that would have turned them into a corpus capable of acting and with a fictive unitary will. A political actor presupposes formal processes by which the decisions made by individuals are attributed to and rendered binding upon the collective whole—therein lies the political fiction of representation. It is only by virtue of such a fiction that the political whole becomes capable of taking action internally and externally, and does not fracture into a multitude of unattributable individual actions. A representative organ in that sense in 1495 was at best the king together with the electors, not, however, the assembled estates as a whole.

Notes

1. RTA MR 5/2, No. 1851, p. 1676 (report by Reinhart Noltz, mayor of Worms). See Reuter, "Worms als Reichstagsstadt," 123–39.
2. RTA MR 5/2, No. 1851, p. 1688.
3. Angermeier, *Reichsreform*; Wiesflecker, *Kaiser Maximilian I.*; see the instructive overview in Moraw, "Der Reichstag zu Worms von 1495," 25–37; Boldt, "1495–1995," 57–70; Isenmann, "Kaiser, Reich und deutsche Nation," 185–227.
4. Angermeier, "Der Wormser Reichstag"; but see his "Einleitung," in RTA MR 1/1, p. 33: Until the seventeenth century, the imperial diets are "not an institution in the Empire, alongside the Empire, or for the Empire, but represent each time the actualization of the Empire under the initiative and leadership of the king." Wiesflecker speaks of the "imperial authority" as the object of the "constitutional conflict" between the king and the imperial estates in *Kaiser Maximilian I.*, 2:224–25. See the fundamental critique by Moraw, "Der Reichstag zu Worms von 1495"; Isenmann, "Städte auf den Reichstagen," esp. 550; for the later period, see Luttenberger, "Reichstage unter Karl V.," 60ff.
5. For the summons to the imperial diet, see RTA MR 5/1, No. 27, p. 127.
6. See the fundamental biography of Maximilian by Wiesflecker, *Kaiser Maximilian I.*, 5 vols., and an abbreviated version, *Maximilian I.*; see also Hollegger, *Maximilian I.*
7. On the imperial diet of 1495, see Moraw, "Der Reichstag zu Worms von 1495" and "Königshof, Hoftag und Reichstag"; Göbel, *Der Reichstag von Worms 1495*; Heinig, "Der Wormser Reichstag von 1495 als Hoftag"; Isenmann, "Kaiser, Reich und deutsche Nation"; Heil, "Verschriftlichung des Verfahrens als Modernisierung" and "Der Reichstag als politisches Kommunikationszentrum"; on the significance of ceremony and rank on the imperial diets of the early sixteenth century, see Luttenberger, "Pracht und Ehre"; Aulinger, *Das Bild des Reichstags*; Willich, "Rangstreit," 37ff.; Lanzinner and Strohmeyer, *Der Reichstag*; see also Zotz, "Der Reichstag als Fest"; Boockmann, *Geschäfte und Geschäftigkeit*.
8. RTA MR 5/2, p. 1681; see also No. 1732, p. 1299 (report from the councilors of electoral Brandenburg to their lord): "Item it has been a long time since there has been such an excellent assembly of the Empire as now."
9. Melville, "'Un bel office.'"
10. Schubert, *Reichstage*; on the medium in general, see Schilling, *Bildpublizistik*; Giesecke, *Buchdruck*; Burkhardt, *Reformationsjahrhundert*. There were two contemporary printed accounts of the imperial diet of 1495, a long version and an abbreviated one: RTA MR 5/2, Nos. 1855a and 1855b, pp. 1689–1706.
11. RTA MR 5/1, No. 27, p. 129.

12. Reuter, "Worms als Reichstagsstadt"; Schenk, "Zähmung der Widerspenstigen?"; Bönnen, "Zwischen Bischof, Reich und Kurpfalz"; for the imperial cities at the Worms diet, see Isenmann, "Städte auf den Reichstagen."
13. The imperial diet therefore plays a central role in the diary of the mayor of Worms, Reinhart Noltz: RTA MR 5/2, pp. 1675–1686, esp. 1676. On the *adventus* in a city in the late Middle Ages, see in general Schenk, *Zeremoniell und Politik*; for the early modern period, see Krischer, *Reichsstädte in der Fürstengesellschaft*.
14. RTA MR 5/1, No. 36, p. 135–36.
15. RTA MR 5/2, No. 1851, p. 1678.
16. On the eagle as the symbol of the king (one-headed) or of the emperor and the Empire (two-headed) since the fourteenth century, see Hye, "Doppeladler"; Gritzner, *Symbole und Wappen*; on heraldry as a political language, see Weber, "Eine eigene Sprache der Politik."
17. The emperor said this already in 1423 about the imperial banner, which he surrendered to the Hereditary Imperial Marshal Pappenheim; see the quote in Gritzner, *Symbole und Wappen*, 119. On the concept of the symbol of presence ("*Präsenzsymbol*"), see Rehberg, "Weltrepräsentanz"; on the coats of arms, see Belting, *Bild-Anthropologie*, 115ff.; Seitter, "Das Wappen als Zweitkörper und Körperzeichen."
18. RTA MR 5/1, No. 53, p. 145; No. 71, p. 155; No. 1851, pp. 1675–83.
19. RTA MR 5/2, No. 1851, p. 1676.
20. In general see Schenk, *Zeremoniell und Politik*.
21. RTA MR 5/2, No. 1851, p. 1678; all this was organized by Hereditary Imperial Marshal Pappenheim. After a prince had been met and escorted to his lodgings, the next day he himself had to make the rounds to pay a visit to everyone who had come out to meet him.
22. See below the section on Lorraine.
23. Heinig, "Der Wormser Reichstag von 1495 als Hoftag," note 48. On the letters of authorisation (*Gewaltbriefe*) of the era of Maximilian, see Lutter, *Politische Kommunikation*, 52ff.; Jucker, *Gesandte, Schreiber, Akten*, 87ff. Some envoys, for example, those of the Bishop of Würzburg, presented themselves to both the Elector of Mainz and to the king, RTA MR 5/2, No. 1734, pp. 1314ff.
24. Dotzauer, "Anrufung," II, 15, 25.
25. RTA MR 5/2, No. 1851, p. 1678–79.
26. RTA MR 5/1, No. 1592, p. 1136.
27. Thus for the first time in 1491; see Isenmann, "Kaiser, Reich und deutsche Nation," 192.
28. *1495—Württemberg wird Herzogtum*, No. 6, 72. See Graf, "Eberhard im Bart," 12–13.
29. There were different variations upon the four-part scheme, and so far historians have not unconvered the precise reasons behind them. See Schubert, "Die Quaternionen"; Müller, *Bilder des Reiches*; "Der Quaternionenadler," in *1495—Kaiser, Reich, Reformen*, 223–25.
30. On membership as the central criterion of organization, see Luhmann, "Funktionen und Folgen formaler Organisation."
31. Through the "Roman months" (*Römermonate*) as the unit of calculation, the ad hoc approval, and more; see Schmid, "Reichssteuern," 164ff.
32. On the special relationship of the free and imperial cities to the king, see the fundamental work of Isenmann, "Reichsstandschaft der Frei- und Reichsstädte."
33. Sieber, *Reichsmatrikelwesen*; Schulze, *Reich und Türkengefahr*; Neu, "Matrikel."

34. On 1486, see RTA MR 1/1, No. 330, p. 373; on 1521, see Schulze and Ott, "Wormser Matrikel"; on 1529, see RTA JR 7/2, pp. 1356–74 (quote p. 1359). The Duke of the Maas probably refers to Masovia; see Sieber, *Reichsmatrikelwesen*, 53ff.; Schmid, "Reichssteuern," 166.
35. RTA MR 5/1, No. 361, No. 469ff. See the seating arrangement in RTA MR 5/2, No. 1592, pp. 1135ff.
36. First draft in RTA MR 5/1, No. 359; objections from the estates in RTA MR 5/1, No. 362, p. 487; detailed draft from the king with modifications from the electors in RTA MR 5/1, No. 361, pp. 469ff.
37. RTA MR 5/1, No. 368, pp. 495ff.
38. RTA JR 2, No. 56, pp. 424–43.
39. RTA MR 3/2, No. 289, p. 1120; No. 307e, p. 1214; Nos. 346a–d, pp. 1356ff.; on the imperial diet of 1491, see RTA MR 5/1, No. 361, p. 471, p. 483; Sieber, *Reichsmatrikelwesen*, 61; Seyboth, *Die Markgraftümer Ansbach und Kulmbach*, 58ff.
40. The basic study with numerous details on the imperial diets of the sixteenth century is Luttenberger, "Pracht und Ehre"; see also Aulinger, *Das Bild des Reichstags*.
41. Such "honor accounts" were kept by various princes and above all by the cities who were concerned about a rank equal to that of the princes. The accounts were managed by the princes' heralds, and in the cities for the most part by the city council's legal advisor; Krischer, *Reichsstädte in der Fürstengesellschaft*, 175–188, esp. 184ff.; the concept of symbolic capital is drawn from Bourdieu, "Ökonomisches Kapital."
42. RTA MR 1/2, No. 910, pp. 880ff.; No. 911, pp. 890ff.; No. 917, pp. 953ff. This latter printed account served as the model for many subsequent ones. Additional, unprinted accounts with detailed lists of attendees can be found in RTA MR 1/2, Nos. 875, 912, 913, 915b (report by the herald Bernhard Sittich, called "Romreich"); see the facsimile in Schottenloher, *Drei Frühdrucke*; in general on the genre, see Schubert, *Reichstage*, 188ff.
43. See Schottenloher, *Drei Frühdrucke*, intro., 17ff., and the facsimile reprint; see also RTA MR 5/2, No. 1855, pp. 1689ff. (in this edition the actual list of participants is left out). According to Schottenloher, both printed accounts probably go back to a common source from a princely chancery. The persevant Ulrich Burckgraf from the margraviate of Brandenburg was probably also the author of another eyewitness account of the Worms diet, which also dealt in detail with questions of rank and status: RTA MR 5/2, No. 1744, pp. 1368ff.
44. On the procession as a form of depicting and perceiving the hierarchical order, see Darnton, "A Bourgeois"; Löther, *Prozessionen*; see also Füssel, *Gelehrtenkultur*, 296–311; Weller, *Theatrum Praecedentiae*, 238ff.
45. RTA MR 5/2, No. 1744, p. 1371; No. 1851, p. 1681.
46. See Löw, *Raumsoziologie*; Füssel, "Rang und Raum"; see examples in Dartmann, Füssel, and Rüther, *Raum und Konflikt*; see also the fundamental reflections in Weller, *Theatrum Praecedentiae*, 32ff.; Füssel, *Gelehrtenkultur*, 73ff.
47. Sturm, *Warhafftig anzaygung* and *Wiewol hievor* (unpaginated). On the printed lists of participants from the diet in Worms in 1521, see also RTA JR 2, pp. 954–55.
48. "Hinc ego non certam potui hic quoque ponere formam, / Sed quam communis sessio habere solet. / Nemo ergo debet, quicumque, sit ille, sedendi / A me hic praescribi iura putare sibi"; Mameranus, *Investitura regalium electoralis dignitatis* (unpaginated).
49. RTA MR 5/1, No. 1598, pp. 1172–73. See the plans for the seating arrangement for the assembly in Frankfurt in 1486 in RTA MR 1/2, No. 922, pp. 983–84; No. 923, pp. 984–85.

50. For the list of participants in the draft of the Imperial Recess, see RTA MR 5/1, No. 1592, p. 1138; for other lists, preserved only in handwritten versions, see RTA MR 5/1, Nos. 1594–95, pp. 1151ff.
51. RTA MR 5/1, No. 1592, pp. 1136ff. At least as far as the cities are concerned, this list is much more precise than the later list by the hereditary imperial marshal.
52. On the assignment of a new seat to the Count of Württemberg, who had been elevated to the rank of a duke, see the section "Elevation in Rank: Württemberg," later in this chapter.
53. Stollberg-Rilinger, "Rang vor Gericht" and "Zeremoniell als politisches Verfahren"; Willich, "Rangstreit"; Annas and Müller, "Kaiser, Kurfürsten und auswärtige Mächte"; Müller, *Théâtre de la préséance*; Zwierlein, "Normativität und Empirie."
54. Thus, for example, in the case of the city of Metz in Frankfurt in 1489, see RTA MR 3/2, Nos. 274a–b, pp. 1056ff.; No. 275a, p. 1059.
55. RTA ÄR 22/2, p. 615; see also the session conflicts in RTA ÄR 22/2, pp. 595–96, 601–2, 736ff.
56. RTA MR 5/2, No. 1736, pp. 1330ff. (report of Brunswick by councilor Vincentius, around 20 June 1495); see the brief commentaries in the seating arrangement list, RTA MR 5/2, No. 1592, p. 1137, as well as in the report from the retinue of the Margrave of Brandenburg, RTA MR 5/2, No. 1744, pp. 1371–72. The Duke of Brunswick was supposed to take his seat behind the Dukes of Bavaria, the Duke of Saxony, and the Margrave of Brandenburg.
57. See in detail Willich, "Rangstreit."
58. RTA MR 5/2, No. 1736, p. 1334.
59. See Schmidt, *Städtetag*; Krischer, *Reichsstädte in der Fürstengesellschaft*.
60. RTA MR 5/2, No. 1797, pp. 1554ff.; see Helmrath, "Sitz und Geschichte." See also the reports by the delegates from Bern, Solothurn, and Fribourg about the honorable place assigned to them, RTA MR 5/2, No. 1803, p. 1599; No. 1804, p. 1600; No. 1806, pp. 1601–2.
61. RTA MR 5/2, No. 1744, p. 1372.
62. On this in general, see Stollberg-Rilinger, "Rang vor Gericht"; see also Isenmann, "Städte auf Reichstagen," 551. It is therefore misleading to say that the seating order "mirrored" or "depicted" the rank order of the Empire (Spieß, "Rangdenken," 42–43); rather, this rank order did not exist in an objectified form beyond the imperial assemblies.
63. Berger, "Anwesenheit und Abwesenheit"; Kieserling, *Kommunikation unter Anwesenden*.
64. See the account (given a literary sheen) by the knight Wilwolt von Schaumburg, RTA MR 5/2, p. 1710. RTA MR 5/2, pp. 1681ff.; see also *1495—Kaiser, Reich, Reformen*, 273–90.
65. On the medial self-staging of the king as knight, especially also in literary form in the epics *Weißkunig*, *Theuerdank*, and *Freydal*, see Müller, *Gedechtnus*.
66. Summons, RTA MR 5/1, No. 27, pp. 127–28. On the character of the Worms diet as a *Hoftag*, see Heinig, "Der Wormser Reichstag von 1495 als Hoftag"; Göbel, *Der Reichstag von Worms 1495*.
67. The distinction arises, for example, from the fact that Pappenheim's register of the diet also includes such "welsche" princes and delegates, of whom it is explicitly stated on the list of the Imperial Recess that they were not summoned nor attended the council. RTA MR 5/1, No. 1592, p. 1138. See Isenmann, "Kaiser, Reich und deutsche Nation," 192ff.
68. Seyboth, "Die Reichstage der 1480er Jahre," 1543ff.

69. In general, see Heinig, "Der Wormser Reichstag von 1495 als Hoftag"; on the concept of procedural autonomy, see Stollberg-Rilinger, *Vormoderne politische Verfahren*, "Einleitung"; drawing the argument on Luhmann, *Legitimation durch Verfahren*. On the emergence of fixed procedural norms of the imperial diets, see above all Isenmann, "Kaiser, Reich und deutsche Nation"; Seyboth, "Die Reichstage der 1480er Jahre." A very precise picture of the procedure is provided by the so-called *reichsstädtische Registratur*, a protocol by the delegates of the Swabian League, Besserer from Ulm and Langenmantel from Augsburg, RTA MR 5/2, No. 1797, pp. 1504ff. By contrast, the procedure is described from the perspective of an outside observer by the Worms mayor Reinhard Noltz, RTA MR 5/2, No. 1851, pp. 1675ff.
70. Seyboth, "Die Reichstage der 1480er Jahre," 525–29.
71. RTA MR 5/2, No. 1851, p. 1677.
72. RTA MR 5/2, No. 1796, p. 1514. That the negotiations were "formally begun" only when the letters of authorization (*Gewaltbriefe*) were verified on 7 April (see Wiesflecker, *Kaiser Maximilian I.*, 2:222) presupposes fixed procedural rules that did not yet exist. Even before that there had already been joint deliberations by all estates.
73. RTA MR 5/2, No. 1797, p. 1515, p. 1521; see No. 1734, pp. 1314ff.
74. For example, RTA MR 5/2, No. 1733, p. 1313: "the other estates were unhappy that the king had invited only three princes jointly with the electors."
75. RTA MR 5/2, No. 1796, pp. 1511–12.
76. On the history of the concept, see Schubert, *König und Reich*, 253ff., 323ff.; Isenmann, "Kaiser, Reich und deutsche Nation," 192ff.; Isenmann, "Städte auf den Reichstagen," 558; Krischer, *Reichsstädte in der Fürstengesellschaft*, 44–59; Conze, "Stand, Klasse."
77. Seyboth, "Die Reichstage der 1480er Jahre," 543–44.
78. Ibid.
79. RTA MR 5/2, No. 1734, p. 1318.
80. RTA MR 5/2, No. 1808, p. 1608; see Heil, "Verschriftlichung des Verfahrens als Modernisierung."
81. On the poll as a ceremonial rule of procedure, see Stollberg-Rilinger, "Zeremoniell als politisches Verfahren," 108ff.; on the praxis in the second half of the sixteenth century, see Rauch, *Traktat über den Reichstag*, 62–63; fundamentally, see Sikora, "Formen des Politischen," esp. 172–73. That the votes were essentially polled in accordance with the seating arrangement also in 1495 emerges from the fact that we read, for example, that the Duke of Brunswick had been passed over in the poll or that the poll had, exceptionally, not been taken according to the seating arrangement; RTA MR 5/2, No. 1736, p. 1333, p. 1335.
82. Schlaich, "Majoritas" and "Mehrheitsabstimmung."
83. RTA MR 2/1, No. 378, p. 481. The polling controversy was settled by treaty in 1529: henceforth, Saxony led the poll in the plenum, Mainz in the council of electors; in general assemblies, they alternated; in the council of princes, Austria and Salzburg alternated: RTA JR 2, No. 4, p. 143; Tetleben, *Protokoll*, 57; see Aulinger, *Das Bild des Reichstags*, 229ff.
84. RTA ÄR 2/2, p. 596. The absence of formality is also indicated by the report of the Basel delegate, in which we read (RTA ÄR 2/2, p. 737) that at the opening session, everyone except for the electors and princes had left the hall, because they could not understand anything about the proposition.
85. RTA MR 5/2, No. 1797, p. 1505; on the participation of the city delegates from the Swiss Confederation, see RTA MR 5/2, Nos. 1803ff., pp. 1599ff.

86. Isenmann, "Städte auf den Reichstagen"; Seyboth, "Die Reichstage der 1480er Jahre," 536; Moraw, "Hoftag und Reichstag," 17–18.
87. RTA MR 5/2, No. 1592, p. 1138.
88. Schmidt, "Die Wetterauer Kuriatstimme": the counts of Wetterau first sent a joint delegate in 1498 to an imperial assembly.
89. See the Metz chronicle of Jean Aubrion, RTA MR 5/2, No. 1809, p. 1609; see RTA MR 5/2, No. 1735, p. 1323.
90. For Bavaria, see RTA MR 5/1, Nos. 1038ff., pp. 848ff.; for Brandenburg, see RTA MR 5/2, No. 1730, p. 1292; for Holstein, see RTA MR 5/1, No. 416, p. 525.
91. See Lutter, *Politische Kommunikation*, 46ff.
92. See Hofmann, *Repräsentation*, 182–90; Müller, *Das imperative und freie Mandat*; Sofsky and Paris, *Figurationen sozialer Macht*, 158ff.; Weiß, *Handeln und handeln lassen*; on mandates in the diplomatic system of the time, see Mattingly, *Renaissance Diplomacy*; Lutter, *Politische Kommunikation*.
93. Formulated thus, for example, in a session conflict in 1524, RTA JR 4, No. 136, p. 568; see likewise in the Golden Bull, chapter XXIX; however, on occasion this was handled differently by the electoral delegates already in the fifteenth century; see on this Annas and Müller, "Kaiser, Kurfürsten und auswärtige Mächte," 109ff.
94. RTA MR 5/2, No. 1733, p. 1304.
95. See chapters 3 and 4.
96. See Hahn, "Geheim"; see also Seyboth, "Die Reichstage der 1480er Jahre," 539ff.
97. RTA MR 2/2, No. 652, p. 934; No. 667, p. 960; No. 729, pp. 1033–34, 1051.
98. RTA MR 2/2, No. 729, p. 1034.
99. RTA MR 5/2, No. 1734, p. 1321; No. 1785, p. 1455; No. 1808, pp. 1608–9.
100. Whether the formula *maiestas imperialis* should be translated as "majesty of the Empire" or "majesty of the emperor" cannot be clearly determined. On this, see Smend, "Formel 'Kaiser und Reich.'"
101. The depiction of 1495 shows the Elector of Brandenburg, although he was not present in person. The king of Bohemia, however, who was not present in person either, is not shown. According to written sources, both men were represented, the king of Bohemia by the hereditary cupbearer (*Erbschenk*) of Limburg, the elector by his brother, the Margrave of Brandenburg-Ansbach, and by the Count of Lindau.
102. Hoffmann, *Die bildlichen Darstellungen des Kurfürstenkollegiums*, 96ff., see the catalog numbers 36, 40–42, 46, 49, 52, 58, 59, 61–69, 72–74, 76–78, 83, 87, 92, 94–97, 99, 100, 114, 127, 162, and 192; see also Schottenloher, *Drei Frühdrucke*, introduction; see also Aulinger, "Die Reichstage des 16. Jahrhunderts im Spiegel bildlicher Quellen."
103. Golden Bull, chapter XXV: that is why crimes against the electors were to be punished like crimes against the crown.
104. RTA MR 5/2, No. 1851, p. 1680; Schottenloher, *Drei Frühdrucke*, 19: square between St. Martin and the Carmelites.
105. In general, see Goez, "Der 'rechte' Sitz."
106. See the description of the imperial diet of 1495 in Senckenberg, *Sammlung*, 4:94–157, here 134; see also RTA MR 5/2, p. 1691; for an especially detailed description of the clothes, for example, on the occasion of the imperial diet of 1486, see RTA MR 1/2, No. 915b, pp. 923–24.
107. Thus in Worms in 1495 in the case of the envoy of the Elector of Brandenburg, Count Johann von Lindau; RTA MR 5/2, No. 1744, p. 1376.

108. See Fillitz, *Die Schatzkammer in Wien*, 24, and "Die Reichskleinodien"; Schlosser, *Reichskleinodien*; Grass, *Reichskleinodien*; Petersohn, "Über monarchische Insignien," 90–91; Kirchweger, "Reichskleinodien"; Rudolph, "Kontinuität und Dynamik," 389ff.
109. RTA MR 5/2, No. 1732, p. 1302: one was still waiting for the pontificalia to be brought from Aachen. RTA MR 5/2, No. 1815, p. 1634: the council of Nuremberg gives permission to its envoys to take the regalia to Aachen with them, if the king intended to perform there the investitures and the coronation of the queen. RTA MR 5/2, No. 1818, p. 1646: the council instructs the envoys to personally return the regalia to Nuremberg.
110. On the significance of clothing for marking out roles, see the reflections by Arlinghaus, "Gesten, Kleidung."
111. RTA MR 5/2, No. 1744, pp. 1374–75; No. 1792, p. 1493.
112. The herald Bernhard Sittich, called "Romreich," asked the Duke of Bavaria to send his court attire to the Frankfurt diet in 1486 so that he would be recognized as belonging and could wear them to this honor: RTA MR 1/2, No. 915, pp. 912–13.
113. Imperial Recess 1495, § 5 (RTA MR 5/1, No. 1593, p. 1143); see Imperial Recess 1497, §§ 8–16 (RTA MR 6, No. 152, pp. 479–87); Freiburg 1498 (RTA MR 6, No. 119, p. 735). The regulations became increasingly more detailed in the subsequent imperial recesses. On dress codes in general, see Bulst and Jütte, "Zwischen Sein und Schein."
114. See also RTA MR 5/2, No. 1792, p. 1493.
115. RTA MR 5/2, No. 1744, p. 1375.
116. Hegel, *Die Chroniken der fränkischen Städte: Nürnberg*, 3:376.
117. Scholarship on the imperial regalia has a long tradition; an overview for the Middle Ages can be found in Petersohn, "Über monarchische Insignien," 69ff.; Grass, *Reichskleinodien*; Schlosser, *Reichskleinodien*; for the early modern period, see Kirchweger, "Reichkleinodien"; Fillitz, "Die Reichskleinodien"; Rudolph, "Kontinuität und Dynamik," 389ff.; Rogge, *Wahl und Krönung*, 96–101. See also chapter 3.
118. Rehberg, "Weltrepräsentanz"; Gumbrecht, "Reflections on Institutions and Re/Presentation"; Petersohn, "Über monarchische Insignien," 87, calls this "fetishism."
119. Golden Bull, chapters II, III, IV, VI, XXI, XXII, XXIII, XXVI, XXVII, XXVIII, and XXIX. An English translation of the Golden Bull is available at http://avalon.law.yale.edu/medieval/golden.asp.
120. All this was summarized in the concepts "curia solempnis, curia regalis sive imperialis" and "actus publicus imperialis." Contemporary German versions say that "uffinbar keisirlichir adir koniglichir hof" (in an imperial or royal assembly) (chapter XXII), that "keisirlichir adir koniglichir hof in wirdekeit gehaltin wird" (a solemn imperial or royal court is held) (chapter XXVI), or that "von allin uffinlichin keisirlichin und koniglichin gededen, an gerichte, lehin zuo lihin, zu dissche eßin, in reden und in allin andirn werckin, adir so in geburit zuosamene komen zuo dedingen umb des richis nuotz und ere" (all public transactions pertaining to the Empire; namely, in courts, while conferring fiefs, when regaling themselves at table, and also in councils and in all other business on account of which they happen or shall happen to come together to treat of the honor or utility of the Empire) (chapter III). Goldene Bulle, *MGH Constitutiones*, 561–631. See Hergemöller, "Die 'solempnis curia,'" 451ff.
121. For an example from the eighteenth century, see Ludewig, *Vollständige Erläuterung*, vol. 2 part 1, 647; see, for example, Willoweit, *Deutsche Verfassungsgeschichte*, 70, who distinguishes the "rational core of the electoral procedure" from the ceremonial.

122. See Zeumer, *Die Goldene Bulle Kaiser Karls IV.*, 28; see especially Kunisch, "Formen symbolischen Handelns"; Schubert, "Erz- und Erbämter"; see also Stollberg-Rilinger, "Verfassungsakt oder Fest?"; Schneidmüller, "Aufführung des Reiches"; Petersohn, "Über monarchische Insignien," esp. 95–96.
123. See the essential Hofmann, *Repräsentation* and "Der spätmittelalterliche Rechtsbegriff"; Podlech, "Repräsentation."
124. See Lupold von Bebenburg, *De iuribus regni et imperii*, 105: "Weil es demnach so eingerichtet wurde, dass bestimmte Fürsten den König und Kaiser wählen, muß man diese Wahl so ansehen, dass sie an der Stelle und mit Vollmacht der Ge- samtheit der Fürsten und des Volks (*omnes principes et alii representantes populum*) gewählt hätte.... Man wird daher nicht sagen können, dass diese Wahl ihnen als Einzelpersonen zusteht, sondern vielmehr als Kollegium oder als Gesamtheit aller Fürsten und des Volks" (Because it was arranged such that certain princes elected the king and emperor, one must regard this election as though they had voted in place of and with the authority of the totality of the princes and the people.... One can therefore not say that this election belonged to them as individuals, but rather as a body or as the totality of all princes and the people). See Hofmann, *Repräsentation*, 228ff.
125. Golden Bull, chapter XXIV.
126. Schubert, "Erz- und Erbämter," calls this "theory of arch offices" a kind of premodern constitutional theory. That this theory has little to do with the causes—still not clearly reconstructed by medievalists—behind the reduction of the royal electors to this circle is a very different question.
127. See the essential Moraw, *Von der offenen Verfassung*, "Versuch," and *Deutscher Königshof, Hoftag und Reichstag*.
128. As one example of many, see Wiesflecker, *Maximilian I.*, 215.
129. Peter von Andlau, *Libellus de Cesarea monarchia*, 278ff. It is therefore misleading if modern translations use the word *Tagungsort* (meeting place) for *locus sessionis* (ibid., 279).
130. See "Schubert, Erz- und Erbämter"; Hergemöller, "Die 'solempnis curia'"; Stollberg-Rilinger, "Verfassungsakt oder Fest?"
131. Heumann and Seckel, *Handlexikon zu den Quellen des römischen Rechts*, s.v. "sollemnis"; *Zedlers Universal-Lexicon*, s.v. "Solennität."
132. On this, see, fundamentally, Althoff, *Spielregeln, Macht der Rituale*, and "Inszenierung verpflichtet."
133. On this, see the example of the Elector of Brandenburg protesting the investiture of the Duke of Pomerania, later in this chapter; Schlaich, "Die 'protestatio'" and "Majoritas"; Becker, "Protestatio."
134. On the feudal system in the Middle Ages, see the fundamental work of Krieger, *Die Lehnshoheit der deutschen Könige*, esp. 426ff.; Keller, "Die Investitur"; Spieß, "Lehn(s)recht, Lehnswesen," "Lehnserneuerung," and "Kommunikationsformen," 277ff.; Althoff and Stollberg-Rilinger, "Rituale der Macht."
135. Willoweit, *Rechtsgrundlagen der Territorialgewalt*, 98ff.; Schönberg, *Recht der Reichslehen*, 90ff., 248ff.; Moser, *Lehens-Verfassung*.
136. See the list of the Worms investitures, RTA MR 5/1, No. 599, pp. 658–82.
137. RTA MR 5/1, Nos. 256–75, pp. 281–304.
138. For example, see the bishop of Geneva, RTA MR 5/1, No. 978, p. 819; the bishop of Regensburg, RTA MR 5/1, No. 991, p. 825; Duke Georg of Lower Bavaria, RTA MR 5/1, No. 1062, p. 859. See Boehmer, *De Investitura per procuratorem*.

139. Thus, Count Haug of Werdenberg, for example, swore the oath before the king, while his brothers swore it before the abbot of Weingarten, RTA MR 5/1, No. 599, p. 667.
140. For example, Duke Otto of Bavaria, Duke Wilhelm of Jülich, and several bishops; see RTA MR 5/2, No. 1793, p. 1493.
141. Wilhelm and Otto of Henneberg; see RTA MR 5/2, No. 1855, p. 1702, 1706.
142. On this, see Roellecke, "Das Ende des römisch-deutschen Kaisertums"; on the concept of authority and authoritative power, see Sofsky and Paris, *Figurationen sozialer Macht*; Popitz, *Phänomene der Macht*.
143. Reichsregimentsplan Articles 3 and 4, RTA MR 5/1, No. 326, p. 337. However, the minor imperial fiefs were to be receivable also from the imperial government.
144. For example, see the reluctance of the bishop of Bamberg to come to the imperial diet in Nuremberg in 1487 in person because it would mean " much cost and hardship" for the bishopric, RTA MR 2/1, No. 489, p. 644.
145. RTA MR 5/2, No. 1727, p. 1286; see also No. 1789, p. 1481.
146. Envoy from Duke Johann of Cleves, RTA MR 5/2, No. 1739, p. 1359; correspondence of the Dukes Georg and Albrecht of Bavaria, RTA MR 5/1, Nos. 1033ff., pp. 845ff.; RTA MR 5/2, Nos. 1749ff., pp. 1387ff., esp. p. 1401. See also how in Frankfurt in 1486 the emperor stalled the bishop of Straßburg with the investiture, RTA MR 1/2, No. 899, pp. 866–67.
147. RTA MR 5/2, No. 1789, p. 1481. With a few princes, Maximilian in the end did agree to investing the envoys; other investitures were made up only at later imperial diets. For example, Albrecht of Bavaria, who was solemny invested only in 1505 in Cologne, RTA MR 5/2, No. 1784, p. 1453; on 1505, see Merlo, "Haus Gürzenich," 42ff.
148. RTA MR 5/2, No. 1732, p. 1302.
149. See Wiesflecker, *Maximilian I.*, 266; for a different viewpoint, see Petersohn, "Über monarchische Insignien," 95–96.
150. On the source, see two princely heraldic accounts in a short and a longer version: RTA MR 5/2, No. 1855, pp. 1689–1706; also in Schottenloher, *Drei Frühdrucke*; additionally, see an eyewitness account from the retinue of the margraviate of Brandenburg (possibly also from the persevant Ulrich Burckgraf): RTA MR 5/2, No. 1744, pp. 1374ff.; see also an account from the Hessian *Landeschronik* of Wigand Gerstenberg: RTA MR 5/2, No. 1856, pp. 1707–8; and brief mentions in the account of the Venetian envoys: RTA MR 5/2, No. 1881, pp. 1776–77, 1784.
151. RTA MR 5/2, No. 1856, p. 1707.
152. On the Council of Constance in 1417, see Richenthal, *Chronik des Constanzer Conzils*, 103ff. On the Frankfurt diet in 1486, see RTA MR 1/2, No. 915b, pp. 913–45. On the solemn banner investiture, see Boehmer, *De investitura per procuratorem*; Bruckauf, *Fahnlehen und Fahnenbelehnung*; Börger, *Belehnungen*; Aulinger, *Das Bild des Reichstages*, 287ff.; Spieß, "Lehnserneuerung"; Petersohn, "Über monarchische Insignien," 74ff. The older distinction between scepter investiture for ecclesiastical princes and banner investiture for secular princes had been lost by now.
153. This *ritus circumequitandi* is attested since Emperor Sigismund. Richenthal, *Chronik des Constanzer Conzils*, 103ff.; see Spieß, "Kommunikationsformen," 280–81; Rödel, "Lehensgebräuche," 1712–13.
154. Francolin, *Kurtzer Bericht*. That no common servants (*Knechte*) and *Spießknaben* were among them is emphasized, for example, by Sturm, *Wahrhafftig anzeygung*.
155. See the wording in the case of Brunswick, for example: RTA MR 5/2, No. 1736, p. 1338; the Brunswick council made a point of adding: "So der König in der Majestät

sitzet, muß man underlassen alle gebuhrlich fürstlich titel." ("When the King is sitting in his majesty, no regular princely titles shall be given to anyone.")
156. RTA MR 5/2, No. 1855, p. 1694: "das rot fenlein, das bedeut die regalia" („The little red flag means the regalia.")
157. The third heir, Margrave Sigmund, had died in Worms during the imperial diet and was solemnly buried there; RTA MR 5/2, No. 1851, p. 1680.
158. RTA MR 5/2, No. 1744, p. 1376–77.
159. Moser, Lehens-Verfassung, 221ff.; see the example of Saxony from the seventeenth century in Lünig, Theatrum Ceremoniale, 2:955ff.
160. RTA MR 5/2, No. 1856, pp. 1707–8. On the ritual element of the despoliation of the banners by the crowd, a ritually conceded act of violence, first attested in 1473, see Francolin, Kurtzer Bericht; Mameranus, Kurtze und eigentliche Verzeychnus, 139, 147; Bruckauf, Fahnlehen und Fahnenbelehnung, 81; Joachim, Von der ehemaligen Gewohnheit, 368ff.; Schenk, Zeremoniell und Politik, 472 ff., proposes a psychoanalytical interpretation.
161. See, for example, RTA MR 5/2, No. 1736, p. 1335. Thus, Councilor Vicentius of Brunswick complained that the Margrave of Brandenburg had taken the place of his brother, the elector, on the royal throne for the sole reason that with the help of this subtlety (suptiligkeit) he would not have to rank behind the Duke of Brunswick.
162. RTA MR 5/2, No. 1744, pp. 1376–77; No. 1855, pp. 1698–99; see Schottenloher, Drei Frühdrucke, 21.
163. Count Eberhard of Württemberg had already been invested with his imperial fief and regalia on 11 April in Worms, though in chamber and without solemnities. When the plan to elevate him to the rank of duke and invest him anew existed is disputed; see Graf, "Eberhard im Bart," 18ff.
164. See also the text of the relevant document, RTA MR 5/1, No. 1168, pp. 914ff.
165. See the account by Werner Keller about the elevation to the dukedom, RTA MR 5/1, No. 1172, pp. 921–22; report from the retinue of the Margrave of Brandenburg, RTA MR 5/2, No. 1744, p. 1377–78; herald report, RTA MR 5/2, No. 1855, pp. 1705–6; likewise, see Schottenloher, Drei Frühdrucke; 1495—Württemberg wird Herzogtum, No. 12, 86–87. See Graf, "Eberhard im Bart," esp. 11ff. on the "rehabilitation of the ceremonial" against the disdain by regional historiography; Schlinker, Fürstenamt und Rezeption, 182ff.
166. RTA MR 5/1, No. 1172, p. 922.
167. See Althoff, "Der friedens-, bündnis- und gemeinschaftsstiftende Charakter"; Völkel, "Öffentliche Tafel"; Stollberg-Rilinger, "Ordnungsleistung."
168. On the concept of social magic, see Bourdieu, "Einsetzungsriten."
169. See the list of those present with seating order in RTA MR 5/2, No. 1592, p. 1137.
170. See the text of the document, RTA MR 5/1, No. 1168, p. 914; see also the reflections on the change of status as the emperor's central and in the end final reserved right in Roellecke, "Das Ende des römisch-deutschen Kaisertums," esp. 100–1.
171. "Hat seine regalia als ein herzog empfangen und wirdet in der session bei der samlung dafur gehalten" ("Received his regalia as duke and is treated as such at the session during the assembly"), writes the envoy from Upper Bavaria, RTA MR 5/2, No. 1778, p. 1445; "ward auf dem tag Herzog und danach hinaufgesetzt nach dem Herzog von Gilch [Jülich]" ("was duke as of that day and was thereafter moved up in seating behind the Duke of Jülich"), RTA MR 5/2, No. 1592, p. 1137.
172. RTA MR 5/2, No. 1744, p. 1377.

173. Moser, TSR, 6:277ff.
174. Gadner, *Chronik Georg Gadners von 1598*, No. 22, 104.
175. RTA MR 5/2, No. 1851, p. 1680.
176. See, for example, RTA JR 1, p. 91, on the coronation of Charles V in Aachen.
177. Golden Bull, chapters XXI and XXII.
178. On the paradox of courtesy, see Althoff, "Inszenierung verpflichtet"; Beetz, *Frühmoderne Höflichkeit*. On the meetings of rulers in the late Middle Ages, see Kintzinger, "Der weiße Reiter" and "Kaiser und König"; on the early modern period, see Rahn, "Grenz-Situationen"; on the modern era, see Paulmann, *Pomp und Politik*.
179. Mohr, *Lothringen*, 119ff.; on the prehistory, see Thomas, "Die lehnsrechtlichen Beziehungen des Herzogtums Lothringen zum Reich"; on the larger context of imperial policy, see Kintzinger, *Westbindungen*, 332ff.
180. Mohr, *Lothringen*, 77; Kintzinger, *Westbindungen*, 334.
181. Sieber, *Reichsmatrikelwesens*, 57.
182. Wiesflecker, *Maximilian I.*, 229; RTA MR 5/1, No. 1068, pp. 861ff.
183. RTA MR 3/1, No. 14a, pp. 174ff. In May 1498, the Electors of Mainz, Trier, and Cologne, as well as the Duke of Jülich-Berg, negotiated with the Duke of Lorraine about a twelve-year agreement, but it never came about; the duke would not allow himself to get drawn into an alliance against the French king. RTA MR 3/1, Nos. 238a–f, pp. 908ff.
184. RTA MR 3/2, No. 264a, p. 1020; No. 264b, p. 1029; on the appraisal in the registers of 1489, see RTA MR 3/2, No. 289, p. 1121; No. 296, p. 1159; No. 300, p. 1184. On the relationship to the French king, see RTA MR 3/2, No. 285, pp. 1106–7: René did not allow the imperial troops to pass through his territory, but he also did not provide the French king with the promised military aid. In 1486, the duke had sent his gratulations to the newly elected Maximilian through a delegation and had referred to himself in the process as "one of the princes of the Empire": RTA MR 1/2, No. 930, p. 1010.
185. Report of 11 May 1495, RTA MR 5/1, No. 1068, pp. 861–63; see Mohr, *Lothringen*, 134ff.
186. In 1354, the counts of Bar had been invested by Emperor Charles IV with the Margraviate of Pont-au-Mousson and given the title of duke. In 1431, these counts of Bar inherited the Duchy of Lorraine, and in 1434 René I was invested with this duchy as a whole by Frederick III.
187. RTA MR 5/1, No. 1068, p. 863; see also RTA MR 5/2, 1787, p. 1468.
188. RTA MR 5/1, Nos. 1069, 1070–72, pp. 863–64.
189. In the Imperial Register of Worms in 1521, the Duke of Lorraine was counted among the uncertain estates. Domke, *Virilstimmen*, 30; Sieber, *Reichsmatrikelwesen*, 57.
190. The debate about this at the imperial diet in Speyer in 1529 was fruitless. Since 1532 the duke had been contesting membership in the Empire; commissions were set up, deductions were drafted, all without result. In 1542, the Empire and France granted Lorraine the status of a free duchy. However, the relevant treaty with the emperor remained vague; whether the duke was a member of the Empire or not still needed to be determined. Since 1567, at the latest, the dukes of Lorraine held a seat and vote at the imperial diets as the margraves of Nomény. See Mohr, *Lothringen*, 134–63.
191. In 1231, Frederick II had granted the Margrave of Brandenburg the feudal sovereignty over Pomerania, while the Duke of Pomerania had been invested as direct imperial vassal by Ludwig the Bavarian in 1338 and Charles IV in 1348. See Lan-

cizolle, *Bildung des preußischen Staats*, 2:545–608; on the investiture of 1338, see Spieß, "Kommunikationsformen," 279, fig. 4; Sieber, *Reichsmatrikelwesen*, 61.
192. See the Straßburg envoy's report, RTA MR 2/2, No. 729, p. 1031.
193. Report from the margravial envoy, RTA MR 2/2, No. 640, pp. 907–8.
194. RTA MR 2/1, No. 477, pp. 637–38; RTA MR 2/2, No. 729, pp. 1030ff.; Riedel, *Codex diplomaticus Brandenburgensis*, 2:332; Hegel, *Chroniken der fränkischen Städte*, 4:381–82; 5:493–94; see Lünig, *Theatrum Ceremoniale*, 2:936; see Seyboth, *Die Markgraftümer Ansbach und Kulmbach*, 61.
195. RTA MR 3/2, No. 289a, p. 1120; No. 296, p. 1158; Seyboth, *Die Markgraftümer Ansbach und Kulmbach*, 63ff.
196. Seyboth, *Die Markgraftümer Ansbach und Kulmbach*, 66ff.; Lancizolle, *Bildung des preußischen Staates*, 4:595ff. Later the content of the treaty was contested. Bogislav claimed that he had been released from the feudal sovereignty of Brandenburg, while the Brandenburgers maintained that they had merely renounced the obligation of renewal each time.
197. In the royal draft and in the list modified by the electors, the Duke of Stettin appeared in the top group along with the electors and the princes; on one occasion he had to pay 3,126 fl, on another occasion 1,200 fl (RTA MR 5/1, No. 361, p. 471, p. 483); see Seyboth, *Die Markgraftümer Ansbach und Kulmbach*, 71ff.
198. RTA MR 5/2, No. 1730, p. 1292.
199. RTA MR 5/2, No. 897, p. 771; No. 1744, p. 1376; No. 1855, pp. 1698–99.
200. RTA MR 6, No. 1, pp. 366–67; see Seyboth, *Die Markgraftümer Ansbach und Kulmbach*, 75ff.; Lancizolle, *Bildung des preußischen Staates*, 4:597–601; Planitz, *Berichte*, 130ff., 134ff., 139ff.; RTA JR 3, pp. 786–87.
201. RTA JR 2, pp. 765–66.
202. RTA JR 2, suppl., p. 113; Feudal Charter of 29 May 1521; RTA JR 2, p. 73; No. 248, pp. 952–53; for the registers, see RTA JR 2, p. 181; p. 197; p. 229; p. 272; p. 429; for Nuremberg, 1522, see RTA JR 3, No. 10, pp. 71–72; Nos. 133–34, pp. 785ff.; for Speyer, 1529, see RTA JR 7/1, p. 735. See Seyboth, *Die Markgraftümer Ansbach und Kulmbach*, 75ff.; Lancizolle, *Bildung des preußischen Staates*, 4:597–604.
203. Lancizolle, *Bildung des preußischen Staates*, 4:601–2.
204. Sturm, *Warhafftig anzaygung*, fol. A iii ff.; see Planitz, *Berichte*, 130ff., 134ff., 139ff. Seyboth, *Die Markgraftümer Ansbach und Kulmbach*, 76, does not mention this event, but considers the conflict as resolved with the Treaty of Grimnitz between Elector Joachim and the two Pomeranian dukes on 26 August 1529.
205. But the imperial chancellor received the written protestation "als ob sy offentlich verlesen worden wäre" ("as though it had been read out publicly"). The background was that Georg of Brandenburg-Ansbach, in contrast to the Elector of Brandenburg, belonged to the party of the Lutheran imperial estates; on this, see chapter 3.
206. But that did not prevent the emperor from affirming the Treaty of Grimnitz a few days later. At the imperial diet in Regensburg in 1541, everything unfolded according to the same scheme as in 1530—the Duke of Pomerania was solemnly invested, and at the ritual the Elector of Brandenburg also took hold of the banner while issuing a formal protest. Conversely, he himself was always invested also with the banners of Pomerania. It was once again this investiture whose precise description the imperial herald published in a printed pamphlet: Landsberger, *Churfürsten*. This contractual arrangement was contested in vain only one more time, following the death of the Duke of Pomerania in 1560. The new duke refused to renew the treaty and in re-

sponse was not invested by the emperor until he relented in 1566; Lancizolle, *Bildung des preußischen Staates*, 4:664–65.
207. Impressive examples in Nolte, *Familie, Hof und Herrschaft*, 315ff.; see also Jucker, *Gesandte, Schreiber, Akten*; in general, see Weitzel, "Schriftlichkeit und Recht"; Keller, "Vom 'heiligen Buch' zur Buchführung"; Ong, *Orality and Literacy*.
208. Verbal note by Gerd Althoff; Grimm and Grimm, *Deutsches Wörterbuch*, 1, col. 99, s.v. "Abschied."
209. See the fundamental Goffman, *Interaction Ritual*.
210. RTA MR 5/2, No. 1737, pp. 1337–38.
211. Grimm and Grimm, *Deutsches Wörterbuch*, 1, col. 99, s.v. "Abschied."
212. On the imperial recesses of the sixteenth century, see Aulinger, *Das Bild des Reichstags*, 248ff.
213. In general, see Moraw, "Versuch"; Isenmann, "Kaiser, Reich und deutsche Nation," 195ff.; Seyboth, "Die Reichstage der 1480er Jahre," 531ff.
214. Isenmann, "Kaiser, Reich und deutsche Nation," 202.
215. Schubert, *König und Reich*, 253–54, 275; Isenmann, "Kaiser, Reich und deutsche Nation," 211.
216. RTA MR 5/2, No. 1593, pp. 1140ff.; Wiesflecker, *Kaiser Maximilian I.*, 2:241 ff.; Seyboth, "Die Reichstage der 1480er Jahre," 531ff.; Heinig, "Der Wormser Reichstag von 1495 als Hoftag." In 1486 the emperor alone had put down the decisions made in a "recess"; in 1487 there had been no final declaration at all; in 1489 the imperial estates had passed a joint recess, but the emperor did not.
217. RTA MR 5/2, No. 1796, pp. 1500ff.; No. 1733, p. 1312. See Heinig, "Der Wormser Reichstag von 1495 als Hoftag"; Wiesflecker, *Kaiser Maximilian I.*, 2:240. The estates of the Swiss Confederation, for example, refused their consent without fundamentally questioning their membership in the Empire. Already during the negotiations at the end of April, one had agreed "that one should report the order as decided upon at this diet to all princes who did not come to this assembly, and to urge them to agree to it. But where they refuse to do so, to hold them to it and to undertake a way of getting them to do so", RTA MR 5/2, No. 1785, p. 1459.
218. RTA MR 5/2, No. 1593, pp. 1140ff., here p. 1140, note 1; Aulinger, *Das Bild des Reichstags*, 251.
219. Moraw, *Von der offenen Verfassung*.
220. Thus, for example, see Schottenloher, *Drei Frühdrucke*, 22.
221. See Luhmann, "Funktionen und Folgen formaler Organisation"; Kieserling, *Kommunikation unter Anwesenden*; a theory of social interaction rules was developed by Goffman, *Interaction Ritual* and *Presentation of Self*.

CHAPTER 2

Cleavage of the Sacral Community
Augsburg, 1530

The Holy Empire

The Empire had been considered holy since the Middle Ages. The Christian religion constituted an all-encompassing symbolic universe, an "absolute interpretive cosmos of the world"[1] that left nothing beyond its grasp. A legitimate sociopolitical order could not be conceived in any way other than being embedded within the divine order. Even though the worldly order was invariably imperfect, a result of the Fall, it did remain connected in every way to the perfect, transcendent order.

This was particularly true of the Holy Roman Empire, for it had been assigned a key role in the divine plan of salvation. The Redeemer had been born under the Roman Empire; the Roman Empire had been the framework for the spread of the Gospel; the Roman Empire was the last of the global empires revealed to the prophet Daniel in a dream, and at the fall of the Roman Empire the eschatological return of the Redeemer was expected.[2] The emperor at the head of this Empire embodied its holiness the same way the pope did as the head of the church. Both men, even in a relationship that was always rife with conflict, formed the keystones in the meaningful structure of the world; next to God, they were themselves the source of all legitimacy, which infused the entire order hierarchically from top to bottom.[3]

One can think of the sacral power of the emperor as "authoritative power."[4] Power is never a quality inherent in the powerful person, nothing substantial, but a reciprocal relationship between individuals. The power of the one is grounded in the need of the other. It is not only a matter of objective means of coercion, but also of reciprocal attribution. Having a reputation of power is already power. That applies especially to "authoritative power," which is based on the basic social need for orientation and recognition. The person to whom it is ascribed embodies the values of the community and has the task of sustaining these values. The others accept him because they, in turn, wish to be acknowledged by him. Authoritative power extends not only to outward actions, but also to the inner attitudes and value convictions of those who submit to it; it generates a "consenting readiness to follow." Authoritative power is therefore by definition legitimate power. Within traditional societies, it is usually institutionalized in specific offices and related back to a supreme source of legitimacy, a *divina auctoritas*. That was so also in the case of the emperor and the Empire. Whoever participated in the Empire could feel like and represent himself as a member of an overall hierarchical order whose sanctity and dignity radiated from the top down into the smallest branches.

The sacral character of the emperor and the Empire was not only a matter of faith, but also—and above all—one of symbolic-ritual practice. A web of ritual acts of obligation and transmission ensured that the institutional order was continually renewed on all levels and related back to the divine source of legitimacy. This order was guaranteed above all by personal oaths. From the election and coronation oath of the emperor himself, to the oaths of the princely throne vassals during investiture and the oaths of homage of their territorial estates (*Landstände*) and subjects, all the way down to the oaths of office by every official—the Empire was held together by a tight-knit network of personal obligations of fealty. The oath established a bond between the person rendering it and the person receiving it, because divine authority itself was being invoked as the third element in the covenant to authenticate the obligation and sanction potential violations.[5]

The sacredness of the Empire was omnipresent. It began with the images: the two heads of the imperial eagle were surrounded by a nimbus as the sign of holiness, and the coats of arms of the members of the Empire were grouped around the picture of the crucified Christ (see figure 3 in chapter 1). The imperial regalia included prominent relics, especially the Holy Cross and the Holy Lance, which, together with the insignia of power (crown, scepter, orb, and sword), virtually embodied the Empire. They constituted a treasure both material and spiritual, in whose effect of grace the members of the Empire participated.[6] The city of Nuremberg, which Emperor Sigismund had privileged as the permanent repository of the imperial regalia, displayed them publicly every year in a paraliturgical act. They were regarded as sacral objects (*Heiligtümer*), and their exhibition was tied to papal indulgences. Above all, the sacredness of the Empire could be experienced in the liturgical acts that accompanied every ritual of rulership. At its core, a sacral ritual consists of the actors invoking the intervention of a transcendental power by performing standardized, symbolically charged scripts, and thereby bringing about a desired effect.[7] That was also the case with the election and coronation of the king of the Romans and the emperor. Such sacral rituals were the "solemn media" by which "the royal government and that of other high lordships are begun, stabilized, and affirmed as an order of God."[8] The anointing of the king, the consecration of the ruler, had a virtually sacramental character. It was performed in the liturgical forms of an episcopal consecration and elevated the ruler above the laity, as had been the case with the Old Testament kings Saul, David, and Solomon.

Pars pro toto, these solemnities united the members of the Empire at every royal succession into a sacral community, a *corpus mysticum*.[9] All the other solemn acts of the Empire functioned in a similar way. It was always necessary to frame them liturgically. The Golden Bull made precise arrangements for this liturgical framework, which had to be enacted by the three ecclesiastical archbishop-electors together with the king or emperor.[10] Acts of lordship and installation on the level of the Empire did not differ fundamentally, in their sacral reference, from every other ritual of transition at every level of the hierarchy. The holiness of the Empire was realized in the liturgical praxis; everything political was sacrally elevated and religiously infused.

In the Empire, the inseparability of political and ecclesiastical order still had a special quality in that there were high ecclesiastical dignitaries whose church office combined simultaneously central rights of political lordship and participation. The entire political system of classification was thus symmetrically doubled: alongside secular electors stood ecclesiastical electors, alongside worldly princes stood religious princes, alongside counts and lords stood princely abbots and abbesses and provosts. At the sessions of the imperial diets, they sat across from one another on separate benches: the ecclesiastical princes as the members of a sacrally consecrated, higher estate to the king's right, the secular princes to his left. That accorded with the metaphor of the *corpus Christi mysticum*, where his right arm represented the spiritual order (*ordo*) of Christendom and his left arm the secular order.

The sacrality of the order of the Empire had consequences also for the deliberations between the emperor and the estates, which, since the late Middle Ages, were usually opened by a mass of the Holy Spirit.[11] The basic principle of political action—consensus—was theologically undergirded. God, it was believed, could not reside in the discord of spirits; only his adversary, the devil, could: *in scissura Deus non est*.[12] An assembly that was inspired by the Holy Spirit could not be divided; only unanimity possessed sacral dignity. *Consensus* and *unanimitas* were virtual synonyms for the teachings of the church.[13] Division was not envisaged in the political-religious symbolic order of the Empire, even though it actually occurred. Intractable and implacable deviation could be interpreted only as heresy, as a crime against the divine and simultaneously worldly majesty.

When the Reformation movement took hold of some of the imperial estates and a profound, conspicuous, and lasting rift opened up between them on the question of the truth of religious faith and religious practice, this was bound to affect the order of the Empire. This raises the following questions: What were the symbolic forms in which this division took place? What did it mean for the representation of political unity—understood as both symbolic-ritual presentation and procedural creation? In what way, and with what consequences, was the religious division integrated into the symbolic order of the Empire and its political processes? How did it change the political confederation without breaking it apart?

The Religious Schism on the Stage of the Imperial Diet

In Augsburg in 1530, the drama of the religious schism was carried onto the great stage of the Empire. To be sure, this was not the first act of the drama—it had already begun at the imperial diet in Worms in 1521, when Charles V had summoned Luther to explain himself and had subsequently placed him under the imperial ban. In the 1520s, the Edict of Worms had proved unenforceable against the will of a group of pro-Luther princes: the Elector of Saxony, the Margrave of Brandenburg-Ansbach, the Landgrave of Hesse, and the Princes of Anhalt and Brunswick-Lüneburg. The emperor, or his deputy Ferdinand, had been forced to compromise and leave the implementation of the edict to the conscience of the territorial lords and city councils.[14] In 1529 in Speyer, the Luther-friendly princes and cities had refused to accept the Imperial Recess enacted by the vast majority of the old-faith estates—it called once again for the enforcement of the ban—and had lodged a formal protest against it.[15] In so doing, they had laid claim to religion as a matter of individual conscience and as a right about which the majority of the assembly could not make a binding decision. To do so they had employed the same instrument that was customary also in other cases—for example, in conflicts over rank and status—to preserve a contrafactual legal claim, thereby keeping a conflict that could not be resolved amicably open and present in ritualized form. Contrary to the usual practice, however, Charles's deputy Ferdinand had refused to accept the document of protest, thereby expressing that he did not recognize the legitimacy of the act.

Expectations about the imperial assembly in Augsburg in 1530 were running particularly high, because the emperor—newly crowned by the pope in Bologna, victorious against France, and in urgent need of aid against the Turks—was planning to attend the diet in person for the first time in nine years. But unlike in Worms in 1521, the last imperial diet with the emperor in attendance, the religious question had become significantly more important to him, even if it still ranked behind his power-political interests. In the imperial summons to the imperial estates as his "incorporated members," we read that the unity in the Empire was to be reestablished "with shared council," with papal holiness and imperial authority. The emperor held out the prospect that he would hear and take into account the "considerations, opinion, and views" of everyone, and "to refrain from everything that has not been rightly construed and done by both parts; through all of us to assume and maintain a single and true religion, and how we all are and fight under one Christ, that is, all of us live in one community, church, and unity."[16] The unity of all under Christ also allowed for only *one* church, *one* political order, and *one* truth. At the imperial diet, Charles V thus wanted to hold court, listen to all sides in his capacity as highest judge, mediator, and patron of the church (in the presence of the papal legate Campeggio), and on this basis restore the unity of the faith. The Elector of Saxony brought along his most important theologians; Luther himself, who was under the imperial ban, corresponded with participants from the neighboring fortress of Coburg.[17]

The submission of the *Confessio Augustana* (Augsburg Confession), which would later become the central doctrinal foundation of the Lutheran Church, and its rejection by Charles V soon made this imperial diet appear as one of the fundamental founding events of Protestantism. Hindsight makes it difficult for us to have an unbiased view of the situation at the time. The entire event always presents itself as a confrontation between the confessional parties, even though those parties were in fact just then in the process of taking shape.[18] For the actors themselves, the permanent confessional schism was by no means foreseeable; they were concerned with reestablishing unity. But the question was whether this unity would arise from a return to obedience toward the imperial majesty or from a free discourse over the truth of Holy Scripture—that is, whether it would be created authoritatively or consensually. The imperial summons suggested vaguely that both approaches could be reconciled, without saying specifically how. However, it was necessary first to gauge the extent to which the accustomed procedures were adequate for dealing with the new conflict. Previously, one had either negotiated compromises at the imperial assemblies or left conflicts in abeyance, while at the same time staging the authority of the whole and the consensus of all members of the Empire. Now, however, this basic consensus about the *maiestas imperialis* itself was being questioned, and the scope and reach of this majesty became an explicit issue. When the emperor interpreted the protest of 1529 as disobedience against his majesty and that of the Empire, he himself put that majesty on the agenda—very much against the intention of the protesters, who were still concerned to present themselves as "faithfully obedient estates." Given the murkiness, unparalleled nature, and openness of the situation, a great deal more than ever before depended on who would be able to define the situation symbolically and assert his interpretation.

For the emperor to give proof of his authority, his personal presence was a fundamental necessity: if there was a remedy against heresy, he wrote to his brother Ferdinand, "then only this, that I appear in person."[19] After all, as we have seen, the *maiestas imperialis* was not an abstract thing that could have been made present at will and without a loss of power through deputies or written communication. The emperor's nine-year absence from the Empire had made that clear.[20] Asserting imperial authority against challenges required the emperor's personal appearance within the circle of the electors. Everyone had to be able to literally *see* the majesty.

Augsburg was the forum at which this fundamental question was to be settled in accordance with the will of the emperor—and that could happen not only verbally, but had to be done also symbolically and ritually. The relationship between a discursive and a symbolic framing of the position was itself the topic of dispute and divergent strategies by the participants. The assembly was from the outset a stage of symbolic demonstrations, on which positions were staked out in nonargumentative ways already before the beginning of the deliberations. Profoundly basic questions were at stake: Who would direct the proceedings? Who would control the public space? Who was a party, who the mediator? And finally, how far did the imperial *maiestas* extend?[21] In other words, the point was to demarcate positions as well as possibilities and limitations of accommodation—to begin with, through spatial positioning in the ceremony and through the visible performance of religious practice, before the verbal arguments even got under way. We have a number of diaries, chronicles, and correspondences that reflect very precisely how the imperial diet of Augsburg was used and perceived by the participants as a crucial venue for symbolic messages. They not only describe, certainly with varying biases, the procedural forms and content of the deliberations, but also pay very careful attention to the details of public actions, and they provide some insights into how contested these details were and how intensely the parties struggled over them.[22]

At the time the diet was announced, the atmosphere was exceedingly tense in many respects. For one, the 1529 protestation by the pro-Luther estates and the conflict of interpretation tied to it were in the air: was this an act of disobedience against the imperial majesty, or a legitimate instrument by the members of the Empire that marked out the limit of their duty of obedience? For another, relations between the emperor and the electors were also tense, because the latter had not been included in the recent imperial coronation in Bologna in keeping with the rules of the Golden Bull. Finally, the city of Augsburg itself was by no means a neutral stage, but had, like almost all the other imperial cities, long since been seized by the Protestant movement.

The citizenry and the council were split into several camps: some adhered to the old faith, some to the Lutherans, and some to the Zwinglians. Although the council of Augsburg had not joined the Protestants at the imperial diet of Speyer in 1529, instead accepting the imperial recess like the old believers, the stance of Augsburg's council elite was in fact no longer unified.[23] To some extent they sympathized with the protesters, but in some ways they also feared an uprising by the "common man," most of whom were leaning toward Protestantism. The horrors of the Peasants' War five years earlier were still vividly in the minds of all the authorities in the Empire. The ritual life of the city, through which the community had traditionally enacted itself as a sacral community, had been disturbed for years by the religious schism. The situation was exacerbated by the participants at the diet, whose theologians were now also preaching in the spirit of the new faith. Moreover, Luther himself had printed a tract with the title *Exhortation to All the Clergy Assembled at the Imperial Diet of Augsburg in 1530*, which, in spite of being banned, was already circulating in the city before the opening of deliberations. If the emperor did in fact wish to bring about a reconciliation, if he wanted to present himself as the sovereign and mediator, not as a party, this presupposed first of all that he gain control of the public sphere.

Charles V tried to exert control already from Italy and later from Innsbruck, and to secure ahead of time in a multitude of ways that this time the protesters would recognize his "sovereignty and majesty, as was proper." For example, he had his councilors indicate to the Elector of Saxony, as the leader of the protesting party, that he could employ his still outstanding enfeoffment as leverage. He demanded that the envoys of the city of Ulm submit ahead of time to his decision "regarding the faith," however it turned out.[24] At the same time he sought, with the help of the government councilors who had also been invited to Augsburg, and who had represented him during his absence, to ensure that he himself would "retain and have sovereignty" in the city.[25] That is why the Augsburg city council had to dismiss the mercenaries it had hired for public security and instead welcome and pay for one thousand imperial soldiers. The imperial quartermasters who had been sent ahead behaved with unusual harshness in taking quarters, or at least that is how many residents perceived it: "completely different from what was ever heard of at imperial diets in Augsburg before." However, it became evident that a power that was dependent on force to assert itself was thereby already demonstrating its weakness. What prevailed was an atmosphere of a latent readiness to use violence on both sides. Different from the splendid Augsburg diets in the past, the word within the citizenry was now that "one did not want to have the emperor."[26]

The Emperor's Entry

Charles V's first appearance on the public stage in Augsburg was his festive entry; it was the subject of the utmost care in staging. Since the beginning of May, the electors of Mainz, Cologne, Saxony, and Brandenburg, as well as numerous secular and ecclesiastical princes, had been gradually arriving in the city with large retinues, among them also the signers of the protestation, who all told made up merely a small minority of the participants at the diet. Charles V himself kept the assembled participants waiting for over two months. He had announced the imperial diet for 8 April but did not arrive outside the city until 14 June—accompanied by a large retinue and the envoys of several European monarchs. Before that, his councilors had negotiated for days with their counterparts of the electors about the modalities of the entry, the sequence in the entrance on horseback, the wording of the welcome speech, and the seating arrangements.[27] With regard to the seating order, the emperor was able to commit the estates to letting their open conflicts rest this time and keeping the seating "safe." In return, he held out the prospect of having all competing claims submitted to him in writing and resolving them once and for all within nine months—in other words, to enact a new kind of Golden Bull, "so that all quarrels on account of the seating would be and remain abolished in the Empire."[28] Although that later turned out to be illusory, initially this was judged a remarkable demonstration of his personal authority: the chancellor of Mainz wrote that on this matter, Charles had found among the princes a willingness to follow that no emperor before him, not even Maximilian, would ever have been allowed to demand.[29] Perhaps this is an indication of how very much it mattered to the imperial princes themselves that the emperor would be able to exercise his mediating role on the religious issue unimpeded in Augsburg.

Of substantial importance to the political constellation at the assembly was the ceremonial status of the papal legate, Cardinal Campeggio, who represented the papal power and to whom the emperor was planning to assign a prominent place on his side—very much in the spirit of his recent concord with the pope.[30] With this he professed from the outset that he would not permit an agreement on the religious question without the Holy See. Thus, when it came to the ceremonial treatment of Campeggio, a question of principle was at stake. In response to a request from the electors, the emperor sent them an instruction with the desired entrance arrangements, in which he expressed the wordy request to accord the papal legate special honor. This directive envisaged, for one, that Charles's brother Ferdinand—King of Hungary and Bohemia and his deputy in the Empire—should ride to his right. This already announced the dynastic claim to succession to the emperorship, which was to be a significant topic at the coming deliberations.[31] For another, and above all, it envisaged that the papal legate should ride to his left. In the process, both Ferdinand and Campeggio were to enter together with the emperor underneath the golden baldachin embroidered with the imperial eagle. This was by no means an insignificant detail—the baldachin was a clear and highly visible sign of majesty. Whoever sat, walked, or rode under it participated visibly in the *maiestas*.[32] At the recent imperial coronation of Charles in Bologna, the two highest powers, the pope and the emperor, had also ridden under the baldachin side by side (figure 5).

In Augsburg, however, this wish was a provocation to the electors. The desired order of the procession clearly violated the rules of the Golden Bull, according to which no one could sit, stand, or walk between the electors and the emperor during solemn acts of the Empire. The electors could be expected to

88 ~: *The Emperor's Old Clothes*

Figure 5. Nicolaus Hogenberg, *Entry of Charles V with Pope Clemens VII into Bologna in 1530 for the Imperial Coronation* (detail), 1532, © Herzog August Bibliothek Wolfenbüttel.

deviate from this only "as a favor, not from any kind of obligation," and Charles was aware of what kind of imposition this was. For some time now, the electors, who elected the king, had been involved in a principled quarrel over rank with the cardinals, who elected the pope.[33] Moreover, as we have seen, they had not been involved in any way in the recent imperial coronation in Bologna, something to which they were entitled by their own interpretation of the Golden Bull. Scepter, sword, and crown had been carried by Italian princes, Spanish and Italian noblemen had made up the coronation procession, and heralds from the Spanish lands had symbolically marked the sovereign act. The entire ritual had enacted Charles's dynastic power, not the majesty of the Empire.

As a result, in Augsburg the electors insisted much more emphatically that their status be made ceremonially visible. The ceremonial role assigned to them threatened their preeminence, their substantive elevation above all others, and their direct proximity to the emperor. Only after lengthy negotiations did they agree to the compromise that the emperor alone would ride under the baldachin, the electors of Mainz and Cologne would ride ahead on the right and left, and the papal legate and Ferdinand would follow him on the right and left outside the baldachin (figure 6); all this, however, on the condition that the emperor formally proclaim (*vivae vocis oraculo*) that he did not intend to create a precedent for the future with this arrangement.

Figure 6. Jörg Breu the Elder, *Entry of Charles V into Augsburg in 1530*, Brunswick, Anton-Ulrich-Museum, Inv. No. 5350b.

The entry procession desired by Charles was thus thwarted by the electors, but even in its modified form it posed a problem for the Protestant estates. Because Charles pushed through the ceremonial staging of papal power as a twin power alongside the imperial one, at least in rudimentary form, he made it difficult for the Protestants to abide by their own interpretation of the situation. In their eyes, after all, the pope embodied the Antichrist who led the eschatological enemies of the Gospel: "party of the pope" and "party of the Gospel," "papists" and "evangelicals" stood diametrically opposed to each other. By contrast, the protesting princes always avoided referring to the emperor himself as their adversary. Instead, they usually attributed hostilities to his Italian (*welsch*) advisors, relatives, or ecclesiastical princes. After all, it was very much in their interest, as members of the Empire, to preserve the authority of the emperor as a conciliator, even if that possibility was increasingly disappearing. They could accept the emperor as mediator, but not the pope.

The dispute over the entry had revealed that the emperor was dependent on the good will of the electors and princes in staging his majesty. An Augsburg chronicle reports tersely that the princes had sent him a message: "if he wished to ride in as was customary from time immemorial, they would ride out to meet His Majesty; if not, they would stay inside. Whereupon the emperor consented."[34] The citizens of Augsburg also did not show much willingness to go out and meet the emperor, which was the customary ritual between a city community and its overlord. The council had to issue an urgent appeal to the two civic societies and the captains of the city neighborhoods to go door to door and prevail upon the citizens one by one to participate.

The actual entry, however, at least as presented in the eyewitness accounts, gave virtually no further indication of all these difficulties. Instead, it was presented as an exceedingly magnificent *adventus*, with hundreds of splendidly uniformed bodyguards and horsemen, drums and trumpets, and the ringing of bells and artillery blasts, as was proper for a newly crowned emperor.[35] A number of broadsheets,[36] including that of the imperial herald Kaspar Sturm, doubled the staging in the mediums of writing and image; Jörg Breu the Elder captured it in an elaborate, ten-part woodcut series.[37] It did not lack for the traditional signs of concord, beginning with the greeting outside the city, where the emperor and the electors dismounted and extended their hands to one other. When seven princes subsequently performed the traditional stirrup service as the emperor remounted his horse, as a sign of submission, there were four Protestants among them, a clear gesture of their willingness to show obedience.[38] Next the emperor and his retinue were escorted into the city, which was ritually demarcated as a graduated space of different legal spheres. At the boundary of the city, the council received the emperor with the city baldachin, which was borne by six councilors. The clergy from all parishes came out to meet the emperor dressed in their vestments and carrying the Blessed Sacrament. Waiting for him at the Church of St. Leonhard were the bishop and the cathedral chapter with the episcopal baldachin, held aloft by six canons. As with every festive *adventus*, an explicit parallel was evoked to Jesus's entry into Jerusalem on Palm Sunday. Charles carried a green branch in his hand and was greeted in the cathedral as the savior with the antiphon of the Easter liturgy, *Advenistis desiderabilis quem expectabamus in tenebris* (You have come, desired one, whom we have waited for in darkness).[39] He prayed bareheaded, kneeling on the bare earth, a successor to Christ simultaneously abased and exalted.[40] All observers highlighted that the Elector of Saxony—no less than the head of the Protestant "party"—was carrying the imperial sword ahead of him during all of this, in keeping with his office as the hereditary imperial marshal. The unpredictable "common man," however, remained excluded; all church doors but one had been barred to him.

Just how difficult the role of the papal legate, in particular, was can be seen from several incidents. Already at the greeting outside the city, he had kept to the side, and like the two other cardinals in the imperial retinue, he had remained seated on his donkey—as a sign of Christian *humilitas*, he was not riding a horse. Observers interpreted this as a sign of his apprehension that he would be denied the proper deference.[41] His fears were not unjustified: when Campeggio had been in Augsburg six years earlier, several citizens had "shown him the donkey with their fingers," that is, they had insulted him with a rude gesture.[42] When he now wished to bless the princes and they kneeled down, the Elector of Saxony demonstratively remained standing and refused the papal legate's blessing. Asked why he was not kneeling down, he is said to have answered: "I bid the rogue a good year!" It was proper to kneel only before God, he declared.[43] In the city, the legate dispensed with blessing the crowd, because, as at least some Protestants believed, he did not want to risk making a fool of himself to the Germans with this Italian custom.[44] It was all the more important to him to be the one who blessed the emperor. One of the broadsheets reported that the archbishop of Salzburg had wanted to give the emperor the blessing in the cathedral: "However, papal legate Compegius [sic] noticed that, and at the hour he also hastened to the altar, pulled the cardinal of Salzburg behind and said that it was his due to give the benediction to His Imperial Majesty, such that the cardinal of Salzburg could not resist but had to let it happen."[45]

Struggle Over the Public Sphere: Seeing versus Hearing

The papal legate's problems had a threefold dimension. First, he had to enforce his precedence over the German princes (including those of the old faith); second, as previously mentioned, he had to assert papal authority as the twin power to the emperor's; third, and more fundamentally, he had to demonstratively uphold the claim of the Roman Church to being the sole source of salvation. Bestowing the blessing was an expression of the priest's role as a mediator between the individual and God, on which the power of the Roman Church was essentially based. In the sacramental act of blessing, the priest, by virtue of his consecrated status and his ecclesiastical office, laid claim to making the divine grace effective in a targeted way. This kind of institutionalized and ritualized, and thereby controllable, mediation of salvation tied to certain conditions was at the heart of what the Protestants were rejecting. The blessing was to them one of the multitude of sacramental and paraliturgical practices they condemned in their entirety as papist abuses: they were not grounded in Holy Scripture and dangerously misled the conscience of believers, because they held out to them the prospect of a false path to God's grace, which could be achieved only by faith. In the lead-up to the imperial diet, the Wittenberg theologians had drawn up a long list of such abuses and sent it along with their elector:

> [P]alms and word blessing, making palm crosses, swallowing palms for various illnesses, Christ riding on the donkey ... , foot washing on Maundy Thursday ... , burying a cross, blessing baptism by dunking the Easter candles and with many ungodly songs, consecrating new fire on Easter eve, making Easter candles, ... blessing sausages, meat and eggs, procession around the church with banners, candles, holy water sprinkler, monstrance; heaven etc., ... sending the Holy Spirit on Pentecost, the festival days of the saints, ... going into the villages with crosses, likewise going around the fields; finally also: Corpus Christi procession with great splendor, banners, candles, etc., setting up decorated altars in all houses etc.

And this list was far from exhaustive.[46] The issue was to strip formulas and gestures, pictures and objects, places and times of any sacrality and disenchant them as purely the work of man. This was a veritable revolution of symbols.

The early Protestant movement acted as a fundamentally antiritualistic movement; it construed a radical opposition between external things and actions on the one hand, and the inner redemptive work of faith and grace on the other.[47] But the symbolic-ritual "externalities" by no means lost all meaning through the Protestant critique—quite the contrary. Though anointing oil and consecrated candles, miracle images and relics, genuflection and gestures of blessing no longer possessed any ritual efficacy in the eyes of the Protestants, precisely to make sure of that they mocked, damaged, or destroyed them.[48] In Augsburg, too, in the 1520s, saints' images had been smeared with cattle blood, and people had publicly "turned their backside" to the consecrated hosts.[49] To be sure, Lutheran theologians—in particular Melanchthon—taught that all mere externalities (*Adiaphora*) mattered nothing before God and conscience, which is why one could leave them to the discretion of each individual.[50] But precisely these externalities represented a provocation to many supporters of the Protestant movement and invited acts of ritual violence. Ceremonies might lose their sacramental efficacy, but they acquired instead an even greater social efficacy in distinguishing and identifying the newly forming groups. That applied not only to the difference between "papists" and "evangelicals," but also to the divergences within the Lutherans and the supporters of the southern German and Swiss reformers.

In Augsburg, all participants, be they town citizens or councilors, princes or theologians, were fully aware of all of this. Charles V was determined to use the symbolic effect of church ceremonies in the public sphere to demonstrate his authority, and to force the Protestants to participate ceremonially in their own marginalization. To that end he employed a clever double strategy, which started from the core of the theological and symbolic clash between the old and new doctrines.

It was no coincidence that the emperor's entry into the city had taken place on 15 June, the day before the Feast of Corpus Christi. When the princes had observed the usual custom of escorting the emperor to his lodgings after the *adventus*, he summoned the Protestant princes and emphatically demanded two things from them: first, that they immediately prohibit their theologians from any preaching; and second, that they participate in person in the Corpus Christi procession the following day.[51] The ban on Protestant preaching and the order to take part in the Feast of Corpus Christi were two corresponding measures by the emperor to control the public realm in his interests and to occupy it symbolically.

Since the High Middle Ages, the rite of the Eucharist had evolved into the heart of Christian religious practice.[52] The exhibition of the consecrated host, in particular, was increasingly cultivated: its elevation as a new, visible high point of the mass, its permanent keeping and display in magnificent monstrances, and above all its public exposure in festive procession. To the faithful, beholding the Body of Christ was especially salvific, which is why the pious sought to see it as often and for as long as possible. The more one did something, it was believed, the more efficacious it was, and this spirit of "quantified piety" also shaped the interactions with the Eucharist.[53] In the fifteenth century this led to a downright inflationary practice of display, which the bishops at their synods sought to stem by restricting the procession with the consecrated host to the Feast of Corpus Christi. Not only did these processions give heightened expression to the entire sacramental system of the old church, they were simultaneously a stage for the social hierarchy, which was measured by the spatial proximity of each individual to the sacral center, the consecrated host.[54] Nowhere else did the order of the old church become so demonstratively and splendidly visible. Small surprise, then, that Corpus Christi processions, in particular, became in many cities the occasion and object of violent conflicts in the wake of the Reformation movement.⁵⁵ Luther had written in 1523 that one should "do away with the houses of sacraments and the procession on the day of Corpus Christi, because it is of no use or value and the sacrament suffers great hypocrisy and mockery from it."⁵⁶ Mockery and hypocrisy he saw in the fact that the outward forms were being performed without inner faith, as the kind of act of deference that one also performed to the secular authorities: "[W]hen you fall down before the altar or the sacrament, bend your knees, bow down, lower your head, look up to the sky, speak with your mouth and whatever else can be done outwardly." And Philipp of Hesse is reported to have said mockingly: "Jesus Christ said that one should eat his body and drink his blood, but not that one should carry him around in alleys."⁵⁷ For Luther the heart of the believer was the real monstrance of the sacrament, "from which much more precious honor comes to it than if you fashioned a monstrance all of gold or the most precious gems."⁵⁸ The ostentatious display was not only devalued but condemned as a downright un-Christian, anti-Christian practice, because it kept people from the true faith while at the same time keeping them imprisoned in a false sense of security.

For the reformers, the core of the sacrament lay in the Word of Christ, the Gospel. A different kind of pious practice corresponded to this view: the *seeing* of the Body should be replaced by the *hearing* of the Word.⁵⁹ Against this background it becomes clear that Charles V's ban on preaching was the measure supplementing the order for the Corpus Christi procession. With it he struck at the heart of the Protestant movement, because the free proclamation of the Gospel was its most basic cause. Philipp of Hesse himself had provocatively demonstrated this symbolically when he and his retinue had ridden into the city with the motto "V.D.M.I.A." on their sleeves: *Verbum Dei Manet In Aeternum* (The Word of God Endures Forever). After initial resistance from the princes, the emperor enforced the prohibition against Protestant preaching by deploying his own preachers and having the ban proclaimed by heralds throughout the city with great ceremony.⁶⁰

Silencing the Protestant preachers in the face of the latent danger of insurrection in the city was one thing; forcing the princes into actively participating in one of the central ceremonies of the old faith was quite another. That the Corpus Christi procession was a deliberate symbolic demonstration was clear to observers on both sides. In Augsburg, the large city procession had already been discontinued since the middle of the 1520s. Thus, the strictly orthodox Augsburg chronicler Clemens Sender wrote that the emperor had ordered the Corpus Christi procession in the knowledge that the Protestant preachers had brought the veneration of the most reverend sacrament to a standstill. Wherever the altar sacrament had been displayed, the Augsburgers had mocked it. That is why Charles V was so invested in celebrating precisely this feast day "in Augsburg before many with great solemnity."⁶¹ Conversely, from the Protestant perspective it was said that the emperor wanted to prevail upon the princes to recognize the Corpus Christi celebration as a true mass through their contribution and presence and against their will. But that would have had the effect of a "tacit renunciation" of the Protestant doctrine before the entire world—whereas they had been summoned to Augsburg precisely to "stand and profess."[62] They knew that the symbolic practice would preempt the discursive engagement of the conflict and in the process rebut the verbal profession from the outset. That is why the Elector of Saxony's theologians advised their lord in principle not to participate. But if he could not entirely avoid service to the emperor, he should perform his duty with "deferential protestation" and refrain from any veneration of the sacrament.[63]

On the morning of 16 June, all of the Protestant princes therefore stayed away from the mass and the procession. Most of the Augsburg citizens also refused to participate, even though the council had called upon every single household to take part. Not a single craft guild joined the procession.[64] By contrast, the emperor and the majority of the participants in the imperial diet celebrated the Feast of Corpus Christi as a solemn act of the entire Empire, not of the city: the Elector of Mainz as imperial arch-chancellor carried the altar sacrament, and six imperial princes held the canopy over it. The emperor, who had donated a large number of expensive wax tapers for this purpose, followed the sacrament as a humble penitent: bareheaded and holding a burning candle.[65] Since the Elector of Saxony was not present at the procession, his court marshal carried the imperial sword ahead of him. The analogy to the festive *adventus* was obvious: the place under the canopy that the emperor himself had occupied the previous day was now taken by the Body of Christ; the solemn forms were the same. The emperor changed position, but the staging remained the same. Where he had the cathedral clergy greet him during the *adventus* as the coming redeemer, he now followed the example of Christ in humility and sacrificial bearing. He benefited from the subtle ambiguity of the *imitatio Christi*: self-abasement constituted simultaneously the most effective exaltation.

Opening Mass

The deliberations of the imperial diet were solemnly opened on 20 June with a mass of the Holy Spirit. The problem of the participation of the Protestant princes arose anew and in a different way, for unlike the Corpus Christi procession, the Holy Spirit mass had been the customary opening ritual since the fifteenth century, which served as the "blessed beginning of the deliberations" and established the unanimity of the participants as a Christian sacral community. But the celebration of the mass was at the very heart of the Protestant criticism and thus also of the impending clashes in Augsburg. The reformers (notwithstanding growing disagreement in their own camp about the character of the Eucharist) denied that the mass was a sacrifice through which the priest alone, by means of its formal performance, was able to bring about salvific effects even without pious participation, *ex opere operato*.[66] They dismissed as "idolatry" such "bought and private masses," with which the faithful sought to win divine grace for themselves and others (living and dead). The celebration of the Eucharist was the symbolic-ritual core of the entire Protestant movement, and at the same time the most contentious issue among the various evangelical currents. However, in all communities, abolishing the liturgy of the Eucharist and allowing the faithful to receive Communion in both forms had been the clearest step toward the Reformation.[67]

The opening mass therefore posed a dilemma for the Protestant princes of the realm. On the one hand, participation could be seen as a veritable "touchstone for the orthodox faith" of the imperial estates.[68] On the other hand, they were concerned not to delegitimize the upcoming deliberations before they had started, since they saw them as the forum for a possible agreement. Moreover, they did not want to arouse suspicion that they denied the real presence of Christ in the sacrament of the altar, something the Zwinglians did. However, three pro-Lutheran princes, among them the Elector of Saxony, had already stayed away from the mass at the imperial diet in Speyer the previous year.[69] In Augsburg the princes did not go that far in the presence of the emperor. Their stance toward the mass was very carefully noted. The Nuremberg delegates wrote back home that "especially" Johann of Saxony, Georg of Brandenburg, Philipp of Hesse, and the Duke of Lüneburg had attended mass and had "served His Imperial Majesty at all ceremonies."[70] But the collection of reports from the Saxon theologian Johannes Aurifaber states that the Elector of Saxony and the Margrave of Brandenburg had participated in the opening mass, while the other Protestant princes had not. We are told that the emperor went to take the Eucharist ("*zum Opfer gegangen*") with all the electors. However, the report explicitly adds that "ours did so with laughter." Contradicting this account, we hear a little later in the same source that only Landgrave Philipp of Hesse did not take Communion, though he had attended the mass.[71] Councilor Tetleben of Mainz reported in greater detail that Philipp did not assume his proper place, entered only for the sermon, left the church afterward, and returned to the choir only at the end in order to escort the emperor to city hall.[72] Given the meticulous arrangement of the seating in the cathedral, this behavior had to come across as extremely provocative. Clemens Sender, who made a careful record of where everyone had taken his rightful place in the church, commented disapprovingly: "Duke Ernst of Lüneburg and the Landgrave of Hesse did not stand in the choir, but took a stroll together in the cathedral church."[73]

Deliberating and Confessing

Participation in the mass, however, was necessary if one wanted to accept the imperial diet as a forum—if only a provisional one—for the religious question. But that was by no means a matter of course. After all, there was no clear and universally accepted procedure for how to handle a conflict of faith. Instead, the procedure itself was the object of the quarrel. Although there was widespread agreement that there was need of a general council as the ultima ratio, the form and composition of that council and its relationship to the pope were deeply contentious.[74] If that was unresolved for now, what role should the imperial assembly play? The participants at the imperial diet were largely in the dark about the course of action the emperor was planning, and they were also not in agreement whether for now they should accept and make use of the forum of an imperial diet in place of a council.[75] The theologians of electoral Saxony were willing to regard the Augsburg assembly provisionally and temporarily as the equivalent of a national council, something they had been calling for in vain for years. However, by his behavior during the mass, Philipp of Hesse had already expressed that he was from the very outset disputing the competency of the emperor and the imperial diet on the religious question.[76]

The wording of the imperial summons suggested various forms—not precisely institutionalized or separate and distinct—in which the desired conciliation could be accomplished. For one, the text evoked the *amicabilis compositio*, the "friendly agreement" that was customary on other issues at the imperial diets, and that, in contrast to an always precarious majority decision, represented the fundamental goal of all political negotiations. It corresponded to the process of the back-and-forth negotiating between the estate groups and the emperor. But this negotiating of a consensus usually rested on a relationship of exchange: it functioned only when all participants could fundamentally expect that they would be able to preserve their interests going forward. Concessions would have to pay off over the long run. Yet arriving at compromises of this kind presupposed that the issue at stake was material or nonmaterial goods that could be balanced out. In this case, however, there were no interests at stake that could be offset against each other, but values and convictions of conscience that were not suitable for horse-trading. As an alternative form of conflict resolution, however, one could also think of the form of a supplication, a deferential request by individual estates of the realm to the sovereign to mediate a conflict.[77] But this presupposed that the emperor would be accepted by all sides as a neutral mediator—and that, precisely, still had to be established in the first place.

One could also think of the conflict as a theological quarrel over the true faith. In that case, one could conceive of more academic forms of engagement: for example, a public disputation, a ritualized, antagonistic debate between scholars, of the kind that had been customary at the major reform councils of the fifteenth century, and for which Johannes Eck had already prepared himself in Augsburg.[78] It was in this way, for example, on the basis of a theological disputation before a large audience in the manner of an academic debate and simultaneously an interrogation, that the council in Zurich had decided to adopt Zwingli's doctrine. Also conceivable was an argumentative discourse among individual scholars and estates in a committee out of the public's gaze, as had been done the previous year at the Marburg Colloquy in an effort to resolve disagreements within the Protestant movement; more so than any other scenario, this would have moved the imperial diet closest to being a national council.[79] In short, there were many possible ways of dealing with this conflict. But the decision in favor of one over another could prejudice the outcome from the outset. At any rate, an unquestioned form equally accepted by all sides did not exist. This procedural uncertainty is something one must bear in mind if one wants to adequately assess the great importance that was attached to the symbolic strategies of all parties involved.

To open the deliberations, the emperor, as usual, invited participants to the great chamber of city hall, which was marked with all the signs of the *maiestas imperialis*. In the *Proposition* he offered once again, in his capacity as "steward and lord protector of the Christian faith," to personally receive in written form the opinions and reciprocal complaints about spiritual and worldly abuses, in order to return to a "unanimous Christian community" and to arrive at a resolution.[80] However, it remained to be seen where and how all of this should happen. To begin with, the very sequence of the topics of deliberation was contested. The Elector of Saxony and his retinue pushed through that the religious question would be discussed before the granting of aid against the Turks. If there was no "agreement," they would abide by their protest and would bring the matter to a universal and free council, meaning one not run by the pope. The second session, once again in the presence of all estates in city hall, therefore now offered the forum for the faith controversy. In the process, the special role of the papal legate as the representative of the pope was emphatically staged, as it had been during the festive entry into the city: the emperor, the king, and the princes went out to meet him as far as the steps of city hall and escorted him to his prominent seat next to King Ferdinand. A chair had been prepared for him "right in front of the emperor, so that he would look straight at the emperor, also entirely draped with golden cloths." He had a silver cross carried ahead of him and sat down "on his chair with great Roman custom," had his letter of accreditation read out, then delivered a long Latin speech "with great ostentation, shouting loudly," a pro-Lutheran observer wrote disagreeably, "thereby showing his papal instructions," and admonished the emperor and princes to restore the old, orderly state of affairs.[81]

Next, the chancellor of Elector Johann of Saxony gave an address as the spokesman of the "opposing party," which was perceived and referred to as such.

Observers spoke of the Elector of Saxony and "his parties, his retinue, his kin," and usually meant by that the four princes who had signed the protestation with him. In the perception of the participants at the diet, the cities hardly played a role. What gave the Protestants weight was the fact that an elector was their leader. As a firmly circumscribed party, "those they called Protestant" had become visible in the ritual act of the protestation. Now they appeared again as a group through the act of the public profession. Most of the contemporary reports barely thought it worth mentioning that the circle of participating cities had changed compared to the diet of Speyer in 1529.

The Saxon chancellor asked permission to read out the articles of faith that Philipp Melanchthon had hastily drawn up on the basis of earlier texts (the later so-called *Confessio Augustana*). How the emperor dealt with this confession of faith reveals just how much the mode of deliberation was now also subject to a symbolic strategy. Charles V rejected the petition to read out the articles and put the Protestants off to another day. The latter asked again "most urgently" to be heard but were again turned down. When the emperor demanded that the document be handed over, the Protestant party in turn refused and insisted once more that it be read out immediately, and again this was turned down. The Protestants were put off to the next day and simply took the document with them.[82]

The emperor had lost the symbolic management of the situation and needed to regain it. He did so by inviting the Protestants to his court the next day to have the articles read out there—namely, in the presence of the other estates, but not in public. In the chamber of his palace he held court as emperor and thus marked his status as a mediator, not as a party to the dispute, which is what he appeared to be during the back-and-forth negotiations at city hall the previous day. The difference was also clear to the Protestants, who still tended to hold, not the emperor himself but his advisors, Ferdinand and especially Campeggio, responsible for the way the events were unfolding: Justus Jonas wrote to Luther that the articles had been read in the emperor's private chamber (*cubiculum*) before a few princes, not in the public assembly. Luther himself later reported that the document had not been read out publicly before the people—its "enemies" had seen to that. Still, on orders from the emperor it had at least been read out before the entire Empire, that is, before all princes and estates (*coram toto imperio, id est: principibus et statibus imperii*), in a loud voice and for three hours.[83] The emperor had the articles handed over to him, but he strictly prohibited the making of any copy, let alone their publication in print, and left it to the orthodox theologians to draft a response. With that he was treating the document demonstratively as a supplication directed solely to him personally and to be answered only by him or on his orders, not as an element of a public and open discourse conducted between two parties of equal standing.

Shortly thereafter (5/6 July), the imperial councilors deliberated extensively with the orthodox estates about the further mode of the conflict. The "Christian" princes, as they called themselves, in no way wanted to act as a party, but saw themselves as mediators and advisors to the emperor. They advised Charles V that he not explicitly address his role as judge in the religious question. For if the Protestants refused to grant him that role, which was to be expected, it would result in "contempt" for the imperial majesty. The important thing was "not to get involved in any disputation" with the Lutherans, but to reject their articles and then prevail upon them in all kindness to relent until a general council clarified the religious question.[84]

If the goal was to maintain the emperor's role as judge, mediator, and patron of the faith under all circumstances, though without explicitly highlighting it, then everything depended on the symbolic staging of the events. The procedural script of the imperial diet was still open enough that Charles V could impart to it the character of an imperial *Hoftag*.[85] Not only did he issue the invitation to the general assemblies at city hall, he also summoned the various estates before himself in his *palatium*—at first only the Protestant princes, then only the orthodox, then the cities; in short, he set the mode of the negotiations. Part of the character of a *Hoftag* was also that the city delegates continued to be largely marginalized as foreign bodies within princely court society, and they were barely informed about the course of events. For example, the correspondence of the Straßburgers shows that the delegates long puzzled over whether they would be asked for their own position on the religious issue, and what to do if they were.[86] In other ways, too, Charles V used every opportunity to set signs of orthodoxy and imperial authority. On the Feast of Saint Ulrich, the patron saint of Augsburg, he again invited the princes explicitly to accompany him to the mass at the Ulrich Monastery;[87] on the Feast of Saint Afra he had a Holy Spirit mass celebrated in the cathedral with all the princes.[88] He observed Saint John's Day with a public High Mass in their presence;[89] he solemnly knighted the mayor and the guild master of the imperial city of Überlingen, who had distinguished themselves as defenders of the old faith, and granted their community new privileges.[90] That the city of Augsburg, on 27 June, had to publicly perform a collective oath of homage to him as the lord of the city was in keeping with the customs of imperial diets, but given the tense atmosphere and the uncertain stance of the council on the religious question, this was also a particularly meaningful act.[91]

Investiture as an Anti-Lutheran Demonstration

In Augsburg, too, the most effective enactment of imperial majesty was the solemn banner investitures within the circle of the electors. On 26 July, that is, between the reading of the *Confessio* (25 June) and its rejection in the *Confutatio* (3 August), the emperor bestowed the regalia upon the Dukes of Pomerania and the Master of the Teutonic Order; later, on 5 September, he invested his brother Ferdinand with the Archduchy of Austria. All of these investitures were politically explosive. The Pomeranian enfeoffment has already been discussed in chapter 1. The investiture of the Master of the Teutonic Order is of particular interest here, since it likewise represented a demonstration of imperial authority in the religious dispute.

The investitures took place in the central communal space, the *Weinmarkt*, in front of the *Metzg* by the city's dancing house, where, as was customary, a wooden scaffold decorated with golden draperies had been erected, and next to it a small house where participants could get dressed.[92] Orthodox chroniclers highlighted the liturgical character of the imperial regalia: alb, stole, diaconal vestments, and "a golden priestly cloak," most sumptuously ornamented and embroidered with the imperial eagle.[93] Another detail struck them as particularly noteworthy: Georg of Brandenburg, Philipp of Hesse, and the sons of the Elector and the Duke of Saxony performed the special ceremonial service of carrying the hem of his robe in the back and on both sides. Three of these men had signed the *Confessio Augustana*.[94] Needless to say, the Elector of Saxony, like the two other electors present, exercised his hereditary office. In this way, the Protestants were coerced into demonstrative participation in the symbolic-ritual message represented by the investiture of the Master of the Teutonic Order. For this was a performative act intended for the Lutherans: the investiture affirmed the doubling of ecclesiastical office and secular lordship, thereby stabilizing one of the pillars of the imperial system that had been fundamentally questioned by Luther's strict separation of spiritual and worldly power and was now one of the central topics of the religious negotiations.[95]

The status of the administrator of the Teutonic Order, Walter of Cronberg, was, in fact, at least as controversial as that of the Dukes of Pomerania, if for very different reasons. The office of the Grand Master of the Teutonic Order in Prussia had originally been held by Albrecht of Brandenburg, who in 1525, upon personal advice from Luther, discarded the Cross of the Order and the habit as the signs of church rank, making him the first ecclesiastical prince to secularize the rulership over his territory. Prussia's Teutonic Knights followed him, and the territorial estates gave him their support.[96] At the same time, however, Albrecht of Brandenburg had the King of Poland enfeoff him and his sons with the Prussian territory as a joint hereditary fief. The Master of the Teutonic Order, Walter of Cronberg, head of the Order within the Empire, lodged a complaint against this at the imperial diet of 1526, arguing that this deprived the Empire of an important member. That claim, however, was highly controversial. For similar to the status of other territories on the periphery of the Empire, the relationship of the Prussian lands of the Teutonic Order to the

Empire was not straightforward. The Order possessed a papal privilege that generally exempted it from the feudal sovereignty of the emperor. However, toward the end of the fifteenth century, the masters of the Order themselves had begun to seek the protection of and membership in the Empire. This was the symptom of a general trend: the Order was getting caught up in the pull of the institutional consolidation that was taking hold of the Empire at the close of the fifteenth century. Already in 1495, the Master of the Teutonic Order had allowed himself to be invested by Maximilian, and had assumed a seat and vote on the bench of the prelates at the imperial diet.[97] And unlike his predecessors, Albrecht of Brandenburg also participated in imperial diets as Grand Master of the Teutonic Order; in Nuremberg in 1524, he had a seat assigned to him on the bench of the ecclesiastical princes, though he had not yet been invested by the emperor, which promptly triggered a seating quarrel with Cronberg, the Master of the Teutonic Order.[98] In the end an investiture by the emperor did not take place at all, since Albrecht had in the meantime decided in favor of the Protestant movement and had been enfeoffed by the Polish king. Thus, when Charles V in Augsburg in 1530 bestowed the regalia and the territory of the Teutonic Order in Prussia on Master Walter of Cronberg, while Albrecht of Brandenburg already held it as a Polish fief, the emperor was claiming a feudal sovereignty that was not supported by any historical tradition. Moreover, the claim that the emperor thereby granted to the Master of the Teutonic Order had no chance to prevail against the estates and subjects in Prussia—nor did Charles subsequently do much to help Walter of Cronberg make his pretensions a reality.[99]

Instead, the ritual of investiture in Augsburg had a very different meaning for the emperor, one that arose from the situation at the imperial diet and can be deduced from the special arrangement of the ritual. He combined the form of investing *ecclesiastical* princes with the scepter, as agreed upon with the pope since the High Middle Ages in the Concordat of Worms, with the manner of investing *secular* princes with the banners and merged the two into a single act. In his account of the scene, councilor Tetleben, a canon in Mainz, noted explicitly "pro memoria: Nota: When the emperor invests publicly, he invests the secular princes with the sword, and the ecclesiastical princes with the scepter. But when the emperor invests in chamber and not publicly, he invests all with the scepter and without the banners."[100] The high medieval distinction between the banner investiture of secular princes and the scepter investiture of ecclesiastical princes had in fact not been observed in this way for quite some time. Rather, the distinction depended on whether the investiture was performed in public (with banners) or in chamber (with scepter). In the investiture of the Master of the Teutonic Order in 1530, however, the old distinction was revived.

The public banner investiture of a simple ecclesiastical prince (not an elector) was at the very least unusual, and at any rate enough to cause a stir. Walter of Cronberg appeared with a large retinue and numerous advocates, who rode around the splendid imperial scaffold three times and asked that he be enfeoffed with the land of Prussia. In the process they argued that Albrecht of Brandenburg had left the Order and forfeited his office; he had not received the office of grand master, "which is properly the fief of the Holy Roman Empire," in a timely manner, and it had therefore reverted back to the Empire.[101] After that, Cronberg appeared in person and handed to the emperor the blood banner (*Blutfahne*) and the banner with the Teutonic Order's Prussian coat of arms. Following the oath upon the evangelary resting in the emperor's lap, he kissed the imperial sword and then touched the scepter—"as though he were a secular as well as an ecclesiastical prince," as the herald's report explicitly stated.[102] The distinction between a scepter and a banner fief was demonstratively taken up to emphasize the dual ecclesiastical-secular character of the lordship over the territory that Albrecht of Brandenburg had de facto transformed into a secular duchy. The Mainz councilor Tetleben explicitly recorded for posterity that the "land of Prussia" had never before been invested under the banners and a still-living grand master had never been deposed, as had now happened here "on account of the Lutheran heresy."[103] In Augsburg, he noted, "there had been a lot of abusive talk about it, for the reason that the one had received the fief, while the other held it and didn't care." For many believed that the investiture of the fief was really the privilege of the King of Poland.[104] So unusual was the case that it became part of the literature on feudal law. Shortly before the end of the empire, Heinrich Gottfried Scheidemantel, a specialist of imperial public law, still referred to it as particularly memorable, "in that all solemnities of the imperial investitures were brought together here."[105]

What the emperor achieved with this ritual innovation was not the actual recovery of the Teutonic Order's lands, but instead a symbolic message to the Protestants, who themselves had to participate prominently in it. Before the eyes of all, the ritual affirmed the link between ecclesiastical office and secular lordship, a fundamental structural element of the empire that Luther had radically questioned and that was also at issue during the deliberations themselves.

Johann of Saxony also had to perform his electoral service during the solemn throne investitures, thus participating in the semblance of consensus that was established by the ritual. Yet he himself had asked in vain for his own investiture on 2 July in an audience with the emperor. Already before the beginning of the imperial diet, Charles V had put him under pressure with the investiture that had been on hold for five years, and he now followed through on his threat: if the elector did not abandon his position on the religious question, he could not reconcile it with his conscience to invest him.[106] Until his death in 1532, Johann was not endowed with any regalia by Charles V, neither publicly nor in chamber, neither in person nor through deputies. The refusal of investiture was attentively registered by contemporaries. It was an extraordinary affront, a visible damage to their territorial rulership, which the Saxon electors sought to compensate for by stepping up strategies of dynastic legitimation—for example, by commissioning sixty diptychs with portraits of all their predecessors.[107] It was three years later that the successor, Johann Frederick of Saxony, was invested in solemn form, namely, by Ferdinand, who had in the meantime been elected king of the Romans, and not by the emperor himself. This was the result of a bargain: Ferdinand solemnly bestowed the regalia on the Elector of Saxony; in return the latter now recognized him as king, something he had previously refused to do. This reciprocal recognition found ritual expression in the unusual act of investiture in Vienna.[108]

Investiture as a Dynastic Demonstration

The investiture of the Master of the Teutonic Order was not the only spectacular banner investiture at this imperial diet. Charles V had not come to Augsburg in 1530 primarily to settle the religious question; more important to him was securing succession to the emperorship for the Habsburg dynasty. Election and inheritance, the two competing principles of succession in Europe, were by no means sharply and unequivocally distinguished; one could imperceptibly pass into the other. The principle of hereditary succession within a family corresponded in general with the principles of the social order and had a high degree of self-evident legitimacy on its side. Although the Golden Bull had enshrined the electoral principle in the Empire, the emperor had ways of influencing his succession by having his son elected king of the Romans already during his lifetime.[109] The Golden Bull, however, did not provide for such an election *vivente Imperatore*. While Emperor Frederick III had his son Maximilian elected king during his lifetime, after Maximilian's death the situation was once again wide open. It was by no means a foregone conclusion in 1519 that another Habsburg would be elected German king in the person of the Spanish monarch Charles. Rather, it was the result of extensive electoral gifts and promises. The goal was to avoid another dangerous and costly interregnum. After Charles V had himself crowned emperor by the pope in Bologna in 1530, the way was now open to have his brother and deputy Ferdinand elected king of the Romans and thus his successor.[110] This had been Ferdinand's goal for a long time, but only now was he able to persuade the emperor to have him elected king instead of his own minor son and heir to the Spanish throne, Philipp. Setting this election in motion was another issue at the imperial diet in Augsburg in 1530.

From the outset, Ferdinand's ceremonial treatment in Augsburg had been a source of conflict. As in the case of the papal legate, his place at the entry into the city and his seat at the deliberations and the mass were a topic of dispute between the emperor and the electors.[111] After all, Ferdinand embodied a number of different roles. First, he was Archduke of Austria; as such, he belonged to the secular princes of the realm, claimed the highest rank among them, and was set apart by a number of special privileges. Second, his brother, the emperor, had appointed him deputy in the Empire during his absence. Third, and finally, he was—on the basis of both hereditary right and election by the estates—King of Bohemia and Hungary and held the electoral office of Bohemia. The Kingdom of Bohemia played a special role, since it cut across the classification system of the Empire. Although the King of Bohemia was an elector and as such among those who chose the king, he was simultaneously a king himself and as such not a member of the realm. He paid no share of the imperial expenses, did not contribute to financing or staffing the Imperial Chamber Court (*Reichskammergericht*) created in 1495, and was not incorporated into the new system of Imperial Districts (*Reichskreise*). That is also why he did not assume a seat in the council of electors during imperial deliberations. Moreover, it was also debatable to what extent Bohemia was an imperial fief. From the Bohemian perspective only the electoral office was bestowed by the emperor, but not lordship over the Bohemian lands.

Ferdinand thus embodied various roles when he appeared at the imperial diet, and these roles entailed varying legal claims. When Charles V wanted him to ride in the most prominent spot during the *adventus*, to his right under the baldachin, it raised the question of what message this was intended to send, what claim was being asserted. The electors feared that the various roles would be inextricably merged to the benefit of the Habsburg dynasty. Above all, it was important to prevent his participation in the electoral council as King of Hungary and Bohemia, since he did not contribute to the Empire's expenses in that capacity. It was only as the Archduke of Austria that he did so. That is why he belonged to the council of princes at the imperial diet and should in no way be seated more prominently than the electors at the opening session. It was thus imperative to define in each instance in what role he was acting in order to prevent the creation of far-reaching precedents for the future, precedents upon which new legal claims could have been construed. And this, in turn, could be ensured only through the most precise ceremonial differentiations.

The emperor's interest at the imperial diet was to extract from the imperial majesty the utmost advantage for the greatness, splendor, and honor of the house of Habsburg. That goal was served by a very special act of investiture on 5 September 1530, which was documented in detail in an official print by the imperial herald Kaspar Sturm:[112] the bestowal of the regalia of the Archduchy of Austria on Ferdinand. The act displayed a whole series of conspicuous deviations from the traditional investiture ritual. Councilor Tetleben of Mainz, among the eyewitnesses who penned the most detailed accounts, commented about this unheard-of staging: there was no one who could remember any such thing.¹¹³ The act of investment followed a very peculiar script, the so-called *Privilegium maius*.¹¹⁴ The latter involved a number of (forged) imperial documents that the Austrian Duke Rudolf IV had fashioned two centuries earlier for his own benefit. They had been expanded further by Frederick III, and they gave the house of Austria a nearly king-like status largely independent of the imperial federation: thereafter, the Austrian lands were tied to the empire only with rights, not with obligations.

Alongside primogeniture, the unity and indivisibility of the lands, and exemption from imperial jurisdiction, the privileges also included a long list of symbolic-ceremonial preferences: the title of archduke, the hereditary office of an imperial master of the hunt (*Reichsjägermeister*), the first place among all the princes, and above all the special modalities of the investiture. Frederick III added, among other things, a right that was otherwise reserved exclusively for the emperor within the Empire, namely, to carry out all kinds of changes in status: to grant a patent of nobility and coat of arms, create doctors, masters, notaries, and judges, declare the illegitimate legitimate and the dishonorable honorable, and carry out demotions in rank.¹¹⁵ Taken together, all of these prerogatives had the goal of fusing the hereditary Austrian lands into a territorial entity and to elevate the rank of the house in Europe above that of all the members of the Empire. The deficits vis-à-vis the electors, which the Duke of Austria was not, were to be more than compensated for. The *Privilegium maius* invented for the lands of the house of Austria an entirely new status that cut across the existing classification system of the Empire. What was missing, though, was the royal title and feudal independence. The circumstance that the hereditary lands still had to be taken as a fief from the Empire therefore had to be downplayed as much as possible; in fact, it had to be reinterpreted as a special privilege, if at all possible.

The investiture ritual served that purpose. However, as we have seen, it had never been performed in the way the *Privilegium maius* envisioned; the archdukes had never insisted on it, and instead had the emperors confirm by charter that omission of the ritual did not in any way detract from their rights.¹¹⁶ They used their privileges more internally against the estates in their lands than externally against the Empire. Only after the house of Habsburg, under Frederick III, held both the imperial dignity and the archduchy did it become possible to fully exploit the symbolic added value of the *Privilegium maius*. But in fact it was only Charles V who made full use of this possibility in Augsburg.

The ritual, as I have noted, was in many respects exceptional.¹¹⁷ To begin with, the act did not take place in the city of Augsburg, but near Wellenburg Castle in the Margraviate of Burgau, that is, on neighboring Austrian territory. There the customary, gold-draped scaffold had been erected in an open field, along with the hut as a changing room. Contrary to the customary ceremonial logic, the emperor and his retinue went out to greet the vassal, and not the other way around. The privilege guaranteed the archdukes that they would receive their fiefs "in their land and on their soil, and were not obligated to do so outside."[118] Many thousands, the imperial herald Kaspar Sturm wrote, had come from the city and the surrounding countryside. As usual, the tournament-like staging of the riding with the banners took place with great material pomp and military outlay before the eyes of the entire court society, which was seated on specially erected bleachers and included the papal legate and delegates from France, Portugal, England, Poland, Venice, Ferrara, and Mantua. The emperor underscored the extraordinary nature of the scene by ordering a court giant and court dwarf to ride out on a real-life camel "as though to a wondrous spectacle"—after all, part of the staging of power was to arouse astonishment.

Initially the act followed the script of the solemn investments as described above: the emperor sat "adorned in majesty" (*in maiestate*) and wore the pontifical regalia. A German, a Burgundian, and a Spanish herald marked out the expanse of his rulership. The electors of Mainz, Saxony, and Brandenburg were present in person, and the others—including Ferdinand, King of Bohemia—were represented by envoys; they held the regalia of the crown, orb, sword, and scepter. The group that rode around the throne was comprised of 350 horsemen of "every nation"—German, Bohemian, Spanish, Hungarian, Croatian—and was led by Georg Truchsess von Waldburg, Ferdinand's governor in Württemberg. That, too, was a deliberate choice, for Charles V had proscribed the Duke of Württemberg and transferred the land to his brother. Four princes of the realm who held fiefs from the crown of Bohemia[119] acted as advocates and asked that the emperor enfeoff King Ferdinand "in the place of His Imperial Majesty and for himself" with all of their lands, be they "inherited, purchased or acquired by the sword." The emperor was thus investing not only his brother, but simultaneously also himself, since the two of them were joint holders of the fiefs of the house of Austria. The emperor, too, was an imperial prince and had to be invested as such; in this instance he was both feudal lord and vassal.[120]

In keeping with the *Privilegium maius*, Ferdinand's appearance was staged in every detail as that of an equal. According to the herald's report, he appeared with a noble retinue of another seven hundred horsemen who were adorned with the red-and-white flags of the house of Austria and carried with them the eighteen feudal banners of the individual territories, including that of the Duchy of Württemberg. Two Austrian heralds accompanied him as living symbols of rulership, for we are told that his privileges allowed him to keep as many heralds as he wished. The hereditary marshal of Austria carried the sword ahead of him as the symbol of judicial power. Ferdinand was dressed in the archducal habit of red velvet edged in ermine, in his hand he carried a scepter, and on his head was the archducal hat, which looked "like the way an ancient crown used to be fashioned."[121] All of this was indistinguishable from an elector's habit. While all others dismounted and knelt before the emperor, he alone, "in accordance with all the privileges and liberties of the princes of Austria, remained seated on his horse," rode up the ramp to the investiture scaffold, doffed the archducal hat, recited the oath on the evangelary, and received the fiefs, still seated high on his horse, by touching along with the emperor every single banner. He did not have to kiss the imperial sword that the Elector of Saxony handed to him; he only had to touch it. After that he turned around and rode back to his tent. While most of the electors remained seated on the scaffold, the emperor changed his clothes and, together with Ferdinand, participated in the great "knightly joust and melee."[122] In the evening they returned to the city and held a banquet, where the royal vassal did not, as usual, appear as a guest, but as the host of the emperor.

The solemn ritual was mirrored by a solemn written confirmation. A few days later, the emperor had a charter drawn up renewing all of the old privileges and affirming them with a gold seal.[123] For contemporaries it was not the charter but the highly singular act that left an impression and made visible the relationship between the house of Austria and the emperorship. That was ensured also by the second-order enactments: the printed and illustrated herald reports of Kaspar Sturm, and Jörg Breus the Elder's pictorial series of eighteen individual woodcuts (figure 7).[124]

In his account, the herald disseminated the fiction that the oldest privileges of the house of Austria were as old as the Roman emperorship itself. The charters inserted into the *Privilegium maius*, most of them granted by Julius Caesar and emperor Nero, which Petrarch and other humanists had already recognized as crude forgeries at first glance, attributed to the Habsburg dynasty a salvific mission.[125] For nearly two thousand years, the herald wrote, the Roman Empire had been maintained undivided by the "Germans." Among them, however, no lineage was as powerful, great, and old as that of the princes of Austria, which had been governing "as long as the Roman Empire has existed so far."[126] But the Empire, in the present "dangerous recent times ... has fallen into great decline, such that it is teetering greatly to the point of falling ... only the most clement blood of Austria will secure it again with God's help." Nobody had won more victories against Turks, pagans, and unbelievers than the Austrian emperors and princes; that is why they were endowed by God with the highest blessings and had been honored by many emperors before all other princes with the highest liberties.

Whether the *Privilegium maius* was entirely or partially forged had long since ceased to matter. Already the recognition by Frederick III had created facts on the ground. Through the enactment, the *Privilegium maius* retroactively acquired much greater authenticity. Now that the content of the charters of liberty had been staged before the eyes of the European noble society, and

Warhafftig anzaygung wie Kaiser Carl der fünft ettlichen Fürsten auff dem Reychstag zů Augspurg im M. CCCCC.XXX. jar gehalten/Regalia vnd Lehen vnder dem fan gelihen/was auch jr Kai. Maie. vnd der selben brů- der Künig Ferdinand zů Hungern vnd Behem ꝛc. Auch anndere Churfürsten / Fürsten vnnd Stende des Reichs für Räthe vnd Adels personen auff solchem Reichstag gehept haben.

Figure 7. Investiture of Archduke Ferdinand by Charles V in 1530. Title-page woodcut from Kaspar Sturm, *Wahrhafftig anzaygung wie Kayser Carl der fünfte ...*, Augsburg 1530, Vienna, Österreichische Nationalbibliothek.

all the princes and delegates had confirmed it by their presence, the question of whether the privilege was real or not was no longer an issue. The Mainz observer Tetleben, no less than a cleric writing in Latin, knew nothing of the forgery. Even Samuel Pufendorf, who denounced the privilege in the seventeenth century as a "serious mutilation of the body of the Empire," was not entirely clear about its authenticity.[127]

The spectacular act of investiture at the imperial diet had a whole host of dimensions of meaning: it affirmed the unique status, rank, and splendor of the house of Austria and its unusual relationship with the Empire; it demonstrated the close ties between imperial title and dynastic rulership in the hands of the Habsburgs; it committed the participants to the problematic transfer of the Duchy of Württemberg to Austria; and it once again assigned the electors and princes—and especially also the Protestants—their places within the overall order of the Empire. With that, the act not least laid the groundwork for the election and coronation of Ferdinand as king of the Romans, which took place in Cologne and Aachen following the end of the imperial diet in Augsburg.[128]

Unfinished Recess

Let us return once more to the religious question at the imperial diet. One month before the unusual investiture of Ferdinand, the orthodox theologians drafted a response to the *Confessio* of the Protestants. Unlike the Protestant document, this *Confutatio* was publicly read out aloud on 3 August in a general assembly of the estates at city hall.[129] It was never handed over in its entirety to the estates either then or later, but only read out in excerpts in all further deliberations. The intent was to prevent it from being printed and discussed point for point, that is, from becoming after all the topic of a public disputation.[130] The mere fact that the Lutherans actually demanded the release of the document so they could verify whether the *Confutatio* was grounded in Holy Scripture was interpreted by some orthodox princes as *lèse majesté*.[131]

The wording of the *Confutatio* repeated what the emperor's symbolic enactment on the diet had already anticipated by explicitly granting the emperor the decision-making power on the religious question. Since the Protestants would not accept that, they had no option but to change the mode of deliberation and switch to negotiations in the manner of a religious colloquy.[132] By way of majority decision, the estates of the realm set up two successive committees, half of whose members were Catholic and half Lutheran. Even if that did not in the end lead to the desired success, it was a momentous symbolic and instrumental step, for this was the first time that the two "parties" faced each other as formal equals at an imperial diet.

But the conflict was not settled in this way, either—as so often, it was simply left unresolved. Already on 6 August, Philipp of Hesse had departed on some pretext against the explicit will of the emperor. After the committees had failed to arrive at an agreement, Charles V, in a separate Religious Recess (*Religionsabschied*) on 22 September, issued an ultimatum to the Protestants to return to the fold of the Roman Church and forbade them to leave the diet. Even though he had the city gates heavily guarded, he was unable to prevent them from departing one by one "without a recess," thereby allowing them to contest that the Imperial Recess (*Reichsabschied*) was binding upon them. Even the council of the city of Augsburg, with whom the emperor had carried on lengthy negotiations, refused to accept the Religious Recess.

The imperial diet continued for quite a bit longer. It was only on 19 November that the entire text of the imperial recess was read out to the estates still present and accepted by the majority, though a minority protested once again. The document contained a long series of other important issues: organizing the enforcement of public order (*Policey*) and the mint, reforming the Imperial Chamber Court (*Reichskammergericht*) and setting up the Imperial Districts (*Reichskreise*), codifying criminal law, and much more—matters that had been deliberated and resolved quietly in various committees, unhampered by the religious quarrels and with the city's public paying little attention. This seems symptomatic of the character of this imperial diet: it was a forum for sober deliberation and decision making about shared problems, as well as the great stage on which fundamental questions of authority and obedience were contested. From the very beginning, the symbolic staging of the relationship between the emperor and the imperial estates had set the framework for any discursive dispute. However, success for the imperial script always presupposed at least the personal presence of the participants. In the end, the staging was thwarted by the fact that the Protestants simply sidestepped the joint recess ritual through their absence. While they had still yielded to a ritual façade of consensus by participating in the investiture of the Master of the Teutonic Order, they now refused such a staging of consensus, which would have bound them to the shared outcome. When modern constitutional historians write that the Augsburg Imperial Recess nevertheless had the "force of law," this is an anachronistic verdict,[133] for it implies that they adopt *one* of several interpretations and presupposes clear rules of conduct accepted ahead of time by all participants. But those rules, precisely, did not exist, and this is why shared rituals of consensus were so important. If those rituals in the end did not materialize, as was the case here, there was no legal basis shared by all.

Interim Summary

At the imperial diet of Augsburg in 1530, symbolic forms of communication played a fundamental role. Ritual conflicts over the Feast of Corpus Christi, the Eucharist, and Protestant preaching characterized the course of the Protestant movement in numerous cities of the Empire in more or less spectacular fashion, similar to Augsburg. Everywhere, the Protestant movement had upset the communal symbolism of unity, which took place in sacral rituals, and in 1530 these processes were by no means completed in most cities. At the imperial diet in Augsburg, the same conflict unfolded on the level of the Empire: its unity as a sacral community, symbolically and ritually created each time by election and coronation, *Hoftage* and imperial diets, was disturbed, and it was an open question how it could be reestablished. Secular and ecclesiastical service, external and internal obedience, symbolic and discursive dispute, religious practice and faith doctrine—in Augsburg in 1530, issues that had previously not been separated now diverged in a controversial way. Reformation doctrine created a conflict and compelled an explicit discussion where previously there had been a self-evident if vague unity, and potential disagreements had been covered up. This created a new and much more complex situation.

In this historically unprecedented situation, deeply divergent interpretations of the situation confronted one another. There was a fundamental disagreement not only about the religious questions themselves, but also about the procedure for managing the conflict and the roles of the participants. The actors tried—each in his own way—to continue acting within the framework of the old order, though they now interpreted it in very different ways. Charles V continued trying to present himself as a mediator, not as a party to the conflict. While the Protestants, in spite of their persistence on the religious question, still sought to portray themselves as obedient subjects of the emperor, they defined the boundaries of their obligation of fealty and the imperial authority differently than he did. And the orthodox estates likewise insisted that they were not a party to the conflict, but advisors to the emperor. Yet the old coordinates were no longer valid, since they presupposed the fundamental unity of secular and ecclesiastical order. This very unity was in question, however, ever since conscience had come into play as the highest authority. Everything, therefore, depended on successful symbolic staging, for whatever was ritually enacted by all bound the participants for the future.

This is why the emperor tried from the outset to gain control of the events with symbolic means, so as to portray himself successfully as judge and mediator, as the supreme ruler and highest authority. Initially the Protestants fit themselves into this symbolic framework and presented themselves in the ceremony as obedient members of the Empire. But it was not made easy for them: the staging of papal power as an authority equal to that of the emperor was something they could not accept. The prohibition of preaching and the Feast of Corpus Christi were intended to coerce the Protestants from the beginning into participating in their own symbolic marginalization. This symbolic management by the emperor stood in contrast to his verbal offer of mediation, gave it the lie, and constrained the leeway of negotiations from the outset. The reading of the *Confessio Augustana* then turned into the stage for a struggle over communicative superiority: the Protestants were concerned with affirming their faith publicly and "loudly," and wanted to enter into an argumentative debate with the opposing party. The orthodox estates, meanwhile, were concerned with preventing precisely any public disputation and any appearance as a party. Putting it in a nutshell, one could say that the emperor and the orthodox bet chiefly on symbolic strategies, while the Protestants bet on discursive ones. In this case, both sides failed in the end.

Obedience toward the emperor now encountered its limit in obedience toward conscience and Holy Scripture. Most of the Protestants eventually demonstrated as much with their departure. By refusing to concede the ritual recess to the emperor, they contested his role as mediator. Lest this lead over the long term to a fragmentation and overthrow of the entire system, it was imperative to find a new organization and introduce a new distinction, namely, between politics and religion. However, this distinction was first drawn in symbolic action: in the differentiation between secular and ecclesiastical service in the sacral acts of the imperial diet.

The solution that emerged for the very first time in the opinion of the theologians of electoral Saxony concerning the Corpus Christi procession, though it by no means prevailed at the time, eventually proved—in a long and conflictual process—to be the only sustainable one.[134] The elector, they wrote, had been invited by the emperor "to perform his office, not the mass or divine service."[135] Service to the emperor had to be performed, while conscience had to decide about worship service. This amounted to a previously unknown distinction between "religion" and "political rule." Subsequently, it became the custom for Protestant princes, if they personally participated in the imperial diets at all, to either skip the mass entirely or at least not participate in the Eucharist. During the election and coronation masses, the practice was also for Protestants to leave during the offertory.[136] This means the conflict remained continually present and visible symbolically, but it did not explode the entire system; instead, it was integrated into the ritual, symbolically incorporated into the staging. In this way, divergent interpretations of the sacred order of the Empire could exist side by side, and at the same time Protestants and Catholics could remain members of a single political body.

This, too, reveals in exemplary fashion the potency of symbolic-ritual acts. Value conflicts that cannot be resolved either by negotiated compromises or authoritative decisions must be endured in every society without threatening its survival.[137] A minimum of communality must be continually reaffirmed, even if clashing values cannot in fact be resolved. That is precisely what the rituals of the Empire accomplished—election and coronation masses, investitures and openings of imperial diets: they staged and preserved a basic consensus that was aimed at the shared order beyond all confessional conflicts. But the year 1530 was a long way from the day when the separation of political obedience and religious freedom of conscience on the part of the imperial estates could have been accepted. It would take another twenty-five years before, for the first time and once again in Augsburg, a contractual agreement was arrived at, one still presented as temporary, the milestone *Pax Augustana* of 1555—and it, too, would not last.[138]

Notes

1. Schlögl, "Der Glaube Alteuropas."
2. Weinfurter, "Wie das Reich heilig wurde"; Müller, *Heiliges Römisches Reich Deutscher Nation*; Moraw, Aretin, and Hammerstein, "Reich," 423–56, 456–86.
3. Sieber-Lehmann, "Verhältnis von Papst und Kaiser."
4. According to Popitz, *Phänomene der Macht*, 132ff.; see Sofsky and Paris, *Figurationen sozialer Macht*, 33ff.
5. Prodi, *Das Sakrament der Herrschaft* and *Glaube und Eid*; Holenstein, "Seelenheil und Untertanenpflicht"; Schreiner, "Iuramentum."
6. Grass, *Reichskleinodien*; Becker and Ruess, *Reichskleinodien*; Petersohn, "Über monarchische Insignien"; Fillitz, "Die Reichskleinodien," 133–61; Kirchweger, "Reichskleinodien."
7. According to Hahn, "Funktionale und stratifikatorische Differenzierung."
8. Thus, the formulation in the preface to the description of the election and coronation of Maximilian II by Habersack; see Edelmayer, *Die Krönung Maximilians II.*, 96. On the election and coronation and their sacral character, see, from the vast literature, Schulte, *Kaiser- und Königskrönungen*; Schramm, *Geschichte des englischen Königtums*; Berbig, "Krönungsritus"; Dotzauer, "Ausformung"; for a brief overview, see Rogge, *Wahl und Krönung*.
9. Hofmann, *Repräsentation*, 121ff.
10. Golden Bull, chapter XXIII.
11. In detail, see Dotzauer, "Anrufung."
12. According to Pope Gregory the Great; see Schreiner, "Wahl, Amtsantritt," 93.
13. Becht, *Pium consensus tueri*, 533–34.
14. In general, see Kohnle and Wolgast, "Die Reichstage der Reformationszeit"; Rabe, *Deutsche Geschichte 1500–1600*; Schilling, *Aufbruch und Krise*; Kohler, *Karl V.*; Lutz et al., *Aus der Arbeit an den Reichstagen*; still worth reading is Ranke, *Reformation*, 546–80.
15. Schlaich, "Majoritas"; Becker, "Protestatio."
16. Förstemann, *Urkundenbuch* 2:3, 7–8; see also Schirrmacher, *Briefe und Acten*, 33–34.
17. On the imperial diet as a whole, see the survey of scholarship on the 450th anniversary by Neuhaus, "Augsburger Reichstag des Jahres 1530"; Immenkötter, *Einheit im Glauben*; Iserloh, *Confessio Augustana und Confutatio*; Aulinger, *Das Bild des Reichstages*, 328–46.
18. Thus, the group of those who had formulated the protestation in 1529 was different from and larger than the one that presented the *Confessio Augustana* in 1530. Especially the southern German cities went a different way in 1530; they did not take part in the committees to deliberate the religious question, and four of them submitted their own professions of faith.
19. Kohler, *Quellen zur Geschichte Karls V.*, 150–51.
20. Roll, *Das zweite Reichsregiment*; on the category of obedience, see Luttenberger, "Friedensgedanke," 63.
21. Scholarship to date has taken no interest in the symbolic-ritual side of the question of resistance. On the discursive side, see most recently especially Haug-Moritz, *Schmalkaldische Bund*; Friedeburg, *Widerstandsrecht*.
22. The relevant volume of the records of the imperial diet has not been published yet; instead, see Förstemann, *Urkundenbuch*; see also the protocol of the councilor of electoral Mainz, Tetleben, *Protokoll*; diaries of the orthodox Augsburg cathedral canon Clemens

Sender, *Chronik*, and the so-called *Langenmantelsche Chronik*, which has a much more positive stance toward the Protestants, and whose author came from one of the Augsburg councilor families; see also the records of the Frankfurt envoy Johannes Aurifaber, Schirrmacher, *Briefe und Acten*; Coelestin, *Historia comitiorum*; correspondences between Protestant theologians and the Nuremberg city envoys, in *Corpus Reformatorum*, vol. 2; correspondence of the Straßburg envoys, in Virck, *Politische Correspondenz*; correspondence of the papal legates, in *Nuntiaturberichte* 1, suppl. vol. 1; Ehses, "Kardinal Lorenzo Campeggio." The number of contemporary publications that appeared about this imperial diet surpasses all the others; Schubert, *Reichstage*, 234, counts more than thirty items. On the sources, see Aulinger, *Das Bild des Reichstages*, 329–30; on the rank conflicts, especially between Salzburg and Magdeburg, see Willich, "Rangstreit," 100ff.

23. On the imperial diet of 1530 from the perspective of the history of Augsburg, see Weller, "Reichsstadt und Reformation," 68ff.; Gottlieb, *Geschichte der Stadt Augsburg*, 391ff., 423ff.; Roth, *Augsburgs Reformationsgeschichte*, 329ff.; most recently, see Gößner, *Weltliche Kirchenhoheit und reichsstädtische Reformation*.

24. For example, see his policy toward electoral Saxony, in Förstemann, *Urkundenbuch*, 1:221–22; for his policy toward Ulm, see *Corpus Reformatorum*, vol.2, No. 714, col. 86–87.

25. *Langenmantelsche Chronik*, 364; see Sender, *Chronik*, 252–53.

26. *Langenmantesche Chronik*, 367.

27. Tetleben, *Protokoll*, 56ff.; Sender, *Chronik*, 262; *Langenmantelsche Chronik*, 368; Förstemann, *Urkundenbuch*, vol. 1, Nos. 83–84, 238ff., 291–92; Schirrmacher, *Briefe und Acten*, 72–73.

28. Tetleben, *Protokoll*, 67 and 57. The polling quarrel between the Electors of Mainz and Saxony was also settled temporarily with a compromise.

29. Tetleben, *Protokoll*, 67.

30. In general, see Müller, "Kardinal Lorenzo Campeggio"; Ehses, "Kardinal Lorenzo Campeggio," 17, 395ff.

31. See the section "Investiture as a Dynastic Demonstration" in this chapter.

32. Förstemann, *Urkundenbuch*, vol. 1, No. 89, 248ff.; Tetleben, *Protokoll*, 60–61; *Corpus Reformatorum*, vol.2, col.106.

33. On the quarrel over rank between the cardinals and the electors, see, for example, Crusius, *De praeeminentia*, book 2, chap. 3; book 4, chaps. 2–3; for the curial ceremonial as an instrument of the papal claim to supremacy, see in general Visceglia and Brice, *Cérémonial et rituel à Rome*; Visceglia, *La città rituale*; Zunckel, "Rangordnungen der Orthodoxie?"

34. *Langenmantelsche Chronik*, 368.

35. Ranke, *Reformation*, 543ff.; Aulinger, *Das Bild des Reichstages*, 328ff.; Weller, "Reichsstadt und Reformation," 86ff.; Förstemann, *Urkundenbuch*, 1:258; on the medieval tradition of the entry, see Schenk, *Zeremoniell und Politik*.

36. Sturm, *Wie die Römische Keiserliche Maiestät* (also in Schirrmacher, *Briefe und Acten*, 54ff.; Förstemann, *Urkundenbuch*, vol. 1, Nos. 92a–b, 257ff.); in detail, see Sender, *Chronik*, 262ff.; in brief, see *Langenmantelsche Chronik*, 368ff.; Aurifaber in Schirrmacher, *Briefe und Acten*, 54ff.; Tetleben, *Protokoll*, 61; Campeggio in *Nuntiaturberichte*, 62ff.; see also Justus Jonas to Martin Luther, 18 June 1530, WA Briefe 5, No. 1590, 366ff. See also Aulinger, *Das Bild des Reichstages*, 329ff.; Schubert, *Reichstage*, 234–35.

37. See above figure 6; *Welt im Umbruch*, No. 91, p. 172; see the drawing of the triumphal procession of Maximilian in Aulinger, *Das Bild des Reichstages*, 85–86; see also Rudolph, "Visuelle Kultur des Reiches."
38. Sender, *Chronik*, 263; Sturm, *Wie die Römische Keiserliche Maiestät*, fol. A iii; namely, the Duke of Lüneburg, the Margrave of Brandenburg, the Landgrave of Hesse, and Count Wolfgang of Anhalt.
39. Sender, *Chronik*, 276; see Kantorowicz, "The 'King's Advent,'" 211–12; see the criticism by the Protestants in Uhlhorn, *Urbanus Rhegius*, 153.
40. Sender, *Chronik*, 277–78, who never misses an opportunity to mention the emperor's special humility and piety.
41. Förstemann, *Urkundenbuch*, 1:258; nothing about this is in Campeggio's own correspondence.
42. Förstemann, *Neues Urkundenbuch*, 156; see Weller, "Reichsstadt und Reformation," 70.
43. Justus Jonas to Luther, WA Briefe 5, 367–68; Schirrmacher, *Briefe und Acten*, 55. When the legate gave his blessing in the cathedral, Philipp of Hesse supposedly ducked behind a candelabra and laughed; see Aulinger, *Das Bild des Reichstages*, 335.
44. Justus Jonas to Luther, WA Briefe 5, 367. Six years earlier Campeggio had already clashed with the citizens of Augsburg; see Roth, *Augsburgs Reformationsgeschichte*, 335.
45. Sturm, *Wie die Römisch Keiserliche Maiestät*, fol. B v. The otherwise very detailed account by the Augsburg cleric Clemens Sender mentions nothing of the sort; Campeggio himself only highlights that he recited the benediction. See *Nuntiaturberichte*, 62.
46. Förstemann, *Urkundenbuch*, 1:100ff., attributes the list to Luther.
47. See, for example, Luther's tract "Von der Freiheit eines Christenmenschen," WA Briefe 7, 20–38; see Hamm, "Normative Zentrierung"; Muir, *Ritual in Early Modern Europe*; Karant-Nunn, *Reformation of Ritual*; Jussen and Koslofsky, *Kulturelle Reformation*; Berns, "Luthers Papstkritik."
48. Schnitzler, *Ikonoklasmus—Bildersturm*; Eire, *War Against the Idols*; Scribner, *Bilder und Bildersturm*.
49. Weller, "Reichsstadt und Reformation," 70; Sender, *Chronik*, 179.
50. See the *Confessio Augustana* itself; see also the previous letters and memoranda for the elector in Förstemann, *Urkundenbuch*, 1:71ff., 103, 110.
51. *Corpus Reformatorum*, vol. 2, col. 107–8; Schirrmacher, *Briefe und Acten*, 58ff.; Förstemann, *Urkundenbuch*, 1:268.
52. Angenendt, *Geschichte der Religiosität*, 491ff., 506; Rubin, *Corpus Christi*, 353ff.
53. Lentes, "Counting Piety"; Hamm, "Einheit und Vielfalt."
54. Rubin, *Corpus Christi*, 353ff.
55. Corpus Christi processions were often the object of confessional provocations; see, for example, Löther, *Prozessionen*, 320ff. This is true also for the period after 1648; see François, *Die unsichtbare Grenze*, 216ff.
56. Luther, "Vom Anbeten des Sakraments des heiligen Leichnams Christi," WA Briefe 11, 431–45, here 445.
57. Grundmann, "Philipp von Hessen."
58. Luther, "Vom Anbeten des Sakraments des heiligen Leichnams Christi," WA Briefe 11, 433.
59. Blickle, *Kommunalisierung und Christianisierung*, 24.
60. Förstemann, *Urkundenbuch*, vol. 1, No. 93, 267–68.
61. Sender, *Chronik*, 277–78, 287. The emperor made other efforts to revive orthodox practice, such as the celebration of Saint John on 24 June, where the Landgrave of Hesse once again attracted attention: "He acted as though he were mad and out of his

mind when the venerable sacrament was lifted during the service; he also did not want to kneel down."
62. Schirrmacher, *Briefe und Acten*, 62–63, 65.
63. Ibid., 65–66; Förstemann, *Urkundenbuch*, 1:267ff.
64. *Corpus Reformatorum*, vol.2, col.106; Schirrmacher, *Briefe und Acten*, 396; see Roth, *Augsburgs Reformationsgeschichte*, 337; Weller, "Reichsstadt und Reformation," 90–91.
65. See Sturm, *Wie die Römische Keiserliche Maiestät*; Grundmann, "Philipp von Hessen," 365–66, 415; *Corpus Reformatorum*, vol.2, col.106.
66. Luther, WA Briefe 11, 431–47; on the Lutherans' understanding of sacraments and signs in the *Confessio Augustana*, see Beinert, "Sakramentsbegriff."
67. Karant-Nunn, *Reformation of Ritual*; Muir, *Ritual in Early Modern Europe*; Wandel, *Eucharist*.
68. Dotzauer, "Anrufung," 16ff.
69. RTA JR 7/1, 547ff.
70. *Corpus Reformatorum*, vol.2, col. 121ff.
71. Schirrmacher, *Briefe und Acten*, 74.
72. Tetleben, *Protokoll*, 68; on Philipp's behavior in the cathedral following the entry, see Aulinger, *Das Bild des Reichstages*, 335 footnote 31.
73. Sender, *Chronik*, 282; see also Grundmann, "Philipp von Hessen," 367.
74. Scholarship has paid remarkably little attention to procedural questions; exceptions are Laubach, "'Nationalversammlung' im 16. Jahrhundert"; Becker, "Verhandlungen"; and for the Reformation period in general, see Luttenberger, "Reichstag unter Karl V."; on the still very open procedural mode at the imperial diet of 1541, see Luttenberger, "Konfessionelle Parteilichkeit."
75. For example, Hesse vs. electoral Saxony or Straßburg vs. Nuremberg: Virck, *Politische Correspondenz*, 457ff., 473; on this, see Laubach, "'Nationalversammlung' im 16. Jahrhundert," 20ff.
76. As it is, it was difficult to clearly distinguish imperial diets and concilia; see Meuthen, *Reichstage und Kirche*. On the assessment by electoral Saxony and Hesse in 1530, see Grundmann, "Philipp von Hessen," 345ff., 361, 363; Becker, "Verhandlungen," 131; Laubach, "'Nationalversammlung' im 16. Jahrhundert."
77. Supplication is mentioned, for example, by Tetleben, *Protokoll*, 75.
78. See Virck, *Politische Correspondenz*, 445–46. On the forms of speech at concilia and imperial diets between an extremely ritualized and a discursively open form, see Helmrath, "Rhetorik und 'Akademisierung.'"
79. Fuchs, *Konfession und Gespräch*, 363–88, on Augsburg, is concerned more with the content than the form of the religious negotiations.
80. Schirrmacher, *Briefe und Acten*, 79–80, Latin version 75ff.; on the opening, see Tetleben, *Protokoll*, 70–71; *Langenmantelsche Chronik*, 373–74; Sender, *Chronik*, 287–88.
81. *Langenmantelsche Chronik*, 374; Sender, *Chronik*, 287–88; for a sketch of the seating arrangement, see Tetleben, *Protokoll*, 76.
82. The most detailed description is in *Langenmantelsche Chronik*, 374ff.; Luther to Cordatus in Zwickau, 6 June 1530, WA Briefe 5, 441–42; Tetleben, *Protokoll*, 74ff.
83. Jonas to Luther, 25 June 1530, WA Briefe 5, 392: "non quidem in tam frequenti consessu, sed in cubiculo Caesaris coram principibus quibusdam." Luther to Cordatus in Zwickau, 6 June 1530, WA Briefe 5, 441–42. See Luther to Hausmann in Zwickau, WA Briefe 5, 440: "confessionam nostram … esse recitatam … coram Cesare et totius imperii principibus et Episcopis publice, tantum exclusa turba vulgi, in ipso palatio Cesaris"; see Schirrmacher, *Briefe und Acten*, 79ff.

84. Tetleben, *Protokoll*, 81ff.
85. Luttenberger, "Reichstag unter Karl V.," 38, speaks of a "strong courtly imprint."
86. Virck, *Politische Correspondenz*, 462ff., 466.
87. Schirrmacher, *Briefe und Acten*, 100; nearly all the princes rode along, except for those of electoral Saxony and Hesse and their retinue.
88. Sender, *Chronik*, 305.
89. Sender, *Chronik*, 287: Philipp of Hesse was present, "He acted as though he were mad and out of his mind when the venerable sacrament was lifted during the service; he also did not want to kneel down."
90. Sender, *Chronik*, 292. The solemn episcopal consecration of the bishop of Constance by the Elector of Mainz could be mentioned: Virck, *Politische Correspondenz*, 467; Tetleben, *Protokoll*, 80–81.
91. Schirrmacher, *Briefe und Acten*, 99; Sender, *Chronik*, 293–94; *Langenmantelsche Chronik*, 379–80; Tetleben, *Protokoll*, 79–80.
92. See chapter 1, section "Conflict: Pomerania."
92. Sturm, *Wahrhafftig anzeygung*; with corrections, see Sturm, *Wiewol hievor*; "Pompa Gualteri Cronbergi" in Coelestin, *Historia comitiorum*, 1:250b; Tetleben, *Protokoll*, 91ff.; in detail, see Sender, *Chronik*, 298ff.; in brief, see *Langenmantelsche Chronik*, 383.
93. Sender, *Chronik*, 299; Tetleben, *Protokoll*, 91; compare the regalia with that of the pope.
94. Sender, *Chronik*, 299 (only the son of the orthodox Duke of Saxony was not among them).
95. Article 28 of the *Confessio Augustana* deals with the episcopate; on the different positions, see Decot, "Confessio Augustana und Reichsverfassung," 29ff.: here the Protestant strategy was supposedly to grant the bishop's jurisdiction, but on the condition that they not burden the conscience of people; in this vein, see also Luther's tract "An die Geistlichen auf dem Augsburger Reichstag," WA Briefe 30/II, 268–356.
96. Herrmann, *Der deutsche Orden unter Walter von Cronberg*; Höß, "Das Reich und Preußen."
97. RTA MR 6:57.
98. RTA JR 3, No. 175, p.842; RTA JR 4, No. 136, pp. 566ff.
99. Cronberg went before the Imperial Chamber Court (*Reichskammergericht*) and obtained the mandate of a ban against Albrecht of Brandenburg; the emperor declared the Cracow feudal treaty with the Polish king as null and void. In 1532, the Imperial Chamber Court imposed the solemn imperial ban first on Albrecht, which he ignored, and later on all of the Prussian territorial estates, because they had not renounced their fealty to him. Enforcing these bans, however, was out of the question; rather, they were repeatedly suspended by the Imperial Chamber Court. Still, the successors of Walter of Cronberg kept alive their claim to the Prussian lands of the Teutonic Order until the end of the empire.
100. Tetleben, *Protokoll*, 91; see also Bruckauf, *Fahnlehen und Fahnenbelehnung*, 87ff.
101. Sturm, *Warhafftig anzeygung*, fol. B ii.
102. Ibid., fol. B iii.
103. Tetleben, *Protokoll*, 93–94: "quia ob heresim lutteranam privatur sua dignitate."
104. *Langenmantelsche Chronik*, 383.
105. Scheidemantel, *Repertorium*, 1:383; Lünig, *Theatrum Ceremoniale*, 2:944–45; Ludewig, *Vollständige Erläuterung*, vol. 2 part 1, 501–2.

106. Elector Johann to Luther, 21 July 1530, Luther, WA Briefe 5:497–98. No. 1658; see Buder, *Nachricht von der Belehnung*, 5ff.; Virck, *Politische Correspondenz*, 477; Schirrmacher, *Briefe und Acten*, 100; Förstemann, *Urkundenbuch*, 1:221–22. Charles also refused to invest his successor, Johann Frederick of Saxony, and it was performed only in 1535 by Ferdinand.
107. See Belting, *Anthropology of Images*, 68.
108. See Buder, *Nachricht von der Belehnung*; Mentz, *Johann Friedrich der Großmütige*, 1:76ff., 2:60ff.; he does not address the investiture at all, even though he recognized that it was the "real main purpose of the costly trip," but takes an interest emphatically only in the "other negotiations." See also Klein, "Politik und Verfassung", 228–29; Kohler, *Antihabsburgische Politik*, 99ff.; Neuhaus, "Königswahl vivente imperatore," 13ff.; Laubach, "Nachfolge im Reich," 30ff.
109. Neuhaus, "Königswahl vivente imperatore."
110. Kohler, *Karl V.*, 205, mentions the concern that someone else might be elected king as a reason for coming to Augsburg; Aulinger, "Einleitung," in RTA JR 10/1, pp. 89ff., 190ff.; see Neuhaus, "Königswahl vivente imperatore"; Laubach, "Nachfolge im Reich"; in general, see also Aulinger, Machoczek, and Schweinzer-Burian, "Ferdinand I. und die Reichstage unter Kaiser Karl V."; Winkelbauer, *Ständefreiheit*, 1:29ff.
111. Tetleben, *Protokoll*, 70, 76–77; see in detail Begert, *Böhmen*, 303ff.
112. Sturm, *Geschichts beschreybung*.
113. Tetleben, *Protokoll*, 138ff.; in brief, see Schirrmacher, *Briefe und Acten*, 256–57; Campeggio in *Nuntiaturberichte*, 124.
114. 1358/59: Lhotsky, *Privilegium maius*; Hödl, "Bestätigung und Erweiterung"; Moraw, "'Privilegium maius'"; Sauter, *Herrschaftsrepräsentation*, 159ff.; Schubert, *Reichstage*, 234.
115. Lhotsky, *Privilegium maius*, 34; Hödl, "Bestätigung und Erweiterung," 234.
116. The investiture is not mentioned either in the literature on the *Privilegium maius* or that on Ferdinand I; see, for example, Kohler, *Ferdinand I.*; Fuchs and Kohler, *Kaiser Ferdinand I.*; Winkelbauer, *Ständefreiheit*. Lhotsky, *Privilegium maius*, 32, even believes that such an investiture "was never really carried out"; he thus overlooks the ritual of 1530 and mentions only the written confirmation of the privilege of 8 September, 1530. But compare Aulinger, *Das Bild des Reichstages*, 342ff.
117. Sturm, *Geschichts beschreybung*; Tetleben, *Protokoll*, 138–39.
118. What follows is based on Sturm, *Geschichts beschreybung*; see also his *Wahrhafftig anzeygung*.
119. The dukes Frederic of Bavaria and Georg of Saxony, Margrave Georg of Brandenburg, and Duke Ottheinrich of the Palatinate.
120. Thus, in Worms in 1495, the estates had demanded from Maximilian "let it be known to them" which lordships he held in fief from the empire, "so that henceforth these would be recognized as fiefs by and received from Roman emperors and kings, as was proper"; Imperial Recess, 1495, Articles 17–18, in RTA MR 5/1, No. 1593, p. 1147; at the assembly in Lindau in 1496, this was on a long list of unfulfilled obligations with which the royal councilors were reproached; see RTA MR 6, No. 121, p. 202. Fundamentally, Emperor Matthias obligated himself in the electoral capitulation of 1612 to request the renewal of his fiefs from the empire like any other vassal.
121. Sturm, *Geschichts beschreybung*; see also Tetleben, *Protokoll*, 138: "factus est ad instar corone regalis."

122. At this German form of the tournament, six knightly packs confronted each other with sword or lance and fought "like a skirmish that would take place in a war and real field." In spite of all the careful staging, the king himself was "once suddenly toppled and thrown down."
123. Lhotsky, *Privilegium maius*, 36–37.
124. "Römischer Kaiserlicher Maiestat Carolj des Fünfften belehnung vber das Haws Osterreich," woodcut by Jörg Breus the Elder, published by Hans Tirol in 1536; see *Welt im Umbruch*, No. 95, 174–75; Essenwein, *Hans Tirol*. The text on the woodcut is largely identical to Sturm, *Geschichts beschreybung*.
125. On the dynastic memorial culture of the Habsburgs, see Müller, *Gedechtnus*; Althoff, "Merowinersage."
126. Sturm, *Geschichts beschreybung*, fol. A ii.
127. Tetleben, *Protokoll*, 139; Pufendorf, *Die Verfassung des deutschen Reiches*, 59. In the interim the documents had been nearly forgotten; Rudolf II had to have the originals searched for in 1597 before renewing them in 1599. They were then reaffirmed in writing in 1665 and 1729; see Lhotsky, *Privilegium maius*, 48ff.
128. On the election, see Neuhaus, "Königswahl vivente imperatore"; Kohler, *Antihabsburgische Politik*; on the coronation, see "Ordnung für die Krönungsfeierlichkeit in Aachen," 98–105; in general, see Kramp, *Krönungen*.
129. Immenkötter, *Confutatio*.
130. This holds also for the *Confessio* of the four southern German imperial cities, the *Tetrapolitana*, and its *Confutatio*; see Virck, *Politische Correspondenz*, 530–31, as well as on the prohibition of a disputation.
131. Sender, *Chronik*, 304.
132. Fuchs, *Konfession und Gespräch*, 364ff.; Immenkötter, "Rahmenbedingungen," 12ff.
133. Neuhaus, "Augsburger Reichstag des Jahres 1530"; for a different viewpoint, see Becker, "Verhandlungen," 149, who rightly opposes an institutional history that is solely "fixated on decisions." On the various stages between the Religious Recess on 22 September and the entire Imperial Recess on 19 November, see Decot, "Confessio Augustana und Reichsverfassung"; Becker, "Verhandlungen."
134. On the deliberations in the estate committee of the imperial diet of 1548, where this separation slowly emerged as a possible solution, see Rabe, *Reichsbund und Interim*, 420; Luttenberger, "Friedensgedanke," 236; Stollberg-Rilinger, "Kneeling Before God—Kneeling Before the Emperor."
135. See memorandum by the councilors of electoral Saxony in Schirrmacher, *Briefe und Actenst*, 65–66; Förstemann, *Urkundenbuch*, 1:267ff.; *Corpus Reformatorum* vol. 2, col. 201.
136. See Dotzauer, "Anrufung" and "Thronerhebung"; Berbig, "Krönungsritus"; Laubach, "Nachfolge im Reich"; Neuhaus, "Königswahl vivente imperatore;" Wanger, *Kaiserwahl und Krönung*; Rudolph, "Kontinuität und Dynamik"; see also chapter 3.
137. See, fundamentally, Luhmann, *Funktionen und Folgen formaler Organisation*, 239ff., 280–81.
138. Gotthard, *Augsburger Religionsfrieden*; Hoffmann et al., *Als Frieden möglich war*; Schilling and Smolinsky, *Augsburger Religionsfrieden 1555*.

CHAPTER 3

More Strife than Ever Before
Regensburg, 1653/54

The Mandate of the Peace of Westphalia

The imperial diet in 1653/54 saw more quarrels than ever before or after, wrote Johann Jakob Moser in the eighteenth century, a specialist in imperial public law who had surveyed the documents more thoroughly than anyone else.[1] At first glance that seems surprising—after all, this was the first imperial diet to be summoned in the wake of the peace treaties of Münster and Osnabrück in 1648. That year is generally seen as a milestone of German constitutional history, indeed of European history in general.[2] After more than thirty years of a destructive "German" war, which had been waged not least over the shape of the Empire, peace had finally come. And the difficult follow-up negotiations about troop withdrawals and other details had also been largely concluded in Nuremberg in 1649/50.[3] Why, then, was the first imperial diet one of conflict and quarrels?

To be sure, the signing of the treaties of Münster and Osnabrück had settled the war between the emperor and the Empire, in one camp, and the monarchs of Sweden and France, in the other; at the same time, the treaties had adopted a multitude of regulations about the state of affairs within the Empire. Among other things, the emperor was now explicitly bound on all important matters by the "common free choice and consent of all the estates of the Empire."[4] But a good deal had still remained open and been put off to the next imperial diet, which, according to Article VIII § 3 of the Treaty of Osnabrück, had to be summoned within six months. The treaty now assigned this diet the central role of putting in place the future shape of the Empire, above all by giving itself a new, fixed form. The procedural questions that were to be resolved once and for all were as old as they were fundamental: How often and how regularly should the imperial diet convene in the future? How should its procedural shortcomings be remedied? To what extent should the majority principle prevail at the diet, that is, to what extent should the minority be obligated by a decision even in the absence of its consent? How should the principle of confessional parity be implemented in the college of electors and in the imperial delegations? What role should the imperial cities play in the consultative proceedings? Should the imperial counts be given a new, fourth voice in the college of princes, and under what conditions should newly elevated princes be admitted there? The imperial diet was thus simultaneously the subject and object of its own reform. In addition, it was tasked with resolving fundamental questions concerning the relationship between emperor, electors, and estates: namely, to what extent the entire imperial diet should henceforth share in the rights previously reserved exclusively for the electors, above all the decision about the election of a king during the emperor's lifetime, the drafting of the electoral capitulation, and the imposition of the imperial ban. And the eternally contentious Imperial Register (Reichsmatrikel) was to be finally adjusted to reflect the changed reality.[5]

The thrust of these changes, which the assembly had been tasked with above all under pressure from Sweden, was obvious: to strengthen and simultaneously equalize the estates of the realm at the expense of the emperor and the electors. To the Swedish peace negotiator Salvius was attributed the statement that "at Osnabrück the beginning has been made to change the Empire, but at the first imperial diet one must overthrow the entire house, and especially the authority of the electors."[6] Others saw the situation exactly the other way around: they continued to see the emperor's pretension to power as the problem. The envoy from Brunswick-Wolfenbüttel maintained that the emperor's foremost goal at this imperial diet was "to turn the aristocratic regime gradually into a monarchical state."[7]

In spite of the peace treaties of Münster and Osnabrück, the situation was thus fluid in the postwar period. What "the Empire" actually was, in what assemblies and by means of what procedures it embodied itself concretely and was collectively capable of acting—this was as ambiguous in praxis as it was contested in theory. During the long period of confessional crisis and war since 1613, there had been only a single imperial diet, namely, in 1640. Instead, the electors had gathered repeatedly as an exclusive group—in 1611, 1627, 1630, 1636, 1640, and 1652—and had made decisions that claimed to be binding upon the whole. This was made possible by the special legal status guaranteed by the Golden Bull: unlike the imperial diet, they could gather also on their own initiative, and in the right to elect the king they had effective leverage against the emperor. For example, on the occasion of the election of Ferdinand III as king of the Romans in 1636, they had extorted from the emperor a long list of concessions and written guarantees of expanded consensus rights and their precedence over all other European princes at the imperial court.[8] For his part, Emperor Ferdinand II had always claimed for himself the right to summon whomever he wanted to. For example, he had by no means invited all estates to the bestowal of the electoral dignity on Maximilian of Bavaria in 1623, even though this was the kind of solemn ritual that traditionally took place at an imperial diet.[9] Imperial diets were thus by no means the only or primary form of decision making in the Empire, nor did they embody the Empire as a whole. To contemporaries it was not at all as clear as it was to later historians that the diets would take place in the same form as in the previous century.[10] Between 1642 and 1645, a committee of the imperial diet had deliberated in Frankfurt am Main about the manner in which the estates of the realm should participate in the peace talks in Münster and Osnabrück, and this had brought into play a host of different variations of action and representation.[11] Here, too, the ultimate issue had always been who represented the Empire as an entity capable of taking action: Was the emperor alone authorized to act for the whole? Were the electors empowered to do so jointly with the emperor? Was it the totality of all estates *in corpore*, that is, in the form of an imperial diet or a committee thereof? Or should every imperial estate deliberate on its own? After all, individual imperial estates had operated independently militarily during the war and had entered into alliances with foreign powers; that is also why they wished to participate in the negotiations as independent *partes belligerantes*, or warring parties.

Eventually, under pressure from foreign powers, the emperor felt compelled to adopt this solution, and in 1645 he invited *all* individual imperial estates to Münster and Osnabrück. With that, one of the central questions over which the war had been fought, and which had to be addressed in the negotiations in the first place, was already predetermined. By sending their delegates individually to the negotiations of the monarchs, the imperial estates appeared as independent actors within the pan-European system of international law that was in the process of taking shape. At the congress itself, however, they still had to assert this status claim in practical terms against the other European potentates—and that was done in no other way than the mode of reciprocal ceremonial treatment, which established a new standard in Münster and Osnabrück (I shall return to this later). Even if the delegates of the imperial estates were treated there in many respects as the delegates of sovereign potentates, it was an open question whether these status claims could be maintained also at an imperial diet vis-à-vis the emperor, and what this meant for the imperial federation—whether the latter would not thereby dissolve into a loose association of individual, independent actors.

A Scholarly Quarrel

Before and during the "German war," there had been not only military but also discursive quarrels over the shape of the Empire. The late sixteenth century saw the emergence of a new learned discipline, the public law of the Empire, *Reichs-*

publizistik or *ius publicum imperii*, which took into account the traditional and continually growing legal material and sought to process it theoretically.[12] The learned men, mostly privy councilors of electors or princes and thus practical men, collected the ever more bewildering array of material generated by the Empire's institutions and organized, systematized, and interpreted it. To that end, the traditional instrumentarium of categories, definitions, and distinctions, derived from Roman and canon law and from classical political theory based on Aristotle, was no longer adequate. One had to devise a new, learned method of presentation and new organizing categories. The strongest impulse behind the new efforts at systematization by the scholars came from a highly influential work: Jean Bodin's 1576 work *Les six livres de la République*.[13] The book triggered intense interpretive debates over the question of what kind of form the Empire had: a monarchical one, an aristocratic one, or—as one could not help but note—neither one. Bodin imposed his categories upon the *Reichspublizisten*: even if they sought to disprove them, they first had to come to terms with them. At the heart of this debate was the concept of *maiestas*, the question of what it consisted of and to whom in the Empire it belonged and in what way.

"Majesty" had once been the label for a very tangible, concrete situation. The emperor, as we have seen, sat *in maiestate*, "in his adornment and dignity," when he performed solemn ritual acts that were symbolically singled out, unfolded in specific forms, and claimed to be valid for the totality. *Maiestas* was a particular, visible quality of persons and their actions. The king or emperor possessed it, and the electors participated in it by walking, standing, or sitting immediately next to him during these solemn acts. Bodin understood the term quite differently. He disconnected it from concrete visual perception and radicalized it by not describing *maiestas* (*souveraineté* in French) in its individual manifestations, but defining it abstractly: as the supreme power, indivisible and uncoupled from the laws (*summa legibus soluta potestas*). Bodin maintained that it was this absolute and supreme power that constituted a body politic (*res publica*) in the first place. This confronted the imperial jurists with considerable problems: How were they to transfer this category to the conventional practice in the Empire by which emperor, electors, and estates worked in concert? After all, the emperor was not able to exercise what Bodin regarded as the most elementary right of majesty—legislation—without the advice and consent of the estates assembled at the imperial diet.

But when it came to assessing the *forma imperii*, it was not only legislation that played a central role, but also the emperor's symbolically and ritually exercised rights of majesty. Those jurists who classified the Empire as a monarchy (but not only they) pointed to the central ritual acts in which the head of the Empire sat *in maiestate*, namely, investitures, the opening of imperial diets, and imperial recesses. The act of investiture made visible something that was difficult to grasp theoretically: the derivation of one right from another. Thus, the Hessian councilor Dietrich Reinking argued in 1619 that the *summa potestas* of the Empire rested solely with the emperor and was identical with his *maiestas*. One could see this from the fact that even the electors received their title from him *humiliter et devote* in the act of investiture. He referred to the princely fiefs as the core and nerves of the imperial body.[14] But Reinking, a man of particular fealty to the emperor, was not the only one who ascribed a monarchical form to the Empire and the *maiestas personalis* to the emperor. The Jena professor Dominikus Arumaeus, one of the founders of *imperial public law* or *Reichspublizistik* as an academic discipline, and the author of the first comprehensive, systematic tractate on the imperial diet, did likewise in 1635. He justified this by noting that only the emperor installed the imperial estates in the act of investiture, and that he was able to summon and end the imperial diet, the heart and shield of the Empire—both of these powers were *insignia supremae potestatis*, signs of his supreme power.[15] Even a scholar like Johannes Limnaeus, who subordinated the 'personal majesty' of the emperor to the 'real majesty' of the Empire as a whole, placed the ritual of investiture at the center of his argument: during the investiture, the emperor was acting in the place and in the name of the Empire as a whole and was imposing on the vassals the obligation of fealty toward the Empire as a whole.[16]

That is why the imperial right of investiture, in particular, was marshaled as the chief argument against Bodin, who had qualified the Empire as a pure aristocracy and had assigned the *maiestas* undivided to the imperial diet alone. The only way Bodin was able to justify his unusual perspective—not shared by most German scholars—was by denying, in an exact inversion, that all symbolic acts, insignia, precedents, honors, and titles had any deeper meaning and efficacy. What was more, he virtually turned the meaning of such symbolism into its opposite by claiming that in well-ordered aristocracies like the Empire, it was "customary to accord the least power to the one who held the highest rank of honor, and vice versa."[17] The most exalted as the least powerful, actual *majesty* and ceremonial sovereignty as opposites—this was a paradox meant to dumbfound the readers; it turned upside down the ways in which contemporaries perceived things and unsettled their confidence in the symbolic readability of the world. Only one German author adopted Bodin's argument: the jurist Philipp Bogislav von Chemnitz, the harshest anti-imperial polemicist in Swedish employ. In his pseudonymous tract against imperial authority, a book that was burned by the executioner in Vienna, he described the emperor's ritually exercised rights of majesty of investiture and elevation in rank as mere fantasies, *simulacra*, which possessed only the semblance of *jura maiestatis*.[18]

By contrast, learned men like Arumaeus described the emperor's power as symbolic power, which was certainly compatible with the consensus rights of the estates at imperial diets and yet did not cease for that reason to constitute the *supreme* power. This was most plausibly illustrated by the old *corpus-caput* metaphor: the political whole, the body of the Empire, was made up of the emperor as the head and the electors or all estates as the limbs. The Empire as a whole, the *corpus mysticum*, was superordinated to its ruler, but only by the head were the limbs united into a whole. This whole was embodied and represented in the "abbreviated" form—as it were—of the imperial diet: "The princes and estates form the imperial body, whose head the emperor is, and when they get together in a *compendium repraesentativum*, one says that the entire Empire is assembled," wrote another important *Reichspublizist*, the Brunswick chancellor Tobias Paurmeister, drawing on the late medieval corporation theory.[19] In his account, the princes and estates have taken the place of the electors; other than that, little had changed compared to medieval theory.

At stake in the debates over the form of the Empire and the possession and exercise of *maiestas*—in images of body and limbs, body and soul, heart and nerves, spring and ocean, top and bottom, high and low—was the interpretation and weighting of the ambiguous and complex historical tradition of how emperor, electors, princes, and estates had for centuries acted in concert, and sometimes in opposition. The sources that the authors drew upon conveyed an archaic image. The view of the imperial diet that was preserved across the dietless reign of Ferdinand II by Arumaeus, Limnaeus, and other scholars was not shaped only by the imperial diets of the late sixteenth century, with their largely sober, businesslike procedural practice, but also by the *Hoftage*, the Golden Bull, and the herald accounts from around 1500. The imperial diet in Augsburg in 1530, in particular, was cited as a popular example. This had to do with the fact that this assembly had played a pivotal role in the history of the *Confessio Augustana*, and its tradition was therefore cultivated with particular care by the Protestants. Numerous illustrated broadsheets recalled the handing over of the *Confessio Augustana* in 1530.[20] Especially the famous historical work of Georg Coelestin kept alive the collective Protestant memory of the imperial diet of 1530.[21] The *Reichspublizistik* was thoroughly shaped by a Protestant bias. The result, paradoxically enough, was that it conveyed an image of the imperial diet from the time of Charles V that was archaic in many ways and conserved the old splendor of imperial majesty.

"Image" should be understood quite literally: the majesty of the Empire existed as an image in people's minds, as a collective imagination that was fed by very concrete, material pictures. On illustrated broadsheets, copper-engraved frontispieces, triumphal arches, patents of nobility—everywhere the Empire continued to be portrayed pars pro toto as the community of the emperor and the electors (now eight in number) (figure 8). Even if concessions were made in the process to modern baroque taste, it is clear that the artists picked up the old pictorial tradition from 1500.[22]

Figure 8. The emperor in the circle of the electors. Single-page broadsheet entitled "Abbildung Unsers heutigen Deutschlands und der höchstgewünschten Vereinigung," copper engraving by Abraham Aubry after Johann Toussin, 1653/54.

The power of the emperor at imperial diets and acts of investiture, the *maiestas imperialis* in the old sense, was an authoritative power—not the kind of instrumental, coercive power that Bodin had in mind. The emperor's last attempt to set up a military executive power of the Empire and to have sole control over it had come to grief in the war. But as the holder of authoritative power, the emperor traditionally guaranteed the entire system of social importance, with himself as the integrating capstone. He alone could create electors, princes, counts, knights, and doctors; he alone could change an illegitimate status into a legitimate one, free bastard children of their stigma, and turn dishonorable persons back into honorable ones.[23] He was the head of the status system; therein lay his authoritative power in the sense described in chapter 1. Such power required visibility to an even greater extent than instrumental power. After all, it consisted precisely in the fact that it was recognized as such by others, and reciprocal recognition could be directly experienced only in public symbolic acts.

The war, however, had profoundly unsettled the entire status system of the Empire. At the first imperial diet following the Peace of Westphalia, against the backdrop of the unresolved procedural questions, which were simultaneously fundamental constitutional questions, the imperative for the emperor was thus to defend his authoritative power. If he wanted to assert himself as the overlord of the Empire's status system, as the source and head of all legitimate status, he had to enact himself symbolically accordingly and prevail upon the other members of the Empire to recognize him in this role in an equally visible way. Here, too, the symbolic action assumed an elementary meaning and significance. And it did so for all sides—what was true for the imperial claims to standing was equally true for the individual members of the realm. Battles over symbolic recognition were also waged by many individual actors on their own behalf—princes, counts, and city councilors were concerned about their own social standing. These issues were interwoven in complex ways with the question of the order of the Empire and the emperor's agenda, and they also had repercussions for Europe as a whole.

The open questions were as follows: Would the rules of procedure and social interaction that prevailed under sovereign monarchs prevail at the imperial diet, thus transforming it into a congress of largely independent potentates? Or would the emperor assert his majesty and celebrate the diet in the old tradition like a *Hoftag*? Given the pressure of the newly ordained confessional parity, what would remain of the sacrality of the Empire, which manifested itself in the orthodox rituals? Would it prove possible to maintain the line separating electors and princes, and the preeminence of the electors? Would the old imperial princes, in turn, be able to set themselves apart from the many new princes that Ferdinand II had elevated to their new dignity during the war? Would electors and princes together fend off the claim of the cities to be treated as equals? In short, would the old hierarchy of the Empire stand its ground, or would it be pulled "into the maelstrom of the leveling of international law?"[24] All of these questions were as much about social standing as they were about political process, and all of them were not only verbally negotiated in the deliberations of the imperial diet, but also—and above all—engaged through the medium of symbolic-ceremonial actions. Only by bearing this in mind can one understand why the imperial diet of 1653/54 was more conflict-ridden than virtually any other that had gone before.

Place, Time, Persons

Emperor Ferdinand III was initially in no hurry to announce the imperial diet within six months, as the Peace of Westphalia stipulated, and to grapple with the participatory claims of the estates. In addition, the Nuremberg negotiations about the implementation questions involving Sweden delayed the summons.[25] The estates, however, were pushing for the peace treaty to be put into practice. The emperor's councilors also advised him to call the imperial diet without delay: otherwise, the estates were threatening to gather somewhere else without him, possibly with support from foreign powers, "and to turn it into a different imperial assembly."[26] Estates gathering on their own initiative could be the beginning of a constitutional revolution: this had happened, for example, at the revolt of the Dutch provinces in 1572. Summoning the estates of the realm and dictating the place and time of their assembly was tantamount to determining whether, when, and where the Empire as a whole made its appearance and could become capable of acting. Even if the emperor, in according with imperial custom, had to ask the electors for their consent, this was nevertheless considered his elementary right of majesty. The Treaty of Osnabrück was now severely restricting that right by prescribing to the emperor when and how he should exercise it. What mattered to the emperor, then, was to stage the imperial diet in such a way that it did not seem like a coerced concession, but as his own, freely made sovereign decision.

Three and a half years after the Peace of Westphalia, on 27 April 1652, the emperor therefore sent out his summons and set 30 October 1652 as the opening date. As the site of the assembly he chose Regensburg, his imperial city, which had a Protestant citizenry, was situated in the midst of the Catholic duchy of Bavaria, and was the residence of a Catholic bishop.[27] After its status as a "royal city" had been decided in 1492, the city had often served as the site of imperial diets, and since 1594 exclusively so. It was close to the Habsburg territories, easy to reach via the Danube, and offered both confessional parties the opportunity to practice their faith. Emperor Rudolf II had even contemplated moving his residence there. That he did not do so in the end illustrated an essential difference between the Empire and most other European monarchies: the residence of the emperor was *not* at the same time the place for the assembly of the estates. Over the long term, the result of this—as we shall see—was that the court of the emperor and the imperial diet turned into two very different things.

As of now, though, that had not yet happened. It was still the case that the imperial court was wherever the emperor happened to be with his courtly retinue. Ferdinand III was now very intent on making sure that the impending imperial diet would become simultaneously an imperial *Hoftag*. He therefore announced that he would appear "in his own person together with his entire court retinue," with his pregnant third wife Eleonora and his son Ferdinand, King of Hungary and Bohemia.[28] This made it "right and proper" that all the electors and princes likewise appear in person. The summons contained the "earnest command to every estate of the realm that you, setting aside all other affairs ... appear in person, surely and unfailingly," in order to secure the peace between the head and limbs of the Empire, among the limbs themselves, and with the foreign crowns, and to deliberate and decide on the issues that had been postponed. Anyone who was prevented from coming in person should send "respectable councilors and delegates with appropriate powers. And even if you should not appear, you will nevertheless be obliged ... to carry out what is decided / alongside the others who are present."[29] At past imperial diets, however, that had not worked very well: neither had the emperor or the princes regularly appeared in person, nor had the binding nature of the decisions been enforced against those absent—above all, that is, against the Protestants.[30] Still, the emperor had always adhered to these norms. Personal absence, even though it had in fact become virtually the rule, was still considered the exception, and to maintain this fiction it was always necessary to offer a ritual apology to the emperor for one's failure to appear.[31] In this way, the norms were stabilized against the transformative power of factual reality.

The form in which the summons were issued revealed not only the rank of the invitee, but also how much importance the emperor attached to his personal appearance: some were presented with a handwritten letter by an envoy of the emperor; others were merely sent a printed form.[32] Seeing as the estates would have a difficult time appearing "with proper honor and dignity" given the burdens of the war, the emperor promised to limit his "courtly retinue as much as possible" and called upon the estates to do likewise.[33] The considerable expenses of a lavish retinue should offer them no reason for staying away. But hardly any of the participants heeded this recommendation, least of all the emperor himself, and yet for many this was not an obstacle—on the contrary. Evidently many of the estates of the realm were fully aware that this imperial diet was to play a key role, and they appeared in person in comparatively large numbers, with the most sumptuous retinues and in the utmost material splendor. In many ways the staging resembled that of Augsburg in 1530—even if by now important changes had taken place.

A New Ceremonial Grammar

The emperor or his delegate to the imperial diet, Volmar, were in charge of overseeing the staging of the events; they had managed to enlist the help of the Elector of Mainz, archchancellor Johann Philipp von Schönborn.[34] Ferdinand III had met with the electors already in September of 1652 in his residence in Prague, where he negotiated very quietly with them about the upcoming imperial diet and his primary concern:[35] the election of his son Ferdinand (IV) as king of the Romans. This meeting had deliberately been staged not as an official imperial solemnity, but as a quasi-private visit by the electors; that is why it had taken place not in an imperial city, but in the emperor's residence. After all, the question of the election of the king had been entrusted to the imperial diet, and one did not wish to officially preempt it. The electors and the emperor had agreed in Prague that they had a shared interest in defending the precedence of the electoral college against the other estates. The majority of the electors signaled the emperor their willingness to elect his son. In return, he granted them—in addition to other benefits—special ceremonial honors. The meeting was especially important to Count Palatine Karl Ludwig, as he had just recovered his electoral title, which his father, the proscribed "Winter King," had forfeited because of his participation in the Bohemian revolt. In August, the count palatine's envoys were invested in Prague; he himself was received with "royal honors" a little while later.[36] This was a central concern of all electors: to receive from the emperor a treatment that was otherwise due only to "crowned heads." With this, the emperor was fulfilling what he already had to promise to the electors in his own electoral capitulation in 1637, and what the foreign monarchs, too, had already accorded them at the congress of the Peace of Westphalia.

Royal honors, *honores regii*, were *the* object of desire. Europe was home to a host of potentates who were not anointed and crowned kings, and to republics who had no monarchical ruler.[37] But some of them were by now playing a role—politically and militarily—that was just as important and independent as that of a monarch: the republics of Venice and the Netherlands, above all, but also some Italian and German vassals of the Empire, for example, the Elector of Brandenburg. The rank to which they laid claim no longer fit into the complex old hierarchy of those who held power—from the pope and emperor to kings, dukes, and counts, all the way down to knights and burgomasters. A new system of political classification was gradually emerging, one that no longer rested on the richly graduated hierarchy of Christendom, but drew only a single distinction: that between sovereigns and subjects. This new, dualistic principle of order slowly pushed itself in front of the old, graduated principle in a lengthy, friction-filled process and began to superimpose itself upon it. However, sovereignty could not yet be conceived in any way other than *royal majesty*; it still seemed entirely bound to the weight of the highest rank among the estates.[38] Efforts to achieve parity with royal status were thus the expression of a long and profound process of leveling and polarization among the European potentates. A distinction was made between those who took each other seriously as sovereign, that is, independent and equal actors under the law of nations, and those who should be regarded as the subjects of others—a process that is generally referred to as the creation of the modern state system.

To be considered sovereigns and the equal of kings, the electors, dukes, margraves, doges, and *Staten Generaal* did not lack for territories, income, soldiers, or subjects, but only three elements: the royal title, the crown, and equal ceremonial treatment by the kings. If they could not attain the crown and royal title, being treated as equals by the "crowned heads" was their highest goal, social recognition the ultimate purpose of all their political striving. The most important medium of this royal-like status now became—alongside personal meetings between the potentates and their written dealings in letters—communication via envoys. The central setting was the solemn audiences of welcoming the envoys and bidding them farewell. They had no other meaning than to display the status that the principals accorded each other. What precisely constituted "royal treatment" was determined by the actual praxis of the most powerful monarchs, especially those of France, Spain, and Sweden. The way in which these kings treated the delegates of foreign powers was how all others wanted to be treated as well; it was they who set the standards.

One precondition for this were the rules of diplomatic representation, the beginnings of which had emerged already in the late Middle Ages, but which were specified with increasing precision around the middle of the seventeenth century.[39] Diplomacy changed in two ways: for one, it became the rule that potentates send each other *permanent* representatives, with the result that a regular system of communication and observation was established between all larger courts. For another, an increasingly precise system of different diplomatic *ranks* emerged. The envoys of different ranks differed first and foremost in their ceremonial treatment. An envoy of the first rank—an *Ambassadeur*—was defined by the fact that he *represented* his lord in the strictest sense of the word, that is, he had to be "accorded as much respect as if his high principal himself were present."[40] An essential requirement was that this representative himself was of high birth and able to display as much splendor as his employer (he had to finance this from his own wealth, which could ruin him financially). For the substantive work of negotiation away from public appearances, a second delegate, the *Secundarius*, was sent along, usually a learned councilor of lower birth who had—instead of a noble title—the title of doctor. The first delegate, however, the principal envoy, had to "represent the sovereignty and wealth" of his principal in a twofold sense: not only were his actions attributed to the employer himself, but the envoy also represented his master in a tangible and perceptible way.

It was precisely this—the ability to send an ambassador as a proxy to a foreign court, where he would receive the highest ceremonial honors—that now developed into the clearest and unequivocal sign of sovereignty, the sign of the reciprocal recognition of kings and potentates as equals.[41] For in the final analysis only that person was sovereign who was recognized as such by other sovereigns—and recognition was manifested in the ceremonial signs of royal-like equality, the *honores regii*. Royal-like treatment was thus a major immaterial good, one that lower-ranking actors like the electors were willing to trade in at any time with the kings for all kinds of other benefits.

The peace congress of Westphalia played a key role in this protracted process of equalization under the law of nations. Leaving aside the reform councils, Münster and Osnabrück had been the first time that delegates of nearly all European potentates and republics had met at close quarters—envoys of actors, that is, who were in fact highly unequal in terms of political power and social status. However, the issue for many actors at this congress was precisely their status as independent subjects under the law of nations. And that status had to be asserted not only abstractly and discursively in the negotiations themselves, but already before that concretely and practically in the ceremonial treatment by the other monarchs. It was not only on paper that the Treaty of Osnabrück granted the electors—indeed, all estates of the realm—the central rights of majesty, namely, to enter into alliances independently, to wage war, and to make peace.[42] At the congress, some of them were already treated by the envoys of the monarchs as independent negotiation partners and enjoyed royal-like *tractement*—though not always and not from all participants.[43] There existed a standard repertoire of signs—shaped largely by the French court—by which a sovereign potentate indicated to an envoy that he regarded his master also as a sovereign potentate. Three things, above all else, were considered "ceremonial rights" since the Peace of Westphalia: the address "Your Excellency" for the envoy; the "first visit," that is, the right to be visited first by the host after the arrival at his residence; and the concession of the "upper hand," that is, precedence and the place on the right hand of the host. Receiving these signs from as many higher-ranking potentates as possible was the ultimate good; granting them to lower-ranking individuals was a strategic political tool.[44]

The system of ceremonial signs that had established itself at the congress subsequently continued in the diplomatic traffic between the courts. For the electors and princes of the Empire, the important thing now was to register precisely the ceremonial honors accorded their envoys, under no circumstances to fall below a level once achieved, and to use every opportunity to negotiate improvements. After all, the ceremonial vocabulary was by no means immune to changes, but was subject to a process of gradual inflation. For example, if one had won the title of "Excellency" and the upper hand for one's principle envoy, the goal was to procure these titles also for the second or even third envoys, the *Secundarii*.

All of this necessitated professional handling. Large courts followed the French model in establishing the office of the *Introducteur des Ambassadeurs*, that is, a master of ceremonies, who, as the French name implied, was in charge of the ceremonial introduction of the ambassadors and solely responsible for the correct *tractement*. Above all, however, one could no longer get by without complete written records. It is no accident that the official ceremonial protocols began at the imperial court in 1652, with the meeting of the electors in Prague; thereafter, the *Obersthofmeisteramt* (Office of the Lord Chamberlain), following the French model, had these protocols drawn up of all solemn occasions.[45] Already the previous year, the emperor had set up his own Court Commission for Ceremonial Questions.[46] In imperial cities this kind of ceremonial bookkeeping had been customary for much longer already, the papal master of ceremonies had been practicing it since the end of the fifteenth century, and at most European princely courts it likewise began in the seventeenth century.[47] One was hoping to avoid in the future what had frequently happened in the past—namely, that in cases of ceremonial conflicts one had "no documents at hand" to be able to invoke earlier precedents.[48] If one court started doing it, the others had to follow suit if they did not want to fall behind. The systematic written record of all solemnities was a result of the heightened attention to the subtleties in the vocabulary and grammar of the ceremonial language, and it in turn contributed to their continual refinement. For it was only in writing that one could preserve a permanent memory of even the smallest details. What had once been recorded as significant was now never forgotten again. Writing reinforced a process that had been under way for some time, a process by which the ceremonial actions between envoys and potentates were clarified, subdivided, and standardized across Europe. Ever more gestures and objects were identified as the smallest significant elements and recorded; fewer and fewer details could be passed over as meaningless. To this day, the dual meaning of the word "protocol" reveals the close link between written record and ceremonial code. This turned the conduct at solemn occasions into an extreme burden for all participants; the possibilities of making mistakes or registering them in others multiplied. The fact that nothing could be forgotten any longer intensified the need to pay attention and constrained the leeway for behavior.

The keeping of such ceremonial books was originally begun by the cities, that is, actors of lower rank, who maintained particularly meticulous records about the honors they had received, and at the same time had to be especially vigilant not to make any mistakes vis-à-vis the princely potentates. That the imperial court now began to do the same reveals that the emperor, too, had become one actor among others, who had to control his own behavior very precisely and could neither dictate nor ignore the increasingly elaborate rules at the European courts.

The accelerated change in the ceremonial language following the Thirty Years' War—ever more precise, complicated, standardized, and thus dangerous—was clearly perceived also by contemporaries. At the beginning of the eighteenth century, the ceremonial experts, who were trying to turn the topic into a science, wrote that only since the Peace of Westphalia had people begun "to treat the ceremonial system with more precision."[49] None other than Gottfried Wilhelm Leibniz described it as a characteristic of the era that people were now "insisting for good reason on the ceremonialia, because formalities are beginning to be considered essentials."[50] With this, Leibniz encapsulated what was also at stake in Regensburg: the form was to be taken for the substance. In borderline and doubtful cases it was the ceremonial *tractement* that decided the current and future status within the international legal system.

Entries, Audiences, Visits

Emperor and electors, princes and counts, prelates and cities—in Regensburg they all had to register anew their quite divergent, frequently competing status claims and reciprocally assert them against others. This happened first of all through the ritual act of welcoming and bidding farewell: through entries, audiences, and visits. These symbolic actions served exclusively to define the reciprocal relationship and thereby marked out the framework for what followed. This was the case wherever rulers encountered each other—whether at an imperial diet, at a court, or at a congress in some third location. The ceremonial elements were in many respects the same, at least at first glance. What mattered now were the fine distinctions.

The assembly in Regensburg in 1653 was simultaneously imperial diet, *Hoftag,* and a congress of envoys. As a result, the events could be interpreted in a variety of ways. From the perspective of the emperor, Regensburg was his court (*Hoflager*); he was the *dominus loci,* received foreign envoys, and granted the estates solemn audience as his vassals or subjects. Many of them came in person instead of sending envoys. At the same time, however, as at a multilateral congress, various actors encountered one another and all were simultaneously hosts and guests, something that was expressed in a complicated interplay of visits and return visits in their respective quarters.[51] The most subtle ceremonial nuances of the treatment that people accorded each other on these occasions showed whether they tended to regard each other as equal negotiating partners or as members of a hierarchical association. That entailed different interpretations of the Empire: anyone who wanted to see it as a loose federation of independent members had to behave at the assembly as at a congress. By contrast, anyone who wanted the Empire to appear as an imperial monarchy had to handle the assembly like a *Hoftag.* The ceremonial interactions contained simultaneously practical answers to the theoretical discourse of the *Reichspublizisten.*

By his very entry in December 1652, the emperor situated the imperial diet firmly within the tradition of the great imperial assemblies of past centuries, the memory of which the jurists and historians had kept alive in their writings. His arrival, accompanied by his wife Eleonora of Mantua and his son Ferdinand, was the object of meticulous planning. The electors of Mainz, Cologne, and Trier and a series of ecclesiastical princes—the bishop of Paderborn, the bishop of Regensburg and Osnabrück, and the abbots of Fulda and Stablo—had already taken quarters in Regensburg; Hereditary Imperial Marshal Pappenheim had made the usual arrangements that turned the city into a special legal sphere for the duration of the imperial diet, and had expelled masterless menials, beggars, "indecent females," and the contagious sick who could have marred the picture of imperial majesty. Like Charles V had done in 1530, the emperor negotiated the modalities of his entry ahead of time with the archchancellor and Elector of Mainz, with both sides sending high-ranking messengers back and forth with written proposals.[52]

The emperor made it clear that he, accompanied by his retinue, would journey only to within a quarter mile of the city "and no farther," where he wished to be met by the electors and princes in keeping with old custom. One question that was the topic of particularly contentious negotiations was whether the imperial *Hartschiere*, his armed guard, should ride immediately behind him or only behind the electors and princes—in other words, whether or not a clear sign of distance was to be established between the carriage of the imperial family and the carriages of the electors. Once again, no one "had the records at hand" to see how the matter had been handled before. As a result, the parties agreed that the entry would not take place in *solemn* but just in simple form. Given an imperial retinue of about three thousand persons[53] and the presence of the "court retainers, servants, second horses, and carriages" of the electors, all decked out in the sumptuous, colorful livery of their lords, it is obvious that "not solemn" by no means meant that the entry would have been modest and devoid of pomp, but only that it did not have law-making, performative character, that is, it should not be considered a precedent for the future.

The ceremony of meeting the emperor largely resembled what had been accorded one hundred and twenty years earlier to Charles V in Augsburg, except that one now rode in carriages instead of on horseback. The participants got out, took off their hats, shook hands in greeting—the imperial estates with "deep reverence"—and exchanged ceremonial welcome speeches. Afterward they rode into the city in the previously agreed-upon order. Waiting at the gate were the city councilors, who fell to their knees, gave a speech, and handed over the keys to the city. The emperor picked the keys up only briefly, returned them immediately, and shook the hand of every councilor.[54] While the bareheaded councilors flanked the emperor and the procession along with the footmen and guards, fusillades from thirty-six canons were fired off as usual at three stations—acoustic signs of lordship and simultaneously controlled military power, intended to recall the horrors of war and transform them into jubilation about the peace. The fact that two serious accidents occurred in the procession was seen as a bad omen for the imperial diet.[55] In the *Ostengasse* a triumphal arch had been erected, whose complex emblematic program one could read about in a broadsheet.[56] In it, Ferdinand was not only celebrated as the hoped-for bringer of peace, a new King Solomon and Emperor Augustus, but he was also depicted in the circle of the electors and reminded that the imperial throne was fortified by good council, *bono consilio*. As the procession passed through the triumphal arch, there was the sound of "beautiful music of all kinds of voices, string music, military drums and trumpets." A schematized picture of the entry, with a meticulous listing of the participants in the precise sequence, was published as an illustrated single-page broadsheet and thus made accessible to a broader, supraregional public (figure 9).[57]

The depiction followed a highly popular pictorial scheme that was customary for solemn entries of every kind from the late sixteenth to the late eighteenth century: the sequence of carriages, horsemen, and guards snaked in long

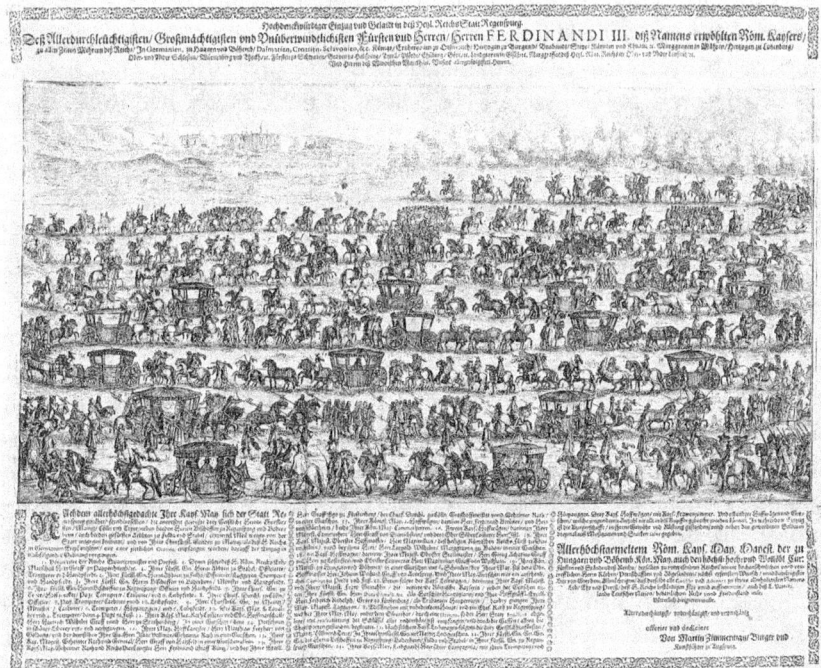

Figure 9. The entry of Ferdinand III into Regensburg on 12 December 1652. Broadsheet by Melchior Küsel, Germanisches Nationalmuseum Nuremberg, Graphische Sammlung.

winding curves toward the city emerging in the distance at the upper edge of the picture. The image created a reality all its own. Nobody who was actually present could have perceived the events in this way. Purged of all distracting incidental details, the picture limits itself to what was significant in terms of the ceremonial message. Even more so than the entry itself, the pictorial type makes it clear and unequivocal what such an arrival was all about: namely, reading a temporal-spatial sequence of individuals as a hierarchical order.

The imperial family took quarters in the episcopal residence. As they were being escorted to their lodgings, a significant ceremonial mistake occurred: the ecclesiastical princes followed the emperor and the electors into the innermost chambers of the residence, the *retirada*. This violated the status boundary between electors and princes and therefore had to be "rectified." The *Oberthofmeister* (lord chamberlain) informed the princes that in the future they were not permitted to enter further than the imperial council chamber. Spatial distances, steps, doors, and thresholds were the vocabulary of the ceremonial language manifested in stone. By creating ever higher staircases and ever longer sequences of rooms, the architects of the residences made possible ever more precisely measured distances in relation to the ruler. The episcopal residence in

Regensburg, too, allowed for at least an elementary distinction between council chamber and *retirada* and thus a distinction between electors and princes. The boundary between estates had to materialize in a visible spatial boundary. That the electors were the "innermost councilors" of the emperor had to be understood very concretely and literally.

Gradually, at greater intervals, additional princes arrived in Regensburg: the Margrave of Baden, the Duke of Württemberg, the Prince-bishops of Münster and Eichstätt, the Elector Karl Ludwig of the Palatinate, the Counts Palatine of Simmern and Neuburg, and finally, in June, the Landgrave of Hesse-Darmstadt. They were at pains not to arrive together and on time, lest it appear that they were coming on command. The customary delayed arrival, the comments noted, was in keeping with their ancient German liberty.[58] The majority of the Protestant estates sent only envoys. A few princes, however, used the presence of the others as an audience and made a great show of their entrances, no matter how much the war had impoverished their territories. Especially the Duke of Württemberg, who had lost his status in the war and had recovered it in the peace treaty, stood out. The ducal couple processed into the city with 200 horses and a retinue of 250 (others estimated 300) persons to the sounds of trumpets, and they had the drums beat—though only when they had arrived at their quarters. The emperor "did not take this too well."[59] Drums and trumpets were part of the exclusive symbolic repertoire of rulership. They surrounded a traveling ruler like a cocoon of sound, preceding him like a widely audible sonorous coat of arms.[60] An exclusive signal is what they were to remain: where the emperor himself was present, he granted this acoustic sign of rulership to no one but the electors. When the Elector of the Palatinate, therefore, entered the city, no one took offense that he let drums and trumpets resound; indeed, the city even had six canons fire three salvos for him. That did not apply to a duke. It was therefore a calculated provocation when Eberhard of Württemberg had the military drums beaten—though only when he arrived in his quarters, just to be on the safe side. He literally announced with drumbeats what was at stake at this imperial diet: leveling out the distinction between electors and princes.

After their arrival, the emperor received all electors and princes as well as all foreign envoys and those from imperial estates at a "solemn audience." These highly formalized inaugural visits followed a strict code and served only to express the reciprocal relationship. They made the gradations according to estate, rank, and favor precisely readable. The instructions given to the envoys drove home most fastidiously the significant distinctions; the envoys knew exactly what they could claim and where they must not yield an inch.[61] When and which court official could one ask for an audience? At what point in time should it be carried out? Did the emperor himself subsequently make a return visit or not? Did the empress also receive the guest? Where would the incoming guest be met, and how far would he be escorted back—at the door of the *retirada* or the audience chamber, at the stairs, at the carriage, or even as far as his own lodgings? Who came out to meet him—the *Obersthofmeister*, a high minister, or merely a footman? Did the emperor remain seated under the canopy, did he stand, or did he even come out to meet the guest—and if so, how many steps? Was the guest allowed to go through the door first and to the right of the emperor, that is, was he given precedence? Did he have to remain standing during the audience, or was he allowed to take a seat across from the emperor—and if so, how did the two chairs differ in form and color? Did the emperor allow him to cover his head, and if so, how long? Did the emperor himself doff his hat during the audience, and if so, when and how often? What titles did the two parties use to address each other? How long did the exchange of the "compliments" last?[62] Did the emperor extend his hand to the guest upon his departure? This was the ceremonial vocabulary that made the display of reverence precisely measurable. Electors in person, for example, were entitled to being received by the *Obersthofmeister* at the door of the carriage, to having the emperor come out five steps in the *Ritterstube* (Knights' Room) to greet them, to wearing the hat, to being received by the empress, and to a return visit by the emperor. Simple princes, let alone counts, lords, or city envoys, were not entitled to any of that; they were the recipients of lesser honors in a precisely graduated manner. The entire audience left no room for spontaneity, nor did it serve the substantive negotiations; rather, it consisted of nothing more than the exchange of precisely calibrated symbolic messages.

Movement came into this system of ceremonial distinctions for several reasons. First, it was not limited to the imperial court, but was practiced at all larger European courts and in all the quarters of envoys. The correspondence of the permanent envoys ensured that each side registered very precisely what was happening at the other courts. If an exception to a rule was made somewhere, others claimed the same exception for themselves: this put the rule in question and it slowly ceased to be one. Almost all actors were eager for exceptions, but especially those whose status was unclear and could be gauged differently according to various classification schemes—like the electors, who were powerful potentates and elected the emperor, while also being imperial vassals.

The emperor himself, however, was fundamentally conservative on ceremonial questions: after all, alongside the pope he was considered the highest-ranking ruler of the Occident, and concessions could only shrink, not increase, the distance separating him from all other actors. Thus, winning a ceremonial exception at the imperial court was as difficult as it was valuable for a potentate. Meanwhile, ever since the Peace of Westphalia, at the latest, the electors, as we have seen, were pursuing the new goal of being treated like "crowned heads." At his court, the emperor had obliged them since time immemorial with special honors and had elevated them clearly above the princes. He was interested in upholding their traditional preeminence, since he depended on them as the men who elected the king. However, treating them like sovereigns could not be in his interest—for that leveled the imperial federation and his own place as its overlord.

However, under pressure from the victorious monarchies, the emperor had found himself compelled in Münster and Osnabrück to treat the envoys from his own vassals just like those from foreign sovereigns. However, that had been a congress of diplomats. Regensburg was an imperial assembly—in the emperor's eyes a considerable difference. What made the situation at this imperial diet especially complicated was that the envoys were not entirely among themselves, as they had been in 1648, but met with many electors and princes who were present in person. At an imperial diet, however, envoys were traditionally supposed to rank *below* the princes present at the diet.[63] Now, if the emperor treated envoys to the diet like the princes themselves, this meant simultaneously that he treated them like envoys from "sovereign lords." He was not willing to do so, for precisely that would have rendered the imperial diet confusingly similar in form to an international congress. This is the point where principles irreconcilable at their core clashed. One group insisted on the equal diplomatic treatment they had just recently been able to push through in Münster and Osnabrück; the others, meanwhile, maintained that the imperial diet followed entirely different rules from a congress with foreign powers.[64] The point for the emperor was to defend the ceremonial logic of the imperial federation against the logic of sovereignty; in other words, to defend the logic of the feudal-legal hierarchy against the logic of diplomatic equality. Many of the innumerable ceremonial conflicts that occupied the actors in Regensburg can be traced back to these competing logics.[65]

The first move was made by the widow of Elector Maximilian I of Bavaria, Maria Anna, a sister of the emperor who was running the government as a regent for her minor son, Ferdinand Maria. Although she was in Regensburg in person, as a woman she had to be represented in the Empire's business by her councilors. There were protracted disputes about the treatment of the six Bavarian envoys at the inaugural audience, masses,[66] and all other public acts. What the regent Maria Anna wanted was for her envoys to be treated as though they represented the elector in person. That was not conceded, in spite of her close kinship with the emperor: the court officials did not address her envoys with the title "Excellency," the lord chamberlain did not meet them at the carriage, and during the audience they were not asked to put their hats back on.[67] The envoys from electoral Brandenburg and electoral Saxony, who arrived a little later, experienced the same; they, too, received markedly lesser treatment than the princes who were at the imperial diet in person, not to mention that accorded the envoys of foreign monarchs.[68]

The quarrel intensified when Elector Karl Ludwig of the Palatinate arrived. Following the imposition of the imperial ban on his father, he had just recently been restored to the electoral dignity, but now he was to content himself with the last, eighth rank in the electoral college in favor of his underage Bavarian cousin.[69] He asserted precedence over all mere electoral envoys and let it be known "that he would rather return home than receive the seat only behind the envoys of his colleagues."[70] The archchancellor had the documents brought from the Mainz archive and found in them an agreement by the electoral college at the 1566 imperial diet in Augsburg that supported the Elector of the Palatinate. That was no surprise, since the Bavarian regent was invoking a new, altered diplomatic practice. She argued that the emperor must not treat the electors worse than he did the foreign Republic of Venice, which, by the standards of European princely society, was after all of lower rank on the estate hierarchy.[71] The emperor, however, was not willing to get involved with the new diplomatic rules in dealing with his own vassals at an imperial diet, and he initially ignored his sister's complaints. The latter, meanwhile, joined forces with the envoys of the electors of Brandenburg and Saxony to continue pursuing their common goal, and they successfully employed the impending royal election as leverage: in Augsburg, where the electors or their envoys resided in May for the election, the latter were now in fact treated the way they had demanded. The Brandenburg envoy Blumenthal wrote to his lord that at the upcoming audience he was "to receive all honor and such treatment as though Your Electoral Highness were present here in person."[72]

From the perspective of most other imperial estates, this seemed like an outrageous innovation, *superbia*, and "vain ambition."[73] Nor did all electors embrace the development of the new rules that was being pushed by Brandenburg, Saxony, and Bavaria. They continued to maintain that they had every right to be given precedence, in principle, over envoys, in keeping with traditional hierarchical culture. Exasperated by their lack of understanding, the ambassador from electoral Brandenburg wrote home "that the electors are not closing ranks rightly, and those who are present believe that it is good that there is a distinction between envoys and them, that is, that their respect is greater than that of the envoys of those absent." The emperor could exploit this, he went on to say, because "on account of this the electors are that much more likely to appear in person and he can obtain greater advantage from their presence than he could in absentia."[74] The personal presence of emperor, princes, and estates conformed to the traditional culture of social interaction in the Empire, a culture the emperor was able to revive one last time in Regensburg in 1653. However, the conflicts over the envoys already revealed that it had no future: the old culture of presence was no longer appropriate to the growing complexity of reality.

The situation was also complicated by the fact that the issue revolved not only around the relationship between the emperor and the members of the Empire and of the latter among themselves, but also around the relationship to the foreign monarchs, who also dispatched their representatives to Regensburg. The many open and unmet status claims rendered the interactions in Regensburg exceedingly difficult or entirely impossible. That became abundantly clear not only when one of the two Brandenburg envoys died in Regensburg and nobody came to his funeral *propter competentias*,[75] but also during the solemn entries of the foreign envoys, most notably the papal nuncio Scipio Pannocchieschi d'Elci, the archbishop of Pisa. The nuncio had arrived outside Regensburg on 13 February 1653 and had planned his solemn entry into the city for 16 February. However, it had to be postponed to 1 March because, as the imperial ceremonial protocol noted with restraint, the nuncio "had invited the lords electors and princes, as well as the ambassadors and envoys, who, because of the unresolved competitions, which it was not feasible to settle this time, would not have been able to get on with one another."[76] In other words, it was impossible to arrange those present into a joint entry procession, as that would have presupposed a resolution of all outstanding ceremonial questions. Another observer reported that two hundred carriages had already been ready to go out and meet the nuncio "when a dispute arose among the carriages, as to which should be the first immediately behind the emperor's, and a number of them already had their orders to force their way in."[77] Because of the threatening tumult among the carriages, the procession of going out to meet the nuncio was eventually terminated, and the emperor decided to have him received at a later time only by the imperial ministers and chamberlains—though with sixteen wagons of six horses each, that is, with the utmost pomp and every kind of conceivable honor. Because of his unresolved status claims vis-à-vis the electors, the nuncio himself subsequently stayed away from the public masses and said he was laid up with a catarrh when he was supposed to celebrate the Maundy Thursday mass and give Communion to the imperial family.[78]

Regensburg made clear that all of these rituals of welcome—entries, audiences, visits, and return visits—were increasingly overtaxed with the task of indicating the status of the actors. After all, the entire status system as such was undergoing a profound transformation. It was of little use to render the signs ever more precise and progressively reduce the leeway for interpretation. On the contrary, the more exact the ceremonial messages, the greater the danger of encountering contradictions and being compelled to suspend public interaction altogether. In essence the same question was always at stake: Would the rules of the Empire's old ceremonial grammar hold, or would the new grammar of sovereignty introduced in Münster and Osnabrück carry the day? Would the Empire remain a hierarchically structured monarchy based on feudal fealty, or was it on the road to becoming a federation of quasi-sovereign potentates? This could not be decided theoretically, but had to be worked out in symbolic praxis on a case-by-case basis. And as always, this question was tied to the question of the holiness of the Empire—this, too, was an issue of stagings and battles over interpretation.

Confessional Enactments

The central public venue of imperial self-staging was the cathedral in Regensburg. Here is where the emperor's family, in the circle of the ecclesiastical electors and princes, regularly attended mass during the many months of its stay in the city. The stage for this had been carefully prepared.[79] First, the bishop had to have the baldachin to the right of the high altar taken down, "because it was not seemly to use it in the presence of His Imperial Majesty." Then an oratorium had been set up for the imperial family in the choir. Reachable from the episcopal residence via a wooden walkway, it was a separate room with windows that removed the family in part from public view and yet secured it the attention of the city's and the court's public. The place assigned to the electors was immediately next to it and was separated by a door from the imperial oratorium. On the other side, also in the choir and reachable by a wooden walkway, the ladies and knights of the Order of the Golden Fleece—that is, the apex of the Habsburg retinue—had their seats, prepared "with a pretty rug." For the imperial princes, however, two benches covered in red satin had been set up "in the center of the church" in front of the high altar. They therefore refused to attend the first mass, because "they would be excluded by this seating from the choir of the church," and they appeared only when two benches were moved to the choir. These quarrels were by no means trivial and vain. Rather, they were driven by two competing ideas about what kind of tableau should be created on the raised, sacrally elevated stage of the choir: the imperial court—the family and the closest court retinue, into which only the electors were incorporated—or the Empire as a community of emperor, electors, and princes.

The Christmas feast in 1652 offered the first opportunity for a major sacral enactment. What was staged was a special spectacle "such as had not happened in two hundred years": the bishop of Regensburg chanted the holy mass "solemnly" in the cathedral, while all three ecclesiastical electors were simultaneously saying masses at three different altars. For the archbishop of Trier this was his first mass; he had just been ordained as a priest. It was an extraordinarily spectacular event, for it had been centuries since the three archbishops of Mainz, Trier, and Cologne had read a mass simultaneously. For them to do so presupposed that they were all, in fact, ordained priests—rather the exception among ecclesiastical imperial princes. A little later, on Epiphany in 1653, the Elector of Cologne festively invested the Elector of Trier with the archiepiscopal pallium in the cathedral of Regensburg in front of the public of the Empire. This demonstrated a new understanding of the office of an ecclesiastical prince, the kind of understanding that been asserting itself slowly—and by no means uniformly—since the Council of Trent.[80]

The message of a triumphally renewed baroque Catholicism was also sent by the other liturgical events: on the second day of Christmas, "at three in the morning, a forty-hour prayer for a blessed imperial diet was begun, which His Papal Holiness had favored with a plenary indulgence." At the end people assembled in the cathedral church to venerate the Blessed Sacrament on their knees—the emperor kneeling on a golden cushion, the king on a reddish-gold one, the electors on red ones, and the princes on the bare floor. The Blessed Sacrament was carried about in solemn procession beneath a baldachin, with the imperial court officials and closest favorites Dietrichstein and Auersperg—clothed, like the emperor himself, in the habit of the Habsburg Order of the Golden Fleece—walking along in the most prominent place to the left and the right.[81]

The mass continued to be the sacral and social center of every community. Where else if not here could social claims of status be made visible and asserted before the eyes of everyone? As with any church, whether in a residence, city, or village, in Regensburg the cathedral was therefore also the most prominent locus of social order, political authority, and confessional piety all in one.[82] With the elaborate sacral enactments the emperor and the Catholic estates co-opted this stage from the outset for themselves. They could do this all the more unimpeded as the Protestant princes had not yet arrived in December of 1652. But even in the period that followed, the imperial family and the Catholic estates, together with the Regensburg bishop Franz Wilhelm von Wartenberg, made a demonstrative public display of piety. For example, on 20 April 1653 the bishop had the bones of the sainted martyr Leontius, a present from Pope Urban VIII, transferred from the church of the Franciscans to the cathedral in Regensburg in a lavish procession attended by the entire secular and religious clergy "and a great mass of the people."[83] The Protestants, with their less ostentatious and visible religious practice, had nothing comparable to counter this dominance of the public space by the imperial court and the Catholic estates present in person, who were in the clear majority at the imperial diet. They could merely engage demonstratively in worldly pleasures on fasting days, as they did, for example, on 7 March, a *quatember* day, when they organized a large joint sled ride, something the imperial court noted with great displeasure.[84]

The venue for the many demonstrations of Catholic religious practice was the episcopal seat of Regensburg, not the imperial city of Regensburg. The two were spatially and confessionally distinguishable. The episcopal and monastic zones of immunity lay as enclaves of orthodoxy in the midst of the communal urban space, which was Protestant, but this in turn lay within an increasingly homogeneous Catholic territory, the Duchy of Bavaria. The Protestant community had therefore been for a long time a haven for many Protestant refugees, who had escaped to there from the re-Catholicization measures of their territorial lords. At the same time, though, the Catholic population of Regensburg was also growing: from the clerics and protected dependents (*Schutzverwandte*) of the bishopric, the Imperial Abbey of St. Emmeram, the Jesuit gymnasium, and several foundations, monasteries, and commanderies (*Kommenden*) of the knightly orders. Catholics and Protestants battled over dominance in the public sphere with elaborate new church constructions and new monasteries. The existence side by side in the same city of two systems of time keeping, the old Julian and the new Gregorian calendar, which worked as signs of confessional affiliation, made the division of the residents in everyday life perceptible to everyone. The city's community had just recently, in 1651, shortly before the imperial diet, separated itself sharply from the growing Catholic population by making the awarding of citizenship dependent on the *Confessio Augustana*.[85] All this casts a revealing light on the tense confessional atmosphere during the imperial assembly.

Four years after the Peace of Westphalia, long regarded as the end of the confessional age and the beginning of an era of religious tolerance and peaceful coexistence,[86] the climate between the confessional groups in the Empire was still characterized by hostility and distrust. The Protestants felt increasingly threatened by the Roman Church ever since a series of spectacular conversions of imperial princes and counts, chief among them Count Palatine Wilhelm of Neuburg in 1613.[87] In the 1650s, in particular, a great many conversion narratives were published in print, aggravating the climate of threat. The imperial court and the ecclesiastical principalities, with their rich sources of social, cultural, and economic capital, exerted a strong attraction and prompted many noblemen in the Empire to return to the Catholic Church. At the same time, the Habsburgs, in their hereditary lands, continued undisturbed the policy of re-Catholicization that had led to war more than thirty years before.[88] For at the congress of Westphalia, the emperor had pushed through his claim to exempt his own lands from the general regulation, according to which the confessional state of the "normal year" 1624 should not be changed by the territorial lord. No agreement had been reached about how much freedom the Protestant subjects of the Habsburgs should have to exercise their religion. In the Treaty of Osnabrück, the Protestant estates had merely reserved the right to intercede peacefully and without violence on behalf of their Austrian fellow believers at a future imperial diet.[89] For that reason, deputies from the Protestant estates of the "land below the Enns" journeyed to Regensburg to present their concerns to the imperial diet, but they were arrested by the emperor and dragged off. The efforts by their princely fellow believers to help them came to naught.[90]

The emperor, it was evident, still felt obligated, because of his office as the head of the Empire and guardian of the true faith, to "eradicate all repugnant beliefs"[91] as long as it was in his power to do so. This was in line with the Habsburg understanding of a *princeps Christianus*, which had been inculcated into him from childhood. God's honor and service were regarded as the highest measure of a Christian government, and the "extermination of the non-Catholics" was the prime maxim that followed from this.[92] The agreements in the Treaty of Osnabrück, which obligated the emperor merely to tolerate the "heretics," therefore violated his "Christian office," or so he believed. The only way he could justify tolerating the Protestants in the Empire before his conscience was by acknowledging that continuing the war would likely "have brought more harm than good."[93] They were still not equal negotiation partners for him. Just how tense the confessional atmosphere was at the imperial diet in Regensburg is revealed by a story that the papal nuncio reported back to Rome. The Protestant heretics, he wrote, were currently gathering their most learned men in Regensburg to defend their false doctrine. According to the nuncio, particular offense had been caused by the recent conversion of Countess Zinzendorf, a wise and learned women who had returned to the true faith, with her husband and her entire surroundings unable to keep her from doing so. In his outrage over this, one of the Protestant preachers in Regensburg had supposedly proclaimed from the pulpit that the emperor and the Jesuits had conspired with all the devils to eradicate the true faith. However, the emperor had initiated inquisitorial proceedings against this preacher.[94]

Against the backdrop of this confessional climate, one can gauge how the public dominance of Catholic piety had to affect the Protestant imperial estates. Although their situation was by now very different from what it had been in Augsburg in 1530, that diet still served them as the model of how to conduct themselves.[95] On the one hand, much as in 1530, they felt under threat in their confessional existence from the imperial policy. On the other hand, by now it was precisely the constitutional order of the Empire, with the emperor at its head, that guaranteed their religious rights with a series of basic laws. Showing fidelity to the emperor and the Empire was thus in the interest of Protestant self-assertion. Paradoxically enough, the Protestants were thus benefiting from the holiness of the Empire (from which the emperor still derived the obligation to exterminate their faith) because it endowed the basic laws of the Empire with sacral legitimation.[96]

Hence, the presence of the Protestants in the cathedral at the fundamental sacral acts of rulership was also in their own interest; indeed, it was a compelling necessity at the Holy Spirit mass that opened the deliberations at the imperial diet, at the election and coronation mass of the king of the Romans, and at the coronation mass of the empress—that is, at the solemn, obligation-creating stagings of the Empire as a sacred order that were performed at the imperial diet in 1653 (and that will be discussed further on). On every occasion, the Protestant princes acted the way they had back in 1530 on the advice of their theologians: they left the church during the Eucharist and returned only at the end of the mass. By now this had become the established practice. The separation during the mass—a kind of ceremonial *itio in partes*—allowed them to benefit from the legitimacy-creating sacrality of the Empire without burdening their conscience. They continued to insist on the position—first developed in 1530—that when it came to sacral imperial solemnities, one had to distinguish political service and religious service, and that the service to the emperor could not be considered tantamount to recognizing the superstitious sacrificial ritual of the mass.[97] For all their anxieties about their own confessional identity, the Protestant princes made a lot of concessions when it came to participation in the courtly festivities and thus the preservation of their political status and social rank. The Protestants participated even in a paraliturgical act of lordship like the Maundy Thursday ritual, when the emperor and the empress publicly washed the feet of twelve poor men and women and served them at table, as a way of demonstrating their charity in imitation of Christ; in fact, along with Cologne and Trier, the Elector of the Palatinate went so far as to serve the dishes to the emperor.[98]

By now, the confessional dualism had been built into the imperial system in manifold ways. It was not only on the ceremonial-liturgical stage that it was repeatedly enacted in ritualized form. Confessional parity had been anchored in various respects also on paper, in the Treaty of Osnabrück.[99] This concerned also the procedures of the deliberations at the diet. To prevent one side from outvoting the other side on religious questions, Catholic and Protestant estates, in cases of conflict, should separate into two sections according to their confessional affiliation, *ire in partes*, and negotiate an amicable agreement with one another: namely, whenever the estates "cannot be seen as one body,"[100] in other words, when they did not form a whole capable of acting. As a result, in 1653/54, the Protestants assembled several times as a separate corpus beyond the boundaries of the councils of the estates.[101] They had already done this on many previous occasions; now, however, it was a right chartered by imperial law. This procedure, too, had a symbolic dimension alongside its instrumental one: it kept the confessional division continually visible and demonstrated a (often merely fictive) community of fellow believers across the boundaries of the estates. After all, two classification criteria were constantly intersecting and overlapping in the Empire: estate affiliation and confessional affiliation. Depending on the circumstances, one could foreground either solidarity with one's peers or solidarity with one's fellow believers. The procedures of the imperial assembly allowed either one or the other principle to become effective: one either separated into the three estate "colleges" or into the confessional *partes*. In either case, one formed various corpora, which then merged back into a uniform corpus only through reciprocal amicable negotiations, *amicabilis compositio*. In this way, the clashing classification principles in the Empire were effective not only subliminally in the heads of the actors, but were always visibly displayed time and again. In short, especially after the Peace of Westphalia, the confessional division was institutionally built into the order of the Empire and symbolically ubiquitous.

Royal Election and Coronation

The election and coronation of the king constituted the procedural and symbolic core of the entire imperial order. "Coronation" stands pars pro toto for a complex sacral inauguration ritual, which consisted of the core elements of anointing, investment with the insignia, enthronement, and acclamation. Such a ritual formed the symbolic center in nearly all European monarchies; it had spread from the Frankish kingdom throughout Europe as *the* ritual of installing a ruler. Crowned heads set themselves fundamentally apart from all other potentates through their sacral consecration. The crown was not only the most important sign of rulership, but—derived therefrom—the epitome and metaphor for the office of the ruler beyond the individuals who held it.[102]

Every change in rule represented a moment of instability and danger that had to be bridged with the most secure and fixed ritual forms. The installation of an individual into the existing system of rulership through a ritual based on customary law or fixed in writing not only legitimized this person as a new holder of power, but also affirmed as legitimate the entire order itself and the roles of all those who participated in it. Throughout Europe, therefore, the ritual of consecrating the ruler constituted the oldest institutional tradition; the ritual form was "the oldest norm."[103] *Ordines*, in which the liturgical formulas, prayers, and chants for the coronation act were recorded, were among the oldest written traditions. The ritual as a whole created a transcendental effect through a series of formalized liturgical acts, namely, the divine sanctioning of the new officeholder.[104] The correct external forms that had to be observed for the ritual to become effective included, not least, the "correctness" of the place and the persons. After all, a ritual never functions without preconditions, but is always embedded within an overall system from which it derives its meaning and efficacy, and which it in turn affirms through its repeated performance. The actors themselves had to be authorized so that they in turn could carry out such a central authorization act—scholars of ritual call this ritual power *agency*. A system that is grounded primarily in ritual and not by way of positive law requires for its stability this kind of agency (seemingly not open to question), that in turn elevates the person holding it above all others. Just as the ritual derived its efficacy from the "right" actors, who were authorized to perform it by consecration, office, and tradition, the actors, conversely, derived their status from their function in this central ritual of rulership. The symbolic-ritual order was like a vault of status claims in which all building blocks supported one another.

In the case of the coronation of the Roman-German king, this order was partly fixed in writing, and partly handed down by customary law. For the royal coronations in the Empire, the Mainz *Ordo* of 1309 (the core of which went back to the tenth century) was still in use, supplemented by the stipulations in the Golden Bull. This spelled out how, where, and by whom the ritual was "correctly" performed.

Even though these forms were in fact by no means unimpeachable, they were felt to be unchangeable. As long as no historical-critical handling of the written tradition existed, it was easy to believe in a timeless continuity. In the case of the Empire, this was the continuity of the Roman imperium in the hands of the elected Frankish-German kings. The imperial coronations of Charlemagne and Otto the Great formed the foundations for the fiction of continuity according to which the Roman imperium had been transferred first to the Franks and then to the "Germans." The coronation of the German king as Roman emperor by the pope in Rome was a liturgical act that took up forms of the episcopal ordination, elevated the emperor above the laity, placed him within the tradition of the Roman Caesars, and endowed him with sacral dignity.[105]

Already in the course of the Middle Ages, the relationship between the elevation of a German king and the Roman imperial coronation had undergone a considerable shift. The right of the seven electors to choose the king had prevailed and had been codified in the Golden Bull of 1356. The rules that had been laid down in that document transformed not only the royal election into a decisive procedure, but at the same time the group of the electors into a political body collectively capable of taking action. The college of electors asserted the claim that by choosing the German king it was also electing the future emperor, thus pushing the role of the papal coronation into the background. In the early modern period, the formerly separated elements of the election of the king by the electors (in Frankfurt as stipulated by the Golden Bull), the coronation of the king (in Aachen as stipulated by the Golden Bull), and the imperial coronation (traditionally by the pope in Rome) slowly intermixed. Maximilian I dispensed entirely with the papal coronation, and after 1508 he called himself "elected Roman emperor." Charles V was the first to codify his promises to the electors in an electoral capitulation (*Wahlkapitulation*) and swore to them the traditional oath even before his royal coronation in Aachen. Only eleven years later did he have himself crowned emperor by the pope in Bologna. Shortly thereafter, he saw to it that in 1531 his brother Ferdinand was elected and crowned king of the Romans "and future emperor" by the electors with papal consent. However, Ferdinand I never received the prospective papal imperial coronation; instead, following his brother's abdication he was proclaimed emperor by the electors.[106] After that there would never be another imperial coronation in Rome. In 1562, Ferdinand's son Maximilian II was elected and crowned king of the Romans and future emperor during his father's lifetime. For the first time, both acts took place in Frankfurt. With this, the previously separate procedures of electing and crowning the German king on the one hand, and crowning the emperor in Rome on the other, were merged for the future into a *single* action sequence. The elected called himself king of the Romans while the emperor was still alive, and after this death he immediately commenced his reign as emperor. This development meant, first, an uncoupling of the Empire from the pope; second, an augmentation of the electors' power through the electoral capitulation issued before the coronation; third, a simultaneous strengthening of dynastic continuity through the principle of election *vivente Imperatore*, that is, during the lifetime of the emperor; and fourth, a further strengthening of the act of election over the act of coronation.

The Protestant jurists of the early seventeenth century had already valorized the election and downgraded the coronation in order to downplay papal influence and the predominantly Catholic sacrality of the ritual.[107] Later historians sharpened their statements into a contrast between the "legal act" of the election and the "empty ceremony" of the coronation. They emphasized the irrelevance of the external forms and lamented the "fetishism" with which people clung, for no reason, to the tangible formalities of the medieval ritual, which no longer had any kind of legally constitutive role.[108] But if one adopts this view, it is impossible to explain why those involved not only continued to adhere to the coronation ritual in its ancient form, but also quarreled intensively over their respective roles in it. When historians complain about the "unclear concepts" and the inconsistent legal classification of the phenomena by the actors at the time, this betrays an anachronistic misunderstanding. For this view presupposes that legal validity can be clearly differentiated from factual practice. However, that is possible only if there are superior, written, universally binding, and enforceable constitutional norms against which factual behavior can be measured. And that, precisely, was not yet the case in the premodern age, or it was only in its beginning stages. Yet if there existed any kind of procedure in the Empire that brought forth universally binding and secure decisions that were accepted a priori, it was the election of the king in accordance with the Golden Bull.

Still, the election did not render the subsequent coronation expendable. The actors themselves took the coronation ritual seriously. Likewise, the scholars who integrated it into their theory of public law did not question its legal quality. They conceived of the coronation as a solemn public act by which the election and the transfer of rulership of the Empire were in a sense renewed— *electio et commissio Imperii quasi renovantur*, in order to bestow divine blessing (*benedictio divina*), stabilize the authority of the elected monarch, and make him known to the people.[109] Even if the coronation had undoubtedly lost importance compared to the election, it is not possible to contrast election and coronation, with the former being a legal act and the latter "mere ritual." Rather, in the early modern era, they still formed an action sequence that was necessary to complete the transfer of rulership.

Election in Augsburg

As it had been for Charles V in 1530, the overriding concern for Ferdinand III in 1653 was securing the dynastic continuity in the house of Habsburg. His twenty-year-old son Ferdinand was to be elected his successor, king of the Romans, on the occasion of the imperial diet. However, the modality of such an election was one of the central points of contention—deferred so far—between the electors and princes that were to be resolved at this imperial diet. That is what the Peace of Westphalia had called for. A few estates disputed that the electors alone were empowered to elect the emperor's successor during his lifetime. With support from Sweden, they had tried unsuccessfully to push through a prohibition of this practice at Osnabrück. Above all, the princes asserted demands for participation in drafting the electoral capitulation, which was now to be permanently established as a kind of perpetual basic imperial law.[110] The Elector of Mainz feared that this would "markedly injure and tear apart the fundamental chief laws of the Holy Empire, bring forth a new form, weaken and nullify the authority and sovereignty of the electors."[111] To prevent this and to defend the traditional preeminence of the electors, the emperor and the electors had agreed on the election of the emperor's son Ferdinand earlier in Prague. It now suited them very well that the solemn reading of the proposition as formal opening of the deliberations had to be continually postponed because Swedish troops had not yet vacated Farther Pomerania. The emperor took advantage of this situation to invite the electors in May to Augsburg for the royal election and to confront the other estates with a fait accompli: "Thus the idea of a reform of the Empire ... perished even before the question could be so much as addressed at the imperial diet."[112]

An election, too, is a symbolic act, not only a technical procedure of decision making.[113] Its purpose is not only to choose a person for an office, but always also to demonstrate the role of the electors themselves, and to affirm the entire system that assigns them this role. That was also the case here. Already the location of the election could be interpreted by observers as a message. The electors or their envoys journeyed to Augsburg to receive the emperor and his son (who, after all, had an electoral vote himself as the King of Bohemia) and carry out the election, while the other estates of the realm remained behind in Regensburg. The justification was that the election business would be too cumbersome in that city; the many foreign guests could hardly be removed from the city for the period of the election, as the Golden Bull stipulated.[114] The papal nuncio reported back to Rome that the electors did not carry out the election under the eyes of the other imperial estates because they wanted to appear completely free in their right of election.[115]

The biconfessional imperial city of Augsburg became for the duration of the election a special, legally, and spatially self-contained area. Following the festive entry of the emperor on 20 May and the act of homage, the city council and the citizenry swore the oath of protection to the archchancellor of Mainz on 30 May, the day before the election.[116] With this oath they pledged to guarantee peace in the city and proceedings free of any threat of violence. All foreigners, among them also the envoys from Poland and Spain, with the exception of the electoral retinue, had to leave the city until the evening before the election. Thereafter the city bailiffs (*Stadtvögte*) brought the archchancellor the keys to the city gates, which remained locked until the end of the election. On the day of the election, the electors of Mainz, Cologne, Trier, the Palatinate, and Bohemia and the electoral envoys from Bavaria, Saxony, and Brandenburg met in city hall. The electors donned their red electoral habit, by which they set themselves visually apart from the envoys, and the group rode in procession— according to a previously negotiated order—to the church of St. Ulrich, with every elector who was participating in person having his electoral sword carried ahead of him. In church everyone took his place at the high altar to attend the mass *De Sancto Spiritu*. The Protestant electors, "not attached to the religion,"[117] left after the Gospel as usual and returned only after the Communion; every time the Catholics knelt, they remained standing. Next all electors swore the oath on the Gospel, as stipulated in the Golden Bull.

The conclave took place in the sacristy. The electors proceeded to this location in precise order, initially still accompanied by three councilors each as witnesses and by two notaries. They sat down in a row of eight identical chairs of red velvet, because now, in the act of election, the envoys for once embodied their lords in the fullest sense of that word. The imperial hereditary marshal brought the keys of the barred city gates into the conclave and locked the door. The Elector of Mainz, as the chief election official, asked whether there was anything "that might be an impediment to this election."[118] Next every elector pledged to affirm the electoral capitulation on oath should he be elected, and to most assuredly submit to the majority decision in the end. This was an especially notable procedure: that the individuals submitted ahead of time to a decision, regardless of its outcome, endowed the decision with a certainty that was otherwise rarely achieved. Then the electoral capitulation—which had already been accepted by all the previous day—was sealed and placed in the conclave on the altar, just as documents had been placed on the altar since time immemorial to symbolically sanction a legal transaction. The notaries made a written protocol of everything that transpired, and three Habsburg councilors witnessed it. Thereafter they left the room, leaving behind only the eight electors. The conclave was now the completely closed-off center of a closed-off city. For forty-five minutes it was a secret room from which nothing penetrated to the outside. Nobody found out about what went on there; no source has handed it down. The exclusion had taken place in several steps, as the circle of those present had been gradually reduced. What was celebrated in this way as a perfect secret was the free choice itself, which belonged solely to the electors.

Once the election had taken place, the councilors and notaries were brought back in first and asked to bring the emperor into the conclave, because his "presence is needed there." Then the Elector of Mainz announced the result to those present, that they had *unanimiter ac nullo discrepante*, unanimously and without any dissent, elected the King of Hungary and Bohemia as king of the Romans, "though for important reasons it had to be kept secret until His Imperial Majesty was present." What came next was the enactment of the authority of the reigning emperor, who consented to the election of his successor even before the latter himself accepted the election.[119] The symbolic framework and the sequence of the acts were highly significant. First, the emperor and his retinue were received at the church door by the eight electors (or rather the electoral envoys) and escorted to a side chapel, "a specially made conclave for this purpose",[120] where he allowed himself to be dressed in the imperial vestments and had the crown placed on his head. Then they jointly proceeded to the electoral conclave, accompanied by the five electoral sword bearers, the holders of the hereditary offices with the imperial regalia, the five heralds (two of the Empire, one each for Hungary, Bohemia, and Austria), and the witnesses. In the conclave a throne had been set up for the emperor next to the altar, where he took his seat while the electors stood facing him with bare heads. Once again the door of the conclave was locked. The Elector of Mainz thanked the emperor for coming and informed him of the result of the election. We then read the following in the ceremonial protocols of the court of Vienna: "But when His Royal Majesty did not wish to agree to the acceptance of this election without the prior knowledge and consent of His Imperial Majesty, that is, his most venerable father, the electors present and the envoys of those absent asked His Imperial Majesty in deepest submission that He condescend not only to most graciously consent to this election, but also to exhort his beloved son to do the same."[121] The emperor expressed his thanks, granted the consent asked for, and promised to ask his son to accept the election and to pledge him his support. Only then did the newly elected king accept the election "in God's name" and thank his father—not the electors—by kissing his hand. There followed the congratulations of the electors and the thanks of the elected, who subsequently swore the oath upon the electoral capitulation, whereby he took off the (Bohemian) crown and touched the Gospel on the altar with two fingers. After the oath, still within the conclave, he was for the first time "proclaimed with the reading of the written form," which those present witnessed and the notaries recorded.

This procedure, inserted between election and proclamation, took into account the fact that the throne was not vacant during the election. The act was arranged in such a way that the electors were not the only ones to appear as actors. Juxtaposed to their conclave was a parallel imperial conclave, where the majesty of the emperor could be enacted in solemn form with everything that pertained to it. At the center of the act stood the emperor, not the newly elected king, who, as a faithfully obedient and submissive son, did only what his father commanded. The emperor injected himself between the choice of the electors and the king's acceptance, so that the son received the office from the hand of his father, not the hands of the electors. If one considers that solemn ritual acts carried out with all the symbols of majesty, and affirmed by the witnesses through their participation, created a high degree of obligatoriness for the future, it becomes clear that this act aimed to visibly strengthen the dynastic element of succession. What was staged here could be interpreted as the right of the emperor to consent to the election of the king. But the actors at the time did not know that yet. Especially the Elector of Brandenburg was concerned that "the constant continuation in a certain house" could impair the freedom of the choice by the electors and could cause the emperorship to degenerate into a hereditary succession to the throne.[122] He had good cause to be worried, since the imperial lord chamberlain (*Obersthofmeister*) and influential courtier Auersperg had let it be known that if the Elector of Brandenburg did not send his envoys to Augsburg in due time, the election could be carried out without him.[123] This reveals just how much the imperial court, in agreement with the archchancellor, had assumed control over the staging of the election and coronation events. The boundaries between the right of election and hereditary right were always fluid, and the transformation from an electoral into a hereditary monarchy was nothing unusual in Europe.[124] If the chosen man, as was the case here, was always also the dynastic successor, the transfer of rulership fluctuated between the hereditary and the electoral right. To protect their unencumbered right of election, the electors had therefore written into the electoral capitulation that, if necessary, they could elect the king of the Romans without imperial consent.[125] In reality, though, the stipulations in the electoral capitulation were not infrequently ignored. The solemn ritual praxis was therefore not an empty show, but an act upon which—circumstances being favorable—one might be able to construct a new legal position.

The first proclamation, which took place still in the conclave, was followed by the graduated presentation of the outcome of the election to a gradually expanded public. First came the courtly public in the church, where the electors seated the king festively on the altar while the Te Deum was chanted, drums were beaten and trumpets sounded, bells were rung, and canons fired from the city's bastions, which made it audible for miles that a new king had been elected. Then the actors took their places at the high altar, the portals of the church were opened, and the crowd assembled outside was admitted. "Before the entire people" the Elector of Mainz acclaimed the king of the Romans for a third time, and the crowd endorsed the election in ritualized form with three cheers of *Vivat Ferdinandus Rex.* Then the city gates were reopened. The other European princely courts were informed of the election either personally by envoys or in writing by messengers; notifications and congratulations were exchanged in a highly ceremonialized form and graduated by rank. The broader European public, finally, was informed of the act through newspapers and periodical journals like the *Theatrum Europaeum*, which devoted great attention to the symbolic-ritual details.[126]

The ceremonial order of individuals in the act of election was precisely spelled out in the Golden Bull to prevent quarrels over rank from ever dividing the college.[127] Now, however, the number of electors had increased. For the first time in three hundred years, the finely calibrated order of the Golden Bull, which assigned everyone a precise place, was thrown out of balance. Since the Peace of Westphalia had transferred to the Duke of Bavaria the electoral honor and thus also the place and office of archsteward previously held by his cousin from the Palatinate, the latter had to content himself with the eighth and final place. Moreover, he no longer possessed an arch office from which the honor of the electors was derived.[128] As a result, Karl Ludwig of the Palatinate had initially continued to bear his old title of archsteward, simply ignoring the fact that the title now belonged to his Bavarian relative and rival, until eventually, after protracted negotiations, a new arch office was created for him, that of archtreasurer. At the imperial diet in Regensburg it was important for him to assert this honor in the most effective way possible, and to compensate for the demotion represented by the eighth place in the college of electors. And so ever since his entry, as we have seen, he was entangled in a dispute with the envoys from the Electress of Bavaria, to whom he did not wish to be subordinated. Above all, it was now unclear which insignia should symbolize his new arch office and what services specifically this would entail during the election and the coronation. The result was that an open conflict broke out during the election proceedings. Karl Ludwig protested *solenniter* during the oath of the electors, because the envoys from the absent electors were given precedence over him. The envoys, however, held their own by arguing that they must be treated like the electors present when playing their role as member of the electoral body.[129] While the emperor was changing, Karl Ludwig was quarreling with the Elector of Trier about the rank order in the escort and complaining about the disadvantage he was suffering from the fact that there still were no regalia for him to carry, even though the emperor had promised him the crown as his heraldic symbol.[130] So when the emperor, following the election, stepped up to the altar before the eyes of the courtly public to pray, Karl Ludwig created a ritual fait accompli by suddenly moving forward and taking the crown from his head. The Brandenburg envoy Blumenthal felt blindsided: "When I had seen this, I likewise stepped forward immediately, such that I also took hold of the Imperial crown, and together with His Electoral Highness of Heidelberg placed it on the velvet cushion prepared for that purpose."[131] Karl Ludwig "took this very badly" and as an affront. However, Blumenthal insisted that placing the crown on the king's head and taking it off, just like dressing and undressing him, was among the tasks of the Brandenburger in his capacity as archchamberlain. When the emperor realized that Blumenthal would "in no way give in" and was determined to also put the crown back on his head, he prevailed upon Karl Ludwig, "in order to prevent a greater scandal in such a place," to yield to the Brandenburger. However, immediately after the election and before the coronation, Karl Ludwig was able to extract from the emperor a clarification of his future role.[132] The emperor in fact not only granted him the "Aachen imperial crown" as a heraldic symbol, but also accorded him the right to carry either the original at the coronation, or, if the king was wearing the original himself, a copy made for that very purpose. And he would carry the crown in his hands instead of on a cushion, something that was especially important to the elector. This is also how Karl Ludwig had himself depicted on broadsheets and portraits later, after the coronation of Leopold I.[133] Sober-minded modern historians have seen this as either personal vanity or archaic fetishism: things in their concrete materialness as veritable magical objects of the electoral craving for prestige. But the struggle over objects and their ritual use was not particularly vain or irrational; rather, it accorded with the logic of the premodern culture of presence. The insignia embodied the majesty of the Empire. And since the privileged electoral participation in the Empire was derived from the arch offices and was manifest in them, the place of every elector within the classification system and the imperial order depended on the performance of the symbolic services and the disposition over the symbolic objects. An honor, however, that was not visible would invariably disappear sooner or later.

The quarrel over the palpable details of the ceremony of the election makes clear that the election by no means had only an instrumental function, that of deciding who would be king, but, inseparably linked to that function, simultaneously possessed high symbolic value. Especially in this first election after the Peace of Westphalia, in a situation that was in many respects open and fluid, the actors had to try and uphold their positions symbolically and ritually: for the electors as a group, the goal was to fend off the right of participation by the other states; for every individual elector, the goal was to preserve his own role in the events; for the emperor, the goal was to stabilize the principle of election *vivente imperatore*. This election not only decided who would be king of the Romans; it also demonstrated who was allowed to vote, according to what right, and within which historical tradition. Above all, the secret act in conclave symbolized—especially when the actual decision had already been negotiated ahead of time—"that the election is in our free will,"[134] namely, solely within the free will of the electors and nobody else.

Coronation in Regensburg

The election was followed by the coronation. The Golden Bull specified Aachen as the place of coronation and the right of the Elector of Cologne to act as consecrator,[135] thus situating every new king within the tradition of Charlemagne and Otto the Great. However, at the coronation of Ferdinand IV, the site was not Aachen but Regensburg, and the consecrator was not the Elector of Cologne but the Elector of Mainz. This coronation reveals in exemplary fashion how flexibly contemporaries handled the ritual tradition, while simultaneously seeking to maintain the old norm in the face of these factual deviations, thereby creating the fiction that the tradition was still continuing—a praxis that is characteristic for the Empire in general.

The year 1653 was by no means the first time that the stipulations of the Golden Bull had been violated. Aachen had last been the coronation site in 1531, when Ferdinand I was elevated as king of the Romans. Since then emperors had departed from this arrangement for various reasons, in each instance "by way of exception." But the council of the city of Aachen never tired of lodging a solemn protest every time against the change in venue, and of having the ancient privilege confirmed in writing time and again. Three imperial regalia were the pledges undergirding Aachen's right as the site of the coronation and the keeper of the Carolingian tradition: a curved sword and a Gospel that were traced back to Charlemagne, and a reliquary with the blood of St. Stephan. The council of Aachen brought these sacred objects, symbols of the presence of the *maiestas Imperii* and embodiments of the unbroken continuity of the emperorship, to every coronation and subsequently returned home with them, exactly what the Nurembergers did with their imperial regalia. In this way, the possession of these objects secured for the Aacheners their regular participation in the coronations and made it easier for them to maintain their claim to being the proper site of the coronation. For it was upon that status that the citizens of Aachen based their rank as the first among the imperial cities, though Cologne traditionally contested it—a dispute that lasted as long as the Empire, was pending before the Imperial Chamber Court for centuries without a decision ever being handed down, and erupted at every coronation banquet as a seating quarrel at the table of the city envoys.[136] To strengthen the Aachen coronation tradition, the city council developed a new strategy in 1653: it advanced a claim to the other imperial insignia, which had been in the possession of the city of Nuremberg since 1423 thanks to an imperial privilege.[137] The justification was still quite terse: Aachen was the coronation city, and the regalia had been kept in Aachen for a long period, though this could hardly be supported with good arguments. Subsequently, this claim led to a protracted debate—carried on in published writings—between the two cities, a debate that challenged the scholars on both sides to reconstruct the history of the imperial regalia in greater detail—with the intent of providing historical justification to their respective claims, though with the eventually counterproductive result that the age of the objects and their ties to Charlemagne became increasingly dubious.[138] Aachen was unable to prevail against Nuremberg with its foray, nor did it succeed in becoming ever again the stage for a coronation. Nevertheless, it continuously maintained its claim with the means of the ritualized protestation until the end of the Empire—one among countless pretensions that, over the centuries, coalesced into an impenetrable thicket of competing claims, and that the *Reichspublizisten* labored to organize and thin out.[139]

The fact that neither Aachen nor even Frankfurt was the coronation city in 1653 but Regensburg had further repercussions. Regensburg was situated neither in the ecclesiastical province of the archbishop of Cologne—like Aachen—nor in that of the archbishop of Mainz—like Frankfurt. In Regensburg, the Elector of Cologne now reasserted his ancient right against Mainz.[140] For both sides an essential interest was at stake. Johann Jakob Moser reported later that "the guards and armed servants of both electors had been given orders to assist their lords with the utmost force, also in the church, were the same to have suffered encroachment on their rights by anyone, so that it could have easily come to a ... bloody tragedy, had not the assiduous care of the emperor prevented such an evil."[141] The emperor decided in the short term in favor of the Elector of Mainz, whereupon his rival from Cologne departed even before the coronation without taking his leave from the emperor. However, *in ipso actu*, during the ritual before the altar, he had his envoy "interject" a solemn *protestatio* to the Mainz rival by rejecting his actions as an unlawful, inflammatory, and violent act, *actum mere turbativum et violentum*.[142] As so often, we encounter here the revealing phenomenon that a competing claim was asserted not merely in writing, but in full form during the performance of a ritual. This reveals once more the kind of efficaciousness that was accorded to the ritual. If a ritual was carried out without dissent, it established a binding claim. That is why the dissent against it always had to be enacted *solemniter* along with the ritual.

After the two electors had received legal backing from prominent scholars, they agreed in 1657 to a compromise that fundamentally affirmed the right of consecration of both archbishops. The right was to be exercised in each case by the man in whose archdiocese the coronation took place; in all other locations, they would take turns. Revealingly enough, historians today explain the quarrel over the coronation right as a strategic calculus on the part of the Elector of Mainz, who was using it to undergird his own "authority to set foreign policy."[143] This implies that the function as consecrator had no value for him as such, but was merely a means to an end. But all electors felt so strongly about their roles at the coronation that they had them specifically confirmed in writing in the electoral capitulations,[144] and as the crown dispute discussed previously between Brandenburg and the Palatinate reveals, they quarreled over them down to the most minute detail.¹⁴⁵ The power of ritual action at the coronation had to be a value in itself to them, because it made visible the foundations of the entire imperial order and their respective places in it.

In Regensburg, the Elector of Mainz asserted himself successfully. It was he who read the mass and recited the liturgical formulas according to the *Ordo* of 1309.¹⁴⁶ In keeping with tradition, the rite began with the prostration, a gesture of total self-abasement, as the oldest Mainz *Ordo* of 960 had already stipulated. The king prostrated himself facedown on the floor in front of the altar. This followed the pattern of all rituals of transition: abasement always preceded the elevation. The higher the *exaltatio*, the lower the preceding *humiliatio*.¹⁴⁷ Next came an act of ritual examination consisting of a number of formulaic questions to the king. By his responses he assumed the duties of his office and affirmed them with an oath. Then the elector turned to the surrounding clerics and princes, who represented the *populus* pars pro toto, and acclaimed the act through their *fiat*. In this way the ritual established a three-sided obligation between God, the king, and "the people." Then the king was disrobed and anointed and blessed like a priest by the archbishop of Mainz. Subsequently he was dressed step-by-step with the vestments and insignia of rulership. Fully attired in the regalia, the newly invested king recited his royal oath upon the Aachen Gospel and received the Eucharist in both forms. All of these elements elevated the king above the laity and endowed him with a sacral, quasi-priestly status. Finally, he took his seat on a throne that had been erected next to the altar and was modeled after the chair of Charlemagne in the cathedral in Aachen, thereby taking possession of the Empire. At this very moment began the Te Deum, drumbeats, trumpet blasts, and canon salvos. Seated on the throne, the king symbolically exercised his future office by knighting a number of cavaliers. This act was a ritual demonstration of his royal authority, the core of which was the power to grant status.¹⁴⁸ The act in the church concluded with the ritualized admission of the elected into the Marienstift monastery in Aachen and the confirmation of the Aachen privileges.

Throughout all of this, the handling of the imperial regalia followed a choreography that had been discussed ahead of time down to every detail, a choreography during which both the electors themselves and their envoys, the holders of the hereditary offices, and the imperial court officials had to pick up, hold, or carry the various sacred objects at different times. In the process the dispute between electoral Palatinate and Brandenburg briefly flared up again, since Elector Frederick William of Brandenburg had once again impressed upon his envoys not to forego the crown service under any circumstances. When the issue of removing the crown from the king's head in front of the altar came up, the count palatine and the envoy Blumenthal therefore "already began to quarrel over this," but they were told that this honor belonged to neither one of them, but to the Elector of Trier.¹⁴⁹

The coronation was followed by the coronation feast in city hall—it, too, followed a fixed ritual script. As with every ritual of transition, the shared meal confirmed the invested individual in his new role.[150] The coronation meal was a symbolic table fellowship of king and people, mediated through the electors or their representatives, who exercised the courtly arch offices on this occasion. While the crowned king was eating at table, a wine fountain had been set up for the citizens in the square before city hall, a whole oxen had been roasted, and a mountain of oats had been heaped up. The hereditary imperial marshal (*Erbmarschall*) fetched a measure of oats for the royal stable, while the hereditary imperial chamberlain (*Erbkämmerer*) brought the hand-washing basin to the king. The hereditary imperial steward (*Erbtruchsess*) and the hereditary imperial cupbearer (*Erbschenk*) took a little from the roasted oxen and the wine fountain and carried it to the royal table; everything else they left for the people.[151] The Elector of the Palatinate exercised his new office of arch-treasurer in person by tossing out coronation coins. While the crowd fought over the surrendered objects, the king, the emperor (not the empress), the electors, and the princes ate the shared meal in the chamber of city hall, strictly arranged and graded according to the rules of the Golden Bull. Each elector had a separate table with a sumptuous credenza, but only the electors who were present in person took their seats there; the others remained empty. The princes had to seat themselves at a long table in the middle of the hall. Hardly anything was actually eaten at this ritual act. The dishes were served by imperial counts, who had previously quarreled vigorously over participation in this service. The entire act was long dismissed by historians as a medieval comic play or "customary imperial nuisance."[152] Of course, contemporaries also experienced all of this as archaic. But that is precisely what constituted the symbolic value of the ritual. The coronation was a staged assertion of continuity, one that made Charlemagne symbolically present at every turn and demonstrated to all the age and sanctity of the emperorship.

The king of the Romans was already king before the coronation and anointing; in the view of the lawyers, as we have seen, he became king through the election. But that did not render the coronation superfluous, for a ritual of installation is never only about the person being installed in his office, but also about those installing him.[153] That was even truer for this election and coronation. Unlike the election, which had taken place in the seclusion of the conclave, the coronation in Regensburg now demonstrated in broad public on the great stage of the imperial diet that the electors were the pillar of the Empire on whom the dignity of the supreme ruler rested.[154] By contrast, the princes had to content themselves with the role of spectators and thus—like it or not— "perform unpaid ceremonial labor."[155] Unless they wanted to absent themselves entirely from the upcoming imperial diet, they had no choice but to contribute to the splendid staging of electoral preeminence by their very presence and to watch their own marginalization. That is why the Princes of Württemberg, Hesse, and Baden offered at least a small sign of their unhappiness at the end. Contrary to custom and in defiance of the explicit order from the hereditary imperial marshal to walk bareheaded on the return from the cathedral to the imperial lodgings, they donned their hats in the procession, and in defiance of the order from Chief Court Marshal Dietrichstein, following the coronation meal they did not proceed on foot with the emperor to his quarters, but disappeared in their coaches. These were pointed gestures of disrespect toward this entire event, by which the emperor and the electors had presented them with a fait accompli on a fundamental constitutional question.[156]

Coronation of the Empress

If the royal coronation was above all an enactment of the exclusive status of the college of electors, the coronation of the empress a few weeks later was a staging of the emperor's court society. Unlike the royal coronation of her stepson, the coronation of Empress Eleonora of Mantua from the house of Gonzaga on 4 August 1653 was, strictly speaking, not a ritual of installation at all. After all, she was the wife of the emperor and thus ipso facto already empress. That accorded with the premodern gender order at all levels of estate-based society—much like the wife of the professor was "Frau Professorin" and the wife of the miller "Frau Müllerin." The emperor and the empress likewise constituted an officeholding couple.[157] Since the dignity of the Roman emperor was acquired by election and not hereditary right, it could not be granted to a woman. Even though no imperial law prohibited it in principle, a woman "could hardly ever entertain any such hope."[158] Only dynastic right of succession made it possible in some monarchies for a woman herself to hold royal power, as for example in the case of Elizabeth of England or Christina of Sweden.[159] By contrast, a woman did not become empress herself but only in her capacity as wife, which is why no coronation at all was in fact required.

Unlike medieval queens, early modern empresses were crowned only in a few instances, and never in a single ritual jointly with their husband.[160] The latter had happened for the last time with Eleonora of Portugal, the wife of Frederick III, in 1452, following their wedding. In 1612, Emperor Matthias was the first to return to this tradition. But different from the event 160 years earlier, his wife, Anna of Tyrol, was crowned in a separate ritual two days after her husband.[161] Ferdinand II had his second wife, Eleonora of Mantua (the Elder), crowned on 7 November 1630 at the electoral assembly in Regensburg as a way of underscoring the resolution to the war of succession over Mantua in his favor; it was thus a dynastic demonstration, entirely independent of his own succession to the throne and the wedding—both events had occurred much earlier. His son Ferdinand III, however, attached importance to having his first wife, Maria Anna of Spain, crowned shortly after his own elevation as king of the Romans. His second wife died young. His third wife, Eleonora of Mantua (the Younger), whom he had married in 1651 and who had just recently—on the day of the royal election in Augsburg—given birth to a daughter, was to be crowned empress in Regensburg. Like his father, Ferdinand III used this ceremony, entirely disconnected from a wedding or change of ruler, for a great dynastic performance on the stage of the Empire.[162]

Unlike in the case of the king, the Golden Bull contained no regulations concerning the coronation of a queen. While the liturgical texts were in line with the medieval coronation *ordines*, the organization of space and persons was not stipulated anywhere. This gave rise to conflicts, but it also opened up much greater leeway and flexibility for the emperor, which Ferdinand III took advantage of.[163] One quarrel that now erupted in the coronation ritual was highly significant: that between the highest female court official, the chief lady chamberlain (*Oberthofmeisterin*), and the imperial princesses and countesses and their daughters. For this was a competition between two different hierarchies and thus also two different systems of ceremonial rules: the hierarchy of the imperial court on the one hand, and that of the Empire on the other.[164] This competition was old, and in Regensburg, too, it had been smoldering the entire time. At liturgical occasions in that city, the high Viennese court officials were assigned the most prominent roles. There had already been repeated clashes over precedence between the female family members of the imperial princes and the ladies of the imperial court.[165] This was now causing unrest on the eve of the coronation of the empress. "The princes are disaffected because, at the coronation of the empress, their children and sisters are to follow on those who hold the court offices, and the counts are sorely dissatisfied because the court ladies are supposed to precede their wives."[166] The hierarchy of the female court offices was a mirror image of that of their husbands; the conflicts of the court ladies therefore reflected those of the men.[167]

The princes and the counts sought to prevail upon the emperor through written petitions not to violate the old custom, which seems to have been on their side.[168] The emperor refused to be drawn into this argument and decided that the chief lady chamberlain (*Oberthofmeisterin*) had to be at the empress's beck and call at all times; she thus had to sit directly behind her throne and walk immediately behind the two princesses, who were carrying the empress's train. He informed the princes coolly that they were free not to have their daughters and sisters participate in the coronation if they had reservations about this arrangement.[169] The imperial counts, who stood at the lower end of the imperial hierarchy and therefore continuously saw their "imperial status and dignity" in peril,[170] likewise did not receive what they wanted: they had to be satisfied with having one imperial countess walking in a row with an imperial court lady and the wife of a chamberlain. This was already a concession that was owed to the "imperial act." As for the rest, the emperor ordered that "the custom at the imperial court would remain in force."[171]

The coronation was staged as a great dynastic solemnity.[172] The emperor and the king of the Romans processed into the cathedral dressed in their vestments and regalia, the emperor with the real Nuremberg crown, the king with a copy.[173] The empress was "very exquisitely draped with many regalia and jewels, and appeared together with her highly respectable ladies,"[174] that is to say, her female household. On the way into the church the long train of her dress was carried by the two imperial princesses of Württemberg and Hesse, and on the way out by the princesses of Palatinate-Simmern and Baden. The two Protestant princesses had to accept that they would have to remain present during the Eucharist, but at least "they moved, as being non-Catholic, a little to the side during Communion."[175] The chief lady chamberlain served the empress throughout in the most prominent place. The emperor presented his wife to the imperial archchancellor, the Elector of Mainz to be crowned. The coronation ceremony itself followed essentially that of the emperor; the liturgy was in line with the medieval *Ordo*: full-body prostration in front of the altar, investment, anointing, and coronation by the Elector and archbishop of Mainz. Four imperial bishops and abbots assisted him. The insignia of the crown, orb, and scepter were those of the emperor himself—the genuine ones, that is, those of Charlemagne, as observers emphasized.[176] The only thing not bestowed upon the empress was the sword, which made visible physical power as the foundation of rulership, and she did not swear a coronation oath.

Contrary to expectations, everything came off peacefully;[177] countesses and princesses assumed the subordinate places assigned to them. The coronation was a clear victory of the Habsburg court over the hierarchy of the Empire and over ancient tradition. The emperor had asserted himself as the ceremonial director on this stage. At the same time, however, another piece was being performed at another venue: sandwiched between the two coronations, the deliberations of the imperial diet had been formally opened with the *Proposition*, the formal presentation of the agenda. Here, too, the question was whether the emperor would assert himself successfully as the head of the status order of the Empire.

Failed Opening

The events in Regensburg in the first half of the year 1653 took place on a front stage and a backstage. The imperial family, electors, and princes had been assembled since the turn of the year along with their large court societies; they had been waiting for months and had been spending a lot of money. They held their separate masses, celebrated weddings, went on sleigh rides and hunting outings, invited one another to banquets and masquerades, watched an opera and Otto von Guericke's vacuum experiment as sensational novelties, and staged the grandiose spectacle of the two coronations. Parallel to this, the princely councilors had already been in session *extraordinarie* since the end of March in the lodgings of Imperial Vice-Chancellor Kurz to deliberate the withdrawal of the Swedes from Pomerania, the upcoming royal election (which they were unable in the end to influence), and not least the modalities of their deliberations. The envoys from electors and cities also met in separate sessions. However, as long as there had been no solemn opening and no reading of the proposition, these assemblies were not considered acts of the Empire, even though they unfolded entirely in keeping with its rules and regulations. The procedural practice had gradually solidified since the early sixteenth century, though without ever having been fixed by treaty or imperial law. The solemn opening with the imperial proposition was followed by the separation into the three estate-based deliberative bodies (*Räte* or *Kurien*) of the electors, princes, and cities, and their interactions. The latter involved a complex, dialogic back and forth between the college of the electors and that of the princes, the outcome of which the cities could then merely join.[178] In the chancellery of the Elector of Mainz, this practice of customary law was put down in writing in 1569 as a guideline for how to conduct the negotiations; in numerous copies it was circulated also within the chanceries of the imperial estates, and since the seventeenth century it had been widely distributed in printed form.[179]

The learned councilors were completely among themselves in the deliberations; "none of the princely persons had appeared."[180] Still, the organizing problems that had bedeviled the imperial diets since time immemorial reared their heads here. After all, the seating order in the deliberations was still a symbolic-ceremonial procedural order that not only ensured an orderly polling of the votes, but at the same time created the exact hierarchical arrangement of the estates.[181] The session conflicts now became more intense than ever before. For now the additional challenge was to put into effect all the changes that had in the meantime occurred among the princes, counts, lords, and prelates in the order of the seats and votes. And since this imperial diet was supposed to rectify the defects of the previous diets, many took the opportunity here to improve their status or settle old scores. One could not begin to think about the other issues up for negotiation until these old and new claims had been transported into an orderly symbolic process.

To get a sense of the variety and nature of the conflicts, it suffices to take a look at the first extraordinary session of the council of princes. A scandal erupted there at the very beginning when the envoys from Palatine-Neuburg and Palatine-Simmern—that is, representatives of competing dynastic lineages—engaged in "tough wrangling" over the taking of their seats, "and nobody wanted to yield to the other, so that they jostled for the place also when sitting down."[182] The envoy from Simmern, who had not received an invitation to the imperial diet even though the Peace of Westphalia had restored to his lord all the holdings lost in the war, would let no one keep him from attending the session standing, and to protest whenever the envoy from the electoral Palatinate gave his vote. A quarrel erupted also over the seats of the secularized bishoprics, which had by now been incorporated into secular territories once and for all.[183] In addition, the many different lines of Ernestine Saxony traditionally fought over the sequence of their votes. An ancient conflict that was given new sustenance was also that between the so-called alternating houses, the principalities of Pomerania, Mecklenburg, Württemberg, Hesse, and Baden, among which there had existed for some time a complicated scheme over the daily alternation of the seats, the details of which were constantly in dispute. In 1640 they had come to an agreement; now, however, the emperor had decreed that Holstein should also be accepted into this session carousel, which once again injected a lot of movement into it. Moreover, the bishops of Eichstätt and Speyer revived their more than one-hundred-year-old quarrel over precedence. New conflict potential was introduced by the Duke of Lauenburg, who wished to be treated like a prince present in person, even though he was merely the younger brother of the governing duke. The Counts of Wetterau opposed the admission of peers from Westphalia and Lower Saxony into their own collective vote.[184] Finally, a protest was also lodged against the first-time participation of four newly elevated princes who had not yet been "solemnly introduced" at the imperial diet.

In most of these cases, the parties involved approached the emperor with memoranda and protestations, including numerous enclosures (copies of documents from earlier imperial diets), and for now kept away from the deliberations so as not to create any fait accompli. But under these circumstances it made no sense to begin the deliberations, because there was a danger that the many absentees would later claim that the decisions made were not binding upon them. That is why the "reintegration of the college" was itself a main topic of the deliberations; the goal was to ensure that the envoys present in Regensburg did in fact appear for the sessions.[185] Some things were therefore "provisionally" settled by majority decision at this time, some things were decided by the emperor by decree, a few issues were settled *in perpetuum* among the parties involved, but much remained in abeyance.

Twelve times the college of princes met in *extraordinarie* until 20 May—the same day the emperor and his son solemnly entered Augsburg for the election—without having "reintegrated" itself and having fundamentally clarified its own participation in the election of the king. The warning of the envoy of Brandenburg "not to put the cart before the horse, to effect the election first and deliberate about it only afterward," went unheeded.[186] For that is precisely what happened: the election and coronation of Ferdinand IV had already taken place when the deliberations of the imperial diet were at long last formally opened.

Only after the Swedes had finally fulfilled the condition of participation at the imperial diet and had withdrawn from Pomerania did the emperor invite the estates to the solemn proposition on 30 June (20 June according to the Protestant calendar), namely, to his residence. He invoked his serious gout, which made it impossible for him to ride a horse, when he chose his lodgings in the bishop's residence as the location for the opening, and not—as was traditional—city hall.[187] As in 1530, this location became once again a bone of contention. It was the wrong stage and the wrong symbolic framework. In the emperor's residence the event would have been subject solely to his direction, which would thus have defined the imperial diet as the emperor's court diet. This significant change of tradition, which had been talked about for months, was not something the imperial estates could accept. For the princes nothing less was at stake than the sovereignty of the emperor, the liberty of the estates, and the preservation of the *status Germaniae*.[188] After all, one had assembled, it was said, to remedy the failings of the previous imperial diets, not to add to them. The princes let it be known that unless the proposition took place *in publico* as per custom, they would "feel little desire to appear."[189] As a result, on the eve of the opening a new imperial order was issued, and the chairs that had already been set up in the *Ritterstube* of the emperor's lodgings were returned to city hall.

The estates and envoys therefore picked up the emperor at his quarters in the morning, as was customary, waited there for two hours in the antechamber until he had taken his breakfast and the first problems of precedence had been resolved, escorted him the few steps from the bishop's residence to the cathedral, where the Holy Spirit mass took place, and from there to city hall across a wooden bridge erected for that very purpose. Observers perceived the events surrounding the procession as not very solemn. The Elector of Cologne had already departed because of the quarrel over the coronation; the bishop of Eichstätt had left Regensburg demonstratively on the day of the opening because he was unwilling to accept the emperor's settlement of his conflict over rank with Speyer, and the "new" princes also stayed away.

The sequencing of persons during the procession seemed "fairly confused, disorderly, muddled."[190] The emperor did not ride on horseback, but was carried in an open litter; the electors and princes were also not mounted, but walked on foot; all the envoys strode ahead haphazardly (*promiscue*), for the princes personally present had previously demanded from the emperor in writing that he provide them precedence over the envoys and forbid them from riding.[191] What was also striking is that neither the emperor nor the electors were wearing their vestments, but "their usual clothes."[192] With that, the opening stood in marked contrast to the election and coronation events shortly

Figure 10. Solemn session of the imperial diet, 1653. Single-page broadsheet entitled *Eigentlicher Abriss der Reichstags-Solennitet, so den 13.–23. Juny Anno 1653 in Regensburg auf dem gewöhnlichen großen Rathauß-Saal, bey Eröffnung der kaiserlichen Proposition angestellet und gehalten worden*, Germanisches Nationalmuseum Nuremberg, Graphische Sammlung.

before. By sitting neither on horseback nor in coaches and not wearing their regalia, the emperor and the electors were visibly downgrading the events in Regensburg city hall. At the election and coronation the majesty of the Empire had been celebrated in all formality by them "exclusively," but not here, in the deliberations with all the other estates. If the emperor was unable to move the opening to his residence, he at least wanted to mark the event as clearly of secondary importance.[193]

The solemn opening session was a spatial depiction of the Empire's classification system. The hereditary imperial marshal had the city hall chamber set up similar to the cathedral, such that the estate gradations became visible in the literal sense of the word: the emperor himself sat at the end wall under the canopy, six steps elevated; two steps elevated to his right and left sat the electors, the Elector of Trier as usual across from him, also elevated two steps. The Elector of the Palatinate had pushed through that he was allowed to sit ahead of the envoys of his electoral colleagues. Elevated only one step stood the benches of the ecclesiastical and secular princes, who were also separated from the imperial counts and the city envoys by a kind of fence. Although the representatives of the princes sat on the seats of their absent lords, they were distinguished from the princes personally present in that they were not allowed to don their hats at any time during the act. A separate cross bench had been set up for the secularized *Hochstifte* of Magdeburg and Lübeck. The newly crowned king of the Romans was symbolically present in the form of the heralds of Bohemia and Hungary. Two imperial heralds and the hereditary imperial marshal with his unsheathed sword marked the act as a formal solemnity of the Empire. Following the reading of the proposition, the emperor himself spoke a few words to the assembled estates. The old logic of personal presence once more governed this opening session. This was in fact the last solemn opening of an imperial diet at which the emperor, the electors, and the princes appeared in person.

Procedural Problems and Status Conflicts

At the first regular session of the individual deliberative bodies three days later—the envoys were now once again entirely among themselves—the problems in the princely council escalated. After all, the very first order of business was to deliberate about the *modus et ordo votandi*. But as long as the order of the votes was not determined, no deliberations could take place—also not about the order of the votes.[194] There was a threat of complete paralysis. To break out of this vicious cycle, all in turn cast their vote, but they protested formally against every contested vote that was cast, with the voting member in turn "re-protesting." The result of this procedure was that the session dragged on from eight in the morning until three in the afternoon.[195]

The envoys had no other choice. The imperial diet was still the *theatrum praecedentiae* of the Empire, the most prominent stage of its political-social hierarchy. The political right to vote and social status, that is, the political constitution and the social order, were simply inseparable, and both were manifested at the imperial diet. Asserting the rank and status of their lord here had by now become even more important than in the previous century, since the protocols now recorded in precise detail the polling order in all of the councils. Unlike at the time of Charles V, it was now possible for all participants to invoke protocols from previous sessions. The seating and voting arrangement (and the sequence of signatures under the imperial recesses) had gradually established itself as the yardstick for the rank order of the imperial estates.[196] As so often, it therefore mattered naught when the vice-chancellor of the Empire emphasized that the seats taken here should not establish a precedent for the future. Ritual protestation and reprotestation were therefore initially the only way for participants to be able to act in concert at all in the face of the countless, unresolved symbolic conflicts.

In countless cases the dispute revolved around who sat and cast his vote where. In some instances the quarrel was even more fundamental: who was allowed to appear at all, that is, who or what was an immediate member of the Empire. After all, unlike the college of the electors, the circle of participants in the college of the princes had always been heterogeneous and open-ended. There was still no formalized membership. To be sure, quite a bit had changed since 1495; because of the Imperial Register (*Reichsmatrikel*) of 1521, much had settled down institutionally. In 1582, it had been decided that seat and vote were henceforth tied to territory, not to individual persons.[197] This meant, on the one hand, that the votes of a house could no longer be multiplied through hereditary divisions. But it also meant that large dynasties combining many territories in one hand carried that many individual votes. In particular, under this arrangement the electors also controlled several votes in the college of the princes.[198] This increasingly distorted the voting ratios in the colleges. Moreover, there were external loyalties. Seated in the imperial diet were envoys from potentates whose centers of power lay outside the Empire. This was by no means unusual; in the following century it would happen with even greater frequency. This was true of the Elector of Brandenburg, who became the sovereign Duke of Prussia in 1656, of the King of Denmark as the Duke of Holstein, and since 1648 also of the King of Sweden. Ever since the Peace of Westphalia had declared the territories of Western Pomerania, Bremen, and Verden to be perpetual imperial fiefs of the Swedish crown, Queen Christina was both things at once: a vassal of the Empire and sovereign queen.[199] The feudal construct made it possible for the territories to come under Swedish rule while at the same time remaining a part of the Empire. The appearance of her representative Bengt Oxenstierna was accordingly conflict-ridden: he was treated only as the envoy of a prince of the realm, but not as a royal envoy, which is what he had demanded.[200]

Finally, the status of the envoy of Lorraine at the imperial diet was ambiguous.[201] In 1653, Duke Charles IV of Lorraine was still on the side of the Spanish king and cousin of the emperor in the war against France. His troops were ravaging the western territories of the Empire and occupying several fortresses, and the duke was demanding substantial financial compensation for their withdrawal. The Lorraine matter was therefore from the beginning an important topic of the estate deliberations and was highly contested between the emperor and the estates. The question was whether Lorraine's envoy should negotiate with the emperor alone, *with* the imperial diet, or even *in* the imperial diet.[202] After all, he could change his roles: as the envoy of the Duke of Lorraine he represented a foreign potentate; as the envoy of the same lord in his capacity as the Count of Nomény he represented an imperial prince. As such he assumed a seat of his own in the college of princes in January of 1654—precisely at the very time when his master, the duke, had invaded the *Reichsstift* of Lüttich with his troops, and this same princely body was deliberating military measures against him. The princes considered this a rude provocation. They ordered the envoy from Lorraine to leave the deliberation chamber, and when he refused and objected, they in turn vacated the chamber and left him behind alone. This case shines a spotlight on the character of the imperial federation and reveals how misleading it is to speak of "imperial borders"; the Duke of Lorraine was both a member and an enemy of the Empire. Over the long term, these structural peculiarities in the composition of the imperial diet invariably exerted a disintegrating effect.

Moreover, ambiguous and contested affiliations continued to exist, namely, within both the college of princes and the college of cities. Whether one was considered an imperial estate or not was still primarily a matter of the tangible assertion of seat and vote. For example, the city of Herford sent envoys to Regensburg, even though the Elector of Brandenburg claimed it as his territorial city and vehemently challenged its place within the college of cities.[203] The physical attempts to assert the seat of Palatinate-Simmern have already been mentioned. And the Count of Schwarzburg had dispatched an envoy to the bench of the imperial counts, even though the Dukes of Saxony considered him their territorial subject (*Landsasse*).[204]

Finally, that the imperial diet was *the* venue for the political-social status order of the Empire is revealed by the dispute over the admission of the "new princes" whom Ferdinand II (under whose government there had been no imperial diet) and Ferdinand III had elevated into the rank of imperial princes: these men had been their Catholic supporters during the war and were now highly influential figures at the imperial court.[205] Their impending admission into the college of princes posed the fundamental question of whether or not the emperor alone could decide on status and rank in the Empire. Electors and princes demanded that it was not sufficient for the emperor to grant the title of prince unilaterally—the new men also had to meet certain conditions to be accepted into the imperial diet. They had to show property that was directly subject to the Empire and fitting for a prince, they had to allow themselves to be assessed for imperial taxes in an imperial district, and, above all, they had to come to an agreement with the old princes about their place in the seating order before they could be "solemnly introduced."[206] Under no circumstances, the majority of the secular princes now demanded, could they simply appear in the deliberations on their own accord.

Historians usually assume that the opposition of the old princes to the new ones was ignited by the fact that the emperor was seeking to acquire more influence over the imperial diet through these status elevations. That is surely not incorrect, though it does not get at the core of the conflict. For the real bone of contention was not *whether*, but rather *where* the new men should take their place in the college of princes.[207] That is what the debates in the sessions of the princely college were about. As the last to join, the newcomers should in principle content themselves with the last seat, since the age of one's house, rank, and name was unquestionably regarded as the most important criteria of rank. However, they now demanded that if present in person, they should have a seat "ahead of all envoys" of the other princes. They were thus asserting the old principle that many old princes themselves also invoked, namely, the principle that the person of rank took precedence over deputies. The new princes were now applying this principle against the old princes. Although the latter did not appear in person at the deliberations, they felt that allowing their envoys to sit and vote behind the Bohemian upstarts would do intolerable harm to their ancient dignity. Above all Elector Frederick William of Brandenburg was clear that "a distinction must be and remain between the old and new princes."[208] Following the first relevant debate in the college of princes, he wrote angrily to his deputies at the imperial diet: "It strikes us as inordinately painful that at the introduction and vote and seating of the Prince of Lobkowitz, against our express order, you behaved so calmly and not only knowingly appeared at this act, but also kept silent during this same act." Instead of merely issuing a written protest after the fact, they should not have yielded to the newcomer from the outset, and should have "publicly protested" then and there. Now, however, there was reason to fear "that ancient princely houses will be insulted and put in danger by this, that they might eventually fall under the power of such new princes and might even be obscured and extinguished."[209] The fear of the electors becomes more plausible if one considers that among the new princes were also the most prominent Habsburg favorites, not least Lord Chamberlain (*Obersthofmeister*) Dietrichstein, who oversaw all the courtly enactments in Regensburg and ensured that the hierarchy of the emperor's court pushed itself ahead of the hierarchy of the Empire. As we have seen, this gave rise to constant conflicts at the processions, solemn masses, and coronation acts. The quarrel over the introduction of the new princes thus revolved around a question of principle: what was at stake was the relationship between the Habsburg court and the order of the Empire. In this case, the electors and old princes were able to have their way after the fact, and to enshrine in the imperial recess that the admission of new princes in the future would be tied to their consent.[210]

The most elementary structure of the Empire, the most essential classification scheme, was given by the three deliberative colleges themselves: electors, princes, and cities. As we have seen, this structure was constantly reproduced at the imperial diets in the hierarchical communication between the colleges, the process by which they related to one another. The separate negotiations in the three hierarchically distinguished groups, colleges, or corpora (*Räte* or *Kurien*) privileged the small but highly closed and exclusive group of the electors and guaranteed them by far the greatest weight in the procedure. The other groups, though they comprised far more members, could do nothing against this. Nascent forms of deliberation spanning the colleges or estates, which had temporarily emerged in the committees in the sixteenth century, had eventually been thwarted by the sustained opposition of the electors, who in the process could have only lost influence.[211]

The council of electors or its director, the archchancellor of Mainz, controlled the entire procedure. He passed the results of the electoral deliberations to the director of the council of princes, an office that alternated between Austria and Salzburg, and asked him for a response. To that end he had the director come to him, not the other way around. Once the two upper colleges had finally reached an agreement after a repeated back and forth of the deliberation results, the archchancellor informed the cities of the outcome. The cities were not asked for their response, but could only join the other two colleges. Their possibilities of exerting influence on the final statement of the estates were minimal.[212] Only in the committees, which were of great importance for the deliberation of complex substantive issues, did the city representatives also have a chance to participate in a meaningful way.

The negotiations at the Congress of Westphalia had begun to dissolve the differences between the three estate groups. The boundary between electors and princes was increasingly threatened by the efforts at parity by the princes, but as we have already seen, it was stabilized above all by the rebuffing of their participation in the royal election and by a multitude of additional symbolic lines of demarcation. At every ceremonial occasion, the electors were keeping watch over the visibility of this boundary. That applied also, and especially, to the procedures by which the bodies related to each other and correlated their activities. Just how much the estate barrier was also in this case conceived not as an abstract boundary, but a concrete, material line in space is revealed by a report from the Brandenburg envoy Blumenthal to the elector. He describes a meeting of the electoral and princely envoys in one room, where the cities presented them with their vote. As usual, the electoral envoys had their seats elevated two steps above the floor, their princely counterparts one step. The princely envoys now stood in the middle of the room and pretended that they could not understand the electoral envoys, asking that they come closer. Whereupon the latter did approach them, as far as possible, without leaving their "elevated" place. This drew a complaint from the director of the princely college: "[I]t was contrary to the reputation of the princes that [the electoral envoys] should stand above; they would not answer until [they] had come down. Since the electoral envoys would not do so, they sat down again; and thus the electors remained in their preeminence."[213]

The boundary between the princes and the cities was far more difficult to overcome than that between the electors and the princes. Here it was not a question of gradation but of a categorical difference. A deep social gap—or better, a real wooden barrier—separated the representatives of the civic communes from all others, even from the envoys of the last prelates and counts at the bottom of the rank order.[214] In a clearly visible way, the barrier separated the space of those who were entitled to full participation from all others, literally the *outsiders*. The representatives of the cities sat where nonparticipating spectators were also allowed to stand. On the contemporary broadsheet, these hierarchical relationships were additionally underscored by the fact that the city envoys, in contrast to all others, were not mentioned by name—in fact, not even the cities they represented were fully listed by name.

The central concern of the elites of the imperial cities was to overcome this hierarchical barrier both literally and figuratively, and to be extended the same respect as the nobility. All policies of the imperial cities in the seventeenth century were pervaded by this goal.[215] The cities did everything they could (including spending considerable financial resources) to gather ceremonial evidence that could support their claim to equal status with the nobility, for example, when the emperor or foreign delegates visited the cities. Especially their struggle for equal participation in the procedures at the imperial diet should also be seen in this context. The solemn proceedings at the imperial diet were not only the most prominent stage of the entire constitutional order. One reason the cities felt that this is where they could most likely push through their claim to status was that they, after all, bore the lion's share of the taxes authorized here. The city envoys had been trying in vain since the sixteenth century to be taken seriously by the two other colleges. They now believed that they had taken a crucial step forward at the Peace of Westphalia: with support from the Swedes, they had been able to have their *votum decisivum* put down in writing—the right, should the two other higher-ranking colleges be in disagreement, to decide the issue with their collective vote, a right that in their view they had always possessed.[216]

This now had to be made good in Regensburg. To that end, the Regensburg council, toward the end of 1652, had prepared the chamber in city hall such that "the barriers set up as of old, by which the honorable cities had been separated from the higher estates," were dismantled and replaced with two benches.[217] When the chamber was inspected in December of 1652, both the lord chamberlain (*Obersthofmeister*) and the Austrian delegate Volmar demanded that either the old barrier be restored or a new gate be erected that once again clearly separated the space of the two higher estates from everyone else. The cities argued that in the Peace of Westphalia they had been given equal status with the other estates with respect to their rights (*iura statuum*), though this did not touch upon the order of dignities (*dignitatum ordo*). The barrier went against this equal treatment (*aequiparatio*); through it, the college of the cities was "bodily excluded" from the others. The difference in *dignitas* between the three estate groups, which was not being touched upon, was already being made sufficiently visible by the difference in the number of steps. The cities were unable to prevail, however; instead, a gate was installed, though it remained unlocked.[218] It was clear to all participants that the wooden barrier was not a trivial externality, but affected the "status and liberty" of the cities in a substantial way: the ceremonial exclusion corresponded to the exclusion from the procedures.[219]

The fact is that the two higher-ranking colleges, in the later deliberations, were simply able to undercut procedurally the claim of the cities to the *votum decisivum* by not including them from the beginning *simultaneo modo* in the negotiations, but as in the past only after they had come to an agreement. In the process they asserted that they did not in any way intend to encroach upon the cities' right of the *votum decisivum*; what was at issue was merely the time at which they could exercise it. They justified their own "liberty to get together about the deliberated imperial acts ahead of others of lower status and background, and ... to seek an agreement with each other" by arguing that, after all, "the imperial constitution, sovereignty, honor, power and dignity of the Holy Roman Empire rested most of all upon their high and inborn status."[220] As for the rest, they denied the cities even the opportunity to assemble in joint deliberations about their concerns. Even though the Protestant electors and princes certainly saw eye to eye with the likewise Protestant-dominated college of the imperial cities (*Städterat*) on many substantive issues, they would not let themselves be tempted into altering the procedures in favor of the cities. In other words, maintaining the hierarchical barrier in the "relational and correlational" procedures was far more important to them than any other concrete issue. And the cities, for their part, were mostly concerned with boosting their hierarchical standing, their *aequiparatio statuum*, to which they were willing—if need be—to subordinate all other political goals.[221] For those lower down in the rank hierarchy, the smaller the political weight of the vote, the greater was—conversely—the symbolic value of the voting right for its holder. Maintaining one's own rank could readily displace the other substantive issues, since questions about the ceremonial procedure were never substantively neutral, but were for their part always concrete questions of high priority.

Unsuccessful Attempts at a Resolution

The session conflicts in Regensburg were in part still the same as at the times of Maximilian I and Charles V. Since then, the competing claims had not diminished, but multiplied. Under Maximilian I the seating order of the imperial assemblies had still been in flux; it had still been able to respond fairly spontaneously and pragmatically to the quarrels and assign seats flexibly depending on the circumstances of a given situation.[222] Subsequently, the seating order had increasingly solidified institutionally—and with it, paradoxically, also the conflicts. For every situational solution held only for the specific imperial diet; the conflicts could erupt anew at every new assembly. As a result, every imperial recess (*Reichsabschied*) since 1526 adopted the stereotypical formula that the adopted seating was not intended to be detrimental to the rights of any estate. But that meant nothing other than placing the conflicts on a permanent footing.

Paradoxically enough, the juridification of the rank conflicts also contributed to preserving them. That is to say, questions of rank and precedence became, as *ius praecedentiae*, a prominent topic of the learned discourse about imperial law.[223] Claims to rank were treated by the jurists as actionable legal claims—and that concerned all levels of society. The scholars documented individual cases, sketched pathways of legal solutions, and tried to reduce the entire matter to certain principles, though this approach quickly encountered its limitations with this *materia difficilis et intricata*. They compiled catalogs of material criteria to assess precedence—age of the family, historical descent, titles, number and size of territories, wealth, and so on. But since all of these criteria were difficult to ascertain or vague, while at the same time being in competition with one another, the most important deciding criteria in the end remained the concrete, demonstrably occupied place, preferably the one in the solemn imperial sessions.[224] But precisely that place was in turn contested—the actors thus found themselves in a vicious cycle.

The attitude of the jurists to the principle of the rank hierarchy was fundamentally ambiguous: on the one hand, they considered the human rank order a reflection of heaven, whose hosts were after all also arranged according to their rank. The fall of the archangel Lucifer appeared to them as the result of the first of all rank conflicts. Ever since equality had come to an end in paradise because of the Fall, the *ordo dignitatum* was considered a highly godly order, the foundation of peace and justice in every human society. It was not up to the discretion of the individual, driven by a false sense of modesty, to simply renounce the rank that was his due, for rank was not a question of courtesy or morality, but a question of law. He who carefully defended his rank, it was said, merely saw to the preservation of the public order.[225] Conversely, for the same reason it was utterly reprehensible to arrogate to oneself, out of "vain ambition and arrogance," a rank to which one was not entitled. But since this precisely was at issue in every individual case, the legal treatment did not lead out of the vicious cycle, but straight into it.

The attempts to solve the problem and fix the order of the estates once and for all were nearly as old as the imperial diets themselves.[226] In the process, all possible paths were taken: the seating order became the object of deliberations at the imperial diets, committees and commissions were charged with the task, it was brought before the Imperial Court Council, it was negotiated before mediation procedures of the imperial estates, and in 1608 Emperor Rudolf II even considered entrusting it to the drawing of lots. Some specific cases were resolved through compromise, in that those involved agreed to a regulated alternation of the seats. Nevertheless, these efforts never succeeded in reducing the potential for conflict. In theory it was clear who was supposed to decide: the emperor was the head and source of the entire status order; granting rank and status was the most crucial of his prerogatives; it was the one in which his authoritative power manifested itself in a special way. With that, the emperor also held the power to define whether a contested claim to rank was a legitimate right or presumptuous ambition. The parties to a quarrel, therefore, usually approached the emperor or his court (the Imperial Court Council) with their supplications and deductions. In fact, though, the emperor was hardly willing and even less so able to play this mediating role. He was aware of the difficulties and did not want to spoil things with the great houses and "incur eternal hatred."[227] That is why for the most part he sought to shunt the issues back to the three colleges of the imperial diet by asking them in turn for their expert opinions. Under the best of circumstances, the latter then made a majority decision, on the basis of which the emperor issued a decree—as in Regensburg in 1653/54 in the cases of Eichstätt/Speyer and Lauenburg.[228] But the problem was this: while the individual estates approached the emperor for arbitration, in most cases they submitted to his decision or to a majority decision by their peers if it suited them. That is what happened, for example, in the case of the bishop of Eichstätt: although he had approached the emperor, he did not accept his decree but departed and waited for an even more favorable occasion to assert his claim. In other words, both the imperial diet itself and the emperor lacked a generalized decision-making power, that is, the power to make decisions that were accepted by all actors as obligatory ahead of time independent of their outcome. As so many other matters, the session problem thus remained fundamentally unresolved at the imperial diets.

The attitude of those involved in this was ambiguous. Everyone lamented the danger to the polity, while at the same time contributing to it with all their might. For example, the Brandenburg councilor Waldeck prophesied to his colleague "la ruine totale de l'Empire" unless the dispute over rank among the princes ceased, even though Brandenburg struggled more vigorously than anyone over rank.[229] There was a social logic to act that no individual imperial estate could avoid.

Solemn Investitures

When it came to questions of rank, it was never only the specific individual conflict that was at stake, but simultaneously also the authority of the emperor as the head and source of the entire imperial order. However, centuries of experience with session conflicts had taught the emperors to hold back on this hopelessly convoluted matter and, when possible, toss the ball back to the colleges themselves. At any rate, for the reasons mentioned the sessions were poorly suited as a venue for staging the emperor's authority. The emperor therefore had to choose other venues to depict himself effectively as the master over the Empire's system of validity: he had to enact the imperial assembly—beyond the deliberative sessions—as a court diet of the old style. As we have seen, he succeeded in doing this with great effect at the two coronations, but also at the exceedingly sumptuous day-to-day life of the court at the many festive masses and baroque diversions (operas and comedies, balls and banquets), for which a new festival hall had been erected ahead of time.[230] Finally, Ferdinand III also resorted to another central ritual of the old court diets: the solemn throne investiture. As mentioned before, influential scholars of imperial law saw in the emperor's feudal sovereignty virtually the chief argument for why the Empire was a real monarchy, and the solemn throne investiture was to them ritual evidence of this. In this respect, too, Ferdinand III was now connecting back to great predecessors like Maximilian I and Charles V.

During the war, many princes had not been properly invested by the emperor. The Peace of Westphalia now specified that the period for renewing the fief would reset on the day the peace was concluded.[231] The form of the throne investiture had changed considerably since the early sixteenth century.[232] The proceedings had shifted from an open space into the closed room of the imperial residence; the dazzling, tournament-like spectacle of the handing over of the banners had been discontinued. The last solemn banner investiture in the open had been that of Elector August of Saxony in Augsburg in 1566.²³³ Since then, the ritual no longer took place in front of the citizenry of an imperial city, but the public of the emperor's court: the doorkeepers "let everyone in," we read.²³⁴ The emperor no longer showed up in his vestments and imperial regalia; instead, all participants appeared in the black Spanish mantles (*Mantelkleid*), the official court attire of Vienna.²³⁵ Of the insignia only the sword was left, whose pommel had to be kissed. Instead, the choreography inside the chamber was embellished in ever more subtle ways; every step and every gesture was recorded.²³⁶ And one thing remained indispensable: the vassal to be invested had to kneel before the throne. It happened once, in 1695, that a princely feudal delegate "had refrained from kneeling at the three reverences before and after the investiture, and he had dared to stand, not in front of the broad stage on the floor … , but on the corner, or the edge of the broad stage." The emperor's response had been irritable. The delegate had to place on record a declaration that the error had occurred, not upon the order of his master, "nor with the intent of introducing something new," let alone "to acquire or gain by trickery an improper prerogative for the future."²³⁷ No such thing would ever happen again.

The fundamental change, however, concerned the participating actors. The electors, with a few exceptions, no longer appeared at all, and even their deputies, the holders of the hereditary imperial offices, had been increasingly replaced—already under Ferdinand I—by the holders of the Habsburg court offices. Only the imperial vice-chancellor as the deputy of the Elector of Mainz was usually present in person. The entire act transformed itself into an almost quotidian event at the emperor's court. Although the participation of the court officials did not happen without conflicts, they revolved primarily around money. The holders of the old hereditary offices were entitled to considerable remuneration for their service at the investiture, which they did not wish to forego. Eventually, with help from their electoral masters, they were able to have their right to these funds put in writing in Ferdinand II's electoral capitulation for all times, even though they were no longer exercising these offices.²³⁸

The most essential change was that the vassals themselves generally no longer appeared in person, while the emperor continued—or rather, now more than ever—to personally carry out *all* throne investitures. In his residence he was the director of the ritual and had the possibility to control the formalities and compel the vassals to adhere to them. From his perspective, the investiture was an imperial boon for which the vassals should be grateful. After all, following every change of ruler they had to petition for a new investiture and "request it from the feudal lord as a benefaction; the vassal is obligated to do this in accordance with the will of the feudal lord."²³⁹ On the other hand, transferring the ritual to his court put the emperor into a structurally difficult situation of wanting something from the vassals that they could also refuse him.²⁴⁰ He did not have the power to prevent personal appearance from becoming the exception and proxy representation the rule. That, however, was by no means unproblematic. After all, the feudal bond was a personal relationship of fealty between the emperor and the vassal that was created by a *physical* oath in words and gestures. The ritual drew its obligatory effect precisely from the personal presence of those involved; through their participation they affirmed the acceptance of what was being ritually staged. It was therefore imperative to establish in a formal way that the oath was effective even if it was not performed by the person it was intended to bind. This happened in that the prince conveyed to his delegates the formal power "to swear the feudal obligation in his soul" (*iurare in eius animam*).[241] Certifying this transfer of will required not only a letter of accreditation; the prince also had to have signed the letter of request (*Mutungsschreiben*) with his own hand.[242] Even though church law since the twelfth century had allowed a person to be represented by an authorized agent—if necessary—in swearing an oath, this kind of proxy representation was always considered problematic.[243] An obligation put in writing and an oath sworn by a proxy was not accorded the same efficacy as a ritual carried out in person. After all, "among most peoples it was properly ordained that oaths were rendered more important, as it were, with special ceremonies, just as the swearing reverence for God must be displayed through certain sacred signs, for example through sacrifice, stepping to the altar, and the like.... For it is surely much more, under solemn ceremonies that indicate the presence of God's majesty not without terror, to call upon God as the witness by oath, than if one does the same in absence through paper and writings, which cannot be shamed nor blush," wrote Samuel Pufendorf, the famous legal scholar.[244] This expressed a twofold mistrust of writing: a person who obligated himself through a mere signature did not experience the same fear of divine sanction as he would during a solemn oath-swearing ritual. And whoever committed perjury through his signature could not reveal himself in the process by physical signs of insincerity. Thus, in the eyes of contemporaries the personal presence at the solemn ritual of swearing an oath could not be simply replaced by writing and proxy representation. The absence of the vassal at the feudal oath was undoubtedly a deficiency.

That the princes no longer appeared in person for the act of investiture thus shifted the relationship to the disadvantage of the emperor. Whenever he alone was present in person at the ritual, it violated the logic of the hierarchy of the estates. After all, a person's high social rank was characterized by the fact that his time and attention were in short supply and valuable. If the princes now placed less importance on meeting with the emperor in person than the latter did on meeting with them, this revealed a structural asymmetry that obviously clashed with the meaning of the ritual.

For this reason, the emperor adhered strictly to the fiction that the personal appearance of the imperial vassals was the norm (even though this had in fact never been the most common form). That goal was served by a special ritualized action element: the emperor demanded that every prince formally excuse his "exceptional" absence, both in writing in the letter of authorization with which his delegate accredited himself, and in the delegate's oral petition for investiture.[245] This ritualized excuse served to maintain the presence of the prince in person as the norm, even if the facts contradicted this; in other words, it served to make the norm resistant to the power of the factual—a phenomenon that we encounter time and again and that is symptomatic for the functioning of the Old Empire. Fixed symbolic-ritual forms served to uphold the norms, however often they were violated in practice. Nobody in fact expected the princes to appear in person to receive their fiefs, but that is precisely the fiction that was created symbolically. At the same time, however, the princes for their part had various possibilities of subverting the norm dictated by the emperor through minute changes in form. Thus, the wording of the excuses conveyed subtle symbolic messages about the reciprocal relationship, depending on how terse or elaborate the justification for the absence was.[246] In short, the ritual of investiture was the stage on which the emperor and the princely vassals symbolically calibrated their reciprocal relationship. At least the emperor had tradition and the legitimacy-conveying authority of his office on his side. But none of that was worth anything as long as it was not visibly acknowledged.

The ritual of investiture took on special meaning above all in cases that constituted irruptions into the status system of the Empire. This was so in 1495 at the elevation of Württemberg into a duchy,[247] in 1548 at the investiture of Moritz of Saxony with the electoral dignity, which Charles V had taken from his cousin Johan Frederick following his defeat in the Schmalkaldic War,[248] and in 1623 at the highly controversial first investiture of Maximilian of Bavaria with the electoral dignity.[249] The secret written pledge to the Bavarian duke two years earlier had by no means been sufficient. All of these cases were unheard-of innovations and were therefore in need of ritual staging to a special degree. In these instances the emperor and the vassal both had a strong interest in seeing that the solemnities take place in all forms and with the participation of as many imperial princes as possible, who attested to their consent by their personal participation. This experience is also what prompted the electors to insert into the electoral capitulation of 1653 that the emperor would no longer be allowed to carry out any new investitures without their consent.[250]

Ferdinand III was aware of the symbolic (and financial) value of the throne investitures. Since 1652, the individual acts were no longer entered only into the imperial feudal register; in addition, at the court in Vienna "a strangely laborious protocol was kept, so as to be able to use and be guided by it in future times and cases."[251] In the new code for the Imperial Court Council, the highest imperial feudal court, all circumstances of investiture were regulated by law in 1654, from the vassal's petition (*Mutung*) to the submission of all necessary documentation to taxes and fees, and anyone who failed to request a new investiture in a timely manner was threatened with prosecution by the imperial exchequer.[252]

When the imperial diet in Regensburg was announced, the Imperial Court Council compiled a list of those invitees who had not yet been enfeoffed.[253] For even though the investiture rituals had been customarily received by delegates in the imperial residence for quite some time, an imperial diet was still considered the most appropriate venue for them. To put it differently, the fact that solemn throne investitures took place at an imperial diet continued to make it appear as a *Hoftag* of the old style. Ferdinand now used the presence of numerous electors and princes to once again stage—before a large public—the ritual of the throne investiture, namely, twice: first on 22 December 1653, of the Count Palatine of Simmern, who had just been restored to his position in the Peace of Westphalia,[254] and then on 4 May 1654, of the highest-ranking member of the Empire, the archchancellor and Elector of Mainz, Johann Philipp von Schönborn.[255] The latter was the first from the southwest German knightly family of Schönborn to attain the electorate of Mainz and thus the highest-ranking office in the Empire, thus laying the basis for the extraordinarily swift rise of his family.[256] He was characterized by great political independence toward the emperor. Because of the experiences of war he distrusted the Habsburgs, and in 1658 he therefore formed what was later called the First Confederation of the Rhine with other imperial estates located on the Rhine and with the king of France. But at the imperial diet of Regensburg he was certainly willing to cooperate with Ferdinand III, because the goal was to defend the electoral right of election against efforts by the princes for equal treatment. For his part, the emperor supported him in the coronation dispute against the Elector of Cologne, as discussed previously in this chapter. Presumably as a quid pro quo, Johann Philipp of Mainz agreed—contrary to the by now long established practice—to ask for and receive his investiture in person.

"As usually happens at the enfeoffment," three noble vassals of the electors genuflected three times as they approached the emperor, who was sitting on the throne in his audience chamber, and asked him on their knees to admit their lord to the investiture, "while His Electoral Grace was ready nearby."[257] The imperial vice-chancellor answered for the emperor that he wanted to "await his personal presence and then grant his desire."[258] Thereupon the elector himself stepped onto the stage accompanied by two princely advocates, the bishop of Regensburg on his right and Prince Lobkowitz on his left, also paid his reverence by genuflecting three times, "His Majesty each time taking off his hat," and then asked on his knees for the investiture, which was bestowed upon him "following the usual custom."[259] The services that the electors themselves had performed during the act were now done by others: the emperor's chief court marshal and the hereditary chamberlain of Hohenzollern (who had been competing for this service for more than a century) jointly held the Gospel, the chief chamberlain the emperor's hat, and the hereditary imperial marshal Pappenheim the unsheathed sword. In deviation from what was customary, however, the elector, "following the oath … does not kiss the sword, but only touches the pommel with his finger, and after the investiture he did not as before and otherwise customary pay his respects, but after paying a new respect he moved a little to the side and accompanied His Imperial Majesty … to his *retirada*." There the Elector of the Palatinate made his appearance—only now. The two men publicly ate their midday meal with the emperor, "and the seating at the table was arranged as previously at other meals."[260] The elector thus received from the emperor a number of special ceremonial favors in return for his willingness to receive his investiture in person. This was, of course unbeknownst to anyone at the time, the last investiture of an elector in person in the history of the Empire, and this act was thus later repeatedly and prominently invoked in the Viennese ceremonial records.[261]

As far as the development of the investiture ritual is concerned, the imperial diet of 1653/54 appears Janus-faced. On the one hand, the emperor succeeded one last time in prevailing upon a high-ranking imperial prince to consent to a solemn investiture, thus staging the imperial diet like an old-style *Hoftag* and himself as the source of the entire status system. On the other hand, missing in the act were the other electors to sit with the emperor *in maiestate* in keeping with tradition. Evidently it was no longer important to them to revive a ritual act during which they had to kneel before the emperor. Ever since the Peace of Westphalia, at the latest, this was no longer compatible with their self-understanding as members of the international community who were the emperor's equals; the ritual manifested too visibly their status as dependent imperial vassals.

Decision-Making Shortcomings

Before the imperial estates had come anywhere close to fulfilling the mandate of the Peace of Westphalia, the emperor already began to prepare for his departure from Regensburg.[262] While the solemn investiture of the Elector of Mainz was taking place on 4 May 1654, the delegates were already drafting the text of the imperial recess (*Reichsabschied*).[263] It was still considered a matter of course that an imperial diet lasted as long as the emperor was present, and that it ended when he departed; this, too, was a mark of the old culture of presence, which was based on the personal presence of the bearers of power. The imperial recess—later referred to as "the most recent" (*Jüngster Reichsabschied*) because there would never be another—was thus also in this instance still an *Abschied* ("leave") in the literal sense, tied to the departure of the emperor.[264]

A few of the problems that had been entrusted to the assembly had been deliberated and resolved in Regensburg, but most had not.[265] The imperial recess contained, to begin with, the text of the Peace of Westphalia, which was explicitly declared to be a fundamental law of the Empire and which subsequently enshrined numerous legal realities as unalterable. One particular success had been the reorganization of the Imperial Chamber Court, long in preparation by a deputation, which made up the better part of the imperial recess. By contrast, what got bogged down was the reform of the executive system, which was intended above all to secure the efficient defense of the Empire against external military attacks. The only consequential regulation that was passed was that the imperial princes no longer had to ask their own territorial estates (*Landstände*) to consent to the taxes devoted to the defense of the realm (§ 180)—a stipulation that largely undermined the old right of the estates in the territories to approve taxes and gave the lords a lever to disempower their territorial estates. Likewise, no final resolution had been found for the fundamental question of whether and how the estates would be allowed to participate in the election of the king of the Romans and the electoral capitulation in the future—the emperor and the electors had successfully put off this issue time and again and thus fended off the attack on the preeminence of the electors. Postponed also was the harmonization of the calendars of Catholics and Protestants (§ 158), the reform of the Imperial Register (*Reichsmatrikel*; § 195), and—as always—a permanent solution of the seating conflicts (§ 196).[266] Moreover, the new regulations that the emperor had issued for his *Hofgericht* and feudal court, the Imperial Court Council, on his own authority as the highest judge of the Empire were not accepted by the imperial diet.[267] Several princes protested in the strongest terms because the order violated the principle of confessional parity. As so often happened, two competing conceptions of the law clashed irreconcilably and permanently: subsequently, the Imperial Court Council operated in accordance with the new order (and Protestants were also among the litigants), even though it had been formally rejected by the Protestant princes at the imperial diet.

Especially the problems that accounted for the imperial diet's shortcomings when it came to decision making were left unresolved. Indeed, the validity of the majority principle was successfully contested when it came to tax questions. This was a central issue that would demonstrate whether the imperial estates individually were willing to subordinate themselves to a decision by the collective even when it went against their own interests. After all, the majority principle is a fundamental decision-making rule that ensures that a collective decision can be made also—and especially—if no consensus can be found on the issue in question. The validity of the majority principle presupposes the generalized willingness of all participants to submit to a decision even before it has been made, and afterward to treat the will of the majority as though it were the will of all. Moreover, majority rule presupposes that all votes are regarded as equal, for only then can they be simply counted and not weighted. In this straightforward sense the majority principle held only in the college of electors when choosing the king. But it had never become the unquestioned, unconditional, and self-evident decision-making principle in the deliberations of the three imperial colleges. To be sure, in most instances the *majora* were adhered to out of habit and pragmatism.[268] But what applied as a majority rule here should not be confused with a majority vote in the strict sense. The polling procedure (*Umfrage*) did not put simple questions up for a vote, but collected complex expressions of opinions in sequence, following the order of ranks. These polls were repeated until a general trend to a consensus shared by the majority began to emerge. The hierarchical weight of the votes played a considerable role in the process. What was considered a majority opinion in the end depended to a considerable degree on the interpretation of the person presiding over the assembly, who summed up the results of the polls. Since a decision could hardly be enforced against the will of powerful estates, any other procedure that completely ignored the weight of the votes would have been utterly meaningless.

If the majority principle thus applied only in a very limited sense already within the colleges, and not at all between them, on essential points touching upon the individual estates in fundamental ways it was questioned in principle. This had been the case with the religious issue.[269] The imperial diet of 1613 had failed because the Catholic majority had tried to force the majority principle upon the Protestant minority. Later, in the Peace of Westphalia, one had drawn from this the conclusion that the two confessional camps should not be able to outvote each other at the imperial diet when it came to matters of faith. The fundamental question about the validity of the *majora* when it came to the authorization of taxes, which had likewise never gone unchallenged, had been postponed in Münster and Osnabrück. Now it was up for discussion again.

The emperor was asking for aid of one hundred *Römermonate*, though he had already exempted the electors at their meeting in Prague before the beginning of the imperial diet to win their votes. The emperor and the electors now jointly advocated that the majority principle be enshrined. The Protestant princes, meanwhile, asserted the old principle that "no estate can vote into another's purse." One had to distinguish between necessary and voluntary taxes, *necessaria* and *voluntaria*; majority decisions could be taken only on *necessaria*. However, the definitive decision of what were necessary and what were voluntary taxes in specific cases could not be left to the *majora*.[270] In this view, every individual estate was bound only to the tax decisions to which it itself had consented. This seemed in accordance with the "ancient German liberty" and was intended to prevent the emperor from instrumentalizing the imperial taxes for his own dynastic interests or even to oppress the Protestants. The Protestant princes, who had been joined by electoral Brandenburg and the cities, also demanded that minority votes in principle had to be included in every *Reichsgutachten*, that is, in the joint resolution of all estates, which was handed over to the emperor at the end of an imperial diet. Although they did not get their way, the emperor and the electors also failed to achieve a resolution about majority decision, since the Protestant princes threatened to simply leave the imperial diet. Even the war taxes asked for were not approved in the end. It was left to everyone whether or not to pay. With that the imperial diet as a whole possessed no capacity for collective action on this elementary issue.

This also meant that the imperial diet was not able to resolve its own procedural problems. Its decision-making shortcomings were not eliminated but intensified; numerous conflicts remained permanently unresolved. For one, this strengthened the emperor's position. For another, and this is why it is part of our discussion, it had repercussions for the role that symbolic-ritual forms of communication played in the Empire, for as we have already encountered in a number of examples, competing claims had to be ritually enacted on every occasion for them to be sustained.

To begin with, the decision-making deficit entailed that the imperial diet did not formally end with the recess and departure of the emperor. After all, it had not resolved the problems it was supposed to according to the Treaty of Osnabrück, which is why the Protestant princes lodged a formal protest one day after the solemn reading of the imperial recess. Thus, so as not to violate the Peace of Westphalia, it was decided that the assembly should convene again exactly two years later, on 17 May 1656, without a new summons and without a new proposition. By definition, this was thus a continuation of the old and not a new imperial diet. In the meantime, the diet was represented by a regular imperial deputation.[271] At least the confessional parties had been able, after heated arguments, to come to an agreement that they would have equal representation on the deputation.[272] The halfhearted end to this imperial diet already indicated the development that the subsequent diet would take (though it did not convene until nearly ten years later), for the same decision-making deficit made the imperial diet of 1663 fully permanent.[273] In the process, this final, "permanent" imperial diet changed its structure very significantly by disconnecting itself completely from the personal presence of the emperor and the estates.

Interim Summary

After the war, the many open questions about the shape of the Empire and the relationship among its various members were dealt with, in part discursively in the deliberations, in part ritually on all public occasions. Precisely because the situation was so open and ambiguous, symbolic demonstrations carried a lot of weight. The point was to create, in a symbolic-ritual way, facts so as to put forth one's own claims and assert them against others. Especially where the deliberations failed to lead to a resolution, it was left to the symbolic acts to define the situation.

The emperor, especially, was able to do this. At his entry, audiences, liturgical feasts, and investitures, above all at the coronations of his son and wife, and even at the royal election, he staged himself—no different than Maximilian I or Charles V had done—as the sacral head of the entire sacred order of the Empire, the source of all legitimate ranks and honors, the highest authority that fed the entire system of social and political status. While his power had been reduced in the previous electoral capitulations to a few clearly defined privileged rights, he was still able to stage his authority as the keystone of the entire system so persuasively that many princes feared he could, like his successors, have a purely monarchical rule in mind. "With enormous effort, Ferdinand III made Regensburg and the imperial court residing there the center of the Empire. The emperor, and nobody else, was master."[274] The electors (with the exception of Brandenburg), fearful of their preeminence, joined him and assisted him in this spectacle. The Protestants among them accepted that by doing so they participated in the old sacredness of the Empire. In return, their exclusive role was confirmed once again for all to see. Before the councils could even deliberate about this, they created a fait accompli with the great rulership rituals of the election and coronation and demonstrated that *they* were still the body that could take action in the name of and in place of the Empire as a whole. In all of this, the imperial diet of 1653/54 appeared once more as a *Hoftag* in the old style, a *solemnis curia* as described in the Golden Bull. The imperial diet was a triumph of the old culture of presence, which rested on the personal, splendid interaction of the "great lords" themselves. Political participation, constitutional legal status, and social rank were still inextricably intertwined.

Yet this was only one side of the coin. The imperial diet had a dual gestalt, for the new logic of sovereignty under the law of nations thrust itself in front of the old logic of the imperial hierarchy. These were two different ceremonial grammars, which—as we have seen—collided time and again. In the logic of the Empire, the electors and princes were vassals of the emperor; in the logic of the state system, however, they asserted the right to be treated as sovereign lords. The Congress of Westphalia had provided the model for this. Ever since, they demanded a certain standard of respectful treatment for themselves, but above all also for their representatives. The ceremony that was accorded to delegates of the first rank was *the* medium in which the status claims of their lords were now negotiated, a medium that became ever more precise and also ever more conflict-laden as a result of the growing use of writing. The system of reference by which the imperial estates were guided in this process was not the Empire, but the community of monarchs and potentates in Europe. The status of the electors and princes in that system depended less on the emperor and more on a third party, the other monarchs. Yet the imperial estates had to maintain their status claims in the ceremonial protocol also in their dealings with the emperor and one another if they wanted to be taken seriously by foreign potentates. A major part of the symbol conflicts in Regensburg was rooted in this constellation.

But the imperial assembly was hopelessly overtaxed with all of these conflicts over the system of political-social classification. On the one hand, all participants had to preserve their claims to status and rank especially here, at this prominent and central *theatrum praecedentiae*. On the other hand, because of its decision-making deficits, the imperial diet was particularly unsuited for resolving the resulting conflicts. The old culture of presence had two kinds of instruments for dealing with such disputes if they could not be settled amicably and consensually: public, ritual protestation or absenteeism. But that led to a communicative dead end. There were countless protestations and reprotestations—but rarely or ever definitive solutions. Virtually all questions of rank and status—from the seating arrangement in the colleges to the exercise of the arch offices—remained unresolved and permanently in abeyance. At the same time, however, they retained the highest priority for those involved.

Given all of this, was the imperial diet truly what Jean Bodin and some historians believed it to be: the "real bearer of the sovereignty of the Empire"?[275] And what could that even mean? The imperial diet was still a stage for the *maiestas imperialis* in the old sense, on which the Empire appeared in all its splendor as a unity of its head and members. It represented the Empire in the sense that it "depicted" it pars pro toto visibly. But the imperial diet was not an entity capable of taking action, one that could have exercised supreme authority over the whole, that is, a body that could have been sovereign in the new sense. It did not represent the Empire such that it could have "established" it through secure decision-making procedures as a uniform political body with a single will—as before, only the electors did so in concert with the emperor. All of the collective rights of participation that the Peace of Westphalia had awarded the imperial diet as a whole and that could have turned it into a bearer of sovereign power existed only on paper. But the limitation of imperial power to a few privileged rights also did not accord with reality, as would become apparent subsequently under Leopold I. Even if the Peace of Westphalia had now been proclaimed a fundamental law of the Empire, this imperial diet was in no way a "constitutive assembly" through which "the Germans" had given themselves "the first written constitution in Europe."[276] This description suggests, after all, that we are dealing with something that was pointing the way to the future. But a modern state constitution is characterized above all by the fact that it contains two things: first, rules that stipulate how final, binding decisions are made; and second, rules that stipulate how law is generated and how, eventually, the constitution itself can be changed.[277] Neither of these things are found in the imperial recess of 1654. Rather, the Treaty of Osnabrück had specified the following: "In order to make provisions that there will be no future disputes concerning the constitution [*in statu politico*], all electors, princes, and estates of the Roman Empire shall be affirmed and confirmed in their old rights, prerogatives, liberties, privileges, the unhindered exercise of territorial sovereignty ... , lordships, regalia, as well as in their possession" (Art. VIII § 1). All of this was to be permanently removed from change. But what if these rights and liberties were mutually incompatible in multifarious ways—if they contradicted one another? How then should each be secured for itself? That precisely was the problem: what had not been settled in an effective and binding manner was a way in which unambiguous decisions could be made and new law created in case of conflict.[278] This shaped the gestalt of the Empire in the subsequent one hundred and fifty years, and it caused parallel worlds to emerge within its shell.

Notes

1. Moser, TSR, 4:367.
2. In general on what follows, see Dickmann, *Westfälischer Frieden*; Duchhardt, *Westfälischer Friede*; Press, *Kriege und Krisen*; Schilling, *Höfe und Allianzen*; Schilling, *Konfessionalisierung und Staatsinteressen*, 565ff.; Münch, *Das Jahrhundert des Zwiespalts*; Burkhardt, *Vollendung und Neuorientierung*; Schmidt, *Geschichte des Alten Reiches*, 177ff.; on the law of nations, see Lesaffer, *Peace Treaties*; Steiger, "Rechtliche Strukturen der europäischen Staatenordnung."
3. Exceptions were the continued occupation of Farther Pomerania—which belonged to Brandenburg—by the Swedes and the incursions by the Duke of Lorraine into northwestern German territories in connection with the ongoing war between Spain and France. See Oschmann, *Nürnberger Exekutionstag*; Neuhaus, "Das Heilige Römische Reich Deutscher Nation."
4. IPO, Art. VIII § 3; English text at http://avalon.law.yale.edu/17th_century/westphal.asp.
5. A basic work on this imperial diet is Müller, *Der Regensburger Reichstag von 1653/54*; see also Aretin, *Das Alte Reich*, 1:172–84; Burkhardt, *Vollendung und Neuorientierung*, 54–62. For an edition of sources based on the protocols of the council of princes, see Meiern, *Comitialia Ratisbonensia*; see also Pfanner, *Historia comitiorum*.
6. Thus wrote the Brandenburg envoy Blumenthal on 1 September 1653 home from Regensburg, *Urkunden und Actenstücke*, 6:283.
7. "Politisches Bedencken über die Regenspurgischen Reichs-Tags-Handlungen," quoted in Meiern, *Comitialia Ratisbonensia*, 147; the author was the envoy to the imperial diet from Brunswick-Wolfenbüttel, Dr. Johann Schwarzkopf; Moser, NTSR, vol. 4, part 1, pp. 3 and 54.
8. Becker, *Kurfürstenrat*; Gotthard, *Säulen*, 276ff.
9. The assembly of 1623 was described as an irregular Imperial Convent (*Reichskonvent*) by Moser, NTSR, 6/1:25. On the investiture of Maximilian, see Kraus, *Maximilian I.*,

129–30; Albrecht, *Auswärtige Politik*, 83ff.; Mußgnug, "Die achte Kurwürde"; Steiner, *Pfälzische Kurwürde*.
10. The imperial laws also contained rules for other forms of assembly in which the Empire could embody itself as an actor: *Reichskreistage*, where the representatives of all imperial districts came together, or *Reichsdeputationstage*, for which an estate committee, a regular Imperial Deputation, was summoned. See Neuhaus, *Reichsständische Repräsentationsformen* and "Von Reichstag(en) zu Reichstag." Reinking, *Tractatus de regimine seculari et ecclesiastico*, 321–22, counts numerous procedural variants.
11. Bierther, *Reichstag von 1640/1641*, 32ff.; Kietzell, "Deputationstag"; Becker, *Kurfürstenrat*, 133ff.; Dickmann, *Westfälischer Frieden*, 163ff.; Stollberg-Rilinger, "Völkerrechtlicher Status."
12. Stolleis, *Geschichte des Öffentlichen Rechts*, and "Glaubensspaltung und öffentliches Recht"; Hammerstein, "Jus publicum Romano-Germanicum"; Hoke, "Emanzipation der deutschen Staatsrechtswissenschaft"; Roeck, *Reichssystem und Reichsherkommen*; Denzer, "Spätaristotelismus"; Friedeburg and Seidler, "Holy Roman Empire"; Schubert, *Reichstage*, 306ff.; Becker, *Kurfürstenrat*, 103ff.
13. Quaritsch, *Souveränität*; Denzer, *Bodin*; on the reception in Germany, see Stolleis, *Geschichte des Öffentlichen Rechts*, 170ff.
14. See Reinking, *De regimine seculari et ecclestiastico*, 199ff., here 203, on the regalia investiture (*Regalienbelehnung*): "in feudis robur et nervos imperii consistere."
15. Arumaeus, *De comitiis*, 1ff.: imperial diets as "cor et clypeus imperii"; 66ff.: the emperor is "causa efficiens" of the imperial diets; 102: "Investitura principalium feudorum Imperatori insignum supremae potestatis specialiter reservatam esse"; compare to Bodin, *Sechs Bücher über den Staat*, 643ff.
16. Limnaeus, *Ius publicum*; detailed documentation in Hoke, *Limnaeus*, 131ff. On the medieval tradition of this distinction, see Kantorowicz, *The King's Two Bodies*. In the seventeenth century it was still difficult to imagine majesty in the abstract, without personal rank and the relevant forms of deference; see Stieve, *Hof-Ceremoniell*, 160–61; Krischer, "Das diplomatische Zeremoniell der Reichsstädte."
17. Bodin, *Sechs Bücher über den Staat*, 386.
18. [Chemnitz], Hippolythus a Lapide, *De ratione status*, book 1, chap.16, pp. 286–98, on investiture: "Videtur hoc simulacrum potius, quaem ius esse maiestatis: quod externa quidem specie magnificum, re tamen ipsa parum potestatis in se continet."
19. Paurmeister, *De iurisdictione imperii Romani*, 1, § 17; see Schubert, *Reichstage*, 495ff.; Becker, *Kurfürstenrat*, 112ff. For the Empire as a *corpus mysticum*, see what is probably the most important *Reichspublizist*, Limnaeus, *Ius publicum*, which shaped the doctrine of the dual majesty; see Hoke, *Limnaeus*.
20. As in 1655 on the one hundredth anniversary of the Peace of Augsburg; see Paas, *German Political Broadsheet*, 158ff., 444–45.
21. Coelestin, *Historia comitiorum*; for 1548, see Spalatin, *Annales reformationis*. Since about 1600, the reading of the *Confessio Augustana* was also depicted in historical images; see Ottomeyer et al., *Altes Reich und neue Staaten*, Essay Volume, 224, fig. 9; 37, fig. 4; 150, fig. 6.
22. Ottomeyer et al., *Altes Reich und neue Staaten*, Catalogue, p. 56, fig. 291; see also the depiction on the honorary arch for Ferdinand III in 1652, ibid., fig. 297; Paas, *German Political Broadsheet*, 115–16, 423–24, 144, 272–73. On the interaction between internal and external images, see the summary in Emich, "Bildlichkeit"; see also Schilling, *Bildpublizistik*; Bredekamp, *Leviathan*; Belting, *Anthropology of Images*.

23. This was the core of the imperial rights, which were left until the end of the Empire as privileges; they all had in common that they concerned interventions in the status system. See Roellecke, "Das Ende des römisch-deutschen Kaisertums."
24. See Becker, Kurfürstenrat, 174, for the development at the Peace Congress of Westphalia.
25. Oschmann, Nürnberger Exekutionstag.
26. Advisory Opinion (Gutachten) by the Imperial Court Council of 30 April 1649, quoted in Müller, Der Regensburger Reichstag von 1653/54, 36.
27. Bishop Franz Wilhelm von Wartenberg was simultaneously the bishop of Osnabrück and had represented the college of electors at the Peace Congress of Westphalia. See Schmid, Geschichte der Stadt Regensburg, 1:148–62; II:710–29, 845–62. Shortly before, in 1651, the civic right had been made dependent on the Protestant confession. On the preparations in the city and tensions between the council and the bishop, which were triggered by the affixing of the episcopal crest, see Gumpelzhaimer, Regensburgs Geschichte, 3:1309ff.
28. Letter to the Regensburg council dated 23 June 1652, HHStA RK RTA 124, fol. 153. For deliberations in July 1651 about the personal appearance, see HHStA RK RTA 122, fol. 183 v- 184 r; for considerations about this in a Privy Council memorandum dated 20 April 1652, see HHStA RK RTA 123. See Müller, Der Regensburger Reichstag von 1653/54, 59ff.; on the person of the emperpor, see Repgen, Ferdinand III.
29. The announcement is in HHStA RK RTA 124; edited in Meiern, Comitialia Ratisbonensia, 6ff.
30. In 1597/98 and 1603 imperial diets took place in Regensburg without the emperor; in 1608 there was an imperial diet in Regensburg without the emperor, broken up without a recess by the quarrel over the majority principle; in 1613 an imperial diet was held with the emperor, but without the protesting estates; and in 1640/41 there was an imperial diet with the emperor, but without the estates hostile to him.
31. See Arumaeus, De comitiis, 40ff.
32. See the list of estates written "de manu, von Hand" in HHStA RK RTA 125, fols. 353–74.
33. Meiern, Comitialia Ratisbonensia, 7; HHStA RK RTA 123. A Privy Council memorandum dated 20 April 1652 had suggested "that the estates appearing in person should limit their comitat as much as possible, and so as to save superfluous expenses not bring along a large retinue."
34. Mentz, Schönborn.
35. See, for example, the memorandum from the imperial councilors on the confidential arrangements between the Austrian directorial envoy Volmar and the Elector of Mainz to avoid predictable ceremonial problems with the electors: HHStA RK RTA 125, fols. 260–67. On the meeting of the electors in Prague, see Gotthard, Säulen, 409ff.
36. HHStA OMeA ZA 1, 1ff.; Merian and Abelin, Theatrum Europaeum, 7:286–87; See Mußgnug, "Die achte Kurwürde," 231; Schubert, "Erz- und Erbämter," 232; Müller, Der Regensburger Reichstag von 1653/54, 55; on the Elector of Brandenburg, who also placed great stock on a royal-like reception, see Urkunden und Actenstücke; see Stollberg-Rilinger, "Höfische Öffentlichkeit" and "Honores regii"; Lünig, Theatrum Ceremoniale, 1:163–64.
37. For the imperial cities, see Krischer, "Das diplomatische Zeremoniell der Reichsstädte"; for the Netherlands, see Heringa, Eer en hoogheid; for Switzerland, see Maissen, Geburt der Republic; for Italy, see Schnettger, Genua; Oresko, "Savoy."

38. Krischer, "Das diplomatische Zeremoniell der Reichsstädte," 5.
39. See Hofmann, *Repräsentation*, 180ff.; Mattingly, *Renaissance Diplomacy*; Roosen, "Early Modern Diplomatic Ceremonial"; Frigo, *Principe, ambasciatori*; Giesey, *Cérémonial et puissance*; Müller, *Gesandtschaftswesen*; Markel, *Rangstufen*; Stollberg-Rilinger, "Höfische Öffentlichkeit" and "Völkerrechtlicher Status"; Krischer, "Gesandtschaftswesen"; Bély and Richefort, *Diplomatie*; Bély, "Souveraineté"; Schilling, *Konfessionalisierung und Staatsinteressen*, 120ff., 160ff.; Wieland, "Diplomaten als Spiegel ihrer Herren?"; Haug-Moritz, "Friedenskongresse."
40. Lünig, *Theatrum Ceremoniale*, 1:368ff.; see Stieve, *Hof-Ceremoniell*, 263ff.; Wicquefort, *L'Ambassadeur*.
41. Wicquefort, *L'Ambassadeur*, 17: "Il n'y a pas de plus illustre marque de la souveraineté" ("There is no clearer sign of sovereignty"); Grotius, *De iure belli ac pacis*, 2:18, 2; see also Leibniz, "De Iure Suprematus" and "Germani Curiosi Admonitiones," 374, for the right to send ambassadors as an indication of the sovereignty of the imperial princes.
42. Asch, "'Ius foederis.'"
43. Stollberg-Rilinger, "Höfische Öffentlichkeit"; Dickmann, "Westfälische Friede," 206ff.; Becker, *Kurfürstenrat*, 169ff.; Christ, "Exzellenz-Titel."
44. Thus, for example, the French envoy granted the electors the "Excellency" title to win them over against Spain: *Urkunden und Actenstücke*, 6:277. See Leibniz, "Germani Curiosi Admonitiones," 369ff.
45. HHStA OMeA ZA, vol. 1ff.; see Hengerer, "Zeremonialprotokolle"; for the diary of the French master of ceremonies, Berlize, see Bély, "Souveraineté"; for the English court, see Finet, *Ceremonies of Charles I*; in general, see Stollberg-Rilinger, "Die Wissenschaft der feinen Unterschiede"; on the diplomatic ceremonial at the curia, see Andretta, "Cerimoniale e diplomazia."
46. On the imperial court, see Hengerer, *Kaiserhof und Adel*; Duindam, *Vienna and Versailles*; Pečar, *Ökonomie der Ehre*.
47. On the imperial cities, see Krischer, *Reichsstädte in der Fürstengesellschaft*; Schenk, *Zeremoniell und Politik*; on Florence, see Trexler, *Libro Ceremoniale*; on the papal curia, see Dykmans, *Cérémonial papal*; Visceglia, *La città rituale*; Visceglia and Brice, *Cérémonial et rituel à Rome*; Bölling, "Causa differentiae"; Zunckel, "Rangordnungen der Orthodoxie?" For other diaries from German courts, see Stollberg-Rilinger, *Hofreisejournal*; Besser, *Schriften*.
48. As at the negotiations over the entry into Regensburg in 1652 between the emperor and the electors, HHStA OMeA ZA 1, 64.
49. Lünig, *Theatrum Ceremoniale*, 1:369, 786ff.; similarly, see Rohr, *Ceremonial-Wissenschafft der großen Herren*, 17; Moser, *Hof-Recht*, 1:32.
50. Leibniz, "Germani Curiosi Admonitiones," 369.
51. For the diplomatic ceremonial of entries, visits, and audiences in general, see Lünig, *Theatrum Ceremoniale*, vol. 1; Rohr, *Ceremoniel-Wissenschafft der großen Herren*; Stieve, *Hof-Ceremoniell*; Vec, *Zeremonialwissenschaft*.
52. All details according to HHStA OMeA ZA 1, 56ff.; HHStA RK RTA 125, fols. 297–311; see also Harrach, *Tagzettel*, 21 December 1652 (though he was in Prague and not himself on-site); report by the Brandenburg envoy, *Urkunden und Actenstücke*, 6:166ff.; report of the papal nuncio Pannochieschi, *Lettere*, fasc. 151; Pfanner, *Historia comitiorum*, 78ff.; *Theatrum Europaeum*, 7:291–94; Paas, *German Political Broadsheet*, 8:117ff.; Gumpelzhaimer, *Regensburg's Geschichte*, 3:1313ff.; see Möseneder, *Feste in Regensburg*, 200–12.

53. See Aretin, *Das Alte Reich*, 1:172ff.; Gumpelzhaimer, *Regensburg's Geschichte*, 3:1312; order of the entry in HHStA OMeA ZA 1, 67ff.
54. HHStA OMeA ZA 1, 71ff.
55. Pfanner, *Historia comitiorum*, 8.
56. Honorary arch for the emperor in Regensburg in Ottomeyer et al., *Altes Reich und neue Staaten*, Catalog, 297–98, fig. 62; Paas, *German Political Broadsheet*, 8:423–24; contemporary description by Balduin, *Poetische Entdeckung der Ehrenpforte*; see Möseneder, *Feste in Regensburg*, 204ff.
57. On the pictorial type, see Rudolph, "Visuelle Kultur des Reiches," 235.
58. Pfanner, *Historia comitiorum*, 8.
59. HHStA OMeA ZA 1, 91–92; Meiern, *Comitialia Ratisbonensia*, 40; *Theatrum Europaeum*, 7:339, speaks of three hundred persons. For the entry of the Elector of the Palatinate with drums and trumpets, see HHStA OMeA ZA 1, 104ff. Later the Duke of Württemberg attracted attention repeatedly through inappropriate acoustic self-presentation: HHStA OMeA ZA 1, 280. On the other hand, the ceremonial protocols emphasize explicitly that the Landgrave of Hesse-Darmstadt in correct fashion did not enter Regensburg with trumpet blasts: HHStA OMeA ZA 1, 200.
60. Berns, "Herrscherliche Klangkunst."
61. See, for example, the instructions for the Brandenburg delegation, *Urkunden und Actenstücke*, 6:149. On Württemberg as an example, see in detail Meiern, *Comitialia Ratisbonensia*, 41ff.
62. Braungart, *Hofberedsamkeit*; Beetz, *Frühmoderne Höflichkeit*.
63. See chapter 2.
64. See Pfanner, *Historia comitiorum*, 41ff.
65. Such as the case of Saxony-Lauenburg; here the brother of the reigning duke appeared as his representative at the imperial diet and demanded to be treated like a prince, not an envoy, something that the emperor granted him by decree: Meiern, *Comitialia Ratisbonensia*, 49, 252–53; Pfanner, *Historia comitiorum*, 285, 318ff. On the new princes, who were concerned about the same issue, see the discussion in the section "Procedural Problems and Status Conflicts" in this chapter.
66. On the symbolic separation of the princes from the princely envoys at mass, see, for example, HHStA OMeA ZA 1, 284.
67. HHStA OMeA ZA 1, 91–101; extensive documentary material on this in HHStA RK RTA 126; see Pfanner, *Historia comitiorum*, 41ff.; Pannochieschi, Lettere, fasc. 151, fol. 51.
68. HHStA OMeA ZA 1, 106–7.
69. Mußgnug, "Die achte Kurwürde."
70. Meiern, *Comitialia Ratisbonensia*, 44; Pannochieschi, Lettere, fasc. 151, fols. 22, 51; Harrach, Tagzettel, 26 January 1653.
71. HHStA OMeA ZA 1, 99–100.
72. *Urkunden und Actenstücke*, 6:228; HHStA OmeA ZA 1, 177ff. See HHStA RK RTA 126, fols. 398ff.
73. See, for example, the tendency in Pfanner, *Historia comitiorum*, 41ff., who wrote from the perspective of Saxony-Weimar; see Moser, NTSR, 6/1:20.
74. *Urkunden und Actenstücke*, 6:260.
75. Ibid., 6:266. Elector Friedrich Wilhelm von Brandenburg, the "Great Elector," was considered by contemporaries as the one man among the electors who treated the cereomonial system with "größter Accuratesse" (the utmost accuracy); Lünig, *The-

atrum Ceremoniale, 1:393. See Becker, *Kurfürstenrat*; Stollberg-Rilinger, "Höfische Öffentlichkeit."
76. HHStA OMeA ZA 1, 139. On the ceremonial treatment of the papal nuncio at the Viennese court, see the fundamental work of Garms-Cornides, "Liturgie und Diplomatie"; on Pannochieschi, see Andretta, "Cerimoniale e diplomazia."
77. Harrach, Tagzettel, 24 February 1653. Nothing of this appears in the report of the papal nuncio himself: Pannochieschi, Lettere, fasc. 151, fols. 104r–v.
78. HHStA OMeA ZA 1, 155. The entry of the Polish envoy later followed the same pattern: HHStA OMeA ZA 1, 144–45. The extraordinary French envoy, on the other hand, was received very coolly, meaning that that no imperial cortège came out to greet him. He had not asked for one, as we read in the ceremonial protocol: HHStA OMEA ZA 1, 279–80.
79. HHStA OMeA ZA 1, 76ff.
80. See Braun, "Seelsorgebischof oder absolutistischer Fürst?"
81. HHStA OMeA ZA 1, 87ff. On the Order of the Golden Fleece as the source of imperial favors, see Hengerer, *Kaiserhof und Adel*, 573ff.
82. On the church as the most prominent place for quarrels over rank, see Peters, "Der Platz in der Kirche"; Weller, *Theatrum Praecedentiae*; Dürr, *Politische Kultur*.
83. HHStA OMeA ZA 1, 163–64; see also Gumpelzhaimer, *Regensburg's Geschichte*, 3:1316.
84. HHStA OMeA ZA 1, 144.
85. See Trapp, "Das evangelische Regensburg."
86. More recent scholarship, however, takes a different viewpoint: Schindling, "Konfessionalisierung"; Holzem, *Frühe Neuzeit*.
87. For an overview of the scholarship, see Siebenhüner, "Glaubenswechsel"; on the Empire, see Mader, "Fürstenkonversionen."
88. Strohmeyer, *Konfessionskonflikt und Herrschaftsordnung*; Winkelbauer, *Ständefreiheit*; Herzig, *Zwang zum wahren Glauben*.
89. IPO, Art. V § 41.
90. For the religious matters on the diet, see Müller, *Der Regensburger Reichstag von 1653/54*, 249ff.; for the Austrian Protestants see ibid., 262ff.; Meiern, *Comitialia Ratisbonensia*; Pfanner, *Historia comitiorum*, 89ff.; Gumpelzhaimer, *Regensburg's Geschichte*, 3:1316.
91. "Considerationes über die Protestirenden den 2./12. Mayo 1653," quoted from Müller, *Der Regensburger Reichstag von 1653/54*, 251–52.
92. "Princeps in compendio," 486–87; Liechtenstein, "Guetachten wegen Education eines jungen Fürsten," 543; see Repgen, "Ferdinand III.," 320–21.
93. "Considerationes über die Protestirenden den 2./12. Mayo 1653," quoted from Müller, *Der Regensburger Reichstag von 1653/54*, 251–52.
94. Pannochieschi, Lettere, fasc. 152, fol. 319r.
95. See, for example, Arumaeus, *De comitiis*, book VII, § 9.
96. On the paradoxes of the imperial constitution according to the Peace of Westphalia, see the basic work of Heckel, "Ius reformandi."
97. See chapter 2.
98. HHStA OMeA ZA 1, 156ff.; on more detail about this ritual, see most recently Scheutz, "Armenspeisung und Gründonnerstags-Fußwaschung."
99. Rules of confessional parity applied to the staffing of the Imperial Chamber Court and four imperial cities; the question had been postponed for the Regular Imperial Deputation.

100. IPO, Art. V § 52: "unum corpus considerari nequunt"; see Heckel, "Itio in partes"; Schlaich, "Majoritas"; Kalipke, "'Weitläuffigkeiten.'"
101. Meiern, *Comitialia Ratisbonensia*; Pfanner, *Historia comitiorum*, 193–94, 279–80.
102. Still worthwhile is Schramm, *Herrschaftszeichen und Staatssymbolik*; for a brief overview, see Rogge, *Wahl und Krönung*; in general, see Duchhardt, *Herrscherweihe*; Wilentz, *Rites of Power*; Weinfurter and Steinicke, *Investitur- und Krönungsrituale*; Kramp, *Krönungen*; *Enzyklopädie der Neuzeit*, s.v. "Herrschaftszeremoniell."
103. Ebel, *Geschichte der Gesetzgebung*.
104. On the concept of ritual, see Hahn, *Kultische und säkulare Riten*; Stollberg-Rilinger, "Symbolische Kommunikation," 502ff., with additional literature.
105. This has been exhaustively studied for the Middle Ages, less so for the early modern period. On royal and imperial coronations in the modern period, see Becker, "Kaiserkrönung"; Reuter-Pettenberg, "Bedeutungswandel"; Berbig, "Krönungsritus"; Dotzauer, "Ausformung" and "Thronerhebung"; Kramp, *Krönungen*; Wanger, *Kaiserwahl und Krönung*; Brockhoff and Matthäus, *Die Kaisermacher*.
106. On this unprecedented act, see Laubach, *Ferdinand I. als Kaiser*; Neuhaus, "Von Karl V. zu Ferdinand I." and "Königswahl vivente Imperatore"; Dotzauer, "Ausformung."
107. See, above all, Limnaeus, *Ius publicum*, 1:2, 4; Moser, TSR, 2:419; see Sellert, "Rechtshistorische Bedeutung," 27ff.
108. See Stutz, "Abstimmungsordnung"; Dotzauer, "Ausformung," 53–54, 73–74, describes the details of the coronation ritual as "unimportant" or "irrelevant," though the act as a whole "cannot be avoided." For a critical view, see Sellert, "Rechtshistorische Bedeutung"; Rudolph, "Kontinuität und Dynamik."
109. Schweder, *Introductio in ius publicum*, 241–42; Vitriarius, *Institutiones iuris publici*, 52–53; see Sellert, "Rechtshistorische Bedeutung," 27ff.
110. Meiern, *Comitialia Ratisbonensia*, 95ff., 99ff.; Pfanner, *Historia comitiorum*, 148ff. In general, see Neuhaus, "Königswahl vivente Imperatore" and "Heiliges Römische Reich Deutscher Nation"; Gotthard, *Säulen*, 485ff.
111. Elector of Mainz, letter dated 22 January 1653, quoted from Neuhaus, "Königswahl vivente Imperatore," 37.
112. Aretin, *Das Alte Reich*, 1:175.
113. See on this now Weller, Wassilowsky, and Dartmann, *Technik und Symbolik vormoderner Wahlverfahren*. See also Schneider and Zimmermann, *Wahlen und Wählen im Mittelalter*; fundamental for modern elections is Edelman, *Symbolic Uses of Politics*.
114. HHStA OMeA ZA 1, 168ff.; see Wanger, *Kaiserwahl und Krönung*, 38ff. Overall on this election, see Meiern, *Comitialia Ratisbonensia*, 203ff.; *Theatrum Europaeum*, 7:354ff.; *Urkunden und Actenstücke*, 6:238ff.; Lünig, *Theatrum Ceremoniale*, 1:1152ff.; Gumpelzhaimer, *Regensburg's Geschichte*, 3:1316ff. The election of 1653 has so far been given little attention, because the king died the following year and never assumed the reins of the government.
115. "Assolutamente liberi," in Pannochieschi, Lettere, fasc. 151, fol. 143r; see also ibid., fol. 274r.
116. Detailed description of the Augsburg election acts can be found in two illustrated broadsheets: Paas, *German Political Broadsheet*, 8:129–30.
117. See the Viennese ceremonial protocol in HHStA OMeA ZA 1, 193.
118. HHStA OMeA ZA 1, 196–97.

119. A similar procedure had been followed for the first time in 1562 at the election of Maximilian II, who was also elected during his father's lifetime; see Dotzauer, "Ausformung," 72.
120. *Theatrum Europaeum*, 7:358; also in Meiern, *Comitialia Ratisbonensia*, we always hear of a second conclave for the emperor.
121. HHStA OMeA ZA 1, 204–5.
122. *Urkunden und Actenstücke*, 6:215, 208.
123. The Elector of Brandenburg supported some of the demands of the Protestant estates and put the emperor under pressure with his electoral vote in order to push through his own territorial demands. That is why he sought to delay the election until the imperial diet had deliberated about it. In the end his envoy Blumenthal ignored this delaying tactic and voted for Ferdinand IV nevertheless; see *Urkunden und Actenstücke*, 6:206ff., 215ff., 238ff.
124. This is how it was, for example, in Bohemia, Denmark, or Hungary; see Neuhaus, "Königswahl vivente imperatore," 6.
125. First in the 1612 Electoral Capitulation of Matthias, Art. 30.
126. See the bibliography in Wanger, *Kaiserwahl und Krönung*, 285ff. Normally elaborate election and coronation diaries would subsequently appear, the production of which took time. Because the king died in the summer of the following year, in this case there is probably no such printed diary, but only illustrated broadsheets. In general on the medial public, see Gestrich, *Absolutismus*; Dölemeyer, "Krönungsdiarien."
127. Kunisch, "Formen symbolischen Handelns"; Annas and Müller, "Kaiser, Kurfürsten und auswärtige Mächte"; Schneidmüller, "Die Aufführung des Reichs"; Stollberg-Rilinger, "Verfassungsakt oder Fest?"; Mußgnug, "Die achte Kurwürde."
128. IPO, Art. IV § 5. Investiture of the envoy from the electoral Palatinate with the eighth electoral honor and the office of the imperial archtreasurer (*Reichserzschatzmeisters*) took place on 5 August 1652; *Theatrum Europaeum*, 7:286–87. See Mußgnug, "Die achte Kurwürde"; Reuter-Pettenberg, "Bedeutungswandel," 80ff.
129. Meiern, *Comitialia Ratisbonensia*, 204: "die praecedentia [ist] ad actus collegiales nicht zu ziehen" ("In collegial acts no one can refer to precedence").
130. HHStA OMeA ZA 1, 209–10; Meiern, *Comitialia Ratisbonensia*, 205; *Urkunden und Actenstücke*, 6:241ff.; Moser, TSR, 2:455; Lünig, *Theatrum Ceremoniale*, 1:1152ff.; see Kugler, *Reichskrone*, 119ff.
131. *Urkunden und Actenstücke*, 6:242; see HHStA OMeA ZA 1, 209–10; Pfanner, *Historia comitiorum*, 274ff.; Lünig, *Theatrum Ceremoniale*, 1:1158–59. Blumenthal had wanted to carry the scepter in place of the Brandenburg archchamberlain, the Count of Hohenzollern; however, it was made clear to him that this was not the job of the electoral representative: *Urkunden und Actenstücke*, 6:241–42. On the old quarrel between electoral envoys and the holders of hereditary offices, see Reuter-Pettenberg, "Bedeutungswandel," 105ff. On the hereditary offices, see Duindam, *The Habsburg Court*.
132. HHStA MEA WK 16.
133. Details in Mußgnug, "Die achte Kurwürde," 233–34; see the depiction on the illustrated broadsheets following the election of Leopold I as emperor in 1658: Paas, *German Political Broadsheet*, 8:244–45, 253, 262–63, 270.
134. Elector of Brandenburg, in *Urkunden und Actenstücke*, 6:215.
135. Golden Bull, chapter XXIV, 1, and chapter IV, 2.

136. Beemelmans, "Der Sessionstreit zwischen Köln und Aachen"; Helmrath, "Sitz und Geschichte."
137. Wanger, *Kaiserwahl und Krönung*, 102ff.; Herkens, *Der Anspruch Aachens auf Krönung der deutschen Könige*; Gsell, *Rechtsstreitigkeiten um den Reichsschatz*, 61ff.; Duchhardt, "Krönungen außerhalb Aachens."
138. Kirchweger, "Reichskleinodien."
139. See, above all, Schweder, *Theatrum historicum praetensionum*.
140. Meiern, *Comitialia Ratisbonensia*, 206–7; Pfanner, *Historia comitiorum*, 273–74; Moser, TSR, 2:455ff.; Pannochieschi, Lettere, fasc. 151, fols. 389ff., 420ff.; see Wallner, "Der Krönungsstreit zwischen Kurköln und Kurmainz"; Sellert, "Rechtshistorischen Bedeutung"; Berbig, "Krönungsritus," 650ff.; Wanger, *Kaiserwahl und Krönung*, 113–14; Schraut, *Schönborn*, 111ff.
141. Moser, TSR, 2:461. The position of the archbishop of Mainz was later buttressed by the famous univeral scholar Hermann Conring.
142. Meiern, *Comitialia Ratisbonensia*, 206–7.
143. Schraut, *Schönborn*, 111. In this case, Mainz and Cologne competed simlutaneously over leadership of the defensive alliance of the Rhenish princes, which was later elaborated into the Confederation of the Rhine under the leadership of Schönborn, the Elector of Mainz.
144. Moser, TSR, 2:437.
145. See below in this chapter.
146. On the coronation act, see HHStA OMeA ZA 1, 230–79; Meiern, *Comitialia Ratisbonensia*, 207ff.; *Theatrum Europaeum* 7:360–61; Gumpelzhaimer, *Regensburg's Geschichte*, 3:1318ff.; see Berbig, "Krönungsritus," 655ff.; Möseneder, *Feste in Regensburg*, 220–29; in general, see Wanger, *Kaiserwahl und Krönung*, 111ff.
147. The classic work is by Gennep, *Rites de passage*; Turner, *Ritual*; on the cultural pattern in the Middle Ages, see Althoff, "Humiliatio—exaltatio."
148. However, the knightly honor thus acquired was no longer considered a true enoblement and had no legal consequences for its holder; see Meiern, *Comitialia Ratisbonensia*, 208.
149. *Urkunden und Actenstücke*, 6:247; Lünig, *Theatrum Ceremoniale*, 1:1159.
150. Althoff, "Der frieden-, bündnis- und gemeinschaftstiftende Charakter"; Stollberg-Rilinger, "Ordnungsleistung"; Ottomeyer and Völkel, *Tafelzeremoniell*; Wanger, *Kaiserwahl und Krönung*, 122ff.; on Frankfurt, see Stahl, "'Im großen Saal des Römers'" and "Ein wahrhafftig Schauspiel."
151. On the arch offices at the coronation meal, see Schubert, "Erz- und Erbämter"; Wanger, "Königswahl und Krönung," 122ff.; Möseneder, *Feste in Regensburg*, 220ff.; as characteristic of the older view, for example, see Sieber, "Volksbelustigungen."
152. Erdmannsdörffer, *Deutsche Geschichte*.
153. Bourdieu, "Einsetzungsriten."
154. Several contemporary illustrated broadsheets about the coronation can be found in Paas, *German Political Broadsheet*, 8:130–38, 433; Möseneder, *Feste in Regensburg*, 220ff. The most widely circulated single-sheet broadsheets show either a sequence of images with nine individual stations of the elevation of the king, or only the central act of coronation, surrounded by the body of the imperial eagle.
155. A formulation by Luhmann, *Legitimation durch Verfahren*, 117.
156. Meiern, *Comitialia Ratisbonensia*, 207; König, *Von denen Teutschen Reichs-Tägen*, 33.
157. Wunder, "Herrschaft und öffentliches Handeln von Frauen in der Gesellschaft."

158. Moser, TSR, 2:327; see ibid., 7:141.
159. Newer literature on the coronation of empresses in the early modern empire does not exist; see only briefly Wanger, *Kaiserwahl und Krönung*, 161ff.; Führer, "Kaiserinnenkrönungen in Frankfurt am Main"; Keller, *Hofdamen*, 142ff. On France, where inheritance law ruled out a female succession to the throne, see Cosandey, *La Reine de France*.
160. Fößel, *Königin im mittelalterlichen Reich*.
161. The last empresses who were crowned in the Old Empire were Eleonora Magdalena Theresia of Pfalz-Neuburg, the wife of Leopold I, in 1690, and Maria Amalia of Austria, the wife of Charles VII, in 1742. Maria Theresia, the wife of Francis I, emphatically rejected her coronation as a comedy; see chapter 4.
162. HHStA OMeA ZA 1, 300–32; Meiern, *Comitialia Ratisbonensia*, 325; *Urkunden und Actenstücke*, 6:259–60; Pannochieschi, Lettere, fasc. 152, fols. 22, 46, 50r, 53r, 88r, 114r; Lünig, *Theatrum Ceremoniale*, 1:1159ff.; *Theatrum Europaeum*, 7:367–68; Moser, TSR, 7:148ff. A description of the coronation appeared as an illustrated broadsheet: *Kurtzer summari- scher Verlauff und Abbildung welcher gestalt ... Eleonora Römische Kayserin ... gecrönet worden*, Augsburg 1653, in Harms and Schilling, *Deutsche illustrierte Flugblätter*, 2:333; Paas, *German Political Broadsheet*, 8:142–43; see Möseneder, *Feste in Regensburg*, 231–32.
163. Pannochieschi, Lettere, fasc. 152, fol. 50r, speaks of the "arbitrio totale" of the emperor in everything that was not specified in the Golden Bull.
164. See Pečar, *Ökonomie der Ehre*, 226ff., 231ff. On the relationship between the imperial princes and the Habsburg court society, see Duindam, *Vienna and Versailles*, 195–96, 210–11, and "The Habsburg Court."
165. HHStA OMeA ZA 1, 111, 134.
166. Brandenburg envoy Blumemberg, report of 11 July, *Urkunden und Actenstücke*, 6:259.
167. Keller, *Hofdamen*; see also Hirschbiegel and Paravicini, *Das Frauenzimmer*.
168. HHStA OMeA ZA 1, 300ff.; see Pannochieschi, Lettere, fasc. 152, fol. 53r. The princes invoked the coronation of Empress Anna; their supplication of 16 July 1653 is printed in Schmidt, *Audientz-Saal*, 72–74; see HHStA OMeA ÄZA 3, No. 3/25; 4, No. 4/9.
169. HHStA OMeA ZA 1, 300ff.; Schmidt, *Audientz-Saal*, 74ff.
170. HHStA OMeA ZA 1, 311; on the imperiled status of the imperial counts in general, see Arndt, *Reichsgrafenkollegium*; Stollberg-Rilinger, "Grafenstand"; Lünig, *Thesaurus iuris*.
171. HHStA OMeA ZA 1, 302ff., 311–12.
172. HHStA OMeA ZA 1, 315–32.
173. HHStA OMeA ZA 1, 319.
174. Lünig, *Theatrum Ceremoniale*, 1:1159.
175. HHStA OMeA ZA 1, 325.
176. HHStA OMeA ZA 1, 323; Pannochieschi, Lettere, fasc. 152, fol. 114r.
177. Scipio Pannochieschi, Lettere, fasc. 152, fol. 114r.
178. In general, see Oestreich, "Die parlamentarische Arbeitsweise"; Aulinger, *Das Bild des Reichstags*; Neuhaus, *Repräsentationsformen*, "Zwänge," and "Wandlungen"; Stollberg-Rilinger, "Zeremoniell als politisches Verfahren"; Heil, "Verschriftlichung des Verfahrens als Modernisierung."
179. Rauch, *Traktat über den Reichstag*; already printed in 1614 in Goldast, *Politische Reichs-Händel*, 926ff.; Lehmann, *Chronica der Freyen Reichsstadt Speyer*, 7:959ff.; Lünig,

Teutsches Reichs-Archiv, 2:3ff.; Arumaeus, *De comitiis*; Ludolph, *Beschreibung eines Reichstags*; see the bibliographic references in Moser, NTSR, 6/1:16ff.; Schubert, *Reichstage*, 243ff.
180. Meiern, *Comitialia Ratisbonensia*, 56ff.
181. In detail on the various conflicts, Meiern, *Comitialia Ratisbonensia*, 44ff., 240ff.; *Akten des Reichserbmarschalls* HHStA RK RTA 126, fol. 270–401; also *Theatrum Europaeum* VII, 334 f.; Moser, TSR 4, 367 ff.
182. Meiern, *Comitialia Ratisbonensia*, 56; IPO, Art. IV § 20. On the conflict over the Palatine territories, see Meiern, *Comitialia Ratisbonensia*, 45ff.; Pfanner, *Historia comitiorum*, 54ff. On this question the emperor supported the Elector of the Palatinate against his relatives in order to strrengthen the electoral influence within the council of princes overall.
183. Magdeburg and Lübeck had separate seats on a cross bench. A contentious point was whether the Protestant princes should hold separate votes for the *Stifte* of Halberstadt, Minden, Verdun, Ratzeburg, and others, which were integrated into their respective territories; see Meiern, *Comitialia Ratisbonensia*, 498–99.
184. See Arndt, *Reichsgrafenkollegium*.
185. Such as the envoys of Brunswick-Wolfenbüttel, according to Meiern, *Comitialia Ratisbonensia*, 76, 98.
186. Meiern, *Comitialia Ratisbonensia*, 101.
187. For the invitation to the court, see HHStA RK RTA 126, fols. 272–73; on the events that transpired, see Meiern, *Comitialia Ratisbonensia*, 234ff.; Pfanner, *Historia comitiorum*, 282ff.; HHStA OMeA ZA 1, 281ff.; *Theatrum Europaeum*, 7:361–62; *Urkunden und Actenstücke*, 6:192–93, 252ff.; Pannochieschi, *Lettere*, fasc. 151, fol. 453r (no mention of any kind of disorder); in general on the proposition, see Küchelbecker, *Nachricht von denen im Heiligen Römischen Reiche gewöhnlichen Reichs-Tagen*, 69ff.
188. Pfanner, *Historia comitiorum*, 282, assigned Württemberg the chief role in the protest; Meiern, *Comitialia Ratisbonensia*, 236, however, gives it to Bavaria.
189. This, in any case, was reported by the *Theatrum Europaeum*, 7:361.
190. Ibid.
191. Meiern, *Comitialia Ratisbonensia*, 233–34, 237.
192. HHStA OMeA ZA 1, 283.
193. See HHStA OMeA ZA 1, 288ff., with a sketch after p. 292. One possible explanation for the wrong date on the broadsheet is that it was printed at a time when the final date was not yet fixed. Moreover, the precise gradation as indicated in the ceremonial protocols is not correctly reflected.
194. The question of who would be the first to hold the directorium—Austria or Salzburg—was traditionally contested, as was the question of which envoys for which territories should cast the vote at what point and what title should be used to call up the individual votes. See HHStA RK RTA 25, fols. 260–67; Meiern, *Comitialia Ratisbonensia*, 240ff.
195. Meiern, *Comitialia Ratisbonensia*, 242ff., where, in addition to the aforementioned rank conflicts, a whole host of others are reported.
196. Heil, "Verschriftlichung des Verfahrens als Modernisierung"; Stollberg-Rilinger, "Zeremoniell als politisches Verfahren"; Sikora, "Der Sinn des Verfahrens."
197. See Domke, *Virilstimmen*.

198. Distribution of votes in Meiern, *Comitialia Ratisbonensia*, 96. See also the above-mentioned case where the Elector of the Palatinate laid claim to holding the votes also of Palatinate-Simmern and Palatinate-Lautern in the college of princes, wherein the emperor supported him by decree; Meiern, *Comitialia Ratisbonensia*, 45ff.
199. IPO, Art. X §§ 2, 6, 7.
200. On the contested status of the Swedish envoy, see Meiern, *Comitialia Ratisbonensia*, 20ff.; Pfanner, *Historia comitiorum*, 9ff.; Moser, NTSR, 6/1:177–78; *Theatrum Europaeum*, 7:334ff.; in general, see Müller, *Der Regensburger Reichstag von 1653/54*, 280–302. On the quarrel between Sweden and Brandenburg over the enactment regarding envoys, see *Urkunden und Actenstücke*, 6:252, 255, 259–60, 264; on the agreement about the sequence of the votes for Western and Eastern Pomerania, see Meiern, *Comitialia Ratisbonensia*, 568–69. See also Leiher, *Rechtliche Stellung der auswärtigen Gesandten*, 40ff. Later, when Sweden was invested, careful attention was paid to the Swedish "*ablegati*" not being treated as royal ambassadors; for example, they were not picked up at their lodgings and so on: HHStA OMeA ZA 2, 973–74 (1661), 990–91, 997 (1662), 1127 (1664).
201. See chapter 1.
202. *Urkunden und Aktenstücke*, 6:409ff., 413; Meiern, *Comitialia Ratisbonensia*, 266ff., 818–19; Gumpelzhaimer, *Regensburg's Geschichte*, 3:1323; in general, see Müller, *Der Regensburger Reichstag von 1653/54*, 351–86; Mohr, *Lothringen*, 373ff.
203. On Herford, see *Urkunden und Actenstücke*, 6:166. Equally precarious was the status of the city of Bremen between imperial estate status and Swedish dominion; see Meiern, *Comitialia Ratisbonensia*, 788ff.
204. On Schwarzburg, see Meiern, *Comitialia Ratisbonensia*, 243.
205. Lobkowitz, Salm, and Eggenberg under Ferdinand II; Auersperg, Dietrichstein, Piccolomini, Weißenwolf, Sinzendorff, and Colloredo under Ferdinand III; to them was added the Protestant Count of Nassau-Hadamar in 1653. See HHStA RK RTA 127, fols. 3–7, 250–62; Müller, *Der Regensburger Reichstag von 1653/54*, 225–31; Klein, "Die Erhebungen in den weltlichen Reichsfürstenstand."
206. This had already been decided at the imperial diet of 1640/41: Meiern, *Comitialia Ratisbonensia*, 248ff., 533ff., 686ff.; Pfanner, *Historia comitiorum*, 311ff.; *Urkunden und Actenstücke*, 7:303–4, 356–62; on the conflict with Lobkowitz, see also Ludewig, *Vollständige Erläuterung*, 2/2, 1484ff.
207. Müller, *Der Regensburger Reichstag von 1653/54*, 228; for a different viewpoint, see Neuhaus, "Das Heilige Römische Reich Deutscher Nation," 22–23.
208. *Urkunden und Actenstücke*, 6:357, report from the imperial diet, 5/15 December 1653.
209. *Urkunden und Actenstücke*, 6:362, Elector to his envoys, 14 December 1653.
210. In the end, the compromise was that the new princes in person would sit ahead of the envoys, but were allowed to vote only after them; see the imperial decree in Meiern, *Comitialia Ratisbonensia*, 264–65; "Fürstenratsprotokoll," in ibid., 859ff. In the electoral capitulation of Ferdinand IV, Art. 45, and in the *Jüngster Reichsabschied* (§ 197), the admission of new princes was tied to the consensus of the estates.
211. Neuhaus, „Von Reichstag(en) zu Reichstag" und "Zwänge"; Oestreich, "Die parlamentarische Arbeitsweise."
212. See Rauch, *Traktat über den Reichstag*, 67–68, 84ff., 116ff.; Isenmann, "Reichsstandschaft der Frei- und Reichsstädte"; see also Oestreich, "Die parlamentarischen Ar-

beitsweise"; Laufs, "Reichsstädte," 35ff.; Krischer, "Das diplomatische Zeremoniell der Reichsstädte" and "Politische Repräsentation und Rhetorik der Reichsstädte."
213. Blumenthal to the electors, 18 September 1653, *Urkunden und Actenstücke*, 6:289.
214. See figure 10, chapter 3.
215. An essential reference here is Krischer, *Reichsstädte in der Fürstengesellschaft*.
216. IPO, Art. VIII § 4; Meiern, *Comitialia Ratisbonensia*, 241, 254ff., 474ff., 522 ff.; Pfanner, *Historia Comitiorum*, 291ff.; see in detail Isenmann, "Reichsstandschaft der Frei- und Reichsstädte"; see also Laufs, "Reichsstädte"; Buchstab, *Reichsstädte*, 142ff.; Müller, *Der Regensburger Reichstag von 1653/54*, 209–24; Krischer, "Politische Repräsentation und Rhetorik der Reichsstädte."
217. According to a report for the college of cities in the city archive in Ulm; quoted in Isenmann, "Reichsstandschaft der Frei- und Reichsstädte," 92.
218. Meiern, *Comitialia Ratisbonensia*, 254ff.; Isenmann, "Reichsstandschaft der Frei- und Reichsstädte," 92.
219. Isenmann, "Reichsstandschaft der Frei- und Reichsstädte," 110.
220. Meiern, *Comitialia Ratisbonensia*, 526.
221. During the negotiations at the Congress of Westphalia, in return for Sweden's help on the question of the *votum decisivum*, the cities had supported the Swedish demand for five million Reichstaler in reparations.
222. See chapter 1.
223. Chasseneuz, *Catalogus gloriae mundi*; Arumaeus, *De comitiis* and *De sessionis praerogativa*; Limnaeus, *Ius publicum*, 1:295ff.; see also Besold, *De praecedentia*; Crusius, *De praeeminentia*; Hellbach, *Meditationes iuris proedriae*; Cocceji, *Disputatio de praecedentia*; Zwantzig, *Theatrum praecedentiae*; and numerous other legal dissertations between 1650 and 1800; comprehensive bibliography in Hellbach, *Handbuch des Rangrechts*. On rank conflicts below the level of imperial estates, see Stollberg-Rilinger, "Rang vor Gericht"; Weller, *Theatrum Praecedentiae*; Füssel, *Gelehrtenkultur*.
224. In detail, see Stollberg-Rilinger, "Zeremoniell als politisches Verfahren," 103ff.
225. See Arumaeus, *De comitiis*, 517ff.: "qui vero ordinem suum tuetur, Rempublicam quantum in se est, defendit."
226. See chapter 1; Moser, TSR, 4:345–80; see Stollberg-Rilinger, "Zeremoniell als politisches Verfahren," 119ff.; Roellecke, "Das Ende des römisch-deutschen Kaisertums."
227. Moser, TSR, 4:377–78.
228. Meiern, *Comitialia Ratisbonensia*, 239–40, 337–38; Moser, TSR, 4:367ff.; Moser, NTSR, 6/1:468ff.
229. *Urkunden und Actenstücke*, 6:253.
230. Möseneder, *Feste in Regensburg*, 200–1.
231. IPO, Art. IV § 50.
232. Stollberg-Rilinger, "Das Reich als Lehnssystem"; Roll, "Archaische Rechtsordnung."
233. See broadsheets in Mameranus, *Kurtze und eigentliche Verzeychnus*; Francolin, *Vera descriptio*; Moser, *Lehens-Verfassung*, 313; Buder, "Investitura," 10.
234. Lünig, *Theatrum Ceremoniale*, 2:937, 942.
235. Ibid., 2:941; Moser, *Lehens-Verfassung*, 322.
236. *Ceremoniale deren Reichs-Fürstliche Belehnungen... betr.*, in HHStA RHR GF TZ 1.
237. HHStA RHR GF TZ 2, fol. 10r, esp. Fiocchi to Modena, 20 May 1695.
238. Moser, "Bericht von dem Streit der Reichs-Erbämter," esp. 159–60, 174–75; electoral capitulation of Ferdinand II, Art. 41; see Moser, *Lehens-Verfassung*, 322, and

Einleitung zu dem Reichs-Hofraths-Prozeß, 11ff.; Lünig, Theatrum Ceremoniale, 2:942; Duindam, "The Habsburg Court."
239. Moser, Einleitung zum Reichs-Hofraths-Prozeß, 15.
240. See, for example, the case of the Ernestines of Saxony in 1559: Buder, "Investitura," 12ff.
241. Moser, Lehens-Verfassung, 255.
242. Ibid., 256–57.
243. Corpus Iuris Canonici, Decretales Gregorii papae IX, book 1, title XXX: De officio legati, chap. VII.
244. Pufendorf, Acht Bücher vom Natur- und Völkerrecht, 1:829–30; Boehmer, De Investitura per procuratorem.
245. Moser, Lehens-Verfassung, 251ff.; Boehmer, De Investitura per procuratorem. According to Beck, "Kurzer Inbegriff," 639, even in the late eighteenth century a proper investiture was supposed to be done in person.
246. Moser, Lehens-Verfassung, 256–57; see a model template for excuses in Cramer, Manuale processus imperialis, 217ff.; for examples, see Noël, "Reichsbelehnungen," 109–10. According to Lünig, Theatrum Ceremoniale, 2:936, only electoral Saxony and electoral Bavaria were exempted from the excuses delivered while kneeling and were also allowed to leave out the titulature when addressing the emperor.
247. See chapter 1.
248. See the herald's report in Mameranus, Investitura regalium electoralis dignitatis.
249. Goetz, Die Politik Maximilians I., No. 8, 26–46; Albrecht, Auswärtige Politik, 69; Steiner, Pfälzische Kurwürde, 77ff.
250. Electoral capitulation of Ferdinand IV of 1653; see Schönberg, Recht der Reichslehen, 113.
251. Moser, Lehens-Verfassung, 327; Hengerer, "Zeremonialprotokolle."
252. Statute of the Imperial Court Council (Reichshofratsordnung) of Ferdinand III, dated 16 March 1654, tit. III, § 8–15, in Sellert, Ordnungen des Reichshofrates, vol. 2, part 2, § 139–44; on the expenses, see Moser, Lehens-Verfassung, 256ff., 279ff.; Beck, "Kurzer Inbegriff," 640ff.
253. HHStA RK RTA 125, fols. 398–419.
254. IPO, Art. IV § 20. On the investiture of Count Palatine Ludwig Philipp von Simmern in person, see HHStA OMeA ZA 1, 350–51; HHStA OMeA ÄZA 4, No. 21, fol. 1r. On the conflict between Electoral Palatinate and Palatinate-Simmern, see Meiern, Comitialia Ratisbonensia, 45ff.; Pfanner, Historia comitiorum, 51ff.; HHStA RK RTA 125, fol. 378r. The emperor had conceded to the Elector of the Palatinate the imperial diet vote of Palatinate-Simmern, even though the Count Palatine of Simmern had tradition on his side. It was therefore very important to the count palatine to be invested again with Simmern only by the emperor. The emperor could take advantage of this and prevail upon him to receive the fief in person. In the Jüngster Reichsabschied (§ 187) the conflict was settled between electoral Palatinate and Simmern.
255. For the investiture of Elector Johann Philipp of Mainz in person by Ferdinand III on 4 May 1654, see HHStA OMeA ZA 1, 367ff.; see HHStA OMeA ÄZA 4, No. 21, fols. 189–90; No. 22, fols. 1r-v; Lünig, Theatrum Ceremoniale, 2:954; Uffenbach, De consilio caesareo-imperiale, 120; Beck, "Kurzer Inbegriff," 639.
256. See Schraut, Schönborn, 15ff., 111ff.
257. HStA OMeA ZA 1, 397; see HHStA OMeA ÄZA 4, No. 21, fols. 189–90.

258. HHStA OMeA ÄZA 4, No. 21, fols. 189–90.
259. HHStA OMeA ZA 1, 368; see HHStA OMeA ÄZA 4, No. 21, fol. 189.
260. HHStA OMeA ÄZA 4, No. 21, fol. 189f.
261. HHStA OMeA ÄZA 4, No. 21 (1653–1709): "Exempla, wo Reichs- und Churfürsten die Reichs-Lehen in persona genohmen." Personal investitures occurred very occasionally even later, but only involving a close client of the imperial house, like Charles of Lorraine as bishop of Osnabrück in 1706, or a lower-ranking prince, like Lamberg with the Landgraviate of Leuchtenberg in 1709.
262. HHStA RK RTA 127, fols. 28ff.
263. HHStA RK RTA 127, fols. 264–82; Moser, NTSR, 6/1:340; Meiern, *Comitialia Ratisbonensia*, 1147. See Müller, *Der Regensburger Reichstag von 1653/54*, 439ff.
264. Advisory opinion of the imperial councilors on the decision of the imperial diet and the departure of the emperor, March 1654, in HHStA RK RTA 127, fols. 28–33. See Moser, TSR, 44:87ff.; in general on the presence of the imperial family at imperial diets, see Moser, NTSR, 6/1:66ff.
265. On the stipulations of the *Jüngster Reichsabschied*, see Müller, *Der Regensburger Reichstag von 1653/54*; Aretin, *Das Alte Reich*, 1:179ff.
266. JRA § 196, text in Buschmann, *Kaiser und Reich*, 2:268–69: the emperor offered, again as always, "to settle all quarrels of session according to everyone's justice in appropriate ways or else to decide according to equity."
267. Sellert, *Ordnungen des Reichshofrates*.
268. Rauch, *Traktat über den Reichstag*; see Sikora, "Der Sinn des Verfahrens"; Schlaich, "Majoritas" and "Mehrheitsabstimmung"; Heckel, "Itio in partes."
269. See chapter 2.
270. HHStA RK RTA 128; Meiern, *Comitialia Ratisbonensia*, 423ff., 440–41, 454 55, 471ff.; Pfanner, *Historia comitiorum*, 477ff.; *Urkunden und Actenstücke*, 6:189, 193, 342, 353; see Müller, *Der Regensburger Reichstag von 1653/54*, 174ff.
271. Schnettger, *Reichsdeputationstag*.
272. The composition of this "ordinari Reichsdeputation," a committee of the three colleges, had been one of the most hotly contested problems of the entire imperial diet, for it, too, had revolved around the preeminence of the electors and around confessional parity; see Müller, *Der Regensburger Reichstag von 1653/54*, 145ff.
273. Burkhardt, "Verfassungsprofil und Leistungsbilanz," sees this decision deficit as the advantage of this assembly, arguing that it led to its institutionalization, thereby making it a precursor of the modern parliament. For a critical perspective on this, see Kampmann, "Der Immerwährende Reichstag."
274. Aretin, *Das Alte Reich*, 1:173–74.
275. See the beginning of this chapter; similarly, see also Schubert, *Reichstage*, 317ff., 323.
276. With a pointedly modernizing formulation, Burkhardt, "Das größte Friedenswerk," 598, following Schindling, *Die Anfänge des Immerwährenden Reichstags*, 15.
277. Vorländer, "Die Verfassung als symbolische Ordnung"; Luhmann, "Verfassung als evolutionäre Errungenschaft."
278. See Haug-Moritz, "Kaisertum und Parität"; Roellecke, "Das Ende des römisch-deutschen Kaisertums."

CHAPTER 4

Parallel Worlds
Frankfurt-Regensburg-Vienna, 1764/65

Epochal Turning Point

The Seven Years' War ended in 1763. "After the war nothing was as before."[1] The weights within the Empire, in Europe, and in the world had been redistributed. In the European theater of war, the Elector of Brandenburg and King of Prussia had defied all expectations in prevailing against the house of Austria, and he had risen from being one of the less important potentates at the periphery of Europe to being a first-rate political actor. As far as the Empire was concerned, the war had also been contested on the level of definitions. The question had been this: Was the King of Prussia waging a war—permissible under the law of nations—against the Queen of Hungary and Bohemia, indeed, a religious war for the Protestant cause? Or was the Elector of Brandenburg violating the imperial peace (*Reichslandfrieden*), which meant that the imperial ban should be imposed upon him? With the imperial estates unable to agree on an interpretation of the conflict, the imperial ban was not invoked. Still, the Empire had entered the war as a collective actor and had mustered an imperial army—with little success—against the King of Prussia. But then individual princes had pulled out again, and in the end the imperial diet had declared the Empire neutral. After the war, two power-political rivals whose territorial centers lay outside of the Empire now faced each other within the imperial federation—a constellation of momentous ambiguity.

The long and expensive war entailed considerable follow-up costs for development within the European states as well (this term had by now established itself[2]). The competitive pressure on the internal structure of the territories had intensified considerably. Not only the defeated monarchies of France and Austria faced imminent national bankruptcy. Brandenburg-Prussia, hated by some and admired by others, presented itself as the new model of success, even though it, too, was financially ruined. Major and minor princes of the Empire felt considerable reform pressure. It was the hour of political reckoning, of counting, saving, and reorganizing. But it was not only the need for reform that was pressing; so was the optimism about reform. A new political discourse had emerged, which looked at states like machines that had to be constructed according to a rational plan. The princes and their ministers—mostly to the applause of the enlightened public—placed a new program on the agenda, one that subordinated all political action to a strict cost-benefit calculus.³ The Empire evaded this kind of rationality. As a result, historians have long devoted their attention almost entirely to the new places where the "growth of state power" could be observed in the seventeenth and eighteenth centuries: Vienna and Berlin, as well as Dresden and Munich, but not Frankfurt or Regensburg. They wrote the history of Austria and Brandenburg-Prussia, but not of the Roman-German Empire as such.

These developments exposed the Empire to growing tensions.⁴ The imbalance between the few large and the many medium-sized and small members of the Empire had worsened. While the imperial federation was for the smaller ones the very condition of their political-social existence, for the larger ones it was partly an obstacle and partly an instrument of their own power politics. The polarization between the hostile great powers created a pull that the smaller powers could hardly avoid. Moreover, the parity rules of the Peace of Westphalia had caused the confessional conflict to pervade the Empire's structure at all levels. It made sense to instrumentalize this conflict, with Brandenbrug-Prussia along with England-Hannover in the north and the Habsburg monarchy in the south representing not only centers of far-flung networks of political-dynastic clients, but also nuclei around which the confessional polarization crystallized.

Where, under these conditions, did the Empire still manifest itself at all? On what stage did it still appear *in corpore*? The symbolic political worlds had diverged. It was now the exception for the Empire to be staged in large-scale, solemn form: at the election and coronation of the emperor or—as in 1764— of the king of the Romans in Frankfurt am Main. In spite of the indebtedness resulting from the war, it was still the case "that at no solemnity and nowhere in the world was such splendor seen as at the election, entry, and coronation of a Roman emperor or king."⁵ Completely separate from this was the day-to-day activity of the Empire, namely, in Regensburg, where the last imperial diet had not disbanded since 1663. The third imperial stage, the emperor's court in Vienna, was primarily a venue for the power and splendor of the house of Austria, though it had by now learned to regard the imperial dignity—which it had lost to a Wittelsbacher between 1742 and 1745—as nothing more than incidental to its status. While the Empire had once been actually present in the places where its head and members assembled in solemn form and in person, the worlds of the emperor and of the imperial estates now separated spatially. Only once, at his coronation, did Joseph II personally appear in his role as king or emperor and sit *in maiestate* in accordance with the regulations of the

Golden Bull, and never again thereafter. Frankfurt am Main, Regensburg, and Vienna must therefore be examined separately as venues of the Empire.

Frankfurt am Main: Ghostly World Theater

In retrospect, after the Old Empire had ceased to exist, the solemn ritual of the royal coronation seemed the symbol and embodiment of a doomed political order. No historian who describes Joseph II's coronation in Frankfurt leaves out the account of Goethe, who witnessed the event as a child and late in life recounted it in great detail in his work *Dichtung und Wahrheit*.[6] In an artistically romanticized refraction, he styled the events into a partly majestic and partly ghostly "world theater. These things gave me much pleasure," he wrote, "as all that took place, no matter of what nature it might be, concealed a certain meaning, indicated some internal relation: and such symbolic ceremonies again, for a moment, represented as living the old Empire of Germany, almost choked to death by so many parchments, papers, and books." (figure 11) The entire event, from the first arrival of the electoral envoys, to the election and coronation, to

Figure 11. The entry of Emperor Francis I and Joseph II into Frankfurt am Main, 1764. Workshop of Martin van Meytens the Younger (Johann Dallinger von Dalling, 1741–1806, et alia), Vienna, around 1765, © KHM, Vienna.

the coronation banquet at the town hall, the *Römer*, is described as a spectacle of increasing dignity, a work of art of the utmost splendor: "A politico-religious ceremony possesses an infinite charm. We behold earthly majesty before our eyes, surrounded by all the symbols of its power; but, while it bends before that of heaven, it brings to our minds the communion of both." About the moment immediately following the coronation, we read that "all seemed only one mass, which, moved by a single will, splendidly harmonious, and thus stepping from the temple amid the sound of the bells, beamed towards us as something holy."[7] What Goethe describes here—in the light of the post-Revolution perspective—is the symbolic enactment of the political body *in actu*, as political theorists from Hobbes to Rousseau had depicted it: a many-headed mass with *one* will, every individual a "hundred-thousandth part of a sovereignty that was now appearing in its full splendor."

Yet Goethe imparts to the festivities, which he compares "not inappropriately with a spectacle," alongside dignified qualities also mildly comical traits. It is above all the clothes through which he makes manifest the ambivalence of the events: old-fashioned Spanish frocks and plumed hats clashed with the fashionable breeches, silk stockings, and shoes appearing underneath in a way that offended the taste of his contemporaries. Only the electoral envoy from Brandenburg, who, "like his King, used to defy all kind of ceremony" and who enjoyed the undisguised sympathy of our observer, set himself apart by the parsimony of his dress, liveries, and equipages.[8] Already Emperor Francis I, at his own coronation twenty years earlier, had appeared "in his strange costume, and seemed to her [his wife], so to speak, like a ghost of Charlemagne," prompting his wife Maria Theresia to "immoderate laughter." Joseph appeared much the same way: "The young king ... in his monstrous articles of dress, with the crown-jewels of Charlemagne, dragged himself along as if he had been in a disguise; so that he himself, looking at his father from time to time, could not refrain from laughing."[9]

As we have seen, for the young Hegel looking back in 1802 the coronation ritual, with its old clothes, also stood pars pro toto for the anachronistic character of the entire structure of the Empire, which rested solely on the "superstition regarding purely external forms." As the most striking indication of the mismatch between the ritual staging and the actual power relationships, he points to the role of the Margrave of Brandenburg: "Even if the Margrave of Brandenburg now has an army of 200,000 troops, his relationship to the German Empire does not seem to have changed since he had fewer than 2,000 regular soldiers in his pay, for the Brandenburg envoy still presents the emperor with oats at his coronation, just as he did in the past."[10] The coronation ritual was an even more grotesque spectacle to later historians: "How might Frederick the Great have performed the task of bringing the emperor washing water and a towel on horseback!"[11] It is all the more remarkable that Frederick the

Great, as the archchamberlain of the Empire, was also present at the coronation through his envoy Plotho, who did not bring the emperor water to wash his hands at the *Römer* (that was the job of the hereditary imperial chamberlain of the Hohenzollerns), but who did help him dress and undress and handed him the scepter. Evidently all participants maintained the normative order of the Empire by publicly participating in the joint ritual, even if they did so through representatives. Nobody took the first step to destroy the collective imagination.

The Stage of the College of Electors

The restoration of peace within the Empire was to be affirmed by the election and coronation of Archduke Joseph as king of the Romans. Both *that* the electors would chose someone *vivente Imperatore* in 1764 and *whom* they would choose had been negotiated ahead of time.[12] Unlike before the war, Habsburg diplomacy had been able to win over all the electors. In the Peace of Hubertusburg, Frederick II had also promised to give his electoral vote to Maria Theresia's oldest son, Joseph. Still, in Frankfurt the ritual of free election and coronation was staged according to the traditional order—though with a few conspicuous deviations.

A lot of movement had come into the college of electors since the end of the seventeenth century. It was not only the Elector of Brandenburg who bore a royal title as of 1701. Since 1697, the Electors of Saxony had been elected kings of Poland on several occasions (though this throne had become vacant in 1763). The Duke of Brunswick-Lüneburg—one of the leaders of those who had sought the parity (*Parification*) of the princes with the electors—had been elevated to the electoral honor by the emperor in 1692; his successors had ascended to the English throne in 1714 and since then had been the leaders of the global power of Great Britain. In return for the granting of this new, ninth electorate, the Habsburgs had pushed through in 1708 that their own electoral vote, the Bohemian one, which had never come into play except at the royal election, was now allowed into all imperial colleges. In 1764 three great European powers, three "crowned heads," were therefore represented in the college of electors. On the other side stood the three ecclesiastical electorates, whose holders came from the nobility (*Stiftsadel*) of the lower Rhine: Breidbach-Bürresheim in Mainz, Königsegg-Rothenfels in Cologne, and Walderdorff in Trier. Their political standing at the head of the imperial hierarchy was in obvious contrast to their social origins in the lower nobility. A clear line of tension thus ran straight through the college of electors.

The establishment of the eighth electorate, but even more so of the ninth, the elevation of Brunswick, had created a precedent that clearly violated the Golden Bull. Unlike in the case of Bavaria and the Palatinate, when the emperor had merely taken the electoral dignity from one man within the dynasty and given it to someone else, this dignity now appeared to have become fundamentally disposable. With this the gates of the competitive dynamic had been thrown wide open. If electors could become kings, princes now wanted to become electors.[13] But the more the order of the Golden Bull was violated, the more carefully it was enacted as a fundamental law of the Empire. The ritual of election and coronation demonstrated an age-old continuity, one that no longer existed, namely, the corporative unity, closed nature, and exclusivity of the college of electors.[14]

The very right of the electors to elect a king of the Romans by their own free decision during the lifetime of the emperor was not enshrined in the Golden Bull. In 1653, the electors had simply confronted the imperial diet with a fait accompli,[15] after which time the right had been contested for decades between the electors and the princes. After the election of Joseph I in 1690, this situation had not occurred again. Now the electoral right of election *vivente Imperatore* was once more up for debate. The electors claimed that, in principle, they could elect a successor possibly without the will of the emperor and during his lifetime. This claim was now to be effectively demonstrated symbolically. It was done through a staging *before* the staging: through the electoral "collegial convent," which was carefully separated from the subsequent "election convent" by symbolic means. The first, the collegial convent, deliberated and decided *whether* one should elect a king of the Romans, and the second, the electoral convent, deliberated and decided *whom* to elect and under what conditions. At the end stood the election day itself, followed a few days later by the coronation.[16]

In keeping with the symbolic order, the Elector of Mainz issued the invitation to this collegial day, namely, for 7 January 1764 in Frankfurt am Main, as provided for in the Golden Bull—the plan to call for the meeting in Augsburg was dismissed again. Hereditary Imperial Marshal Pappenheim personally saw to it that the city was prepared in the traditional way as the venue. The electors sent high-ranking multimember electoral deputations; after 1711, none of them had appeared in person at such deliberations. The spectacle was staged in front of a European public—the pope, the kings of France, Spain, Portugal, Sweden, Naples, and the Dutch States General sent envoys to Frankfurt. On 6 February, the collegial convent was opened *en cérémonie* in the town hall, the *Römer*, with everything that appertained to it: six-horse state carriages, parading city militias, and music. The very first thing that was settled there was the ceremonial order of the visits, return visits, processions, and sessions that followed. The challenge was to defend the status claims of the college of electors as a whole against the foreign powers, the other princes, and not least against the heterogeneity within it.[17]

The emperor himself sent the Prince of Liechtenstein as a high-ranking commissioner. He entered Frankfurt in great pomp, performed the lengthy and highly formalized program of the ceremonies of welcome and notification with the city council and the envoys, and was eventually brought to the third session of the convent of electors in the *Römer* with all solemnities, including twenty six-horse state carriages and the salute of one hundred canons. There he presented the imperial proposition, that is to say, he posed the formal question to the convent of electors of whether and how the election of the king of the Romans should be carried out. Then he was escorted back to his lodgings equally festively, where he entertained the electoral envoys with a ceremonial meal. Two days later the electoral convent met again in city hall, made its decision about the election, and drafted its response to the emperor.

Next the collegial convent transformed itself into an electoral convent. Looking at the whole affair from an instrumental perspective, this could have been done with little effort, since the location and participants were the same. This was *not* an instrumental procedure, however, but an event of pure symbolism. A clear break was therefore enacted to symbolically separate the two assemblies. For one, it was only now that the envoy from electoral Mainz formally invited the electors to the electoral convent. Exceptionally, as was emphasized apologetically, the messengers were not dispatched to the courts of the electors, but only to the electoral delegations present in Frankfurt. For another, the imperial commissioner staged his departure by leaving the city in the most solemn fashion. For one day he repaired to Darmstadt along with his entire retinue and then returned quietly to Frankfurt as a private man. This was done solely "to indicate in this way to the public the end of the imperial commission."[18] The ceremonial distinction between the collegial and the electoral convent was the only way to convey the constitutionally relevant message that the electors—and they alone—had the right to decide about the need to elect a king of the Romans, and that they did not have to proceed to the election without further ado simply upon the emperor's request.

The electoral convent that followed served above all to deliberate about the electoral capitulation. The electoral delegations proceeded to the ten sessions that took place in accordance with the previously agreed ceremonial order "with their entire retinue in splendor."[19] When the deliberations neared their end, the old electoral capitulation having been adopted without restrictions, the ecclesiastical electors arrived in Frankfurt in person one by one. The secular electors, however, continued to be represented by their electoral envoys—including Maria Theresia as the Queen of Bohemia. But she was not the only one who was absent—contrary to all custom, neither the emperor nor the candidate himself were personally present at the election. Instead, the Prince of Liechtenstein had himself legitimated once again as commissioner in electoral Mainz one day before the election—in case "the election should fall upon His Royal Highness, the Archduke Joseph."[20] The fiction of the open outcome to the election was thus maintained by all participants, even though the man to be elected was already waiting beyond the city walls.

The election procedure took place on 27 March in Frankfurt in accordance with the Golden Bull and the most recent agreements of the electoral convent, in all solemn form and with the greatest pomp.²¹ In the emperor's stead, Liechtenstein was brought into the conclave "with great ceremony," where he granted the "imperial and paternal consent" to the election. Then, in place of Joseph, the electoral envoy from electoral Bohemia pronounced the oath on the electoral capitulation by swearing upon "the soul of the king of the Romans." The staging of the election was entirely in the hands of the Elector of Mainz. Two things were symbolically enacted in Frankfurt (as they already had been in 1653): the closed corporate character of the electoral college, and the exclusive electoral authority of the electors—not only the competency to select a successor to the throne, but also to decide whether there should be an election at all and under what conditions.

To preserve the college of electors as an entity capable of taking action across all internal tensions, following the election and coronation the Association of Electors (*Kurverein*) was renewed, that is, the old Agreement of 1558 was confirmed by oath.²² In 1558 the electors had pledged to one another that they would allow neither the religious split nor rank conflicts to divide them. The agreement, which in the final analysis reached back all the way to 1338, consisted of a personal allegiance by each member; when he died, it ceased to exist. The last renewal had occurred in 1745. Of the members at that time, only the Queen of Bohemia, Maria Theresia, and Frederick II of Prussia were still alive. That is why the four electors who were now present in person in Frankfurt, those of Mainz, Trier, Cologne, and the Palatinate, assembled with the envoys of the others on 7 April for an "illustrious meeting," where the text of the *Kurverein* of 1558 was read out. Here one elector would swear the oath to the next one: first Mainz to Bohemia, the last surviving member of the old *Kurverein* of 1745, then Trier to Mainz, the Palatinate to Trier, and so on, so that all were tied to one another and to the old alliance of 1745 in an unbroken chain of personal obligations. Apart from electoral Brandenburg, this left only electoral Brunswick, whose envoy had no special authorization for this act, and it made up the oath in October in Regensburg in proper form. In everything the participants observed "the traditional manner of performing the oath based on the directives and regulations of the Golden Bull Art. II § 2."²³ Ritually the fiction of an unbroken chain of tradition reaching back into the fourteenth century was created. In short, Frankfurt was the stage on which the old order of the Empire was invoked and affirmed on oath.

Absences

And yet, the absence of the imperial family during all of the electoral happenings was a symbolic message that no one could misread. The Elector of

Mainz had in vain expressed his concerns about this situation, but at least he obtained an imperial declaration that this would not establish a precedent for the future.[24] Maria Theresia had remained in Vienna, while Francis I and the two archdukes Joseph and Leopold had set out on 12 March and had arrived in Heusenstamm, outside the gates of Frankfurt, on 23 March. There they had taken lodgings in a castle of the Schönborn family, waited for the election, and in the meantime received electors and foreign envoys for informal audiences. What is revealing is that—unlike in 1653—the continuous ceremonial protocols of the Habsburg court were carried on in Vienna during the entire election and coronation journey, and that virtually no notice was taken of the events in Frankfurt.[25] This meant that the court was not where the emperor was—the court remained where the empress-queen was in residence.

From the perspective of the successor himself, the entire event was bothersome and unpleasant. Joseph was mourning his recently deceased wife, and he could muster no interest at all in the office intended for him, which he regarded as "disagreeable and useless"[26]—to say nothing of the many ceremonial troubles within his own retinue and vis-à-vis the electoral college. To the very end, negotiations went back and forth between Heusenstamm and Frankfurt concerning the ceremony; at issue were countless details, from the entry all the way to the liveries of the archduke's bodyguard. With a mixture of nervousness and disdain, Joseph was waiting for the final stage directions. Even an angel would lose patience over the ceremonial questions, he wrote to his mother: "pour moi ... c'est une vraie comedie" (for me ... it is a real comedy).[27]

In Heusenstamm, the emperor and the elected king received the "solemn notification" of the election from the hereditary imperial marshal Pappenheim and from the brother of the Elector of Cologne. That not only the father received the news but the son as well, and the latter from a different messenger, had previously been decided by the electors explicitly and against custom. This, too, was a symbolic message of constitutional significance, for it was intended "to further affirm that a king of the Romans could be elected also *invito Imperatore*" (i.e., without the emperor's will).[28] Next came the entry into the city, which outdid all the splendor displayed until then in every possible respect—in terms of time and space, as well as the persons involved and the sumptuous furnishings.[29] All bells were rung for two hours, three hundred canons were fired, and ninety-five six-horse state carriages drove up. First, the new king personally reaffirmed the electoral capitulation in the cathedral: his obligations to the traditional rights and liberties of electors and estates had the highest priority and could not be affirmed only by his deputy.

However, apart from the three ecclesiastical electors, no electors and princes were present in person during the solicitation—with one exception, as the *Obersthofmeister* of Vienna, Khevenhüller-Metsch, noted disapprovingly. The old Prince of Anhalt-Zerbst, while completely devoted to the imperial court, made a deranged impression in "appearance and deportment" and had only a "very dirty" and—worse still—"borrowed country equipage" with him, yet "he could not be dissuaded and rode in it in his princely rank, namely, as the first and only prince of the old houses present at the public entry."[30] Such contrasts, which disturbed the courtly splendor in a way that was considered embarrassing, appear repeatedly in the records of the participants. The imperial-royal court society felt it was unreasonable that they would have to forego their accustomed comfort in the cramped conditions of the old imperial city. The emperor and the king held only a makeshift court in their quarters, received visitors in their lodgings with card games, concerts, and dinners, and eagerly awaited the end of the solemnities.

A latent tension existed between the imperial court and the college of electors, which became visible at the ceremonial occasions in spite of all the careful prior agreements. At the public events in Frankfurt, the Elector of Mainz was largely in charge of the staging, but at the audiences in his quarters it was the emperor who set the rules. Already in Heusenstamm he had used this to coerce the three ecclesiastical electors to pay their formal respects also to his sons, Joseph and Leopold. However, that meant that they were asked something that no foreign potentate had to do, and it contravened their primary concern: to be treated by the emperor like kings. The Elector of Mainz had sought to prevent this during the preliminary negotiations, but he made no headway. To conceal the ceremonial defeat and save face, he had no choice but to stage the visit with the two archdukes as a completely spontaneous idea of his own. The Elector of Cologne did likewise with *grimaces et affectations*; only their colleague from Trier visited the princes *sans affecter la surprise*, without feigning surprise.[31]

In Frankfurt, where the electoral envoys had to appear before the emperor for a solemn audience, both sides continued the strategy of gaining ceremonial ground with all means. The bone of contention was the "Spanish reverence" on bent knee, which the emperor demanded from the electoral envoys in his written regulation but not from the envoys of foreign monarchs.[32] "But since the reverence on bent knee in this regulation was very offensive to the delegation from electoral Bavaria, Saxony, and the Palatinate, and especially to electoral Brandenburg," the Brunswick envoys wrote to their lord, the King of England, it was the subject of protracted negotiations. "Yet the imperial court did not wish to yield the least bit on this, and the delegation from electoral Brandenburg, to which the others could not accord any priority, would not even entertain the proposed compromises. Thus they found themselves compelled to act united in refusing the reverence on bent knee."[33] The delegation from electoral Bavaria was the first to be summoned to an audience, and "was the first to suffer this steadfast decision." Although it had previously been stated that the emperor would not appear in the official Spanish mantle (*Mantelkleid*), and the envoys therefore also had to appear *in Campagne Gala*—according to the courtly code, *en campagne* was the formula for the reduced level of formality that prevailed at the pleasure residences in the countryside and gave greater leeway to dress—the imperial court marshal surprised them upon their arrival with the announcement that things would be different now. They thus had to fetch their mantles (*Mantelkleider*) in all haste to change on the lower floor of the imperial quarters, which they regarded as a shrewdly arranged embarrassment. The other envoys were given a timely warning, allowing them to appear in the requested ceremonial attire. While the imperial *Obersthofmeister* passed this "considerable confusion" off as a misunderstanding, which even the envoy from electoral Bohemia had been unable to prevent, the envoys were convinced that this was the emperor's payback for their steadfast refusal to pay their respects on bent knee. But even after this incident they were not willing to do it.

A few days after the election, on 3 April, Joseph was crowned king of the Romans with all traditional pomp in the Cathedral of St. Bartholomew in Frankfurt.[34] The highly formalized handling of the imperial regalia, which represented the ritual continuity with Charlemagne, continued to be the object of old and new rank conflicts. For example, the deputies from Aachen and Nuremberg quarreled again over who would be the first to bring their regalia into the cathedral,[35] even though the insignia and relics had long since become the object of critical historical scholarship by the time of Joseph II's coronation. As early as 1630, Johann Müllner, the Nuremberg council clerk, had disputed the authenticity of the relics and had questioned the age of the insignia and regalia.[36] His tract had been published in 1742. That the imperial crown, the sword, and the regalia did not really go back to Charlemagne was hardly a point of contention among eighteenth-century scholars. Their symbolic interpretation had become the topic of mere "academic pedantry."[37] Yet how the regalia were specifically interpreted, the age one ascribed to them and whether they were venerated as sacred, hardly played a role any longer in practice. What mattered is that they elevated the person who was allowed to handle them above all others, and this had turned them into the preferred objects of the general competition for prestige.

The same was true of the performance of the arch offices at the coronation meal. On the one hand, they were described as "contemptible tifles and trivialities," as a "court game" and "eye service," that really had no business being in a legal code like the Golden Bull.[38] On the other hand, however, they remained the object of protracted conflicts between the old and new electors.[39] The chief reason was that the emperor had created the new electoral dignity for Brunswick in 1692 and needed an arch office for it. It was very convenient, then, that the imperial ban was imposed on the Elector of Bavaria in the War of the Spanish Succession and his office as steward reverted back to the Elector of the Palatinate, to whom it had, after all, originally belonged. His office as treasurer was thereby freed up for Brunswick. But when the Elector of Bavaria was later restored to all of his offices and dignities, he demanded the office of steward back from his Palatinate colleague, who in turn challenged Brunswick for the office of treasurer. But the new elector refused to go along and relinquish title and symbol until he had been given a new, adequate arch office. The efforts by the imperial court to find such an office for Brunswick filled numerous file cabinets. The court contemplated the hereditary banner office, but Württemberg claimed it as an old title, and invented an archhuntmaster office, which it tried in vain to depict as something attractive. In 1764 this conflict had been going on for fifty years and was still unresolved. At the coronation and the meal, the arch officer of the Palatinate, Sinzendorff, exercised the office of treasurer.[40] At every opportunity, however, electoral Palatinate and electoral Brunswick issued protestations and reprotestations, for example, when the contested titles were publically announced at the imperial diet.

This highly typical conflict over symbols shows three things. First, within the exceedingly complicated structure of the Empire, nearly everything was connected to everything else, and nearly everything was taken equally seriously, which means that any change triggered chain reactions of secondary problems. Second, once something had become the object of competition for symbolic capital, such a competitive struggle unleashed its own dynamism and no one could simply avoid it. That was especially true of the arch offices. Third, the case is characteristic of the structural impossibility of resolving nearly any of these conflicts. Often it was only the death of one party that put an end to them. And so it was here: the contest over the office of treasurer ended only when the Bavarian Wittelsbacher died out.

The endless struggle of the secular electors over the arch offices at the coronation stood in stark contrast, however, to the fact that they avoided being present in person. Revealingly enough, the Elector of the Palatinate arrived in Frankfurt exactly one day after the coronation, while the others did not show up at all. The situation was paradoxical. The arch offices were services that—much like the "reverence on bent knee"—symbolized the reverential subordination of the electors to the emperor. This message was to be avoided at all costs. At the same time, though, the arch offices also symbolized the electors' elevated status above all other princes and were therefore traditionally prime investments in symbolic capital.[41] Moreover, the multiplication of the electoral dignities had turned them into objects of a competitive struggle. Renouncing such a prestigious object would have been regarded as a public defeat—even by the King of England. The social logic of princely society thus put the electors into a situation of having to pursue two contradictory goals: first, wanting to hold the arch offices at all costs, and second, under no circumstances to exercise them in person.

As a result they absented themselves from the coronation meal. In keeping with the traditional arrangement, in the festive hall of the *Römer* the emperor and king dined at the front wall elevated four steps. Table service was performed by forty-four imperial counts in person in a precisely regulated sequence; these counts placed great stock in this office, for it made their direct membership in the Empire visible and set them symbolically apart from other, new counts.[42] On both sides of the opposite end of the hall, and elevated one step, separate tables had been laid for the nine electors, sumptuous sideboards had been set up, and canopies had been hung. In the center of the hall, on level ground, stood the large table for the princes, also sumptuously laid. But only the three ecclesiastical electors sat in their seats; all other chairs remained empty, since the envoys of the other electors had no access to the *Römer*—they "usually eat together at the place of the envoy from electoral Saxony, who was staying nearby."[43] The princes themselves had been staying away from the coronation banquets since 1742, because the emperor was ignoring their claim to be treated the same as the electors. Still, the dishes were served also for the secular electors and princes, as though they were present.

Serving those absent created the symbolic fiction that they were present; its purpose was to maintain their appearance as the norm, no matter how often they violated it. This imparted something eerie to the scene, at least in the account of Goethe, who had gained access to the hall as a young boy:

> [T]he buffets and tables of all the temporal electors, which were, indeed, magnificently ornamented, but without occupants, made one think of the misunderstanding which had gradually arisen for centuries between them and the head of the Empire … and if the greater part of the hall assumed a sort of spectral appearance, by so many invisible guests being so magnificently attended, a large unfurnished table in the middle was still more sad to look upon; for there, also, many covers stood empty, because all those who had certainly a right to sit there had, for appearance' sake, kept away, that on the greatest day of honor they might not renounce any of their honor, if, indeed, they were then to be found in the city.[44]

Later, the emperor had the workshop of his court painter Martin van Meytens create a sequence of large-format paintings of the coronation events, one of which depicts the coronation meal (figure 12). One has to look very closely to find the empty seats in this painting. The artist made them almost disappear in the overcrowded courtly scenery of the Frankfurt council hall—but only almost. Upon second look, the bustle of courtiers, servants, and spectators makes the empty chairs appear all the more bizarre. The picture illustrates both the norm and its violation, since it depicts the ideal arrangement of the seats and that they were in fact empty.

When the procedure of the coronation had been prepared in writing in Vienna ahead of time based on old ceremonial documents, value had also been placed on maintaining the normative order, even though it was expected that it would be violated again. The procedure was provided for in case the worldly

Figure 12. The coronation meal of Joseph II in the *Römer*, 1764. Workshop of Martin van Meytens the Younger, Vienna, around 1764, © KHM, Vienna.

electors and princes did appear in person. To be sure, the Viennese councilor Wolfscron, who was in charge of planning, had initially written very realistically: "At the table of the imperial princes which has already been prepared, nobody is eating." Later this had to be changed *per dictaturam* of the chief court marshal: "nobody is eating" was crossed out, and in its stead the following correction was inserted in the margin: "the present imperial princes eat."[45] After all, the Viennese stage directions for 1764, which built on the cases of 1653 and 1690, were supposed to represent the norm for the next time. That is why here, too, it was important to hold on to the expectation of the personal appearance of the princes in the face of a contrary reality.

The crowned king, meanwhile, barely took note of all of this; for him the meal was too long, and afterward he was happy to have gotten through it without major embarrassments. His relationship to his own coronation was exceedingly ambivalent: it fluctuated between uneasiness and detached observation. He detested "all the difficulties and awkwardness attached to such ceremonies," he wrote to his mother.[46] Time and again he reflected in his letters the contrast between his emotional state—grief over his recently deceased wife—and the demands of the ritual staging, which he wanted to get over with as quickly as possible. At the same time, though, he also registered that the ritual possessed a certain infectious emotional power. In spite of everything, he experienced the coronation as *superbe et auguste*. He was especially taken with the cheering crowds. One could see that the Elector of Mainz had been present with all his heart. His father, too, the emperor, of whom it was usually said that he stood aloof from the Viennese court ceremonies, had not been able to escape the effect of the spectacle and, like many of the participants, could not hold back his tears. The way in which Joseph reported back to Vienna about the ritual attests to a culture—anything but self-evident—of writing about one's emotions and talking about one's inner life. He observed the events with very different eyes than a herald, master of ceremonies, or *Obersthofmarschall* would have, and he noted every sign of emotional involvement in himself and others. Very much unlike older accounts of such rituals, which focused on what was outwardly visible and recorded, in formulaic terms, at best the appropriate signs of joy or sorrow,[47] the relationship between the internal and the external, of reality and appearance, had become a fundamental problem. A criterion of inner sincerity and authenticity was asserting itself, measured against which the old rituals were in danger of losing their credibility, for if it was not sufficient for them to be performed in a formally correct way, and if what mattered was their emotionally persuasive force, it was easy for them to go awry and turn into something ridiculous.

The emperor and the king soon set out on their return to Vienna (10 April). Joseph II would never again return to Frankfurt either as king or emperor. Following the death of his father and his own ascension to the throne the following year, he did not receive the acclamation of the citizens of Frankfurt and the other imperial cities in person, but sent a commissioner.[48] To be sure, he later undertook lengthy travels through his hereditary lands as well as the Empire and Europe, but these were political expeditions driven by technical aspects of his governance; they served to broaden his knowledge and were entirely different from the traditional journey of a ruler. Joseph always embarked on these travels incognito, without a large retinue and no ceremonial accompaniment, without drums, trumpets, and gun salutes, without state carriages, guards

(*Hatschiere*), and parading citizen militias. The purpose of these trips was to see, not to be seen. They were motivated by a new understanding of rulership, namely, the notion that governance needed the ruler's knowledge more so than his demonstrative physical presence. Joseph never again undertook a journey like the election and coronation trip to Frankfurt, where 450 horses had to be changed at every postal station.

Regensburg: Ambiguities

During the coronation of the king of the Romans, the imperial assembly was meeting elsewhere: in Regensburg. On its return from Frankfurt to Vienna, the court society, traveling on the Danube, passed by the city. The emperor and the king showed themselves on their splendid boats while the citizens fired seventy canons and mortars and rang all the bells in their honor. Nobody expected that they would stop at the imperial city or even enter. People were already pleased, we read, that the lords, in spite of the poor weather, showed themselves at the railing from a distance and waved.[49]

On the occasion of the Peace of Hubertusburg in 1763, the city fathers in Regensburg had held a double festive celebration and minted commemorative coins, for it was now exactly one hundred years that the last imperial diet had assembled here.[50] Emperor Leopold I could not get around summoning the imperial diet in 1662, far later than planned, because, much like Maximilian I nearly two centuries earlier, he had felt compelled to do so by the acute threat to his lands from the Turks.[51] At the beginning of 1664, after the diet had already been in session for one year, the emperor, the imperial archchancellor of Mainz, and a number of electors and princes had come to Regensburg in person once more—for the last time, as it would turn out. They had departed again in May to leave the deliberations to their representatives, who had remained entirely among themselves ever since. With one exception during the Wittelsbach intermezzo of 1742–45, no ruler appeared in person at the imperial diet ever again.

The agenda in 1663 had essentially been the same as in 1653/54. Time and again, efforts were made to take up the "postponed matters" (*negotia remissa*) from last time and to negotiate them. Especially the formulation of the permanent electoral capitulation, which would have curtailed the privileges of the electors in a central point, was a major issue. Another matter was to establish a modern organization for the defense of the Empire that did justice to the general trend toward standing armies. Yet the deliberations got bogged down or failed repeatedly; although individual decisions were made, an imperial recess was never issued. Nevertheless, the envoys stayed put, primarily because new wars and crises necessitated new negotiations, and because the assembly proved a valuable instrument to the emperor for bringing his influence to bear and a useful forum for exchanging information between the courts.[52]

On the question of whether, and in what sense, this "permanent imperial diet" (*Immerwährender Reichstag*) was a symbolic embodiment of the Empire as a whole, opinions diverged as widely already in the eighteenth century as they have among modern constitutional historians. Some continued to speak of the *comitia Imperii* in the plural, "where the head and members of the Holy Empire together are regarded as and considered one corpus,"[53] and they described the imperial diet as an assembly of emperor and estates where the "*summa maiestas* resides."[54] If the Peace of Westphalia was the guide, the imperial diet was the institution that combined the emperor and the estates into a body capable of acting and doing so with *one* will. These descriptions always had in mind the picture of a living body. For example, we read that "the marvelous great body of our German state is animated in all its members chiefly through the imperial diets."[55] The instructions given to the French envoy to Regensburg in 1754 also stated that the imperial diet was the source of the legislative power, because the head and the members formed one political body. But the instructions simultaneously pointed out that every individual *state* of a German prince barely differed from that of a sovereign.[56] How did these contradictory statements go together? There were just as many voices who believed that "the Empire is erroneously regarded as a single autonomous state." Instead, one had to see it as a "collection of many free states which have combined into a certain system" in order to recognize its intelligent order.[57]

In short, the Empire was a puzzle to observers. Ever since the concept of "state" had established itself and become a theoretical yardstick of reality, the Empire presented itself to outsiders more than ever as a shifting image: sometimes as *one* state, sometimes as the sum of many individual states.[58] Depending on which perspective one chose, the imperial diet appeared as a traditional assembly of the estates or as a congress under the law of nations. After all, many foreign potentates were also keeping permanent delegations there. The choice one made was a matter of perspective, an ascription, the assertion of a particular validity. Experts of the complicated matter wisely rejected this option and preferred to dispense entirely with a theoretical concept for the "irregular body resembling a monstrosity," as the famous formulation of Samuel Pufendorf put it.[59] But one thing was clear to everyone: without an imperial diet there was no Empire. The year 1765 saw the appearance of a sensational little tract entitled *Von dem deutschen Nationalgeist* (Of the German National Spirit), which denounced the failings of the imperial constitution with patriotic intent and at the behest of the emperor. It came from the pen of Friedrich Carl von Moser, the son of the famous *Reichspublizist*. We read there that the imperial diet was "the only bond that ties together the various German lands:

should it rupture completely, Germany would turn into a map of many islands torn away from solid land, whose inhabitants lacked the ferries and bridges to maintain communication among themselves."[60]

Later historians described the permanent imperial diet with as much diversity as contemporaries back then. For a long time, it was seen as a sad or ridiculous event, because it was so completely out of line with how one envisaged the functioning organ of a powerful national state.[61] Later, when the German power state was utterly discredited and one had to look around for other, peaceful patterns of political identification in Germany history, the tables were turned and the permanent imperial diet was seen as a model—whether as a legislative organ that was especially progressive because it was continually in session,[62] or as an organ of a transnational federation similar to the modern unified Europe or an international organization like the United Nations.[63] The imperial diet was described as an "early form of the parliament" and as the "representation of the German people vis-à-vis the head of the Empire,"[64] even as "our modern Bundestag in its nascent stage,"[65] endowed with comprehensive competencies. As an organ that shared and controlled government, it supposedly confronted the "executive" in the form of the emperor and the Viennese imperial chancery, who were "responsible for foreign policy."[66] It is obvious that in the process the constitutional legal categories of the nineteenth century were transferred to the Old Empire, as though it had been a deliberately designed constitutional system with clearly demarcated competencies. While the countless ceremonial quarrels had been highlighted in the eighteenth and nineteenth centuries as an indication of the hopeless ridiculousness of the entire thing, now there was the opposite tendency to excuse them as marginal phenomena typical of their age or to simply ignore them—with the more or less subliminal intent to cast the Empire as a highly functional entity and thus find in it a historical legacy for the present.

These approaches do not do justice to the phenomena. Instead, what is needed is to endure and take seriously their fundamental ambiguity. The Empire was not unequivocal—also and especially so in the eighteenth century. It was not an objectively given fact; it had no existence independent of the acts, perceptions, and ascriptions of contemporaries. Trying to resolve and settle the divergent and competing interpretations from a modern perspective misses the point: the point is precisely to make them visible. The imperial diet itself was a hybrid creature that allowed for different interpretations. The external forms in which it presented itself—the place, time, and appearance of the actors—was perceived by outside observers in a variety of ways. Within the medium of symbolic action, the actors kept the same conflicts going that already existed in 1653/54—namely, the character of the imperial convention as a whole and the status of each individual within it.

A Gloomy Place

The external shape of the imperial diet was in many ways still that of the seventeenth or even the sixteenth century. The imperial city was still the host of the assembly; the envoys with their families still formed "a kind of republic of their own" in relationship to the community of the imperial city.[67] Meetings were held in the same city hall chamber as in the sixteenth century; the throne of the emperor stood three steps higher, under a canopy, and a step lower were the red velvet chairs for the electors. City hall had not changed. But next to it, the community, in an effort to demonstrate its autonomy as an imperial city, which was constantly under threat from Bavaria, had built a new, modern city hall, one that dwarfed the neighboring structure and made it look literally old (figure 13).[68]

This was noted by all travelers who, on their way through the large residences, stopped over in Regensburg. It was commonplace in contemporary travel literature to point out the archaic, cramped space and gloominess of the old Regensburg city hall. Travelers experienced the place as they expected to, based on their guidebooks, and they reproduced this impression in their letters and accounts. Their comments are therefore strikingly similar. This view was also shaped by the images reproduced in many learned works about the imperial diet. The main hall in which all three colleges of the estates assembled (*Re- und Correlationssaal*, figure 14) and the primary and secondary chambers of the

Figure 13. Old and new city halls in Regensburg. Oil on canvas, Historisches Museum der Stadt Regensburg, Inv. No. AB 274.

Figure 14. Andreas Geyer, *Re- und Correlationssaal des Regensburger Reichstags*, around 1725.

three colleges appeared in stylized barrenness: low, dark, and almost entirely devoid of decoration.[69]

Even though the large city hall chamber had not changed since the seventeenth century, it now made a completely different impression in the illustrations; indeed, it no longer seems to be the same room. The main reason was that since the rulers no longer appeared there in person, it was always depicted empty, without any people. The throne under the canopy was always vacant. Without the presence of the individuals of high rank, the chamber forfeited its lordly aura.

If one bears in mind that institutions were embodied above all in buildings and that architecture was the most impressive instrument of the baroque representation of lordship, it becomes understandable how the chamber of the imperial diet in Regensburg struck contemporaries. While the imperial princes—from a King of Saxony-Poland in Dresden to a Prince-Bishop of Würzburg, all the way down to an imperial abbot in Salem—displayed all manner of gold and glittering pomp in their residences, the Empire as such had no authoritative architecture at all. For that it lacked either money or the consensus of the imperial estates, or both.[70] Instead, participants made do with the provisional arrangements of the imperial city, which might once have been suited to the temporary character of the old imperial diets, but which, now that the assembly had become a stationary, permanent institution, inevitably had to be experienced as anachronistic.

But it was not only architectural taste that had changed—the criteria of what constituted a well-ordered community and a sensible government were by now also different. Both architecture and political theory were guided by the ideal of planned, systematic regularity arising from the spirit of geometry. Travelers who considered themselves modern and enlightened, therefore, took the condition of the imperial city in general and of the city hall in particular as symbolic of the Empire as a whole, "pitiful, sad, and old-fashioned";[71] in their eyes Regensburg was "a gloomy, melancholy city caught up within itself. ... Nothing gives a more vivid image of the mournful body of the imperial constitution that it holds in safekeeping than it."[72] That "the decrepit state of the building of the estate assembly has a notable connection with the duration of the imperial system" became a virtual truism: the imperial hall "is like the German Empire itself, old, rambling, and dilapidated," wrote the Berlin publisher Friedrich Nicolai; another travel writer described the city hall as "very old, empty, gloomy," as full of nooks and crannies "as the German imperial constitution itself."[73]

Joseph II evidently saw it in much the same way. Not only did he not set foot in the city on his coronation journey, he did not go there after he ascended to the throne, nor did he receive the homage of the citizens in person. Later he only visited it once, in May 1781, and he did so strictly incognito, that is, without any of the solemnities that characterized his role as emperor. He made no festive entry and did not participate in a solemn session of the imperial diet, but was shown around city hall the way one tours a historical attraction. We are told that the Elector of Mainz, as the highest-ranking envoy, acted as his guide and complained about the decrepit state of the building during the tour, to which the emperor responded: "Eh bien! Si la maison s'écroule, le recès de l'Empire sera fait" (If the house falls down, the Imperial Recess is finished), a historical allusion drawing on the metaphorical meaning of the word *Reichsgebäude* ("imperial edifice").[74]

The emperor was no longer physically present in Regensburg as such, only symbolically—through his permanent representative, the principal commissioner (*Principalcommissar*). The place where the latter resided when in Regensburg—which was at most a few months out of the year—stood in marked contrast to the old city hall. It was not, as before, the bishop's residence, but a sumptuous baroque palace at Emmeram Square. The principal commissioner, Alexander Ferdinand von Thurn und Taxis, whom Francis I had appointed as early as 1748 and who himself had just recently risen to the rank of imperial prince, had rented the building of the Reichsstift Sankt Emmeram and the so-called Freisinger Hof and had renovated them into a splendid residence fit for a prince.[75] It included an audience hall in which the emperor was symbolically present through his portrait, a canopy, and a red carpet on which stood a throne of gold brocade. Here the principal commissioner received homages and congratulations in the emperor's stead; here he received foreign envoys for audiences. In this palace he celebrated the dynastic *Galatage*, that is, the birthdays and name day festivals of the imperial family as well as memorial services if someone in the imperial house died. This turned his residence into a kind of mirror of the imperial court. What regularly took place here several times a year with great ceremony and imparted structure to the life of the envoys were not festivals of the Empire, but family festivals of the Habsburg-Lorraine dynasty (with which the Thurn und Taxis dynasty itself had been linked by marriage since 1745).[76] The principal commissioner communicated with "the Empire" by receiving the directorial envoy from electoral Mainz in his palace *nomine imperii*. By contrast, he made no appearance at the imperial diet in city hall. Nor did he have any reason to, since there was no longer a festive opening or a recess.

Putting the imperial diet on a permanent footing had the result that in Regensburg separate worlds came into contact, even if some of the actors were the same: here the court life of the imperial representative, with weekly dinners, assemblies, and concerts, with theater, opera, dance, and pleasant conviviality; there the austere happenings of the deliberations of the imperial diet in city hall. Foreign travelers observed two sets of customs, language, and behavior.[77] Critics of the imperial diet played one off against the other: "One has to admit that much less has been done to ensure that excellent delegations deliberate for the common good of the Holy Roman Empire of the German Nation, than that they can eat and dance with propriety and convenience," wrote Nicolai.[78] The imperial assembly itself, meanwhile, no longer staged itself in solemn public form. "If the principal commissioner were not here with his court, the opera, comedies, hunts, balls, and fireworks, one wouldn't even know that the imperial diet was in session in the city."[79] And if an imperial prince did in fact come to Regensburg in person, as Duke Karl Eugen von Württemberg did, he visited only the court of the Prince of Thurn und Taxis and ignored the imperial assembly.[80]

Representations

The culture of presence of the old *Hoftag* was gone.[81] The personal presence of the bearers of power, both the emperor and the imperial estates, was completely replaced by representatives. Even the bishop of Regensburg, who after all resided in that city in person, sent an envoy to represent him at the imperial diet. Much of the communication took place through the ritualized exchange of written documents. What is notable is not only that the princes no longer appeared in person—after all, they had rarely done so even in previous centuries. More significant still was that they no longer apologized for their absence in their envoys' letters of accreditation.[82] With that, personal presence was abandoned not only de facto, but also as a norm. Even Hereditary Imperial Marshal Pappenheim, who, as the deputy of the imperial archmarshal and Elector of Saxony, was responsible for the logistics and internal jurisdiction of the imperial diet, sent as his representative a lower-ranking official, the imperial quartermaster, or even a mere clerk (*Kanzlist*) and appeared in person only on rare and exceptional occasions.

The office of the principal commissioner was considered "the first and noblest office ... which His Imperial Majesty had to bestow within the Empire."[83] He was the representative of the emperor in the full sense of the word, that is, his actions were attributed to the emperor, and he had to be treated as though he were the emperor himself. Upon the emperor's death his office expired, and his appointment had to be renewed by the successor to the throne. It was his task "to support the office of the emperor with éclat,"[84] something that entailed considerable cost and required that he possess substantial wealth of his own, since remuneration was sparse and irregular. The day-to-day business, however, was the responsibility of the *Concommissar* (co-commissioner), a learned man of lower rank. The principal commissioner was for good reason not described as *ambassadeur*, as an envoy of the first rank, the kind monarchs used to send to other monarchs, but as a commissioner, that is, a deputy sent by a ruler to his subjects. The difference was a fundamental one, and it was manifested entirely in the medium of symbolic-ceremonial treatment.[85] The emperor still did not negotiate with the estates in the same way he did with other monarchs, as between equals. That is why the principal commissioner held audiences, but he himself did not pay any visits; he received *hommages* from the members of the diet instead of the *simples égards*, the treatment that was due between sovereigns.[86]

But if the imperial estates had to put up with this, they insisted that the principal commissioner had to be of princely status.[87] The birth rank of an officeholder was still a symbol of the value accorded the office. Office and person were still not clearly distinct; high offices still required high-ranking individuals as officeholders. The electors and princes therefore took it as an affront that the emperor expected them to show imperial honors to a principal commissioner who had a lesser status than they did. In their eyes this expressed that the emperor did not value this office highly enough—and thus also not the members of the imperial diet as a whole. This was the case with Alexander Ferdinand von Thurn und Taxis. The family had been elevated to princely rank by the emperor in 1695, but it had not yet been accepted by the imperial diet—it was thus one of the titular princely families without an imperial territory of their own, from whom the old families continued to set themselves apart carefully. When Alexander Ferdinand was the first member of this family to be appointed principal commissioner by Charles VII in 1742, and then again by Francis I in 1748 and by Joseph II in 1765, this violated the rule of appointing only "real" imperial princes to this office. Even though—or perhaps because—the house subsequently experienced a rapid social ascent, with the Thurn und Taxis office of imperial post master upgraded to a throne fief in 1744, and Alexander Ferdinand even marrying into the house of Lorraine in 1745, the princes resisted accepting him as an equal in the princely council (*Fürstenrat*). This resulted in the awkward and embarrassing situation that he officiated as principal commissioner but was rejected as a member of the council of imperial princes. After his envoy to the imperial diet (for he had himself represented as well) had been nevertheless solemnly introduced into the council of princes in 1754, the envoys of the old princes lodged a formal protest every time the vote of the Princes of Thurn und Taxis was called for in the deliberations. It was only in 1785 that Alexander Ferdinand's son and successor acquired an imperial territory and thus fulfilled the requirements for admission into the council of princes.[88] The French envoy Du Buat penned his assessment of the principal commissioner in 1772: to the administration of the business of the imperial diet he meant less than nothing, *moins que zero*, but he occupied his rank with dignity and zeal, *digneté et chaleur*[89]—but that, precisely, is what it was all about.

Even if the princes complained about the low birth rank of the imperial representatives, they themselves acted hardly any different from the emperor when it came to authorizing envoys for the imperial diet. On the contrary, ever since the imperial diet had become permanent, the estate rank of the envoys (*Comitialgesandte*) had tended to decline steadily.[90] Regensburg was regarded as a less than reputable and desirable posting for envoys. Anyone who had been an ambassador to the court of a monarch and was then sent to Regensburg considered that a demotion. For example, Joseph II expressed to Freiherr von Gleichen, who had been a Danish envoy to several European courts, "his astonishment at how he ... could have become accustomed to being in Regensburg."[91] No less a figure than Montesquieu, who had come to Regensburg on a trip through Europe, noted in his travel account: "The posts in Regensburg are all filled with envoys who are not highly thought of by their lords or have fallen into disfavor. They no longer enjoy the confidence of their princes, and therefore they also no longer have their interests at heart, but seek only ease or the benefactions they can extract from the court in Vienna."[92] We encounter similar verdicts repeatedly in contemporary descriptions of the imperial diet, and especially authors who were patriotic about the Empire deeply lamented this situation. Above all they criticized that the imperial estates did not have enough money to support the imperial diet. "Because of their low salaries," the envoys had to live "very withdrawn. They do not spread much light. They live from the stipend: with this capital they economize as much as wealth and the dignity of their courts permit." Even the envoys from large houses and foreign ministers "live very quietly."[93]

Most of all, however, many imperial estates did not send any representatives of their own, but engaged others to exercise their vote. For example, the envoy from electoral Mainz at times cast nearly twenty votes, among them several electoral ones. It has been reckoned that in 1764, 35 envoys held 161 votes.[94] The individual mandates changed frequently and were the object of jealous competition among those who held them. A comment in 1763 from Karg von Bebenburg, the envoy from electoral Cologne, conveys a sense of how complicated the situation was:

> The accreditation of the envoy from princely Anhalt, von Pfau, to exercise the vote of Holstein-Gottorp also deserves a brief comment, especially since this vote, prior to the last holder, Zweig, was represented by von Schwarzenau of Baden-Durlach, but then it had been transferred to Baron von Teuffel from the Duchy of Württemberg; after the deaths of the Russian Empress Elizabeth and of Peter III, it was returned to von Schwarzenau, though after only two months it was taken away again and finally assigned to the above-mentioned von Pfau from Anhalt.[95]

The goal was not simply to collect as many mandates as possible, but as many high-ranking ones as possible. To keep the allocation of rank among the envoys from being constantly disturbed, an attempt was made to introduce the rule that each envoy could only assume the rank of his primary employer, and that this rank could not be improved upon through subsequent, higher-ranking mandates.[96] As so often, however, this rule was invoked only by those who benefited from it; no agreement about it was ever reached. To save money, some posts of envoys were often left vacant for extended periods. Even outside of the already lengthy recesses, both the principal commissioner and the other envoys traveled frequently, especially to the neighboring courts in Munich and Vienna, which they could comfortably reach with the weekly postal ship. During their absence the legation secretaries looked after their affairs and reported back to them about the goings-on. However, it was forbidden to admit the secretaries into the councils to take minutes of the proceedings in the absence of the envoys, because contemporaries were fully aware of the danger that in the end only the representatives of the representatives would be sitting in the deliberations.[97] In addition to the poor pay, the accumulation of votes, and the frequent absenteeism, observers criticized that many envoys were dependent on the house of Austria and were instructed to always vote in its interests—in fact, one envoy had foolishly declared as much "in the public imperial assembly," that is, he had accidently unmasked the strenuously maintained fiction of independent voting to be just that.[98] For everyone knew that a large number especially of the ecclesiastical and the new princes had a close client relationship with the house of Habsburg. Finally, critics deplored that the secrecy of deliberations was not maintained; indeed, printed newspapers reported matters of the imperial diet "that the common man should not know about." One legation secretary had gone so far as to sell protocols of the deliberations to foreign ministers.[99]

The starkest disrespect was shown the representatives of the cities. For reasons of cost, all imperial cities had themselves represented by a few Regensburg councilors who were already on-site. "No business is transacted" with them, we are told, and "no social intercourse of any kind is cultivated."[100] "The college of the imperial cities consists mostly of magistrates from the imperial city of Regensburg, and these 'deputies' or 'minor envoys,' as they were called, are too uninteresting to deserve even a few comments," wrote Ompteda, the envoy from electoral Brunswick.[101] The college of the imperial cities was considered a "bell without a clapper," after it had failed—in spite of its formal *votum decisivum*—to be included in the proceedings with the two higher colleges. The cities had no choice but to regularly follow the two higher estates in their vote. When they failed to do so on one occasion, the envoys of the electors lodged an outraged complaint about the "contrary conduct" of the councilors.[102] In short, the envoys of the imperial diet were few in number, poorly paid, often absent, and subject to political influence from third parties. These aspects were interconnected. Both the imperial princes and the emperor demonstrated in this way their lack of respect for the imperial diet, while at the same time contributing to a further decline in its reputation.

Notifications

The self-perception of the envoys stood in sharp contrast to this state of affairs. They saw themselves as *ambassadeurs* at a diplomatic congress and postured as courtly cavaliers. The fact that they no longer accompanied their "high lord principals" as councilors, as had been the case in the sixteenth and to some extent also in the seventeenth centuries, but represented them in the fullest sense, was also manifested by a change in dress. At the imperial diet in 1715, the old, long, black scholar's mantel had been exchanged for colorful, courtly *alamode* dress with a sword. This had caused more than a minor stir. The jurist Johann Joachim Müller, a learned expert of the old imperial diets, published a satirical tract with the title *Pallium exulans in comitiis* in which he mocked the envoys' slavish imitation of courtly behavior. His yardstick was the imperial assemblies from the era of Maximilian, when the learned, bourgeois councilors had confidently set themselves apart from their lords with their own dress. With the *alamode* dress, however, people were only making fools of themselves. On the one hand, the change in dress was in line with the general trend toward the aristocratization of academic attire. On the other hand, at the imperial diet it also entailed the message that the envoys thought of themselves not as learned councilors, but as diplomats within Europe's princely society.[103] They laid claim to the status of envoys of the first rank—which was considered the surest sign of the sovereignty of their employers and manifested itself in the *honores regii*.

As we have seen, the reason behind the problems at the imperial assembly was that the status system of the Empire did not fit with the system of the European law of nations—that is, that the imperial diet moved back and forth between being an international congress and an assembly of estates. On the one hand, all imperial estates wanted to be treated according to the rules of diplomatic intercourse like sovereigns and thus have their envoys treated as *ambassadeurs*. On the other hand, some were not willing to concede that privilege to others under any circumstances. The order of the imperial diet preserved the old classification scheme of electors, princes, counts, prelates, and cities. But the symbolic boundaries between these estate groups were under constant pressure from below and had to be constantly defended from the top. Added to this was a wealth of new, more subtle symbolic distinctions. As already in 1653/54, the issue at the permanent imperial diet was demarcating the old from the new princes, the old from the new counts. What further complicated the situation was the fact that a few imperial estates—electors and princes—were simultaneously European monarchs and that other foreign kings were also maintaining permanent delegations at the imperial diet.

The most important public stage for all status definitions were the elaborate notification rituals by which the envoys introduced themselves and acknowledged each other in their official roles. As far as the registrations, letters of accreditation, audiences, visits, and countervisits were concerned, the situation had by no means eased since the imperial diet of 1653/54 with the complete absence of the "high potentates"—quite the opposite. The ceremonial conflicts at the imperial diet had in fact become permanent, just like the diet itself. There was no longer *one* solemn beginning for all and *one* ending, but a continuous coming and going. Since the mandates changed frequently and the envoys were often absent for longer periods of time, formal notifications were always on the agenda, and at stake in each one was the status that people did or did not accord each other. In 1764 it occurred on average two to three times a month that envoys either arrived, returned from a trip, or took on a new mandate and therefore had to formally legitimize themselves.[104] Each instance required the sort of ceremonies of mutual recognition that were customary in diplomatic relations at the courts and congresses. A newly arriving envoy handed his accreditation over to the Mainz directorium and requested an audience with the principal commissioner. He was received by the latter for the solemn introductory visit with all extravagance *en cérémonie* and *en gala* and presented the credentials of his court. Afterward he had his arrival announced to all other envoys, "he placed himself into the public," as it was said, was given an official welcoming present by the city, received the first visit from the other envoys, and then paid them a return visit. At least, that was the norm, but it rarely functioned this way, for all of these issues were the subject of perennial conflicts.

At the center of the status system stood the principal commissioner, to whom all new arrivals had to report and deliver their credentials, and from whom they had to request a solemn audience. For his part, he never paid a countervisit. His institutional counterpart was the directorial envoy from electoral Mainz, who ran the imperial diet and before whom all envoys had to first legitimize themselves with a letter of accreditation, which he then conveyed to the entire imperial diet *per dictaturam*, that is, by formally dictating it to the chancery clerks. In principle, every envoy then had to announce himself to all others, receive the first visit, and pay a countervisit: a barely manageable web of ceremonial contacts between everyone and thus an equally unmanageable field of potential conflicts.[105] No wonder that the ceremonial of the visits was "almost always contentious."[106] The relevant questions were: Who indicates his arrival to whom and in what way? Who conveys the letter of legitimation—the envoy himself, the legation secretary, or a mere chancery secretary? What is the form of address—"Excellency" (*Exzellenz*), "Most Serene Highness" (*Durchlauchtigst*), or simply "Serene Highness" (*Durchlaucht*)? Who receives the first visit from whom and in what way? With one or several two-horse or six-horse state carriages? What is the value of the city's welcoming gift, and how is it presented? There was no limit to the multiplication of differentiations. The standards of the reciprocal ceremonial *tractements* that had been developed in the seventeenth century between sovereign potentates were still valid, but they had been considerably refined. Alongside the title of "Excellency," first visit, and the right to sit and walk on the host's right side (*Oberhand*), everything could become a symbol of distinction. The electoral envoys were set apart from the princely envoys by, among other things, the fact that the principal commissioner came forward to greet them not only at the threshold of the audience chamber, but in the middle of the antechamber, and that their chairs during the audience were allowed to rest on the red carpet with the front legs—but *only* the front legs! Electoral and princely envoys quarreled for years over red or black velvet chairs at the table of the principal commissioner, and accepted as the consequence of this disagreement that any relations between them ground to a complete halt for a longer period.[107] An "entire army of ceremonial disputes" extended "even to the fringes on the armchairs or chairs, to knife, fork, and spoon, whether those should be ornate or smooth, to the covered goblets [*Deckelgläser*], whether or not the electoral envoys should drink from them with the princely envoys, and the like."[108]

We are dealing with a series of interconnected permanent conflicts that merely manifested themselves in ever new forms. All of these conflicts were the subject of the deliberations in the imperial colleges and gave rise to a wealth of relevant collegial decrees. At the top of the imperial hierarchy, the primary concern continued to be that the electors wished to be treated as the equals of kings—especially those who had not been able to transform themselves into European monarchs. The chasm between crowned and uncrowned heads ran right through the college of electors and was constantly putting the solidarity of the electors as an estate to the test. As a result, the electoral envoys had already agreed in 1701, and then again in 1726, to always accord each other royal honors while insisting on them collectively vis-à-vis third parties, but under no circumstances to grant the princes the same. This in turn meant a permanent conflict with the princely envoys, and as a result the two groups paid no visits to each other. An additional bone of contention was that the principal commissioner not only favored the electoral envoys, but worse still, included the envoys from Austria and Burgundy in this preferential treatment—after all, they were Habsburg envoys like himself. The other "secular, old princely" envoys were in a state of continuous protest against this. They fought permanently on several fronts: for parity with the electors, against the collective preferential treatment of the ecclesiastical princes,[109] and against the convergence of the new princes and the counts.[110] Moreover, it was important to prevent the envoys of imperial princes who were also foreign kings—namely, the Dukes of Western Pomerania and of Holstein—from claiming elevated ceremonial treatment for themselves. This is what happened in 1763/64—an attempt that caused quite a stir and provoked "a few barbed writings," but that could be nipped in the bud.[111] To jointly preserve their ceremonial interests, the princely envoys had formed into an organization (i.e., they had formed an estate within an estate) to collectively articulate their protests anew at every solemn opportunity. Moreover, they avoided every occasion to meet their rivals, be it at visits or at the table of the principal commissioner.

The demarcation of the "old princes" had its counterpart in the efforts by the envoy of the counts (there was in fact only one) "to equal the electoral and princely envoys in luster," that is to say, to ride to a visit in a six-horse carriage, to hand over his notifications not in person but through a secretary, and so on.[112] This was part of the encompassing strategy of the old houses of imperial counts, on the one hand, to set themselves apart as an estate from imperial knights and mere titular counts, and on the other, to present themselves as peers and the equals of the princes. As we have seen, that end was served not only by their ceremonial role at the royal coronation, but also by their symbolic presence at the imperial diet.[113] The electors and princes rebuffed this by granting the envoys of counts only the status of "deputies" (*Deputierte*)—a term that was used to describe the delegations from subjects to their overlords.

For outsiders, the thicket of ceremonial conflicts was impenetrable and its compelling logic incomprehensible. For example, at the beginning of the century the English traveler Lady Wortley Montagu wrote with bemusement how difficult the envoys and their wives made life for themselves with the quarrels over rank, and how they would rather refrain from attending any social event than yield an inch on their demands. Ceremony was the sole topic of conversation; everything revolved around the title of "Excellency." Lady Montagu had proposed simply addressing everyone as "Excellency," in which case everyone would be called such reversely. We are told that this was received with indignation. Her practice "of being equally polite to everyone," and her recommendation to solve the problems through equal treatment across the board, had been taken as a particular form of arrogance.[114]

Something seemingly very similar happened in the case of the French envoy Chavigny, who saw the ceremony "with entirely different eyes than one customarily does here."[115] He had been given a lower envoy rank by his court, which was taken as a disparagement of the imperial diet. By sending him not as an *ambassadeur*, but merely as a *ministre plenipotentiaire*, the French king indicated that he was not willing to treat the electors and princes as equal sovereigns. The electoral envoys therefore agreed not only to refuse to grant Chavigny the title of "Excellency," but also to inflict a whole series of further ceremonial humiliations on him, namely, "that they would receive him at his visit only at the top of the stairs and escort him back out only to the third stair, while he would have to receive them down below at the carriage and then escort them back there again."[116] Everyone assumed that the upshot of this would be to make any type of public interaction impossible for the French envoy. The same had already happened to Chavigny's predecessor: because the envoy rank he held was too low, he had never been received in three years and had been completely ignored by everyone. It thus came as a great surprise that the new French envoy did everything the electoral envoys demanded of him. But their ceremonial triumph was brief, for they discovered that he showed the same courtesy to the princely envoys and—scandalously—to the deputies of the city of Regensburg. When the latter wanted to present the usual gift, "they found the French minister at the door, and he received them (not without bewilderment) at the carriage, virtually forced precedence [*Oberhand*] upon them, and gave them the title of Excellency with much prodigality."[117] It is not surprising that the city councilors found so much deference disconcerting: the profligate use of the contested ceremonial signs did not elevate the participants, but instead cut the ground from under the entire symbolic system. What was accorded to everyone without differentiation ceased being a mark of distinction. The instructions to the French delegation clearly reveal that Chavigny's behavior was calculated and not the result of naïveté. This was a subtle strategy to devalue the entire ceremonial arsenal, and to render the claim of the delegates of the imperial diet to be treated like royal ambassadors ridiculous through an *excès d'honneurs*.[118]

The envoys (*Comitialgesandte*) expected to be taken seriously as the ambassadors of sovereign powers especially in their dealings with the representatives of foreign crowns, but precisely that did not happen. They responded in turn by not treating the foreigners as equals. The French envoys put up with this for decades. Only in the 1740s did they gradually begin to withdraw their concessions. For example, Baron von Mackau avoided escorting the envoy of electoral Mainz back to the bottom of the stairs at his visit by feigning an attack of gout. The Comte Du Buat surprised the electoral envoys by making up some excuse to refuse receiving them.[119] Eventually, following the end of the Seven Years' War, the French, Russian, and English envoys agreed to undertake a joint effort to obtain full ceremonial honors for themselves. Their plan completely failed. The three ministers soon found the entire imperial diet united against them in rare unanimity. Even the King of England seemed to have remembered that he was the Elector of Brunswick and showed solidarity with his peers. At the electoral assembly in Frankfurt (*Kollegialtag*) on the occasion of the election of the king in the spring of 1764, the electors agreed once more to be united on the ceremonial question and not to yield also vis-à-vis foreign monarchs.[120] Their solidarity was soon put to the test when the foreign ambassadors at the court of Vienna, on the occasion of the marriage between Joseph II and Princess Maria Josepha of Bavaria, did not wish to treat the envoy from electoral Bavaria like an ambassador. The latter approached the emperor and the college of electors for support; pamphlets were published; the uproar in Regensburg was considerable.[121] The right to royal honors was defended as an "important part of the electoral competencies"; it was supposedly based on the oldest imperial constitutions and had been affirmed at the peace congresses, for whatever was accorded in the ceremonies there in terms of rank and honor assumed "the nature of treaties."[122] In the end the foreign envoys relented—evidently the matter was not important enough to them. Within the Empire, on the other hand, there was a willingness to dispense entirely with one's presence rather than cast one's own ceremonial standards in question. The French court was perplexed why those in Regensburg were not flattered that the king of France even deemed the imperial diet worthy of a permanent delegation.[123] But the Regensburg perspective was entirely preoccupied with itself and found that "the presence of said foreign ministers at this general imperial assembly is not at all necessary and often creates more confusion than genuine advantage."[124]

Un petit manège des grandes vanités

The imperial diet had turned into a curiosity within European princely society. Even the great imperial patriot Johann Jakob Moser castigated the "heavy amount of far-reaching ceremonial quarrels and trivialities, which strike me as revolting and foreign nations as truly incomprehensible," that he was forced to deal with. "But as long as His Imperial Majesty and the estates of the Empire do not see fit to place the imperial assembly, in view of certain circumstances, on the very footing that is now customary at nearly all congresses of the European sovereigns, ceremonial science is a necessary evil for someone who has to deal with German matters of state, but especially with matters of the imperial diet."[125] The Regensburg envoys (*Comitialgesandte*) took the international ceremonial code, with its subtle and minute distinctions, to an extreme, while the European potentates had long since abandoned it at their international congresses. In Ryswick, Utrecht, Cambrai, and Soissons, they had freed themselves of the burden of signs by giving their envoys the lesser status of mere plenipotentiaries and had not "observed any ceremony" in order to be able to negotiate that much more effectively with one another. Moser maintained that this did not detract in any way from their power and reputation in the *res publica gentium*. But if this already applied to the largest assemblies of the most powerful European potentates, it should apply even more so to relations among the imperial estates, which was of no relevance to outsiders. The imperial diet, he asserted, was useless as a stage for asserting status claims in Europe's princely society. After all, the manner in which the envoys treated one another there was "nevermore taken as a model by the other powers." Moser saw straight through the communicative vicious circle of the competition over rank and status. In Regensburg, too, he advised, someone had to simply make the beginning and lead by example to break out of it. One of the great and eminent envoys should be the first to "preempt the others with courtesy," according them all the requested honors and demanding nothing in return; then the others could follow suit without losing face.

Moser was an exceedingly sober scholar of strict Pietistic devoutness, anything but a courtier. He considered ceremony a mere "work of shadows" and the envoys slaves of their own fantasies. From his perspective, "great ministers" did not owe their personal dignity and honor to the ceremony accorded them. But that precisely was the case with the envoys of the imperial diet, for most of them were not "great ministers" outside of the imperial diet. Almost all of them owed their status solely to their rank as envoys. Their personal honor consisted of the acts of deference accorded them as ambassadors. For example, it was said that the electoral envoy Karg von Bebenburg had "no other fatherland than the imperial diet," as his father and grandfather had also been envoys. And this was said about the envoy Oexle, who held the votes of several ecclesiastical princes: "He would be nothing if he were not an envoy to the imperial diet."[126]

The envoys borrowed the symbolic capital of their masters and drew on it for their own social self-portrayal, which was that much easier to do, as office and person could still hardly be separated. This was evident upon their death. An exact code of hierarchical gradations generally applied to funeral celebrations, starting with the number and rank of the participants in the funeral procession and extending to the quality of the mourning clothes and the weight of the candles at the public viewing. If envoys died while exercising their office in Regensburg, and most remained in office until their death, they were buried in a manner that reflected the rank of their employer, not their own birth rank. For example, we are told that the funeral festivities for the envoy of the Elector of Saxony in 1764 took place in the most solemn form, "as if it were the elector himself."[127] The conflicts over rank carried over seamlessly on the burial grounds: for example, the fact that the legation secretary of the Wetterau Association of Imperial Counts (*Wetterauer Grafenverein*), that is, the lowest-ranking representative of the lowest-ranking member of the college of princes, was buried with a six-horse state carriage sparked protest from the electoral and princely envoys.[128]

A phenomenon that can be generally observed is that representatives, in their dealings with one another far away from their masters, develop their own social sphere. Their actions become uncoupled from the concerns of those they represent and follow a logic all their own, one that not least serves the social identity of the representatives.[129] That was true also in Regensburg, where it gave rise to a paradoxical development. On the one hand, the task of the *representative* envoys was to *embody* the political-social role of their lords in the fullest sense of that word. This conveyed to them a far greater dignity than their own social status would have ever been able to. Personifying their lords, therefore, had to be for them a concern of the highest priority. On the other hand, the interest of their lords to have their status embodied at the imperial diet waned more and more, because they had now developed other stages and forms for doing so at their courts. The upshot was that they sent fewer envoys to Regensburg, and those they did send were of lower status. This created a feedback effect: the lower the social origins of the envoys, the more importance the latter placed on representing the status of their lords. The envoys' own social interest in the display of rank grew in inverse proportion to the interests that the "high principals" themselves could muster for it. Outsiders perceived this mismatch: to them, the imperial assembly seemed increasingly like a *petit manège* of very vain little men.[130]

Ritualized Deliberations

The permanent imperial diet cannot be adequately understood unless one assesses it on the basis of the social logic of the society of envoys: as the *theatrum praecedentiae* not only of the imperial estates themselves, but also—and above all—of their representatives. But how did the assembly present itself as a decision-making organ? How had the deliberative and decision-making procedures developed ever since the imperial diet became permanent?

I have already noted that the hierarchy of the Empire had changed in many respects. Many barons and counts had become princes, a few princes had become electors, and a few electors had become kings. In the college of princes, too, as we have seen, there were envoys of imperial princes who were simultaneously kings: the King of Sweden held the lordship over a part of Western Pomerania, the King of Denmark was Duke of Holstein-Glückstadt, the Duchess of Holstein-Gottorp was the Czarina of Russia. By now, many princes combined the votes of many individual imperial territories—through conquest, marriage, inheritance, or secularization. The King of Prussia and Elector of Brandenburg, for example, simultaneously held the votes of Magdeburg, Halberstadt, Minden, Kammin, Eastern Pomerania, and East Frisia, not to mention a series of smaller countships. The house of Habsburg held the votes of Bohemia, Austria, Burgundy, and Nomény, territories that were nearly completely exempt from obligations toward the Empire as a whole. The colleges of the imperial diet had thus become increasingly heterogeneous over the course of time—for one through the accumulation of territories by the major powers, for another through the new reception of Habsburg favorites of lesser power. Alongside the great potentates, who had assembled numerous seats, sat princelings with small territories, *territoriuncula*, as well as prince-bishops and prince-abbots who owed their independent existence entirely to the patronage of the imperial dynasty.[131]

Although the situation of territorial lordship was in constant flux, the seats at the imperial diet remained nominally always the same. Even seats that were permanently vacant—because their holders had long ceased considering themselves part of the Empire, like the bishop of Besançon, or because they did not accept the rank they held there, like the Duke of Savoy, by now King of Sardinia and Sicily—remained on all member lists and summonses.[132] All seats and votes had been frozen, as it were, where they had stood in the sixteenth century. Over time, the order within the imperial diet had thus ceased to correspond to any order outside of it. The old classification system of the three colleges cut across the status system of the European potentates, with which it was simultaneously interwoven in multifarious ways. If kings had votes in the college of electors and in the college of princes down to the bench of counts, their status within the European system of power obviously had little to do with their status in the imperial system. But the traditional order of the Empire continued to lead a tenacious symbolic existence—on paper in the procedural rituals of the imperial assembly.

In learned handbooks, the imperial diet was traced back to the court assemblies (*Hoftage*) of Charlemagne[133] and described in the forms of the sixteenth century. Writers still posited the traditional procedural script with a solemn opening and recess, even though the last opening dated back a hundred years and no one seriously expected a recess any longer. At its core, the deliberative procedure did in fact still adhere to the forms of the sixteenth century.[134] However, the imperial assembly communicated with the emperor solely through the highly ceremonialized exchange of written documents between the principal commissioner and the directorial envoy from electoral Mainz, who acted in the name (*nomine imperii*) of the Empire. He received imperial commission decrees as deliberation guidelines and formally passed them on to the imperial assembly *per dictaturam*, by dictating them to the chancery clerks of the delegations. The deliberations themselves took place either in plenary session (though this was now rare) or separately in the three colleges. The directorium announced in writing what the deliberations would be about. The decisions by the various colleges were first compared between the two higher estates in the traditional relation and correlation procedures and combined—or not—into a joint *conclusum*. This *conclusum* of the electors and princes was passed on to the college of the cities, who could join it or not. If the result was a joint *conclusum* by all three colleges, the envoy from electoral Mainz handed it as a resolution of the imperial estates (*Reichs-Gutachten*) to the principal commissioner, who conveyed it to the emperor. If the emperor assented, the principal commissioner in turn notified the envoy of electoral Mainz in a commission decree, and the latter published it formally as an imperial decision (*Reichs-Schluss*). The sessions of the imperial diet were recorded in protocols by all members, and the protocols were carefully archived. Even though they were, strictly speaking, subject to the secrecy of deliberations, they were frequently published in printed form. The imperial assembly was no longer an arcane realm; secrecy was not only impossible, but often not even desired.[135]

Only a very small part of what was discussed in the imperial assembly in writing and verbally was initiated by the emperor and took place in the strict form described above. In addition to the imperial decrees, a wealth of other written documents reached imperial dictation (*Reichs-Dictatur*), also in the form of printed texts that were distributed to the envoys. These were above all the *Promemorias* of individual estates or private individuals, which made some concern or another the topic of deliberation or merely wanted to bring some news, opinion, or protest to the attention of "the Empire." On the occasion of the election and coronation of Joseph II alone, more than forty printed documents reached the imperial diet over the course of 1764—from congratulatory compliments to the decisions of the imperial colleges, the text of the electoral capitulation, and fundamental theoretical treatises about the election of the king of the Romans.[136] In the eighteenth century, the imperial assembly had evolved into a first-rate center for the general exchange of information; from here, news spread to the courts, cities, and universities by way of journals and the correspondence of the envoys. Anyone with a political concern could have it "made public" by way of the imperial assembly.[137]

Important committees of political communication were the two confessional bodies that cut across the three colleges and were composed of the envoys from all Protestant or Catholic estates.[138] After all, when it came to religion, which was a matter of definition and could potentially be anything, the Peace of Westphalia stipulated that decisions could be made only by the amicable agreement of the two confessional parties—or not at all. The two corpora were therefore a permanent embodiment of the confessional dichotomy of the Empire. But only the *corpus evangelicorum* was publicly visible. Its directory—the director was, bizarrely enough, the Elector of Saxony, who had in the meantime converted to Catholicism—received all the complaints from Protestant inhabitants of the Empire who felt impeded in the free exercise of their religion. The imperial envoy from electoral Saxony made all of these *gravamina* officially public in writing.[139] Regardless of whether or not the complaints were deliberated, a public stage had been provided on which the rights of the Protestant coreligionists were permanently kept in awareness, Catholic princes were denounced as despots, and the great Protestant princes (which in this instance included the Elector of Saxony, who was considered "institutionally" Protestant) could be presented as the protectors of the lesser princes. The confessional bodies were the institutional form around which the political polarization between Austria and Prussia could crystallize in the imperial assembly.

The actual deliberative procedures in the three colleges made up only a very minor part of the overall proceedings at the imperial diet. Deliberations took place at most during six months of the year; the rest of the time was taken up by breaks for Christmas, carnival, Easter, Pentecost, and harvest. The directorium could extend the recess at will if nothing important was up for debate, if many envoys were absent, or if the deliberations were blocked for some reason or another. It could happen that no session took place for years.[140] As it was, during formal session periods participants were summoned to deliberations on only two days per week. And if envoys gathered in city hall in a plenary session or in their colleges, formal deliberations did not always take place by any means. While this had once been seen as the exception and had been criticized, it slowly became customary in the eighteenth century. As Johann Jakob Moser wrote: "Now it often happens that people gather 10, 20, 50 times or more without anything being placed in proper proposition or deliberation."[141] And even if a "real deliberation" took place, it rarely took the old form of the ceremonial session and polling, but often *in circulo*, that is, the envoys stood "pell-mell around the directorial table" and voted without any order.[142]

There were good reasons for this. The old formal session was still a place of the utmost significance, a symbolic core of the imperial constitution. Here the Empire acted *in corpore*; here was a place where the traditional order was symbolically and ritually enshrined against all de facto changes. In a sense, the envoys were enacting a historical tableau of the sixteenth century when they sat in formal order and conducted a poll. Here all the votes that had been vacant for centuries were called out. The envoys who held multiple votes appeared in multiple roles; sometimes they had to run back and forth between the electoral and the princely colleges, and in fact they could end up having to cast opposing votes.[143] The session was simultaneously still the locus where competing claims to rank clashed and had to be asserted. When it came to the seating order, as well, the fact that the imperial diet had become permanent had by no means settled the order of the hierarchical relationships once and for all nor resolved the quarrels over rank. On the contrary, in the electoral college the changed composition had added new conflicts, and in the princely college the old session conflicts had become permanent and ritually frozen in place, as it were. That had been done by means of the so-called alternating stanzas. To outsiders this was a strange way of avoiding an unambiguous rank order of seats and votes by having the sequence of votes change at regular intervals.[144] Every day or every week, seats were taken and votes were polled according to a different pattern; when all stanzas had been completed, the whole thing started over. The stanzas followed an exceedingly complicated scheme composed of many individual agreements that had been negotiated over time. After all, almost all imperial estates quarreled with their respective neighbors over rank: six old princely houses alternated according to an intricate scheme, into which Holstein had also been admitted most recently after long negotiations; Austria, Salzburg, and Burgundy traded the chairmanship in the princely council; the many lines of the house of Saxony and the house of Brunswick alternated; the Palatinate and Bavaria did the same; the bishoprics of Münster, Lüttich, and Osnabrück alternated, as did Würzburg and Worms, as well as the new princely houses and the benches of the counts. In the city college, Aachen and Cologne, Lübeck and Worms, and Rottweil and Überlingen continued to alternate, to name only the most prominent cities. The further down one went in the imperial hierarchy, the more striking was the incongruity between the complexity of the polling arrangement and the weight of the votes in the deliberative and decision-making procedures. It was not the case, as one might assume, that the conflicts over rank were pursued so vigorously because real political influence was at stake. On the contrary, the relevance of the votes of the counts, for example, to a *conclusum* of the princely college tended toward zero, but that made no difference to the attention that a count's envoy devoted to his vote and its place in the sequence. And this applied not only to the votes at the lower end of the hierarchy, but also to the procedure as a whole. The ever more subtle refinements and ramifications of the *ceremonalia* went along with the increasing insignificance of the matters that actually came up for discussion and the waning efficiency of the decision making. The form itself was one of the most important issues. The less the imperial assembly was in session at all, the more it was preoccupied with itself. Measured by rational-utilitarian criteria, this cannot be explained. It makes sense only out of the communicative logic of the whole. I shall illustrate this with the electoral and coronation year of 1764.

Organized Hypocrisy

What, then, transpired at the Regensburg imperial diet in 1764, when Joseph II was elected and crowned king of the Romans? What did "the Empire" do in the place where it "was regarded as and considered a single body"?[145] What was deliberated on, and what was decided?[146]

From the outset, the year was dominated by the royal election. Not much had been deliberated since the beginning of the year: a promise was made that a petition from Count Pappenheim for a reimbursement of expenses, which had been on the table since 1753, would be "brought into a proper proposition" in the future; a decision was made to henceforth "compliantly" support the Regensburg city council in its struggle against the game of hazard; to repair the Phillipsburg fortress, the diet held out the prospect of 2,500 gulden from the Empire's operating fund (which was empty at that time, however).[147] All of this was deliberated and decided formlessly *in circulo*. However, before all three colleges agreed, on 27 February, to take leave until 30 April for carnival holidays, one proper session did take place in the princely college. The acting director for that day, the envoy from Salzburg, read out a rescript in which the emperor informed the principal commissioner that the electors in Frankfurt had decided to hold a royal election.[148]

The envoy from Salzburg formally submitted the document for deliberation, with the words that it was beyond doubt that the estate of the imperial princes would "most happily participate" in the election and would "demand to declare this patriotic sentiment to His Royal Majesty." It now had plenty of opportunity to do so. The envoys of the princes voted by rank in accordance with the second stanza of the alternating scheme, with twenty-two absent and seven permanently vacant votes also called up. Austria set the tone: what was to be decided here consisted of "a preceding expression of thanks to His Imperial Majesty, then a patriotic declaration of how completely convinced said council of imperial princes is of the great utility of the planned election, and finally, the addition of a most devoted wish that the election be speedily announced."[149] Salzburg added loquaciously that one should express to the emperor "the proper, most humble thanks for the repeated display of the imperial-fatherly, most beneficent disposition and demonstrated solicitude" in the form of a proper *conclusum*. The envoys of all Catholic princes joined with more or less concise statements and always voted "like Austria" or "like Salzburg." The envoys of the Protestant princes likewise assented. However, many of them would not be deterred from repeating the same matter once again with extravagant rhetoric. The envoy from small Brandenburg-Ansbach remarked as an aside why they were doing so: because it was "a very exceptional pleasure to give their consenting declaration by dint of their right of freely giving their vote ... [we are] in favor, however" that the election of the king of the Romans be undertaken soon.[150] Everyone, with the "most approving patriotic sentiment" and "the greatest pleasure," was casting his "free vote" in accordance with the "voting right of the Peace Treaty (of Westphalia)." Revealingly enough, only the two envoys from Holstein—that is, the Danish king and the Russian czarina—remained aloof from this procedure and cast their votes outside of the session *in circulo*. Thereafter the Salzburg envoy formulated the wording of the decision, at which point the others tweaked it a little and then charged him with handing the congratulatory letter to the principal commissioner. Finally, it was decided to send a collegial writing to the Elector of Mainz, in which the college of princes expressed its desire for the new electoral capitulation. Two days later the city council met for the same reason and likewise passed a *conclusum gratulatorium*.[151]

This session of the college of princes is significant. It was the only gathering (out of a total of five) throughout the entire assembly period from the beginning of January to the end of April 1764 that was held in the old form of a proper session. The protocol and the decision were published in writing. On the surface it seemed to be only about congratulating the emperor on the upcoming royal election of his son and to thank him for it. In fact, however, something else was at stake: namely, to symbolically stage *in actu* the order of the Empire itself, which defined the estate of imperial princes as a whole and accorded all of its component parts—down to the last imperial court and prelate—a share in the Empire. How else could the princely estate have manifested itself as such? But what the college of princes had to forego was the claim—still advanced in 1653—of actually participating in negotiating the new electoral capitulation. Like the cities, the princes had not been invited to the electoral negotiations in Frankfurt. They had to content themselves with sending their "most humble proposal" to that city in writing, as a supplication like anybody else.[152] In this document, however, they declared their proposals to be an expression of their constitutional right to participate in all matters of the Empire. But the message of this writing was no match for the message of the symbolic-ceremonial staging in Frankfurt: only the electors carried out the election business. News of the election and coronation was conveyed to the imperial diet a week later through a decree from the emperor. The announcement was made on 13 April at an extraordinary session during the recess. The imperial diet passed a congratulatory declaration, in which it most devotedly expressed "the most fervently cultivated joy" about this "universally pleasant event, fruitful for maintaining the most highly esteemed peace and warding off harmful divisions and errors."[153]

The electoral assembly in Frankfurt had adopted the old electoral capitulation of Francis I unchanged; in addition, however, it had expressed a few wishes to the emperor. Among them was the request to finally implement the visitation of the Imperial Chamber Court, which had been held out unsuccessfully for decades and was urgently needed because of numerous grievances.[154] Following the recess in June and July, electoral Mainz did in fact put this issue to the three colleges for deliberation.[155] On 6 August an imperial decree arrived in Regensburg announcing the visitation for 1 January of the following year and calling upon the imperial assembly to create a deputation for court.

Although the most recent Imperial Recess of 1654 (*Jüngster Reichsabschied*) had regulated the composition of such an imperial deputation very precisely, this regulation no longer fit, because the number of members in the college of electors and the confessional composition of the college of princes had changed since then. But this problem, as urgent as it was explosive, was not deliberated in the end: first, the assembly recessed again on 3 August until 22 October; second, the ability of the imperial assembly to make decisions following the recess was completely blocked, as a conflict had erupted over the imperial vote of the Prince-Bishopric of Osnabrück. The Catholic cathedral chapter and the Protestant Elector of Brunswick, who was King of England and father of the recently born candidate for the office of bishop, quarreled over who would be regent. The two great Protestant powers of Brunswick and Brandenburg had put this conflict to the *corpus evangelicorum*, and it had resulted in a formal *itio in partes*, a separation of the two confessional parties. As long as there was no amicable agreement about Osnabrück's vote, it was impossible to engage in formal deliberation and decision making in the imperial assembly. But that also made it impossible to assemble the imperial deputation for the urgently needed visitation of the Imperial Chamber Court. The date when it was to begin its work, 1 January 1765, came and went without anything happening. Nothing further transpired until the death of Emperor Francis I and the succession of Joseph II on 18 August 1765. Then there was another recess until the beginning of November. To be sure, the day-to-day business continued; numerous writings, complaints, requests, and appeals from the imperial courts to the imperial diet were received by the directorate; credentials were issued; felicitations and compliments were drafted; the colleges met on matters of their own, for example, to protest against the high wood prices in Bavaria or fend off the attacks of the foreign envoys on the ceremonial standards.[156] But as far as the imperial assembly *in corpore* was concerned, the symbolic embodiment of the Empire as a collective whole capable of taking action, this body was paralyzed. At least for the years 1764 and 1765, one could hardly say "that this both marvelous and great body of our German state is animated in all its parts chiefly through the imperial diets."[157]

The events of these years reveal in exemplary fashion the structural defects of the imperial assembly lamented by the imperial patriots in the eighteenth century[158] (and which are not the invention of pro-Prussian historians in the nineteenth century). The imperial diet was effective as a hub for the exchange of news or the locus of informal networks of the great powers, but not what it should have been as stipulated by the Peace of Westphalia and other fundamental laws of the Empire: the joint decision-making organ of the emperor and the imperial estates on all important matters—legislating, levying taxes, conducting war, negotiating alliances with foreign powers, and so on. To be sure, the matters considered to be within the purview of the imperial assembly did not become fewer in number. On the contrary, all of the issues assigned to it by the *Jüngster Reichsabschied* in 1654 were still unfinished; new religious complaints were constantly added; appeals from the imperial courts to the imperial diet became ever more frequent. Yet all of these matters accumulated without being resolved.

The decision-making weakness was structural and grounded in the order of the Empire as a whole. For while the fundamental laws of the Empire explicitly guaranteed every single right of every single member of the Empire, in countless instances these rights clashed. Although the fundamental imperial laws provided mechanisms of conflict resolution and adjudication, these procedures could not guarantee that every member of the Empire would in fact accept the outcome if it went against him. And if a member rejected the result of a procedure, there was no further mechanism to determine what to do next. After all, among the contested issues that resisted resolution was also the question of who had the final say on constitutional matters. The relationship between the imperial diet and the imperial courts in the eighteenth century makes this clear: if one party was unhappy with the adjudication of one of the two imperial courts, it could appeal to the imperial diet. Whether such appeals were permissible was controversial, however, and required a decision by the imperial diet. And in the final analysis such a decision was possible only through an amicable consensus, and such a consensus is precisely what did not exist. Nothing that was binding could be decided over the will of the great and mighty potentates, which is what some members of the Empire were. The result, as evident at the imperial assembly of 1764, was the growing accumulation of unresolved conflicts and the painstaking symbolic-ritual preservation of all old claims. This situation was proverbial: "Protestando convenimus, conveniendo competimus, competendo consulimus, in confusion concludimus, conclusa rejicimus, et salute patriae consideramus" (Protesting we assemble, in the assembly we quarrel, quarreling we deliberate, in confusion we decide, the decisions we discard, the welfare of the fatherland we pursue), it is said in Diderot's famous *Encyclopédie* about the imperial assembly.[159]

In all of this, everyone agreed, the issue was always the welfare and unity of the whole. Some participants certainly called this obvious disconnect between talk and action by its name. For example, the envoy Trauttmannsdorff penned these words in 1785 as he reflected back over his many years as the envoy of electoral Bohemia to the imperial diet: "The affairs that can be dealt with in Regensburg are limited merely to everyday business of the Empire, otherwise everyone there is highly ignorant of all events in Europe; even the issues pertaining to the everyday imperial deliberation are mostly of no importance and of utter indifference to the Most Eminent Imperial Court." However, he advised his successor "to arrange his conduct and, if necessary, his unavoidable speech at all times in accordance with the utmost impartiality," and to "give yourself the appearance that, as a link in a chain, you do not consider even topics of lesser importance, in reference to the preservation of the whole, as so unimportant that they do not deserve the most mature deliberation."[160]

The difference between the envoys' way of talking and their actions stood out everywhere. The more glaring the decision-making shortcomings, the more talk there was of a "German patriotic mind-set," of zeal for the "unity and welfare of the beloved German fatherland," of the "sacred bond between the head and the limbs." Using a modern term, one can describe this as "organizational hypocrisy."[161] This does not simply mean hypocrisy in the moral sense, since the problem cannot be adequately grasped as an individual moral failing. Instead, we are dealing with institutionalized hypocrisy, that is to say, a hypocrisy that is embedded in the structure of the institution, is virtually compelled by it, and is therefore collectively practiced. This kind of structural pretense occurs when institutions make irreconcilable claims upon individuals, creating what one might call a permanent "double-bind" situation. If that happens, speech and actions move on parallel tracks only loosely connected. This makes it possible to uphold the norms of the institution even as members (must) constantly violate them in their actions. The hypocrite pays his respects to a norm that he is violating. Hypocrisy is a "long-term investment" in the norm.[162]

This is precisely what was happening in the Empire in the eighteenth century. Institutionalized hypocrisy reflected and responded to the unresolvable contradiction between two fundamental values: unity under the emperor on the one hand, and freedom of the members on the other. Every newly accredited envoy gave expression to this clash of values in his stereotyped inaugural compliment to the imperial diet: in the name of his principal, he promised to reconcile "different duties"—by paying "reverence to the highest ruler himself, and steadfast devotion to the high co-estates [Mit-Stände] ... ; to the entire Empire, however, through genuinely supportive means removed from self-interest, and tireless vigilance before its sovereignty, peace, and welfare; finally, with no less respect for his own interests through ... the staunch representation of the privileges and liberties belonging to his old princely estate and religion."[163] Generally, however, these duties were irreconcilable. If one de facto pursued the interests of one's own court, the norm of unity was rhetorically maintained all the more floridly. The unresolvable and fundamental conflict of values created a dual reality, which Hegel captured in his formulation that Germany "is not a state and yet is a state."[164] The structural paradox was that the unity of the whole under the emperor's authority guaranteed the preservation of the rights and liberties of the individual (small) members, while the liberty of the (great) members constantly ran counter to and endangered the unity of the whole. Both aspects were mutually interdependent and yet could not exist simultaneously—a kind of political uncertainty principle. In short, there was not merely the *one*—unambiguous—reality of the Empire; there were multiple realities. This ambiguity, which compelled all participants into hypocrisy, was a structural characteristic of the imperial order in its late phase.

Vienna: The Empire at the Emperor's Court

A dual role was also played by Vienna, the third venue of the Empire, the emperor's residence. Some called Vienna the "capital of all of Germany."[165] In Vienna itself, however, one spoke of "journeying into the Empire."[166] From the Austrian perspective, the Empire was outside; imperial policy was foreign policy—already for contemporaries in the eighteenth century and even more so for later historians.[167] The house of Austria had held a particularly independent status vis-à-vis the imperial federation for quite some time—Ferdinand I's enfeoffment with the archduchy in 1530 had already demonstrated as much.[168] Over time, the focal point of the vast Habsburg territorial complex shifted more and more as the expanse of the hereditary lands situated outside of the Empire grew ever larger. Finally, the relationship of the house of Habsburg to the imperial office had also changed significantly after the death of Charles VI in 1740, when for the first time in three centuries the successor to the throne was not a Habsburg, but Charles VII from the Bavarian house of Wittelsbach. When the husband of Maria Theresia of Habsburg, Francis Stephan of Lorraine, was elected emperor in 1745 following the War of the Austrian Succession, she had refused to be crowned empress, and as we have seen, she did not appear at the election and coronation of her son twenty years later. For the house of Habsburg, the imperial dignity was now only accidental, even if it still had great symbolic value.[169]

To what extent was Vienna at all a stage of the Empire and not merely the residence of the Habsburg monarchy? To what extent was the Empire symbolically present there? Crown, scepter, sword, orb, and vestments—materializations of the imperial dignity—were not kept in Vienna but in Nuremberg, and the imperial throne stood in Aachen. Nor was Vienna ever the stage for a solemn *Hoftag,* a *curia solemnis* of the Empire, as described in the Golden Bull—for that, the emperor had to "journey into the Empire," something he did in the eighteenth century for his election and coronation. The electors never exercised their offices at the Viennese court, and their hereditary representatives (the hereditary officials) were generally also replaced by court officials from the hereditary lands.[170] The Habsburg court had its own hierarchy of ranks, which had nothing to do with that of the Empire. Already since the early seventeenth century, no princes of the Empire were in the emperor's courtly retinue any longer; instead, like foreign monarchs, they sent their envoys. After all, for quite some time the electors and princes had been concerned with asserting the symbolic grammar of foreign affairs in their dealings with the emperor.

Nevertheless, the imperial residence continued to be a stage of the Empire: for one, the imperial vice-chancellor, as the representative of the archchancellor of Mainz, resided there and established the symbolic presence of the Empire;[171] for another, the emperor was still the highest judge and feudal lord, an office he no longer exercised at solemn *Hoftage* in the Empire, but exclusively at his residence in Vienna. The Imperial Court Council (Reichshofrat), the governing council and simultaneously the emperor's highest court of law, sat in the Hofburg; it was the organ through which the emperor exercised his office.[172] Most of all, however, by now the solemn investiture of every imperial prince took place exclusively at the Viennese court before the throne and by the emperor in person. The investiture of the Italian and the nonprincely German imperial vassals was carried out by the Imperial Court Council. Symbolic markers ensured that the actions of the emperor (or the empress) could be distinguished from those of the sovereign monarch (or queen) of the Habsburg hereditary lands.

In 1764, however, Joseph was, first of all, not a sovereign monarch—as king of the Romans he was merely the successor to the throne. That changed on 18 August of the following year, when his father died suddenly and he became emperor immediately and without any further ceremony. But it changed only in part, for the death of his father made Joseph emperor of the Holy Roman-German Empire and nothing more. He was the first emperor who had no sovereign rights of his own. His father had been Duke of Lorraine, but in 1735 he had exchanged that territory for the Grand Duchy of Tuscany. Joseph had renounced this grand duchy in favor of his brother Leopold. All the other Habsburg hereditary lands were under the sole rule of his mother. Although this violated the traditional gender order, which was regarded as a natural order, the problem was circumvented by seeing and treating Maria Theresia as a man by virtue of a legal fiction.[173] But an emperor without any territorial rule of his own—that *was* a problem: it did not accord with the renown and the rank of the imperial dignity as the secular pinnacle of European Christendom. The problem was discussed in court conferences and memoranda, and like Maria Theresia herself, participants came to the conclusion that she would have to appoint her son coregent. That happened without any ritual act, without territorial diets (*Landtage*), solely through a written declaration by Maria Theresia and a written counterdeclaration by Joseph. Documents replaced any kind of ritual. This expressed that it was at the sovereign's free discretion if and when she would install her oldest son with the right that would pass to him after her death in any case.

Still, the new constellation was a problem for the symbolic order at court, for the ceremonial rank hierarchy had made visible how the imperial dignity and the regency over the hereditary lands were related. As emperor, Joseph stood in rank above all others; that was beyond question. Even the son's natural duty of obedience toward his mother did not change this. As coregent in the hereditary lands, however, he played a different role: here he was expected to subordinate himself to his mother in his decisions and rank. Externally, meanwhile, before the eyes of the subjects and the foreign courts, it was important to portray the shared regency as "perfect harmony and unanimity," from which one expected the "most fruitful consequences in enhancing the renown at home and abroad."[174]

But when it came to the daily enactment of the relationship between the imperial dignity and the royal dignity of the hereditary lands, the devil was in the details. For example, should Maria Theresia continue, as was customary, to receive all foreign ambassadors to a solemn audience twice in a row, once as the emperor's widow and once as queen of her own territories? How should her royal household behave toward that of the emperor? Should Maria Theresia vacate her residence in the Hofburg to make room for the emperor? Most difficult was the question of the place Joseph's second wife, who was nothing less than the "reigning" empress, should assume within the hierarchy. In the final analysis, all of these issues always revolved around a decision of symbolic priority—that of the imperial office or that of the house of Habsburg. In the logic of the Empire, the "reigning" empress should have precedence over the emperor's widow. On the other hand, there were good reasons for making an exception in this case, lest Maria Theresia, as the "matriarch of the arch house" and sovereign queen of "one of the leading European powers," relinquish any of its rights. Joseph, out of "complete filial reverence" for his mother, accorded her precedence over his wife; he was then reproached for undermining the imperial dignity and risked displeased reactions within the Empire. The court conference that dealt with the problem was stumped, as the case had no historical precedent, and there was nothing about it in the imperial laws. Various ways out of the dilemma were contemplated. One suggestion was that every public meeting between the two women be avoided. That was out of the question, however, for it would have meant that the emperor's widow could no longer show herself at the public table. Another possibility for keeping the rank issue in abeyance was to always proceed by the rules of hospitality, according to which the host granted precedence to the guest. This, too, did not seem very practical, as it would have required that the emperor's widow and the empress constantly take turns treating each other as a guest in their shared residence, which would have created an unforeseeable multitude of problems of definition. It was therefore suggested to simply give the emperor's widow precedence ipso facto, and to keep the interpretation of this measure deliberately open, "thus leaving to the public the judgment whether this arose merely from filial respect or also from other causes." The conference could not reach an agreement and in the end left the whole matter to the "most sovereign decision." Joseph himself, as it would turn out, had no problem with it. All the subtle considerations of the councilors did not interest him: he made the succinct decision that the empress-queen took precedence over his wife always and everywhere, and he left everything else to his mother.[175]

That was hardly a surprise. As we have seen, Joseph despised ritual and ceremony. For the courtiers in Vienna it was a horror that he "regards everything resembling a ceremony as an embarrassment."[176] Already in his very first memorandum he had elevated a strict cost-benefit calculation to the highest guiding principle of how to act. His basic economistic attitude was opposed to the courtly practice of the ostentatious waste of both time and material goods. It is well-known that Joseph began his reign as emperor with a few spectacular acts of demonstrative antiritualism. He abolished the *Galas* for dynastic name days and birthdays, dispensed with the washing of the feet on Maundy Thursday, and—following the Protestant model—cleaned up the church's feast calendar.[177] His low regard for ceremonial forms manifested itself most clearly—as it usually does—in dress. To the horror of court society, he ignored the courtly dress code by appearing on nearly all occasions, following in the footsteps of his admired exemplar Frederick of Prussia, in military uniform, even when he was wearing the collar of the Order of the Golden Fleece.[178] The court officials Ulfeld and Khevenhüller tried in vain to keep him from doing so. They were concerned above all with preventing the overthrow of the courtly rank order. On solemn occasions, the Spanish *Mantelkleid* made visible membership in the closer circles of court society. If the emperor himself now wore a military uniform, this elevated the status of those who held military commissions, yet these men as such had no place of their own within the court hierarchy. But lord chamberlain Khevenhüller also argued that the *Mantelkleid* was the "imperial dress." It was worn during all imperial solemnities and marked the actions of the emperor in his capacity as emperor. The legibility of the world was at risk if the *Mantelkleid* lost its character as a marker of distinction. How, Ulfeld asked, could Turkish envoys properly kiss the hem of the imperial cloak if the emperor was no longer wearing it? And above all, the emperor must not snub the foreign ambassadors and the feudal envoys of the imperial princes; after all, these ceremonies were "quasi-contracts" that he could not break unilaterally. In December of 1765, on the occasion of the first throne investiture he performed, Joseph had already caused great vexation among the envoys of the Prince-Bishop of Lüttich by appearing *en campagne*. Before the ceremony, the envoys had asked the lord chamberlain whether they were supposed to appear for the solemn investiture "like tailors before His Imperial Majesty," and in keeping with the regulations they came dressed in long mourning cloaks.[179] Later this earned them a "sharp rebuke" from their principals for having put up with the emperor's violation of form without objecting. But Joseph ignored the horrified protests of the court officials, and in November of 1766 he issued a decree that prohibited the Spanish *Mantelkleid* outright for the court household. This did not by any means signify an indifference to external formalities. On the contrary, one cannot *not* communicate symbolically, as a somewhat modified truism of communications theory would have it. Especially the relinquishing of a symbol was a symbolic message. Joseph was taking the *Mantelkleid* seriously by prohibiting it. In the spirit of Enlightenment philosophy, his goal was to send a signal against the rule of "tradition and prejudice," and to demystify the reverence-commanding courtly structures as mere conventions that could be readily abolished. His antiritualistic campaign had the character of a deliberate symbolic revolution.

But what did it mean for the imperial dignity if the emperor distanced himself from the symbolic system on which his office rested? It would become clear that Joseph misunderstood the character of the imperial dignity, even though he took the office very seriously—at least at the beginning of his reign. In November 1766, he addressed a list of twenty-one questions to State Chancellor Kaunitz, Imperial Vice-Chancellor Colloredo, and State Minister Pergen on how the imperial authority could be restored within the Empire and by what reasonable "system" fractured imperial politics could be shaped in the future without causing all too much expense to the arch house.[180] The three memoranda he received in response discussed in detail "the advantage to be drawn from the imperial crown" for the house of Habsburg: whether through the high renown connected with it, or through the political and financial capital that could be extracted from it directly or indirectly. The usefulness of the imperial dignity seemed anything but minor, provided it was possible to make the imperial estates well-disposed through a reputation of friendship and impartiality and thus "lull them to sleep, as it were" as potential enemies.[181] The ministers had a very clear sense that symbolic capital could be converted into political capital. Rank and dignity, too, were objects of their cost-benefit calculations. In the eyes of Austrian State Chancellor Kaunitz, the status of the emperor as "first sovereign" among all the Christian crowned heads, his rank as "patron of Christendom, highest judge," and "political ruler of so many great and renowned princes" were privileges that were "of incalculable value as long as human passions rule." The emperor's right to control the status system of the Empire put him in a position "to make use for his benefit of the jealousy, distinction, fear, and all other passions of the estates."[182]

The chief pillars of imperial power in the Empire, on this there was consensus, were the supreme judicial sovereignty and the feudal bond. But precisely these foundational pillars—imperial justice and the feudal system—were decaying, which meant that the entire edifice of the Empire seemed in danger of collapsing. That is why Joseph embarked on a vigorous policy of reform in the first year of his reign as emperor: through commission decrees he sought to invigorate the legislative activity of the imperial diet, he set about to reform the Imperial Court Council, and he carried out the visitation of the Imperial

Chamber Court, which had been delayed for decades.[183] Finally, he also endeavored to revive the throne investitures, which had ground almost to a complete halt for two decades. It would turn out, however, that he overestimated the office of the emperor and his—at best—authoritative power. He exercised his office as though it was the government of a princely state, and in so doing he failed across the board.

The End of Throne Investitures

Only a year before the outbreak of the French Revolution, Johann Stefan Pütter, the leading German legal theorist of the eighteenth century, penned the following words: "One of the most solemn occasions at which, in Vienna, the union of the diverse members of the Empire under one supreme ruler is most visible is the investiture that every holder of an imperial fief is obligated to receive."[184] It was still universally agreed that the personal feudal bond constituted the core of the imperial federation. The question was, however, what role the ritual of investiture played in this. After all, the princes exercised their territorial lordship already *before* their formal investiture, along with the associated right to a seat and vote at the imperial diet. By posing this question, the scholars were distinguishing the right from the ritual.

Their positions were controversial. For example, one jurist from Brandenburg maintained, back in the seventeenth century, that the imperial vassals held a *superioritas territorialis sive potestas autocratica* within their territories. All that followed from the investiture was that they were obligated to show fealty toward the Empire. The act of investiture did not establish the right to the fief and did not transfer the right of ownership of the fief, but merely "represented" the transfer of the feudal object through signs *solennitatis causa*. Essential the ritual was not.[185] The solemnities of the investiture served, for one, to illustrate the dignity of the matter and, for another, to provide public testimony of the procedure.[186] Johann Jakob Moser saw the situation differently: "The investiture is a solemn act by which the feudal lord grants the vassal the right to the ownership and enjoyment of his fief, or also confirms him in the true ownership of his fief." "The effect of an investiture lies in the fact that it is a public, mutual recognition." Even if the exercise of territorial sovereignty did not depend on the ritual, "the investiture is not a mere ceremony, as some recent authors wish to assert, but a solemn testimony and, respectively, affirmation that the fiefs themselves, with all their rights, have passed from the emperor and the Empire to the vassal, also that it is not the full property of the vassals, but, like all other fiefs, bound to the emperor and the Empire with a special obligation (from which the allodial holdings are exempt)."[187] And the Habsburg court jurist Christian August von Beck, in his lectures instructing the future emperor Joseph II, asserted succinctly: "Investiture is a solemn act by which the feudal lord truly transfers the fief to the vassal in return for the promise of fealty and feudal services. Through the same the vassal acquires a right to the ownership of the fief."[188] Finally, there was the historicizing explanation by the Brunswick court councilor Boehmer, who saw the ritual as a relic of a bygone age. The feudal relationship, he argued, was established by a mutual contract, and that contract was the investiture. The solemn symbolic act served to express the serious intent of the two parties. It had been introduced a long time ago, when the secret of writing was still unknown, and remained because ceremonies and signs indicated the seriousness and determination much more powerfully and were remembered better than words.[189]

By contrast, Joseph's ministers considered it "certain and incontrovertible that the most essential bond between the head and the members and the entire German imperial constitution rests on the receipt of the fief and the *juramentum fidelitatis* that must be sworn."[190] Imperial Vice-Chancellor Colloredo maintained that the feudal relationship gave the emperor "great adornment and even greater advantage." For him, the essential aspect of this bond was the "public assumption of obligation and the oath," which had to be insisted upon under any and all circumstances. The mere issuance of an imperial letter of confirmation was by no means sufficient. Rather, foregoing the oath *coram throno* was for the vassals the first step to complete independence. The "omission of their most respectful fief investitures" served the princes "to completely evade their subordination and thereby introduce ... a kind of equality between the emperor and the Empire."[191]

The legal controversy was patently connected to a fundamental question of ritual theory. Those who, like Moser and Beck, emphasized the feudal bond saw in the investiture a performative ritual that "brought about" the obligation it designated. By contrast, those who sought to marginalize the feudal bond, like the scholars from Brandenburg and Brunswick, regarded investiture as an anachronistic "mere ceremony" that had only illustrative character and could be readily replaced by a written contract. But that raised the following question: What remained of the "primary bond that solidifies the imperial constitution and the coherence between the head and the members"[192] if it ceased to be publicly manifested by ritual? Did it not require a performative act to maintain the institutional fiction of the Empire?[193] What if one could no longer *see* the imperial bond at all?

Since the sixteenth century, acts of investiture, which still became due every time either the lord or vassal changed, had made up no small part of the day-to-day life of the court at the imperial residence in Vienna.[194] Under Francis I, a scheme for the act was prescribed, the details of which bore the traces of past struggles for precedence and symbolic conflicts.[195] Under this scheme, the director of the entire process was the lord chamberlain, to whom the delegations had to report and with whom they had to resolve any possible "difficulties." He determined the day and hour of the arrival, which was to take place with no more than twenty six-horse carriages. So-called *Fiocchi*, tassels on the horse blankets, were explicitly prohibited in the wake of a grave conflict about them.[196] The setting for the event was the Hofburg in Vienna, since the envoys had successfully resisted being received at Laxenburg or another summer residence.[197] The Swiss Guard paraded in the Inner Court; only the carriage of the first envoy was allowed to drive up there, while all others had to stop at the Burgplatz (figure 15).

The prescribed dress for clerics was long cassocks and mantels, for laymen, as we have seen, black Spanish *Mantelkleider* without sword. The envoys and their retinues proceeded up the staircase, with nobody coming down to meet them, and passed the guard house, where the Residence Guards (*Hartschiergarde*) formed an honor guard and the pages and house officers awaited them. In the first antechamber they were greeted by the chief chamberlain (*Oberstkämmerer*). The investiture act took place in the second antechamber. The emperor appeared with the "chamberlains, privy councilors, hereditary and chief court officials, as well as the chief court marshal with the unsheathed state sword carried before him, and accompanied by the two captains of the House Guard, and were seated, head covered, in the throne prepared there." (figure 16) Only then were the feudal envoys admitted. "The envoys, as soon as they were

Figure 15. Salomon Kleiner, *Entry of the Envoys into the Hofburg in Vienna, Inner Court*. Vienna, Österreichische Nationalbibliothek, © ÖNB Bildarchiv, Vienna, NB 902.35b-A/B.

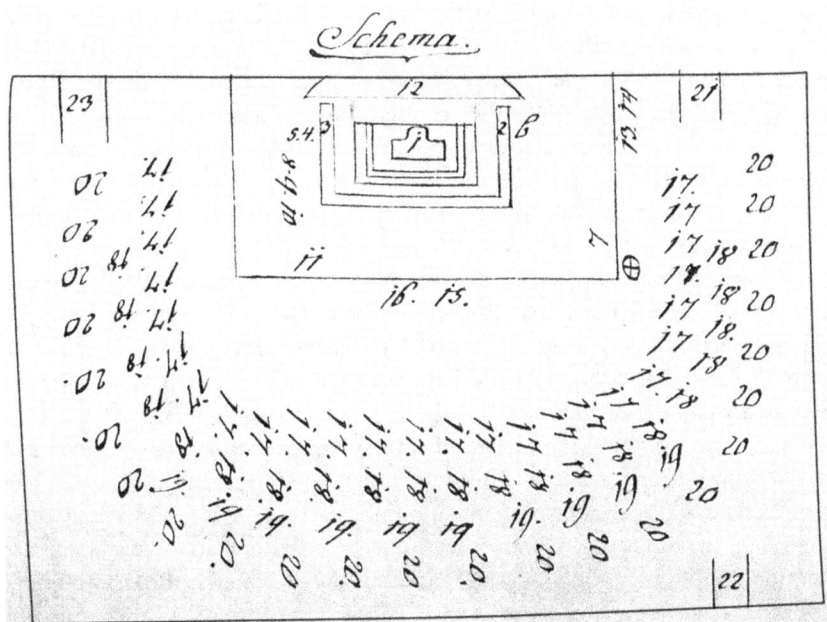

Figure 16. Diagram of the throne investiture of Liege at the Viennese court, 12 December 1765. Vienna, HHStA OMeA ZA 30, fol. 377v.

one step within the door, performed the first, genuflecting Spanish reverence, but thereupon immediately the first genuflection on two knees"; in the middle of the room they carried out "the other Spanish reverence, and thereupon the second genuflection on both knees"; and at the first step before the throne "the third Spanish reverence, and then the third genuflection on both knees on level ground, and they remain on both knees in front of the above-mentioned group on the elevated ground."[198] Still kneeling they requested that the absence of their principals be excused before the highly formalized sequence of performative speeches and gestures unfolded with numerous additional genuflections. The place of the Elector of Mainz was taken by the imperial vice-chancellor; those of the other ecclesiastical electors were taken by the high court officials, however.[199] In the end the departure took place like the entry—an excess of repeated simple genuflections and kneeling on both knees. All of this occurred in front of a large audience: privy councilors, imperial chamberlains, foreign ministers, various gentlemen, and other observers. It was important "that everyone who wants and can get in be let in … so that the entire world sees that one has to receive the fiefs kneeling before His Imperial Majesty."[200]

At least, this was the norm. That the princes, with very few exceptions,[201] no longer performed this spectacle in person has already been mentioned. In other respects, as well, the Imperial Court Council had long been lamenting the flouting of the rules, especially that the prescribed dates were not being observed. After all, considerable income for the imperial court depended on them, from the feudal taxes and chancery fees down to the gratuities for the doorkeepers. Although the 1659 Rules of the Imperial Court Council prescribed that the Imperial Court Treasury should proceed harshly in such cases, the lawyers repeatedly complained that nobody was afraid of possible sanctions. Moser noted critically that the treasury in any case took action only against smaller vassals, "and in many cases it does nothing."[202]

Moreover, the original rank of the feudal envoys tended to decline, much like that of the envoys to the imperial diet. The proper thing, from the imperial perspective, was to send a high-ranking princely subvassal, for ecclesiastical princes a member of the cathedral chapter. The emperor had found himself repeatedly compelled to issue explicit regulations about this. As early as 1688, a decree had been published to the effect that the envoys for the acceptance of the fief should be at least of old lordly or knightly estate; anything else was "not appropriate to imperial respect and authority."[203] Instead, envoys were increasingly sent "who have seen neither the imperial court nor other courts and are coming to this task accidentally and innocently." For example, the Brandenburg court jurist Ludewig, not without anti-Habsburg spite, mocked the numerous faux pas and mistakes of the feudal envoys who, intimidated by the imperial pomp, gave the courtiers plenty of opportunity for ridicule: "Now one of them turns mute during the speech; now crazy; now confused; now he gets stuck in the mantel; now he forgets a reverence, or he never learned to do it, or in other ways does not know how to behave properly." The lower the social rank of the feudal envoys, the more they tried, conversely, to gain symbolic capital from the ceremony—at least according to Ludewig, who remarked that "a princely investiture rarely takes place now without the feudal envoys themselves seeking to place into the hands of the newspaper and new history writers an account to hand down to posterity the memory of this event and their name."[204] The solemn throne investiture boosted the symbolic capital only of subordinate envoys; the princely vassals themselves saw it at most as an unpleasant duty.

Yet by the time Joseph ascended to the throne, the problem was even more serious: by now, the electors and the old secular princes were refusing to even send envoys to the investiture. This crisis had been triggered by the weak Wittelsbach emperor Charles VII (1742–45). In order to be elected he had had to make considerable concessions and thus also relinquish ceremonial positions that the Habsburg emperors had defended for centuries.[205] For example, in return for his vote, he promised Frederick II of Prussia in a secret agreement— this was the original ceremonial sin, so to speak—that his envoy would be allowed to accept the Brandenburg imperial fiefs not in the chamber, but in the *retirada*, that is, in one of the emperor's intimate private chambers, and in the process he did not have to kneel or excuse his principal; he was even exempted from the feudal dues. However, no throne investiture took place at all during his brief emperorship, which was marked by the War of the Austrian Succession. At the subsequent electoral convent, when Francis Stephan of Lorraine was supposed to be chosen, the crowned electors of Saxony and Brunswick now demanded, as was to be expected, the same ceremonial concessions that had been given to Brandenburg. Immediately the uncrowned electors of Cologne, Bavaria, and the Palatinate banded together and demanded the "same change in ceremony." This in turn set off a veritable spiral of refusals.

Once a year and a day since the succession had passed and the investitures were due, Francis I showed that he was determined to move against the lapses with sanctions.[206] In response the envoys of the three elector-kings submitted petitions for postponement. But a new symbolic detail aroused the ire of the imperial court: the writings had not been drafted by the electors themselves, but by their envoys. The Imperial Court Council firmly rejected this "unusual novelty" and demanded that the imperial fiefs be "properly requested" by the electors and princes themselves, "signed by their own hand."[207] The personal signature was the silk thread—as it were—that still held up the fiction that the investiture ritual was a personal interaction between the feudal lord and the vassals.

"After much negotiating" only the two ecclesiastical electors of Mainz and Trier accepted investiture in 1748 in the traditional way through envoys, but in return they demanded from the emperor the written promise that he would "not yield anything contrary to the old observance" in his dealings with the others. In return for the solemn investitures, which the emperor hoped would set an example, the electors were rewarded with all sorts of demonstrative favors.[208] But as it would turn out, these were the very last electoral investitures ever. Francis I was determined not to make any more ceremonial concessions. A rumor at court had it "that if one of His [i.e., the emperor's] state ministers, whoever it may be, should venture to speak to Him about some changes or reductions of the ceremonies during the acceptance of an imperial fief ... they should be immediately dismissed from their offices without further ado and be and remain dismissed."[209] In 1749, the emperor issued a resolution in which he ordered the renewal of the fief within three months, noting that the electoral capitulation obligated him, after all, "not to detract the least from the Empire and from the successors in the imperial office." And he threatened "that otherwise the harsher ordinances prescribed in their feudal rights and imperial statutes would be pursued against everyone."[210] At the same time, the Imperial Court Council circulated a document among the envoys in Vienna that was intended to persuade the tardy electors and princes with arguments.[211] It all but pleaded that preserving the acceptance of the fief had to be in their own interests, since the act established a bond not only with the emperor, but also with the Empire as the totality of all its members. Omitting the investiture would lead to the general "separation and fragmentation" of the Empire. It also appealed to the princes' consciousness of rank and hierarchy: the omission of the investitures put in doubt the precedence of the emperor over all other European powers, and with that the members of the Empire also lost their special status. The council held out the prospect of its special favor to everyone who made a beginning by receiving the fief. In short, one could not allow "the prerogative of imperial authority still remaining through the investiture, the only one, as it were, to become diminished."[212]

His insistence put Francis I in a trap of his own making. The more he tried to prevail upon the electors to receive their fiefs, the more attention the whole issue attracted, and the more powerless he proved himself to be.[213] He could not risk carrying out the threatened sanctions. Behind closed doors, it had long been said at the European courts that "it is almost impossible to understand why the imperial court wishes to cling [to the whole investiture business], seeing as it can compel neither the King of Prussia nor others."[214] By now the old secular princely dynasties had also agreed to await a decision on the matter before receiving their fiefs, to avoid being slighted vis-à-vis the electors. The situation was that "each tossed the ball to the other, and nobody wanted to be the first with the reception of the fief."[215] Only the ecclesiastical and lesser princes still accepted investiture at the Viennese court. And the imperial counts—at the other end of the hierarchy, in a gray zone between princes and imperial knights—tried, for their part, to derive symbolic capital from the situation. After all, for some time now they had been pursuing the strategy, in various venues, to shift the estate boundaries and push through their claim that they actually belonged to the estate of the imperial princes since time immemorial. They now undergirded this historically with the argument that in the fifteenth century some counts had still been accorded solemn investiture with banners, just like the princes.[216] The investitures quarrel was therefore very convenient for them: they offered to be invested in person by the emperor before the throne, though without success.

The conflict over the throne investitures dragged on through the entire reign of Francis I. He offered ever new compromises, which were answered with ever new evasions and delaying tactics. For example, Maria Theresia, as the Electress of Bohemia, offered to make the beginning and be invested in the traditional form by her husband, but even this did not persuade the other princes. In 1764, when Francis I needed the votes of the electors for the election of his son as king, he accommodated them to the point of dispensing their envoys from kneeling before the throne for their electoral lands; the only thing he still insisted on was the apology for their personal absence.[217] Most were willing to go along only on the condition that they alone would enjoy this ceremonial privilege, while the other princes "should remain in their category." But that continued the vicious circle, since the princes for their part refused to receive their fiefs as long as they were not put on an equal status with the electors.

This was the completely deadlocked situation when Joseph II ascended to the throne.[218] As the "enemy of all trivialities of an unnecessary ceremonial and Asian pomp, which no longer fits into our century," he couldn't care less whether or not the feudal envoys kneeled, excused their principals, or kissed the pommel of the sword. He considered the struggles over the ceremonial details a mere pretext for no longer having to receive the investiture at all. But for all his disdain for external forms, ritual was also to him an "indispensable necessity," without which the entire body "would have no coherence."[219] That is why he accommodated the electors on all issues in 1769. But even that did not help: new demands were simply made, new evasions sought out. Eventually, Joseph took an unprecedented measure. In January 1787, he issued a decree ordering all his subjects that "from now on and in the future ... the genuflecting reverences and the kneeling itself by everyone and in all cases shall cease entirely, and thus nobody, whoever he may be ... shall kneel any longer in the future, because this is not a suitable action between humans, but must remain reserved entirely toward God." At first this decree had nothing to do with the quarrel over investitures, but resulted from "the respect that the emperor believed he owed to the least of his subjects as fellow human beings."[220] In January 1788, another decree had to explicitly point out that the prohibition of kneeling also applied to throne investitures.[221] There followed a rapid sequence of decisions by the Imperial Court Council, which formally summoned the individual princes to receive their fiefs and set dates for them to do so.[222] Now there could be no further excuses to refuse the investiture; all significant ceremonial details had been abolished. Hardly anything was left of the traditional investiture ritual[223]—apart from the fees (*Laudemien*) and taxes that had to be paid, and that had by now multiplied several times over because of the changes in ruler that had occurred, and that presumably were a not inconsiderable motivation behind Joseph's tough stance. But this, too, made no difference: too obvious was the hopelessness of forcing anything against the will of the powerful members of the Empire. Joseph recognized the impasse. In the summer of the same year, he suddenly and unexpectedly suspended all further actions on the investiture matter[224] and thus saved himself another and final demonstration of imperial impotence. And that is how the history of the imperial throne investitures came to an end.

The investiture conflict was about more than vain externalities. That was confirmed also by the behavior of those who advocated the "deleterious principle that the investiture consisted of a mere ceremony" on which the imperial system did not depend.[225] For if the electors and princes had in fact considered the investiture ritual an empty form, they would not have tried to avoid it at all costs. Instead, their behavior bore out the observers who took this position: "Needless to say, no imperial prince could simply omit the receipt of the fief without dissolving the bond between the head and the members and shattering the entire imperial system."[226] Along with the ritual they also refused the feudal obligations themselves, which were created by this performative act, and only by it: they refused to recognize the emperor as the sovereign and highest judge and destroyed the authoritative power of his office. In so doing they knocked out the symbolic keystone of the imperial edifice.

Notes

1. Kunisch, *Friedrich der Große*, 443; in general, see Duchhardt, *Balance of Power*; Demel, *Reich, Reformen und sozialer Wandel*, 264ff.
2. Koselleck, "Staat."
3. Reinhard, "Wachstum der Staatsgewalt" and *Geschichte der Staatsgewalt*; Stollberg-Rilinger, *Staat als Maschine*.
4. In general, see Demel, *Reich, Reformen und sozialer Wandel*, 283ff.; Aretin, *Das Alte Reich*, 3:122ff.; Gotthard, *Das Alte Reich*, 139ff.; Schmidt, *Geschichte des Alten Reiches*, 245ff.
5. Moser, NTSR, 2:351.
6. Goethe, *Dichtung und Wahrheit*. Werke 9:180ff.; English text: http://www.gutenberg.org/cache/epub/5733/pg5733.html. See, for example, Matthäus and Brockhoff, *Die Kaisermacher*; Beales, *Joseph II*, 110ff.; Beetz, "Überlebtes Welttheater."
7. Goethe, *Dichtung und Wahrheit*. Werke 9:202.
8. Ibid., 182ff., 189–90, 209.
9. Ibid., 203; see Joseph's own account: Arneth, *Correspondenz*, 66.
10. Hegel, "Die Verfassung Deutschlands," 86, though he mixes up the office of the marshal and that of the chamberlain.
11. Schulte, *Kaiser- und Königskrönungen*, 89: "Jealousy, calculation, and self-love drives the representatives to the place, not devotion to the emperor and the empire, not a deep love for the state. One could not reform the political-religious event; the old piece was played out as it had been handed down."
12. Beales, *Joseph II*, 110ff.
13. Aretin, *Das Alte Reich*, 2:54ff.; Schnath, *Geschichte Hannovers*; Pelizaeus, *Aufstieg Württembergs und Hessens*.
14. On what follows, see HHStA OMeA ZA Sonderreihe 15: „Ceremonialien anläßlich der Krönung Josephs II.," ZA 29 (1763–1764); "Reise Journal des ersten Kaysers. Wahlbotschafters Fürsten Joseph Wenzel von Liechtenstein verfaßt von seinem Legations Sekretär F. Joseph von Löschenkohl vom 18. Jänner bis 30. März 1764," HHStA RK WK 88; Leopold, *Journal du voyage*; Arneth, *Correspondenz*; Khevenhüller-Metsch, *Tagebuch*, 1764–1767; see also the official printed diaries: Seitz, *Vollständiges Diarium*; *Prächtiger und feyerlicher Einzug*; Oertel, *Reichstags-Diarium*, 7:751ff., 792ff.
15. See chapter 3; see Neuhaus, "Königswahl vivente imperatore"; Scheel, "Die Stellung der Reichsstände."
16. Moser, NTSR, 2:707ff.; Oertel, *Reichstags-Diarium*, 7:792ff.
17. On the content of the *conclusum* of 1764, see Moser, NTSR, 2:100ff.; Moser, TSR, Additions, 1:356ff.
18. "Diarium Löschenkohl," HHStA RK WK 88 (9 March).
19. Details in Oertel, *Reichstags-Diarium*, 7:801ff.

20. This was the official formulation: "Diarium Löschenkohl," HHStA RK WK 88 (26 March).
21. See the description in Seitz, *Vollständiges Diarium*, vol. 1; HHStA OMeA ZA, Sonderreihe 15: „Ceremonialien anläßlich der Krönung Josephs II."; Oertel, *Reichstags-Diarium*, 7:808ff.
22. Faber et al., *Neue europäische Staatscanzley*, 8:49ff.; Oertel, *Reichstags-Diarium*, 7:838ff.; on 1558, see Gotthard, *Säulen*, 37ff.
23. Faber et al., *Neue europäische Staatscanzley*, 8:56.
24. Moser, NTSR, 2:718.
25. See vol. 29 of the ceremonial protocols of the Viennese court for the year 1764 (HHStA OMeA ZA 29); a separate document records the ceremonial of the election and coronation journey (HHStA OMeA ZA Sonderreihe 15).
26. Joseph to the Duke of Parma, 11 December 1763, quoted from Arneth, *Geschichte Maria Theresia's*, 507.
27. Arneth, *Correspondenz*, 53, 61; Leopold, *Journal du voyage*, 26ff.; Khevenhüller-Metsch, *Tagebuch*, 1764–1767, 11ff.
28. Report by the envoys from electoral Brunswick, Busch and Gemmingen, to the king of England, 27 March 1764 (HHStA RK WK 88).
29. A separate description of this was published; see *Prächtiger und feyerlicher Einzug*.
30. Khevenhüller-Metsch, *Tagebuch*, 1764–1767, 14.
31. Ibid., 12–13.
32. Ibid., 16–17; see Arneth, *Correspondenz*, 48; correspondence of the election envoys of electoral Brunswick, HHStA RK WK 88; in general, see Moser, TSR, Zusätze, 280ff.; Moser, NTSR, 2:100ff.
33. Letter from the election envoys of electoral Brunswick to the king of England, 3 April 1764 (HHStA RK WK 88).
34. "Ceremonialien anläßlich der Krönung Josephs II. von Wirkl. Hofrat Wolfscron zusammengetragen aus den Hofprotocollen der Jahre 1653 und 1690 und für 1764 zugerichtet," HHStA OMeA ZA Sonderreihe 15; Seitz, *Vollständiges Diarium*, vol. 3; Leopold, *Journal du voyage*, 68ff.; Oertel, *Reichstags-Diarium*, 7:820ff. On the coronations in Frankfurt in general, see Brockhoff and Matthäus, *Die Kaisermacher*; Bauer, "Wahl und Krönung"; Wanger, *Kaiserwahl und Krönung*, 102ff.
35. Thus, for the first time in 1745, HHStA OMeA ZA Sonderreihe 15, fols.11v–12r. On the quarrel between Nuremberg and Aachen, see chapter 3.
36. Published in 1742 by Johannes Paul Roeder and in 1789 by Christoph Theophil von Murr: *Codex historcus testimoniorum*; all of the learned literature on this topic is listed there. Regarding the regalia, see ibid. 452-53 (Müllner).–By contrast, Ludewig, *Vollständige Erläuterungen*, 2:292ff., 617ff., insists on the Carolingian origins of crown, scepter, and orb. See Petersohn, "Über monarchische Insignien"; Kirchweger, "Die Reichskleinodien."
37. Rohr, *Ceremoniel-Wissenschafft der großen Herren*, 594.
38. Ludewig, *Vollständige Erläuterungen*, 2/1, 647.
39. König, *Von denen Teutschen Reichs-Tägen*, 294ff.; Moser, TSR, 2:271ff.; Moser, NTSR, 2:340ff.; Oertel, *Reichstags-Diarium*, 7:825ff.; HHStA GF TZ 3, Kurbraunschweigische Belehnungs- und Erzamtssache; see Wanger, *Kaiserwahl und Krönung*, 122ff.
40. Leopold, *Journal du voyage*, 70, 78, 86; Seitz, *Vollständiges Diarium*, vol. 3; Oertel, *Reichstags-Diarium*, 7:828.
41. For the Middle Ages, see Althoff and Witthöft, "Les services symboliques."

42. Lünig, *Thesaurus Juris*; see Stollberg-Rilinger, "Grafenstand."
43. Seitz, *Vollständiges Diarium*, vol. 3; see Stahl, "'Im großen Saal des Römers.'"
44. Goethe, *Dichtung und Wahrheit*. Werke 9:207.
45. Ceremonialien anläßlich der Krönung Josephs II. von Wirkl. Hofrat Wolfscron zusammengetragen aus den Hofprotocollen der Jahre 1653 und 1690 und für 1764 zugerichtet, HHStA OMeA ZA Sonderreihe 15, fol. 71v.
46. Arneth, *Correspondenz*, 74ff.
47. For the Middle Ages, see Althoff, "Körper, Emotionen, Rituale."
48. For Frankfurt, see *Ausführliche Beschreibung*; for Regensburg, see Möseneder, *Feste in Regensburg*, 377ff.
49. Gumpelzhaimer, *Regensburgs Geschichte*, 3:1650ff.
50. Möseneder, *Feste in Regensburg*, 367ff.
51. Schindling, *Anfänge des Immerwährenden Reichstags*, 63ff.; Aretin, *Das Alte Reich*, 1: 217ff.; see also Luttenberger, "Der Immerwährende Reichstag zu Regensburg."
52. See, in detail, Friedrich, *Drehscheibe*.
53. König, *Von denen Teutschen Reichs-Tägen*, 31; see Moser, TSR, 43:403ff., with an exhaustive bibliography of all learned writings about the imperial diets; Moser, NTSR, 6/1–6/2.
54. Franken, *Von der neuesten Beschaffenheit*, 122.
55. Menzel, *Neuestes Teutsches Reichs-Tags-Theatrum*, from Moser, TSR, 43:416; Moser, NTSR, 6/1:23.
56. "C'est là que réside la source du pouvoir législatif, par l'union du chef et des membres qui forment un corps politique ... L'etat d'un prince d'Allemagne ... ne diffère que peu de celui d'un souverain": Auerbach, "Diète Germanique," in *Recueil des instructions*, 226; see Externbrink, *Friedrich der Große*, 81.
57. See, for example, Riesbeck, *Briefe*, 78; by contrast, see a critical view, for example, in Diderot and D'Alembert, *Encyclopédie*, s.v. "Empire germanique."
58. On the place of "state" within state theory in the eighteenth century, see Stolleis, *Geschichte des Öffentlichen Rechts*; Roeck, *Reichssystem und Reichsherkommen*.
59. Pufendorf, *Die Verfassung des deutschen Reiches*, 198–99.
60. Moser, *National-Geist*, quoted in NTSR, 6/1:32; Moser, "Neujahrs-Wunsch"; see Burgdorf, *Reichskonstitution*, 191ff.
61. See the older historiography with a Prussian, nation-state imprint; on the history of scholarship in general, see Schindling, "Kaiser, Reich und Reichsverfassung"; Schnettger, "Reichsverfassungsgeschichtsschreibung."
62. See above all Burkhardt, "Verfassungsprofil und Leistungsbilanz" and "Das größte Friedenswerk"; for a critical take on this perspective, see Kampmann, "Der Immerwährende Reichstag."
63. For example, see Kimminich, "Der Regensburger Reichstag"; Hartmann, *Geschichte des Heiligen Römischen Reiches*; most recently, see the critical Nicklas, "Müssen wir das Alte Reich lieben?"
64. Fürnrohr, *Der Immerwährende Reichstag*, and "Der Immerwährende Reichstag," 687.
65. Boll, *Reichstagsmuseum*, 31, out of sense of local Regensburg patriotism.
66. Härter, *Reichstag und Revolution*, 35, 40, 44; Corterier, "Der Reichstag"; see a measured assessment by Becker, "Recht und Politik auf dem Immerwährenden Reichstag."
67. Wekhrlin, *Anselmus Rabiosus Reise durch Oberdeutschland*, 61–62.
68. See Küchelbecker, *Nachricht von denen im Heiligen Römischen Reiche gewöhnlichen Reichs-Tagen*, 158ff.

69. For example, see König, *Von denen Teutschen Reichs-Tägen*; Küchelbecker, *Nachricht von denen im Heiligen Römischen Reiche gewöhnlichen Reichs-Tagen*; Lünig, *Theatrum Ceremoniale*, vol. 2; Moser, TSR, vol. 44.
70. This applied also to the Imperial Chamber Court, which in Wetzlar also had to make do with a paltry and inadequate provisional arrangement; see Hausmann, *Fern vom Kaiser*.
71. Küttner, *Reise durch Deutschland*, 4:476–77.
72. Wekhrlin, *Anselmus Rabiosus Reise durch Oberdeutschland*, 61; Riesbeck, *Briefe*, 73ff., also calls Regensburg gloomy and melancholy; see also Riederer and Schuhbauer, "'… eine finstere, melancholische und in sich selbst vertiefte Stadt'"; Burgdorf, *Weltbild*, 27ff.
73. Nicolai, *Reise*, 2:348–49, Additions to the second volume, 5; Schulz, *Reise nach Warschau*, 186–87.
74. Nicolai, *Reise*, Additions to the second volume, 7.
75. Reidel, "Die Residenz der kaiserlichen Prinzipalkommissare"; Piendl, "Die fürstliche Residenz"; in general, see Piendl, "Prinzipalkommissariat und Prinzipalkommissare"; Möseneder, *Feste in Regensburg*, 351ff.; Gumpelzhaimer, *Regenburgs Geschichte*, 3:1611.
76. Gala days are described in König, *Von denen Teutschen Reichs-Tägen*, 112ff.; Kayser, *Versuch einer kurzen Beschreibung*, 51–52.
77. See, for example, Riesbeck, *Briefe*, 73ff.; Keyssler, *Reisen*; Freytag, "Vom Sterben"; Reiser, *Stadtleben*. Historical scholarship, too, liked to and still likes to keep the two things—court life and imperial politics—separate; see, for example, Styra, "Der Immerwährende Reichstag in der Regensburger Geschichtsschreibung."
78. Nicolai, *Reise*, 2:349ff., 402–3.
79. Riesbeck, *Briefe*, 73; see Wekhrlin, *Anselmus Rabiosus Reise durch Oberdeutschland*, 61–62, for one example of many.
80. Uhland, *Tagbücher*, where the imperial assembly is not mentioned at all.
81. In general on the following, see Moser, TSR, vol. 44; Moser, NTSR, 6/1; König, *Von denen Teutschen Reichs-Tägen*; Franken, *Von der neuesten Beschaffenheit*; Küchelbecker, *Nachricht von denen im Heiligen Römischen Reiche gewöhnlichen Reichs-Tagen*; Keyssler, *Neueste Reisen durch Deutschland*; Bülow, *Über Geschichte und Verfassung*.
82. König, *Von denen Teutschen Reichs-Tägen*, 132–33.
83. Moser, TSR, 44:362, 364; Moser, NTSR, 6/1:66ff.; Franken, *Von der neuesten Beschaffenheit*, 17ff.; König, *Von denen Teutschen Reichs-Tägen*, 112ff.; see Piendl, "Prinzipalkommissariat und Prinzipalkommissare"; Freytag, "Alexander Ferdinand von Thurn und Taxis."
84. Franken, *Von der neuesten Beschaffenheit*, 14.
85. Lünig, *Theatrum Ceremoniale*, 1:1049ff.; Moser, NTSR, 6/1:91ff., 125ff.; König, *Von denen Teutschen Reichs-Tägen*, 156ff.; Piendl, "Prinzipalkommissariat und Prinzipalkommissare."
86. Baron Mackau, 1757–63, French envoy to the imperial diet, quoted from Externbrink, *Friedrich der Große*, 81.
87. Moser, TSR, 44:214ff.; Moser, NTSR, 6/1:82ff.; König, *Von denen Teutschen Reichs-Tägen*, 66ff.
88. For Alexander Ferdinand's biography, see Freytag, "Alexander Ferdinand von Thurn und Taxis"; on the introduction into the council of princes, see Franken, *Von der neuesten Beschaffenheit*, 86ff.
89. *Recueil des instructions*, 335; see Trauttmannsdorff, quoted in Aretin, *Heiliges Römisches Reich*, 2:109.

90. Moser, NTSR, 6/1:182–83; Nicolai, *Reise*, 2:391; Trautmannsorff, quoted in Aretin, *Heiliges Römisches Reich*, 2:119. Beginning in 1717 the envoys were listed in continuously appearing official calendars, at first separately under the title "Fortflorirender Reichs-Convent," later as part of the "Regensburgischer Comitialkalender"; also published in Oertel, *Reichstags-Diarium*. See Bauer, *Repertorium territorialer Amtskalender*, 39ff.
91. According to the statement by Nicolai, *Reise*, Additions to the second volume, 6. In Brandenburg-Prussia it proved difficult in 1753 to fill the post of envoy to Regensburg because the position was so poorly paid; several individuals turned down the job: *Allgemeine Deutsche Biographie*, 26:312–17, s.v. "Plotho, Erich Christoph."
92. "Les places de Ratisbonne étoient toutes occupées par des ministers dont les princes étoient dégoutés, ou qui étoient disgraciés. Ils n'avoient point la confiance de leurs maîtres, & eux n'avoient point à coeur leurs interêts & ne cherechoient que le repos ou les douceurs qu'ils pouvoient tirer de la cour de Vienne." Montesquieu, *Oeuvres complètes*, 1284. Additional pieces of evidence in Ulbert, "Französische Gesandtenberichte"; Externbrink, *Friedrich der Große*, 72ff.; Göller, "Sir George Etherege und Hugh Hughes."
93. Riesbeck, *Briefe*, 73ff.; Wekhrlin, *Anselmus Rabiosus Reise durch Oberdeutschland*, 63; Trauttmannsdorff, in Aretin, *Heiliges Römisches Reich*, 2:119; Moser, NTSR, 6/1:196.
94. Rohr, "Der deutsche Reichstag," 37; see Aretin, *Das Alte Reich*, 1:141.
95. Karg von Bebenburg to the Elector of Cologne, 11 December 1763, HStA Düsseldorf, Kurköln VI, Reichssachen, No. 878, fol. 9r.
96. König, *Von denen Teutschen Reichs-Tägen*, 341ff.; Moser, NTSR, 6/1:223.
97. Keyssler, *Reisen*, 1437–38; König, *Von denen Teutschen Reichs-Tägen*, 135–36.
98. Keyssler, *Reisen*, 1438; Riesbeck, *Briefe*, 73ff.; see Trauttmannsdorff, edited in Aretin, *Heiliges Römisches Reich*, 2:107–19.
99. Moser, NTSR, 6/1:345–46; Friedrich, *Drehscheibe*, 504ff., 510 (quote); Ulbert, "Französische Gesandtenberichte."
100. Trauttmannsdorff, edited in Aretin, *Heiliges Römisches Reich*, 2:118.
101. Ompteda, "Versuch einer Skizze," 71.
102. Keyssler, *Reisen*, 1439–40; see Krischer, "Reichsstädte."
103. Müller, "Pallium exulans in comitiis"; on the introduction of the *alamode* dress, see Moser, NTSR, 6/1:216; *Recueil des instructions*; in general, see Füssel, *Gelehrtenkultur*, 378ff.; Kühlmann, *Gelehrtenrepublik und Fürstenstaat*, 109.
104. Oertel, *Reichstags-Diarium*, 7:1764.
105. On what follows, see Moser, TSR, vols. 44–45; Moser, NTSR, 6/1–6/2; for the most detailed account, see König, *Von denen Teutschen Reichs-Tägen*, 66ff., 156ff.; see also Franken, *Von der neuesten Beschaffenheit*, 50ff.; Küchelbecker, *Nachricht von denen im Heiligen Römischen Reiche gewöhnlichen Reichs-Tagen*, 214ff.; Keyssler, *Reisen*, 1430ff.; precedents in Lünig, *Theatrum Ceremoniale*, 1:1412.
106. Moser, NTSR, 6/1:220.
107. Stollberg-Rilinger, "Ordnungsleistung."
108. "Reflexiones über die Ceremoniel-Streitigkeiten auf dem Reichs-Convent," in Moser, TSR, 45:89–94.
109. König, *Von denen Teutschen Reichs-Tägen*, 195ff.; "Reflexiones eines Unpartheyischen über die Reichs-Tägliche Rang- und Ceremoniel-Disputen," in Moser, *Teutsches Staats-Archiv*, 4:139–49; see Stollberg-Rilinger, "Ordnungsleistung."

110. König, *Von denen Teutschen Reichs-Tägen*, 188ff.
111. Moser, NTSR, 6/1:177ff.; Faber et al., *Neue europäische Staatscanzley*, 11:225–37; 15:390–400; 20:113; Oertel, *Reichstags-Diarium*, 6:646ff., 691, 707; correspondence of the envoy Karg from electoral Cologne: HStA Düsseldorf, Kurköln VI, Reichssachen, No. 896, Verhandlungen betr. Gesandtschaftlichen Ceremoniels 1763–1765, fols. 95–101.
112. Moser, NTSR, 6/1:197; Moser, TSR, 45:89–90; König, *Von denen Teutschen Reichs-Tägen*, 205ff.; Franken, *Von der neuesten Beschaffenheit*, 57ff.; see Stollberg-Rilinger, "Grafenstand."
113. In Regensburg this long-term strategy of estate politics was pursued by a single actor, the envoy Wilhelm Friedrich Pistorius, who represented three of the four colleges of counts from 1742 to 1778. See Arndt, *Reichsgrafenkollegium*, 256ff.; Stollberg-Rilinger, "Grafenstand"; collection of all relevant tractates in Lünig, *Thesaurus Juris*.
114. Montagu, *Reisebriefe*, 17–18.
115. Keyssler, *Reisen*, 1433–34; *Recueil des instructions*, 325ff. (overview of the development of the relationship since the beginning of the century in the instructions for the French envoy Bulkeley in 1771); König, *Von denen Teutschen Reichs-Tägen*, 156ff.; see also Ulbert, "Französische Gesandtenberichte," 149ff.
116. Keyssler, *Reisen*, 1434.
117. Ibid.
118. *Recueil des instructions*, 326: "cet excès d'honneurs les faisait dégénérer en dérision. Il colorait sa facilité par un sophisme, en disant qu'il n'était qu'un particulier chargé de rendre témoignage aux sentiments du Roi."
119. *Recueil des instructions*, 326ff.
120. *Recueil des instructions*, 327ff.; see Rohr, "Der deutsche Reichstag," 59ff.; Faber et al., *Neue europäische Reichskanzley*, 11:225–37; Oertel, *Reichstags-Diarium*, 6:646ff., 691, 707; Moser, NTSR, 6/1:178ff.
121. HStA Düsseldorf, Kurköln VI, Reichssachen, No. 896, Verhandlungen betr. gesandtschaftlichen Ceremoniels 1763–1765, fols. 1–81.
122. Printed pro memoria of electoral Bavaria, Munich 1765, HStA Düsseldorf, Kurköln VI, Reichssachen, No. 720, fols. 1–4.
123. *Recueil des instructions*, 330.
124. Letter by envoy Karg to the Elector of Cologne, 26 April 1763, HStA Düsseldorf, Kurköln VI, Reichssachen, No. 878, fol. 2v; see the judgment of Trauttmannsdorff, in Aretin, *Heiliges Römisches Reich*, 2:109.
125. Moser, TSR, 43:449; on what follows, see Moser, TSR, 45:88–94.
126. According to the French envoy Du Buat: "Karg n'a point d'autre patrie que la Diète; Oexle ne serait rien, s'il n'était pas un Ministre Comitial," *Recueil des instructions*, 337, 342.
127. Gumpelzhaimer, *Regensburg's Geschichte*, 3:1677. On the role of funerals in the symbolic demonstration of status, see Weller, *Theatrum Praecedentiae*, 230ff.
128. Franken, *Von der neuesten Beschaffenheit*, 107.
129. See Sofsky and Paris, *Figurationen sozialer Macht*.
130. *Recueil des instructions*, 337: "la Diète, le petit manège par lequel on trompe et l'on fait parler das Cours comme on veut, la petite adresse qui attire des présents ou des bienfaits, la très grande vanité d'un petit homme." Similar assessment by Trauttmannsdorff, in Aretin, *Heiliges Römisches Reich*, 2:107–19.

131. On the imbalance of the votes, see König, *Von denen Teutschen Reichs-Tägen*, 341ff.
132. Moser, NTSR, 6/1:151ff. Some princes tried in vain to obtain additional votes for their individual territories, in part by invoking earlier rights, in part by invoking new acquisitions; see König, *Von denen Teutschen Reichs-Tägen*, 341.
133. Moser, NTSR, 6/1:35; Küchelbecker, *Nachricht von denen im Heiligen Römischen Reiche gewöhnlichen Reichs-Tagen*, 9–10.
134. The following is according to Moser, NTSR, 6/1:338ff.; 6/2:1ff.; König, *Von denen Teutschen Reichs-Tägen*, 375ff.; Küchelbecker, *Nachricht von denen im Heiligen Römischen Reiche gewöhnlichen Reichs-Tagen*, 173ff.; Franken, *Von der neuesten Beschaffenheit*, 67ff.; see Aretin, *Das Alte Reich*, 1:130 ff.; Härter, *Reichstag und Revolution*, 51ff.; Corterier, "Der Reichstag"; Rohr, "Der deutsche Reichstag," 31ff.; Burkhardt, "Verfassungsprofil und Leistungsbilanz"; in detail most recently, see Friedrich, *Drehscheibe*, 125ff.
135. Friedrich, *Drehscheibe*, 516ff.; Gestrich, *Absolutismus*; still fundamental is Habermas, *The Structural Transformation of the Public Sphere*; most recently, see Schlögl, "Politik beobachten."
136. Recorded in Oertel, *Reichstags-Diarium*, 7:720ff., 749ff., 792.
137. In detail, see Friedrich, *Drehscheibe*.
138. Schlaich, "Majoritas"; Heckel, "Itio in partes"; Kalipke, "Weitläuffigkeiten."
139. The religious gravamina is also regularly published in Oertel, *Reichstags-Diarium*.
140. As in 1692–97, 1747–50, and 1780–85. Moser, NTSR, 6/1:451ff.; Franken, *Von der neuesten Beschaffenheit*, 96ff.
141. Moser, NTSR, 6/1:488.
142. Moser, NTSR, 6/1:487; 6/2:11–12.
143. Though this was de facto rare; see Aretin, *Das Alte Reich*, 1:130ff.; Franken, *Von der neuesten Beschaffenheit*, 76; for example, see Karg von Bebenburg, in *Recueil des instructions*, 337.
144. König, *Von denen Teutschen Reichs-Tägen*, 375ff.; Franken, *Von der neuesten Beschaffenheit*, 78ff.
145. König, *Von denen Teutschen Reichs-Tägen*, 31.
146. The following according to Oertel, *Reichstags-Diarium*, vol. 7; Faber et al., *Neue europäische Staatscanzley*, vols. 10–13; see Rohr, "Der deutsche Reichstag," 54ff.
147. Oertel, *Reichstags-Diarium*, 7:718ff.
148. Faber et al., *Neue europäische Staatscanzley*, 10:312ff.
149. Ibid., 10:316.
150. Ibid., 10:321ff.
151. Oertel, *Reichstags-Diarium*, 7:720.
152. Faber et al., *Neue europäische Staatscanzley*, 10:336ff.; see Moser, TSR, additions to vol. 2, 426ff.
153. Oertel, *Reichstags-Diarium*, 7:729ff., 746.
154. See Rohr, "Der deutsche Reichstag," 71ff.; Aretin, *Das Alte Reich*, 3:135ff.
155. Oertel, *Reichstags-Diarium*, 7:747, 774ff.
156. Ibid., 7:945ff.; see Rohr, "Der deutsche Reichstag," 82ff. The blockade caused by the Osnabrücker Kapitelstreit (Osnabrück Chapter Quarrel) was not resolved until June 1766.
157. Menzel, *Neuestes Teutsches Reichs-Tags-Theatrum*, quoted by Moser, TSR, 43:416; Moser, NTSR, 6/1:23.
158. Moser, NTSR, 6/1:338ff.

159. Diderot and D'Alembert, *Encyclopédie*, s.v. "Empire Germanique." Other articles praised the decision-making weakness, because it prevented the Empire from setting the tone in Europe; see Malettke, "Die Perzeption des Alten Reiches in der 'Encyclopédie.'"
160. Trauttmannsdorff to Kaunitz, 20 May 1785, in Aretin, *Heiliges Römisches Reich*, 2:108–9.
161. Brunsson, *The Organization of Hypocrisy*; Meyer and Rowan, "Institutionalized Organizations"; Ortmann, *Fiktionen und Organisationen*, 91–114.
162. A variation upon a formulation of Ortmann, *Fiktionen und Organisationen*, 111.
163. König, *Von denen Teutschen Reichs-Tägen*, 328–29.
164. Hegel, "Die Verfassung Deutschlands," 62.
165. Riesbeck, *Briefe*, 133, 138; for other quotes, see Duindam, "The Habsburg Court."
166. Khevenhüller-Metsch, *Tagebuch*, 1764–1767, 198.
167. Mikoletzky, *Kaiser Joseph II.*, 21; see Klueting, *Das Reich und Österreich*.
168. See chapter 2.
169. For what follows, see Aretin, *Das Alte Reich*, 3:113ff.; Arneth, *Geschichte Maria Theresia's*; Blanning, *Joseph II*, 147ff.; Beales, *Joseph II*.
170. Duindam, *Vienna and Versailles* and "The Habsburg Court"; Pečar, *Ökonomie der Ehre*; Hengerer, *Kaiserhof und Adel*.
171. Aretin, *Das Alte Reich*, 1:122ff.; Kretschmayr, "Das deutsche Reichsvizekanzleramt." The conflict potential in this role was reflected not least in numerous symbolic conflicts between the imperial vice-chancellor and the highest court officials. This deserves a separate chapter and had to be left out here.
172. Sellert, *Reichshofrat und Reichskammergericht*; Scheurmann, *Frieden durch Recht*; Ehrenpreis, *Kaiserliche Gerichtsbarkeit*; Aretin, *Das Alte Reich*, 1:85ff.; 3:122ff.; Rauscher, "Recht und Politik."
173. Expert opinion by councilor Koller, in Khevenhüller-Metsch, *Tagebuch*, 1764–1767, 388ff.
174. Presentation by *Staatskanzler* (State Chancellor) Kaunitz about the court conference on 12 September 1765, HHStA OMeA, ZA 30, fols. 261–85, here 262v; further, expert opinion by *Hofkammerrat* (court chamber councilor) Festetics, *Reichshofrat* (imperial court councilor) Bartenstein, and *Hofrat* (court councilor) Koller, edited in Khevenhüller-Metsch, *Tagebuch*, 1765–1767, 381–93.
175. HHStA OMeA ZA 30, fols. 284r–v.
176. Khevenhüller-Metsch, *Tagebuch*, 1764–1767, 196.
177. See Beales, *Joseph II*, 95ff., 156ff.
178. Presentation by Ulfeld on 4 November 1766, edited in Khevenhüller-Metsch, *Tagebuch*, 1765–1767, 518–22; 150–51, 156, 159, 207; see Kurzel-Runtscheiner, "Vom 'Mantelkleid' zu Staatsfrack und Waffenrock"; Haupt, "Die Aufhebung des spanischen Mantelkleides durch Kaiser Joseph II."
179. Khevenhüller-Metsch, *Tagebuch*, 1764–1767, 159, 519; HHStA OMeA ZA 30, fols. 376ff.
180. The *deliberanda* of Joseph and the memoranda of state chancellor Kaunitz and imperial vice-chancellor Colloredo are edited in Khevenhüller-Metsch, *Tagebuch*, 1764–1767, 479–518; the memorandum of Pergen is in Pergen, "Denkschrift"; on this, see Beales, *Joseph II*, 119ff.; Aretin, *Das Alte Reich*, 3:121ff. See Joseph's own memorandum of 1767/68: Conrad, "Verfassung und politische Lage"; and see the later memorandum by Trauttmannsdorff, in Aretin, *Heiliges Römisches Reich*, 2:107ff.

181. Pergen, "Denkschrift," 163.
182. Kaunitz, in Khevenhüller-Metsch, *Tagebuch*, 1765–1767, 502–3.
183. Aretin, *Das Alte Reich*, 3:124 ff., and "Reichshofrat und Reichskammergericht in den Reformplänen Josephs II."; Rauscher, "Recht und Politik"; Rohr, "Der deutsche Reichstag," 90ff.
184. Pütter, *Entwickelung*, 3:219; similarly, see Scheidemantel, *Repertorium*, 1:337–54, s.v. "Belehnung."
185. Seyfert and Müller, *De jure investiendi*, 1:3; 5:1–2: "essentiale enim feudi fides est." "hic ritus essentialis non est."
186. Ibid.: "tam ad illustrandam rei ipsius dignitatem, quam publici rei sic revera gestae testimonium"; "ita etiam per investituram solennem quasi traditur res feudalis, & per eam publicatur quasi & in externam componitur perfectionem." The inverstiture was compared to a wedding which is perfect only with the priest's blessing.
187. Moser, *Lehens-Verfassung*, 313, 341.
188. Beck, "Kurzer Inbegriff," 634.
189. Boehmer, *De indole et natura expectativae et investiturae feudalis*, 45ff.: "Feudum per solam investituram constitui." "Investitura ... solennem contractum feudalem denotat (58)." "Itaque symbolorum rationem in investitura in eo contineri apparet, ut, eis adhibitis, de seria utriusque. contrahentis voluntate constet (72)."
190. Kaunitz, in Khevenhüller-Metsch, *Tagebuch*, 1765–1767, 516; almost verbatim by Colloredo, in Khevenhüller-Metsch, *Tagebuch*, 1765–1767, 496; Conrad, "Verfassung und politische Lage," 169.
191. Colloredo, in Khevenhüller-Metsch, *Tagebuch*, 1764–1767, 496ff., with reference to the imperial vassalage of the Italian city republic of Genua. On the Italian imperial fiefs, see Schnettger, "Das Alte Reich und Italien" and "Rang, Zeremoniell, Lehnssysteme."
192. Colloredo, Referat 1766, HHStA RK GF TZ 1, fol. 36r.
193. See Rehberg, "Stabilisierende 'Fiktionalität,'" 406.
194. On what follows, see Noël, "Reichsbelehnungen"; Schönberg, *Das Recht der Reichslehen*; Aretin, *Das Alte Reich*, 1:79ff.; Schnettger, "Rang, Zeremoniell, Lehnssysteme"; Fröschl, "'Das organisierte Chaos'"; Steiger, "Rechtliche Strukturen der europäischen Staatenordnung"; Stollberg-Rilinger, "Das Reich als Lehnssystem"; Roll, "Archaische Rechtsordnung."
195. For the form of the throne investiture fixed after 1746, see Ceremoniale Deren Reichs-Thron-Belehnungen und Investituren, wann solche durch Gevollmächtigte empfangen werden, betreffend, HHStA RHR GF TZ 1; Uffenbach, *De excelsissimo consilio caesareo-imperiale*, 113ff.; Cramer, *Manuale processus imperialis*, 227ff.; Ludewig, *Vollständige Erläuterungen*, 2/2, 1170ff.; Scheidemantel, *Repertorium*, 1:337–54, s.v. "Belehnung"; Lünig, *Theatrum Ceremoniale*, 2:936ff.; Moser, *Lehens-Verfassung*, 311ff.
196. On the *Fiocchi* and the arrival, 1729, see HHStA RHR GF TZ 2, fols. 1–10; Moser, *Lehens-Verfassung*, 321ff.
197. Moser, *Einleitung zum Reichs-Hofrats-Prozeß*, 8ff.; Ludewig, *Vollständige Erläuterungen*, 2/2, 1328.
198. HHStA RHR GF TZ 1, Ceremoniale 5r–6v.
199. The relationship between the imperical vice-chancellor and the *Obersthofmeister* was also always fraught with the potential for conflict; see HHStA RK GF TZ 1.

200. This is what Charles VI had ordained; HHStA OMeA ÄZA Karton 26, fol. 12r; see Duindam, *Vienna and Versailles*, 169.
201. The great exception, the investiture of the Duke of Lorraine with the territory (*Hochstift*) of Osnabrück in 1706, was carefully documented in the ceremonial files, for example, HHStA OMeA ÄZA 4, "Exempla, wie Lehen in Person genommen."
202. Moser, *Lehens-Verfassung*, 239ff.: "Fere omnes Vasalli hunc terminum negligunt, sine ullo caducitatis metu." Sellert, *Ordnungen des Reichshofrates*, 2:142–43.
203. HHStA OMeA ÄZA 3, No. 37; Sellert, *Ordnungen des Reichshofrates*, 2:140–41; Lünig, *Theatrum Ceremoniale*, 2:963; Moser, *Lehens-Verfassung*, 255–56.
204. Ludewig, *Vollständige Erläuterungen*, 2/2:1198.
205. Reconstruction of the crisis-ridden development by Colloredo, "Referat Act. 25. April 1766 die Kayl. Thron Belehnung und derselben Ceremoniel betreffend", HHStA RHR GF TZ 2, fols. 28–49; see also the anonymous memorandum, "Hergang und Stand deren Kur- und Fürstlichen Reichs-Thronbelehnungen, vom Jahr 1740 bis Ende 1787", verfasset im December 1787, HHStA RHR GF TZ 1; printed reports include Reuß, *Teutsche Staatskanzlei*, part 22; *Über die Irrungen*; Schmid, *Berichte*, 286–87.
206. Emperor's decree of 7 February 1746, according to which "all fiefs must be received within a month following recognition, all requisita must be properly presented, accreditations issued with clausula jurandi in animan, and the tax must be paid ahead of time"; Moser, *Lehens-Verfassung*, 278; again on 18 April 1749, Moser, *Lehens-Verfassung*, 320.
207. Colloredo, Referat, HHStA RHR GF TZ 2, fol. 33v.
208. Ibid., fol. 35r.
209. Report of the envoy of the electoral Palatinate, Vienna 21 March 1749, HStA Düsseldorf, Kurköln VI, Reichssachen, No. 1655.
210. Moser, *Lehens-Verfassung*, 320; Resolutio Caesarea, die Thron-Lehen im heiligen Röm. Reich betr., 13 August 1749, HHStA RHR GF TZ 1, No. 146.
211. "General-Gründe, so samtliche hohe Fürsten und Stände, so noch bißhero die Thron Belehnungen nicht genommen, allerdings vermögen sollten, sich hierzu zu bequemen", printed in Moser, *Lehens-Verfassung*, 305ff.
212. Ibid.
213. Ibid., 310.
214. Austrian envoy in Munich to Ulfeld in Vienna, 26 December 1747, Schmid, *Berichte*, No. 136, p. 736–37; on this see also Schmid, *Berichte*, Nos. 48, 60, 69, 85, 89, 125, 127.
215. Colloredo, Referat, HHStA RHR GF TZ 2, fol. 36r–v.
216. *Beweis, daß die Reichslehnbaren immediaten Graf- und Herrschaften ohnzweifentliche Fahnen- und Thronlehen seyen*; see Moser, *Lehens-Verfassung*, 328; Bruckauf, *Fahnlehen und Fahnenbelehnung*, 104ff.; Arndt, *Reichsgrafenkollegium*, 256ff.; Stollberg-Rilinger, "Grafenstand."
217. "Hergang und Stand deren Kur- und Fürstlichen Reichs Thronbelehnungen vom Jahr 1740 bis Ende 1787," 1787, HHStA RHR GF TZ 2, fol. 2r; Colloredo, Referat, HHStA RHR GF TZ 2, fol. 43r–v.
218. Colloredo had prepared his presentation about this. On the further events, see "Hergang und Stand deren Kur- und Fürstlichen Reichs Thronbelehnungen vom Jahr 1740 bis Ende 1787," 1787, HHStA RHR GF TZ, fols. 2ff.; Reuß, *Teutsche Staats-*

kanzlei, part 22:343ff.; Moser, Lehens-Verfassung, 296ff.; Über die Irrungen, 9ff.; see Noël, "Reichsbelehnungen," 114ff.
219. Conrad, "Verfassung und politische Lage," 169.
220. Text in Reuß, Teutsche Staatskanzlei, part 20:454ff.; see 22:334.
221. Ibid., 22:347; Über die Irrungen, 11.
222. Über die Irrungen, 16; "Reichshofrats-Conclusa," Über die Irrungen, 43ff.
223. See Denmark's taking of Holstein as a fief, one of the very last princely investitures, on 7 February 1788, in Reuß, Teutsche Staatskanzlei, part 23:259; Über die Irrungen, 35; and in 1789, the investitures of Freising, Regensburg, Lübeck, and Osnabrück, in Reuß, Teutsche Staatskanzlei, part 23:261–62.
224. Reuß, Teutsche Staatskanzlei, part 23:260.
225. Colloredo, Referat, HHStA RHR GF TZ 2, fol. 37r–v.
226. Reuß, Teutsche Staatskanzlei, part 22:321.

Conclusion
The Symbolic Logic of the Empire

A Culture of Presence

The aim of this book was to lay out the constitutional history of the Old Empire from the vantage point of its symbolic language. The question was how the Empire as a whole was *represented* across three centuries of the early modern period, namely, in both senses of the word. For a political entity to exist, it needs a procedural *creation* and a symbolic *depiction* of its unity. Both aspects are encompassed under the term "representation." At first glance, the two dimensions of this concept—political representation, on the one hand, and symbolic representation, on the other—hardly seem to have anything to do with each other, as they usually fall within the purview of different scholarly disciplines. Constitutional history deals with processes of political representation, that is, with processes of attribution that turn the actions of individual persons into the actions of the entire political entity. By contrast, cultural studies, art history, and literature deal with symbolic representation, that is, with the phenomena of pictorial, literary, and performative depiction and embodiment.[1] The thesis I have tried to develop in this book is that these two dimensions of representation in the Old Empire were originally indissolubly connected and only gradually developed along separate tracks. In the beginning, in Worms in 1495, the Empire had become symbolically manifested in the personal presence of the emperor, the electors, and the princes, and had been capable of taking action (even if on a limited scale) as a whole. In the end, in 1764, the symbolic depiction of the Empire had taken on a life of its own as a romantic spectacle in Frankfurt, and the creation of a collective actor in Regensburg had become virtually impossible.

The Empire of the late Middle Ages and early modern period obeyed the logic of a culture of presence, that is, it was integrated into a whole through the fact that the actors assembled *in person* at the same place from time to time. Its order was performatively created time and again by being publicly staged pars pro toto.[2] This was done in symbolic-ritual, festive, and formal (in the language of the time: *solemn*) acts, which were elevated over the flow of everyday life by a multitude of symbolic markers: above all coronations, feudal investitures, and the openings and closings of imperial diets. The external forms were essential, for the order established by these rituals was concrete, not abstract. One had to be able to see it: *majesty* or *status*, *possession* or *Abschied (recess)* were taken quite literally. The institutional structure of the whole came alive anew every time in "solemn acts of category-creation."[3] Empire and imperial estate, emperor, Roman king, elector, imperial prince, imperial count, imperial city, and so on—ritual acts revealed and affirmed what and who these were. By taking place in repeatable (but by no means unchangeable) forms, these acts pointed beyond a given moment in time and linked them to the past and the future. While they changed the status of specific individuals, they simultaneously affirmed the persistence of the order as a whole across time and created reliable expectations. The representation of the Empire rested on identity, not on proxy representation. The assembly of emperor, electors, and princes *was* the Empire, namely, in a dual sense: the solemn act not only made visible the majesty of the Empire and *depicted* it, making it perceptible to the senses, but also *created* it in the technical-legal sense, that is, what these men decided or carried out in certain forms was considered binding and as having been decided and carried out by the entire Empire as a political body. This applied not only to the solemn rituals of installation, election or coronation, and feudal investiture, but also to the decisions by the imperial assembly, that is, all the acts that had already been performed in the Middle Ages at a royal *Hoftag*, a *solemnis curia*.

Of course, the order that was enacted and created did not exist without preconditions. Rather, it rested on a complex substructure composed of the access by members of the Empire to economic resources and physical means of coercion, of the social capital of kinship, friendship, patronage, and so forth. All of these things were necessary but not sufficient conditions for the institutional order of the Empire. They all had to be converted into symbolic capital, at least now and then, and had to be made publicly visible and asserted. What exactly the Empire was, who was part of it, where its internal and external boundaries ran, and how it was capable of taking action—all this was still relatively open and available around 1500; it could be newly calibrated case by case and depended on actual practice. Abstract and unequivocal formal criteria of affiliation did not exist. The cases of Lorraine and Pomerania show how flexible and open to interpretation the lines of demarcation still were.

A fairly small power gradient existed between emperor, electors, and princes, because they all controlled similar resources and lordship over third parties. The relationship among them was determined not only by instrumental coercive power. A legitimate exercise of power by a sovereign was tied fundamentally to the consensus and participation of others. The office of the emperor did not endow him with any rights of lordship, but with authoritative power—that is, a power that rested on the need for mutual recognition. The authority of the emperor formed the capstone of the institutional system; his office embodied the age, sacredness, and dignity of the whole. The members of the Empire had a fundamental interest in the recognition of this authority, as long as their own recognition, self-understanding, and the legitimacy of their own elevated status was simultaneously dependent on it.

The logic of the culture of presence was a logic of honor and renown.[4] The rank and status of "high persons" had to be continually asserted before the eyes of all and acknowledged by others through finely graded forms of deference. Preserving rank and honor was a motivation for action with high priority and simultaneously great potential for conflict, since the views about the precise place of an individual within the system of the whole diverged in many cases. The deliberations of the imperial diet also continued to be shaped by these conflicts over rank. They, too, served not only the procedural creation of political decisions, but always also the symbolic depiction of the status of all participants.

The social rank and political status of the members of the Empire could plainly not be separated one from the other. The members' political participation in the Empire depended on their status as rulers and therefore presupposed a high degree of economic and social capital. That is why they had to make their status visible through material splendor and demonstrative prodigality. This applied not only to each individual ruler, but also to the majesty of the Empire as a whole. Majesty had to be visible, that is, it required the marshaling of a large and high-ranking retinue, costly materials, and artistic perfection. What was demonstrated was the profligate handling of space and time, money, goods, and retinues. If the world was to be readable, lordship had to go hand in hand with wealth; the highest-ranking monarch had to display the greatest splendor. It was irritating if lower-ranking individuals expended more pomp than was proper for them, but also if high-ranking individuals or their representatives were unable to display the appropriate splendor.

The ritual acts of the Empire established obligations. It was in keeping with the logic of the culture of presence that these obligations were still tied in large measure to personal presence. Only he who was present in person professed his assent to what was being formally decided and ritually staged.[5] The institutional development of the Empire, its integration into a whole capable of taking action, depended quite crucially on the extent to which it proved possible to overcome this principle of personal presence and obligate also the absent. This succeeded at various times to different degrees, but never completely—which had much to do with the fact that there were only anemic efforts toward the establishment of a centralized coercive power. Procedures of proxy representation were practiced, but they functioned only incompletely, and they were seen as an exception to the rule. Symptomatic of that was that envoys always had to excuse the absence of their principles and that they were not allowed to take their place during solemn acts. Even more, envoys in the deliberations never received complete authorization to act for their principles, with the result that the imperial assembly as a whole did not develop any procedural autonomy, no independent corporate capacity for action.

The relationship that linked the members of the Empire with the sovereign and to one another was a personal relationship of fealty, which was ritually established by the coronation oath, the feudal oath, or the oath of homage. The obligation created by such an act was all-encompassing and vague. It bound the entire person as such, not as the bearer of a specific, clearly defined institutional role. The fact that these obligations were symbolically and ritually created and not spelled out in writing offered leeway for divergent interpretations.

Of course, the imperial constitution did not consist solely of symbolic-ritual acts, but also of a few norms fixed in writing, chief among them the Golden Bull. But written *fundamental laws*—strictly speaking, they were contracts, not laws—had a status different from what seems obvious today. To contemporaries, ritual and contract seemed closely related: rituals were seen as nonwritten, tacit contracts, and contracts were seen as rituals fixed in writing. Both rested on the consensual foundation of two parties and established reciprocal obligations.[6] In most cases the two came together: ritual act and written document supplemented each other. But the norm fixed in writing by no means stood a priori above obligations ritually assumed. Instead, claims documented in writing were often inferior to actual ritual practice,[7] since people initially placed less trust in the written word than in ritual. This was in keeping with the logic of the culture of presence: after all, writing disconnected the entire procedure from the presence of the individuals, who guaranteed its truth and obligatory nature. A wealth of information that is conveyed by the personal communication of those present is lost in the written medium. It therefore requires institutional techniques of authorization and staging to endow a written text with the same authority that persons themselves possess. There was also need of well-practiced techniques for collecting, organizing, and preserving written documents in order to fully utilize the possibilities offered by writing. As the examples from the Worms diet showed, none of this was yet self-evidently the case around 1500. That is why writing could in no way take the place of ritual acts.

It accorded with the logic of the culture of presence and the political weight of the members of the Empire that those present had to negotiate compromises and come to a consensual agreement for a decision to be reached. To be sure, in the late Middle Ages formal procedures were developed that were intended to bring about decisions collectively binding upon all members of the Empire even when no consensus existed. But these procedures never achieved such a degree of obligation that *all* participants accepted the decisions *in advance*—that is, also in case a decision did not accord with their wishes and will. Powerful imperial estates, above all, could not be forced to take this position. Instead, time and again one was dependent on the negotiating of compromises. If unanimity could not be created in this way, the conflict in question remained in most cases unresolved. Although there was no lack of effort to change this, these efforts failed, because the emperor and the imperial estates were unable to agree, and because there was no authority that could have pushed through a decision over the objections of dissenters. Thus, the fact that conflicts were not solved through decisions was and remained a structural feature of the Empire.

In case of an open conflict within the imperial assembly, there were two basic options for participants: to depart or lodge a solemn protest. This is what happened with the most serious conflict that occupied the imperial diets, the religious schism, and with the countless rank and status conflicts among the members of the Empire. If such conflicts could not be resolved for the reasons given, there was a symbolic way out: the competing claims were maintained side by side in ritualized form. In a sense, the conflicts were symbolically costaged in the solemn enactments. If two competing parties simultaneously took hold of the banners at the investiture, if the sequence of the votes in the imperial diet changed day by day, if the Protestants temporarily left the church during the coronation mass—such behavior was always prompted by the same symbolic strategy. The competing points of view were symbolically staged and thus remained visible, but one could still continue to act in concert. The same happened if a norm was violated and there was no chance of penalizing the violation and compelling adherence to the norm. In these cases, one likewise employed symbolic means to secure the norm contrafactually: solemn protestations, ritualized excuses, severability clauses, gestures of dissent. A particularly significant example is the norm enshrined in the Golden Bull that the king should be crowned in Aachen. In the early modern period, this norm was not honored a single time after 1531, but the city maintained it by having the privilege confirmed in writing at every coronation and admitted the newly crowned emperor as a canon into the Marienstift. In short, the existence of countless mutually contradicting claims that were preserved in writing and symbolically and ritually was a characteristic of the Empire. Nevertheless, an elementary consensus existed, and it was the essential achievement of the ritual acts of the Empire (coronations, investitures, opening masses, and sessions of the imperial diet) to stage this fundamental consensus, a consensus beyond the countless competing claims, unresolved conflicts, and persistent violations of the norms: the consensus, namely, about the existence of the imperial order itself as a political body composed of head and limbs.

Writing

For various reasons, the Old Empire, as it presented itself around 1500, had only a limited capacity to act as a whole. The members of the Empire were and remained only weakly integrated into a unity. A strong orientation toward consensus, weak coercive power, and the nonresolution of conflicts were simultaneously the causes and consequences of this state of affairs. And that is why—so my thesis contends—the logic of the culture of presence in the Empire persisted and was not eliminated by writing and proxy representation. However, the advance of writing and the practice of proxy representation were not without an effect on the representation of the Empire. Rather, both factors caused the rise of the parallel worlds described in chapter 4.

For quite some time, all institutions of the Empire had been generating mountains of written and printed paper. The deliberations at the imperial diet were recorded and archived; gradually the transactions of all imperial institutions were put into writing. Scholars for their part doubled and tripled this mass of writing by making everything that was going on within the imperial institutions and between members of the Empire a topic of learned collections, publications, and discussion.[8] Every legal claim was thoroughly examined in legal dissertations, documented in collections of sources, and historically buttressed. Attempts were made to channel this flood of written material in bibliographic reference works, handbooks, encyclopedias, and compendia. This learned collection was by no means merely a reflection of what already existed. The scholars did more than just preserve. By subjecting everything that was transmitted in writing to their grasp, they also altered the character of the fabric of norms. Not only could legal claims be more easily demonstrated and substantiated. By collecting and recording them, they were brought into a systematic, abstract order, and the whole was given a coherence it otherwise did not possess; at the same time, the written collection also made fully apparent what kinds of contradictions and unresolved conflicts the whole contained.

The Empire manifested itself also in ink and paper, and therein lay its primary experiential reality for scholars. If it did not have its own architecture of power in which it was manifestly represented as a whole, it could instead be depicted as an Empire of books. A frontispiece copper engraving (figure 17) in a handbook about the "the permanent imperial diet in Regensburg" illustrates this. The Empire is staged as a palace of books and files, the law of the Empire as an awe-inspiring edifice of writing. The fundamental imperial laws on the right, the imperial resolutions on the left are presented as though on two altars, surrounded by room-high drawers full of sealed documents and shelves full of massive folios. In the middle a passage opens into a bright, well-proportioned palace and through it to the outside. "For emperor and Empire," *pro Caesare et*

Figure 17. Title-page copper engraving from Johann Carl König, *Abhandlungen von denen Teutschen Reichs-Tägen*, Nuremberg, 1738.

Imperio, reads the inscription on the cartouche above the door. *Acta comitialia*, files, have taken the place here of the *actus solennes*, the solemn acts.

But in fact the public of writing by no means replaced the symbolic-ritual public even then; the written preservation of the norms did not displace the symbolic-ritual staging. On the contrary, the rituals and ceremonies became themselves the subject of writing, contractual fixation, and legal scholarship. Printing potentiated the public of the solemn enactments in large, illustrated festive books. Rituals and ceremonies were painstakingly recorded, documented in print, and systematized *more geometrico*. The ceremonial place of every individual when walking, standing, sitting, and voting, their titles, address, and greetings, became the stuff of learned law, which gave rise to a new subdiscipline, the *Ius praecedentiae*.[9] Ritual acts were not only equivalents of written contracts, but were in turn also regulated in treaties and privileges. The result was that all details of the external forms remained continuously present. It was hardly possible any longer to react flexibly to changed circumstances, as had still been the case under Maximilian I. What was true for the legal claims of the members of the Empire as a whole was true also for all symbolic-ritual details:

> Through imperial recesses, peace treaties, electoral capitulations, *Hausverträge*, decisions by the imperial courts, and so on, the political property of every member of the German body politic is carefully determined. The careful attention to all of this extended—with the most punctilious religiosity—to everything and everyone, and years of efforts were devoted to seemingly unimportant matters, for example, titles, the arrangements in walking, standing, and sitting, the color of some furniture and the like. From this side one must attribute the best organization to the German state.[10]

Characteristic for the order of the Empire was that there was no boundary beyond which such symbolic-ritual claims could have been neglected, and no procedure that would have made it possible to distinguish between important and less important matters. Since, in the logic of the culture of presence, the symbolic-ritual details of walking, standing, sitting, address, and so on defined the status of an individual and manifested the order of the whole, nobody believed they could relinquish them without endangering their own status. Every advance against the most minor detail always raised the fundamental *quaestio status*; the order of the whole always seemed to be at stake. The Peace of Westphalia reinforced this peculiarity of the imperial order by explicitly protecting *all* existing rights, liberties, and privileges of all members of the Empire against changes.[11] Everything was connected to everything else and was preserved in the same punctilious way. But new claims were continually added, and new conflicts constantly erupted. The order could not be frozen in place—the imperial diet of 1653/54, with its wealth of new status conflicts, illustrates this vividly. But the procedures that would have made it possible to make binding decisions among the countless competing claims functioned less and less. The "discrepancy between the need for change in the imperial constitution and its capacity for change" grew ever larger,[12] the thicket of "pretensions" grew ever denser, the handling of the problem ever more complicated. Hardly anyone could still keep track of it all; imperial law turned into an *arcanum* of specialists.[13]

What this led to in day-to-day dealings became evident in Regensburg in the eighteenth century. The ever subtler elaborations in the ceremonial grammar of visits and countervisits, the ever more complicated strophes in the alternation schemes at the sessions of the imperial diet—there was no limit to fine and minute differentiations. At the same time, managing the problems always moved within the same framework, namely, that of the old culture of presence. Cultural sociologists have observed similar phenomena in other cultures and eras: a progressive elaboration of always the same patterns of behavior, virtuosic variations and elaborated refinements within a framework of action that remained the same. "Existing forms and means were reused, modified, diversified, and refined, and taken to the very limit of what was existentially possible."[14] The same behavioral strategies that gave rise to the problems were also deployed to solve these problems, which produced a kind of feedback loop. We are dealing with a "reaction to structural changes that did not lead to the adjustment of structures that were becoming obsolete to changed conditions, but which, on the contrary, must be described as the expansion, intensification, refinement, and enhanced significance of the old structures that were becoming obsolete."[15] This is also how it was in the Empire in the eighteenth century: in their attempt to solve structural problems, the actors created ever new, more complicated problems, which they in turn tried to solve in the same manner, and in this way they maneuvered themselves ever deeper into a communicative dead end. However, this level of action was not the only one—on other levels, actions followed different rules. The highly artificial and formalized way of interacting had a false bottom. The main actors were aware—as the quote from the envoy of electoral Bohemia, Trauttmannsdorff, showed[16]—that they were moving simultaneously in two parallel worlds. What was enacted in one world with the greatest meticulousness and dead seriousness could be derided as a comedy in the other.

Proxy Representation

This development can be understood only if one takes the dynamic of representation into consideration. The system of permanent representatives, as it was perfected in Europe in the seventeenth century, allowed the potentates to communicate in symbolic form about their reciprocal status claims without meeting in person. The communication system could be maintained also in the absence of the potentates; indeed, it could be further refined. The electors and princes were now for their part members of European princely society and therefore participated in this new diplomatic system. At the same time, though, they were vassals of the emperor and members of the Empire, and here a different ceremonial logic applied. Thus, the struggle over the shape of the Empire—feudal hierarchy under the imperial sovereign or federation of quasi-sovereign potentates—was played out not least at the level of ceremony involving envoys. The imperial assembly in Regensburg and the throne investitures at the imperial court were the most prominent stages for this struggle.

In Regensburg, the envoys were entirely among themselves since 1664. That changed a lot of things. As long as at least a few princes had been present in person and had been accompanied by their learned councilors, the spheres between "own persons" and mere authorized agents had remained clearly separated symbolically. The envoys were clearly distinct from the princes in person in every respect—in their clothes, equipages, servants, habitus, and ceremonial treatment. Now, in the seventeenth century, with the Peace of Westphalia representing a milestone in this process, diplomatic representation through envoys of the first rank (*ambassadeurs*) became a central symbolic instrument in the development of the new system of sovereign actors. The principals demanded that their envoys appear with as much splendor and pomp as they themselves did, and they pushed through that they were also treated the same way as they were, for precisely that was considered the clearest sign of their full recognition as sovereigns, as the *plus illustre marque de la souveraineté*. For that purpose, however, the envoys themselves had to be of high birth rank and have considerable means at their disposal. For the substantive work they had learned councilors by their side. This systemic doubling kept the separation of the hierarchical spheres between noble representatives and bourgeois, at most newly ennobled councilors always visible. This forbade the learned men from confusing the portrayal of their own person with the portrayal of their "high principals." This symbolic code corresponded to the transition period during which the circle of sovereigns of equal standing was just then being reshaped.

While this system of diplomatic signs persisted in the eighteenth century, it also revealed its glaring weaknesses: it made unperturbed negotiations over rank conflicts extremely difficult. That is why the European potentates gradually learned to circumvent the communicative problems: they used round tables, lesser envoy ranks, and so on—that is, symbolic means that freed the actors from the burden of rank symbolism if their political interests demanded it with sufficient urgency. Only at the imperial diet in Regensburg was the opposite the case: here one still tried to enforce the ceremonial rules of the system of envoys under the law of nations when the actors in international dealings were already starting to cast it off. All imperial estates, down to the prelates and counts, indeed even the cities, advanced the claim to be treated like sovereign lords.

Precisely because their representatives in Regensburg were completely among themselves, and precisely because they themselves had much lower birth status, they placed the greatest weight on the most precise status representations of their principals. But since these potentates were simultaneously enacting their own status demonstrations on very different stages, they invested fewer and fewer resources in their Regensburg delegations. Yet the envoys themselves barely disposed of their own economic resources, as the envoys of the high nobility still did in the seventeenth century, and thus they could not even remotely display the material splendor that the representation of the great princes invariably demanded. What they were left with were only the ceremonial titles, the gestures of sovereignty, the number of paces, the seat at the table, the sequence of visits, and the gravity of the formulas of address. They guarded these all the more zealously, for they knew that they were acting on behalf of their "high lord principals." Their own concern of social self-presentation disappeared behind their high office, and their actions seemed to them all the more legitimate, as they were, after all, acting in the interest of the princes themselves. That is why the envoys offered what was to outsiders the ridiculous sight of lower-ranking individuals who performed in front of each other the spectacle of high-ranking individuals in accordance with the old ceremonial rules. They obeyed the logic of the culture of presence, whose foundations were no longer in place.

In the eighteenth century, the Empire no longer had a uniform locus. It no longer manifested itself by having all estates assemble at a particular time on a shared stage with the sovereign, to jointly enact the *maiestas imperialis* with solemnity and splendor. To be sure, on the one hand, the ritual acts of election and coronation still existed—but most rulers stayed away. On the other hand, there was still an emperor—yet he no longer met with the estates in person, but had withdrawn to his residence at the periphery of the Empire, and the princes did everything they could to avoid having to kneel in front of him and swear the feudal oath, not even through their representatives. Finally, there was still an imperial diet—but when it lost its character as a specific event, it also lost the splendor and presence of the rulers, and it was less able than ever before to make collectively binding decisions. It was only on paper, in the compendia of the imperial jurists, that the Empire as a whole was put into a more or less coherent and systematic order.

At the same time, however, a different development was taking place on another level. In their residences, the great electors and princes deployed the splendor of their own majesty, whether or not they were kings, and in international relations they acted in every respect like sovereigns. Their actions were shaped by a structural ambiguity, since the question that had been posed at the imperial diet of 1653/54—whether the Empire was a loose federation of independent potentates or a hierarchy under the emperor and electors—was never decided. Instead, two competing interpretations of the Empire, two behavioral maxims, and two symbolic languages existed permanently side by side. These often intersected and constantly gave rise to new causes for conflict: on the one hand, the egalitarian grammar of diplomatic business, according to which sovereigns treated each other as equals and gave expression to this through the *honores regii*; on the other hand, the hierarchical grammar of the Empire, with imperial majesty and electoral preeminence, a hierarchy of estates down to the most minor counts and prelates, with investiture rituals and the performance of arch offices—in short, the old grammar of the culture of presence. For the actors it meant that unambiguous behavior was not possible. They found themselves constantly confronted by irreconcilable behavioral orientations. The many memoranda at this time invoked the dilemma and sought ways to reconcile the unity of the whole and the "veneration of the highest sovereign" with the "freedom of the members." The Empire, as Friedrich Carl von Moser put it, was a "political puzzle" that could not be solved in a rigorous and logical way.[17] Others called it a chimera, a hybrid entity with a dual nature, one that could not be grasped conceptually.

This dual reality is revealed in exemplary fashion in the events surrounding the election and coronation in Frankfurt am Main in 1764. It was not the case that the great imperial princes simply treated this old ritual with disdain or even ignored it. The kings who had led the war against the house of Habsburg, the electors who declined to appear in person at the coronation because they were afraid they would have to kneel—they were simultaneously the same who quarreled for decades about which regalia their envoys were allowed to hand over at the coronation. Electoral Brunswick and electoral Brandenburg themselves maintained the institutional fiction of the old imperial order in ritual with great meticulousness; indeed, they still fought over their places within it, while they simultaneously—on other stages—worked to undermine it. Equally divided was the Queen of Bohemia between her roles as sovereign potentate, member of the electoral college, and empress. The stance of the actors could not be unambiguous, for they both were and were not members of the Empire. But all participants aligned their public conduct with the fiction of the Empire as long as they assumed that others would do likewise. It was this thoroughly ambiguous situation that made clear and unambiguous conduct impossible, and instead all but compelled a structural hypocrisy. This was not a moral failing on the part of individuals, but something in which all actors participated more or less involuntarily.

At the same time, however, new standards of sincerity and authenticity, of unambiguousness and simplicity, developed. These drew upon very diverse, old and new sources: Pietistic devoutness and contempt for all worldly externalities, rationalistic cost-benefit calculations, a strict spirit of systematics, and a new pathos of naturalness. All this led to the demystification of the imperial solemnities: the old clothes seemed like a ridiculous costume, the arch offices like trifles, the entire coronation a comedy, the imperial assembly like the arena of little vain men, and the throne investiture as the "empty shadow play of vain ceremonies."[18] That all of this nevertheless continued to be staged, and that participants even quarreled over it, seemed intolerable once one began to measure the Empire against the criteria of a philosophical system: "The old forms… do not express the true state of affairs; the two are split and contradictory, and have no reciprocal truth."[19]

No Final Act

Four acts on the stage of the Empire are the subject of this book—what is missing is the final act. For when the Empire came to an end, there was no solemn enactment. When people speak about the end of the Empire, it is usually captured in the formulation that Francis II "put down the imperial crown." But this is a purely metaphorical way of speaking that does not correspond to any concrete act. The imperial crown was not literally taken off the way it had been placed on the head at the coronation; there was no inverse ritual, no solemn divestiture, no performative act of abdication—unlike in the Middle Ages, when Louis the Pious placed his insignia back upon the altar in a solemn ritual, or when Pope Celestine V took off his vestments and sat down on the steps in front of his vacant throne. A ritual would have integrated the abdication into the continuing order and bridged the rupture symbolically. But Francis II did not simply abdicate personally to make it possible for someone else to succeed him: instead, he dissolved the institutional order itself. It was not done forcefully and spectacularly (even if it happened under the threat of Napoleon's army). The emperor was not led to the scaffold; the imperial body was not literally decapitated, as was the French monarchy. The end of the Empire did not take place symbolically and ritually, but in writing. It perished with the stroke of a pen: it simply ceased to exist as an institutional reality. That is also why, in contrast to the fall of the monarchy in France, there were no pictures of the event, either real or imaginary. The end of the Empire is a medial blank space.[20]

Instead, there were two written declarations. The imperial estates that had joined Napoleon to form the Confederation of the Rhine declared in a written document that they dissociated themselves "from their previous bond with the German imperial body," and they justified it by saying that "the bond that was supposed to unite the various members of the German body politic to date is no longer adequate for this purpose, or rather, it has in fact already been dissolved."[21] This proclamation was read out in the imperial assembly on 1 August 1806.[22] The emperor for his part declared the following a few days later (6 August) in a written document, which was read out in Regensburg: "We regard the bond, which has up to now united Us to the body politic of the

German Empire, as severed; that We consider the office and honor of Supreme Head of the Empire as lapsed owing to the union of the confederate Estates of the Rhine, and that We are thereby released from all duties undertaken with regard to the German Empire and the Imperial Crown worn and the Imperial rule conducted, on its account, as resigned, as is hereby done." At the same time, he absolved all members and servants of the Empire "from their duties by which they were bound to Us by the constitution as legal Supreme Head of the Empire."[23] Even if he sought to deflect the responsibility for this step from himself, the emperor did note that with his declaration the Empire ceased to exist. Without the head, the body no longer existed.

All of these events unfolded under pressure from the Napoleonic troops. The revolutionary wars had previously already dissolved the order within the Empire; they had driven some to flight, and others into the arms of Napoleon. As early as 1803, a proper imperial deputation had, in a formally correct way, dissolved the most elementary legal principles of the imperial order, dissolved small territories, secularized spiritual territories, and divided the remaining assets among the great powers. Within the forms of imperial law, one had begun to abolish imperial law. Initially, one had still pretended that this was being done for the good of and to save the whole, and one had employed the traditional metaphors. The dispossessions were supposedly intended to "give new life" to the imperial constitution, by "removing the weak parts of the system and solidifying its chief basic pillars," proclaimed the declaration of the princes of the Confederation of the Rhine. But in truth, to stay faithful to the metaphor, they had long since begun to build their own, new palaces out of the blocks of the old structure.

Toward the end, the process of redistribution and enrichment accelerated. The old competition over titles and honors assumed inflationary forms: princes became electors, electors became kings. Even the imperial dignity was pulled into the maelstrom of the impetuous dynamic. In the face of the new imperial titles of the French and the Russians, Francis II, as the sovereign of his hereditary lands, gave himself the title of Emperor of Austria. As early as October of 1800, he had the imperial crown secretly transported from Regensburg—where it had been taken to safety from the advancing revolutionary troops—to his treasury in Vienna. This violation against the rather marginal and "merely symbolic-seeming" privilege of the city of Nuremberg from 1424 was in fact revealing. It casts a light upon the entire happenings, for as we have seen, the order of the Empire all but consisted of an endless plethora of such individual rights and privileges; these rights and privileges were all so closely interconnected that important ones could simply not be distinguished from unimportant ones. Rather, in the eyes of those who held these rights, the status question depended on each and every one, and all of them had so far been always carefully maintained symbolically—even, and especially, if they were violated time and again, as in the case of the Aachen coronation right, for example. That is why it was highly significant that the emperor now had the imperial regalia disappear into his treasury.

The authority of the emperor was the symbolic capstone of the imperial constitution. Constitutional historians have referred to Francis's declaration in response to Napoleon's pressure that the Empire was dissolved as a breach of the imperial constitution, and scholars quarreled long over whether he was allowed to do so, indeed, if he even *could* do so or whether the Empire did not in fact continue to exist because the dissolution had not been legal.[24] About this there is no doubt: the imperial constitution did not envisage its own abolition. But how should a legal order continue to exist if nobody's expectations and actions were guided by it?

It was easy to destroy the institutional fiction of the Empire with the stroke of a pen, since its capacity for collective action had already been destroyed. Hegel had described this with the greatest precision in his constitutional tract of 1802. It was fully evident when the declaration of withdrawal by the princes of the Confederation of the Rhine was read out aloud at the imperial diet on 1 August 1806: only sixteen envoys (*Comitialgesandte*) listened impotently to the reading; nobody did anything against it, either in the imperial diet or anywhere else. The bizarre situation in Regensburg becomes clear if one considers that some of the envoys present held mandates from new sovereigns and from enemies of Napoleon simultaneously.[25] How was such an assembly supposed to act as the representative organ of the whole? How could it have imparted to "the body of our German state the animation in all its members," which was the function the scholars of imperial law ascribed to it?[26]

This is not to say that contemporaries were not aghast—namely, about how easy it was to destroy the institutional order. At one blow it became apparent that it was a ritually created fiction. The imperial order lost the aura of objectivity and appeared as a "mere thing of the mind" (*blosses Gedankending*).[27] It is true of every institutional order that it functions only as long as all believe in its functioning and make this the premise of their actions—or at least impute as much to one another. The normative edifice of the imperial constitution collapsed that much more easily because for a long time none of the great potentates were guided in their behavior by it and also no longer expected as much from others. Now it became clear how ambiguous the behavior of the participants had been for a long time. The main actors themselves had smiled condescendingly at the symbolic staging of the *maiestas imperialis* as an anachronistic spectacle. And yet, the contradictory web of norms that made up the imperial constitution had been maintained with great—and ever rising—meticulousness by being ritually staged time and again. The creation and portrayal of the Empire had long since ceased to be congruent, but had created a dual reality that constantly forced all participants into institutional hypocrisy. Napoleon liberated them from it all.

Notes

1. See Hofmann, *Repräsentation*; Chartier, *Unvollendete Vergangenheit*; Rehberg, "Weltrepräsentanz."
2. Kieserling, *Kommunikation unter Anwesenden*; Martschukat and Patzold, *Geschichtswissenschaft*; Stollberg-Rilinger, "Symbolische Kommunikation"; Holenstein, *Huldigung*.
3. Bourdieu, "Einsetzungsriten."
4. In general, see Schreiner and Schwerhoff, "Introduction," in Schreiner and Schwerhoff, *Verletzte Ehre*.
5. Althoff, *Spielregeln* and *Macht der Rituale*.
6. Mohnhaupt, "Vertragskonstruktion und fingierter Vertrag."
7. Weitzel, "Schriftlichkeit und Recht"; Bohn, *Schriftlichkeit und Gesellschaft*; Schlögl, "Politik beobachten"; see examples in Mostert and Schulte, *Trust in Writing*; Dartmann and Keller, "Inszenierungen von Ordnung."
8. See chapter 3; Stolleis, *Geschichte des Öffentlichen Rechts*; Hammerstein, *Jus und Historie*; Roeck, *Reichssystem und Reichsherkommen*; on the theoretical debates, see Burgdorf, *Reichskonstitution*; for a bibliography, see Pütter, *Litteratur des teutschen Staatsrechts*.
9. Vec, *Zeremonialwissenschaft*; see Stollberg-Rilinger, "Die Wissenschaft der feinen Unterschiede" and "Rang vor Gericht"; Weller, *Theatrum Praecedentiae*; Krischer, *Reichsstädte in der Fürstengesellschaft*.
10. Hegel, "Die Verfassung Deutschlands," 29, see also 21.
11. IPO, Art. VIII § 1; see chapter 3.
12. Haug-Moritz, "Kaisertum und Parität."
13. Aretin, *Das Alte Reich*, 1:26.
14. Luhmann, *Gesellschaftsstruktur und Semantik*, 87–88, 98.
15. See Winterling, "'Krise ohne Alternative,'" on similar phenomena in the Roman imperial period. Hegel already pointed to the parallel between the latter and the late phase of the Empire; see his "Die Verfassung Deutschlands," 85.
16. See section on "Organized Hypocrisy" in chapter 4.
17. Moser, *Von dem Deutschen national-Geist*, 6.
18. Pütter, *Patriotische Abbildung*, 30.
19. Hegel, "Die Verfassung Deutschlands," 92.
20. On the phenomena of the abdication of the ruler, see in general Richter, *Thronverzicht*; especially Schieder, "'Ay no; no ay,'" on abdication as a "medial blank space"; Kleinheyer, "Die Abdankung des Kaisers." On the end of the Empire, see Burgdorf, *Weltbild*; for a survey of the scholarship, see Härter, "Zweihundert Jahre"; Nicklas, "Müssen wir das Alte Reich lieben?"
21. Hofmann, *Quellen zum Verfassungsorganismus*, No. 70a, 392–93.
22. Dramatically recounted in Burgdorf, *Weltbild*, 120ff.
23. English text at http://en.wikisource.org/wiki/Abdication_of_Francis_II,_Holy_Roman_Emperor.
24. Kleinheyer, "Die Abdankung des Kaisers," 124ff.; Burgdorf, *Weltbild*, 128ff.
25. Burgdorf, *Weltbild*, 131ff., 173ff.
26. Moser, TSR, 43:416.
27. Kant, "Metaphysik der Sitten," 450 (about the nobility).

~: BIBLIOGRAPHY :~

Archival Sources

Haus-, Hof- und Staatsarchiv Wien (HHStA Vienna)

Reichshofrat (RHR)
  Gratialia et Feudalia, Fürstliche Thronbelehnungen (GF FT), Karton 3
  Gratialia et Feudalia, Thronbelehnungen und Zeremonialanstände (GF TZ), Kartons 1,2,3
Reichskanzlei (RK)
  Wahl- und Krönungsakten (WK), Kartons 77–88 (1763–65)
  Reichstagsakten (RTA), Kartons 125, 126, 127, 128
Oberhofmeisteramt (OMeA)
  Zeremonialakten (ZA), Protokolle, vol. 1 (1652–59); vol. 29 (1763–64); vol. 30 (1765); Sonderreihe, vol. 15 (1764)
  Ältere Zeremonialakten (ÄZA), Kartons 3, 4, 21, 26, 34
Mainzer Erzkanzlerarchiv (MEA)
  Wahl- und Krönungsakten (WK), Karton 16

Österreichisches Staatsarchiv, Allgemeines Verwaltungsarchiv

Familienarchiv Harrach, Karton 441 (referenced in notes as Harrach, Tagzettel)

Österreichische Nationalbibliothek Wien

Handschriftenabteilung, Cod. ser. no. 12.178, *Journal du voyage que j'ai fait avec sa Majesté L'Empereur et mon frère Joseph de Vienne à Franckforth pour Le couronnement du Roi des Romains au 1764* (referenced in notes as Leopold, *Journal du voyage*)

Hauptstaatsarchiv Düsseldorf (HStA Düsseldorf)

Kurköln VI, Reichssachen, Nos. 878, 896, 1655

Biblioteca Apostolica Vaticana (BAV)

Segretaria di Stato, Germania, Fasc. 151, Lettere di Mon. Nunt. [Scipio Pannochieschi, Erzbischof von Pisa] in Vienna 1653; Fasc. 152, Lettere di Mon. Nunt. All'Imperatore [aus Regensburg 1653] (referenced in notes as Pannochieschi, Lettere)

Published Sources

Andlau, Peter von. *Libellus de Caesarea monarchia (1469): Kaiser und Reich* (Latin and German). Edited by Rainer A. Müller. Frankfurt am Main, 1998.

Arneth, Alfred Ritter von. *Geschichte Maria Theresia's.* Vol. 7, *Maria Theresia's Letzte Regierungszeit, 1: 1763–1780.* 1876; repr., Osnabrück, 1971.

———. *Maria Theresia und Joseph II.: Ihre Correspondenz samt Briefen Joseph's an seinen Bruder Leopold.* Vol. 1, *1761–1772.* Vienna, 1867.

Arumaeus, Dominicus. *Commentarius iuridico-historico-politicus de comitiis Romano-Germanici Imperii.* Jena, 1635.

———. *De sessionis praerogativa.* Basilea, 1622.

Ausführliche Beschreibung aller bey der im Allerhöchsten Namen Ihro Röm. Kayserl. Majestät Joseph des Andern durch den Herrn Grafen von Pergen Excellenz als Allerhöchst dem verordneten Herrn Stell-Vertreter in der Kayserl. Freyen Reichs-Stadt Frankfurt Rath und Bürgerschaft angenommenen Huldigung.... Frankfurt, 1766.

Balduin, Christoph Adolph. *Poetische Entdeckung der Ehrenpforte, welche Ferdinand dem Dritten zu Regenspurg aufgerichtet worden.* Regensburg, 1653.

Bebenburg, Lupold von. *De iuribus regni et imperii: Über die Rechte von Kaiser und Reich.* Edited by Jürgen Miethke. Bibliothek des deutschen Staatsdenkens 14. Munich, 2005.

Beck, Christian August von. "Kurzer Inbegriff des deutschen Lehensrechts" (1757). In *Recht und Verfassung in der Zeit Maria Theresias: Die Vorträge zum Unterricht des Erzherzogs Joseph im Natur- und Voelkerrecht sowie im deutschen Staats- und Lehnrecht,* edited by Hermann Conrad. Cologne and Opladen, 1964.

"Beschreibung des Reichs-Tags von 1495." In *Senckenbergische Sammlung von ungedruckt- und raren Schriften,* vol. 4, 94–197. Frankfurt am Main, 1751.

Besold, Christoph. *De praecedentia et sessionis praerogativa.* Straßburg, 1641.

Besser, Johann von. *Preußische Krönungs-Geschichte: Oder Verlauf der Ceremonien, mit welchen ... Herr Friderich der Dritte, Marggraf und Churfürst zu Brandenburg die königliche Würde des von ihm gestiffteten Königreichs Preussen angenommen, und sich und seine Gemahlin, ... als König und Königin einweihen lassen ... ; aufs sorgfältigste beschrieben, und der Nachwelt ... in Kupfern ... vorgestellet ...* Cöln an der Spree, 1712.

———. *Schriften.* Vol. 3, *Ceremonial-Acta.* Edited by Peter-Michael Hahn, redacted by Vinzenz Czech and Holger Kürbis. Heidelberg, 2009.

Beweis, daß die Reichslehnbaren immediaten Graf- und Herrschaften ohnzweifentliche Fahnen- und Thronlehen seyen. Oehringen, 1743.

Bodin, Jean. *Sechs Bücher über den Staat* (1576). Translated and with an introduction by Bernd Wimmer, edited by and with a foreword by Peter-Cornelius Mayer-Tasch. Munich, 1981–86.

Boehmer, Georg Ludwig. *De Indole et natura expectativae et investiturae feudalis et de hujus renovatione.* Göttingen, 1747.

———. *De Investitura per procuratorem.* Göttingen, 1761.

Buder, Christian Gottlieb. "De Investitura feudorum imperii in camera." In *Amoenitates juris feudalis,* 12–19. Jena, 1741.

———. *Nachricht von der Belehnung Johann Friedrichs zu Sachsen, geschehen vor dem Röm. Könige Ferdinand dem Ersten zu Wien im Jahr 1535.* Jena, 1755.

Bulla aurea Karoli IV. imperatoris anno MCCCLVI promulgata (1356). Edited by Wolfgang D. Fritz. MGH Fontes iuris antiqui in us. schol. 11. Weimar, 1992.

Bülow, Heinrich Wilhelm von. *Über Geschichte und Verfassung des gegenwärtigen Reichstages.* 2 vols. Regensburg, 1792.
Buschmann, Arno, ed. *Kaiser und Reich: Verfassungsgeschichte des Heiligen Römischen Reiches Deutscher Nation vom Beginn des 12. Jahrhunderts bis zum Jahre 1806 in Dokumenten.* 2 vols., 2nd, expanded ed. Baden-Baden, 1994.
Chasseneuz, Barthélemy de. *Catalogus gloriae mundi: In Qvo Mvlta Praeclara De Praerogativis, Praeeminentijs, Maioritate ... continentur ... Opvs ... In XII. Libros diuisum ...* Frankfurt am Main, 1579.
[Chemnitz, Bogislaus Philipp von]. *Hippolithus a Lapide, Dissertatio de ratione status in Imperio nostro Romano-Germanico.* 1640.
Cocceji, Heinrich von. *Disputatio de praecedentia.* Heidelberg, 1681.
Coelestin, Georg. *Historia comitiorum anno M. D. XXX. augustae celebratorum.* Frankfurt an der Oder, 1597.
Conrad, Hermann, ed. "Verfassung und politische Lage des Reiches in einer Denkschrift Josephs II. von 1767/68." In *Festschrift Nikolaus Grass zum 60. Geb. dargebracht,* edited by Louis Carlen and Fritz Steinegger, vol. 1, 161–85. Innsbruck and Munich, 1974.
Corpus Iuris Canonici. Edited by Ludwig Emil Richter and Emil Friedberg, 2nd. edition. Leipzig, 1879.
Corpus Reformatorum. Vol. 2, *Philipp Melanchthon, Opera quae supersunt omia.* Edited by Karl Gottlieb Bretschneider. Halle, 1835.
Cramer, Johann Friedrich. *Manuale Processus Imperialis Sive Compendiosa Introductio Ad Praxin Augustissimi Judicii Caesareo-Imperialis Aulici: In qva Modus agendi, procurandi, advocandi & dijudicandi causas tam Justitiae, qvam gratiae ... exponitur.* Nuremberg and Stuttgart, 1704.
Crusius, Jacob Andreas. *Tractatus politico-juridico-historicus de praeeminentia, sessione, praecedentia et universo iure proedrias.* Four books in one volume. Bremen, 1666.
Deutsche Reichtagsakten, Ältere Reihe. *Deutsche Reichstagsakten unter Kaiser Friedrich III.* Vol. 2, part 2, *1471.* Edited by Helmut Wolff. Göttingen, 1999.
Deutsche Reichstagsakten, Jüngere Reihe. *Deutsche Reichstagsakten unter Kaiser Karl V.* Vol. 1. Edited by August Kluckhohn. Gotha, 1893.
———. *Deutsche Reichtagsakten unter Kaiser Karl V.* Vol. 2. Edited by Adolf Wrede. Gotha, 1896.
———. *Deutsche Reichstagsakten unter Kaiser Karl V.* Vol. 3. Edited by Adolf Wrede. Gotha, 1901.
———. *Deutsche Reichstagsakten unter Kaiser Karl V.* Vol. 4. Edited by Adolf Wrede. Gotha, 1905.
———. *Deutsche Reichstagsakten unter Kaiser Karl V.* Vol. 7, parts 1–2. Edited by Johannes Kühn. Stuttgart, 1935.
———. *Deutsche Reichstagsakten unter Kaiser Karl V.* Vol. 10, *Der Reichstag zu Regensburg und die Verhandlungen über einen Friedstand mit den Protestanten in Schweinfurt und Nürnberg 1532.* Edited by Rosemarie Aulinger. Göttingen, 1992.
Deutsche Reichstagsakten, Mittlere Reihe. *Deutsche Reichstagsakten unter Maximilian I.* Vol. 1, parts 1–2, *Reichstag zu Frankfurt 1486.* Edited by Heinz Angermeier. Göttingen, 1989.
———. *Deutsche Reichstagsakten unter Maximilian I.* Vol. 2, parts 1–2, *Reichstag zu Nürnberg 1487.* Edited by Reinhard Seyboth. Göttingen, 2001.
———. *Deutsche Reichstagsakten unter Maximilian I.* Vol. 3, parts 1–2, *1488–1490.* Edited by Ernst Bock. Göttingen, 1972–73.

———. Deutsche Reichstagsakten unter Maximilian I. Vol. 5, *Reichstag zu Worms 1495: Akten, Urkunden und Korrespondenzen*. Edited by Heinz Angermeier. Göttingen, 1981.

———. Deutsche Reichtagsakten unter Maximilian I. Vol. 6, *Reichstage von Lindau, Worms und Freiburg 1496–1498*. Edited by Heinz Gollwitzer. Göttingen, 1979.

Diderot, Denis, Le Rond D'Alembert, and Jean Baptiste. *Encyclopédie ou Dictionnaire raisonné des sciences, des arts et des métiers*. Paris, 1751–80; repr., Stuttgart, 1966.

Duchhardt, Heinz, and Franz-Josef Jakobi, eds. *Der Westfälische Frieden: Das münstersche Exemplar des Vertrags zwischen Kaiser/Reich und Frankreich vom 24. Oktober 1648*. Vol. 1, *Faksimile*; vol. 2, *Einführung, Transkription, Übersetzung*. Wiesbaden, 1996.

Edelmayer, Friedrich, ed. *Die Krönungen Maximilians II. zum König von Böhmen, Römischer König und König von Ungarn (1562/63): Nach der Beschreibung von Hans Habersack*. Fontes rerum Austriacarum: Abt. 1, 13. Vienna, 1990.

Ehses, Stephan, ed. "Kardinal Lorenzo Campeggio auf dem Reichstage von Augsburg 1530." *Römische Quartalschrift* 17 (1903): 383–406; 18 (1904): 358–84; 19 (1905): 129–52; 20 (1906): 54–80; 21 (1907): 114–39.

Essenwein, August von, ed. *Hans Tirol, Holzschnitt darstellend die Belehnung König Ferdinands I. mit den österreichischen Erbländern durch Kaiser Karl V. auf dem Reichstage zu Augsburg am 5. September 1530*. . . . Frankfurt am Main, 1887.

Faber, Anton [Christian Leonhard Leucht], and Johann Christoph von Gritschke, eds. *Neue europäische Staatscanzley welche die wichtigsten öffentlichen Angelegenheiten, vornemlich des Deutschen Reiches in sich fasset*. Vols. 8–20. Ulm, Frankfurt am Main, and Leipzig, 1764–67.

Finet, John. *Ceremonies of Charles I: the note books of John Finet, 1628-1641*. Edited by Albert Joseph Loomie. Fordham MI, 1987.

Förstemann, Karl Eduard, ed. *Neues Urkundenbuch zur Geschichte der evangelischen Kirchen-Reformation*. Hamburg, 1942.

———, ed. *Urkundenbuch zu der Geschichte des Reichstags zu Augsburg im Jahre 1530*. 2 vols. Halle, 1833; repr., Osnabrück, 1966.

Francolin, Johann von. *Vera descriptio quomodo Sa. Cae. Maximilianus secundus etc. in suis primis Augustae habitis . . . concessit*. Augsburg, 1566.

———. *Kurtzer Bericht Welcher gestalt von . . . Keyser Maximilian, . . . dem andern, Der Churfürst Hertzog Augustus zu Sachssen, . . . Reichs Lehen vnd Regalien, auff den jtzigen jrer Kay. May. ersten Reichstag, alhier zu Augspurg, den 23. Aprilis, offentlich . . . empfangen*. Erfurt, 1566.

Franken, Heinrich Gottlieb. *Nachricht von der neuesten Beschaffenheit eines Reichs-Tags im Heiligen Römischen Reich und Abriß einer hinlänglichen Reichs-Tags-Bibliothek*. Regensburg, 1760.

Gadner, Gerorg. *Chronik Georg Gadners von 1598, in: 1495—Württemberg wird Herzogtum: Dokumente aus dem Hauptstaatsarchiv Stuttgart zu einem epochalen Ereignis*. Edited by Stephan Molitor. Stuttgart, 1995.

Goethe, Johann Wolfgang. *Aus meinem Leben: Dichtung und Wahrheit (1811–1833)*. Edited by Erich Trunz, vols. 9–10, Hamburger ed. Munich, 1981.

Goetz, Walter, ed. *Die Politik Maximilians I. von Baiern und seiner Verbündeten, 1618–1651*. Vol. 2, part 1. Briefe und Akten zur Geschichte des Dreißigjährigen Krieges, N.F. 2,1. Munich, 1942.

Goldast, Melchior. *Politische Reichs-Händel, Das ist / Allerhand gemeine Acten / Regimentssachen / und Weltliche Discursen: Das gantze heilige Römische Reich, . . . insonderheit aber das geliebte Vatterland teutscher Nation betreffendt*. Frankfurt am Main, 1614.

Goldene Bulle. In *MGH Constitutiones et acta publica iperatorum et regum*, vol. 11, *Dokumente zur Geschichte des Deutschen Reiches und seiner Verfassung 1354–1356*, edited by Wolfgang D. Fritz, 561–631. Weimar, 1992.
Grotius, Hugo. *De iure belli ac pacis: Drei Bücher vom Recht des Krieges und des Friedens* (1625). Die Klassiker des Voelkerrechts 1. Tübingen, 1950.
Gumpelzhaimer, Gottlieb Christian. *Regensburg's Geschichte, Sagen und Merkwürdigkeiten: Von den ältesten bis auf die neuesten Zeiten, in einem Abriss aus den besten Chroniken, Geschichtsbüchern, und Urkunden-Sammlungen (1830–38)*. 4 vols. Regensburg, 1984.
Hammerstein, Notker, ed. *Staatslehre der frühen Neuzeit*. Bibliothek der Geschichte und Politik 16. Frankfurt am Main, 1995.
Harms, Wolfgang, and Michael Schilling, eds. *Deutsche illustrierte Flugblätter des 16. und 17. Jahrhunderts*. 7 vols. Tübingen (vol. 2: Munich), 1985–97.
Hegel, Georg Friedrich Wilhelm. "Die Verfassung Deutschlands" (1802). In *Politische Schriften*, with an afterword by Jürgen Habermas. Frankfurt am Main, 1966.
———. *Political Writings*. Translated by Lawrence Dickey and Hugh B. Nisbet. Cambridge, 1999.
Hegel, Karl, ed. *Die Chroniken der fränkischen Städte: Nürnberg*. Vols. 3–4. Göttingen, 1961. *Die Chroniken der deutschen Städte vom 14. bis ins 16. Jahrhundert*, vol. 10.
———, ed. *Die Chroniken der schwäbischen Städte: Augsburg*. Vol. 5. Leipzig, 1896. *Die Chroniken der deutschen Städte vom 14. bis ins 16. Jahrhundert*, vol. 25.
Heine, Heinrich. *Deutschland, ein Wintermärchen* (1844). Edited by Werner Bellmann. Stuttgart, 2006.
Hellbach, Johann Christoph Theodor. *Meditationes juris proedriae moderni oder Abhandlungen von den heutigen Rechten des Ranges, Vorzugs und Vorsitzes*. Leipzig, 1742.
Hellbach, Johann Cristian von. *Handbuch des Rangrechts in welchem die Literatur und Theorie nebst einem Promtuar ueber die praktischen Grundsaetze desselben, ingleichen die neuesten vorzueglichen Rangordnungen im Anhange enthalten sind*. Erfurt, 1804.
Herder, Johann Gottfried. "Über die Reichsgeschichte: Ein historischer Spaziergang" (1769). In *Herders Sämmtliche Schriften*, edited by Bernard Suphan, vol. 3, 462–71. Berlin, 1878.
Hofmann, Hanns Hubert, ed. *Quellen zum Verfassungsorganismus des Heiligen Römischen Reiches deutscher Nation 1495–1815*. Freiherr-vom-Stein-Gedächtnisausgabe 13. Darmstadt, 1976.
"Instrumentum Pacis Osnabrugense." In *Der Westfälische Frieden: Das Münstersche Exemplar des Vertrags zwischen Kaiser / Reich und Frankreich vom 24. Oktober 1648*. Vol. 1, *Faksimile*; vol. 2, *Einführung, Transkription, Übersetzung*. Edited by Heinz Durchhardt and Franz-Josef Jakobi. Wiesbaden, 1996.
Immenkötter, Herbert, ed. *Die Confutatio der Confessio Augustana vom 3. August 1530*. 2nd ed. Corpus catholicorum 33. Münster, 1981.
Joachim, Johann F. *Von der ehemaligen Gewohnheit bei Reichsbelehnungen die Fahnen über den kaiserlichen Lehnstuhl herabzuwerffen*. In *Fortgesetzte Sammlung vermischter Anmerckungen, in welchen unterschiedene in die Staats- und Lehen-Rechte wie auch in die Geschichte gehörige Sachen abgehandelt werden*, edited by Johann F. Joachim, vol. 2, 349–87. Halle, 1753.
Der Jüngste Reichsabschied von 1654: Abschied der Römisch Kaiserlichen Majestät und gemeiner Stände, welcher auf dem Reichstag zu Regensburg im Jahr Christi 1654 aufgerichtet ist. Edited by Adolf Laufs. Quellen zur neueren Geschichte 32. Bern, 1975.

Kant, Immanuel. "Metaphysik der Sitten" (1797). In *Werke*, edited by Wilhelm Weischedel, vol. 13. Frankfurt am Main, 1968.

Kayser, Albrecht Christoph. *Versuch einer kurzen Beschreibung der Kaiserlichen freyen Reichsstadt Regensburg*. Regensburg, 1797; repr., Regensburg, 1995.

Keyssler, Johann Georg. *Johann Georg Keyßlers Reisen durch Deutschland, Böhmen, Ungarn, die Schweiz, Italien und Lothringen: In welchem der Zustand und das Merkwürdigste dieser Länder beschrieben, und vermittelst der Natürlichen, Gelehrten und Politischen Geschichte, der Mechanik, Mahler-, Bau- und Bildhauerkunst, Münzen und Alterthümer, wie auch mit verschiedenen Kupfern erläutert wird*. 2 vols. Hannover, 1776.

———. *Neueste Reisen durch Deutschland, Böhmen, Ungarn, die Schweiz, Italien und Lothringen . . . .* 2 vols. Hannover, 1740–41.

Khevenhüller-Metsch, Johann Josef. *Aus der Zeit Maria Theresias: Tagebuch des Fürsten Johann Josef Khevenhüller-Metsch, Kaiserlichen Obersthofmeisters, 1742–1776*. Edited by Rudolf Graf Khevenhüller-Metsch. 7 vols. Vienna and Leipzig, 1907–25.

Kohler, Alfred, ed. *Quellen zur Geschichte Karls V*. Ausgewählte Quellen zur deutschen Geschichte der Neuzeit 15. Darmstadt, 1990.

König, Johann Carl. *Gründliche Abhandlung von denen Teutschen Reichs-Tägen überhaupt und dem noch fürwährenden zu Regensburg insbesondere, erschienen Teil 1*. Nuremberg, 1738.

Küchelbecker, Johann Basilius. *Nachricht von denen im Heiligen Römischen Reiche gewöhnlichen Reichs-Tagen, Insbesondere aber von der Verfassung der fürwährenden Reichs-Versammlung zu Regensburg . . . .* Leipzig, 1742.

Küttner, Carl Gottlob. *Reise durch Deutschland, Daenemark, Schweden, Norwegen und einen Theil von Italien: In den Jahren 1797, 1798, 1799*. 4 vols. Leipzig, 1801.

Landsberger, Lorenz. *Churfürsten / Fürsten / Gaistlich vnd weltlich / . . . so bey der Rö. Kay. vnd Kü. Mayestet auff de(m) Reychstag zu Regenspurg gewesen sind . . . Item des Hertzogen vo(n) Pom(m)ern Lehens empfahlung . . . .* Augsburg, 1541.

"Langenmantelsche Chronik: Der Reichstag zu Augsburg im Jahre 1530." In *Die Chroniken der deutschen Städte vom 14. bis 16. Jahrhundert*, published by the Historische Commission der Königlichen Akademie der Wissenschaften, vol. 25, 361–401. Leipzig, 1896.

Lapide, Hippolythus. See Chemnitz, Philipp Bogislav von.

Lehmann, Christoph. *Chronica der Freien Reichsstadt Speyer*. Frankfurt am Main, 1662 (1st ed., 1612).

Leibniz, Gottfried Wilhelm. "Caesarini Fuerstenerii de Jure Suprematus ac Legationis Principum Germaniae" (1677). In *Sämtliche Schriften und Briefe*, Akademie-Ausgabe, 4th series, *Politische Schriften*, 2nd vol., 3–277. Berlin, 1963.

———. "Germani Curiosi Admonitiones" (1677). In *Sämtliche Schriften und Briefe*, Akademie-Ausgabe, 4th series, *Politische Schriften*, 2nd vol., 367–78. Berlin, 1963.

Liechtenstein, Gundacker von. "Guetachten wegen Education eines jungen Fürsten . . ." (after 1648). In *Staatslehre der Frühen Neuzeit: Die Entwicklung der deutschen Staatslehre vom Beginn der Neuzeit bis zur Aufklärung*, edited by Notker Hammerstein, 543–66. Bibliothek der Geschichte und Politik 16; Bibliothek deutscher Klassiker 130. Frankfurt am Main, 1995.

Limnaeus, Johannes. *Ius publicum Imperii Romano-Germanici*. 6 vols. Agentorati, 1629–80.

Ludewig, Johann Peter. *Vollständige Erläuterung der Güldenen Bulle*. 2 parts in 3 vols. With an introduction and edited by Hans Hattenhauer. Frankfurt am Main and Leipzig, 1752; repr., Hildesheim, Zürich, and New York, 2005.

Ludolph, Georg Melchior von. *Beschreibung eines Reichstags wie er im Heiligen Römischen Reich gehalten wird.* Frankfurt am Main and Leipzig, 1751.

Lünig, Johann Christian. *Capitulationes imperatorum et regum Romano-Germanorum, Caroli V., Ferdinandi I., Maximiliani II., Rudolphi II., Matthiae, Ferdinandi II., Ferdinandi III.* 3rd ed. Argentorati, 1674.

———. *Des Teutschen Reichs-Archivs ... oder Germania sacra diplomatica.* 24 vols. Leipzig, 1711–22.

———. *Theatrum Ceremoniale Historico-Politicum oder Historisch- und Politischer Schau-Platz Aller Ceremonien....* 3 parts in 2 vols. Leipzig, 1719–20.

———, ed. *Thesaurus Juris derer Grafen und Herren des Heiligen Römischen Reichs, worinn von deren Ursprunge, Wachsthum, Praerogativen und Gerechtsamen gehandelt.* Frankfurt am Main and Leipzig, 1725.

Luther, Martin. *Werke: Kritische Gesamtausgabe.* Weimar, 1883ff.

Mameranus, Nikolaus. *Investitura regalium electoralis dignitatis nonnullorumque aliorum Dominiorum Mauritii ducis Saxoniae 24. Febr. Anno 1548 Augustae facta.* Augsburg, 1548.

———. *Kurtzer Bericht welcher Gestalt Kayser Carl der fünfft den Hertzog Moritzen, Churfürst zu Sachssen, mit dem Ertzmarschallen Ampt, und der Chur zu Sachssen ... auff dem Reychs Tage zu Augspurg, offentlich ... belehnet hat.* Augsburg, 1548.

———. *Kurtze und eigentliche Verzeychnus der Teilnehmer am Reichstag zu Augsburg 1566.* Repr., Neustadt an der Aisch, 1985.

Meiern, Johann Gottfried von, ed. *Acta comitialia Ratisbonensia publica: Oder Regensburgische Reichstags-Handlungen und Geschichte von den Jahren 1653 u. 1654.* Leipzig, 1738.

Menzel, Karl Philipp. *Neuestes Teutsches Reichs-Tags-Theatrum; Das ist: Ausführlicher Bericht von allen demjenigen, so auf der noch fürwährenden Versammlung der Röm. Kayserlichen Majestät, auch Chur-Fürsten, Fürsten und Ständen des Heiligen Römischen Reichs in der Stadt Regensburg vorgangen: Mit angefügten Kayserlichen Decreten, Reichs-Gutachten, Memorialien, und anderen ... communicierten Schrifften.* Nuremberg, 1733.

Merian, Matthaeus, and Johann Philipp Abelin, eds. *Theatrum Europaeum.* 21 vols. Frankfurt am Main, 1643–1738.

Montagu, Lady Mary Wortley. *Reisebriefe (1716–1718).* Edited by Max Bauer. Berlin and Leipzig, n.d.

Montesquieu, Charles de. *Oeuvres complètes.* Edited by André Masson. Vol. 2. Paris, 1950.

Moser, Friedrich Carl von. "Bericht von dem Streit der Reichs-Erbämter mit denen Kayserlichen Hofämtern ... vom Jahr 1356 bis 1745." In *Kleine Schriften*, vol. 4, 1–176. Frankfurt am Main, 1753.

———. *Von dem Deutschen national-Geist.* 1765.

———. *Deutsches Hof-Recht.* 2 vols. Frankfurt am Main, 1761.

———. "Neujahrs-Wunsch an den Reichs-Tag zu Regensburg, 1765." In *Neues Patriotisches Archiv für Deutschland* 1 (1792): 293–398.

Moser, Johann Jakob. *Einleitung zu dem Reichs-Hofraths-Prozeß.* Frankfurt am Main and Leipzig, 1734.

———. *Neues Teutsches Staatsrecht.* 20 vols. and 3 suppl. vols. 1766–82; repr., Osnabrück, 1967.

———. *Von der Teutschen Lehens-Verfassung.* 1774; repr., Osnabrück, 1967. Also published as *Neues Teutsches Staatsrecht*, vol. 9).

———, ed. *Teutsches Staats-Archiv, oder Sammlung derer neuest- und wichtigsten Reichs-, Crays- und anderer Handlungen, Deductionen, Urtheile derer höchsten Reichs-Gerichte.* Vol. 4. Frankfurt and Leipzig, 1756.

———. *Teutsches Staatsrecht*. 50 vols., 2 suppl. vols., and reg. Nuremberg, 1737–54.
Müller, Johann Joachim. *Des Heiligen Römischen Reichs teutscher Nation Reichstags-Theatrum*. 3 vols. Jena, 1713–19.
———. "Pallium exulans in comitiis." In *Juristisch-historische Electa: Worinnen zuförderst die Staats-Geschäfte bey dem noch fortwehrenden Reichs-Tage zu Regensburg . . . .* Vol. 2. Jena, 1727.
Murr, Christian Theophilus von, ed. *Johannis Paulli Roederi Codex historicus testimoniorum locuplentissimorum des fatis klinodiorum augustalium*. Frankfurt am Main and Leipzig, 1789.
Nicolai, Friedrich. *Beschreibung einer Reise durch Deutschland und die Schweiz im Jahre 1781: Nebst Bemerkungen über Gelehrsamkeit, Industrie, Religion und Sitten*. 12 vols. Berlin and Stettin, 1783–96.
Nuntiaturberichte aus Deutschland 1533–1559 nebst ergänzenden Aktenstücken. Section 1, 1. Suppl. vol. 1530–31, *Legation Lorenzo Campeggios 1530–1531 u. Nuntiatur Girolamo Aleandros 1531*. Edited by Gerhard Müller. Graz and Tübingen, 1963.
Oertel, Christian Gottfried. *Reichstags-Diarium oder zuverläßige Nachricht von dem was unter der Regierung Kaisers Franz des Ersten auf dem Allgemeinen Deutschen Reichs-Tage an Legitimationen der Gesandtschaften . . . und in die Reichs-Händel einschlagenden bekannt gewordenen Schriften von 1745–1765 sich ergeben*. Vol. 6, 1762/63; vol. 7, 1764/65. Regensburg, 1766.
Ompteda, Ludwig Freiherr von. "Versuch einer Skizze der damaligen vortrefflichen Comitial-Gesandten zu Regensburg" (1792). In *Irrfahrten und Abenteuer eines mittelständischen Diplomaten*, 58–71. Leipzig, 1894.
"Ordnung für die Krönungsfeierlichkeit in Aachen." In *Quellentexte zur Aachener Geschichte*, vol. 3, *Die Aachener Königs-Krönungen*, edited by Walter Kaemmerer, 98–105. Aachen, 1961.
Paas, John Roger, ed. *The German Political Broadsheet 1600–1700*. Vol. 8, 1649–1661. Wiesbaden, 2005.
Paine, Thomas. "Rights of Man" (1791). *Writings*, edited by M.C. Conway, vol. 2. New York, 1902.
Paurmeister, Tobias. *De iurisdictione imperii Romani: Libri II, in quibus nobilissimum hoc iuris publici caput, . . . dilucide explicatur, et ad statum praesentem reipublicae a forma ac membris suis, . . . accurate descriptae accomodatur*. Hannover, 1608.
Pergen, Johann Anton Graf von. "Denkschrift über die Bedeutung des römischen Kaiserkrone für das Haus Österreich." In *Gesamtdeutsche Vergangenheit: Festgabe für Heinrich Ritter von Srbik zum 60. Geburtstag am 10. November 1938*, edited by Hans von Voltelini, 152–68. Munich, 1937.
Pfanner, Tobias. *Historia comitiorum imp. celebratorum. . . 1652, 1653 et 1654*. Jena, 1694.
Planitz, Hans von der. *Berichte aus dem Reichsregiment in Nürnberg 1521–1523*. Hildesheim, 1979; repr., Leipzig, 1899.
Prächtiger und feyerlicher Einzug Ihro Röm.-Kaiserlichen und Römisch-Königlichen Majestät wie solcher in des heil: Röm. Reichs Wahls-Stadt Frankfurt, den 29ten Märtz 1764 gehalten worden. Frankfurt am Main, 1764.
"Princeps in compendio" (1632). In *Staatslehre der Frühen Neuzeit: Die Entwicklung der deutschen Staatslehre vom Beginn der Neuzeit bis zur Aufklärung*, edited by Notker Hammerstein, 453–540. Bibliothek der Geschichte und Politik 16; Bibliothek deutscher Klassiker 130. Frankfurt am Main, 1995.
Pufendorf, Samuel. *Acht Bücher vom Natur- und Völkerrecht*. 2 vols. Frankfurt am Main, 1711; repr., Hildesheim, 2001.

———. *Die Verfassung des deutschen Reiches* (1667). Edited and translanted by Horst Denzer. Bibliothek des deutschen Staatsdenkens 4. Frankfurt am Main and Leipzig, 1994.
Pütter, Johann Stephan. *Historische Entwickelung der heutigen Staatsverfassung des Teutschen Reichs.* 3 vols. Göttingen, 1786–87.
———. *Litteratur des teutschen Staatsrechts.* 3 vols. Göttingen, 1776–83; repr., Frankfurt am Main, 1965.
———. *Patriotische Abbildung des heutigen Zustandes beyder höchsten Reichsgerichte....* [Göttingen], 1749.
Rauch, Karl, ed. *Traktat über den Reichstag im 16. Jahrhundert: Eine offiziöse Darstellung aus der Kurmainzischen Kanzlei.* Quellen und Studien zur Verfassungsgeschichte des Deutschen Reiches in Mittelalter und Neuzeit 1. Weimar, 1905.
Recueil des instructions données aux ambassadeurs et ministres de France depuis des Traités de Westphalie jusqu'à la Révolution Française. Vol. 18, *Diète germanique.* Edited by Bertrand Auerbach. Paris, 1912.
"Reflexiones eines Unpartheyischen über die Reichs-Tägliche Rang- und Ceremoniel-Disputen." In *Teutsches Staats-Archiv,* edited by Johann Jacob Moser, vol. 4, 139–49. Frankfurt and Leipzig, 1751.
Reinkingk, Theodor von. *Tractatus de regimine seculari et ecclesiastico: Exhibens brevem et methodicam iuris publici delineationem ac praecipuarum controversiarum, circa hodiernum Sacri Imperii Romani statum ac gubernationem ... resolutionem; cum indice capitum, rerum et verborum.* 5th ed. Frankfurt am Main, 1651.
Reuß, Johann Anton, ed. *Teutsche Staatskanzlei.* 15 vols. Ulm and Stettin, 1785–99.
Richenthal, Ulrich. *Chronik des Constanzer Conzils 1414–1418.* Edited by M. R. Buck. Tübingen, 1882.
Riedel, Adolph Friedrich. *Codex diplomaticus Brandenburgensis: Sammlung der Urkunden, Chroniken und sonstigen Quellenschriften für die Geschichte der Mark Brandenburg und ihrer Regenten.* 2 vols. Berlin, 1838–45.
Riesbeck, Johann Kaspar. *Briefe eines reisenden Franzosen über Deutschland an seinen Bruder zu Paris.* Zurich, 1783; repr., Berlin, 1976.
Roeder, Johannes Paul. *Codex historicus ... de fatis klinodiorum augustalium Norimbergae adservatorum....* Frankfurt and Leipzig, 1789.
Rohr, Julius Bernhard von. *Einleitung zur Ceremonial-Wissenschaft der großen Herren.* Berlin, 1729; repr., Leipzig, 1990.
———. *Einleitung zur Ceremonial-Wissenschaft der Privat-Personen.* Berlin, 1728; repr., Leipzig, 1990.
Scheidemantel, Heinrich Gottfried. *Repertorium des Teutschen Staats- und Lehnrechts.* 4 vols. Leipzig, 1782–95.
Schiller, Friedrich. *Deutsche Größe: Ein unvollendetes Gedicht Schillers 1801.* Facsimile of the manuscript on behest of the Goethe Gesellschaft, with an explanatory essay by Bernhard Suphan. Weimar, 1902.
Schirrmacher, Friedrich Wilhelm, ed. *Briefe und Acten zu der Geschichte des Religionsgesprächs zu Marburg 1529 und des Reichstags zu Augsburg 1530 nach der Handschrift des Joh. Aurifaber.* Gotha, 1876.
Schmid, Alois, ed. *Die Berichte der diplomatischen Vertreter des Kaiserhofes aus München an die Staatskanzlei zu Wien während der Regierungszeit des Kurfürsten Max III. Joseph.* Vol. 2, *1747–49.* Munich, 2000.
Schmidt, Sigismund. *Der eröffnete Teutsche Audientz-Saal / darinnen die gebräuchlichsten Curialien und Ceremonien enthalten seynd / Welche bey Käys. und Kön. Wahl und Crönungs-Solen[n]itäten beobachtet zu werden pflegen....* Frankfurt am Main, 1697.

Schottenloher, Otto. *Drei Frühdrucke zur Reichsgeschichte*. Veröffentlichungen der Gesellschaft für Typenkunde des XV. Jahrhunderts, Wiegendruckgesellschaft, Series B, 2. Mainz, 1486 and 1493; repr., Leipzig, 1938.

Schulz, Joachim Christoph Friedrich. *Reise nach Warschau: Eine Schilderung aus den Jahren 1791–1793*. Frankfurt am Main, 1996.

Schweder, Christoph H. von. *Introductio in ius publicum Imperii Romano-Germanici novissimum* (1st ed., 1681). 7th ed. Stuttgart, 1711.

———. *Theatrum historicum praetensionum et controversiarum illustrium in Europa: Historischer Schauplatz der Ansprüche und Streitigkeiten hoher Potentaten und anderer regierenden Herrschafften in Europa*. Leipzig, 1712.

Seitz, Philipp Johann Nepomuk. *Vollständiges Diarium Von der ... Krönung Des ... Herrn Josephs des Andern, Erwählten und gekrönten Römischen Königes, ... Von Ihro Kurfürstlichen Gnaden zu Mainz, Dem ... Herrn Emerich Joseph, des Heil: Stuhls zu Mainz Erzbischoffen, ... Zum Römischen Könige ... feierlich gesalbet und gekrönet worden ....* 3 vols. Mainz, 1767–71.

Sellert, Wolfgang, ed. *Die Ordnungen des Reichshofrates: 1550–1766*. 2 vols. Quellen und Forschungen zur höchsten Gerichtsbarkeit im alten Reich 8. Cologne, Weimar, and Vienna, 1980–90.

Senckenberg, Heinrich Christian von. *Sammlung von ungedruckt- und raren Schriften, zu Erläuterung des Staats- des gemeinen Bürgerlichen und Kirchen-Rechts*. Edited by Johann Erasmus Senckenberg. Vols. 1–4. Frankfurt am Main, 1745–51.

Sender, Clemens. *Die Chronik von Clemens Sender von den ältesten Zeiten der Stadt bis zum Jahre 1536*. Die Chroniken der deutschen Städte vom 14. bis ins 16. Jahrhundert 23. Leipzig, 1894.

Seyfert, Carl Andreas (Resp.), and Peter Müller (Praes.). *De iure investiendi status Imperii Germanici-Romani: Von Reichs-Belehnungen*. Jena, 1685.

Spalatin, Georg. *Annales reformationis, oder Jahr-Bücher von der Reformation Lutheri*. Edited by Ernst Salomon Cyprian. Leipzig, 1718.

Stieve, Gottfried. *Europäisches Hof-Ceremoniell*. 2nd ed. Leipzig, 1723.

Stollberg-Rilinger, Barbara, and André Krischer, ed. *Das Hofreisejournal des Kurfürsten Clemens August von Köln 1719–1745*. Ortstermine 12. Siegburg, 2000.

Sturm, Kaspar. *Geschichts beschreybung kaiser Karls V. belehnung umb das erzherzogtum Oesterreich, sampt anzeigung der fürstlichen ritterspiele in zeit des reichstags im 1530. jahr zu Augsburg gehalten*. n.p. [Augsburg], n.d. [1530].

———. *Kayserlicher Maiestat Einreyttung zu München / ... Wie kayserliche May. von den Churfürsten vnd Fürsten / in jrer Mayestat eynreyttung vor Augspurg den XV. Junij entpfangen ist. ....* n.p. [Nuremberg], n.d. [1530].

———. *Warhafftig anzaygung wie Kaiser Carl der fünft ettlichen Fürsten auff dem Reychstag zu Augspurg im M.CCCCC.XXX. jar gehalten, Regalia und Lehen under dem fan gelihen, was auch jr Kai. Maie. und derselben brüder ... Fürsten unnd Stende des Reichs für Räthe und Adelspersonen auff solchem Reichstag gehept haben*. Augsburg, 1530.

———. *Wie die Römische Keiserliche Majestät von Innsbruck aus zu Schwaz, München und 1530 zu Augsburg eingeritten, summarie beschrieben*. n.p. [Augsburg], n.d. [1530].

———. *Wiewol hievor in dreyen underschidlichen büchlein beschriben, und im Truck außgangen, Wie die Rö. Kai. Maie. von Inßpruck auß, zu Schwartz, München, und volgends auff angesetzten Reichstag, Anno etc. 1530. zu Augspurg eingeritten ....* Augsburg, 1530.

Tetleben, Valentin von. *Protokoll des Augsburger Reichstages 1530*. Edited with an introduction by Herbert Grundmann. Göttingen, 1958.

Theatrum Europaeum: Oder ausführlich fortgeführte Friedens- und Kriegsbeschreibung und was mehr von denckwürdigsten Geschichten in Europa, vornemlich aber in Hoch- und Nieder-Teutschland ... sich begeben haben. Vols. 1–21. Frankfurt am Main, 1646–1734.

Trexler, Richard, ed. *The Libro Ceremoniale of the Florentine Republic by Francesco Filarete and Angelo Manfidi.* Travaux d'humanisme et renaissance 165. Geneva, 1978.

Über die Irrungen, welche in Ansehung der Reichsbelehnungen überhaupt, ... , zwischen Kaiserlicher Majestät, dem Reichshofrath, und der Reichshofcanzley an einem, dann den H. R. Kurfürsten und alt fürstlichen Häusern am andern Theile, oberalten, Mit Beylagen. Nuremberg, 1791.

Uffenbach, Johann Christoph von. *Tractatus singularis et methodicus de excelsissimo consilio caesareo-imperiale aulico, Vom Kayserlichen Reichs-Hoff-Rath.* Frankfurt am Main, 1700.

Uhland, Robert, ed. *Tagbücher seiner Rayßen ... in den Jahren 1783–1791 vom Herzog Carl Eugen selbsten beschrieben.* Tübingen, 1968.

Urkunden und Actenstücke zur Geschichte des Kurfürsten Friedrich Wilhelm von Brandenburg. 23 vols. Berlin, 1864–1930.

Virck, Hans, ed. *Politische Correspondenz der Stadt Straßburg im Zeitalter der Reformation.* Vol. 1, *1517–1530.* Straßburg, 1882.

Vitriarius, Philipp Reinhard. *Institutiones juris publici Romano-Germanici selectae.* Leiden, 1686; repr., Nuremberg and Leipzig, 1727.

Wekhrlin, Wilhelm Ludwig. *Anselmus Rabiosus Reise durch Oberdeutschland.* Bibliothek des 18. Jahrhunderts. 1778; repr., Munich, 1988.

Wicquefort, Abraham de. *L'Ambassadeur et ses fonctions.* 2 vols. (1st ed., 1676). Amsterdam, 1746.

Zedler, Johann Heinrich, ed. *Großes vollständiges Universal-Lexicon aller Wissenschaften und Künste....* Halle and Leipzig, 1732–54.

Zeumer, Karl, ed. *Die Goldene Bulle Kaiser Karls IV.* 2 vols. Quellen und Studien zur Verfassungsgeschichte des Deutschen Reiches in Mittelalter und Neuzeit 2. Weimar, 1908; repr., Hildesheim, 1972.

Ziegler, Christoph, ed. *Wahl-Capitulationes, welche mit denen Römischen Kaysern und Königen, dann des H. Röm.Reichs Churfürsten als dessen vordersten Gliedern und Grund-Säulen ... Geding- und Pacts-weise auffgerichtet, vereiniget und verglichen ....* Frankfurt am Main, 1711.

Zwantzig, Zacharias. *Theatrum praecedentiae, oder Eines Theils illustrer Rang-Streit, Andern Theils illustre Rang-Ordnung ....* Berlin, 1706.

Literature

1495—Kaiser, Reich, Reformen: Der Reichstag zu Worms; Ausstellung des Landeshauptarchivs Koblenz in Verbindung mit der Stadt Worms zum 500jährigen Jubiläum des Wormser Reichstags von 1495. Koblenz, 1995.

1495—Württemberg wird Herzogtum: Dokumente aus dem Hauptstaatsarchiv Stuttgart zu einem epochalen Ereignis. Edited by Stephan Molitor. Stuttgart, 1995.

1648—Krieg und Frieden in Europa. Published by the Veranstaltungsgesellschaft 350 Jahre Westfälischer Friede. Münster, 1998.

Albrecht, Dieter. *Die auswärtige Politik Maximilians von Bayern: 1618–1635.* Schriftenreihe der Historischen Kommission bei der Bayerischen Akademie der Wissenschaften 6. Göttingen, 1962.

———, ed. *Regensburg—Stadt der Reichstage: Vom Mittelalter zur Neuzeit.* Regensburg, 1994.

Allgemeine Deutsche Biographie. Published by the Historische Commission bei der Königl. Akademie der Wissenschaften. 56 vols. Leipzig, 1875–1912; repr., 1967–71.

Althoff, Gerd. "Freiwilligkeit und Konsensfassaden: Emotionale Ausdrucksformen in der Politik des Mittelalters." In *Pathos, Affekt, Gefühl: Die Emotionen in den Künsten,* edited by Klaus Herding and Bernhard Stumpfhaus, 145–61. Berlin, 2004.

———. "Der frieden-, bündnis- und gemeinschaftsstiftende Charakter des Mahles im früheren Mittelalter." In *Essen und Trinken in Mittelalter und Neuzeit: Vorträge eines interdisziplinären Symposions vom 10.-13. Juni 1987 an der Justus-Liebig-Universität Gießen,* edited by Irmgard Bitsch, 13–26. Sigmaringen, 1987.

———. "Gefühle in der öffentlichen Kommunikation des Mittelalters." In *Emotionalität: Zur Geschichte der Gefühle,* edited by Claudia Bentien, Anne Fleig, and Ingrid Kasten, 82–99. Literatur—Kultur—Geschlecht; Kleine Reihe 16. Vienna, 2000.

———. "Herrscherbegegnung oder: Inszenierung verpflichtet—Zum Verständnis ritueller Akte bei Papst-Kaiser-Begegnungen im 12. Jahrhundert." *Frühmittelalterliche Studien* 35 (2001): 61–84.

———. "Humiliatio—exaltation: Zur Genealogie eines rituellen Verhaltens- und Erzählmusters." In *Text und Kontext: Fallstudien und theoretische Begründungen einer kulturwissenschaftlich angeleiteten Mediävistik,* edited by Jan-Dirk Müller, 39–51. Schriften des Historischen Kollegs. Munich, 2005.

———. "Körper, Emotionen, Rituale." In *MedienRevolutionen,* edited by Ralf Schell, transcript, 13–36. Bielefeld, 2006.

———. *Die Macht der Rituale: Symbolik und Herrschaft im Mittelalter.* Darmstadt, 2003.

———. *Spielregeln der Politik im Mittelalter: Kommunikation in Frieden und Fehde.* Darmstadt, 1997.

———. "Studien zur habsburgischen Merowingersage." *Mitteilungen des Instituts für österreichische Geschichtsforschung* 87 (1979): 71–100.

Althoff, Gerd, and Barbara Stollberg-Rilinger. "Rituale der Macht in Mittelalter und Früher Neuzeit." In *Die neue Kraft der Rituale,* edited by Axel Michaels, 141–77. Heidelberg, 2007.

Althoff, Gerd, and Christiane Witthöft. "Les services symboliques entre dignité et contrainte." *Annales* 58 (2003): 1293–1318.

Andretta, Stefano. "Cerimoniale e diplomazia pontificia nel XVII secolo." In *Cérémonial et rituel à Rome (XVIe–XIXe siècles),* edited by Maria Antonietta Visceglia and Catherine Brice, 201–222. Rome, 1997.

Angenendt, Arnold. *Geschichte der Religiosität im Mittelalter.* 3rd ed. Darmstadt, 2005.

Angermeier, Heinz. *Die Reichsreform 1410–1555: Die Staatsproblematik in Deutschland zwischen Mittelalter und Gegenwart.* Munich, 1984.

———. "Der Wormser Reichstag 1495—ein europäisches Ereignis." *Historische Zeitschrift* 261 (1995): 739–68.

Annas, Gabriele, and Heribert Müller. "Kaiser, Kurfürsten und auswärtige Mächte: Zur Bedeutung der Goldenen Bulle im Rahmen von Reichsversammlungen und Konzilien des 15. Jahrhunderts." In *Die Kaisermacher; Frankfurt am Main und die Goldene Bulle. 1356–1806. Eine Ausstellung des Instituts für Stadtgeschichte. Frankfurt am Main, 30. September 2006 bis 14. Januar 2007,* edited by Evelyn Brockhoff and Michael Matthäus, 106–29. Frankfurt am Main, 2006.

Aretin, Karl Ottmar von. *Das Alte Reich 1648–1806*. Vol. 1, *Föderalistische oder hierarchische Ordnung (1648–1684)*; vol. 2, *Kaisertradition und österreichische Großmachtpolitik (1684–1745)*; vol. 3, *Das Reich und der österreichisch-preußische Dualismus (1745–1806)*. Stuttgart, 1993–97.

———. "Das Alte Reich, eine Föderation?" In *Faszinierende Frühneuzeit: Reich, Frieden, Kultur und Kommunikation 1500–1800, Festschrift für Johannes Burkhardt zum 65. Geburtstag*, edited by Wolfgang E. J. Weber and Regina Dauser, 15–26. Berlin, 2008.

———. *Heiliges Römisches Reich: 1776–1806; Reichsverfassung und Staatssouveränität*. 2 vols. Veröffentlichungen des Instituts für Europäische Geschichte, Mainz, Abteilung Universalgeschichte 38. Wiesbaden, 1967.

———. "Reichshofrat und Reichskammergericht in den Reformplänen Josephs II." In *Friedenssicherung und Rechtsgewährung*, edited by Bernhard Diestelkamp and Ingrid Scheuermann, 51–82. Bonn and Wetzlar, 1997.

Arlinghaus, Franz-Josef. "Gesten, Kleidung und die Etablierung von Diskursräumen im städtischen Gerichtswesen (1350–1650)." In *Kommunikation und Medien in der Frühen Neuzeit*, edited by Johannes Burkhardt and Christine Werkstetter, 461–98. Munich, 2005.

Arndt, Johannes. *Das niederrheinisch-westfälische Reichsgrafenkollegium und seine Mitglieder (1653–1806)*. Veröffentlichungen des Instituts für Europäische Geschichte Mainz 133; Beiträge zur Sozial- und Verfassungsgeschichte des Alten Reiches 9. Mainz, 1991.

Asch, Ronald G. "Estates and Princes after 1648: The Consequences of the Thirty Years War." *German History* 6 (1988): 113–32.

———. "The 'ius foederis' Re-examined: The Peace of Westphalia and the Constitution of the Holy Roman Empire." In *Peace Treaties and international Law in European History: From the Late Middle Ages to World War One*, edited by Randall Lesaffer, 319–37. Cambridge, 2004.

Aulinger, Rosemarie. *Das Bild des Reichstages im 16. Jahrhundert: Beiträge zu einer typologischen Analyse schriftlicher und bildlicher Quellen*. Schriftenreihe der Historischen Kommission bei der Bayerischen Akademie der Wissenschaften 18. Göttingen, 1980.

———. "Die Reichstage des 16. Jahrhunderts im Spiegel bildlicher Quellen." In *Der Reichstag: Kommunikation—Wahrnehmung—Öffentlichkeiten*, edited by Maximilian Lanzinner and Arno Strohmeyer, 313–41. Göttingen, 2006.

Aulinger, Rosemarie, Ursula Machoczek, and Silvia Schweinzer-Burian. "Ferdinand I. und die Reichstage unter Kaiser Karl V. (1521–1555)." In *Kaiser Ferdinand I.: Aspekte eines Herrscherlebens*, edited by Martina Fuchs and Alfred Kohler, 87–122. Münster, 2003.

Bauer, Thomas. "Wahl und Krönung." In *FFM 1200: Traditionen u. Perspektiven einer Stadt*, edited by Lothar Gall, 153–82. Sigmaringen, 1994.

Bauer, Volker. "Höfische Gesellschaft und höfische Öffentlichkeit im Alten Reich: Überlegungen zur Mediengeschichte des Fürstenhofs im 17. und 18. Jahrhundert." *Jahrbuch für Kommunikationsgeschichte* 5 (2003): 29–68.

———. *Repertorium territorialer Amtskalender und Amtshandbücher im Alten Reich*. Vol. 4. Frankfurt am Main, 2005.

Beales, Derek Edward Dawson. *Joseph II*. Vol. 1, *In the Shadow of Maria Theresa* (only 1 vol. published). Cambridge, 1997.

Becht, Michael. *Pium consensum tueri: Studien zum Begriff "consensus" im Werk von Erasmus von Rotterdam, Philipp Melanchthon und Johannes Calvin*. Reformationsgeschichtliche Studien und Texte 144. Münster, 2000.

Becker, Hans-Jürgen. "Kaiserkrönung." In *Handwörterbuch zur deutschen Rechtsgeschichte*, edited by Adalbert Erler, vol. 2, 555–61. Berlin, 1978.

———. "Protestatio, Protest: Funktion und Funktionswandel eines rechtlichen Instruments." *Zeitschrift für Historische Forschung* 5 (1978): 385–412.

———. "Recht und Politik auf dem Immerwährenden Reichstag zu Regensburg." In *Reichsstadt und Immerwährender Reichstag (1663–1806): 250 Jahre Haus Thurn und Taxis in Regensburg*, 235–51. Thurn-und-Taxis-Studien 20. Kallmünz, 2001.

Becker, Hans-Jürgen, and Karl-Heinz Ruess, eds. *Die Reichkleinodien: Herrschaftszeichen des Heiligen Römischen Reiches*. Schriften zur staufischen Geschichte und Kunst 16. Göppingen, 1997.

Becker, Winfried. *Der Kurfürstenrat: Grundzüge seiner Entwicklung in der Reichsverfassung und seine Stellung auf dem Westfälischen Friedenskongreß*. Schriftenreihe der Vereinigung zur Erforschung der Neueren Geschichte e.V. 5. Münster, 1973.

———. "Die Verhandlungen der Reichsstände über die Confessio Augustana als Ringen um Einheit und Kirchenreform." In *Confessio Augustana und Confutatio: Der Augsburger Reichstag 1530 und die Einheit der Kirche—Internationales Symposium der Gesellschaft zur Herausgabe des Corpus Catholicorum in Augsburg vom 3.-7. September 1979*, edited by Erwin Iserloh, 127–54. Münster, 1980.

Beemelmans, Wilhelm. "Der Sessionsstreit zwischen Köln und Kölnischen Aachen." *Jahrbuch des Geschichtsvereins Köln* 18 (1926): 65–110.

Beetz, Manfred. *Frühmoderne Höflichkeit: Komplimentierkunst und gesellschaftliche Rituale im altdeutschen Sprachraum*. Stuttgart, 1990.

———. "Überlebtes Welttheater: Goethes autobiographische Darstellung der Wahl und Krönung Josephs II. in Frankfurt am Main. 1764." In *Zeremoniell als höfische Ästhetik in Spätmittelalter und Früher Neuzeit*, edited by Jörg Jochen Berns and Thomas Rahn, 572–99. Tübingen, 1995.

Begert, Alexander. *Böhmen, die böhmische Kur und das Reich vom Hochmittelalter bis zum Ende des alten Reiches: Studien zur Kurwürde und staatsrechtlichen Stellung Böhmens*. Historische Studien 475. Husum, 2003.

Beinert, Wolfgang. "Der Sakramentsbegriff der Confessio Augustana." In *Confessio Augustana und Confutatio: Der Augsburger Reichstag 1530 und die Einheit der Kirche—Internationales Symposium der Gesellschaft zur Herausgabe des Corpus Catholicorum in Augsburg vom 3.-7. September 1979*, edited by Erwin Iserloh, 440–42. Münster, 1980.

Belting, Hans. *An Anthropology of Images. Picture, Medium, Body*. Princeton, 2014.

Bély, Lucien. "Souveraineté et souverains: La question du cérémonial dans les relations internationales à l'époque moderne." *Annuaire-Bulletin de la Société de l'Histoire de France*, 1993, 27–43.

Bély, Lucien, and Isabelle Richefort, eds. *L'invention de la diplomatie: Moyen Age, les Temps modernes*. Paris, 1998.

Berbig, Hans Joachim. "Der Krönungsritus im Alten Reich (1648–1806)." *Zeitschrift für bayerische Landesgeschichte* 38 (1975): 639–700.

Berger, Peter L. "Anwesenheit und Abwesenheit. Raumbezüge sozialen Handelns." *Berliner Jahrbuch für Soziologie*, 1995, 99–111.

Berger, Peter L., and Thomas Luckmann. *The Social Construction of Reality: A Treatise in the Sociology of Knowledge*. New York 1966.

Berns, Jörg Jochen. "Die Festkultur der deutschen Höfe zwischen 1580 und 1730—eine Problemskizze in typologischer Absicht." *Germanisch-romanische Monatsschrift*, n.s., 34 (1984): 295–311.

---. "Herrscherliche Klangkunst und höfische Hallräume: Zur zeremoniellen Funktion akustischer Zeichen." In *Zeichen und Raum: Ausstattung und höfisches Zeremoniell in den deutschen Schlössern der frühen Neuzeit*, 49–64. Munich and Berlin, 2006.

---. "Luthers Papstkritik als Zeremoniellkritik: Zur Bedeutung des päpstlichen Zeremoniells für das fürstliche Hofzeremoniell der Frühen Neuzeit." In *Zeremoniell als höfische Ästhetik in Spätmittelalter und Früher Neuzeit*, edited by Jörg Jochen Berns, 157–73. Tübingen, 1995.

---. "Der nackte Monarch und die nackte Wahrheit: Auskünfte der deutschen Zeitungs- und Zeremoniellschriften des späten 17. und frühen 18. Jahrhunderts zum Verhältnis von Hof und Öffentlichkeit." In *Daphnis* 11 (1982): 315–49.

Bertelli, Sergio. *The King's Body: Sacred Rituals of Power in Medieval and Early Modern Europe*. Pennsylvania, 2001.

Bierther, Kathrin. *Der Regensburger Reichstag von 1640/1641*. Regensburger historische Forschungen 1. Kallmünz, 1971.

Blänkner, Reinhard. "Integration durch Verfassung? Die 'Verfassung' in den institutionellen Symbolordnungen des 19. Jh. in Deutschland." In *Integration durch Verfassung*, edited by Hans Vorländer, 213–36. Wiesbaden, 2001.

---. "Verfassung als symbolische Ordnung: Zur politischen Kultur des Konstitutionalismus in Deutschland 1790–1840." In *Marianne—Germania: Deutsch-französischer Kulturtransfer im europäischen Kontext, 1789–1914*, edited by Etienne François, 157–82. Leipzig, 1998.

Blanning, Timothy C. W. *Joseph II*. London and New York, 1994.

Blickle, Peter. *Kommunalisierung und Christianisierung: Voraussetzungen und Folgen der Reformation 1400–1600*. Berlin, 1989.

Blockmans, Wim, ed. *Emperor Charles V 1500–1558*. London, 2002.

Bohn, Cornelia. *Schriftlichkeit und Gesellschaft: Kommunikation und Sozialität in der Neuzeit*. Opladen, 1999.

Boldt, Hans. "1495–1995: Der Reichstag zu Worms in der deutschen Verfassungsgeschichte." In *1495—Kaiser, Reich, Reformen: Der Reichstag zu Worms; Ausstellung des Landeshauptarchivs Koblenz in Verbindung mit der Stadt Worms zum 500jährigen Jubiläum des Wormser Reichstags von 1495*. Koblenz, 1995.

---. *Deutsche Verfassungsgeschichte: Politische Strukturen und ihr Wandel*. Munich, 1984.

---. *Einführung in die Verfassungsgeschichte: Zwei Abhandlungen zu ihrer Methodik und Geschichte*. Düsseldorf, 1984.

Boll, Walter. *Reichstagsmuseum*. 3rd ed. Sammlungen der Stadt Regensburg 9. Regensburg, 1968.

Bölling, Jörg. "Causa differentiae: Rang- und Präzedenzregelungen für Fürsten, Herzöge und Gesandte im vortridentinischen Papstzeremoniell." In *Rom und das Reich vor der Reformation*, edited by Nikolaus Staubach and Peter Land, 147–96. Frankfurt am Main, 2004.

---. *Das Papstzeremoniell der Renaissance: Texte—Musik—Performanz*. Frankfurt am Main, 2006.

Bönnen, Gerold. "Zwischen Bischof, Reich und Kurpfalz: Worms im späten Mittelalter (1250–1520)." In *Geschichte der Stadt Worms*, edited by Gerold Bönnen, 193–261. Stuttgart, 2005.

Boockmann, Hartmut. *Geschäfte und Geschäftigkeit auf dem Reichstag im späten Mittelalter*. Schriften des Historischen Kollegs 17. Munich, 1988.

Börger, Robert. *Belehnungen der deutschen geistlichen Fürsten nach dem Wormser Konkordat*. Leipziger Studien aus dem Gebiet der Geschichte 1. Leipzig, 1901.

Bourdieu, Pierre. "Einsetzungsriten." In *Was heißt sprechen? Die Ökonomie des sprachlichen Tausches*, 84–93. Vienna, 1990.

———. *The Logic of Practice*. Translated by Richard Nice. Stanford, CA, 1990.

———. "Ökonomisches Kapital, kulturelles Kapital, soziales Kapital." In *Soziale Ungleichheiten*, edited by Reinhard Kreckel, 183–98. Göttingen, 1983. English translation: "The forms of capital." In Handbook of Theory and Research for the Sociology of Education, edited by J. Richardson, 241–258. New York, 1986.

Brady, Thomas A. *German Histories in the Age of Reformations, 1400–1650*. Cambridge, 2009.

Brandi, Karl. *Kaiser Karl V. Werden und Schicksal einer Persönlichkeit und eines Weltreiches*. 8th ed. Frankfurt am Main, 1986.

Braun, Bettina. "Seelsorgebischof oder absolutistischer Fürst? Die Fürstbischöfe in der Spätphase des Alten Reichs zwischen Anspruch und Wirklichkeit." In *Geistliche Staaten im Nordwesten des Alten Reiches*, edited by Bettina Braun, Frank Göttmann, and Michael Ströhmer, 87–116. Paderborner Beiträge zur Geschichte 13. Paderborn, 2003.

Braungart, Georg. *Hofberedsamkeit: Studien zur Praxis höfisch-politischer Rede im deutschen Territorialabsolutismus*. Tübingen, 1988.

Bredekamp, Horst. *Thomas Hobbes / Der Leviathan: Das Urbild des modernen Staates und seine Gegenbilder 1651–2001*. Berlin, 2002.

Brockhoff, Evelyn, and Michael Matthäus, eds. *Die Kaisermacher: Frankfurt am Main und die Goldene Bulle. 1356–1806. Eine Ausstellung des Instituts für Stadtgeschichte. Frankfurt am Main, 30. September 2006 bis 14. Januar 2007*. Frankfurt am Main, 2006.

Bruckauf, Julius. *Fahnlehen und Fahnenbelehnung im alten deutschen Reiche*. Leipziger historische Abhandlungen 3. Leipzig, 1907.

Brunner, Otto. *Land und Herrschaft: Grundfragen der territorialen Verfassungsgeschichte Österreichs im Mittelalter*. 5th ed. 1965; repr., Darmstadt, 1984. Published in English as *Land and Lordship: Structures of Governance in Medieval Austria*, translated by Howard Kaminsky and James van Horn Melton. Philadelphia, 1992.

Brunsson, Nils. *The Organization of Hypocrisy: Talk, Decisions and Actions in Organizations*. 2nd ed. Copenhagen, 2002.

Buchstab, Günter. *Reichsstädte, Städtekurie und Westfälischer Friedenskongreß*. Münster, 1976.

Bulst, Neithard, and Robert Jütte, eds. "Zwischen Sein und Schein: Kleidung und Identität in der ständischen Gesellschaft." *Saeculum* 44 (1993): 1–112.

Burgdorf, Wolfgang. *Reichskonstitution und Nation: Verfassungsreformprojekte für das Heilige Römische Reich Deutscher Nation im politischen Schrifttum von 1648 bis 1806*. Veröffentlichungen des Instituts für Europäische Geschichte Mainz 173. Mainz, 1998.

———. *Ein Weltbild verliert seine Welt: Der Untergang des Alten Reiches und die Generation 1806*. Munich, 2006.

Burkhardt, Johannes. "Das größte Friedenswerk der Neuzeit: Der Westfälische Frieden in neuer Perspektive." *Geschichte in Wissenschaft und Unterricht* 49 (1998): 592–612.

———. *Das Reformationsjahrhundert: Deutsche Geschichte zwischen Medienrevolution und Institutionenbildung 1517–1617*. Stuttgart, 2002.

———. "Verfassungsprofil und Leistungsbilanz des Immerwährenden Reichstags: Zur Evaluierung einer frühmodernen Institution." In *Reichsständische Libertät und habsburgisches Kaisertum*, edited by Heinz Durchhardt, 151–83. Mainz, 1999.

———. *Vollendung und Neuorientierung des frühmodernen Reiches: 1648–1763*. Gebhardt Handbuch der deutschen Geschichte 11. Stuttgart, 2006.

Cassirer, Ernst. *Philosophie der symbolischen Formen.* 3 vols. Hamburg, 2001–2. Also published as *Gesammelte Werke: Hamburger Ausgabe,* edited by Birgit Recki, vols. 11–13.
Chartier, Roger. *Cultural History: Between Practices and Representations.* Ithaca, NY, 1988.
———. *Die unvollendete Vergangenheit: Geschichte und die Macht der Weltauslegung.* Berlin, 1989.
Christ, Günter. "Der Exzellenz-Titel für die kurfürstlichen Gesandten auf dem Westfälischen Friedenskongreß." *Parliaments, Estates and Representation* 19 (1999): 89–102.
———. *Praesentia Regis: Kaiserliche Diplomatie und Reichskirchenpolitik vornehmlich am Beispiel des Zeremoniells für die kaiserlichen Wahlgesandten in Würzburg und Bamberg.* Wiesbaden, 1975.
Conze, Werner. "Stand, Klasse." In *Geschichtliche Grundbegriffe: Historisches Lexikon zur politisch-sozialen Sprache in Deutschland,* edited by Otto Brunner, Werner Conze, and Reinhart Koselleck, vol. 6, 200–17. Stuttgart, 1990.
Corterier, Peter. "Der Reichstag: Seine Kompetenzen und sein Verfahren in der zweiten Hälfte des 18. Jahrhunderts." Dissertation, Bonn, 1972.
Cosandey, Fanny. *La Reine de France: Symbole et pouvoir XVe–XVIIIe siècle.* Paris, 2000.
Coy, Jan Philip, Benjamin Marschke, and David Warren Sabean, eds. *The Holy Roman Empire Reconsidered.* Spektrum: Publications of the German Studies Association 1. New York and Oxford, 2010.
Daniel, Ute. "Clio unter Kulturschock: Zu den aktuellen Debatten der Geschichtswissenschaft." Parts 1 and 2. *Geschichte in Wissenschaft und Unterricht* 48 (1997): 195–219 and 259–78.
———. *Kompendium Kulturgeschichte: Theorien, Praxis, Schlüsselwörter.* Frankfurt am Main, 2001.
Darnton, Robert. "A Bouregois Puts His World in Order: The City as a Text." In *The Great Cat Massacre, and Other Episodes in French Cultural History,* 107–43. New York, 1984.
Dartmann, Christoph, Marian Füssel, and Stefanie Rüther, eds. *Raum und Konflikt: Zur symbolischen Konstituierung gesellschaftlicher Ordnung in Mittelalter und Früher Neuzeit.* Münster, 2004.
Dartmann, Christoph, and Hagen Keller. "Inszenierungen von Ordnung und Konsens: Privileg und Statutenbuch in der symbolischen Kommunikation mittelalterlicher Rechtsgemeinschaften." In *Zeichen—Rituale—Werte,* edited by Gerd Althoff, 201–23. Münster, 2004.
Decot, Rolf. "Confessio Augustana und Reichsverfassung: Die Religionsfrage in den Reichstagsverhandlungen des 16. Jahrhunderts." In *Im Schatten der Confessio Augustana: Die Religionsverhandlungen des Augsburger Reichstages 1530 im historischen Kontext,* edited by Herbert Immekötter, 19–49. Münster, 1997.
Demel, Walter. *Reich, Reformen und sozialer Wandel: 1763–1806.* Gebhardt Handbuch der deutschen Geschichte 12. Stuttgart, 2005.
Denzer, Horst, ed. *Jean Bodin: Verhandlungen der Internationalen Bodin-Tagung in München.* Münchener Studien zur Politik 18. Munich, 1973.
———. "Spätaristotelismus, Naturrecht und Reichsreform: Politische Ideen in Deutschland 1600–1750." In *Pipers Handbuch der politischen Ideen,* edited by Iring Fetscher and Herfried Münkler, vol. 3, 233–74. Munich and Zürich, 1985.
Dickmann, Fritz. *Der Westfälische Frieden.* 7th ed. Münster, 1998.
———. "Der Westfälische Friede und die Reichsverfassung." In *Forschungen und Studien zur Geschichte des Westfälischen Friedens,* edited by Max Braubach, 5–32. Schriftenreihe der Vereinigung zur Erforschung der Neueren Geschichte 1. Münster, 1965.

Dilcher, Gerhard. "Vom ständischen Herrschaftsvertrag zum Verfassungsgesetz." *Der Staat* 27 (1988): 161–93.
Dölemeyer, Barbara. "Reichsrecht, politische Propaganda und Festbeschreibung in den Wahl- und Krönungsdiarien." In *Die Kaisermacher: Frankfurt am Main und die Goldene Bulle—1356–1806*, edited by Evelyn Brockhoff and Michael Matthäus, 140–51. Frankfurt am Main, 2006.
Domke, Waldemar. *Die Virilstimmen im Reichs-Fürstenrath von 1495 bis 1654*. Breslau, 1882.
Dörner, Andreas. *Politainment: Politik in der medialen Erlebnisgesellschaft*. Frankfurt am Main, 2001.
———. *Politischer Mythos und symbolische Politik: Der Hermannsmythos—zur Entstehung des Nationalbewußtseins der Deutschen*. Reinbek, 1996.
Dotzauer, Winfried. "Anrufung und Messe vom Heiligen Geist bei Königswahl und Reichstagen in Mittelalter und Früher Neuzeit." Part 1, *Archiv für mittelrheinische Kirchengeschichte* 33 (1981): 11–44; part 2, *Archiv für mittelrheinische Kirchengeschichte* 34 (1982): 11–36.
———. "Die Ausformung der frühneuzeitlichen deutschen Thronerhebung: Stellenwert, Handlung und Zeremoniell unter dem Einfluß von Säkularisation und Reformation." *Archiv für Kulturgeschichte* 68 (1986): 25–80.
———. "Die Entstehung der frühneuzeitlichen deutschen Thronerhebung: Säkularisation und Reformation." In *Herrscherweihe und Königskrönung im frühneuzeitlichen Europa*, edited by Heinz Durchhardt, 1–20. Wiesbaden, 1983.
Duchhardt, Heinz. *Balance of Power und Pentarchie: Internationale Beziehungen 1700–1785*. Handbuch der Geschichte der Internationalen Beziehungen 4. Paderborn, 1997.
———. *Deutsche Verfassungsgeschichte 1495–1806*. Stuttgart, 1991.
———, ed. *Herrscherweihe und Königskrönung im frühneuzeitlichen Europa*. Schriften der Mainzer Philosophischen Fakultätsgesellschaft 8. Wiesbaden, 1983.
———. "Krönungen außerhalb Aachens: Die Habsburger bis 1806." In *Krönungen: Könige in Aachen. Geschichte und Mythos. Katalog der Ausstellung in zwei Bänden*, edited by Mario Kramp, vol. 2, 636–42. Mainz, 2000.
———, ed. *Der Westfälische Friede: Diplomatie—politische Zäsur—kulturelles Umfeld—Rezeptionsgeschichte*. Historische Zeitschrift: Beihefte, n.s., 26. Munich, 1998.
Duchhardt, Heinz, and Matthias Schnettger, eds. *Reichsständische Libertät und Habsburgisches Kaisertum*. Mainz, 1999.
Duhamelle, Christophe. *La frontière au village: Une identité catholique allemande au temps des Lumières*. Paris, 2012.
Duindam, Jeroen. "The Habsburg Court in Vienna: Kaiserhof or Reichshof?" In *The Holy Roman Empire 1495–1806: A European Perspective*, edited by R. J. W. Evans and Peter H. Wilson, 91–119. Leiden, 2012.
———. *Vienna and Versailles: The Courts of Europes Dynastic Rivals, 1550–1780*. Cambridge, 2003.
Dürr, Renate. *Politische Kultur in der Frühen Neuzeit*. Gütersloh, 2006.
Dykmans, Marc. *Le cérémonial papal de la fin du moyen âge à la Renaissance*. 4 vols. Vatican City, 1977–85.
Ebel, Wilhelm. *Geschichte der Gesetzgebung in Deutschland*. 2nd ed., 1958; exp. repr. ed., Göttingen, 1988.
Edelman, Murray. *The Symbolic Uses of Politics*. Urbana, 1985.

———. *Politik als Ritual: Die symbolische Funktion staatlicher Institutionen und politischen Handelns.* With a foreword by Claus Offe and an afterword by Frank Nullmeier. 3rd, expanded ed. Frankfurt am Main and New York, 2005.

Ehrenpreis, Stefan. *Kaiserliche Gerichtsbarkeit und Konfessionskonflikt: Der Reichshofrat unter Rudolf II.; 1576–1612.* Schriftenreihe der Historischen Kommission bei der Bayerischen Akademie der Wissenschaften 72. Göttingen, 2006.

Eichhorn, Karl Friedrich. *Deutsche Staats- und Rechtsgeschichte.* 5th, improved ed. Göttingen, 1844.

Eire, Carlos M. *War Against the Idols: The Reformation of Warship from Erasmus to Calvin.* New York, 1986.

Emich, Birgit. "Bildlichkeit und Intermedialität in der frühen Neuzeit: Eine interdisziplinäre Spurensuche." *Zeitschrift für Historische Forschung* 35 (2008): 31–56.

Enzyklopädie der Neuzeit. Edited by Friedrich Jaeger. 15 vols. Stuttgart, 2005–2011.

Erdmannsdörffer, Bernhard. *Deutsche Geschichte vom Westfälischen Frieden bis zum Regierungsantritt Friedrichs des Grossen: 1648–1740.* 2 vols. 1932; repr., Wiesbaden, 1962.

Evans, Robert J. W., Michael Schaich, and Peter H. Wilson, eds. *The Holy Roman Empire 1495–1806.* Studies of the German Historical Institute London. Oxford, 2011.

Evans, Robert J. W., and Peter H. Wilson, eds. *The Holy Roman Empire, 1495–1806: A European Perspective.* Leiden, 2011.

Externbrink, Sven. *Friedrich der Große, Maria Theresia und das Alte Reich: Deutschlandbild und Entscheidungsprozesse in der Außenpolitik Frankreichs im Siebenjährigen Krieg.* Berlin, 2006.

Fillitz, Hermann. "Die Reichskleinodien: Ein Versuch zur Erklärung ihrer Entstehung und Entwicklung." In *Heilig, römisch, deutsch: Das Reich im mittelalterlichen Europa; Internationale Tagung zur 29. Ausstellung des Europarates und Landesausstellung Sachsen-Anhalt,* edited by Bernd Schneidmüller, 133–61. Dresden, 2006.

———. *Die Schatzkammer in Wien.* Vienna and Munich, 1964.

Fößel, Amalie. *Die Königin im mittelalterlichen Reich: Herrschaftsausübung, Herrschaftsrechte, Handlungsspielräume.* Mittelalter-Forschungen 4. Sigmaringen, 2000.

Foucault, Michel. *The Order of Things.* New York, 1970.

François, Etienne. *Die unsichtbare Grenze: Protestanten und Katholiken in Augsburg 1648–1806.* Abhandlungen zur Geschichte der Stadt Augsburg, n.s., 33. Sigmaringen, 1991.

Frevert, Ute. "Neue Politikgeschichte: Konzepte und Herausforderungen." In *Neue Politikgeschichte: Perspektiven einer historischen Politikforschung,* edited by Ute Frevert and Heinz-Gerhard Haupt, 7–26. Frankfurt am Main, 2005.

Freytag, Rudolf. "Das Prinzipalkommissariat des Fürsten Alexander Ferdinand von Thurn und Taxis." *Jahrbuch des Historischen Vereins Dillingen* 25 (1912): 1–26.

———. "Vom Sterben des immerwährenden Reichstags." *Verhandlungen des Historischen Vereins für Oberpfalz und Regensburg* 84 (1934): 185–235.

Friedeburg, Robert von. *Widerstandsrecht und Konfessionskonflikt: Notwehr und gemeiner Mann im deutsch-britischen Vergleich 1530–1669.* Schriften zur europäischen Rechts- und Verfassungsgeschichte 27. Berlin, 1999.

Friedeburg, Robert von, and Michael J. Seidler. "The Holy Roman Empire of the German Nation." In *European Political Thought, 1450–1700,* vol. 1, 102–55. New Haven, CT, and London, 2008.

Friedrich, Susanne. *Drehscheibe Regensburg: Das Informations- und Kommunikationssystem des Immerwährenden Reichstags um 1700.* Colloquia Augustana 23. Berlin, 2007.

Frigo, Daniela. *Principe, ambasciatori e "jus gentium."* Rome, 1991.
Fröschl, Thomas. "'Das organisierte Chaos': Lehnswesen und Feudalsystem als Ordnungsprinzipien im Heiligen Römischen Reich." In *Die Fürstenberger: 800 Jahre Herrschaft und Kultur in Mitteleuropa*, edited by Erwein H. Eltz and Arno Strohmeyer, 39–44. Kronenburg, 1994.
Fuchs, Martina, and Alfred Kohler, eds. *Kaiser Ferdinand I.: Aspekte eines Herrscherlebens.* Münster, 2003.
Fuchs, Thomas. *Konfession und Gespräch: Typologie und Funktion der Religionsgespräche in der Reformationszeit.* Norm und Struktur 4. Cologne et al., 1995.
Führer, Jochen A. "Kaiserinnenkrönungen in Frankfurt am Main." In *Die Kaisermacher: Frankfurt am Main und die Goldene Bulle—1356–1806*, edited by Evelyn Brockhoff and Michael Matthäus, 294–305. Frankfurt am Main, 2006.
Fürnrohr, Walter. "Der Immerwährende Reichstag—die Repräsentation des Alten Reiches." *Geschichte in Wissenschaft und Unterricht* 15 (1964): 684–700.
———. *Der Immerwährende Reichstag zu Regensburg: Das Parlament des alten Reiches—Zur 300-Jahrfeier seiner Eröffnung 1663.* Regensburg, 1963.
Füssel, Marian. *Gelehrtenkultur als symbolische Praxis: Rang, Ritual und Konflikt an der Universität der Frühen Neuzeit.* Darmstadt, 2006.
———. "Rang und Raum: Gesellschaftliche Kartographie und die soziale Logik des Raumes an frühneuzeitlichen Universitäten." In *Raum und Konflikt: Zur symbolischen Konstituierung gesellschaftlicher Ordnung in Mittelalter und Früher Neuzeit*, edited by Christoph Darmann, Marian Füssel, and Stefanie Rüther, 175–97. Münster, 2004.
Füssel, Marian, and Thomas Weller, eds. *Ordnung und Distinktion: Praktiken sozialer Repräsentation in der ständischen Gesellschaft.* Münster, 2005.
Gagliardo, John. *Germany Under the Old Regime 1600–1790.* London, 1991.
———. *Reich and Nation: The Holy Roman Empire as Idea and Reality 1763–1806.* Bloomington, IN, 1980.
Garms-Cornides, Elisabeth. "Liturgie und Diplomatie: Zum Zeremoniell des Nuntius am Wiener Kaiserhof im 17. und 18. Jahrhundert." In *Kaiserhof—Papsthof (16.—18. Jahrhundert)*, 125–46. Vienna, 2006.
Gennep, Arnold van. *Les rites de passage* (1st ed., 1909). Paris, 1981.
Gestrich, Andreas. *Absolutismus und Öffentlichkeit: Politische Kommunikation in Deutschland zu Beginn des 18. Jahrhunderts.* Göttingen, 1994.
Geyken, Frauke. *Gentlemen auf Reisen: Das britische Deutschlandbild im 18. Jahrhundert.* Frankfurt am Main, 2002.
Giddens, Anthony. *The Constitution of Society: Outline of the Theory of Structuration.* Cambridge, 1984.
Giesecke, Michael. *Der Buchdruck in der frühen Neuzeit: Eine historische Fallstudie über die Durchsetzung neuer Informations- und Kommunikationstechnologien.* 4th ed. Frankfurt am Main, 2006.
Giesey, Ralph E. *Cérémonial et puissance souveraine: France XVe–XVIIe siècles.* Paris, 1987.
Göbel, Christina. *Der Reichstag von Worms 1495: Zwischen Wandel und Beharrung; Eine verfassungs- und institutionengeschichtliche Ortsbestimmung.* Marburg, 1996.
Goez, Hans-Werner. "Der 'rechte' Sitz: Die Symbolik von Rang und Herrschaft im hohen Mittelalter im Spiegel der Sitzordnung." In *Symbole des Alltags, Alltag der Symbole: Festschrift für Harry Kühnel zum 65. Geburtstag*, edited by Gertrud Blaschitz, Helmut Hundsbichler, Gerhard Jaritz, and Elisabeth Vavra, 11–47. Graz, 1992.
Goffman, Erving. *Interaction Ritual: Essays on Face-to-Face Behaviour.* New York, 1967.

———. *The Presentation of Self in Everyday Life*. New York, 1959.
Göller, Karl Heinz. "Sir George Etherege und Hugh Hughes als englische Gesandte am Reichstag." In *Regensburg, Stadt der Reichstage: Vom Mittelalter zur Neuzeit*, edited by Dieter Albrecht, 143–66. Schriftenreihe der Universität Regensburg, n.s., 21). Regensburg, 1994.
Gößner, Andreas. *Weltliche Kirchenhoheit und reichsstädtische Reformation: Die Augsburger Ratspolitik des "milten und mitleren weges" 1520–1534*. Colloquia Augustana 11. Berlin, 1999.
Gotthard, Axel. *Das Alte Reich 1495–1806*. Geschichte kompakt. 3rd ed. Darmstadt, 2006.
———. *Der Augsburger Religionsfrieden*. Reformationsgeschichtliche Studien und Texte 148. Münster, 2004.
———. *Säulen des Reiches: Die Kurfürsten im frühneuzeitlichen Reichsverband*. Vols. 1–2. Historische Studien 457. Husum, 1999.
Gottlieb, Gunther, Wolfram Baer, Josef Becker, Josef Bellot, Karl Filser, Pankraz Fried, Wolfgang Reinhard, and Bernhard Schimmelpfennig. *Geschichte der Stadt Augsburg: Von der Römerzeit bis zur Gegenwart*. Stuttgart, 1984.
Götzmann, Jutta. "Kaiserliche Legitimation im Bildnis." In *Heiliges Römisches Reich Deutscher Nation 962–1806: Altes Reich und neue Staaten 1495 bis 1806*, edited by Heinz Schilling, Werner Heun, and Jutta Götzmann, 257–71. Dresden, 2006.
Graf, Klaus. "Eberhard im Bart und die Herzogserhebung 1495." In *1495—Württemberg wird Herzogtum: Dokumente aus dem Hauptstaatsarchiv Stuttgart zu einem epochalen Ereignis*, edited by Stephan Molitor, 9–43. Stuttgart, 1995.
Grass, Nikolaus. *Reichskleinodien: Studien aus rechtshistorischer Sicht*. Graz, 1965.
Greyerz, Kaspar von, and Kim Siebenhüner, eds. *Religion und Gewalt: Konflikt, Rituale, Deutungen (1500–1800)*. Veröffentlichungen des Max-Planck-Instituts für Geschichte 215. Göttingen, 2006.
Grimm, Jakob, and Wilhelm Grimm, eds. *Deutsches Wörterbuch*. Vols. 1–16. Leipzig, 1845–1954.
Gritzner, Erich. *Symbole und Wappen des alten deutschen Reichs*. Leipziger Studien aus dem Gebiet der Geschichte 8,3. Leipzig, 1902.
Gross, Hans. *Empire and Sovereignty: A History of the Public Law Literature in the Holy Roman Empire 1599–1804*. Chicago, 1973.
Großmann, Georg Ulrich, ed. *Von deutscher Not zu höfischer Pracht 1648–1701: Ausstellungskatalog*. Nuremberg and Cologne, 1998.
Grothe, Ewald. *Zwischen Geschichte und Recht: Deutsche Verfassungsgeschichtsschreibung 1900–1970*. Munich, 2005.
Grundmann, Herbert. "Landgraf Philipp von Hessen auf dem Augsburger Reichstag 1530." In *Aus den Reichstagen des 15. und 16. Jh. Festgabe dargebracht der Bayrischen Historischen Kommission zur Feier ihres 100jährigen Bestehens*, 341–423. Göttingen, 1957.
Gsell, Klemens. *Die Rechtsstreitigkeiten um den Reichsschatz: Das Rechtsproblem aus rechtshistorischer und aktueller Sicht*. Erlangen and Nuremberg, 1999.
Gumbrecht, Hans Ulrich. "Ten Brief Reflections on Institutions and Re/Presentation." In *Institutionalität und Symbolisierung: Verstetigungen kultureller Ordnungsmuster in Vergangenheit und Gegenwart*, edited by Gert Melville, 69–76. Cologne, Weimar, and Vienna, 2001.
Habermas, Jürgen. *The Structural Transformation of the Public Sphere: An Inquiry into a Category of Bourgeois Society*. Translated by Thomas Burger with the assistance of Frederick Lawrence. Cambridge, MA, 1989.

Hahn, Alois. "Funktionale und stratifikatorische Differenzierung und ihre Rolle für die gepflegte Semantik: Zu Niklas Luhmanns 'Gesellschaftsstruktur und Semantik.'" *Kölner Zeitschrift für Soziologie und Sozialpsychologie* 33 (1981): 345–60.

———. "Geheim." In *Das Geheimnis am Beginn der europäischen Moderne*, edited by Gisela Engel, Britta Rang, Klaus Reichert, and Heide Wunder, 21–42. Frankfurt am Main, 2002.

———. "Kultische und säkulare Riten und Zeremonien in soziologischer Sicht." In *Anthropologie des Kults: Die Bedeutung des Kults für das Überleben des Menschen*, 51–81. Freiburg, Basel, and Vienna, 1977.

Hamm, Berndt. "Einheit und Vielfalt der Reformation—oder: Was die Reformation zur Reformation machte." In *Reformationstheorien: Ein kirchenhistorischer Disput über Einheit und Vielfalt der Reformation*, edited by Berndt Hamm, Bernd Moeller, and Dorothea Wendebourg, 57–127. Göttingen, 1995.

———. "Normative Zentrierung im 15. und 16. Jahrhundert: Beobachtungen zur Religiosität, Theologie und Ikonologie." *Zeitschrift für Historische Forschung* 26 (1999): 163–202.

Hammerstein, Notker. "Jus public Romano-Germanicum." In *Diritto e potere nella storia Europea: Atti in onore di Bruno Paradisi—Quarto Congresso internazionale della Soc. Italiana di storia del diretto*, 717–53. Florence, 1982.

———. *Jus und Historie: Ein Beitrag zur Geschichte des historischen Denkens an deutschen Universitäten im späten 17. und 18. Jahrhundert*. Göttingen, 1972.

Härter, Karl. *Reichstag und Revolution 1789–1806: Die Auseinandersetzung des immerwährenden Reichstagz zu Regensburg mit den Auswirkungen der Französischen Revolution auf das Alte Reich*. Göttingen, 1992.

———. "Zweihundert Jahre nach dem europäischen Umbruch von 1803: Neuerscheinungen zur Reichsdeputationshauptschluß, Säkularisationen und Endphase des Alten Reiches." *Zeitschrift für Historische Forschung* 33 (2006): 89–115.

Hartmann, Peter C. *Kulturgeschichte des Heiligen Römischen Reiches 1648 bis 1806*. Cologne, 2001.

Haug-Moritz, Gabriele. "Die Friedenskongresse von Münster und Osnabrück (1643–1648) und Wien (1815/15) als 'deutsche' Verfassungskongresse: Ein Vergleich in verfahrensgeschichtlicher Perspektive." *Historisches Jahrbuch* 124 (2004): 125–78.

———. "Kaisertum und Parität: Reichspolitik und Konfession nach dem Westfälischen Frieden." *Zeitschrift für historische Forschung* 19 (1992): 445–82.

———. *Der Schmalkaldische Bund 1530–1541/42: Eine Studie zu den genossenschaftlichen Strukturelementen der politischen Ordnungs des Heiliges Römisches Reiches Deutscher Nation*. Leinfelden-Echterdingen, 2002.

———, ed. *Verfassungsgeschichte des Alten Reiches*. Basistexte Frühe Neuzeit. Stuttgart, 2014.

Hausmann, Jost, ed. *Fern vom Kaiser: Städte und Stätten des Reichskammergerichts*. Cologne, Weimar, and Vienna, 1995.

Haupt, Herbert. "Die Aufhebung des spanischen Mantelkleides durch Kaiser Joseph II.—ein Wendepunkt im höfischen Zeremoniell." In *Österreich zur Zeit Kaiser Josephs II., Mitregent Kaiserin Maria Theresias, Kaiser und Landesfürst*, 79–81. Vienna, 1980.

Heckel, Martin. "Itio in partes: Zur Religionsverfassung des Heiligen Römischen Reiches Deutscher Nation." *Zeitschrift der Savigny-Stiftung für Rechtsgeschichte: Kanonistische Abteilung* 64 (1978): 180–308.

———. "Ius reformandi: Auf dem Weg zum 'modernen' Staatskirchenrecht im Konfessionellen Zeitalter." In *Gesammelte Schriften: Staat, Kirche, Recht, Geschichte*, vol. 5, 135–84. Tübingen, 2004.

Heil, Dietmar. "Der Reichstag als politisches Kommunikationszentrum." In *Kommunikation und Medien in der Frühen Neuzeit*, edited by Johannes Burkhardt and Christine Werkstetter, 249–65. HZ-Beihefte, n.s., 40. Munich, 2005.

———. "Verschriftlichung des Verfahrens als Modernisierung des Reichstags (1495–1586)." In *Der Reichstag: Kommunikation, Wahrnehmung, Öffentlichkeiten*, edited by Maximilian Lanzinner and Arno Strohmeyer, 55–76. Göttingen, 2006.

Heiliges Römisches Reich Deutscher Nation 962–1806: Altes Reich und neue Staaten 1495 bis 1806. Edited by Heinz Schilling, Werner Heun, and Jutta Götzmann. 2 vols. Dresden, 2006.

Heinig, Paul-Joachim. "Der Wormser Reichstag von 1495 als Hoftag." *Zeitschrift für historische Forschung* 33 (2006): 337–57.

Heller, Hermann. *Staatslehre*. Edited by Gerhart Niemeyer. 4th ed. Leiden, 1970.

Helmrath, Johannes. "Rhetorik und 'Akademisierung' auf den deutschen Reichstagen im 15. und 16. Jahrhundert." In *Im Spannungsfeld von Recht und Ritual: Soziale Kommunikation in Mittelalter und Früher Neuzeit*, edited by Heinz Durchhardt, 423–46. Cologne, Weimar, and Vienna, 1997.

———. "Sitz und Geschichte: Köln im Rangstreit mit Aachen auf den Reichstagen des 15. Jahrhunderts." In *Stadt und Bistum in Kirche und Reich des Mittelalters: Festschrift für Odilo Engels zum 65. Geburtstag*, edited by H. Vollrath and Stefan Weinfurter, 719–60. Cologne, Weimar, and Vienna, 1993.

Hengerer, Mark. *Kaiserhof und Adel in der Mitte des 17. Jahrhunderts: Eine Mikrogeschichte der Macht in der Vormoderne*. Konstanz, 2004.

———. "Die Zeremonialprotokolle und weitere Quellen zum Zeremoniell des Kaiserhofes im Wiener Haus-, Hof- und Staatsarchiv." In *Quellenkunde der Habsburgermonarchie (16.–18. Jh.): Ein exemplarisches Handbuch*, edited by Josef Pauser, Martin Scheutz, and Thomas Winkelbauer, 76-93. Vienna and Munich, 2004.

Hergemöller, Bernd-Ulrich. "Die 'solempnis curia' als Element der Herrschaftsausübung in der Spätphase Karls IV. (1360–1376)." In *Deutscher Königshof, Hoftag und Reichstag im späteren Mittelalter*, edited by Peter Moraw, 451–76. Stuttgart, 2002.

Heringa, Jan. *De eer en hoogheid van de staat: Over de plaats der Verenigde Nederlanden in het diplomatieke leven de zeventiende eeuw*. Groningen, 1961.

Herkens, Rudolf. *Der Anspruch Aachens auf Krönung der deutschen Könige nach 1531, Mikrofiche-Ausgabe*. Bonn, 1959.

Herrmann, Axel. *Der Deutsche Orden unter Walter von Cronberg (1525–1543): Zur Politik und Struktur des "Teutschen Adels Spitale" im Reformationszeitalter*. Quellen und Studien zur Geschichte des Deutschen Ordens 35. Bonn, 1974.

Herzig, Arno. *Der Zwang zum wahren Glauben: Rekatholisierung vom 16. bis zum 18. Jh*. Göttingen, 2000.

Heumann, Hermann Gottlieb, and Emil Seckel, eds. *Handlexikon zu den Quellen des römischen Rechts*. 11th ed. Graz, 1971.

Hirschbiegel, Jan, and Werner Paravicini. *Das Frauenzimmer: Die Frau bei Hofe in Spätmittelalter und Früher Neuzeit*. Stuttgart, 2000.

Hödl, Günther. "Die Bestätigung und Erweiterung der österreichischen Freiheitsbriefe durch Kaiser Friedrich III." In *Fälschungen im Mittelalter*, vol. 3, 225–46. MGH-Schriften 33. Hannover, 1988.

Hoffmann, Carl A., Markus Johanns, Annette Kranz, Christof Trepesch, and Oliver Zeidler, eds. *Als Frieden möglich war—450 Jahre Augsburger Religionsfrieden, Begleitband zur Ausstellung im Maximilianmuseum Augsburg*. Regensburg, 2005.

Hoffmann, Paul. *Die bildlichen Darstellungen des Kurfürstenkollegiums von den Anfängen bis zum Ende des Heiligen Römischen Reiches (13.–18. Jh.)*. Bonn, 1976.

Hofmann, Hasso. *Repräsentation: Studien zur Wort- und Begriffsgeschichte von der Antike bis zum 19. Jahrhundert*. Berlin, 1974.

———. "Der spätmittelalterliche Rechtsbegriff der Repräsentation in Reich und Kirche." In *Höfische Repräsentation: Das Zeremoniell und die Zeichen*, edited by Helga Ragotzky and Horst Wenzel, 17–42. Tübingen, 1990.

Hoke, Rudolf. "Die Emanzipation der deutschen Staatsrechtswissenschaft von der Zivilitik im 17. Jahrhundert." *Der Staat* 15 (1976): 211–30.

———. *Die Reichsstaatsrechtslehre des Johannes Limnaeus: Ein Beitrag zur Geschichte der deutschen Staatsrechtswissenschaft im 17. Jh*. Untersuchungen zur deutschen Staats- und Rechtsgeschichte, n.s., 9. Aalen, 1968.

Holenstein, André. *Die Huldigung der Untertanen: Rechtskultur und Herrschaftsordnung 800–1800*. Stuttgart, 1991.

———. "Seelenheil und Untertanenpflicht: Zur gesellschaftlichen Funktion und theoretischen Begründung des Eides in der ständischen Gesellschaft." In *Der Fluch und der Eid: Die metaphysische Begründung gesellschaftlichen Zusammenlebens und politischer Ordnung in der ständischen Gesellschaft*, edited by Peter Blickle, 11–63. Berlin, 1993.

Hollegger, Manfred. *Maximilian I. (1459–1519): Herrscher und Mensch einer Zeitenwende*. Stuttgart, 2005.

Holzem, Andreas, ed. *Die Frühe Neuzeit und der Umbruch ins 19. Jahrhundert (1550–1848)*. Paderborn, 2007.

Höß, Irmgard. "Das Reich und Preußen in der Zeit der Umwandlung des Ordenslandes in das Herzogtum." In *Aus der Arbeit an den Reichstagen unter Kaiser Karl V.: 7 Beiträge zu Fragen der Forschung und Edition*, edited by Heinrich Lutz, 130–57. Göttingen, 1986.

Hye, Franz-Heinz. "Der Doppeladler als Symbol für Kaiser und Recht." *Mitteilungen des Instituts für Österreichische Geschichte* 81 (1973): 63–100.

Immenkötter, Herbert. "Die Rahmenbedingungen der Augsburger Religionsverhandlungen." In *Im Schatten der Confessio Augustana: Die Religionsverhandlungen des Augsburger Reichstages 1530 im historischen Kontext*, edited by Herbert Immenkötter, 10–18. Münster, 1997.

———. *Um die Einheit im Glauben: Die Unionsverhandlungen des Augsburger Reichstages im August und September 1530*. 2nd ed. Münster, 1974.

Isenmann, Eberhard. *Die deutsche Stadt im Spätmittelalter 1250–1500: Stadtgestalt, Recht, Stadtregiment, Kirche, Gesellschaft, Wirtschaft*. Stuttgart, 1988.

———. "Kaiser, Reich und deutsche Nation am Ausgang des 15. Jahrhunderts." In *Ansätze und Diskontinuität deutscher Nationsbildung im Mittelalter*, edited by Joachim Ehlers, 185–227. Sigmaringen, 1989.

———. "Die Städte auf den Reichstagen im ausgehenden Mittelalter." In *Deutscher Königshof, Hoftag und Reichstag im späteren Mittelalter*, edited by Peter Moraw, 547–77. Stuttgart, 2002.

———. "Zur Frage der Reichsstandschaft der Frei- und Reichsstädte." In *Stadtverfassung, Verfassungsstaat, Pressepolitik: Festschrift für Eberhard Naujoks zum 65. Geburtstag*, edited by Franz Quarthal and Wilfried Setzler, 91–110. Sigmaringen, 1980.

Iserloh, Erwin, ed. *Confessio Augustana und Confutatio: Der Augsburger Reichstag 1530 und die Einheit der Kirche*. Münster, 1980.

Jucker, Michael. *Gesandte, Schreiber, Akten: Politische Kommunikation auf eidgenössischen Tagsatzungen im Spätmittelalter*. Zurich, 2004.

Jussen, Bernhard. *Die Macht des Königs: Herrschaft in Europa vom Frühmittelalter bis in die Neuzeit.* Munich, 2005.

Jussen, Bernhard, and Craig Koslofsky, eds. *Kulturelle Reformation: Sinnformationen im Umbruch 1400–1600.* Göttingen, 1999.

Kalipke, Andreas. "'Weitläufftigkeiten und Bedencklichkeiten': Die Behandlung konfessioneller Konflikte am Corpus Evangelicorum. Kulturwissenschaftliche Perspektiven." *ZHF* 35 (2008): 405–47.

Kampmann, Christoph. "Der Immerwährende Reichstag als 'erstes stehendes Parlament'? Aktuelle Forschungsfragen und ein deutsch-englischer Vergleich." *Geschichte in Wissenschaft und Unterricht* 55 (2004): 646–62.

Kantorowicz, Ernst H. "The 'King's Advent' and the Enigmatic Panels in the Doors of Santa Sabina." *The Art Bulletin* 26 (1944): 207–31.

———. *The King's Two Bodies: A Study in Mediaeval Political Theology.* Princeton, NJ, 1957.

Karant-Nunn, Susan C. *The Reformation of Ritual: An Interpretation of Early Modern Germany.* London, 1997.

Kaufmann, Thomas. *Konfession und Kultur: Lutherischer Protestantismus in der zweiten Hälfte des Reformationsjahrhunderts.* Spätmittelalter und Reformation, n.s., 29. Tübingen, 2006.

Keller, Hagen. "Vom 'heiligen Buch' zur Buchführung: Lebensfunktionen der Schrift im Mittelalter." *Frühmittelalterliche Studien* 26 (1992): 1–31.

———. "Die Investitur: Ein Beitrag zum Problem der 'Staatssymbolik' im Hochmittelalter." *Frühmittelalterliche Studien* 279 (1993): 51–86.

———. "Urkunde und Buch in der symbolischen Kommunikation mittelalterlicher Rechtsgemeinschaften und Herrschaftsverbände." *Jahrbuch der historischen Forschung in der BRD* 2004 (2005): 41–51.

Keller, Katrin. *Hofdamen: Amtsträgerinnen im Wiener Hofstaat des 17. Jahrhunderts.* Vienna, Cologne, and Weimar, 2005.

Kieserling, André. *Kommunikation unter Anwesenden: Studie über Interaktionssysteme.* Frankfurt am Main, 1999.

Kietzell, Roswitha von. "Der Frankfurter Deputationstag von 1642–1645: Eine Untersuchung der staatsrechtlichen Bedeutung dieser Reichsversammlung." *Nassauische Annalen* 83 (1972): 99–117.

Kimminich, Otto. "Der Regensburger Reichstag als Grundlage eines europäischen Friedensmodells." In *Regensburg—Stadt der Reichstage,* edited by Dieter Albrecht, 109–26. Regensburg, 1980.

Kintzinger, Martin. "Kaiser und König: Das römisch-deutsche Reich und Frankreich im Spätmittelalter." In *Auswärtige Politik und internationale Beziehungen im Mittelalter (13.–16. Jh.),* edited by Dieter Berg, Martin Kintzinger, and Pierre Monnet, 113–36. Bochum, 2002.

———. "Der weiße Reiter: Formen internationaler Politik im Spätmittelalter." *Frühmittelalterliche Studien* 37 (2003): 315–53.

———. *Westbindungen im spätmittelalterlichen Europa.* Stuttgart, 2000.

Kirchweger, Franz. "Die Reichskleinodien in Nürnberg in der Frühen Neuzeit (1525–1796): Zwischen Glaube und Kritik, Forschung und Verehrung." In *Heiliges Römische Reich Deutscher Nation 962–1806: Altes Reich und neue Staaten 1495 bis 1806,* edited by Heinz Schilling, Werner Heun, and Jutta Götzmann, 187–99. Dresden, 2006.

Klein, Thomas. "Die Erhebung in den weltlichen Reichsfürstenstand 1550–1806." *Blätter für deutsche Landesgeschichte* 122 (1986): 137–92.

Klein, Thomas. "Politik und Verfassung von der Leipziger Teilung bis zur Teilung des ernestinischen Staates (1485-1572). In *Geschichte Thüringens*, edited by Hans Patze and Walter Schlesinger. 3rd. vol. Cologne and Graz, 1967.

Kleinheyer, Gerd. "Die Abdankung des Kaisers." In *Wege der europäischen Rechtsgeschichte: Karl Kroeschell zum 60. Geburtstag*, edited by Gerhard Köbler, 124–45. Frankfurt am Main, 1988.

Klueting, Harm. *Das Reich und Österreich 1648–1740*. Historia profana et ecclesiastica 1. Münster, 1999.

Kohler, Alfred. *Antihabsburgische Politik in der Epoche Karls V. Die reichsständische Opposition gegen die Wahl Ferdinands I. zum römischen König und gegen die Anerkennung seines Königtums (1524–1534)*. Göttingen, 1982.

——— . *Ferdinand I. 1503–1564: Fürst, König, Kaiser*. Munich, 2003.

——— . *Karl V. 1500–1558: Eine Biographie*. Munich, 1999.

Kohnle, Armin, and Eike Wolgast. "Die Reichstage der Reformationszeit." In *Theologische Realenzyklopädie*, edited by Gerhard Müller, vol. 28, 457–70. Berlin, 1997.

Koschorke, Albrecht. *Der fiktive Staat: Konstruktionen des politischen Körpers in der Geschichte Europas*. Frankfurt am Main, 2007.

Koschorke, Albrecht, Thomas Frank, and Susanne Lüdemann. *Des Kaisers neue Kleider: Über das Imaginäre politischer Herrschaft—Texte, Bilder, Lektüren*. Frankfurt am Main, 2002.

Koselleck, Reinhart. "Begriffsgeschichtliche Probleme der Verfassungsgeschichtsschreibung." In *Gegenstand und Begriffe der Verfassungsgeschichtsschreibung*, 7–21. Berlin, 1983.

——— . "Staat: 'Staat' im Zeitalter revolutionärer Bewegung." In *Geschichtliche Grundbegriffe: Historisches Lexikon zur politisch-sozialen Sprache in Deutschland*, edited by Otto Brunner, Werner Conze, and Reinhart Koselleck, vol. 6, 25–64. Stuttgart, 2004.

Kramp, Mario, ed. *Krönungen: Könige in Aachen—Geschichte und Mythos, Katalog zur Ausstellung*. 2 vols. Mainz, 2000.

Kraus, Andreas. *Maximilian I. Bayerns großer Kurfürst*. Graz, 1990.

Kraus, Hans-Christof, and Thomas Nicklas, eds. *Geschichte der Politik*. Historische Zeitschrift: Beihefte, n.s., 44. Munich, 2007.

Kretschmayr, Heinrich. "Das deutsche Reichsvizekanzleramt." *Archiv für Österreichische Geschichte* 84 (1898): 381–501.

Krieger, Karl-Friedrich. *Die Lehnshoheit der deutschen Könige im Spätmittelalter (1200–1437)*. Aalen, 1979.

Krischer, André. "Das diplomatische Zeremoniell der Reichsstädte, oder: Was heißt Stadtfreiheit in der Fürstengesellschaft." *Historische Zeitschrift* 281 (2007): 1–30.

——— . "'Ein nothwendig Stück der Ambassaden': Zur politischen Rationalität des diplomatischen Zeremoniells bei Kurfürst Clemens August." *Annalen des Historischen Vereins für den Niederrhein* 205 (2002): 161–200.

——— . "Das Gesandtschaftswesen und das vormoderne Völkerrecht." In *Rechtsformen Internationaler Politik: Theorie, Norm und Praxis vom 12. bis 18. Jahrhundert*, edited by Martin Kintzinger and Michael Jucker, 197–240. Berlin, 2011.

——— . "Inszenierung und Verfahren auf den Reichstagen der Frühen Neuzeit." In *Politische Versammlungen und ihre Rituale: Repräsentationsformen und Entscheidunhgsprozesse des Reichs und der Kirche im späten Mittelalter*, edited by Jörg Peltzer, Gerald Schwedler, and Paul Töbelmann, 181–205. Ostfildern, 2009.

——— . "Politische Repräsentation und Rhetorik der Reichsstädte auf dem Reichstag nach 1648." In *Politische Redekultur in der Vormoderne: Die Oratorik europäischer Parlamente* in *Spätmittelalter und Früher Neuzeit*, edited by Johannes Helmrath and Jörg Feuchter, 135–48. Frankfurt am Main and New York, 2008.

———. *Reichsstädte in der Fürstengesellschaft: Politischer Zeichengebrauch in der Frühen Neuzeit*. Darmstadt, 2006.

Kühlmann, Wilhelm. *Gelehrtenrepublik und Fürstenstaat: Entwicklung und Kritik des deutschen Späthumanismus in der Literatur des Barockzeitalters*. Studien und Texte zur Sozialgeschichte der Literatur 3. Tübingen, 1982.

Kugler, Georg Johannes. *Die Reichskrone*. 2nd, revised, and expanded edition. Sammlung Die Kronen des Hauses Österreich 5. Vienna, 1986.

Kümin, Beat. "Political Culture in the Holy Roman Empire." *German History* 27, no. 1 (2009): 131–44.

Kunisch, Johannes. "Formen symbolischen Handelns in der Goldenen Bulle von 1356." In *Vormoderne politische Verfahren*, edited by Barbara Stollberg-Rilinger, 263–80. Berlin, 2001.

———. *Friedrich der Große: Der König und seine Zeit*. Munich, 2004.

Kurzel-Runtscheiner, Monica. "Vom 'Mantelkleid' zu Staatsfrack und Waffenrock: Anfänge und Entwicklung der Ziviluniform in Österreich." In *Die zivile Uniform als symbolische Kommunikation: Kleidung zwischen Repräsentation, Imagination und Konsumption in Europa vom 18. bis zum 21. Jahrhundert*, edited by Elisabeth Hackspiel-Mikosch and Stefan Haas, 81–97. Stuttgart, 2006.

Lancizolle, Karl Wilhelm von. *Geschichte der Bildung des preußischen Staats. Erster Theil. Erste (und zweite) Abtheilung*. Berlin, 1828.

Landwehr, Achim. "Diskurs—Macht—Wissen: Perspektiven einer Kulturgeschichte des Politischen." *Archiv für Kulturgeschichte* 85 (2003): 71–117.

Lanzinner, Maximilian, and Arno Strohmeyer, eds. *Der Reichstag: Kommunikation, Wahrnehmung, Öffentlichkeiten*. Göttingen, 2006.

Laubach, Ernst. *Ferdinand I. als Kaiser: Politik und Herrschaftsauffassung des Nachfolgers Karls V.* Münster, 2001.

———. "Karl V., Ferdinand I. und die Nachfolge im Reich." *Mitteilungen des Österreichischen Staatsarchivs* 29 (1976): 1–51.

———. "'Nationalversammlung' im 16. Jahrhundert: Zu Inhalt und Funktion eines politischen Begriffs." *Mitteilungen des Österreichischen Staatsarchivs* 38 (1983): 1–48.

Laufs, Adolf. "Die Reichsstädte auf dem Regensburger Reichstag 1653/54." *Die alte Stadt: Zeitschrift für Stadtgeschichte, Stadtsoziologie und Denkmalpflege* 1 (1974): 23–48.

Leiher, Nikolaus. *Die rechtliche Stellung der auswärtigen Gesandten beim Immerwährenden Reichstag zu Regensburg: Eine rechtshistorische Untersuchung unter Auswertung der Schriften zum Ius Publicum des Alten Reiches*. Aachen, 2003.

Lentes, Thomas. "Counting Piety in the Late Middle Ages." In *Ordering Medieval Society: Perspectives on Intellectual and Practical Modes of Shaping Social Relations*, edited by Bernhard Jussen, 55–91. Philadelphia, 2001.

Lesaffer, Randal, ed. *Peace Treaties and International Law in European History: From the Late Middle Ages to World War One*. New York, 2004.

Lhotsky, Alphons. *Privilegium maius: Die Geschichte einer Urkunde*. Munich, 1957.

Lhotta, Roland, ed. *Die Integration des modernen Staates: Zur Aktualität der Integrationslehre von Rudolf Smend*. Staatsverständnisse 8. Baden-Baden, 2005.

Löther, Andrea. *Prozessionen in spätmittelalterlichen Städten: Politische Partizipation, obrigkeitliche Inszenierung, städtische Einheit*. Cologne, Weimar, and Vienna, 1999.

Löw, Martina. *Raumsoziologie*. Frankfurt am Main, 2001.

Luhmann, Niklas. *Ausdifferenzierung des Rechts: Beiträge zu Rechtstheorie und Rechtssoziologie*. Frankfurt am Main, 1981.

———. *Funktionen und Folgen formaler Organisation*. Berlin, 1964.

———. *Gesellschaftsstruktur und Semantik: Studien zur Wissenssoziologie*. Vol. 1. Frankfurt am Main, 1980.

———. *Legitimation durch Verfahren*. Soziologische Texte 66. Neuwied, 1969.

———. *Rechtssoziologie*. 2 vols. Reinbek bei Hamburg, 1972.

———. "Verfassung als evolutionäre Errungenschaft." *Rechtshistorisches Journal* 9 (1990): 176–220.

Luttenberger, Albrecht Pius. "Friedensgedanke und Glaubensspaltung: Aspekte kaiserlicher und ständischer Reichspolitik 1521–1555." In *Suche nach Frieden: Politische Ethik in der Frühen Neuzeit*, edited by Norbert Brieskorn, 201–40. Stuttgart, 2002.

———. "Der Immerwährende Reichstag zu Regensburg, das europäische Mächtesystem und die politische Ordnung des Reichs." In *Reichsstadt und Immerwährender Reichstag (1663–1806): 250 Jahre Haus Thurn und Taxis in Regensburg*, 11–23. Thurn-und-Taxis-Studien 20. Kallmünz, 2001.

———. "Konfessionelle Parteilichkeit und Reichstagspolitik: Zur Verhandlungsführung des Kaisers und der Stände in Regensburg 1541." In *Fortschritte der Geschichtswissenschaft durch Reichstagsaktenforschung*, edited by Heinz Angermeier and Erich Meuthen, 64–101. Göttingen, 1988.

———. "Pracht und Ehre: Gesellschaftliche Repräsentation und Zeremoniell auf dem Reichstag." In *Alltag im 16. Jahrhundert: Studien zu Lebensformen in mitteleuropäischen Städten*, edited by Alred Kohler and Heinrich Lutz, 291–326. Munich, 1987.

———. "Reichspolitik und Reichstag unter Karl V.: Formen zentralen politischen Handelns." In *Aus der Arbeit an den Reichstagen unter Kaiser Karl V.: 7 Beiträge zu Fragen der Forschung und Edition*, edited by Heinrich Lutz, 18–68. Göttingen, 1986.

Lutter, Christina. *Politische Kommunikation an der Wende vom Mittelalter zur Neuzeit: Die Beziehung zwischen der Republik Venedig und Maximilian I. (1495–1508)*. Vienna, 1998.

Lutz, Heinrich, and Alfred Kohler, eds. *Aus der Arbeit an den Reichstagen unter Kaiser Karl V.: Sieben Beiträge zu Fragen der Forschung und Edition*. Schriftenreihe der Historischen Kommission bei der Bayerischen Akademie der Wissenschaften 26. Göttingen, 1986.

Mader, Eric-Oliver. "Fürstenkonversionen zum Katholizismus in Mitteleuropa im 17. Jahrhundert: Ein systematischer Ansatz in fallorientierter Perspektive." *Zeitschrift für Historische Forschung* 34 (2007): 403–40.

Maissen, Thomas. *Die Geburt der Republik: Politisches Selbstverständnis und Repräsentation*. Göttingen, 2002.

Malettke, Klaus. "Die Perzeption des Alten Reiches in der 'Encyclopédie.'" In *Altes Reich, Frankreich und Europa: Politische, philosophische und historische Aspekte des französischen Deutschlandbildes im 17. und 18. Jahrhundert*, edited by Olaf Asbach, Klaus Malettke, and Sven Externbrink, 279–98. Berlin, 2001.

Markel, Erich H. *Die Entwicklung der diplomatischen Rangstufen*. Erlangen, 1951.

Martschukat, Jürgen, and Steffen Patzold, eds. *Geschichtswissenschaft und "performative turn": Ritual, Inszenierung und Performanz vom Mittelalter bis zur Neuzeit*. Cologne, Weimar, and Vienna, 2003.

Matthäus, Michael, and Evelyn Brockhoff, eds. *Die Kaisermacher: Frankfurt am Main und die Goldene Bulle—1356–1806*. 2 vols. Frankfurt am Main, 2006.

Mattingly, Garrett. *Renaissance Diplomacy*. London, 1955; repr., New York, 1988.

Mazohl-Wallnig, Brigitte. *Zeitenwende 1806: Das Heilige Römische Reich und die Geburt des modernen Europa.* Vienna, Cologne, and Weimar, 2005.

Melville, Gert. "'Un bel office': Zum Heroldswesen in der spätmittelalterlichen Welt des Adels, der Höfe und der Fürsten." In *Deutscher Königshof, Hoftag und Reichstag im späteren Mittelalter,* edited by Peter Moraw, 291–321. Stuttgart, 2002.

Mentz, Georg. *Johann Friedrich der Großmüthige 1503–1554.* 3 vols. Jena, 1903–8.

———. *Johann Philipp von Schönborn: Kurfürst von Mainz, Bischof von Würzburg und Worms, 1605–1673—Ein Beitrag zur Geschichte des siebzehnten Jahrhunderts.* 2 vols. Jena, 1896–99.

Mergel, Thomas. "Überlegungen zu einer Kulturgeschichte der Politik." *Geschichte und Gesellschaft* 28 (2002): 574–606.

Merlo, Johann J. "Haus Gürzenich zu Köln, sein Saal und dessen Feste." *Annalen des Historischen Vereins für den Niederrhein* 43 (1885): 1–79.

Meuthen, Erich, ed. *Reichstage und Kirche: Kolloquium der Historischen Kommission bei der Bayerischen Akademie der Wissenschaften, München 9. März 1900.* Göttingen, 1991.

Meyer, John W., and Brian Rowan. "Institutionalized Organizations: Formal Structure as Myth and Ceremony." In *The New Institutionalism in Organizational Analysis,* edited by Paul J. Di Maggio and Walter W. Powell, 41–62. Chicago, 1991.

Meyer, Thomas. *Die Inszenierung des Scheins: Voraussetzungen und Folgen symbolischer Politik.* Frankfurt am Main, 1992.

———. *Politik als Theater: Die neue Macht der Darstellungskunst.* Berlin, 1998.

Mikoletzky, Lorenz. *Kaiser Joseph II.: Herrscher zwischen den Zeiten.* Persönlichkeit und Geschichte 107. Göttingen, 1990.

Mohnhaupt, Heinz. "Von den 'leges fundamentales' zur modernen Verfassung in Europa." *Ius commune* 25 (1998): 121–58.

———. "Vertragskonstruktion und fingierter Vertrag zur Sicherung von Normativität: Gesetz, Privileg, Verfassung." In *Gesellschaftliche Freiheit und vertragliche Bindung in Rechtsgeschichte und Philosophie,* edited by Jean-Francois Kervégan und Heinz Mohnhaupt, 1–33. Frankfurt am Main, 1999.

Mohnhaupt, Heinz, and Dieter Grimm. "Verfassung." *Geschichtliche Grundbegriffe: Historisches Lexikon zur politisch-sozialen Sprache in Deutschland,* edited by Otto Brunner, and Werner Conze, and Reinhart Koselleck, vol. 6, 831–99. Stuttgart, 1990.

———. *Verfassung: Zur Geschichte des Begriffs von der Antike bis zur Gegenwart.* Schriften zur Verfassungsgeschichte 47. Berlin, 2002.

Mohr, Walter. *Geschichte des Herzogtums Lothringen.* Vol. 4. Saarbrücken, 1986.

Moraw, Peter, ed. *Deutscher Königshof, Hoftag und Reichstag im späten Mittelalter.* Stuttgart, 2002.

———. "Hoftag und Reichstag von den Anfängen im Mittelalter bis 1806." In *Parlamentsrecht und Parlamentspraxis in der Bundesrepublik Deutschland: Ein Handbuch,* edited by Hans-Peter Schneider and Wolfgang Zeh, 3–47. Berlin and New York, 1989.

———. "Die Kurfürsten, der Hoftag, der Reichstag und die Anfänge der Reichsverwaltung." In *Deutsche Verwaltungsgeschichte,* vol. 1, *Vom Spätmittelalter bis zum Ende des Reiches,* edited by Kurt Jeserich, Hans Pohl, and Georg-Christoph von Unruh, 53–65. Stuttgart, 1983.

———. "Das 'Privilegium maius' und die Reichsverfassung." In *Fälschungen im Mittelalter,* 201–24. Hannover, 1988.

———. *Von der offenen Verfassung zu gestalteter Verdichtung: Das Reich im späten Mittelalter 1250–1490.* Berlin, 1985.

———. "Der Reichstag zu Worms von 1495." In *1495—Kaiser, Reich, Reformen: Der Reichstag zu Worms; Ausstellung des Landeshauptarchivs Koblenz in Verbindung mit der Stadt Worms zum 500jährigen Jubiläum des Wormser Reichstags von 1495*. Koblenz, 1995.

———. "Über den Hof Kaiser Karls IV." In *Deutscher Königshof, Hoftag und Reichstag im späteren Mittelalter*, 77–103. Stuttgart, 2002.

———. "Versuch über die Entstehung des Reichstags." In *Politische Ordnungen und soziale Kräfte im Alten Reich*, edited by Hans-Ulrich Wehler, 1–36. Wiesbaden, 1980.

Moraw, Peter, Karl Otmar von Aretin, and Notker Hammerstein. "Reich." In *Historisches Lexikon zur politisch-sozialen Sprache in Deutschland*, edited by Otto Brunner, Werner Werner, and Reinhart Koselleck, vol. 5, 423–86. Stuttgart, 1984.

Moraw, Peter, and Volker Press. "Probleme der Sozial- und Verfassungsgeschichte des Heiligen Römischen Reiches im späten Mittelalter und der Frühen Neuzeit, 13.–18. Jahrhundert." *Zeitschrift für Historische Forschung* 2 (1975): 95–108.

Möseneder, Karl, ed. *Feste in Regensburg: Von der Reformation bis in die Gegenwart*. Regensburg, 1986.

Mostert, Marco, and Petra Schulte, eds. *Trust in Writing: Papers from the Fifth Utrecht Symposium on Medieval Literacy*. Utrecht Studies in Medieval Literacy 13. Turnhout, 2008.

Muir, Edward. *Civic Ritual in Renaissance Venice*. Princeton, NJ, 1981.

———. *Ritual in Early Modern Europe*. 2nd ed. Cambridge, 2005.

Müller, Andreas. *Der Regensburger Reichstag von 1653/54: Eine Studie zur Entwicklung des Alten Reiches nach dem Westfälischen Frieden*. Europäische Hochschulschriften III, 511. Frankfurt am Main, 1992.

Müller, Christoph. *Das imperative und freie Mandat: Überlegungen zur Lehre von der Repräsentation des Volkes*. Leiden, 1966.

Müller, Gerhard. "Kardinal Lorenzo Campeggio, die römische Kurie und der Augsburger Reichstag 1530." In *Causa Reformationis: Beiträge zur Reformationsgeschichte und zur Theologie Martin Luthers*, edited by Gottfried Maron and Gottfried Seebaß, 111–30. Gütersloh, 1989.

Müller, Heribert. *Théâtre de la préséance: Les ducs de Bourgogne face aux grandes assemblées dans le Saint-Empire*. Conférences annuelles de l'Institut Historique Allemand 13. Ostfildern, 2007.

Müller, Jan-Dirk. *Gedechtnus: Literatur und Hofgesellschaft um Maximilian I*. Forschungen zur Geschichte der älteren deutschen Literatur 2. Munich, 1982.

Müller, Klaus. *Das kaiserliche Gesandtschaftswesen im Jahrhundert nach dem Westfälischen Frieden 1648–1740*. Bonn, 1976.

Müller, Rainer A., ed. *Bilder des Reiches*. Sigmaringen, 1997.

———. *Heiliges Römisches Reich Deutscher Nation: Anspruch und Bedeutung des Reichstitels in der frühen Neuzeit*. Eichstätter Hochschulreden 75. Regensburg, 1990.

Münch, Paul. *Das Jahrhundert des Zwiespalts: Deutschland 1600–1700*. Stuttgart, 1999.

Münkler, Herfried. "Die Visibilität der Macht und die Strategien der Machtvisualisierung." In *Macht der Öffentlichkeit—Öffentlichkeit der Macht*, edited by Gerhard Köhler, 213–30. Baden-Baden, 1995.

Mußgnug, Dorothee. "Die Achte Kurwürde." In *Humaniora: Medizin—Recht—Geschichte. Festschrift für Adolf Laufs zum 70. Geburtstag*, edited by Bernd-Rüdiger Kern, Elmar Wadle, Klaus-Peter Schroeder and Christian Katzenmeier, 219–49. Berlin, 2006.

Nicklas, Thomas. "Müssen wir das Alte Reich lieben? Texte und Bilder zum 200. Jahrestag eines Endes; Revision der Literatur des Erinnerungsjahres 2006." *Archiv für Kulturgeschichte* 89 (2007): 447–74.

Neu, Tim. "Matrikel." *Enzyklopädie der Neuzeit*, edited by Friedrich Jaeger, vol. 7. Stuttgart and Weimar, 2008.

Neuhaus, Helmut. "Der Augsburger Reichstag des Jahres 1530: Ein Forschungsbericht." *Zeitschrift für Historische Forschung* 9 (1982): 167–211.

———. "Das Heilige Römische Reich Deutscher Nation am Ende des Dreißigjährigen Krieges (1648–1654)." In *Nachkriegszeiten—Die Stunde Null als Realität und Mythos in der deutschen Geschichte: Acta Hohenschwangau 1995*, edited by Stefan Krimm and Wieland Zirbs, 10–33. Munich, 1996.

———. "Von Karl V. zu Ferdinand I.: Herrschaftsübergang im Heiligen Römischen Reich 1555–1558." In *Recht und Reich im Zeitalter der Reformation: Festschrift für Horst Rabe*, edited by Christine Roll, 417–40. Frankfurt am Main, 1997.

———. *Das Reich in der Frühen Neuzeit*. Enzyklopädie deutscher Geschichte 42. Munich, 1997.

———. "Von Reichstag(en) zu Reichstag: Reichsständische Beratungsformen von der Mitte des 16. bis zur Mitte des 17. Jahrhunderts." In *Reichsständische Libertät und habsburgisches Kaisertum*, edited by Heinz Duchhardt, 135–49. Mainz, 1999.

———. *Reichsständische Repräsentationsformen im 16. Jahrhundert: Reichstag, Reichskreistag, Reichsdeputationstag*. Schriften zur Verfassungsgeschichte 33. Berlin, 1982.

———. "Die Römische Königswahl vivente imperatore in der Neuzeit: Zum Problem der Kontinuität in einer frühneuzeitlichen Wahlmonarchie." In *Neue Studien zur frühneuzeitlichen Reichsgeschichte*, edited by Johannes Kunisch, 1–53. Berlin, 1997.

———. "Wandlungen der Reichstagsorganisation in der ersten Hälfte des 16. Jahrhunderts." In *Neue Studien zur frühneuzeitlichen Reichsgeschichte*, edited by Johannes Kunisch, 113–40. Berlin, 1987.

———. "Zwänge und Entwicklungsmöglichkeiten reichsständischer Beratungsformen in der zweiten Hälfte des 16. Jahrhunderts." *Zeitschrift für Historische Forschung* 10 (1983): 279–98.

Noël, Jean-François. "Zur Geschichte der Reichsbelehnungen im 18. Jahrhundert." *Mitteilungen des Österreichischen Staatsarchivs* 21 (1968): 106–22.

Nolte, Cordula. *Familie, Hof und Herrschaft: Das verwandtschaftliche Beziehungs- und Kommunikationsnetz der Reichsfürsten am Beispiel der Markgrafen von Brandenburg-Ansbach*. Ostfildern, 2005.

Nullmeier, Frank. "Nachwort." In *Politik als Ritual: Die symbolische Funktion staatlicher Institutionen und politischen Handelns*, by Murray Edelman, 3rd, expanded edition. Frankfurt am Main and New York, 2005.

Oestreich, Gerhard. "Zur parlamentarischen Arbeitsweise der deutschen Reichstage unter Karl V. (1519–1556): Kuriensystem und Ausschussbildung." In *Die geschichtlichen Grundlagen der modernen Volksvertretung: Die Entwicklung von den mittelalterlichen Korporationen zu den modernen Parlamenten*, vol. 2, *Reichsstände und Landstände*, edited by Heinz Rausch, 242–78. Wege der Forschung 469). Darmstadt, 1974.

Ong, Walter J. *Orality and Literacy: The Technologizing of the World*. London and New York, 1993.

Oresko, Robert. "The House of Savoy in Search for a Royal Crown." In *Royal and Republican Sovereignty in Early Modern Europe: Essays in Memory of Ragnhild Hatton*, edited by Robert Oresko, G. C. Gibbs, and H. M. Scott, 272–350. Cambridge, 1997.

Ortmann, Günther. *Als ob. Fiktionen und Organisationen*. Wiesbaden, 2004.

Oschmann, Antje. *Der Nürnberger Exekutionstag 1649–1650: Das Ende des Dreißigjährigen Krieges in Deutschland*. Schriftenreihe der Vereinigung zur Erforschung der Neueren Geschichte e.V. 17. Münster, 1991.

Ottomeyer, Hans, Jutta Götzmann, Ansgar Reiss, Heinz Schilling, and Werner Heun, eds. *Heiliges Römisches Reich Deutscher Nation 962 bis 1806: Altes Reich und neue Staaten* 2 vols. Dresden, 2006.

Ottomeyer, Hans, and Michaela Völkel, eds. *Die öffentliche Tafel: Tafelzeremoniell in Europa 1300–1900.* Wolfratshausen, 2002.

Pangerl, Irmgard, Martin Scheutz, and Thomas Winkelbauer, eds. *Der Wiener Hof im Spiegel der Zeremonialprotokolle (1652–1800): Eine Annäherung.* Innsbruck, 2007.

Paravicini, Werner. "Zeremoniell und Raum." In *Zeremoniell und Raum*, edited by Werner Paravicni, 11-36. Sigmaringen, 1997.

Paulmann, Johannes. *Pomp und Politik: Monarchenbegegnungen in Europa zwischen Ancien Régime und Erstem Weltkrieg.* Paderborn, 2000.

Pečar, Andreas. *Die Ökonomie der Ehre: Der höfische Adel am Kaiserhof Karls VI. (1711–1740). Symbolische Kommunikation in der Vormoderne.* Darmstadt, 2003.

Pelizaeus, Ludolf. *Der Aufstieg Württembergs und Hessens zur Kurwürde 1692–1803.* Frankfurt am Main, 2000.

Peters, Jan. "Der Platz in der Kirche: Über soziales Rangdenken im Spätfeudalismus." *Jahrbuch für Volkskunde und Kulturgeschichte* 28 (1985): 77–106.

Petersohn, Jürgen. "Über monarchische Insignien und ihre Funktion im mittelalterlichen Reich." *Historische Zeitschrift* 266 (1998): 47–96.

Piendl, Max. "Die fürstliche Residenz in Regensburg im 18. und beginnenden 19. Jahrhundert." In *Thurn und Taxis—Studien*, vol. 3, *Beiträge zur Kunst—und Kulturpflege im Hause Thurn und Taxis, 1963, Jubiläumsband gewidmet zum 70. Geburtstag von Fürst Joseph von Thurn und Taxis*, edited by Max Piendl, 47–125. Kallmünz, 1963.

———. "Prinzipalkommissariat und Prinzipalkommissare am Immerwährenden Reichstag." In *Regensburg, Stadt der Reichstage: Vom Mittelalter zur Neuzeit*, edited by Dieter Albrecht, 167–84. Schriftenreihe der Universität Regensburg, n.s., 21. Regensburg, 1994.

Podlech, Adalbert. "Repräsentation." In *Geschichtliche Grundbegriffe: Historisches Lexikon zur politisch-sozialen Sprache in Deutschland*, edited by Otto Brunner, Werner Conze, and Reinhart Koselleck, 509–47. Stuttgart, 1984.

Popitz, Heinrich. *Phänomene der Macht*. 2nd ed. Tübingen, 1999.

Press, Volker. *Kriege und Krisen, Deutschland 1600–1715.* Die neue deutsche Geschichte 5. Munich, 1991.

Prodi, Paolo. *Glaube und Eid: Treueformeln, Glaubensbekenntnisse und Sozialdisziplinierung zwischen Mittelalter und Neuzeit.* Schriften des Historischen Kollegs: Kolloquien 28. Munich, 1993.

———. *Das Sakrament der Herrschaft: Der politische Eid in der Verfassungsgeschichte des Okzidents.* Schriften des Italienisch-Deutschen Historischen Instituts in Trient 11. Berlin, 1997.

Quaritsch, Helmut. *Souveränität: Entstehung und Entwicklung des Begriffs in Frankreich und Deutschland vom 13. Jh. bis 1806.* Schriften zur Verfassungsgeschichte 38. Berlin, 1986.

Rabe, Horst. *Deutsche Geschichte 1500–1600: Das Jahrhundert der Glaubensspaltung.* Munich, 1991.

———. *Reichsbund und Interim: Die Verfassungs- und Religionspolitik Karls V. und der Reichstag von Augsburg 1547/1548.* Cologne and Vienna, 1971.

Rahn, Thomas. *Festbeschreibung: Funktion und Topik einer Textsorte am Beispiel der Beschreibung höfischer Hochzeiten (1568–1794).* Tübingen, 2006.

———. "Grenz-Situationen des Zeremoniells in der Frühen Neuzeit." In *Die Grenze: Begriff und Inszenierung*, edited by Markus Bauer, 177–206. Berlin, 1997.

Ranke, Leopold von. *Deutsche Geschichte im Zeitalter der Reformation*. Edited by P. Jachimsen. 6 vols. Munich, 1925–26.
Rappaport, Roy A. "The Obvious Aspects of Ritual." In *Ecology, Meaning, and Religion*, 175–221. Berkeley CA, 1979.
Rauscher, Peter. "Recht und Politik: Reichsjustiz und oberstrichterliches Amt des Kaisers im Spannungsfeld des preußisch-österreichischen Dualismus (1740–1785)." *Mitteilungen des Österreichischen Staatsarchivs* 46 (1998): 269–309.
Rehberg, Karl-Siegbert. "Institutionen als symbolische Ordnungen: Leitfragen zur Theorie und Analyse institutioneller Mechanismen." In *Die Eigenart der Institutionen*, ed. Gerhard Goehler, 47–84. Baden-Baden, 1994.
———. "Institutionenwandel und die Funktionsveränderung des Symbolischen." In *Institutionenwandel*, edited by Gerhard Goehler, 94–118. Opladen, 1997.
———. "Die stabilisierende 'Fiktionalität' von Präsenz und Dauer: Institutionelle Analyse und historische Forschung." In *Institutionen und Ereignis: Über historische Praktiken und Vorstellungen gesellschaftlichen Ordnens*, edited by Reinhard Blänkner and Bernhard Jussen, 381–407. Göttingen, 1998.
———. "Weltrepräsentanz und Verkörperung: Institutionelle Analyse und Symboltheorien—eine Einführung in systematische Absicht." In *Institutionalität und Symbolisierung: Verstetigungen kultureller Ordnungsmuster in Vergangenheit und Gegenwart*, edited by Gert Melville, 3–49. Cologne, Weimar, and Vienna, 2001.
Reichsstadt und Immerwährender Reichstag (1663–1806): 250 Jahre Haus Thurn und Taxis in Regensburg; Beiträge des Regensburger Herbstsymposions zur Kunstgeschichte und Denkmalpflege vom 17. bis 22. November 1998. Thurn-und-Taxis-Studien 20; Regensburger Herbstsymposion zur Kunstgeschichte und Denkmalpflege 5. Kallmünz, 2001.
Reidel, Hermann. "Die Residenz der kaiserlichen Prinzipalkommissare am Immerwährenden Reichstag." In *Reichsstadt und Immerwährender Reichstag (1663–1806): 250 Jahre Haus Thurn und Taxis in Regensburg*, 165–74. Thurn-und-Taxis-Studien 20. Kallmünz, 2001.
Reinhard, Wolfgang. "Frühmoderner Staat und deutsches Monstrum: Die Entstehung des modernen Staates und das Alte Reich." *Zeitschrift für Historische Forschung* 29 (2002): 339–57.
———. *Geschichte der Staatsgewalt: Eine vergleichende Verfassungsgeschichte Europas von den Anfängen bis zur Gegenwart*. Munich, 1999.
———, ed. *Krumme Touren: Anthropologie kommunikativer Umwege*. Veröffentlichungen des Instituts für Historische Anthropologie e.V. 10. Vienna, Cologne, and Weimar, 2007.
———. "Das Wachstum der Staatsgewalt. Historische Reflexionen." *Der Staat* 31 (1992): 59–75.
———. "Was ist europäische politische Kultur? Versuch zur Begründung einer politischen historischen Anthropologie." *Geschichte und Gesellschaft* 27 (2001): 593–616.
Reiser, Rudolf. *Adliges Stadtleben im Barockzeitalter: Internationales Gesandtenleben auf dem Immerwährenden Reichstag zu Regensburg—Ein Beitrag zur Kultur- und Gesellschafts-Geschichte der Barockzeit*. Munich, 1969.
Repgen, Konrad. "Ferdinand III. (1637–1657)." In *Dreißigjähriger Krieg und Westfälischer Friede: Studien und Quellen*, edited by Franz Bosbach and Christoph Kampmann, 319–43, 319–43. Rechts- und staatswissenschaftliche Veröffentlichungen der Görres-Gesellschaft, n.s., 81. Paderborn, 1998.
Reuter, Fritz. "Worms als Reichstagsstadt." In *1495—Kaiser, Reich, Reformen: Der Reichstag zu Worms; Ausstellung des Landeshauptarchivs Koblenz in Verbindung mit der Stadt*

Worms zum 500jährigen Jubiläum des Wormser Reichstags von 1495, 123–39. Koblenz, 1995.

Reuter-Pettenberg, Helga. "Bedeutungswandel der römischen Königskrönung in der Neuzeit." Dissertation, Cologne, 1963.

Richter, Susan, and Dirk Dirbach, eds. *Thronverzicht: Die Abdankung in Monarchien vom Mittelalter bis in die Neuzeit*. Cologne, Weimar, and Vienna, 2010.

Riederer, Günter, and Thomas Schuhbauer. "'… eine finstere, melancholische und in sich selbst vertiefte Stadt': Blicke von innen und außen." In *Regensburg: Historische Bilder einer Reichsstadt*, edited by Lothar Kolmer and Fritz Wiedemann, 260–83. Regensburg, 1994.

Rödder, Andreas. "Klios neue Kleider: Theoriedebatten um eine Kulturgeschichte der Politik in der Moderne." *Historische Zeitschrift* 283 (2006): 657–88.

Rödel, Volker. "Lehensgebräuche." In *Handwörterbuch zur deutschen Rechtsgeschichte*, edited by Adalbert Erler and Erich Schmidt, vol. 2, 1712–14. Berlin, 1978.

Roeck, Bernd. *Reichssystem und Reichsherkommen: Die Diskussion über die Staatlichkeit des Reiches in der politischen Publizistik des 17. und. 18. Jahrhunderts*. Veröffentlichungen des Instituts für Europäische Geschichte Mainz: Abteilung Universalgeschichte 112. Stuttgart, 1984.

Roellecke, Gerd. "Das Ende des römisch-deutschen Kaisertums und der Wandel der europäischen Gesellschaft." In *Heiliges Römisches Reich und moderne Staatlichkeit*, edited by Wilhelm Brauneder, 93–109. Frankfurt am Main, 1993.

Rogge, Jörg. *Die deutschen Könige im Mittelalter—Wahl und Krönung*. Geschichte Kompakt. Darmstadt, 2006.

Rohr, Theodor. "Der deutsche Reichstag vom Hubertusburger Frieden bis zum Bayerischen Erbfolgekrieg (1763–1778)." Dissertation, Bonn, 1968.

Roll, Christine. "Archaische Rechtsordnung oder politisches Instrument? Überlegungen zur Bedeutung des Lehnswesens im frühneuzeitlichen Reich." *Zeitenblicke* 6 (2007), http://www.zeitenblicke.de/2007/1/roll/index_html, URN: urn:nbn:de:0009-9-8133 (accessed 10.05.2007).

———. *Das zweite Reichsregiment 1521–1530: Ständische Regierung oder kaiserliche Regentschaft?* Cologne, Weimar, and Vienna, 1995.

Roosen, William. "Early Modern Diplomatic Ceremonial: A Systems Approach." *Journal of Modern History* 52 (1980): 452–76.

Roth, Friedrich. *Augsburgs Reformationsgeschichte*. Vol. 1, *1517–1530*. Munich, 1901.

Rubin, Miri. *Corpus Christi: The Eucharist in Late Medieval Culture*. Cambridge, 2004.

Rudolph, Harriet. "Kontinuität und Dynamik: Ritual und Zeremoniell bei Krönungsakten im Alten Reich—Maximilian II., Rudolf II. und Matthias in vergleichender Perspektive." In *Investitur- und Krönungsrituale: Herrschaftseinsetzungen im kulturellen Vergleich*, edited by Marion Steinicke and Stefan Weinfurter, 377–99. Cologne, Weimar, and Vienna, 2005.

———. "Die visuelle Kultur des Reiches: Kaiserliche Einzüge im Medium der Druckgraphik (1500–1800)." In *Heiliges Römische Reich Deutscher Nation 962–1806. Altes Reich und neue Staaten 1495 bis 1806*, vol. 1, *Essays*, edited by Heinz Schilling, Werner Heun, and Jutta Götzmann, 231–41. Dresden, 2006.

Sauter, Alexander. *Fürstliche Herrschaftsrepräsentation: Die Habsburger im 14. Jahrhundert*. Ostfildern, 2003.

Scheel, Gerhard. "Die Stellung der Reichsstände zur Römischen Königswahl seit den Westfälischen Friedensverhandlungen." In *Forschungen zu Staat und Verfassung. Festgabe für Fritz Hartung*, 113–32. Berlin, 1958.

Schenk, Gerrit Jasper. "Zähmung der Widerspenstigen? Die Huldigung der Stadt Worms 1494 zwischen Text, Ritual und Performanz." *Paragrana* 12 (2003): 223–56.

———. *Zeremoniell und Politik: Herrschereinzüge im spätmittelalterlichen Reich.* Forschungen zur Kaiser- und Papstgeschichte des Mittelalters, Beiheft, 21. Cologne, Weimar, and Vienna, 2003.

Scheurmann, Ingrid, ed. *Frieden durch Recht: Das Reichskammergericht von 1495 bis 1806.* Mainz, 1994.

Scheutz, Martin. "'Der vermenschte Heiland': Armenspeisung und Gründonnerstags-Fußwaschung am Wiener Kaiserhof." In *Ein zweigeteilter Ort? Hof und Stadt in der Frühen Neuzeit,* edited by Susanne Claudine Pils, 189–253. Innsbruck, 2005.

Schieder, Michael. "'Ay, no; no, ay; for I must nothing be.' Die Abdankung des Monarchen – eine Leerstelle in der Herrscherikonographie." In *Thronverzicht. Die Abdankung in Monarchien vom Mittelalter bis in die Neuzeit,* edited by Susan Richter and Dirk Dirbach, Cologne, Weimar, and Vienna, 2010.

Schilling, Heinz. "Das Alte Reich: Ein teilmodernisiertes System als Ergebnis der partiellen Anpassung an die frühmoderne Staatsbildung in den Territorien und den europäischen Nachbarländern." In *Imperium Romanum—Irregulare Corpus—Teutscher Reichs-Staat: Das Alte Reich im Verständnis der Zeitgenossen und der Historiographie,* edited by Matthias Schnettger, 279–91. Mainz, 2002.

———. *Aufbruch und Krise: Deutschland 1517–1648.* Das Reich und die Deutschen 5. Berlin, 1988.

———. *Höfe und Allianzen: Deutschland 1648–1763.* Siedler deutsche Geschichte 6. Munich, 1998.

———. *Konfessionalisierung und Staatsinteressen: Internationale Beziehungen 1559–1660.* Handbuch der Geschichte der internationalen Beziehungen 2. Paderborn, 2007.

Schilling, Heinz, and Heribert Smolinsky, eds. *Der Augsburger Religionsfrieden 1555.* Gütersloh, 2007.

Schilling, Michael. *Bildpublizistik in der Frühen Neuzeit: Aufgaben und Leistungen des illustrierten Flugblattes in Deutschland bis um 1700.* Tübingen, 1990.

Schindling, Anton. *Die Anfänge des Immerwährenden Reichstags zu Regensburg: Ständevertretung und Staatskunst nach dem Westfälischen Frieden.* Mainz, 1991.

———. "Kaiser, Reich und Reichsverfassung 1648–1806: Das neue Bild vom Alten Reich." In *Altes Reich, Frankreich und Europa: Politische, philosophische und historische Aspekte des französischen Deutschlandbildes im 17. und 18. Jahrhundert,* edited by Olaf Ansbach, Klaus Malettke, and Sven Externbrink, 25–54. Berlin, 2001.

———. "Konfessionalisierung und Grenzen von Konfessionalisierbarkeit." In *Die Territorien des Reichs um Zeitalter der Reformation und Konfessionalisierung,* edited by Anton Schindling and Walter Ziegler, vol.7, 9–44. Münster, 1997.

———. "Der Westfälische Frieden und der Reichstag." In *Politische Ordnungen und soziale Kräfte im Alten Reich,* edited by Hermann Weber, 113–53. Veröffentlichungen des Instituts für Europäische Geschichte Mainz, Abteilung Universalgeschichte, 8. Wiesbaden, 1980.

Schlaich, Klaus. "Majoritas, protestatio, itio in partes, corpus evangelicorum: Das Verfahren im Reichstag des Heiligen Römischen Reiches Deutscher Nation nach der Reformation." *Zeitschrift der Savigny-Stiftung für Rechtsgeschichte: Kanonistische Abteilung* 94 (1977): 264–99; 95 (1978): 139–79.

———. "Die Mehrheitsabstimmung im Reichstag zwischen 1495 und 1613." *Zeitschrift für Historische Forschung* 10 (1983): 299–340.

———. "Die 'protestatio' beim Reichstag in Speyer von 1529 in verfassungsrechtlicher Sicht." In *Gesammelte Schriften: Staat, Kirche, Recht, Geschichte*, 49–64. Tübingen, 1997.
Schlinker, Steffen. *Fürstenamt und Rezeption: Reichsfürstenstand und gelehrte Literatur im späten Mittelalter*. Cologne, Weimar, and Vienna, 1999.
Schlögl, Rudolf. "Der frühneuzeitliche Hof als Kommunikationsraum: Interaktionstheoretische Perspektiven der Forschung." In *Geschichte und Systemtheorie: Exemplarische Fallstudien*, edited by Frank Becker, 185–225. Frankfurt am Main and New York, 2004.
———. "Der Glaube Alteuropas und die Moderne Welt: Zum Verhältnis von Säkularisation und Säkularisierung." In *Zerfall und Wiederbeginn: Vom Erzbistum zum Bistum Mainz (1792/97–1830)—Ein Vergleich, Festschrift für Friedhelm Jürgensmeier*, edited by Walter G. Rödel and Regina E. Schwerdtfeger, 63–82. Würzburg, 2002.
———. "Politik beobachten: Öffentlichkeit und Medien in der Frühen Neuzeit." *Zeitschrift für Historische Forschung* 35 (2008): 581–616.
———. "Symbole in der Kommunikation: Zur Einführung." In *Die Wirklichkeit der Symbole: Grundlagen der Kommunikation in historischen und gegenwärtigen Gesellschaften*, edited by Rudolf Schlögl, Bernhard Giesen, and Jürgen Osterhammel, 9–38. Konstanz, 2004.
———. "Vergesellschaftung unter Anwesenden." In *Interaktion und Herrschaft: Die Politik der frühneuzeitlichen Stadt*, 9–60. Konstanz, 2004.
Schlosser, Julius. *Die deutschen Reichskleinodien*. Vienna, 1920.
Schmale, Wolfgang. "Constitution, Constitutionnel." In *Handbuch politisch-sozialer Grundbegriffe in Frankreich 1680–1820*, edited by Rolf Reichardt, vol. 12, 31–63. Munich, 1992.
Schmid, Peter. *Geschichte der Stadt Regensburg*. 2 vols. Regensburg, 2000.
———. "Reichssteuern, Reichsfinanzen und Reichsgewalt in der ersten Hälfte des 16. Jahrhunderts." In *Säkulare Aspekte der Reformationszeit*, edited by Heinz Angermeier, 153–98. Munich, 1983.
Schmidt, Georg. "Das frühneuzeitliche Reich: Sonderweg und Modell für Europa oder Staat der Deutschen Nation." In *Imperium Romanum—Irregulare Corpus—Teutscher Reichs-Staat: Das Alte Reich im Verständnis der Zeitgenossen und der Historiographie*, edited by Matthias Schnettger, 247–77. Mainz, 2002.
———. *Geschichte des alten Reiches: Staat und Nation in der Frühen Neuzeit—1495–1806*. Munich, 1999.
———. *Der Städtetag in der Reichsverfassung: Eine Untersuchung zur korporativen Politik der Freien und Reichsstädte in der ersten Hälfte des 16. Jahrhunderts*. Stuttgart, 1984.
———. "Die Wetterauer Kuriatstimme auf dem Reichstag." In *Stände und Gesellschaft im Alten Reich*, 93–109. Stuttgart, 1989.
Schmidt, Peter. "Die gotische Ruine der Reichsverfassung." *Weimarer Beiträge* 35 (1989): 745–58.
Schnath, Georg. *Geschichte Hannovers im Zeitalter der neunten Kur und der englischen Sukzession: 1674–1714; im Anschluß an Adolf Köcher's unvollendete "Geschichte von Hannover und Braunschweig 1648–1714."* 4 vols. Hildesheim, 1938–82.
Schneider, Reinhard, and Harald Zimmermann, eds. *Wahlen und Wählen im Mittelalter*. Vorträge und Forschungen 37. Sigmaringen, 1990.
Schneidmüller, Bernd. "Die Aufführung des Reichs: Zeremoniell, Ritual und Performanz in der Goldenen Bulle von 1356." In *Die Kaisermacher: Frankfurt am Main und die Goldene Bulle—1356–1806*, edited by Evelyn Brockhoff and Michael Matthäus, 76–94. Frankfurt am Main, 2006.

Schnettger, Matthias. "Das Alte Reich und Italien in der Frühen Neuzeit." *Quellen und Forschungen aus italienischen Archiven und Bibliotheken* 79 (1999): 344–420.

———, ed. *Kaiserliches und päpstliches Lehnswesen in der Frühen Neuzeit. Zeitenblicke* 6,1. Cologne, 2007. Available at http://www.zeitenblicke.de/2007/1/ (accessed 15 June 2007).

———. "Von der 'Kleinstaaterei' zum 'komplementären Reichs-Staat': Die Reichsverfassungsgeschichtsschreibung seit dem Zweiten Weltkrieg." In *Geschichte der Politik: Alte und neue Wege*, edited by Hans-Christof Kraus and Thomas Nicklas, 129–54. Munich, 2007.

———. *"Principe sovrano" oder "civitas imperialis"? Die Republik Genua und das Alte Reich in der Frühen Neuzeit (1556–1797)*. Veröffentlichungen des Instituts für Europäische Geschichte Mainz: Abteilung für Universalgeschichte 209; Beiträge zur Sozial- und Verfassungsgeschichte des Alten Reiches 17. Mainz, 2006.

———. "Rang, Zeremoniell, Lehnssysteme: Hierarchische Elemente im europäischen Staatensystem der Frühen Neuzeit." In *Die frühneuzeitliche Monarchie und ihr Erbe: Festschrift für Heinz Duchhardt zum 60. Geburtstag*, edited by Ronald G. Asch, Johannes Arndt, and Matthias Schnettger, 179–95. Münster, Munich, and Berlin, 2003.

———. *Der Reichsdeputationstag von 1655–1663: Kaiser und Stände zwischen Westfälischem Frieden und Immerwährendem Reichstag*. Münster, 1996.

Schnitzler, Norbert. *Ikonoklasmus—Bildersturm: Theologischer Bilderstreit und ikonoklastisches Handeln während des 15. und 16. Jahrhunderts*. Munich, 1996.

Schönberg, Rüdiger Freiherr von. *Das Recht der Reichslehen im 18. Jahrhundert: Zugleich ein Beitrag zu den Grundlagen der bundesstaatlichen Ordnung*. Heidelberg and Karlsruhe, 1977.

Schramm, Percy Ernst. *Geschichte des englischen Königtums im Lichte der Krönung*. 2 vols. Weimar, 1937.

———. *Herrschaftszeichen und Staatssymbolik: Beiträge zu ihrer Geschichte vom dritten bis zum sechzehnten Jahrhundert*. 3 vols. Stuttgart, 1954–56.

Schraut, Sylvia. *Das Haus Schönborn—eine Familienbiographie: Katholischer Reichsadel 1640–1840*. Paderborn, 2004.

Schreiner, Klaus. "Iuramentum Religionis: Entstehung, Geschichte und Funktion des Konfessionseides der Staats- und Kirchendiener im Territorialstaat der frühen Neuzeit." *Der Staat* 24 (1985): 211–46.

———. "Wahl, Amtsantritt und Amtsenthebung von Bischöfen: Rituelle Handlungsmuster, rechtlich normierte Verfahren, traditionsgestützte Gewohnheiten." In *Vormoderne politische Verfahren*, edited by Barbara Stollberg-Rilinger, 73–117. Berlin, 2001.

Schreiner, Klaus, and Gerd Schwerhoff, eds. *Verletzte Ehre: Ehrkonflikte in Gesellschaften des Mittelalters und der Frühen Neuzeit*. Cologne, Weimar, and Vienna, 1996.

Schubert, Ernst. "Erz- und Erbämter am hoch- und spätmittelalterlichen Königshof." In *Deutscher Königshof, Hoftag und Reichstag im späteren Mittelalter*, edited by Peter Moraw, 191–237. Stuttgart, 2002.

———. *König und Reich: Studie zur spätmittelalterlichen deutschen Verfassungsgeschichte*. Göttingen, 1979.

———. "Die Quaternionen: Entstehung, Sinngehalt und Folgen einer spätmittelalterlichen Deutung der Reichsverfassung." *Zeitschrift für Historische Forschung* 20 (1993): 1–63.

Schubert, Friedrich Hermann. *Die deutschen Reichstage in der Staatslehre der frühen Neuzeit*. Schriftenreihe der Historischen Kommission bei der Bayerischen Akademie der Wissenschaften 7. Göttingen, 1966.

Schulte, Aloys. *Die Kaiser- und Königskrönungen zu Aachen: 813–1531.* 1924; repr., Darmstadt, 1965.
Schulze, Winfried. "Augsburg und die Reichstage im späten 16. Jahrhundert." In *Welt im Umbruch: Augsburg zwischen Renaissance und Barock,* vol. 1, 43–49. Augsburg, 1980.
———. *Reich und Türkengefahr im späten 16. Jahrhundert: Studien zu den politischen und gesellschaftlichen Auswirkungen einer äußeren Bedrohung.* Munich, 1978.
Schulze, Winfried, and Thomas Ott. "Wormser Matrikel, Reichsmatrikel." In *Handwörterbuch zur deutschen Rechtsgeschichte,* edited by Erich Schmidt, vol. 5, 1530–36. Berlin, 1998.
Schütz, Alfred. *Der sinnhafte Aufbau der sozialen Welt: Eine Einleitung in die verstehende Soziologie.* Frankfurt am Main, 1993.
Scribner, Robert, ed. *Bilder und Bildersturm im Spätmittelalter und in der frühen Neuzeit.* Wolfenbütteler Forschungen 46. Wiesbaden, 1990.
Scribner, Robert, and C. Scott Dixon. *The German Reformation.* 2nd ed. Basingstoke, 2003.
Seitter, Walter. "Das Wappen als Zweitkörper und Körperzeichen." In *Die Wiederkehr des Körpers,* edited by Dietmar Kamper and Christoph Wulf, 299–312. Frankfurt am Main, 1982.
Sellert, Wolfgang. "Zur rechtshistorischen Bedeutung der Krönung und des Streites um das Krönungsrecht zwischen Mainz und Köln." In *Herrscherweihe und Königskrönung im frühneuzeitlichen Europa,* edited by Heinz Durchhardt, 21–32. Wiesbaden, 1983.
———, ed. *Reichshofrat und Reichskammergericht, ein Konkurrenzverhältnis.* Quellen und Forschungen zur höchsten Gerichtsbarkeit im Alten Reich 34. Cologne, Weimar, and Vienna, 1999.
Seyboth, Reinhard. *Die Markgraftümer Ansbach und Kulmbach unter der Regierung Markgraf Friedrichs des Älteren (1486–1515).* Schriftenreihe der Historischen Kommission bei der Bayerischen Akademie der Wissenschaften 24. Göttingen, 1985.
———. "Die Reichstage der 1480er Jahre." In *Deutscher Königshof, Hoftag und Reichstag im späteren Mittelalter,* edited by Peter Moraw, 519–46. Stuttgart, 2002.
Siebenhüner, Kim. "Glaubenswechsel in der frühen Neuzeit: Chancen und Tendenzen einer historischen Konversionsforschung." *Zeitschrift für Historische Forschung* 34 (2007): 243–72.
Sieber, Friedrich. "Volksbelustigungen bei deutschen Kaiserkrönungen." *Archiv für Frankfurts Geschichte und Kunst,* 3rd. series, 11 (1913): 3–106.
Sieber, Johannes. *Zur Geschichte des Reichsmatrikelwesens im ausgehenden Mittelalter (1422–1521).* Leipziger Historische Abhandlungen 24. Leipzig, 1911.
Sieber-Lehmann, Claudius. "Warum es für das Verhältnis von Papst und Kaiser kein erfolgreiches Denkmodell gab." In *Die Macht des Königs: Herrschaft in Europa vom Frühmittelalter bis in die Neuzeit,* edited by Bernhard Jussen, 150–64. Munich, 2005.
Sikora, Michael. "Formen des Politischen: Der frühmoderne deutsche Reichstag in systemtheoretischer Perspektive." In *Geschichte und Systemtheorie,* edited by Frank Becker, 157–84. Frankfurt am Main, 2004.
———. "Der Sinn des Verfahrens: Soziologische Deutungsangebote." In *Vormoderne politische Verfahren,* edited by Barbara Stollberg-Rilinger, 25–51. Berlin, 2001.
Smend, Rudolf. "Zur Geschichte der Formel 'Kaiser und Reich' in den letzten Jahrhunderten des alten Reiches." In *Staatsrechtliche Abhandlungen und andere Aufsätze,* 2nd ed., 9–18. Berlin, 1968.
———. *Verfassung und Verfassungsrecht.* Munich, 1928.

Soeffner, Georg, and Drik Tänzler, eds. *Figurative Politik: Zur Performanz der Macht in der modernen Gesellschaft*. Opladen, 2002.

Sofsky, Wolfgang, and Rainer Paris. *Figurationen sozialer Macht*. Frankfurt am Main, 1994.

Spieß, Karl-Heinz. "Kommunikationsformen im Hochadel und am Königshof im Spätmittelalter." In *Formen und Funktionen öffentlicher Kommunikation im Mittelalter*, edited by Gerd Althoff, 261–90. Vorträge und Forschungen 51. Stuttgart, 2001.

———. "Lehnserneuerung." In *Handwörterbuch der deutschen Rechtsgeschichte*, vol. 2, 1708–10. Berlin, 1978.

———. "Lehn(s)recht, Lehnswesen." In *Handwörterbuch der deutschen Rechtsgeschichte*, vol. 2, 1725–41. Berlin, 1978.

———. "Rangdenken und Rangstreit im Mittelalter." In *Zeremoniell und Raum*, edited by Werner Paravicini, 39–61. Sigmaringen, 1997.

Stahl, Patricia. "'Im großen Saal des Römers ward gespeiset im höchsten Grade prächtig': Zur Geschichte der kaiserlichen Krönungsbankette in Frankfurt am Main." In *Die öffentliche Tafel: Tafelzeremoniell in Europa 1300–1900*, edited by Hans Ottomeyer and Michaela Völkel, 58–71. Wolfratshausen, 2002.

———. "Ein wahrhafftig Schauspiel und fürtrefflich Mahl: Die kaiserlichen Krönungsbankette im Frankfurter Römer." In *Die Kaisermacher: Frankfurt am Main und die Goldene Bulle—1356–1806*, edited by Evelyn Brockhoff and Michael Matthäus, 282–93. Frankfurt am Main, 2006.

Steiger, Heinhard. "Rechtliche Strukturen der europäischen Staatenordnung 1648–1792." *Zeitschrift für ausländisches öffentliches Recht und Völkerrecht* 59 (1999): 609–47.

Steiner, Jürgen. *Die pfälzische Kurwürde während des Dreißigjährigen Krieges (1618–1648)*. Speyer, 1985.

Steinicke, Marion, and Stefan Weinfurter, eds. *Investitur- und Krönungsrituale: Herrschaftseinsetzungen im kulturellen Vergleich*. Cologne, Weimar, and Vienna, 2005.

Stollberg-Rilinger, Barbara. "Der Grafenstand in der Reichspublizistik." In *Dynastie und Herrschaftssicherung in der Frühen Neuzeit: Geschlechter und Geschlecht*, edited by Heide Wunder, 29–54. Zeitschrift für Historische Forschung 28. Berlin, 2002.

———. *Das Heilige Römische Reich Deutscher Nation: Vom Ende des Mittelalters bis 1806*. Munich, 2006.

———. "Höfische Öffentlichkeit: Zur zeremoniellen Selbstdarstellung des brandenburgischen Hofes vor dem europäischen Publikum." *Forschungen zur brandenburgischen und preußischen Geschichte*, n.s., 7 (1997): 147–76.

———. "Honores regii: Die Königswürde im zeremoniellen Zeichensystem der Frühen Neuzeit." In *Dreihundert Jahre Preußische Königskrönung: Eine Tagungsdokumentation*, edited by Johannes Kunisch, 1–26. Berlin, 2002.

———. "Kneeling Before God–Kneeling Before the Emperor". in: *Resonances. Historical Essays on Continuity and Change*, edited by Nils Holger Petersen, 149–172. Turnhout, 2011.

———. "Ordnungsleistung und Konfliktträchtigkeit der höfischen Tafel." In *Zeichen und Raum: Ausstattung und höfisches Zeremoniell in den deutschen Schlössern der Frühen Neuzeit*, edited by Peter-Michael Hahn and Ulrich Schütte, 103–22. Rudolstädter Forschungen zur Residenzkultur 3. Munich and Berlin, 2006.

———. "Rang vor Gericht: Zur Verrechtlichung sozialer Rangkonflikte in der frühen Neuzeit." *Zeitschrift für Historische Forschung* 28 (2001): 385–418.

———. "Das Reich als Lehnssystem." In *Heiliges Römisches Reich Deutscher Nation 962–1806: Altes Reich und neue Staaten 1495 bis 1806*, edited by Heinz Schilling, Werner Heun, and Jutta Götzmann, 55–67. Dresden, 2006.

---. *Der Staat als Maschine: Zur politischen Metaphorik des absoluten Fürstenstaats* (Historische Forschungen, 30). Berlin, 1986.

---. "Symbolische Kommunikation in der Vormoderne: Begriffe, Thesen, Forschungsperspektiven." *Zeitschrift für Historische Forschung* 31 (2004): 489–527.

---. "Verfassungsakt oder Fest?" In *Die Kaisermacher: Frankfurt am Main und die Goldene Bulle—1356–1806*, edited by Evelyn Brockhoff and Michael Matthäus, 94–105. Frankfurt am Main, 2006.

---. "Völkerrechtlicher Status und zeremonielle Praxis auf dem Westfälischen Friedenskongreß." In *Rechtsformen internationaler Politik: Theorie, Norm und Praxis vom 12. bis zum 18. Jahrhundert*, edited by Martin Kintzinger and Michael Jucker, 147–64. Berlin, 2011.

---, ed. *Vormoderne politische Verfahren.* Zeitschrift für Historische Forschung 25. Berlin, 2001.

---, ed. *Was heißt Kulturgeschichte des Politischen?* Zeitschrift für Historische Forschung 35. Berlin, 2005.

---. "Die Wissenschaft der feinen Unterschiede: Das Präzedenzrecht und die europäischen Monarchien vom 16. bis zum 18. Jh." *Majestas* 10 (2002): 125–50.

---. "Zeremoniell als politisches Verfahren: Rangordnung und Rangstreit als Strukturmerkmale des frühneuzeitlichen Reichstags." *Zeitschrift für Historische Forschung* 19 (1997): 91–132.

---. "Die zeremonielle Inszenierung des Reiches oder: Was leistet der kulturalistische Ansatz für die Reichsverfassungsgeschichte?" In *Imperium Romanum—Irregulare Corpus—Teutscher Reichs-Staat: Das Alte Reich im Verständnis der Zeitgenossen und der Historiographie*, edited by Matthias Schnettger, 233–46. Mainz, 2002.

---. "Zeremoniell, Ritual, Symbol: Neue Forschungen zur symbolischen Kommunikation in Spätmittelalter und Früher Neuzeit." *Zeitschrift für historische Forschung* 27 (2000): 389–405.

Stolleis, Michael. *Geschichte des Öffentlichen Rechts*. Vol. 1, *Reichspublizistik und Policeywissenschaft: 1600–1800*. Munich, 1988.

---. "Glaubensspaltung und Öffentliches Recht in Deutschland." In *Staat und Staatsräson in der Frühen Neuzeit*, 268–97. Frankfurt am Main, 1990.

---. "'Konfessionalisierung' oder 'Säkularisierung' bei der Entstehung des frühmodernen Staates." *Ius commune* 20 (1993): 1–23.

---. *Staat und Staatsräson in der frühen Neuzeit: Studien zur Geschichte des Öffentlichen Rechts*. Suhrkamp-Taschenbuch Wissenschaft 878. Frankfurt am Main, 1990.

Strohmeyer, Arno. *Konfessionskonflikt und Herrschaftsordnung: Widerstandsrecht bei den österreichischen Ständen (1550–1650)*. Mainz, 2006.

Stutz, Ulrich. "Die Abstimmungsordnung der Goldenen Bulle." *Zeitschrift der Savigny-Stiftung für Rechtsgeschichte, Germanistische Abteilung* 43 (1922): 217–66.

Styra, Peter. "Der Immerwährende Reichstag in der Regensburger Geschichtsschreibung." In *Reichsstadt und Immerwährender Reichstag (1663–1806): 250 Jahre Haus Thurn und Taxis in Regensburg*, 25–33. Thurn-und-Taxis-Studien 20. Kallmünz, 2001.

Thomas, Heinz. "Die lehnrechtlichen Beziehungen des Herzogtums Lothringen zum Reich von der Mitte des 13. bis zum Ende des 14. Jahrhunderts." *Rheinische Vierteljahrsblätter* 38 (1974): 166–202.

Trapp, Eugen. "Das evangelische Regensburg." In *Geschichte der Stadt Regensburg*, edited by Peter Schmidt, vol. 2, 845–62. Regensburg, 2000.

Turner, Victor. *Das Ritual: Struktur und Anti-Struktur*. Frankfurt am Main, 1989.

Uhlhorn, Gerhard. *Urbanus Rhegius: Leben und ausgewählte Schriften.* Leben u. ausgew. Schriften der Väter und Begründer der lutherischen Kirche 7. Elberfeld, 1861.
Ulbert, Jörg. "Der Reichstag im Spiegel französischer Gesandtenberichte (1715–1723)." In *Altes Reich, Frankreich und Europa: Politische, philosophische und historische Aspekte des französischen Deutschlandbildes im 17. und 18. Jahrhundert,* edited by Olaf Asbach, 145–69. Berlin, 2001.
Vann, James Allan, ed. *The Old Reich: Essays on German Political Institutions 1495–1806.* Brussels, 1974.
Vec, Miloš. *Zeremonialwissenschaft im Fürstenstaat: Studien zur juristischen und politischen Theorie absolutistischer Herrschaftsrepräsentation.* Studien zur europäischen Rechtsgeschichte 106. Frankfurt am Main, 1998.
Visceglia, Maria Antonietta. *La città rituale: Roma e le sue cerimonie in età moderna.* Rome, 2002.
Visceglia, Maria Antonietta, and Catherine Brice, eds. *Cérémonial et rituel à Rome (XVIe–XIXe siècles).* Rome, 1997.
Völkel, Markus. "The 'Historical Consciousness' of the Holy Roman Empire of the German Nation (16th–18th Century)." In *The Holy Roman Empire,* edited by R. J. W. Evans, Michael Schaich, and Peter H. Wilson, 323-346. Oxford, 2008.
Völkel, Michaela. "Die öffentliche Tafel an den europäischen Höfen der frühen Neuzeit." In *Die öffentliche Tafel: Tafelzeremoniell in Europa 1300–1900,* edited by Hans Ottomeyer and Michaela Völkel, 10–21. Wolfratshausen, 2002.
Vorländer, Hans. "Integration durch Verfassung? Die symbolische Bedeutung der Verfassung im politischen Integrationsprozeß." In *Integration durch Verfassung,* edited by Hans Vorländer, 9–40. Wiesbaden, 2002.
———. "Die Verfassung als symbolische Ordnung: Perspektiven einer kulturwissenschaftlich-institutionalistischen Verfassungstheorie." In *Politik und Recht,* edited by Michael Becker and Ruth Zimmerling, 229–49. Wiesbaden, 2006.
———. *Die Verfassung: Idee und Geschichte.* 2nd, rev. ed. Munich, 2004.
Walker, Mack. *Johann Jakob Moser and the Holy Roman Empire of the German Nation.* Chapel Hill, NC, 1989.
Wallner, Günter. "Der Krönungsstreit zwischen Kurköln und Kurmainz (1653–1657)." Dissertation, Mainz, 1968.
Wandel, Lee Palmer. *The Eucharist in the Reformation: Incarnation and Liturgy.* Cambridge and New York, 2006.
Wanger, Bernd Herbert. *Kaiserwahl und Krönung im Frankfurt des 17. Jahrhunderts: Darstellung anhand der zeitgenössischen Bild- und Schriftquellen und unter besonderer Berücksichtigung der Erhebung des Jahres 1612.* Studien zur Frankfurter Geschichte 34. Frankfurt am Main, 1994.
Weber, Christoph Friedrich. "Eine eigene Sprache der Politik: Heraldische Symbolik in italienischen Stadtkommunen des Mittelalters." *Zeitschrift für Historische Forschung* 33 (2006): 523–64.
Weick, Karl E. *Der Prozeß des Organisierens.* Frankfurt am Main, 1995.
Weinfurter, Stefan. "Wie das Reich heilig wurde." In *Die Macht des Königs: Herrschaft in Europa vom Frühmittelalter bis in die Neuzeit,* edited by Bernhard Jussen, 190–204. Munich, 2005.
Weiß, Johannes. *Handeln und handeln lassen: Über Stellvertretung.* Opladen, 1998.
Weitzel, Jürgen. "Schriftlichkeit und Recht." In *Schrift und Schriftlichkeit: Ein interdisziplinäres Handbuch,* edited by Hartmut Günther and Otto Ludwig, vol. 1, 610–19. Berlin, 1994.

Weller, Thomas. "Reichsstadt und Reformation." State examination thesis (unprinted), Cologne, 1999.

———. *Theatrum Praecedentiae: Zeremonieller Rang und gesellschaftliche Ordnung in der frühneuzeitlichen Stadt—Leipzig 1500–1800*. Darmstadt, 2006.

Weller, Thomas, Günther Wassilowsky, and Christoph Dartmann, eds. *Technik und Symbolik vormoderner Wahlverfahren*. Beiheft der Historischen Zeitschrift 52. Munich, 2010.

Welt im Umbruch: Augsburg zwischen Renaissance und Barock. Vol. 1, *Zeughaus*. Edited by Bruno Bushart. Augsburg, 1980.

Whaley, Joachim. *Germany and the Holy Roman Empire 1493-1806*. 2 vols. Oxford, 2012.

Wieland, Christian. "Diplomaten als Spiegel ihrer Herren? Römische und florentinische Diplomatie zu Beginn des 17. Jahrhunderts." *Zeitschrift für Historische Forschung* 31 (2004): 359–79.

———. *Fürsten, Freunde, Diplomaten: Die römisch-florentinischen Beziehungen unter Paul V. (1605–1621)*. Cologne, Weimar, and Vienna, 2004.

Wiesflecker, Hermann. *Kaiser Maximilian I*. 5 vols. Munich, 1971–86.

———. *Maximilian I.: Die Fundamente des habsburgischen Weltreichs*. Vienna and Munich, 1991.

Wilentz, Sean. *Rites of Power: Symbolism, Ritual and Politics since the Middle Ages*. Philadelphia, 1985.

Willich, Thomas. "Der Rangstreit zwischen den Erzbischöfen von Magdeburg und Salzburg sowie den Erzherzogen von Österreich: Ein Beitrag zur Verfassungsgeschichte des Heiligen Römischen Reichs Deutscher Nation, ca. 1460–1535." *Mitteilungen der Gesellschaft für Salzburger Landeskunde* 134 (1994): 7–166.

Willoweit, Dietmar. *Deutsche Verfassungsgeschichte: Vom Frankenreich bis zur Teilung Deutschlands—Ein Studienbuch*. 2nd ed. Munich, 1992.

———. *Rechtsgrundlagen der Territorialgewalt, Landesobrigkeit, Herrschaftsrechte und Territorium in der Rechtswissenschaft der Neuzeit*. Cologne and Vienna, 1975.

Wilson, Peter. *The Holy Roman Empire 1495-1806*. 2nd. edition. Basingstoke, 2011.

Windler, Christian. "Tribut und Gabe: Mediterrane Diplomatie als interkulturelle Kommunikation." *Saeculum* 51 (2000): 24–56.

Winkelbauer, Thomas. *Ständefreiheit und Fürstenmacht. Geschichte Österreichs*. Edited by Herwig Wolfram. Vol. 6, 2 parts. Vienna, 2003.

Winterling, Aloys. "'Krise ohne Alternative' im Alten Rom." In *Christian Meier zur Diskussion*, edited by Monika Bernett, Wilfried Nippel, and Aloys Winterling, 219–39. Stuttgart, 2008.

Wunder, Heide. "Herrschaft und öffentliches Handeln von Frauen in der Gesellschaft der Frühen Neuzeit." In *Frauen in der Geschichte des Rechts: Von der frühen Neuzeit bis zur Gegenwart*, edited by Ute Gerhard, 27–54. Munich, 1997.

Zotz, Thomas. "Der Reichstag als Fest: Feiern, Spiele, Kurzweil." In *Der Kaiser in seiner Stadt: Maximilian I. und der Reichstag zu Freiburg 1498*, edited by Hans Schadeck, 146–71. Freiburg, 1998.

Zunckel, Julia. "Rangordnungen der Orthodoxie? Päpstlicher Suprematieanspruch und Wertewandel im Spiegel der Präzedenzkonflikte am heiligen römischen Hof in post-tridentinischer Zeit." In *Werte und Symbole im frühneuzeitlichen Rom*, edited by Günther Wassilowsky and Wolf Hubert, 101–28. Münster, 2005.

Zwierlein, Cornel. "Normativität und Empirie: Denkrahmen der Präzedenz zwischen Königen auf dem Basler Konzil, am päpstlichen Hof (1564) und in der entstehenden Politikwissenschaft (bis 1648)." *Historisches Jahrbuch* 125 (2005): 101–32.

INDEX

Albrecht of Brandenburg, Elector and Archbishop of Mainz (1490–1545), 86, 87, 89, 95, 107
Albrecht III Achilles, Elector of Brandenburg (1414–1486), 58
Albrecht, called *der Beherzte*, Duke of Saxony (1443–1500), 29, 50
Albrecht IV, called *der Weise*, Duke of Bavaria (1447–1508), 36, 49
Albrecht of Brandenburg-Ansbach, Grand Master of Teutonic Knights, Duke of Prussia (1490–1568), 101, 102, 103
Alexander IV., Papst (1430–1503), 15
Andersen, Hans Christian (1805–1875), 2, 5
Andlau, Peter von (ca. 1420–1480), 46
Anna of Tyrol (1585–1618), 161
Anna Katharina von Kyrburg, Duchess of Wurttemberg (1614–1655), 163
Anton Günther I, Count of Schwarzburg-Sondershausen (1620–1666), 170
Arumaeus, Dominikus (1579–1634), 125, 126
Auersperg, Johann Weikhard Count of (1615–1677), 144, 154
Augsburg, Bishop, *See* Christopher of Stadion.
August, Elector of Saxony (1526–1586), 178
Augustus (63 b.c.–14 a.d.), Roman Emperor, 136
Aurifaber, Joannes (c. 1519–1575), 96

Bamberg, Bishop, *See* Henry III, Groß von Trockau.
Beck, Christian August von (1720–1783), 250, 251
Berthold von Henneberg, Elector and Archbishop of Mainz (1442–1504), 15, 20, 21, 33, 34, 35, 38, 39, 50, 51, 56, 57, 58, 59, 61, 64, 66
Bianca Maria Sforza (between 1472 and 1474–1510), 53
Blumenthal, Joachim Friedrich Baron of (1607–1657), 141, 155, 156, 159, 173
Bodin, Jean (1529 or 1530–1596), 124, 125, 127, 187
Boehmer, Georg Ludwig (1715–1797), 251
Bogislav X., Duke of Pommern-Stettin (1454–1523), 26, 58, 59, 60
Breidbach zu Bürresheim, Emmerich Joseph von, Elector and Archbishop of Mainz (1707–1774), 207, 208, 210, 211, 212, 217
Brück, Gregor von, called Heyns(e) (lat. Pontanus) (1485–1557), 98, 99
Burgkmair, Hans, the Elder (1473–1531), 23
Burkgraf, Ulrich (dates unknown), 26

Campeggio, Lorenzo (1474–1539), 84, 87, 89, 91, 98, 99, 104, 107
Charlemagne, Emperor (747–814), 1, 30, 41, 43, 56, 149, 157, 158, 159, 160, 163, 206, 213, 236
Charles IV, Emperor (1316–1378), 44
Charles V, Emperor (1500–1558), 10, 59, 60, 61, 62, 83, 84, 85, 86, 87, 88, 89, 90, 91, 92, 93, 94, 95, 96, 97, 98, 99, 100, 101, 102, 103, 104, 105, 106, 107, 108, 109, 110, 111, 112, 113, 126, 135, 136, 149, 151, 169, 175, 177, 180, 186
Charles VI, Emperor, 245
Charles VII, Albrecht, Emperor (1697–1745), 225, 245, 254
Charles VII, King of France (1403–1461), 56

Charles VIII, King of France (1470–1498), 15, 49, 57
Charles II Caspar von der Leyen-Hohengeroldseck, Elector and Bishop of Trier (1618–1676), 135, 143, 147, 152, 155, 159, 168
Charles I Louis, Elector of the Palatinate (1618–1680), 130, 131, 138, 140, 141, 147, 152, 155, 159, 160, 168, 182
Charles IV Theodore, Elector of the Palatinate, since 1777 Elector of Bavaria (1724–1799), 210, 213, 214, 255
Charles I, Duke of Savoy (1468–1490), 24
Charles IV, Duke of Lorraine and Bar (1604–1675), 170
Charles II Eugene, Duke of Wurttemberg (1728–1793), 224
Charles of Outremont, Bishop of Liège (died 1771), 248
Casimir, Margrave of Brandenburg-Ansbach (1481–1527), 69
Catherine II, the Great, Czarina of Russia (1729–1796), 240, 241
Cologne, Archbishops and Electors, See Clemens August I of Bavaria, Hermann IV of Hesse, Hermann V von Wied, Maximilian Frederick of Königsegg-Rothenfels, Maximilian Henry of Bavaria

Eric I, Duke of Brunswick-Calenberg (1470–1540), 63
Ernest II of Saxony, Archbishop of Magdeburg (1464–1513), 30
Ernest I, called *der Bekenner*, Duke of Brunswick-Lüneburg (1497–1546), 96

Ferdinand I, Emperor (1503–1564), 60, 83, 84, 87, 89, 98, 99, 101, 104, 105, 107, 108, 109, 110, 149, 150, 157, 178, 245
Ferdinand II, Emperor (1578–1637), 122, 126, 128, 161, 170, 178
Ferdinand III, Emperor (1608–1657), 10, 122, 128, 129, 130, 135, 136, 137, 138, 139, 140, 141, 142, 144, 145, 146, 147, 151, 152, 153, 154, 155, 156, 158, 160, 161, 162, 163, 165, 166, 168, 170, 171, 176, 178, 180, 181, 182, 183, 184, 185, 186
Ferdinand IV, Roman King (1633–1654), 129, 130, 135, 151, 153, 154, 155, 156, 157, 159, 160, 162, 163, 165, 168
Ferdinand II, King of Naples (1469–1496), 34
Ferdinand Maria, Elector of Bavaria (1636–1679), 140, 141
Francis I Stephen, Emperor (1708–1765), 205, 206, 207, 208, 209, 211, 212, 213, 214, 215, 217, 218, 223, 225, 233, 240, 241, 242, 245, 251, 255, 256
Francis II, Emperor (1768–1835), 281, 282
Francis William of Wartenberg, Bishop of Regensburg and Osnabrück (1593–1661), 129, 135, 143, 144, 181
Frederick III, Emperor (1415–1493), 15, 17, 29, 33, 58, 104, 106, 108, 161
Frederick I, King of Denmark and Norway and Duke of Holstein (1471–1533), 36
Frederick III, King of Denmark and Norway (1609–1670), 169
Frederick II, the Great, King of Prussia (1712–1786), 203, 206, 207, 210, 248, 254, 256
Frederick V, called *der Gute*, King of Denkmark and Norway (1723–1766), 240
Frederick August II, Elector of Saxony and King of Poland (1696–1763), 255
Frederick August III, called *der Gerechte*, Elector, later King of Saxony (1750–1827), 235
Frederick August, Infant of Great Britain and Bishop of Osnabrück (1763–1827), 242
Frederick III, called *der Weise*, Elector of Saxony (1463–1525), 49, 50, 52, 54, 55, 56, 83
Frederick V, *called* Winter King, Elector Palatine and King of Bohemia (1596–1632), 131

Frederick William I, called *Großer Kurfürst*, Elector of Brandenburg (1620–1688), 131, 141, 154, 159, 169, 170, 171
Frederick V, Margrave of Brandenburg-Ansbach (1460–1536), 26, 30, 42, 50, 51, 52, 56, 58, 63, 83
Frederick August, Prince of Anhalt-Zerbst (1734–1793), 221
Fulda, Abbot, *See* Joachim von Gravenegg

Galen, Christoph Bernhard von, Bishop of Münster (1606–1678), 138
George II August, King of Great Britain and Ireland (1683–1760), 255
George III William Frederick, King of Great Britain and Ireland (1738–182), 212, 214, 233, 242
George called *der Reiche*, Duke of Bavaria (1455–1503), 36, 49
George called *der Fromme or der Bekenner*, Margrave of Brandenburg-Ansbach (1484–1543), 61, 96, 101
George II, Landgrave of Hesse-Darmstadt (1605–1661), 138, 161
Geyer, Andreas (died 1712), 222
Gleichen, William Frederick Baron of (1717–1783), 226
Goethe, Johann Wolfgang von (1749–1832), 205, 206, 215
Gravenegg, Joachim von, Abbot of Fulda (died 1671), 135

Hegel, Georg Wilhelm Friedrich (1770–1831), 1, 5, 9, 206, 244, 293
Henry I, the Elder, Duke of Brunswick-Lüneburg (1463–1513), 29, 30, 50, 52, 61, 63
Henry III, Groß von Trockau, Bishop of Bamberg (before 1451–1501), 29
Heinrich II Österreicher, Abbot of Schussenried (died 1505), 36
Herder, Johann Gottfried (1744–1803), 8, 9
Hermann IV of Hesse, called *der Friedsame*, Elector and Archbishop of Cologne (1450–1508), 50, 55, 56

Hermann V von Wied, Elector and Archbishop of Cologne (1477–1552), 86, 89
Hobbes, Thomas (1588–1679), 206
Hogenberg, Nicolaus (c. 1500–1539), 88
Hohenzollern, Hereditary Imperial Chamberlains, 207

Innocent X, Pope (1574–1655), 144

Johann I Nestor, Elector of Brandenburg (1484–1535), 59, 60, 86, 107
Johann I, called Hans, King of Denmark, Norway and Sweden (1455–1513), 28
Johann II of Baden, Elector and Archbishop of Trier (1430–1503), 51, 56
Johann IV Cicero, Elector of Brandenburg (1455–1499), 25, 36, 37, 49, 50, 52, 57, 58, 59
Johann called *der Beständige*, Elector of Saxony (1468–1532), 84, 86, 91, 95, 96, 98, 99, 101, 103, 107, 108, 123
Johann Frederick I, called *der Großmütige*, Elector of Saxony (1503–1554), 104, 180
Johann George I, Elector of Saxony (1585–1656), 141
Johann II, Duke of Cleves-Mark (1458–1521), 49
Johann I, Count Palatine and Duke of Bavaria (1459–1509), 31
Johann III of Dalberg, Bishop of Worms (1455–1503), 18
Jonas, Justus, the Elder (1493–1555), 99
Joseph I, Emperor (1678–1711), 208
Joseph II, Emperor (1741–1790), 10, 204, 205, 206, 207, 209, 210, 211, 212, 213, 216, 217, 218, 223, 225, 226, 233, 237, 239, 242, 246, 247, 248, 249, 250, 251, 254, 255, 256, 257

Karg von Bebenburg, Johann Friedrich (1709–1773), 227, 234
Kaunitz-Rietberg, Wenzel Anton Prince of (1711–1794), 249
Khevenhüller-Metsch, John Joseph Prince of (1706–1776), 211, 248

König, Johann Karl (1705–1753), 275
Kurz von Senftenau, Ferdinand Sigmund, Count (1592–1659), 164, 169, 178, 181

Leibniz, Gottfried Wilhelm (1646–1716), 134
Leopold I, Emperor (1640–1705), 156, 218, 225
Leopold II, Emperor (1747–1792), 211, 212, 246
Liechtenstein, Joseph Wenzel Prince of (1696–1772), 208, 209
Liège, Bishop, *See* Karl von Outremont
Lothar Friedrich of Metternich-Burscheid, Archbishop and Elector of Mainz and Bishop of Speyer (1617–1675), 165
Louis I, the Pious, King of the Franks (778–840), 281
Louis XIV, King of France (1638–1715), 181
Ludwig IV, called *der Bayer*, Emperor (1282–1347), 232
Ludwig Philipp, Count Palatine of Simmern (1602–1655), 138, 181
Luther, Martin (1483–1546), 83, 84, 86, 94, 99, 101, 103

Mackau, Louis Eleonor Baron von (1727–1767), 233
Magdeburg, Bishop, *See* Ernest II of Saxonia
Mainz, Archbishops and Electors, *See* Albrecht of Brandenburg, Berthold of Henneberg, Emmerich Joseph von Breidbach zu Bürresheim, John Frederick Charles of Ostein, John Philip of Schönborn, Lothair Frederick of Metternich-Burscheid
Mameranus, Nicolaus (1500– c. 1567), 28
Maria Anna of Spain (1606–1646), 162
Maria Theresia, Empress (1717–1780), 203, 206, 207, 209, 210, 211, 245, 246, 247, 248, 256, 280
Maria Josepha of Bavaria, Empress (1739–1767), 233

Maria Anna of Austria, Electress and Regent of Bavaria (1610–1665), 140, 141, 155
Maria Isabella of Bourbon-Parma, Archduchess of Austria (1741–1763), 211, 217, 247
Maria Eleonora of Brandenburg, Countess Palatine-Simmern (1607–1675), 163
Matthäus Lang von Wellenburg, Archbishop of Salzburg (1468–1540), 91
Matthias, Emperor (1557–1619), 161
Maximilian I, Emperor (1459–1519), 10, 15, 16, 17, 18, 19, 26, 30, 33, 34, 36, 40, 41, 42, 43, 48, 49, 55, 56, 58, 59, 64, 68, 87, 102, 104, 175, 177, 186, 218, 228, 276
Maximilian II, Emperor (1527–1576), 149, 150
Maximilian Heinrich, Elector and Archbishop of Cologne (1621–1688), 135, 143, 147, 152, 158, 166, 181
Maximilian Friedrich von Königsegg-Rothenfels, Elector and Archbishop of Cologne (1708–1784), 207, 210, 211, 212
Maximilian I, Elector of Bavaria (1573–1651), 122, 140, 180
Maximilian II Emanuel, Elector of Bavaria (1662–1726), 213
Maximilian III Joseph, Elector of Bavaria (1727–1777), 255
Melanchthon, Philipp (1497–1560), 92, 99
Meytens, Martin van (1695–1770), 205, 215, 216
Montagu, Lady Mary Wortley (1689–1762), 231
Montesquieu, Charles-Louis de Secondat, Baron de la Brède (1688 or 89–1755), 226
Moraw, Peter, historian (1935–2013), 6
Moritz, Elector of Saxony (1521–1553), 180
Moser, Friedrich Carl von (1723–1798), 219, 280
Moser, Johann Jakob (1701–1785), 121, 158, 233, 234, 238, 250, 251, 254

Müller, Johann Joachim (died 1731), 228
Müllner, Johann (1565–1643), 213
Münster, Bishop, *See* Christoph Bernhard von Galen

Napoleon I Bonaparte, Emperor of France (1769–1821), 281, 282, 283
Nicolai, Friedrich (1733–1811), 223, 224
Noltz, Reinhart, Mayor of Worms, 15, 18, 20

Ompteda, Dietrich Heinrich Ludwig von (1746–1803), 228
Ostein, Johann Friedrich Karl von, Elector and Archbishop of Mainz (1689–1763), 255
Otto II, Count Palatine-Mosbach and Duke of Bavaria (1435–1499), 30
Otto III, Count of Henneberg-Aschach (1437–1502), 48, 50
Oxenstierna, Bengt Gabrielsson (1623–1702), 169

Paderborn, Bishop, *See* Dietrich Adolf von der Recke
Paine, Thomas (1737–1809), 5
Pannochieschi d'Elci, Scipio, Bishop of Pisa (died 1670), 142, 146, 152
Pappenheim, Hereditary Imperial Marshals, 19, 21, 28, 30, 34, 42, 43, 52, 91, 135, 160, 161, 168, 182, 208, 211, 225, 240
Paurmeister, Tobias (1555–1616), 126
Pergen, Johann Anton, Count of (1725–1814), 249
Petrarca, Francesco (1304–1374), 108
Peter III Fjodorowitsch, Czar of Russia (1728–1762), 227
Philip I, King of Castile (1478–1506), 28
Philip II, King of Spain (1527–1598), 104
Philip IV, King of Spain (1605–1665), 170
Philipp, Elector of the Palatinate (1448–1508), 28, 50
Philipp Wilhelm, Elector of the Palatinate, Count Palatinate-Neuburg (1615–1690), 138

Philipp I, called *der Großmütige*, Landgrave of Hesse (1504–1567), 83, 94, 96, 97, 101, 110
Plotho, Erich Christoph, Baron of (1707–1788), 207
Pufendorf, Samuel von (1632–1694), 109, 179, 219
Pütter, Johann Stefan (1725–1807), 250

Ranke, Leopold von (1795–1886), 11
Recke, Dietrich Adolf von der, Bishop of Paderborn (1601–1661), 135
Regensburg, Bishop, *See* Franz Wilhelm, Count of Wartenberg
Reinking, Dietrich (Theodor) (1590–1664)
René II of Anjou, Duke of Lorraine (1451–1508), 21, 52, 54, 55, 56
Reppin, Lord of, 52
Rousseau, Jean-Jacques (1712–1778), 206
Rudolph II, Emperor (1552–1612), 129, 176
Rudolph IV, Duke of Austria (1339–1365), 106
Rugen, Jorg, Herald, 22, 23

Salvius, John Adler (1590–1652), 122
Salzburg, Archbishops, *See* Matthäus Lang von Wellenburg, Sigmund II von Hollenegg
Scheidemantel, Heinrich Gottfried (1739–1788), 103
Schenk von Castell, Marquard II, Bishop of Eichstätt (1605–1685), 138, 165, 166, 176
Schönborn, Franz Georg von, Elector and Archbishop of Trier (1682–1756), 255
Schönborn, Johann Philipp von, Elector and Archbishop of Mainz (1605–1673), 130, 135, 141, 143, 151, 152, 154, 157, 158, 163, 164, 172, 181, 182, 218
Schussenried, Abbot, *See* Henry II
Schwarzkopf, Johann
Sender, Clemens (1475–1537)
Sigismund, Emperor (1368–1437)
Sigismund I, King of Poland (1467–1548)

Stablo, Prince-abbot, *See* Wilhelm II of Bavaria
Stadion, Christoph von, Bishop of Augsburg (1478–1543), 91
Sturm, Kaspar (1475–1552)

Tetleben, Valentin, Capitular of Mainz, Bishop of Hildesheim (1488 or 1489–1551), 102, 103, 105, 106, 109
Thurn und Taxis, Alexander Ferdinand Prince of (1704–1773), 223, 225, 226, 241
Thurn und Taxis, Charles Anselm Prince of (1733–1805), 226
Trautmannsdorf, Ferdinand Count of (1749–1828), 253, 277
Trier, Archbishops and Electors, *See* Franz George von Schönborn, John II of Baden, John Philip von Walderdorff, Charles II Caspar von der Leyen-Hohengeroldseck

Ulfeld, Anton Corfiz Count of, 248
Ulrich, Duke of Wurttemberg (1487–1550), 107
Urban VII, Pope (1568–1644), 144

Vicentius, Ravennas, 29

Vladislav II, King of Bohemia (1456–1516), 24
Volmar, Isaak, Baron of Rieden (1582–1662), 130, 174

Waldburg-Zeil, George III Truchsess von (1488–1531), 107
Waldeck, Count of, 177
Walderdorff, Johann Philipp von, Elector and Archbishop of Trier (1701–1768), 207, 210, 212
Wilhelm IV, Duke of Jülich (1455–1511), 63
Wilhelm, Margrave of Baden (1593–1677), 138, 161
Wilhelm II, Landgrave of Hesse (1469–1509), 50, 51
Wilhelm III, Landgrave of Hesse (1471–1500), 50
Wilhelm II of Bavaria, Prince-Abbot of Stablo and Malmedy (died 1657), 135
Wilhelm IV, Count of Henneberg-Schleusingen (1478–1559), 48, 50
Wolfgang Wilhelm, Count Palatine-Neuburg (1578–1663), 145
Wolkenstein, Veit, Baron of (died 1498 or 99), 52
Worms, Bishop, *See* John III of Dalberg

www.ingramcontent.com/pod-product-compliance
Lightning Source LLC
Chambersburg PA
CBHW072143100526
44589CB00015B/2071